Microsoft®
Visual
C++® 6.0
Run-Time
Library
Reference

PUBLISHED BY
Microsoft Press
A Division of Microsoft Corporation
One Microsoft Way
Redmond, Washington 98052-6399

Library of Congress Cataloging-in-Publication Data
Microsoft Visual C++ 6.0 Reference Library / Microsoft Corporation.
      p.   cm.
   Includes index.
   ISBN 1-57231-865-1
   1. C++ (Computer program language)   2. Microsoft Visual C++.
 I. Microsoft Corporation.
 QA76.73.C153M4977   1998
 005.26'8--dc21   98-14785
                                       CIP

Printed and bound in the United States of America.

2 3 4 5 6 7 8 9 WCWC 3 2 1 0 9

Distributed in Canada by Penguin Books Canada Limited.

A CIP catalogue record for this book is available from the British Library.

Microsoft Press books are available through booksellers and distributors worldwide. For further information about international editions, contact your local Microsoft Corporation office or contact Microsoft Press International directly at fax (425) 936-7329. Visit our Web site at mspress.microsoft.com.

Acquisitions Editor: Eric Stroo
Project Editor: Maureen Williams Zimmerman

Part No. 097-0001949

Microsoft®

Visual
C++® 6.0
iostream
Library
Reference

Contents

Contents

Introduction

Microsoft Visual C++ contains the C++ iostream class library, which supports object-oriented input and output. This library follows the syntax that the authors of the C++ language originally established and thus represents a de facto standard for C++ input and output.

About the iostream Documentation

Chapter 1, "iostream Programming," provides information you need to get started using iostream classes. After reading this material, you will begin to understand how to write programs that process formatted text character streams and binary disk files and how to customize the library in limited ways. The chapter includes advanced information on how to derive iostream classes and create custom multiparameter "manipulators." These topics will get you started on extending the library and doing specialized formatting. You will also learn about the relationship between the iostream classes and their subsidiary buffer classes. You can then apply some of the iostream library design principles to your own class libraries.

Chapter 2, "Alphabetic Microsoft iostream Class Library Reference," begins with a detailed class hierarchy diagram. The iostream class library reference follows, arranged by classes in alphabetic order. Each class description includes a summary of each member, arranged by category, followed by alphabetical listings of member functions (public and protected), overloaded operators, data members, and manipulators.

Public and protected class members are documented only when they are normally used in application programs or derived classes. See the class header files for a complete listing of class members.

iostream Programming

This chapter begins with a general description of the iostream classes and then describes output streams, input streams, and input/output streams. The end of the chapter provides information about advanced iostream programming.

What a Stream Is

Like C, C++ does not have built-in input/output capability. All C++ compilers, however, come bundled with a systematic, object-oriented I/O package, known as the iostream classes. The "stream" is the central concept of the iostream classes. You can think of a stream object as a "smart file" that acts as a source and destination for bytes. A stream's characteristics are determined by its class and by customized insertion and extraction operators.

Through device drivers, the disk operating system deals with the keyboard, screen, printer, and communication ports as extended files. The iostream classes interact with these extended files. Built-in classes support reading from and writing to memory with syntax identical to that for disk I/O, which makes it easy to derive stream classes.

Input/Output Alternatives

This product provides several options for I/O programming:

- C run-time library direct, unbuffered I/O
- ANSI C run-time library stream I/O
- Console and port direct I/O
- The Microsoft Foundation Class Library
- The Microsoft iostream Class Library

The iostream classes are useful for buffered, formatted text I/O. They are also useful for unbuffered or binary I/O if you need a C++ programming interface and decide not to use the Microsoft Foundation classes. The iostream classes are an object-oriented I/O alternative to the C run-time functions.

You can use iostream classes with the Microsoft Windows operating system. String and file streams work without restrictions, but the character-mode stream **objects cin**, **cout**, **cerr**, and **clog** are inconsistent with the Windows graphical user interface. You can also derive custom stream classes that interact directly with the Windows environment. If you link with the QuickWin library, however, the **cin, cout, cerr,** and **clog** objects are assigned to special windows because they are connected to the predefined files **stdin**, **stdout**, and **stderr**.

You cannot use iostream classes in tiny-model programs because tiny-model programs cannot contain static objects such as cin and cout.

The iostream Class Hierarchy

The class hierarchy diagram at the beginning of Chapter 2 shows some relationships between iostream classes. There are additional "member" relationships between the **ios** and **streambuf** families. Use the diagram to locate base classes that provide inherited member functions for derived classes.

Output Streams

An output stream object is a destination for bytes. The three most important output stream classes are ostream, ofstream, and ostrstream.

The **ostream** class, through the derived class ostream_withassign, supports the predefined stream objects:

- **cout**   standard output

- **cerr**   standard error with limited buffering

- **clog**   similar to **cerr** but with full buffering

Objects are rarely constructed from **ostream** or **ostream_withassign**; predefined objects are generally used. In some cases, you can reassign predefined objects after program startup. The **ostream** class, which can be configured for buffered or unbuffered operation, is best suited to sequential text-mode output. All functionality of the base class, **ios**, is included in **ostream**. If you construct an object of class **ostream**, you must specify a **streambuf** object to the constructor.

The ofstream class supports disk file output. If you need an output-only disk, construct an object of class **ofstream**. You can specify whether **ofstream** objects accept binary or text-mode data before or after opening the file. Many formatting options and member functions apply to **ofstream** objects, and all functionality of the base classes **ios** and **ostream** is included.

If you specify a filename in the constructor, that file is automatically opened when the object is constructed. Otherwise, you can use the **open** member function after invoking the default constructor, or you can construct an **ofstream** object based on an open file that is identified by a file descriptor.

Like the run-time function **sprintf**, the ostrstream class supports output to in-memory strings. To create a string in memory using I/O stream formatting, construct an object of class **ostrstream**. Because **ostrstream** objects are write-only, your program must access the resulting string through a pointer to **char**.

Constructing Output Stream Objects

If you use only the predefined **cout, cerr,** or **clog** objects, you don't need to construct an output stream. You must use constructors for:

- File streams
- String streams

Output File Stream Constructors

You can construct an output file stream in one of three ways:

- Use the default constructor, then call the **open** member function.

```
ofstream myFile; // Static or on the stack
myFile.open( "filename", iosmode );

ofstream* pmyFile = new ofstream; // On the heap
pmyFile->open( "filename", iosmode );
```

- Specify a filename and mode flags in the constructor call.

```
ofstream myFile( "filename", iosmode );
```

- Specify an integer file descriptor for a file already open for output. You can specify unbuffered output or a pointer to your own buffer.

```
int fd = _open( "filename", dosmode );
ofstream myFile1( fd ); // Buffered mode (default)
ofstream myFile2( fd, NULL, 0 ); // Unbuffered mode ofstream
myFile3( fd, pch, buflen); // User-supplied buffer
```

Output String Stream Constructors

To construct an output string stream, you can use one of two ostrstream constructors. One dynamically allocates its own storage, and the other requires the address and size of a preallocated buffer.

- The dynamic constructor is used like this:

```
char* sp;
ostrstream myString;
mystring << "this is a test" << ends;
sp = myString.str();  // Get a pointer to the string
```

The **ends** "manipulator" adds the necessary terminating null character to the string.

- The constructor that requires the preallocated buffer is used like this:

```
char s[32];
ostrstream myString( s, sizeof( s ) );
myString << "this is a test" << ends; // Text stored in s
```

Using Insertion Operators and Controlling Format

This section shows how to control format and how to create insertion operators for your own classes. The insertion (<<) operator, which is preprogrammed for all standard C++ data types, sends bytes to an output stream object. Insertion operators work with predefined "manipulators," which are elements that change the default format of integer arguments.

Output Width

To align output, you specify the output width for each item by placing the **setw** manipulator in the stream or by calling the **width** member function. This example right aligns the values in a column at least 10 characters wide:

```
#include <iostream.h>

void main()
{
    double values[] = { 1.23, 35.36, 653.7, 4358.24 };
    for( int i = 0; i < 4; i++ )
    {
        cout.width(10);
        cout << values[i] << '\n';
    }
}
```

The output looks like this:

```
    1.23
    35.36
    653.7
    4358.24
```

Leading blanks are added to any value fewer than 10 characters wide.

To pad a field, use the **fill** member function, which sets the value of the padding character for fields that have a specified width. The default is a blank. To pad the column of numbers with asterisks, modify the previous **for** loop as follows:

```
for( int i = 0; i < 4; i++ )
{
    cout.width( 10 );
    cout.fill( '*' );
    cout << values[i] << endl
}
```

The **endl** manipulator replaces the newline character ('\n'). The output looks like this:

```
******1.23
*****35.36
*****653.7
***4358.24
```

To specify widths for data elements in the same line, use the **setw** manipulator:

```
#include <iostream.h>
#include <iomanip.h>

void main()
{
    double values[] = { 1.23, 35.36, 653.7, 4358.24 };
    char *names[] = { "Zoot", "Jimmy", "Al", "Stan" };
    for( int i = 0; i < 4; i++ )
        cout << setw( 6 )  << names[i]
            << setw( 10 ) << values[i] << endl;
}
```

The **width** member function is declared in IOSTREAM.H. If you use **setw** or any other manipulator *with arguments*, you must include IOMANIP.H. In the output, strings are printed in a field of width 6 and integers in a field of width 10:

```
  Zoot       1.23
 Jimmy      35.36
    Al      653.7
  Stan    4358.24
```

Neither **setw** nor **width** truncates values. If formatted output exceeds the width, the entire value prints, subject to the stream's precision setting. Both **setw** and **width** affect the following field only. Field width reverts to its default behavior (the necessary width) after one field has been printed. However, the other stream format options remain in effect until changed.

Alignment

Output streams default to right-aligned text. To left align the names in the previous example and right align the numbers, replace the **for** loop as follows:

```
for ( int i = 0; i < 4; i++ )
    cout << setiosflags( ios::left )
        << setw( 6 )  << names[i]
        << resetiosflags( ios::left )
        << setw( 10 ) << values[i] << endl;
```

The output looks like this:

```
Zoot        1.23
Jimmy      35.36
Al         653.7
Stan      4358.24
```

The left-align flag is set by using the setiosflags manipulator with the ios::left enumerator. This enumerator is defined in the ios class, so its reference must include the ios:: prefix. The resetiosflags manipulator turns off the left-align flag. Unlike **width** and **setw**, the effect of **setiosflags** and **resetiosflags** is permanent.

Precision

The default value for floating-point precision is six. For example, the number 3466.9768 prints as 3466.98. To change the way this value prints, use the setprecision manipulator. The manipulator has two flags, ios::fixed and ios::scientific. If ios::fixed is set, the number prints as 3466.976800. If ios::scientific is set, it prints as 3.4669773+003.

To display the floating-point numbers shown in Alignment with one significant digit, replace the **for** loop as follows:

```
for ( int i = 0; i < 4; i++ )
    cout << setiosflags( ios::left )
         << setw( 6 )
         << names[i]
         << resetiosflags( ios::left )
         << setw( 10 )
         << setprecision( 1 )
         << values[i]
         << endl;
```

The program prints this list:

```
Zoot         1
Jimmy     4e+001
Al        7e+002
Stan      4e+003
```

To eliminate scientific notation, insert this statement before the **for** loop:

```
cout << setiosflags( ios::fixed );
```

With fixed notation, the program prints with one digit after the decimal point.

```
Zoot        1.2
Jimmy      35.4
Al         653.7
Stan      4358.2
```

If you change the **ios::fixed** flag to **ios::scientific,** the program prints this:

```
Zoot     1.2e+000
Jimmy    3.5e+001
Al       6.5e+002
Stan     4.4e+003
```

Again, the program prints one digit after the decimal point. If *either* **ios::fixed** or **ios::scientific** is set, the precision value determines the number of digits after the decimal point. If neither flag is set, the precision value determines the total number of significant digits. The **resetiosflags** manipulator clears these flags.

Radix

The **dec**, **oct**, and **hex** manipulators set the default radix for input and output. For example, if you insert the **hex** manipulator into the output stream, the object correctly translates the internal data representation of integers into a hexadecimal output format. The numbers are displayed with digits "a" through "f" in lowercase if the ios::uppercase flag is clear (the default); otherwise, they are displayed in uppercase. The default radix is **dec** (decimal).

Output File Stream Member Functions

Output stream member functions have three types: those that are equivalent to manipulators, those that perform unformatted write operations, and those that otherwise modify the stream state and have no equivalent manipulator or insertion operator. For sequential, formatted output, you might use only insertion operators and manipulators. For random-access binary disk output, you use other member functions, with or without insertion operators.

The open Function for Output Streams

To use an output file stream (ofstream), you must associate that stream with a specific disk file in the constructor or the **open** function. If you use the **open** function, you can reuse the same stream object with a series of files. In either case, the arguments describing the file are the same.

When you open the file associated with an output stream, you generally specify an **open_mode** flag. You can combine these flags, which are defined as enumerators in the **ios** class, with the bitwise OR (|) operator.

Flag	Function
ios::app	Opens an output file for appending.
ios::ate	Opens an existing file (either input or output) and seeks the end.

(continued)

(continued)

Flag	Function
ios::in	Opens an input file. Use **ios::in** as an **open_mode** for an **ofstream** file to prevent truncating an existing file.
ios::out	Opens an output file. When you use **ios::out** for an **ofstream** object without **ios::app, ios::ate,** or **ios::in, ios::trunc** is implied.
ios::nocreate	Opens a file only if it already exists; otherwise the operation fails.
ios::noreplace	Opens a file only if it does not exist; otherwise the operation fails.
ios::trunc	Opens a file and deletes the old file (if it already exists).
ios::binary	Opens a file in binary mode (default is text mode).

Three common output stream situations involve mode options:

- Creating a file. If the file already exists, the old version is deleted.

```
ostream ofile( "FILENAME" );  // Default is ios::out
ofstream ofile( "FILENAME", ios::out ); // Equivalent to above
```

- Appending records to an existing file or creating one if it does not exist.

```
ofstream ofile( "FILENAME", ios::app );
```

- Opening two files, one at a time, on the same stream.

```
ofstream ofile();
ofile.open( "FILE1", ios::in );
// Do some output
ofile.close(); // FILE1 closed
ofile.open( "FILE2", ios::in );
// Do some more output
ofile.close(); // FILE2 closed
// When ofile goes out of scope it is destroyed.
```

The put Function

The **put** function writes one character to the output stream. The following two statements are the same by default, but the second is affected by the stream's format arguments:

```
cout.put( 'A' ); // Exactly one character written
cout << 'A'; // Format arguments 'width' and 'fill' apply
```

The write Function

The **write** function writes a block of memory to an output file stream. The length argument specifies the number of bytes written. This example creates an output file stream and writes the binary value of the Date structure to it:

```
#include <fstream.h>

struct Date
{
    int mo, da, yr;
};

void main()
{
    Date dt = { 6, 10, 92 };
    ofstream tfile( "date.dat" , ios::binary );
    tfile.write( (char *) &dt, sizeof dt );
}
```

The **write** function does not stop when it reaches a null character, so the complete class structure is written. The function takes two arguments: a **char** pointer and a count of characters to write. Note the required cast to **char*** before the address of the structure object.

The seekp and tellp Functions

An output file stream keeps an internal pointer that points to the position where data is to be written next. The **seekp** member function sets this pointer and thus provides random-access disk file output. The **tellp** member function returns the file position. For examples that use the input stream equivalants to **seekp** and **tellp**, see The seekg and tellg Functions.

The close Function for Output Streams

The **close** member function closes the disk file associated with an output file stream. The file must be closed to complete all disk output. If necessary, the **ofstream** destructor closes the file for you, but you can use the **close** function if you need to open another file for the same stream object.

The output stream destructor automatically closes a stream's file only if the constructor or the **open** member function opened the file. If you pass the constructor a file descriptor for an already-open file or use the **attach** member function, you must close the file explicitly.

Error Processing Functions

Use these member functions to test for errors while writing to a stream:

Function	Return value
bad	Returns **TRUE** if there is an unrecoverable error.
fail	Returns **TRUE** if there is an unrecoverable error or an "expected" condition, such as a conversion error, or if the file is not found. Processing can often resume after a call to **clear** with a zero argument.
good	Returns **TRUE** if there is no error condition (unrecoverable or otherwise) and the end-of-file flag is not set.
eof	Returns **TRUE** on the end-of-file condition.
clear	Sets the internal error state. If called with the default arguments, it clears all error bits.
rdstate	Returns the current error state.

The ! operator is overloaded to perform the same function as the **fail** function. Thus the expression

```
if( !cout)...
```

is equivalent to

```
if( cout.fail() )...
```

The **void***() operator is overloaded to be the opposite of the ! operator; thus the expression

```
if( cout)...
```

is equal to

```
if( !cout.fail() )...
```

The **void***() operator is not equivalent to **good** because it doesn't test for the end of file.

The Effects of Buffering

The following example shows the effects of buffering. You might expect the program to print please wait, wait 5 seconds, and then proceed. It won't necessarily work this way, however, because the output is buffered.

```
#include <iostream.h>
#include <time.h>

void main()
```

```
{
    time_t tm = time( NULL ) + 5;
    cout << "Please wait...";
    while ( time( NULL ) < tm )
        ;
    cout << "\nAll done" << endl;
}
```

To make the program work logically, the **cout** object must empty itself when the message is to appear. To flush an **ostream** object, send it the **flush** manipulator:

```
cout << "Please wait..." << flush;
```

This step flushes the buffer, ensuring the message prints before the wait. You can also use the **endl** manipulator, which flushes the buffer and outputs a carriage return-linefeed, or you can use the **cin** object. This object (with the **cerr** or **clog** objects) is usually tied to the **cout** object. Thus, any use of **cin** (or of the **cerr** or **clog** objects) flushes the **cout** object.

Binary Output Files

Streams were originally designed for text, so the default output mode is text. In text mode, the newline character (hexadecimal 10) expands to a carriage return-linefeed (16-bit only). The expansion can cause problems, as shown here:

```
#include <fstream.h>
int iarray[2] = { 99, 10 };
void main()
{
    ofstream os( "test.dat" );
    os.write( (char *) iarray, sizeof( iarray ) );
}
```

You might expect this program to output the byte sequence { 99, 0, 10, 0 }; instead, it outputs { 99, 0, 13, 10, 0 }, which causes problems for a program expecting binary input. If you need true binary output, in which characters are written untranslated, you have several choices:

- Construct a stream as usual, then use the setmode member function, which changes the mode after the file is opened:

```
ofstream ofs ( "test.dat" );
ofs.setmode( filebuf::binary );
ofs.write( char*iarray, 4 ); // Exactly 4 bytes written
```

- Specify binary output by using the ofstream constuctor mode argument:

```
#include <fstream.h>
#include <fcntl.h>
#include <io.h>
```

```
int iarray[2] = { 99, 10 };
void main()
{
    ofstream os( "test.dat", ios::binary );
    ofs.write( iarray, 4 ); // Exactly 4 bytes written
}
```

- Use the binary manipulator instead of the setmode member function:

```
ofs << binary;
```

Use the text manipulator to switch the stream to text translation mode.

- Open the file using the run-time _open function with a binary mode flag:

```
filedesc fd = _open( "test.dat",
                _O_BINARY | _O_CREAT | _O_WRONLY );
ofstream ofs( fd );
ofs.write( ( char* ) iarray, 4 ); // Exactly 4 bytes written
```

Overloading the << Operator for Your Own Classes

Output streams use the insertion (<<) operator for standard types. You can also overload the << operator for your own classes.

The **write** function example showed the use of a Date structure. A date is an ideal candidate for a C++ class in which the data members (month, day, and year) are hidden from view. An output stream is the logical destination for displaying such a structure. This code displays a date using the **cout** object:

```
Date dt( 1, 2, 92 );
cout << dt;
```

To get **cout** to accept a Date object after the insertion operator, overload the insertion operator to recognize an **ostream** object on the left and a Date on the right. The overloaded << operator function must then be declared as a friend of class Date so it can access the private data within a Date object.

```
#include <iostream.h>

class Date
{
    int mo, da, yr;
public:
    Date( int m, int d, int y )
    {
        mo = m; da = d; yr = y;
    }
    friend ostream& operator<< ( ostream& os, Date& dt );
};
```

```
ostream& operator<< ( ostream& os, Date& dt )
{
    os << dt.mo << '/' << dt.da << '/' << dt.yr;
    return os;
}

void main()
{
    Date dt( 5, 6, 92 );
    cout << dt;
}
```

When you run this program, it prints the date:

```
5/6/92
```

The overloaded operator returns a reference to the original **ostream** object, which means you can combine insertions:

```
cout << "The date is" << dt << flush;
```

Writing Your Own Manipulators Without Arguments

Writing manipulators that don't use arguments requires neither class derivation nor use of complex macros. Suppose your printer requires the pair <ESC>[to enter bold mode. You can insert this pair directly into the stream:

```
cout << "regular " << '\033' << '[' << "boldface" << endl;
```

Or you can define the bold manipulator, which inserts the characters:

```
ostream& bold( ostream& os ) {
    return os << '\033' << '[';
}
cout << "regular " << bold << "boldface" << endl;
```

The globally defined bold function takes an **ostream** reference argument and returns the **ostream** reference. It is not a member function or a friend because it doesn't need access to any private class elements. The bold function connects to the stream because the stream's << operator is overloaded to accept that type of function, using a declaration that looks something like this:

```
ostream& ostream::operator<< ( ostream& (*_f)( ostream& ) ); {
    (*_f)( *this );
    return *this;
}
```

You can use this feature to extend other overloaded operators. In this case, it is incidental that bold inserts characters into the stream. The function is called when it is inserted into the stream, not necessarily when the adjacent characters are printed. Thus, printing could be delayed because of the stream's buffering.

Input Streams

An input stream object is a source of bytes. The three most important input stream classes are istream, ifstream, and istrstream.

The **istream** class is best used for sequential text-mode input. You can configure objects of class **istream** for buffered or unbuffered operation. All functionality of the base class, **ios**, is included in **istream**. You will rarely construct objects from class **istream**. Instead, you will generally use the predefined **cin** object, which is actually an object of class istream_withassign. In some cases, you can assign cin to other stream objects after program startup.

The **ifstream** class supports disk file input. If you need an input-only disk file, construct an object of class **ifstream**. You can specify binary or text-mode data. If you specify a filename in the constructor, the file is automatically opened when the object is constructed. Otherwise, you can use the **open** function after invoking the default constructor. Many formatting options and member functions apply to **ifstream** objects. All functionality of the base classes **ios** and **istream** is included in **ifstream**.

Like the library function **sscanf**, the **istrstream** class supports input from in-memory strings. To extract data from a character array that has a null terminator, allocate and initialize the string, then construct an object of class **istrstream**.

Constructing Input Stream Objects

If you use only the **cin** object, you don't need to construct an input stream. You must construct an input stream if you use:

- File stream

- String stream

Input File Stream Constructors

There are three ways to create an input file stream:

- Use the **void**-argument constructor, then call the **open** member function:

```
ifstream myFile; // On the stack
myFile.open( "filename", iosmode );

ifstream* pmyFile = new ifstream; // On the heap
pmyFile->open( "filename", iosmode );
```

- Specify a filename and mode flags in the constructor invocation, thereby opening the file during the construction process:

```
ifstream myFile( "filename", iosmode );
```

- Specify an integer file descriptor for a file already open for input. In this case you can specify unbuffered input or a pointer to your own buffer:

```
int fd = _open( "filename", dosmode );
ifstream myFile1( fd );  // Buffered mode (default)
ifstream myFile2( fd, NULL, 0 );  // Unbuffered mode
ifstream myFile3( fd, pch, buflen );  // User-supplied buffer
```

Input String Stream Constructors

Input string stream constructors require the address of preallocated, preinitialized storage:

```
char s[] = "123.45";
double amt;
istrstream myString( s );
myString >> amt; // Amt should contain 123.45
```

Using Extraction Operators

The extraction operator (>>), which is preprogrammed for all standard C++ data types, is the easiest way to get bytes from an input stream object.

Formatted text input extraction operators depend on white space to separate incoming data values. This is inconvenient when a text field contains multiple words or when commas separate numbers. In such a case, one alternative is to use the unformatted input member function getline to read a block of text with white space included, then parse the block with special functions. Another method is to derive an input stream class with a member function such as GetNextToken, which can call istream members to extract and format character data.

Testing for Extraction Errors

Output error processing functions, discussed in "Error Processing Functions," apply to input streams. Testing for errors during extraction is important. Consider this statement:

```
cin >> n;
```

If n is a signed integer, a value greater than 32,767 (the maximum allowed value, or MAX_INT) sets the stream's **fail** bit, and the **cin** object becomes unusable. All subsequent extractions result in an immediate return with no value stored.

Input Stream Manipulators

Many manipulators, such as **setprecision**, are defined for the **ios** class and thus apply to input streams. Few manipulators, however, actually affect input stream objects. Of those that do, the most important are the radix manipulators, **dec, oct**, and **hex**, which determine the conversion base used with numbers from the input stream.

On extraction, the **hex** manipulator enables processing of various input formats. For example, c, C, 0xc, 0xC, 0Xc, and 0XC are all interpreted as the decimal integer 12. Any character other than 0 through 9, A through F, a through f, x, and X terminates the numeric conversion. Thus the sequence "124n5" is converted to the number 124 with the ios::fail bit set.

Input Stream Member Functions

Input stream member functions are used for disk input. The member functions include:

- The open Function
- The get Function
- The getline Function
- The read Function
- The seekg and tellg Functions
- The close Function

The open Function for Input Streams

If you are using an input file stream (**ifstream**), you must associate that stream with a specific disk file. You can do this in the constructor, or you can use the **open** function. In either case, the arguments are the same.

You generally specify an **open_mode** flag when you open the file associated with an input stream (the default mode is **ios::in**). For a list of the **open_mode** flags, see "The open Function." The flags can be combined with the bitwise OR (|) operator.

To read a file, first use the **fail** member function to determine whether it exists:

```
istream ifile( "FILENAME", ios::nocreate );
if ( ifile.fail() )
// The file does not exist ...
```

The get Function

The unformatted **get** member function works like the >> operator with two exceptions. First, the **get** function includes white-space characters, whereas the extractor excludes white space when the **ios::skipws** flag is set (the default). Second, the **get** function is less likely to cause a tied output stream (**cout**, for example) to be flushed.

A variation of the **get** function specifies a buffer address and the maximum number of characters to read. This is useful for limiting the number of characters sent to a specific variable, as this example shows:

```
#include <iostream.h>

void main()
{
   char line[25];
   cout << " Type a line terminated by carriage return\n>";
   cin.get( line, 25 );
   cout << ' ' << line;
}
```

In this example, you can type up to 24 characters and a terminating character. Any remaining characters can be extracted later.

The getline Function

The getline member function is similar to the **get** function. Both functions allow a third argument that specifies the terminating character for input. The default value is the newline character. Both functions reserve one character for the required terminating character. However, **get** leaves the terminating character in the stream and **getline** removes the terminating character.

The following example specifies a terminating character for the input stream:

```
#include <iostream.h>

void main()
{
   char line[100];
   cout << " Type a line terminated by 't'" << endl;
   cin.getline( line, 100, 't' );
   cout << line;
}
```

The read Function

The **read** member function reads bytes from a file to a specified area of memory. The length argument determines the number of bytes read. If you do not include that argument, reading stops when the physical end of file is reached or, in the case of a text-mode file, when an embedded **EOF** character is read.

This example reads a binary record from a payroll file into a structure:

```
#include <fstream.h>
#include <fcntl.h>
#include <io.h>

void main()
{
    struct
    {
        double salary;
        char name[23];
    } employee;

    ifstream is( "payroll", ios::binary | ios::nocreate );
    if( is ) {   // ios::operator void*()
        is.read( (char *) &employee, sizeof( employee ) );
        cout << employee.name << ' ' << employee.salary << endl;
    }
    else {
        cout << "ERROR: Cannot open file 'payroll'." << endl;
    }
}
```

The program assumes that the data records are formatted exactly as specified by the structure with no terminating carriage-return or linefeed characters.

The seekg and tellg Functions

Input file streams keep an internal pointer to the position in the file where data is to be read next. You set this pointer with the **seekg** function, as shown here:

```
#include <fstream.h>

void main()
{
    char ch;

    ifstream tfile( "payroll", ios::binary | ios::nocreate );
    if( tfile ) {
        tfile.seekg( 8 );       // Seek 8 bytes in (past salary)
```

```
        while ( tfile.good() ) { // EOF or failure stops the reading
            tfile.get( ch );
            if( !ch ) break; // quit on null
            cout << ch;
        }
    }
    else {
        cout << "ERROR: Cannot open file 'payroll'." << endl;
    }
}
```

To use **seekg** to implement record-oriented data management systems, multiply the fixed-length record size by the record number to obtain the byte position relative to the end of the file, then use the **get** object to read the record.

The **tellg** member function returns the current file position for reading. This value is of type **streampos**, a **typedef** defined in IOSTREAM.H. The following example reads a file and displays messages showing the positions of spaces.

```
#include <fstream.h>

void main()
{
    char ch;
ifstream tfile( "payroll", ios::binary | ios::nocreate );
    if( tfile ) {
        while ( tfile.good() ) {
            streampos here = tfile.tellg();
            tfile.get( ch );
            if ( ch == ' ' )
                cout << "\nPosition " << here << " is a space";
        }
    }
    else {
        cout << "ERROR: Cannot open file 'payroll'." << endl;
    }
}
```

The close Function for Input Streams

The close member function closes the disk file associated with an input file stream and frees the operating system file handle. The ifstream destructor closes the file for you (unless you called the **attach** function or passed your own file descriptor to the constructor), but you can use the **close** function if you need to open another file for the same stream object.

Overloading the >> Operator for Your Own Classes

Input streams use the extraction (>>) operator for the standard types. You can write similar extraction operators for your own types; your success depends on using white space precisely.

Here is an example of an extraction operator for the Date class presented earlier:

```
istream& operator>> ( istream& is, Date& dt )
{
    is >> dt.mo >> dt.da >> dt.yr;
    return is;
}
```

Input/Output Streams

An **iostream** object is a source and/or a destination for bytes. The two most important I/O stream classes, both derived from **iostream**, are fstream and strstream. These classes inherit the functionality of the **istream** and **ostream** classes described previously.

The **fstream** class supports disk file input and output. If you need to read from and write to a particular disk file in the same program, construct an **fstream** object. An **fstream** object is a single stream with two logical substreams, one for input and one for output. Although the underlying buffer contains separately designated positions for reading and writing, those positions are tied together.

The **strstream** class supports input and output of in-memory strings.

Custom Manipulators with Arguments

This section describes how to create output stream manipulators with one or more arguments, and how to use manipulators for non-output streams.

- Output Stream Manipulators with One Argument (int or long)

- Other One-Argument Output Stream Manipulators

- Output Stream Manipulators with More Than One Argument

- Custom Manipulators for Input and Input/Output Streams

- Using Manipulators with Derived Stream Classes

Output Stream Manipulators with One Argument (int or long)

The iostream class library provides a set of macros for creating parameterized manipulators. Manipulators with a single **int** or **long** argument are a special case. To create an output stream manipulator that accepts a single **int** or **long** argument (like **setw**), you must use the **OMANIP** macro, which is defined in IOMANIP.H. This example defines a fillblank manipulator that inserts a specified number of blanks into the stream:

```
#include <iostream.h>
#include <iomanip.h>

ostream& fb( ostream& os, int l )
{
    for( int i=0; i < l; i++ )
        os << ' ';
    return os;
}

OMANIP(int) fillblank( int l )
{
    return OMANIP(int) ( fb, l );
}

void main()
{
    cout << "10 blanks follow" << fillblank( 10 ) << ".\n";
}
```

The IOMANIP.H header file contains a macro that expands **OMANIP(int)** into a class, **__OMANIP_int,** which includes a constructor and an overloaded **ostream** insertion operator for an object of the class. In the previous example, the fillblank function calls the **__OMANIP_int** constructor to return an object of class **__OMANIP_int.** Thus, fillblank can be used with an **ostream** insertion operator. The constructor calls the fb function. The expression **OMANIP(long)** expands to another built-in class, **__OMANIP_long**, which accommodates functions with a long integer argument.

Other One-Argument Output Stream Manipulators

To create manipulators that take arguments other than **int** and **long**, you must use the **IOMANIPdeclare** macro, which declares the classes for your new type, as well as the **OMANIP** macro.

The following example uses a class money, which is a **long** type. The setpic manipulator attaches a formatting "picture" string to the class that can be used by the overloaded stream insertion operator of the class money. The picture string is stored as a static variable in the money class rather than as data member of a stream class, so you do not have to derive a new output stream class.

```
#include <iostream.h>
#include <iomanip.h>
#include <string.h>

typedef char* charp;
IOMANIPdeclare( charp );

class money {
private:
   long value;
   static char *szCurrentPic;
public:
   money( long val ) { value = val; }
   friend ostream& operator << ( ostream& os, money m ) {
      // A more complete function would merge the picture
      // with the value rather than simply appending it
      os << m.value << '[' << money::szCurrentPic << ']';
         return os;
   }
   friend ostream& setpic( ostream& os, char* szPic ) {
      money::szCurrentPic = new char[strlen( szPic ) + 1];
         strcpy( money::szCurrentPic, szPic );
         return os;
   }
};
char *money::szCurrentPic;  // Static pointer to picture

OMANIP(charp) setpic(charp c)
{
   return OMANIP(charp) (setpic, c);
}

void main()
{
   money amt = 35235.22;
   cout << setiosflags( ios::fixed );
   cout << setpic( "###,###,###.##" ) << "amount = " << amt << endl;
}
```

Output Stream Manipulators with More Than One Argument

The following example shows how to write a manipulator, fill, to insert a specific number of a particular character. The manipulator, which takes two arguments, is similar to setpic in the previous example. The difference is that the character pointer type declaration is replaced by a structure declaration.

```
#include <iostream.h>
#include <iomanip.h>
```

```
struct fillpair {
      char ch;
        int  cch;
};

IOMANIPdeclare( fillpair );

ostream& fp( ostream& os, fillpair pair )
{
   for ( int c = 0; c < pair.cch; c++ ) {
        os << pair.ch;
   }
   return os;
}

OMANIP(fillpair) fill( char ch, int cch )
{
   fillpair pair;

   pair.cch = cch;
   pair.ch  = ch;
   return OMANIP (fillpair)( fp, pair );
}

void main()
{
   cout << "10 dots coming" << fill( '.', 10 ) << "done" << endl;
}
```

This example can be rewritten so that the manipulator definition is in a separate program file. In this case, the header file must contain these declarations:

```
struct fillpair {
      char ch;
      int  cch;
};
IOMANIPdeclare( fillpair );
ostream& fp( ostream& o, fillpair pair );
OMANIP(fillpair) fill( char ch, int cch );
```

Custom Manipulators for Input and Input/Output Streams

The **OMANIP** macro works with **ostream** and its derived classes. The **SMANIP**, **IMANIP**, and **IOMANIP** macros work with the classes ios, istream, and iostream, respectively.

Using Manipulators with Derived Stream Classes

Suppose you define a manipulator, xstream, that works with the ostream class. The manipulator will work with all classes derived from **ostream**. Further suppose you need manipulators that work only with xstream. In this case, you must add an overloaded insertion operator that is not a member of **ostream**:

```
xstream& operator<< ( xstream& xs, xstream& (*_f)( xstream& ) ) {
    (*_f)( xs );
    return xs;
}
```

The manipulator code looks like this:

```
xstream& bold( xstream& xs ) {
    return xs << '\033' << '[';
}
```

If the manipulator needs to access xstream protected data member functions, you can declare the bold function as a friend of the xstream class.

Deriving Your Own Stream Classes

Like any C++ class, a stream class can be derived to add new member functions, data members, or manipulators. If you need an input file stream that tokenizes its input data, for example, you can derive from the ifstream class. This derived class can include a member function that returns the next token by calling its base class's public member functions or extractors. You may need new data members to hold the stream object's state between operations, but you probably won't need to use the base class's protected member functions or data members.

For the straightforward stream class derivation, you need only write the necessary constructors and the new member functions.

The streambuf Class

Unless you plan to make major changes to the iostream library, you do not need to work much with the streambuf class, which does most of the work for the other stream classes. In most cases, you will create a modified output stream by deriving only a new streambuf class and connecting it to the ostream class.

Why Derive a Custom streambuf Class?

Existing output streams communicate to the file system and to in-memory strings. You can create streams that address a memory-mapped video screen, a window as defined by Microsoft Windows, a new physical device, and so on. A simpler method is to alter the byte stream as it goes to a file system device.

A streambuf Derivation Example

The following example modifies the **cout** object to print in two-column landscape (horizontal) mode on a printer that uses the PCL control language (for example, Hewlett-Packard LaserJet printer). As the test driver program shows, all member functions and manipulators that work with the original **cout** object work with the special version. The application programming interface is the same.

The example is divided into three source files:

- HSTREAM.H — the LaserJet class declaration that must be included in the implementation file and application file

- HSTREAM.CPP — the LaserJet class implementation that must be linked with the application

- EXIOS204.CPP — the test driver program that sends output to a LaserJet printer

HSTREAM.H contains only the class declaration for hstreambuf, which is derived from the **filebuf** class and overrides the appropriate **filebuf** virtual functions.

```
// hstream.h - HP LaserJet output stream header
#include <fstream.h> // Accesses filebuf class
#include <string.h>
#include <stdio.h> // for sprintf

class hstreambuf : public filebuf
{
public:
    hstreambuf( int filed );
    virtual int sync();
    virtual int overflow( int ch );
    ~hstreambuf();
private:
    int column, line, page;
    char* buffer;
    void convert( long cnt );
    void newline( char*& pd, int& jj );
    void heading( char*& pd, int& jj );
    void pstring( char* ph, char*& pd, int& jj );
};
ostream& und( ostream& os );
ostream& reg( ostream& os );
```

HSTREAM.CPP contains the hstreambuf class implementation.

```
// hstream.cpp  - HP LaserJet output stream
#include "hstream.h"
```

```
const int REG  = 0x01;    // Regular font code
const int UND  = 0x02;    // Underline font code
const int CR   = 0x0d;    // Carriage return character
const int NL   = 0x0a;    // Newline character
const int FF   = 0x0c;    // Formfeed character
const int TAB  = 0x09;    // Tab character
const int LPP  = 57;      // Lines per page
const int TABW = 5;       // Tab width

// Prolog defines printer initialization (font, orientation, etc.
char prolog[] =
{ 0x1B, 0x45,                         // Reset printer
  0x1B, 0x28, 0x31, 0x30, 0x55,       // IBM PC char set
  0x1B, 0x26, 0x6C, 0x31, 0x4F,       // Landscape
  0x1B, 0x26, 0x6C, 0x38, 0x44,       // 8 lines per inch
  0x1B, 0x26, 0x6B, 0x32, 0x53};      // Lineprinter font

// Epilog prints the final page and terminates the output
char epilog[] = { 0x0C, 0x1B, 0x45 };   // Formfeed, reset

char uon[] = { 0x1B, 0x26, 0x64, 0x44, 0 };  // Underline on
char uoff[] = { 0x1B, 0x26, 0x64, 0x40, 0 }; // Underline off

hstreambuf::hstreambuf( int filed ) : filebuf( filed )
{
   column = line = page = 0;
   int size = sizeof( prolog );
   setp( prolog, prolog + size );
   pbump( size );   // Puts the prolog in the put area
   filebuf::sync(); // Sends the prolog to the output file
   buffer = new char[1024]; // Allocates destination buffer
}

hstreambuf::~hstreambuf()
{
   sync(); // Makes sure the current buffer is empty
   delete buffer; // Frees the memory
   int size = sizeof( epilog );
   setp( epilog, epilog + size );
   pbump( size );   // Puts the epilog in the put area
   filebuf::sync(); // Sends the epilog to the output file
}
int hstreambuf::sync()
{
   long count = out_waiting();
   if ( count ) {
      convert( count );
   }
   return filebuf::sync();
}
```

```
int hstreambuf::overflow( int ch )
{
    long count = out_waiting();
    if ( count ) {
        convert( count );
    }
    return filebuf::overflow( ch );
}
// The following code is specific to the HP LaserJet printer

// Converts a buffer to HP, then writes it
void hstreambuf::convert( long cnt )
{
    char *bufs, *bufd; // Source, destination pointers
    int j = 0;

    bufs = pbase();
    bufd = buffer;
    if( page == 0 ) {
        newline( bufd, j );
    }
    for( int i = 0; i < cnt; i++ ) {
        char c = *( bufs++ );  // Gets character from source buffer
        if( c >= ' ' ) {          // Character is printable
            * ( bufd++ ) = c;
            j++;
            column++;
        }

else if( c == NL ) {            // Moves down one line
            *( bufd++ ) = c;      // Passes character through
            j++;
            line++;
            newline( bufd, j ); // Checks for page break, etc.
    }
        else if( c == FF ) {     // Ejects paper on formfeed
            line = line - line % LPP + LPP;
            newline( bufd, j ); // Checks for page break, etc.
    }
        else if( c == TAB ) {    // Expands tabs
            do {
                *( bufd++ ) = ' ';
                j++;
                column++;
            } while ( column % TABW );
    }
```

```
            else if( c == UND ) { // Responds to und manipulator
                pstring( uon, bufd, j );
            }
            else if( c == REG ) { // Responds to reg manipulator
                pstring( uoff, bufd, j );
            }
        }
    setp( buffer, buffer + 1024 ); // Sets new put area
    pbump( j ); // Tells number of characters in the dest buffer
}

// simple manipulators - apply to all ostream classes
ostream& und( ostream& os ) // Turns on underscore mode
{
    os << (char) UND; return os;
}

ostream& reg( ostream& os ) // Turns off underscore mode
{
    os << (char) REG; return os;
}

void hstreambuf::newline( char*& pd, int& jj ) {
// Called for each newline character
    column = 0;
    if ( ( ( line % ( LPP*2 ) ) == 0 ) { // Even page
        page++;
        pstring( "\033&a+0L", pd, jj );  // Set left margin to zero
        heading( pd, jj );               // Print heading
        pstring( "\033*p0x77Y", pd, jj );// Cursor to (0,77) dots
    }
    if ( ( ( line % LPP ) == 0 ) && ( line % ( LPP*2 ) ) != 0 ) {
    //  Odd page; prepare to move to right column
        page++;
        pstring( "\033*p0x77Y", pd, jj ); // Cursor to (0,77) dots
        pstring( "\033&a+88L", pd, jj );  // Left margin to col 88
    }
}

void hstreambuf::heading( char*& pd, int& jj ) // Prints heading
{
    char hdg[20];
    int i;

    if( page > 1 ) {
        *( pd++ ) = FF;
        jj++;
    }
```

```
   pstring( "\033*p0x0Y", pd, jj ); // Top of page
   pstring( uon, pd, jj );          // Underline on
   sprintf( hdg, "Page %-3d", page );
   pstring( hdg, pd, jj );
   for( i=0; i < 80; i++ ) {         // Pads with blanks
       *( pd++ ) = ' ';
       jj++;
   }
   sprintf( hdg, "Page %-3d", page+1 ) ;
   pstring( hdg, pd, jj );
   for( i=0; i < 80; i++ ) {         // Pads with blanks
       *( pd++ ) = ' ';
       jj++;
   }
   pstring( uoff, pd, jj ); // Underline off
}
// Outputs a string to the buffer
void hstreambuf::pstring( char* ph, char*& pd, int& jj )
{
   int len = strlen( ph );
   strncpy( pd, ph, len );
   pd += len;
   jj += len;
}
```

EXIOS204.CPP reads text lines from the cin object and writes them to the modified cout object.

```
// exios204.cpp
// hstream Driver program copies cin to cout until end of file
#include "hstream.h"

hstreambuf hsb( 4 ); // 4=stdprn

void main()
{
   char line[200];
   cout = &hsb; // Associates the HP LaserJet streambuf to cout
   while( 1 ) {
       cin.getline( line, 200 );
       if( !cin.good() ) break;
       cout << line << endl;
   }
}
```

Here are the main points in the preceding code:

- The new class `hstreambuf` is derived from **filebuf**, which is the buffer class for disk file I/O. The **filebuf** class writes to disk in response to commands from its associated **ostream** class. The `hstreambuf` constructor takes an argument that corresponds to the operating system file number, in this case 1, for **stdout**. This constructor is invoked by this line:

```
hstreambuf hsb( 1 );
```

- The **ostream_withassign** assignment operator associates the hstreambuf object with the **cout** object:

```
ostream& operator =( streambuf* sbp );
```

  This statement in EXIOS204.CPP executes the assignment:

```
cout = &hsb;
```

- The `hstreambuf` constructor prints the prolog that sets up the laser printer, then allocates a temporary print buffer.

- The destructor outputs the epilog text and frees the print buffer when the object goes out of scope, which happens after the exit from **main**.

- The **streambuf** virtual **overflow** and **sync** functions do the low-level output. The `hstreambuf` class overrides these functions to gain control of the byte stream. The functions call the private `convert` member function.

- The `convert` function processes the characters in the `hstreambuf` buffer and stores them in the object's temporary buffer. The **filebuf** functions process the temporary buffer.

- The details of convert relate more to the PCL language than to the iostream library. Private data members keep track of column, line, and page numbers.

- The und and reg manipulators control the underscore print attribute by inserting codes 0x02 and 0x03 into the stream. The convert function later translates these codes into printer-specific sequences.

- The program can be extended easily to embellish the heading, add more formatting features, and so forth.

In a more general program, the `hstreambuf` class could be derived from the **streambuf** class rather than the **filebuf** class. The **filebuf** derivation shown gets the most leverage from existing iostream library code, but it makes assumptions about the implementation of **filebuf**, particularly the **overflow** and **sync** functions. Thus you cannot necessarily expect this example to work with other derived **streambuf** classes or with **filebuf** classes provided by other software publishers.

Alphabetic Microsoft iostream Class Library Reference

iostream Class Hierarchy Diagram:

ios
- istream
  - istrstream
  - istream_withassign
  - ifstream
- ostream
  - ofstream
  - ostream_withassign
  - ostrstream

iostream
- fstream
- strstream
- stdiostream

streambuf   iostream_init
- filebuf
- strstreambuf
- stdiobuf

iostream Class List

Abstract Stream Base Class

ios	Stream base class.

Input Stream Classes

istream	General-purpose input stream class and base class for other input streams.
ifstream	Input file stream class.
istream_withassign	Input stream class for **cin**.
istrstream	Input string stream class.

Output Stream Classes

ostream	General-purpose output stream class and base class for other output streams.
ofstream	Output file stream class.
ostream_withassign	Output stream class for **cout**, **cerr**, and **clog**.
ostrstream	Output string stream class.

Input/Output Stream Classes

iostream	General-purpose input/output stream class and base class for other input/output streams.
fstream	Input/output file stream class.
strstream	Input/output string stream class.
stdiostream	Input/output class for standard I/O files.

Stream Buffer Classes

streambuf	Abstract stream buffer base class.
filebuf	Stream buffer class for disk files.
strstreambuf	Stream buffer class for strings.
stdiobuf	Stream buffer class for standard I/O files.

Predefined Stream Initializer Class

Iostream_init	Predefined stream initializer class.

class filebuf

#include <fstream.h>

The **filebuf** class is a derived class of **streambuf** that is specialized for buffered disk file I/O. The buffering is managed entirely within the Microsoft iostream Class Library. **filebuf** member functions call the run-time low-level I/O routines (the functions declared in IO.H) such as **_sopen**, **_read**, and **_write**.

The file stream classes, **ofstream**, **ifstream**, and **fstream**, use **filebuf** member functions to fetch and store characters. Some of these member functions are virtual functions of the **streambuf** class.

The reserve area, put area, and get area are introduced in the **streambuf** class description. The put area and the get area are always the same for **filebuf** objects. Also, the get pointer and put pointers are tied; when one moves, so does the other.

Construction/Destruction — Public Members

filebuf
Constructs a **filebuf** object.

~filebuf
Destroys a **filebuf** object.

Operations — Public Members

open
Opens a file and attaches it to the **filebuf** object.

close
Flushes any waiting output and closes the attached file.

setmode
Sets the file's mode to binary or text.

attach
Attaches the **filebuf** object to an open file.

Status/Information — Public Members

fd
Returns the stream's file descriptor.

is_open
Tests whether the file is open.

See Also

ifstream, ofstream, streambuf, strstreambuf, stdiobuf

Member Functions

filebuf::attach

filebuf* attach(filedesc *fd* **);**

Attaches this **filebuf** object to the open file specified by *fd*.

Return Value

The function returns **NULL** when the stream is already attached to a file; otherwise it returns the address of the **filebuf** object.

Parameter

fd

> A file descriptor as returned by a call to the run-time function **_open** or **_sopen**. **filedesc** is a **typedef** equivalent to **int**.

filebuf::close

filebuf* close();

Flushes any waiting output, closes the file, and disconnects the file from the **filebuf** object.

Return Value

If an error occurs, the function returns **NULL** and leaves the **filebuf** object in a closed state. If there is no error, the function returns the address of the **filebuf** object and clears its error state.

See Also

filebuf::open

filebuf::fd

filedesc fd() const;

Returns the file descriptor associated with the **filebuf** object; **filedesc** is a **typedef** equivalent to **int**.

Return Value

The value is supplied by the underlying file system. The function returns **EOF** if the object is not attached to a file.

See Also

filebuf::attach

filebuf::filebuf

filebuf();
filebuf(filedesc *fd* **);**
filebuf(filedesc *fd*, **char* pr, int** *nLength* **);**

Parameters

fd

A file descriptor as returned by a call to the run-time function **_sopen**. **filedesc** is a
typedef equivalent to **int**.

pr

Pointer to a previously allocated reserve area of length *nLength*.

nLength

The length (in bytes) of the reserve area.

Remarks

The three filebuf constructors are described as follows:

filebuf()

Constructs a **filebuf** object without attaching it to a file.

filebuf(filedesc)

Constructs a **filebuf** object and attaches it to an open file.

filebuf(filedesc, char*, int)

Constructs a **filebuf** object, attaches it to an open file, and initializes it to use a
specified reserve area.

filebuf::~filebuf

~filebuf();

Remarks

Closes the attached file only if that file was opened by the **open** member function.

filebuf::is_open

int is_open() const;

Return Value

Returns a nonzero value if this **filebuf** object is attached to an open disk file identified by a
file descriptor; otherwise 0.

See Also

filebuf::open

filebuf::open

filebuf* open(const char* *szName***, int** *nMode***, int** *nProt* **= filebuf::openprot);**

Opens a disk file and attaches it with this **filebuf** object.

Return Value

If the file is already open, or if there is an error while opening the file, the function returns **NULL**; otherwise it returns the **filebuf** address.

Parameters

szName

> The name of the file to be opened during construction.

nMode

> An integer containing mode bits defined as **ios** enumerators that can be combined with the OR (|) operator. See the ofstream constructor for a list of the enumerators.

nProt

> The file protection specification; defaults to the static integer **filebuf::openprot**, which is equivalent to the operating system default (**filebuf::sh_compat** for MS-DOS). The possible values of *nProt* are:
>
> - **filebuf::sh_compat**   Compatibility share mode (MS-DOS only).
> - **filebuf::sh_none**   Exclusive mode — no sharing.
> - **filebuf::sh_read**   Read sharing allowed.
> - **filebuf::sh_write**   Write sharing allowed.
>
> You can combine the **filebuf::sh_read** and **filebuf::sh_write** modes with the logical OR (||) operator.

See Also

filebuf::is_open, filebuf::close, filebuf::~filebuf

filebuf::setmode

int setmode(int *nMode* **= filebuf::text);**

Parameter

nMode
> An integer that must be one of the static **filebuf** constants. The *nMode* parameter must have one of the following values:

> - **filebuf::text**   Text mode (newline characters translated to and from carriage return-linefeed pairs under MS-DOS).

> - **filebuf::binary**   Binary mode (no translation).

Return Value

The previous mode if there is no error; otherwise 0.

Remarks

Sets the binary/text mode of the stream's **filebuf** object.

See Also

ios binary manipulator, ios text manipulator

class fstream

#include <fstream.h>

The **fstream** class is an **iostream** derivative specialized for combined disk file input and output. Its constructors automatically create and attach a **filebuf** buffer object.

See filebuf class for information on the get and put areas and their associated pointers. Although the **filebuf** object's get and put pointers are theoretically independent, the get area and the put area are not active at the same time. When the stream's mode changes from input to output, the get area is emptied and the put area is reinitialized. When the mode changes from output to input, the put area is flushed and the get area is reinitialized. Thus, either the get pointer or the put pointer is null at all times.

Construction/Destruction — Public Members

fstream
> Constructs an **fstream** object.

~fstream
> Destroys an **fstream** object.

Operations — Public Members

open
> Opens a file and attaches it to the **filebuf** object and thus to the stream.

close
> Flushes any waiting output and closes the stream's file.

setbuf
> Attaches the specified reserve area to the stream's **filebuf** object.

setmode
> Sets the stream's mode to binary or text.

attach
> Attaches the stream (through the **filebuf** object) to an open file.

Status/Information — Public Members

rdbuf
> Gets the stream's **filebuf** object.

fd
> Returns the file descriptor associated with the stream.

is_open
> Tests whether the stream's file is open.

See Also

ifstream, ofstream, strstream, stdiostream, filebuf

Member Functions

fstream::attach

void attach(filedesc *fd* **);**

Attaches this stream to the open file specified by *fd*.

Parameter

fd

A file descriptor as returned by a call to the run-time function **_open** or **_sopen**; **filedesc** is a **typedef** equivalent to **int**.

Remarks

The function fails when the stream is already attached to a file. In that case, the function sets **ios::failbit** in the stream's error state.

See Also

filebuf::attach, fstream::fd

fstream::close

void close();

Remarks

Calls the **close** member function for the associated **filebuf** object. This function, in turn, flushes any waiting output, closes the file, and disconnects the file from the **filebuf** object. The **filebuf** object is not destroyed.

The stream's error state is cleared unless the call to **filebuf::close** fails.

See Also

filebuf::close, fstream::open, fstream::is_open

fstream::fd

filedesc fd() const;

Remarks

Returns the file descriptor associated with the stream. **filedesc** is a **typedef** equivalent to **int**. Its value is supplied by the underlying file system.

See Also

filebuf::fd, fstream::attach

fstream::fstream

fstream();
fstream(const char* *szName*, **int** *nMode*, **int** *nProt* = **filebuf::openprot);**
fstream(filedesc *fd* **);**
fstream(filedesc *fd*, **char*** *pch*, **int** *nLength* **);**

Parameters

szName
> The name of the file to be opened during construction.

nMode
> An integer that contains mode bits defined as **ios** enumerators that can be combined with the bitwise OR (|) operator. The *nMode* parameter must have one of the following values:

- **ios::app** The function performs a seek to the end of file. When new bytes are written to the file, they are always appended to the end, even if the position is moved with the **ostream::seekp** function.

- **ios::ate** The function performs a seek to the end of file. When the first new byte is written to the file, it is appended to the end, but when subsequent bytes are written, they are written to the current position.

- **ios::in** The file is opened for input. The original file (if it exists) will not be truncated.

- **ios::out** The file is opened for output.

- **ios::trunc** If the file already exists, its contents are discarded. This mode is implied if **ios::out** is specified, and **ios::ate**, **ios::app**, and **ios:in** are not specified.

- **ios::nocreate** If the file does not already exist, the function fails.

- **ios::noreplace** If the file already exists, the function fails.

- **ios::binary** Opens the file in binary mode (the default is text mode).

> Note that there is no **ios::in** or **ios::out** default mode for **fstream** objects. You must specify both modes if your **fstream** object must both read and write files.

nProt
> The file protection specification; defaults to the static integer **filebuf::openprot**, which is equivalent to the operating system default, **filebuf::sh_compat**, under MS-DOS. The possible *nProt* values are as follows:

- **filebuf::sh_compat** Compatibility share mode (MS-DOS only).

- **filebuf::sh_none** Exclusive mode — no sharing.

- **filebuf::sh_read**   Read sharing allowed.

- **filebuf::sh_write**   Write sharing allowed.

The **filebuf::sh_read** and **filebuf::sh_write** modes can be combined with the logical OR (||) operator.

fd
   A file descriptor as returned by a call to the run-time function **_open** or **_sopen**. **filedesc** is a **typedef** equivalent to **int**.

pch
   Pointer to a previously allocated reserve area of length *nLength*. A **NULL** value (or *nLength* = 0) indicates that the stream will be unbuffered.

nLength
   The length (in bytes) of the reserve area (0 = unbuffered).

Remarks

The four **fstream** constructors are:

- **fstream()**   Constructs an **fstream** object without opening a file.

- **fstream(const char*, int, int)**   Contructs an **fstream** object, opening the specified file.

- **fstream(filedesc)**   Constructs an **fstream** object that is attached to an open file.

- **fstream(filedesc, char*, int)**   Constructs an **fstream** object that is associated with a **filebuf** object. The **filebuf** object is attached to an open file and to a specified reserve area.

All **fstream** constructors construct a **filebuf** object. The first three use an internally allocated reserve area, but the fourth uses a user-allocated area. The user-allocated area is not automatically released during destruction.

fstream::~fstream

~fstream();

Remarks

Flushes the buffer, then destroys an **fstream** object, along with its associated **filebuf** object. The file is closed only if it was opened by the constructor or by the **open** member function.

The **filebuf** destructor releases the reserve buffer only if it was internally allocated.

fstream::is_open

int is_open() const;

Return Value

Returns a nonzero value if this stream is attached to an open disk file identified by a file descriptor; otherwise 0.

See Also

filebuf::is_open, fstream::open, fstream::close

fstream::open

void open(const char* *szName***, int** *nMode***, int** *nProt* **= filebuf::openprot);**

Opens a disk file and attaches it to the stream's **filebuf** object.

Parameters

szName

The name of the file to be opened during construction.

nMode

An integer containing mode bits defined as **ios** enumerators that can be combined with the OR (|) operator. See the **fstream** constructor for a list of the enumerators. There is no default; a valid mode must be specified.

nProt

The file protection specification; defaults to the static integer **filebuf::openprot**. See the **fstream** constructor for a list of the other allowed values.

Remarks

If the **filebuf** object is already attached to an open file, or if a **filebuf** call fails, the **ios::failbit** is set. If the file is not found, then the **ios::failbit** is set only if the **ios::nocreate** mode was used.

See Also

filebuf::open, fstream::fstream, fstream::close, fstream::is_open

fstream::rdbuf

filebuf* rdbuf() const;

Remarks

Returns a pointer to the **filebuf** buffer object that is associated with this stream. (This is not the character buffer; the **filebuf** object contains a pointer to the character area.)

fstream::setbuf

streambuf* setbuf(char* *pch*, **int** *nLength*);

Attaches the specified reserve area to the stream's **filebuf** object.

Return Value

If the file is open and a buffer has already been allocated, the function returns **NULL**; otherwise it returns a pointer to the **filebuf** cast as a **streambuf**. The reserve area will not be released by the destructor.

Parameters

pch
> A pointer to a previously allocated reserve area of length *nLength*. A **NULL** value indicates an unbuffered stream.

nLength
> The length (in bytes) of the reserve area. A length of 0 indicates an unbuffered stream.

fstream::setmode

int setmode(int *nMode* = **filebuf::text**);

Sets the binary/text mode of the stream's **filebuf** object. It can be called only after the file is opened.

Return Value

The previous mode; –1 if the parameter is invalid, the file is not open, or the mode cannot be changed.

Parameter

nMode
> An integer that must be one of the following static **filebuf** constants:
>
> - **filebuf::text** Text mode (newline characters translated to and from carriage-return-linefeed pairs).
>
> - **filebuf::binary** Binary mode (no translation).

See Also

ios binary manipulator, ios text manipulator

class ifstream

#include <fstream.h>

The **ifstream** class is an **istream** derivative specialized for disk file input. Its constructors automatically create and attach a **filebuf** buffer object.

The **filebuf** class documentation describes the get and put areas and their associated pointers. Only the get area and the get pointer are active for the **ifstream** class.

Construction/Destruction — Public Members

ifstream
> Constructs an **ifstream** object.

~ifstream
> Destroys an **ifstream** object.

Operations — Public Members

open
> Opens a file and attaches it to the **filebuf** object and thus to the stream.

close
> Closes the stream's file.

setbuf
> Associates the specified reserve area to the stream's **filebuf** object.

setmode
> Sets the stream's mode to binary or text.

attach
> Attaches the stream (through the **filebuf** object) to an open file.

Status/Information — Public Members

rdbuf
> Gets the stream's **filebuf** object.

fd
> Returns the file descriptor associated with the stream.

is_open
> Tests whether the stream's file is open.

See Also

filebuf, streambuf, ofstream, fstream

Member Functions

ifstream::attach

void attach(filedesc *fd* **);**

Attaches this stream to the open file specified by *fd*.

Parameter

fd

    A file descriptor as returned by a call to the run-time function **_open** or **_sopen**; **filedesc** is a **typedef** equivalent to **int**.

Remarks

The function fails when the stream is already attached to a file. In that case, the function sets **ios::failbit** in the stream's error state.

See Also

filebuf::attach, ifstream::fd

ifstream::close

void close();

Remarks

Calls the **close** member function for the associated **filebuf** object. This function, in turn, closes the file and disconnects the file from the **filebuf** object. The **filebuf** object is not destroyed.

The stream's error state is cleared unless the call to **filebuf::close** fails.

See Also

filebuf::close, ifstream::open, ifstream::is_open

ifstream::fd

filedesc fd() const;

Return Value

Returns the file descriptor associated with the stream; **filedesc** is a **typedef** equivalent to **int**. Its value is supplied by the underlying file system.

See Also

filebuf::fd, ifstream::attach

ifstream::ifstream

ifstream();
ifstream(const char* *szName***, int** *nMode* **= ios::in, int** *nProt* **= filebuf::openprot);**
ifstream(filedesc *fd* **);**
ifstream(filedesc *fd***, char*** *pch***, int** *nLength* **);**

Parameters

szName

The name of the file to be opened during construction.

nMode

An integer that contains mode bits defined as **ios** enumerators that can be combined with the bitwise OR (|) operator. The *nMode* parameter must have one of the following values:

- **ios::in**   The file is opened for input (default).

- **ios::nocreate**   If the file does not already exist, the function fails.

- **ios::binary**   Opens the file in binary mode (the default is text mode).

Note that the **ios::nocreate** flag is necessary if you intend to test for the file's existence (the usual case).

nProt

The file protection specification; defaults to the static integer **filebuf::openprot** that is equivalent to **filebuf::sh_compat**. The possible *nProt* values are:

- **filebuf::sh_compat**   Compatibility share mode.

- **filebuf::sh_none**   Exclusive mode — no sharing.

- **filebuf::sh_read**   Read sharing allowed.

- **filebuf::sh_write**   Write sharing allowed.

To combine the **filebuf::sh_read** and **filebuf::sh_write** modes, use the logical OR (||) operator.

fd

A file descriptor as returned by a call to the run-time function **_open** or **_sopen**; **filedesc** is a **typedef** equivalent to **int**.

pch

Pointer to a previously allocated reserve area of length *nLength*. A **NULL** value (or *nLength* = 0) indicates that the stream will be unbuffered.

nLength

The length (in bytes) of the reserve area (0 = unbuffered).

Remarks

The four **ifstream** constructors are:

- **ifstream()**   Constructs an **ifstream** object without opening a file.

- **ifstream(const char***, **int, int)**   Contructs an **ifstream** object, opening the specified file.

- **ifstream(filedesc)**   Constructs an **ifstream** object that is attached to an open file.

- **ifstream(filedesc, char***, **int)**   Constructs an **ifstream** object that is associated with a **filebuf** object. The **filebuf** object is attached to an open file and to a specified reserve area.

All **ifstream** constructors construct a **filebuf** object. The first three use an internally allocated reserve area, but the fourth uses a user-allocated area.

ifstream::~ifstream

~ifstream();

Remarks

Destroys an **ifstream** object along with its associated **filebuf** object. The file is closed only if it was opened by the constructor or by the **open** member function.

The **filebuf** destructor releases the reserve buffer only if it was internally allocated.

ifstream::is_open

int is_open() const;

Return Value

Returns a nonzero value if this stream is attached to an open disk file identified by a file descriptor; otherwise 0.

See Also

filebuf::is_open, ifstream::open, ifstream::close

ifstream::open

void open(const char* *szName*, **int** *nMode* **= ios::in, int** *nProt* **= filebuf::openprot);**

Parameters

szName
    The name of the file to be opened during construction.

nMode

> An integer containing bits defined as **ios** enumerators that can be combined with the OR (|) operator. See the ifstream constructor for a list of the enumerators. The **ios::in** mode is implied.

nProt

> The file protection specification; defaults to the static integer **filebuf::openprot**. See the **ifstream** constructor for a list of the other allowed values.

Remarks

Opens a disk file and attaches it to the stream's **filebuf** object. If the **filebuf** object is already attached to an open file, or if a **filebuf** call fails, the **ios::failbit** is set. If the file is not found, then the **ios::failbit** is set only if the **ios::nocreate** mode was used.

See Also

filebuf::open, ifstream::ifstream, ifstream::close, ifstream::is_open, ios::flags

ifstream::rdbuf

filebuf* rdbuf() const;

Return Value

Returns a pointer to the **filebuf** buffer object that is associated with this stream. (This is not the character buffer; the **filebuf** object contains a pointer to the character area.)

ifstream::setbuf

streambuf* setbuf(char* *pch***, int** *nLength* **);**

Attaches the specified reserve area to the stream's **filebuf** object.

Return Value

If the file is open and a buffer has already been allocated, the function returns **NULL**; otherwise it returns a pointer to the **filebuf**, which is cast as a **streambuf**. The reserve area will not be released by the destructor.

Parameters

pch

> A pointer to a previously allocated reserve area of length *nLength*. A **NULL** value indicates an unbuffered stream.

nLength

> The length (in bytes) of the reserve area. A length of 0 indicates an unbuffered stream.

ifstream::setmode

int setmode(int *nMode* **= filebuf::text);**

Return Value

The previous mode; −1 if the parameter is invalid, the file is not open, or the mode cannot be changed.

Parameters

nMode
> An integer that must be one of the following static **filebuf** constants:
> - **filebuf::text**   Text mode (newline characters translated to and from carriage return-linefeed pairs).
> - **filebuf::binary**   Binary mode (no translation).

Remarks

This function sets the binary/text mode of the stream's **filebuf** object. It may be called only after the file is opened.

See Also

ios binary manipulator, ios text manipulator

class ios

#include <iostream.h>

As the iostream class hierarchy diagram shows, **ios** is the base class for all the input/output stream classes. While **ios** is not technically an abstract base class, you will not usually construct **ios** objects, nor will you derive classes directly from **ios**. Instead, you will use the derived classes **istream** and **ostream** or other derived classes.

Even though you will not use ios directly, you will be using many of the inherited member functions and data members described here. Remember that these inherited member function descriptions are not duplicated for derived classes.

Data Members (static) — Public Members

basefield
> Mask for obtaining the conversion base flags (**dec**, **oct**, or **hex**).

adjustfield
> Mask for obtaining the field padding flags (**left**, **right**, or **internal**).

floatfield
> Mask for obtaining the numeric format (**scientific** or **fixed**).

Construction/Destruction — Public Members

ios
> Constructor for use in derived classes.

~ios
> Virtual destructor.

Flag and Format Access Functions — Public Members

flags
> Sets or reads the stream's format flags.

setf
> Manipulates the stream's format flags.

unsetf
> Clears the stream's format flags.

fill
> Sets or reads the stream's fill character.

precision
> Sets or reads the stream's floating-point format display precision.

width
> Sets or reads the stream's output field width.

Status-Testing Functions — Public Members

good
Indicates good stream status.

bad
Indicates a serious I/O error.

eof
Indicates end of file.

fail
Indicates a serious I/O error or a possibly recoverable I/O formatting error.

rdstate
Returns the stream's error flags.

clear
Sets or clears the stream's error flags.

User-Defined Format Flags — Public Members

bitalloc
Provides a mask for an unused format bit in the stream's private flags variable (static function).

xalloc
Provides an index to an unused word in an array reserved for special-purpose stream state variables (static function).

iword
Converts the index provided by **xalloc** to a reference (valid only until the next **xalloc**).

pword
Converts the index provided by xalloc to a pointer (valid only until the next xalloc).

Other Functions — Public Members

delbuf
Controls the connection of **streambuf** deletion with **ios** destruction.

rdbuf
Gets the stream's **streambuf** object.

sync_with_stdio
Synchronizes the predefined objects **cin, cout, cerr,** and **clog** with the standard I/O system.

tie
Ties a specified ostream to this stream.

Operators — Public Members

operator void*
> Converts a stream to a pointer that can be used only for error checking.

operator !
> Returns a nonzero value if a stream I/O error occurs.

ios Manipulators

dec
> Causes the interpretation of subsequent fields in decimal format (the default mode).

hex
> Causes the interpretation of subsequent fields in hexadecimal format.

oct
> Causes the interpretation of subsequent fields in octal format.

binary
> Sets the stream's mode to binary (stream must have an associated **filebuf** buffer).

text
> Sets the stream's mode to text, the default mode (stream must have an associated **filebuf** buffer).

Parameterized Manipulators

(**#include <iomanip.h>** required)

setiosflags
> Sets the stream's format flags.

resetiosflags
> Resets the stream's format flags.

setfill
> Sets the stream's fill character.

setprecision
> Sets the stream's floating-point display precision.

setw
> Sets the stream's field width (for the next field only).

See Also

istream, ostream

Member Functions

ios::bad

int bad() const;

Return Value

Returns a nonzero value to indicate a serious I/O error. This is the same as setting the **badbit** error state. Do not continue I/O operations on the stream in this situation.

See Also

ios::good, ios::fail, ios::rdstate

ios::bitalloc

static long bitalloc();

Remarks

Provides a mask for an unused format bit in the stream's private flags variable (static function). The **ios** class currently defines 15 format flag bits accessible through **flags** and other member functions. These bits reside in a 32-bit private **ios** data member and are accessed through enumerators such as **ios::left** and **ios::hex.**

The bitalloc member function provides a mask for a previously unused bit in the data member. Once you obtain the mask, you can use it to set or test the corresponding custom flag bit in conjunction with the ios member functions and manipulators listed under "See Also."

See Also

ios::flags, ios::setf, ios::unsetf, ios setiosflags manipulator, ios resetiosflags manipulator

ios::clear

void clear(int *nState* **= 0);**

Parameter

nState

If 0, all error bits are cleared; otherwise bits are set according to the following masks (**ios** enumerators) that can be combined using the bitwise OR (|) operator. The *nState* parameter must have one of the following values:

- **ios::goodbit**   No error condition (no bits set).

- **ios::eofbit**   End of file reached.

- **ios::failbit**   A possibly recoverable formatting or conversion error.
- **ios::badbit**   A severe I/O error.

Remarks

Sets or clears the error-state flags. The **rdstate** function can be used to read the current error state.

See Also

ios::rdstate, ios::good, ios::bad, ios::eof

ios::delbuf

void delbuf(int *nDelFlag* **);**
int delbuf() const;

Parameter

nDelFlag

A nonzero value indicates that **~ios** should delete the stream's attached **streambuf** object. A 0 value prevents deletion.

Remarks

The first overloaded **delbuf** function assigns a value to the stream's buffer-deletion flag. The second function returns the current value of the flag.

This function is public only because it is accessed by the **Iostream_init** class. Treat it as protected.

See Also

ios::rdbuf, ios::~ios

ios::eof

int eof() const;

Return Value

Returns a nonzero value if end of file has been reached. This is the same as setting the **eofbit** error flag.

ios::fail

int fail() const;

Return Value

Returns a nonzero value if any I/O error (not end of file) has occurred. This condition corresponds to either the **badbit** or **failbit** error flag being set. If a call to **bad** returns 0, you can assume that the error condition is nonfatal and that you can probably continue processing after you clear the flags.

See Also

ios::bad, ios::clear

ios::fill

char fill(char *cFill* **);**
char fill() const;

Return Value

The first overloaded function sets the stream's internal fill character variable to *cFill* and returns the previous value. The default fill character is a space.

The second **fill** function returns the stream's fill character.

Parameter

cFill
    The new fill character to be used as padding between fields.

See Also

ios setfill manipulator

ios::flags

long flags(long *lFlags* **);**
long flags() const;

Return Value

The first overloaded **flags** function sets the stream's internal flags variable to *lFlags* and returns the previous value.

The second function returns the stream's current flags.

Parameter

lFlags
    The new format flag values for the stream. The values are specified by the following bit masks (**ios** enumerators) that can be combined using the bitwise OR (|) operator. The *lFlags* parameter must have one of the following values:

- **ios::skipws**   Skip white space on input.

- **ios::left**   Left-align values; pad on the right with the fill character.

- **ios::right**   Right-align values; pad on the left with the fill character (default alignment).

- **ios::internal** Add fill characters after any leading sign or base indication, but before the value.

- **ios::dec** Format numeric values as base 10 (decimal) (default radix).

- **ios::oct** Format numeric values as base 8 (octal).

- **ios::hex** Format numeric values as base 16 (hexadecimal).

- **ios::showbase** Display numeric constants in a format that can be read by the C++ compiler.

- **ios::showpoint** Show decimal point and trailing zeros for floating-point values.

- **ios::uppercase** Display uppercase A through F for hexadecimal values and E for scientific values.

- **ios::showpos** Show plus signs (+) for positive values.

- **ios::scientific** Display floating-point numbers in scientific format.

- **ios::fixed** Display floating-point numbers in fixed format.

- **ios::unitbuf** Cause **ostream::osfx** to flush the stream after each insertion. By default, **cerr** is unit buffered.

- **ios::stdio** Cause **ostream::osfx** to flush stdout and stderr after each insertion.

See Also

ios::setf, ios::unsetf, ios setiosflags manipulator, ios resetiosflags manipulator, ios::adjustfield, ios::basefield, ios::floatfield

ios::good

int good() const;

Return Value

Returns a nonzero value if all error bits are clear. Note that the **good** member function is not simply the inverse of the **bad** function.

See Also

ios::bad, ios::fail, ios::rdstate

ios::init

Protected →

void init(streambuf* *psb* **);**

END Protected

Parameter

psb
> A pointer to an existing streambuf object.

Remarks

Associates an object of a **streambuf**-derived class with this stream and, if necessary, deletes a dynamically created stream buffer object that was previously associated. The **init** function is useful in derived classes in conjunction with the protected default **istream**, **ostream**, and **iostream** constructors. Thus, an **ios**-derived class constructor can construct and attach its own predetermined stream buffer object.

See Also

istream::istream, ostream::ostream, iostream::iostream

ios::ios

ios(streambuf* *psb* **);**

Parameter

psb
> A pointer to an existing streambuf object.

Remarks

Constructor for **ios**. You will seldom need to invoke this constructor except in derived classes. Generally, you will be deriving classes not from **ios** but from **istream, ostream,** and **iostream**.

ios::~ios

virtual ~ios();

Remarks

Virtual destructor for **ios**.

ios::iword

long& iword(int *nIndex* **) const;**

Parameter

nIndex
> An index to a table of words that are associated with the **ios** object.

Remarks

The **xalloc** member function provides the index to the table of special-purpose words. The **pword** function converts that index to a reference to a 32-bit word.

See Also

ios::xalloc, ios::pword

ios::precision

int precision(int *np* **);**
int precision() const;

Return Value

The first overloaded **precision** function sets the stream's internal floating-point precision variable to *np* and returns the previous value. The default precision is six digits. If the display format is scientific or fixed, the precision indicates the number of digits after the decimal point. If the format is automatic (neither floating point nor fixed), the precision indicates the total number of significant digits.

The second function returns the stream's current precision value.

Parameter

np
    An integer that indicates the number of significant digits or significant decimal digits to be used for floating-point display.

See Also

ios setprecision manipulator

ios::pword

void*& pword(int nIndex **) const;**

Parameter

nIndex
    An index to a table of words that are associated with the **ios** object.

Remarks

The **xalloc** member function provides the index to the table of special-purpose words. The **pword** function converts that index to a reference to a pointer to a 32-bit word.

See Also

ios::xalloc, ios::iword

ios::rdbuf

streambuf* rdbuf() const;

Return Value

Returns a pointer to the **streambuf** object that is associated with this stream. The **rdbuf** function is useful when you need to call **streambuf** member functions.

ios::rdstate

int rdstate() const;

Return Value

Returns the current error state as specified by the following masks (**ios** enumerators):

- **ios::goodbit**   No error condition.
- **ios::eofbit**   End of file reached.
- **ios::failbit**   A possibly recoverable formatting or conversion error.
- **ios::badbit**   A severe I/O error or unknown state.

The returned value can be tested against a mask with the AND (**&**) operator.

See Also

ios::clear

ios::setf

long setf(long *lFlags*);
long setf(long lFlags, long lMask);

Return Value

The first overloaded **setf** function turns on only those format bits that are specified by 1s in *lFlags*. It returns a **long** that contains the previous value of all the flags.

The second function alters those format bits specified by 1s in *lMask*. The new values of those format bits are determined by the corresponding bits in *lFlags*. It returns a **long** that contains the previous value of all the flags.

Parameters

lFlags

> Format flag bit values. See the "flags member function" for a list of format flags. To combine these flags, use the bitwise OR (|) operator.

lMask

> Format flag bit mask.

See Also

ios::flags, ios::unsetf, ios setiosflags manipulator

ios::sync_with_stdio

static void sync_with_stdio();

Remarks

Synchronizes the C++ streams with the standard I/O system. The first time this function is called, it resets the predefined streams (**cin, cout, cerr, clog**) to use a **stdiobuf** object rather than a **filebuf** object. After that, you can mix I/O using these streams with I/O using **stdin, stdout**, and **stderr**. Expect some performance decrease because there is buffering both in the stream class and in the standard I/O file system.

After the call to **sync_with_stdio**, the **ios::stdio** bit is set for all affected predefined stream objects, and **cout** is set to unit buffered mode.

ios::tie

ostream* tie(ostream* *pos*);
ostream* tie() const;

Return Value

The first overloaded **tie** function ties this stream to the specified **ostream** and returns the value of the previous tie pointer or **NULL** if this stream was not previously tied. A stream tie enables automatic flushing of the **ostream** when more characters are needed, or there are characters to be consumed.

By default, **cin** is initially tied to **cout** so that attempts to get more characters from standard input may result in flushing standard output. In addition, **cerr** and **clog** are tied to **cout** by default.

The second function returns the value of the previous tie pointer or **NULL** if this stream was not previously tied.

Parameter

pos

> A pointer to an **ostream** object.

ios::unsetf

long unsetf(long *lFlags* **);**

Return Value

Clears the format flags specified by 1s in *lFlags*. It returns a **long** that contains the previous value of all the flags.

Parameter

lFlags
    Format flag bit values. See the "flags member function" for a list of format flags.

See Also

ios::flags, ios::setf, ios resetiosflags manipulator

ios::width

int width(int *nw* **);**
int width() const;

Return Value

The first overloaded **width** function sets the stream's internal field width variable to *nw*. When the width is 0 (the default), inserters insert only the number of characters necessary to represent the inserted value. When the width is not 0, the inserters pad the field with the stream's fill character, up to *nw*. If the unpadded representation of the field is larger than nw, the field is not truncated. Thus, *nw* is a minimum field width.

The internal width value is reset to 0 after each insertion or extraction.

The second overloaded **width** function returns the current value of the stream's width variable.

Parameter

nw
    The minimum field width in characters.

See Also

ios setw manipulator

ios::xalloc

static int xalloc();

Return Value

Provides extra **ios** object state variables without the need for class derivation. It does so by returning an index to an unused 32-bit word in an internal array. This index can subsequently be converted into a reference or pointer by using the **iword** or **pword** member functions.

Any call to **xalloc** invalidates values returned by previous calls to **iword** and **pword**.

Operators

ios::adjustfield

static const long adjustfield;

Remarks

A mask for obtaining the padding flag bits (**left, right**, or **internal**).

Example

```
extern ostream os;
if( ( os.flags() & ios::adjustfield ) == ios::left ) .....
```

See Also

ios::flags

ios::basefield

static const long basefield;

Remarks

A mask for obtaining the current radix flag bits (**dec, oct,** or **hex**).

Example

```
extern ostream os;
if( ( os.flags() & ios::basefield ) == ios::hex ) .....
```

See Also

ios::flags

ios::floatfield

static const long floatfield;

Remarks

A mask for obtaining floating-point format flag bits (**scientific** or **fixed**).

Example

```
extern ostream os;
if( ( os.flags() & ios::floatfield ) == ios::scientific ) .....
```

See Also

ios::flags

ios::operator void*

operator void* () const;

An operator that converts a stream to a pointer that can be compared to 0.

Return Value

The conversion returns 0 if either **failbit** or **badbit** is set in the stream's error state. See "rdstate" for a description of the error state masks. A nonzero pointer is not meant to be dereferenced.

See Also

ios::good, ios::fail

ios::operator !

int operator !() const;

Return Value

Returns a nonzero value if either **failbit** or **badbit** is set in the stream's error state. See "rdstate" for a description of the error state masks.

See Also

ios::good, ios::fail

Manipulators

ios& binary

binary

Remarks

Sets the stream's mode to binary. The default mode is text.

The stream must have an associated **filebuf** buffer.

See Also

ios text manipulator, ofstream::setmode, ifstream::setmode, filebuf::setmode

ios& dec

dec

Remarks

Sets the format conversion base to 10 (decimal).

See Also

ios hex manipulator, ios oct manipulator

ios& hex

hex

Remarks

Sets the format conversion base to 16 (hexadecimal).

See Also

ios dec manipulator, ios oct manipulator

ios& oct

oct

Remarks

Sets the format conversion base to 8 (octal).

See Also

ios dec manipulator, ios hex manipulator

ios& text

text

Sets the stream's mode to text (the default mode).

Remarks

The stream must have an associated **filebuf** buffer.

See Also

ios binary manipulator, ofstream::setmode, ifstream::setmode, filebuf::setmode

resetiosflags

SMANIP(long) resetiosflags(long *lFlags* **);**

#include <iomanip.h>

Parameter

lFlags
> Format flag bit values. See the "flags member function" for a list of format flags.
> To combine these flags, use the OR (|) operator.

Remarks

This parameterized manipulator clears only the specified format flags. This setting remains in effect until you change it.

setfill

SMANIP(int) setfill(int *nFill* **);**

#include <iomanip.h>

Parameter

nFill
> The new fill character to be used as padding between fields.

Remarks

This parameterized manipulator sets the stream's fill character. The default is a space. This setting remains in effect until the next change.

setiosflags

SMANIP(long) setiosflags(long *lFlags* **);**

#include <iomanip.h>

Parameter

lFlags

Format flag bit values. See the "flags member function" for a list of format flags. To combine these flags, use the OR (|) operator.

Remarks

This parameterized manipulator sets only the specified format flags. This setting remains in effect until the next change.

setprecision

SMANIP(int) setprecision(int np);

#include <iomanip.h>

Parameter

np

An integer that indicates the number of significant digits or significant decimal digits to be used for floating-point display.

Remarks

This parameterized manipulator sets the stream's internal floating-point precision variable to *np*. The default precision is six digits. If the display format is scientific or fixed, then the precision indicates the number of digits after the decimal point. If the format is automatic (neither floating point nor fixed), then the precision indicates the total number of significant digits. This setting remains in effect until the next change.

setw

SMANIP(int) setw(int *nw* **);**

#include <iomanip.h>

Parameter

nw

The field width in characters.

Remarks

This parameterized manipulator sets the stream's internal field width parameter. See the "width member function" for more information. This setting remains in effect only for the next insertion.

class iostream

#include <iostream.h>

The **iostream** class provides the basic capability for sequential and random-access I/O. It inherits functionality from the **istream** and **ostream** classes.

The **iostream** class works in conjunction with classes derived from **streambuf** (for example, **filebuf**). In fact, most of the **iostream** "personality" comes from its attached **streambuf** class. You can use **iostream** objects for sequential disk I/O if you first construct an appropriate **filebuf** object. More often, you will use objects of classes **fstream** and **strstream**.

Derivation

For derivation suggestions, see the **istream** and **ostream** classes.

Public Members

iostream
   Constructs an **iostream** object that is attached to an existing **streambuf** object.

~iostream
   Destroys an **iostream** object.

Protected Members

iostream
   Acts as a **void**-argument **iostream** constructor.

See Also

istream, **ostream**, **fstream**, **strstream**, **stdiostream**

Member Functions

iostream::iostream

Public →

iostream(streambuf* *psb* **);**

END Public

Protected →

iostream( );

END Protected

Parameter

psb

A pointer to an existing **streambuf** object (or an object of a derived class).

Remarks

Constructs an object of type **iostream**.

See Also

ios::init

iostream::~iostream

virtual ~iostream();

Remarks

Virtual destructor for the **iostream** class.

class Iostream_init

#include <iostream.h>

The **Iostream_init** class is a static class that initializes the predefined stream objects **cin, cout, cerr**, and **clog**. A single object of this class is constructed "invisibly" in response to any reference to the predefined objects. The class is documented for completeness only. You will not normally construct objects of this class.

Public Members

Iostream_init
   A constructor that initializes **cin, cout, cerr**, and **clog**.

~Iostream_init
   The destructor for the **Iostream_init** class.

Member Functions

Iostream_init::Iostream_init

Iostream_init();

Remarks

Iostream_init constructor that initializes **cin, cout, cerr**, and **clog**. For internal use only.

Iostream_init::~Iostream_init

~Iostream_init();

Remarks

Iostream_init destructor. For internal use only.

class istream

#include <iostream.h>

The **istream** class provides the basic capability for sequential and random-access input. An **istream** object has a **streambuf**-derived object attached, and the two classes work together; the **istream** class does the formatting, and the **streambuf** class does the low-level buffered input.

You can use **istream** objects for sequential disk input if you first construct an appropriate **filebuf** object. More often, you will use the predefined stream object **cin** (which is actually an object of class **istream_withassign**), or you will use objects of classes **ifstream** (disk file streams) and **istrstream** (string streams).

Derivation

It is not always necessary to derive from **istream** to add functionality to a stream; consider deriving from **streambuf** instead, as illustrated in "Deriving Your Own Stream Classes," earlier in this book. The **ifstream** and **istrstream** classes are examples of **istream**-derived classes that construct member objects of predetermined derived **streambuf** classes. You can add manipulators without deriving a new class.

If you add new extraction operators for a derived **istream** class, then the rules of C++ dictate that you must reimplement all the base class extraction operators. See the "Derivation" section of class **ostream** for an efficient reimplementation technique.

Construction/Destruction — Public Members

istream
> Constructs an **istream** object attached to an existing object of a **streambuf**-derived class.

~istream
> Destroys an **istream** object.

Prefix/Suffix Functions — Public Members

ipfx
> Check for error conditions prior to extraction operations (input prefix function).

isfx
> Called after extraction operations (input suffix function).

Input Functions — Public Members

get
> Extracts characters from the stream up to, but not including, delimiters.

getline
> Extracts characters from the stream (extracts and discards delimiters).

read
> Extracts data from the stream.

ignore
> Extracts and discards characters.

peek
> Returns a character without extracting it from the stream.

gcount
> Counts the characters extracted in the last unformatted operation.

eatwhite
> Extracts leading white space.

Other Functions — Public Members

putback
> Puts characters back to the stream.

sync
> Synchronizes the stream buffer with the external source of characters.

seekg
> Changes the stream's get pointer.

tellg
> Gets the value of the stream's get pointer.

Operators — Public Members

operator >>
> Extraction operator for various types.

Protected Members

istream
> Constructs an **istream** object.

Manipulators

ws
> Extracts leading white space.

See Also

streambuf, ifstream, istrstream, istream_withassign

Member Functions

istream::eatwhite

void eatwhite();

Remarks

Extracts white space from the stream by advancing the get pointer past spaces and tabs.

See Also

istream ws manipulator

istream::gcount

int gcount() const;

Remarks

Returns the number of characters extracted by the last unformatted input function. Formatted extraction operators may call unformatted input functions and thus reset this number.

See Also

istream::get, istream::getline, istream::ignore, istream::read

istream::get

int get(); &
istream& get(char* *pch*, **int** *nCount*, **char** *delim* = '\n');
istream& get(unsigned char* *puch*, **int** *nCount*, **char** *delim* = '\n');
istream& get(signed char* *psch*, **int** *nCount*, **char** *delim* = '\n');
istream& get(char& *rch*);
istream& get(unsigned char& *ruch*);
istream& get(signed char& *rsch*);
istream& get(streambuf& *rsb*, **char** *delim* = '\n');

Parameters

pch, puch, psch
    A pointer to a character array.

nCount
    The maximum number of characters to store, including the terminating **NULL**.

delim
> The delimiter character (defaults to newline).

rch, ruch, rsch
> A reference to a character.

rsb
> A reference to an object of a **streambuf**-derived class.

Remarks

These functions extract data from an input stream as follows:

Variation	Description
get();	Extracts a single character from the stream and returns it.
get(char*, int, char);	Extracts characters from the stream until either *delim* is found, the limit *nCount* is reached, or the end of file is reached. The characters are stored in the array followed by a null terminator.
get(char&);	Extracts a single character from the stream and stores it as specified by the reference argument.
get(streambuf&, char);	Gets characters from the stream and stores them in a **streambuf** object until the delimiter is found or the end of the file is reached. The **ios::failbit** flag is set if the **streambuf** output operation fails.

In all cases, the delimiter is neither extracted from the stream nor returned by the function. The **getline** function, in contrast, extracts but does not store the delimiter.

See Also

istream::getline, istream::read, istream::ignore, istream::gcount

istream::getline

istream& getline(char* *pch*, **int** *nCount*, **char** *delim* = '\n');
istream& getline(unsigned char* *puch*, **int** *nCount*, **char** *delim* = '\n');
istream& getline(signed char* *psch*, **int** *nCount*, **char** *delim* = '\n');

Parameters

pch, puch, psch
> A pointer to a character array.

nCount
> The maximum number of characters to store, including the terminating **NULL**.

delim
> The delimiter character (defaults to newline).

Remarks

Extracts characters from the stream until either the delimiter *delim* is found, the limit *nCount*–1 is reached, or end of file is reached. The characters are stored in the specified array followed by a null terminator. If the delimiter is found, it is extracted but not stored.

The **get** function, in contrast, neither extracts nor stores the delimiter.

See Also

istream::get, istream::read

istream::ignore

istream& ignore(int *nCount* **= 1, int** *delim* **= EOF);**

Parameters

nCount

> The maximum number of characters to extract.

delim

> The delimiter character (defaults to **EOF**).

Remarks

Extracts and discards up to *nCount* characters. Extraction stops if the delimiter *delim* is extracted or the end of file is reached. If *delim* = **EOF** (the default), then only the end of file condition causes termination. The delimiter character is extracted.

istream::ipfx

int ipfx(int *need* **= 0);**

Return Value

A nonzero return value if the operation was successful; 0 if the stream's error state is nonzero, in which case the function does nothing.

Parameter

need

> Zero if called from formatted input functions; otherwise the minimum number of characters needed.

Remarks

This input prefix function is called by input functions prior to extracting data from the stream. Formatted input functions call **ipfx(0)**, while unformatted input functions usually call **ipfx(1)**.

Any **ios** object tied to this stream is flushed if *need* = 0 or if there are fewer than *need* characters in the input buffer. Also, **ipfx** extracts leading white space if **ios::skipws** is set.

See Also

istream::isfx

istream::isfx

void isfx();

Remarks

This input suffix function is called at the end of every extraction operation.

istream::istream

Public →

istream(streambuf* *psb*);

END Public

Protected →

istream( );

END Protected

Parameter

psb
    A pointer to an existing object of a **streambuf**-derived class.

Remarks

Constructs an object of type **istream**.

See Also

ios::init

istream::~istream

virtual ~istream();

Remarks

Virtual destructor for the **istream** class.

istream::peek

int peek();

Return Value

Returns the next character without extracting it from the stream. Returns **EOF** if the stream is at end of file or if the **ipfx** function indicates an error.

istream::putback

istream& putback(char *ch* **);**

Parameter

ch
> The character to put back; must be the character previously extracted.

Remarks

Puts a character back into the input stream. The **putback** function may fail and set the error state. If *ch* does not match the character that was previously extracted, the result is undefined.

istream::read

istream& read(char* *pch*, **int** *nCount* **);**
istream& read(unsigned char* *puch*, **int** *nCount* **);**
istream& read(signed char* *psch*, **int** *nCount* **);**

Parameters

pch, puch, psch
> A pointer to a character array.

nCount
> The maximum number of characters to read.

Remarks

Extracts bytes from the stream until the limit *nCount* is reached or until the end of file is reached. The **read** function is useful for binary stream input.

See Also

istream::get, istream::getline, istream::gcount, istream::ignore

istream::seekg

istream& seekg(streampos *pos* **);**
istream& seekg(streamoff *off*, **ios::seek_dir** *dir* **);**

Parameters

pos

The new position value; **streampos** is a **typedef** equivalent to **long**.

off

The new offset value; **streamoff** is a **typedef** equivalent to **long**.

dir

The seek direction. Must be one of the following enumerators:

- **ios::beg** Seek from the beginning of the stream.
- **ios::cur** Seek from the current position in the stream.
- **ios::end** Seek from the end of the stream.

Remarks

Changes the get pointer for the stream. Not all derived classes of **istream** need support positioning; it is most often used with file-based streams.

See Also

istream::tellg, ostream::seekp, ostream::tellp

istream::sync

int sync();

Synchronizes the stream's internal buffer with the external source of characters.

Return Value

EOF to indicate errors.

Remarks

Synchronizes the stream's internal buffer with the external source of characters. This function calls the virtual **streambuf::sync** function so you can customize its implementation by deriving a new class from **streambuf**.

See Also

streambuf::sync

istream::tellg

streampos tellg();

Gets the value for the stream's **get** pointer.

Return Value

A **streampos** type, corresponding to a **long**.

See Also

istream::seekg, ostream::tellp, ostream::seekp

Operators

istream::operator >>

istream& operator >>(char* *psz* **);**
istream& operator >>(unsigned char* *pusz* **);**
istream& operator >>(signed char* *pssz* **);**
istream& operator >>(char& *rch* **);**
istream& operator >>(unsigned char& *ruch* **);**
istream& operator >>(signed char& *rsch* **);**
istream& operator >>(short& *s* **);**
istream& operator >>(unsigned short& *us* **);**
istream& operator >>(int& *n* **);**
istream& operator >>(unsigned int& *un* **);**
istream& operator >>(long& *l* **);**
istream& operator >>(unsigned long& *ul* **);**
istream& operator >>(float& *f* **);**
istream& operator >>(double& *d* **);**
istream& operator >>(long double& *ld* **);** (16-bit only)
istream& operator >>(streambuf* *psb* **);**
istream& operator >>(istream& (* *fcn* **)(istream&));**
istream& operator >>(ios& (* *fcn* **)(ios&));**

Remarks

These overloaded operators extract their argument from the stream. With the last two variations, you can use manipulators that are defined for both **istream** and **ios**.

Manipulators

istream& ws

ws

Remarks

Extracts leading white space from the stream by calling the **eatwhite** function.

See Also

istream::eatwhite

class istream_withassign

#include <iostream.h>

The **istream_withassign** class is a variant of **istream** that allows object assignment.
The predefined object cin is an object of this class and thus may be reassigned at run time
to a different **istream** object. For example, a program that normally expects input from
stdin could be temporarily directed to accept its input from a disk file.

Predefined Objects

The **cin** object is a predefined object of class ostream_withassign. It is connected to **stdin**
(standard input, file descriptor 0).

The objects **cin, cerr**, and **clog** are tied to **cout** so that use of any of these may cause **cout**
to be flushed.

Construction/Destruction — Public Members

istream_withassign
    Constructs an **istream_withassign** object.

~istream_withassign
    Destroys an istream_withassign object.

Operators — Public Members

operator =
    Indicates an assignment operator.

See Also

ostream_withassign

Member Functions

istream_withassign::istream_withassign

istream_withassign(streambuf* *psb* **);**
istream_withassign();

Parameter

psb
    A pointer to an existing object of a **streambuf**-derived class.

Remarks

The first constructor creates a ready-to-use object of type **istream_withassign**, complete
with attached **streambuf** object.

The second constructor creates an object but does not initialize it. You must subsequently
use the second variation of the **istream_withassign** assignment operator to attach the

streambuf object, or use the first variation to initialize this object to match the specified **istream** object.

See Also

istream_withassign::operator =

istream_withassign::~istream_withassign

~istream_withassign();

Remarks

Destructor for the **istream_withassign** class.

Operators

istream_withassign::operator =

istream& operator =(const istream& *ris* **);**
istream& operator =(streambuf* *psb* **);**

Remarks

The first overloaded assignment operator assigns the specified **istream** object to this **istream_withassign** object.

The second operator attaches a **streambuf** object to an existing **istream_withassign** object, and it initializes the state of the **istream_withassign** object. This operator is often used in conjunction with the **void**-argument constructor.

Example

```
char buffer[100];
class xistream; // A special-purpose class derived from istream
extern xistream xin; // An xistream object constructed elsewhere

cin = xin; // cin is reassigned to xin
cin >> buffer; // xin used instead of cin
```

Example

```
char buffer[100];
extern filedesc fd; // A file descriptor for an open file
filebuf fb( fd ); // Construct a filebuf attached to fd

cin = &fb;     // fb associated with cin
cin >> buffer; // cin now gets its intput from the fb file
```

See Also

istream_withassign::istream_withassign

class istrstream

#include <strstrea.h>

The **istrstream** class supports input streams that have character arrays as a source. You must allocate a character array before constructing an **istrstream** object. You can use **istream** operators and functions on this character data. A get pointer, working in the attached **strstreambuf** class, advances as you extract fields from the stream's array. Use **istream::seekg** to go backwards. If the get pointer reaches the end of the string (and sets the **ios::eof** flag), you must call **clear** before **seekg**.

Construction/Destruction — Public Members

istrstream
> Constructs an **istrstream** object.

~istrstream
> Destroys an **istrstream** object.

Other Functions — Public Members

rdbuf
> Returns a pointer to the stream's associated **strstreambuf** object.

str
> Returns a character array pointer to the string stream's contents.

See Also

strstreambuf, streambuf, strstream, ostrstream

Member Functions

istrstream::istrstream

istrstream(char* *psz* **);**
istrstream(char* *pch***, int** *nLength* **);**

Parameters

psz
> A null-terminated character array (string).

pch
> A character array that is not necessarily null terminated.

nLength
> Size (in characters) of *pch*. If 0, then *pch* is assumed to point to a null-terminated array; if less than 0, then the array length is assumed to be unlimited.

Remarks

The first constructor uses the specified *psz* buffer to make an **istrstream** object with length corresponding to the string length.

The second constructor makes an **istrstream** object out of the first *nLength* characters of the *pch* buffer.

Both constructors automatically construct a **strstreambuf** object that manages the specified character buffer.

istrstream::~istrstream

~istrstream();

Remarks

Destroys an **istrstream** object and its associated **strstreambuf** object. The character buffer is not released because it was allocated by the user prior to **istrstream** construction.

istrstream::rdbuf

strstreambuf* rdbuf() const;

Return Value

Returns a pointer to the **strstreambuf** buffer object that is associated with this stream. Note that this is not the character buffer itself; the **strstreambuf** object contains a pointer to the character area.

See Also

istrstream::str

istrstream::str

char* str();

Return Value

Returns a pointer to the string stream's character array. This pointer corresponds to the array used to construct the **istrstream** object.

See Also

istrstream::istrstream

class ofstream

#include <fstream.h>

The **ofstream** class is an **ostream** derivative specialized for disk file output. All of its constructors automatically create and associate a **filebuf** buffer object.

The **filebuf** class documentation describes the get and put areas and their associated pointers. Only the put area and the put pointer are active for the **ofstream** class.

Construction/Destruction — Public Members

ofstream
> Constructs an **ofstream** object.

~ofstream
> Destroys an **ofstream** object.

Operations — Public Members

open
> Opens a file and attaches it to the **filebuf** object and thus to the stream.

close
> Flushes any waiting output and closes the stream's file.

setbuf
> Associates the specified reserve area to the stream's **filebuf** object.

setmode
> Sets the stream's mode to binary or text.

attach
> Attaches the stream (through the **filebuf** object) to an open file.

Status/Information — Public Members

rdbuf
> Gets the stream's **filebuf** object.

fd
> Returns the file descriptor associated with the stream.

is_open
> Tests whether the stream's file is open.

See Also

filebuf, streambuf, ifstream, fstream

Member Functions

ofstream::attach

void attach(filedesc *fd* **);**

Parameter

fd

> A file descriptor as returned by a call to the run-time function **_open** or **_sopen**; **filedesc** is a **typedef** equivalent to **int**.

Remarks

Attaches this stream to the open file specified by *fd*. The function fails when the stream is already attached to a file. In that case, the function sets **ios::failbit** in the stream's error state.

See Also

filebuf::attach, ofstream::fd

ofstream::close

void close();

Remarks

Calls the close member function for the associated **filebuf** object. This function, in turn, flushes any waiting output, closes the file, and disconnects the file from the **filebuf** object. The **filebuf** object is not destroyed.

The stream's error state is cleared unless the call to **filebuf::close** fails.

See Also

filebuf::close, ofstream::open, ofstream::is_open

ofstream::fd

filedesc fd() const;

Return Value

Returns the file descriptor associated with the stream. **filedesc** is a **typedef** equivalent to **int**. Its value is supplied by the underlying file system.

See Also

filebuf::fd, ofstream::attach

ofstream::is_open

int is_open() const;

Return Value

Returns a nonzero value if this stream is attached to an open disk file identified by a file descriptor; otherwise 0.

See Also

filebuf::is_open, ofstream::open, ofstream::close

ofstream::ofstream

ofstream();
ofstream(const char* *szName*, **int** *nMode* = **ios::out, int** *nProt* = **filebuf::openprot);**
ofstream(filedesc *fd* **);**
ofstream(filedesc *fd*, **char*** *pch*, **int** *nLength* **);**

Parameters

szName
    The name of the file to be opened during construction.

nMode
    An integer that contains mode bits defined as **ios** enumerators that can be combined with the bitwise OR (|) operator. The *nMode* parameter must have one of the following values:

- **ios::app**   The function performs a seek to the end of file. When new bytes are written to the file, they are always appended to the end, even if the position is moved with the **ostream::seekp** function.

- **ios::ate**   The function performs a seek to the end of file. When the first new byte is written to the file, it is appended to the end, but when subsequent bytes are written, they are written to the current position.

- **ios::in**   If this mode is specified, then the original file (if it exists) will not be truncated.

- **ios::out**   The file is opened for output (implied for all **ofstream** objects).

- **ios::trunc**   If the file already exists, its contents are discarded. This mode is implied if **ios::out** is specified and **ios::ate, ios::app**, and **ios:in** are not specified.

- **ios::nocreate**   If the file does not already exist, the function fails.

- **ios::noreplace**   If the file already exists, the function fails.

- **ios::binary**   Opens the file in binary mode (the default is text mode).

nProt

The file protection specification; defaults to the static integer **filebuf::openprot** that is equivalent to **filebuf::sh_compat.** The possible *nProt* values are:

- **filebuf::sh_compat**   Compatibility share mode.

- **filebuf::sh_none**   Exclusive mode; no sharing.

- **filebuf::sh_read**   Read sharing allowed.

- **filebuf::sh_write**   Write sharing allowed.

To combine the **filebuf::sh_read** and **filebuf::sh_write** modes, use the logical OR (‖) operator.

fd

A file descriptor as returned by a call to the run-time function **_open or _sopen;** **filedesc** is a **typedef** equivalent to **int.**

pch

Pointer to a previously allocated reserve area of length *nLength*. A **NULL** value (or *nLength* = 0) indicates that the stream will be unbuffered.

nLength

The length (in bytes) of the reserve area (0 = unbuffered).

Remarks

The four **ofstream** constructors are:

Constructor	Description
ofstream()	Constructs an **ofstream** object without opening a file.
ofstream(const char*, int, int)	Contructs an **ofstream** object, opening the specified file.
ofstream(filedesc)	Constructs an **ofstream** object that is attached to an open file.
ofstream(filedesc, char*, int)	Constructs an **ofstream** object that is associated with a **filebuf** object. The **filebuf** object is attached to an open file and to a specified reserve area.

All **ofstream** constructors construct a **filebuf** object. The first three use an internally allocated reserve area, but the fourth uses a user-allocated area. The user-allocated area is not automatically released during destruction.

ofstream::~ofstream

~ofstream();

Remarks

Flushes the buffer, then destroys an **ofstream** object along with its associated **filebuf** object. The file is closed only if was opened by the constructor or by the **open** member function.

The **filebuf** destructor releases the reserve buffer only if it was internally allocated.

ofstream::open

void open(const char* *szName***, int** *nMode* **= ios::out, int** *nProt* **= filebuf::openprot);**

Parameters

szName
    The name of the file to be opened during construction.

nMode
    An integer containing mode bits defined as **ios** enumerators that can be combined with the OR (|) operator. See the "**ofstream** constructor" for a list of the enumerators. The **ios::out** mode is implied.

nProt
    The file protection specification; defaults to the static integer **filebuf::openprot**. See the "**ofstream** constructor" for a list of the other allowed values.

Remarks

Opens a disk file and attaches it to the stream's **filebuf** object. If the **filebuf** object is already attached to an open file, or if a **filebuf** call fails, the **ios::failbit** is set. If the file is not found, the **ios::failbit** is set only if the **ios::nocreate** mode was used.

See Also

filebuf::open, ofstream::ofstream, ofstream::close, ofstream::is_open

ofstream::rdbuf

filebuf* rdbuf() const;

Return Value

Returns a pointer to the **filebuf** buffer object that is associated with this stream. (Note that this is not the character buffer; the **filebuf** object contains a pointer to the character area.)

Example

```
extern ofstream ofs;
int fd = ofs.rdbuf()->fd(); // Get the file descriptor for ofs
```

ofstream::setbuf

streambuf* setbuf(char* *pch***, int** *nLength* **);**

Attaches the specified reserve area to the stream's **filebuf** object.

Return Value

If the file is open and a buffer has already been allocated, the function returns **NULL**; otherwise it returns a pointer to the **filebuf** cast as a **streambuf**. The reserve area will not be released by the destructor.

Parameters

pch
> A pointer to a previously allocated reserve area of length *nLength*. A **NULL** value indicates an unbuffered stream.

nLength
> The length (in bytes) of the reserve area. A length of 0 indicates an unbuffered stream.

ofstream::setmode

int setmode(int *nMode* **= filebuf::text);**

Return Value

The previous mode; –1 if the parameter is invalid, the file is not open, or the mode cannot be changed.

Parameter

nMode
> An integer that must be one of the following static **filebuf** constants:
>
> - **filebuf::text** Text mode (newline characters translated to and from carriage return – linefeed pairs).
> - **filebuf::binary** Binary mode (no translation).

Remarks

This function sets the binary/text mode of the stream's **filebuf** object. It may be called only after the file is opened.

See Also

ios binary manipulator, ios text manipulator

class ostream

#include <iostream.h>

The **ostream** class provides the basic capability for sequential and random-access output. An **ostream** object has a **streambuf**-derived object attached, and the two classes work together; the **ostream** class does the formatting, and the **streambuf** class does the low-level buffered output.

You can use **ostream** objects for sequential disk output if you first construct an appropriate **filebuf** object. (The **filebuf** class is derived from **streambuf**.) More often, you will use the predefined stream objects **cout, cerr,** and **clog** (actually objects of class **ostream_withassign**), or you will use objects of classes **ofstream** (disk file streams) and **ostrstream** (string streams).

All of the **ostream** member functions write unformatted data; formatted output is handled by the insertion operators.

Derivation

It is not always necessary to derive from **ostream** to add functionality to a stream; consider deriving from **streambuf** instead, as illustrated in "Deriving Your Own Stream Classes," earlier in this book. The **ofstream** and **ostrstream** classes are examples of **ostream**-derived classes that construct member objects of predetermined derived **streambuf** classes. You can add manipulators without deriving a new class.

If you add new insertion operators for a derived **ostream** class, then the rules of C++ dictate that you must reimplement all the base class insertion operators. If, however, you reimplement the operators through inline equivalence, no extra code will be generated.

Construction/Destruction — Public Members

ostream
> Constructs an **ostream** object that is attached to an existing **streambuf** object.

~ostream
> Destroys an **ostream** object.

Prefix/Suffix Functions — Public Members

opfx
> Output prefix function, called prior to insertion operations to check for error conditions, and so forth.

osfx
> Output suffix function, called after insertion operations; flushes the stream's buffer if it is unit buffered.

Unformatted Output — Public Members

put
> Inserts a single byte into the stream.

write
> Inserts a series of bytes into the stream.

Other Functions — Public Members

flush
> Flushes the buffer associated with this stream.

seekp
> Changes the stream's put pointer.

tellp
> Gets the value of the stream's put pointer.

Operators — Public Members

operator <<
> Insertion operator for various types.

Manipulators

endl
> Inserts a newline sequence and flushes the buffer.

ends
> Inserts a null character to terminate a string.

flush
> Flushes the stream's buffer.

See Also

streambuf, ofstream, ostrstream, cout, cerr, clog

Example

```
class xstream : public ostream
{
public:
    // Constructors, etc.
    // ........
    inline xstream& operator << ( char ch ) // insertion for char
    {
        return (xstream&)ostream::operator << ( ch );
    }
    // ........
    // Insertions for other types
};
```

Member Functions

ostream::flush

ostream& flush();

Remarks

Flushes the buffer associated with this stream. The **flush** function calls the **sync** function of the associated **streambuf**.

See Also

ostream flush manipulator, streambuf::sync

ostream::opfx

int opfx();

Return Value

If the **ostream** object's error state is not 0, **opfx** returns 0 immediately; otherwise it returns a nonzero value.

Remarks

This output prefix function is called before every insertion operation. If another **ostream** object is tied to this stream, the **opfx** function flushes that stream.

ostream::osfx

void osfx();

Remarks

This output suffix function is called after every insertion operation. It flushes the **ostream** object if **ios::unitbuf** is set, or **stdout** and **stderr** if **ios::stdio** is set.

ostream::ostream

Public →

ostream(streambuf* *psb*);

END Public

Protected →

ostream( );

END Protected

Parameter

psb

 A pointer to an existing object of a **streambuf**-derived class.

Remarks

Constructs an object of type **ostream**.

See Also

ios::init

ostream::~ostream

virtual ~ostream();

Remarks

Destroys an **ostream** object. The output buffer is flushed as appropriate. The attached **streambuf** object is destroyed only if it was allocated internally within the **ostream** constructor.

ostream::put

ostream& put(char *ch* **);**

Parameter

ch

 The character to insert.

Remarks

This function inserts a single character into the output stream.

ostream::seekp

ostream& seekp(streampos *pos* **);**
ostream& seekp(streamoff *off***, ios::seek_dir** *dir* **);**

Parameters

pos

 The new position value; **streampos** is a **typedef** equivalent to **long**.

off

 The new offset value; **streamoff** is a **typedef** equivalent to **long**.

dir
> The seek direction specified by the enumerated type **ios::seek_dir**, with values including:
>
> - **ios::beg**   Seek from the beginning of the stream.
> - **ios::cur**   Seek from the current position in the stream.
> - **ios::end**   Seek from the end of the stream.

Remarks

Changes the position value for the stream. Not all derived classes of **ostream** need support positioning. For file streams, the position is the byte offset from the beginning of the file; for string streams, it is the byte offset from the beginning of the string.

See Also

ostream::tellp, istream::seekg, istream::tellg

ostream::tellp

streampos tellp();

Return Value

A **streampos** type that corresponds to a **long**.

Remarks

Gets the position value for the stream. Not all derived classes of **ostream** need support positioning. For file streams, the position is the byte offset from the beginning of the file; for string streams, it is the byte offset from the beginning of the string. Gets the value for the stream's put pointer.

See Also

ostream::seekp, istream::tellg, istream::seekg

ostream::write

ostream& write(const char* *pch***, int** *nCount* **);**
ostream& write(const unsigned char* *puch***, int** *nCount* **);**
ostream& write(const signed char* *psch***, int** *nCount* **);**

Parameters

pch, puch, psch
> A pointer to a character array.

nCount
> The number of characters to be written.

Remarks

Inserts a specified number of bytes from a buffer into the stream. If the underlying file was opened in text mode, additional carriage return characters may be inserted. The **write** function is useful for binary stream output.

Operators

ostream::operator <<

ostream& operator <<(char *ch* **);**
ostream& operator <<(unsigned char *uch* **);**
ostream& operator <<(signed char *sch* **);**
ostream& operator <<(const char* *psz* **);**
ostream& operator <<(const unsigned char* *pusz* **);**
ostream& operator <<(const signed char* *pssz* **);**
ostream& operator <<(short *s* **);**
ostream& operator <<(unsigned short *us* **);**
ostream& operator <<(int *n* **);**
ostream& operator <<(unsigned int *un* **);**
ostream& operator <<(long *l* **);**
ostream& operator <<(unsigned long *ul* **);**
ostream& operator <<(float *f* **);**
ostream& operator <<(double *d* **);**
ostream& operator <<(long double *ld* **);** (16-bit only)
ostream& operator <<(const void* *pv* **);**
ostream& operator <<(streambuf* *psb* **);**
ostream& operator <<(ostream& (*fcn*)(ostream&) **);**
ostream& operator <<(ios& (*fcn*)(ios&) **);**

Remarks

These overloaded operators insert their argument into the stream. With the last two variations, you can use manipulators that are defined for both **ostream** and **ios**.

Manipulators

ostream& endl

endl

Remarks

This manipulator, when inserted into an output stream, inserts a newline character and then flushes the buffer.

ostream& ends

ends

Remarks

This manipulator, when inserted into an output stream, inserts a null-terminator character. It is particularly useful for **ostrstream** objects.

ostream& flush

flush

Remarks

This manipulator, when inserted into an output stream, flushes the output buffer by calling the **streambuf::sync** member function.

See Also

ostream::flush, streambuf::sync

class ostream_withassign

#include <iostream.h>

The **ostream_withassign** class is a variant of **ostream** that allows object assignment. The predefined objects **cout**, **cerr**, and **clog** are objects of this class and thus may be reassigned at run time to a different **ostream** object. For example, a program that normally sends output to **stdout** could be temporarily directed to send its output to a disk file.

Predefined Objects

The three predefined objects of class **ostream_withassign** are connected as follows:

cout
> Standard output (file descriptor 1).

cerr
> Unit buffered standard error (file descriptor 2).

clog
> Fully buffered standard error (file descriptor 2).

Unit buffering, as used by **cerr**, means that characters are flushed after each insertion operation. The objects **cin**, **cerr**, and **clog** are tied to **cout** so that use of any of these will cause **cout** to be flushed.

Construction/Destruction — Public Members

ostream_withassign
> Constructs an **ostream_withassign** object.

~ostream_withassign
> Destroys an **ostream_withassign** object.

Operators — Public Members

operator =
> Assignment operator.

See Also

istream_withassign

Member Functions

ostream_withassign::ostream_withassign

ostream_withassign(streambuf* *psb* **);**
ostream_withassign();

Parameter

psb

A pointer to an existing object of a **streambuf**-derived class.

Remarks

The first constructor makes a ready-to-use object of type **ostream_withassign**, with an attached **streambuf** object.

The second constructor makes an object but does not initialize it. You must subsequently use the **streambuf** assignment operator to attach the **streambuf** object, or use the **ostream** assignment operator to initialize this object to match the specified object.

See Also

ostream_withassign::operator =

ostream_withassign::~ostream_withassign

~ostream_withassign();

Remarks

Destructor for the **ostream_withassign** class.

Operators

ostream_withassign::operator =

ostream& operator =(const ostream&_os);
ostream& operator =(streambuf*_sp);

Remarks

The first overloaded assignment operator assigns the specified **ostream** object to this **ostream_withassign** object.

The second operator attaches a **streambuf** object to an existing **ostream_withassign** object, and initializes the state of the **ostream_withassign** object. This operator is often used in conjunction with the **void**-argument constructor.

Example

```
filebuf fb( "test.dat" );  // Filebuf object attached to "test.dat"
cout = &fb;         // fb associated with cout
cout << "testing"; // Message goes to "test.dat" instead of stdout
```

See Also

ostream_withassign::ostream_withassign, cout

class ostrstream

#include <strstrea.h>

The **ostrstream** class supports output streams that have character arrays as a destination. You can allocate a character array prior to construction, or the constructor can internally allocate an expandable array. You can then use all the **ostream** operators and functions to fill the array.

Be aware that there is a put pointer working behind the scenes in the attached **strstreambuf** class. This pointer advances as you insert fields into the stream's array. The only way you can make it go backward is to use the **ostream::seekp** function. If the put pointer reaches the end of user-allocated memory (and sets the **ios::eof** flag), you must call **clear** before **seekp**.

Construction/Destruction — Public Members

ostrstream
> Constructs an **ostrstream** object.

~ostrstream
> Destroys an **ostrstream** object.

Other Functions — Public Members

pcount
> Returns the number of bytes that have been stored in the stream's buffer.

rdbuf
> Returns a pointer to the stream's associated **strstreambuf** object.

str
> Returns a character array pointer to the string stream's contents and freezes the array.

See Also

strstreambuf, streambuf, strstream, istrstream

Member Functions

ostrstream::ostrstream

ostrstream();

ostrstream(char* *pch*, **int** *nLength*, **int** *nMode* **= ios::out);**

Parameters

pch
> A character array that is large enough to accommodate future output stream activity.

nLength

> The size (in characters) of *pch*. If 0, then *pch* is assumed to point to a null-terminated array and **strlen(** *pch* **)** is used as the length; if less than 0, the array is assumed to have infinite length.

nMode

> The stream-creation mode, which must be one of the following enumerators as defined in class **ios**:

- **ios::out**   Default; storing begins at *pch*.

- **ios::ate**   The *pch* parameter is assumed to be a null-terminated array; storing begins at the NULL character.

- **ios::app**   Same as **ios::ate.**

Remarks

The first constructor makes an ostrstream object that uses an internal, dynamic buffer.

The second constructor makes an ostrstream object out of the first nLength characters of the pch buffer. The stream will not accept characters once the length reaches nLength.

ostrstream::~ostrstream

~ostrstream();

Remarks

Destroys an **ostrstream** object and its associated **strstreambuf** object, thus releasing all internally allocated memory. If you used the **void**-argument constructor, the internally allocated character buffer is released; otherwise, you must release it.

An internally allocated character buffer will not be released if it was previously frozen by an **str** or **strstreambuf::freeze** function call.

See Also

ostrstream::str, strstreambuf::freeze

ostrstream::pcount

int pcount() const;

Return Value

Returns the number of bytes stored in the buffer. This information is especially useful when you have stored binary data in the object.

ostrstream::rdbuf

strstreambuf* rdbuf() const;

Return Value

Returns a pointer to the **strstreambuf** buffer object that is associated with this stream.
This is not the character buffer; the **strstreambuf** object contains a pointer to the
character area.

See Also

ostrstream::str

ostrstream::str

char* str();

Return Value

Returns a pointer to the internal character array. If the stream was built with the **void**-
argument constructor, **str** freezes the array. You must not send characters to a frozen
stream, and you are responsible for deleting the array. You can, however, subsequently
unfreeze the array by calling **rdbuf->freeze(0).**

If the stream was built with the constructor that specified the buffer, the pointer contains
the same address as the array used to construct the **ostrstream** object.

See Also

ostrstream::ostrstream, ostrstream::rdbuf, strstreambuf::freeze

100 iostream Library Reference

class stdiobuf

#include <stdiostr.h>

The run-time library supports three conceptual sets of I/O functions: iostreams (C++ only), standard I/O (the functions declared in STDIO.H), and low-level I/O (the functions declared in IO.H). The **stdiobuf** class is a derived class of **streambuf** that is specialized for buffering to and from the standard I/O system.

Because the standard I/O system does its own internal buffering, the extra buffering level provided by **stdiobuf** may reduce overall input/output efficiency. The **stdiobuf** class is useful when you need to mix iostream I/O with standard I/O (**printf** and so forth).

You can avoid use of the **stdiobuf** class if you use the **filebuf** class. You must also use the stream class's **ios::flags** member function to set the **ios::stdio** format flag value.

Construction/Destruction — Public Members

stdiobuf
> Constructs a **stdiobuf** object from a **FILE** pointer.

~stdiobuf
> Destroys a **stdiobuf** object.

Other Functions — Public Members

stdiofile
> Gets the file that is attached to the **stdiofile** object.

See Also

stdiostream, filebuf, strstreambuf, ios::flags

Member Functions

stdiobuf::stdiobuf

stdiobuf(FILE* *fp* **);**

Parameter

fp
> A standard I/O file pointer (can be obtained through an **fopen** or **_fsopen** call).

Remarks

Objects of class **stdiobuf** are constructed from open standard I/O files, including **stdin**, **stdout**, and **stderr**. The object is unbuffered by default.

stdiobuf::~stdiobuf

~stdiobuf();

Remarks

Destroys a **stdiobuf** object and, in the process, flushes the put area. The destructor does not close the attached file.

stdiobuf::stdiofile

FILE* stdiofile();

Remarks

Returns the standard I/O file pointer associated with a **stdiobuf** object.

class stdiostream

#include <stdiostr.h>

The **stdiostream** class makes I/O calls (through the **stdiobuf** class) to the standard I/O system, which does its own internal buffering. Calls to the functions declared in STDIO.H, such as **printf**, can be mixed with **stdiostream** I/O calls.

This class is included for compatibility with earlier stream libraries. You can avoid use of the **stdiostream** class if you use the **ostream** or **istream** class with an associated **filebuf** class. You must also use the stream class's **ios::flags** member function to set the **ios::stdio** format flag value.

The use of the **stdiobuf** class may reduce efficiency because it imposes an extra level of buffering. Do not use this feature unless you need to mix iostream library calls with standard I/O calls for the same file.

Construction/Destruction — Public Members

stdiostream
  Constructs a **stdiostream** object that is associated with a standard I/O **FILE** pointer.

~stdiostream
  Destroys a **stdiostream** object (virtual).

Other Functions — Public Members

rdbuf
  Gets the stream's **stdiobuf** object.

See Also

stdiobuf, ios::flags

Member Functions

stdiostream::rdbuf

stdiobuf* rdbuf() const;

Return Value

Returns a pointer to the **stdiobuf** buffer object that is associated with this stream. The **rdbuf** function is useful when you need to call **stdiobuf** member functions.

stdiostream::stdiostream

stdiostream(FILE* *fp* **);**

Parameter

fp

> A standard I/O file pointer (can be obtained through an **fopen** or **_fsopen** call). Could be **stdin**, **stdout**, or **stderr**.

Remarks

Objects of class **stdiostream** are constructed from open standard I/O files. An unbuffered **stdiobuf** object is automatically associated, but the standard I/O system provides its own buffering.

Example

```
stdiostream myStream( stdout );
```

stdiostream::~stdiostream

~stdiostream();

Remarks

This destructor destroys the **stdiobuf** object associated with this stream; however, the attached file is not closed.

class streambuf

#include <iostream.h>

All the iostream classes in the ios hierarchy depend on an attached **streambuf** class for the actual I/O processing. This class is an abstract class, but the iostream class library contains the following derived buffer classes for use with streams:

- **filebuf**   Buffered disk file I/O.

- **strstreambuf**   Stream data held entirely within an in-memory byte array.

- **stdiobuf**   Disk I/O with buffering done by the underlying standard I/O system.

All streambuf objects, when configured for buffered processing, maintain a fixed memory buffer, called a reserve area, that can be dynamically partitioned into a get area for input, and a put area for output. These areas may or may not overlap. With the protected member functions, you can access and manipulate a get pointer for character retrieval and a put pointer for character storage. The exact behavior of the buffers and pointers depends on the implementation of the derived class.

The capabilities of the iostream classes can be extended significantly through the derivation of new **streambuf** classes. The **ios** class tree supplies the programming interface and all formatting features, but the **streambuf** class does the real work. The **ios** classes call the **streambuf** public members, including a set of virtual functions.

The **streambuf** class provides a default implementation of certain virtual member functions. The "Default Implementation" section for each such function suggests function behavior for the derived class.

Character Input Functions — Public Members

in_avail
    Returns the number of characters in the get area.

sgetc
    Returns the character at the get pointer, but does not move the pointer.

snextc
    Advances the get pointer, then returns the next character.

sbumpc
    Returns the current character, and then advances the get pointer.

stossc
    Moves the get pointer forward one position, but does not return a character.

sputbackc
    Attempts to move the get pointer back one position.

sgetn
    Gets a sequence of characters from the streambuf object's buffer.

Character Output Functions — Public Members

out_waiting
> Returns the number of characters in the put area.

sputc
> Stores a character in the put area and advances the put pointer.

sputn
> Stores a sequence of characters in the **streambuf** object's buffer and advances the put pointer.

Construction/Destruction — Public Members

~streambuf
> Virtual destructor.

Diagnostic Functions — Public Members

dbp
> Prints buffer statistics and pointer values.

Virtual Functions — Public Members

sync
> Empties the get area and the put area.

setbuf
> Attempts to attach a reserve area to the **streambuf** object.

seekoff
> Seeks to a specified offset.

seekpos
> Seeks to a specified position.

overflow
> Empties the put area.

underflow
> Fills the get area if necessary.

pbackfail
> Augments the **sputbackc** function.

Construction/Destruction — Protected Members

streambuf
> Constructors for use in derived classes.

Other Protected Member Functions — Protected Members

base
> Returns a pointer to the start of the reserve area.

ebuf
> Returns a pointer to the end of the reserve area.

blen
> Returns the size of the reserve area.

pbase
> Returns a pointer to the start of the put area.

pptr
> Returns the put pointer.

epptr
> Returns a pointer to the end of the put area.

eback
> Returns the lower bound of the get area.

gptr
> Returns the get pointer.

egptr
> Returns a pointer to the end of the get area.

setp
> Sets all the put area pointers.

setg
> Sets all the get area pointers.

pbump
> Increments the put pointer.

gbump
> Increments the get pointer.

setb
> Sets up the reserve area.

unbuffered
> Tests or sets the **streambuf** buffer state variable.

allocate
> Allocates a buffer, if needed, by calling **doalloc**.

doallocate
> Allocates a reserve area (virtual function).

See Also

streambuf::doallocate, streambuf::unbuffered

Member Functions

streambuf::allocate

Protected →

int allocate();

END Protected

Return Value

Calls the virtual function **doallocate** to set up a reserve area. If a reserve area already exists or if the **streambuf** object is unbuffered, **allocate** returns 0. If the space allocation fails, **allocate** returns **EOF**.

See Also

streambuf::doallocate, streambuf::unbuffered

streambuf::base

Protected →

char* base() const;

END Protected

Return Value

Returns a pointer to the first byte of the reserve area. The reserve area consists of space between the pointers returned by **base** and **ebuf**.

See Also

streambuf::ebuf, streambuf::setb, streambuf::blen

streambuf::blen

Protected →

int blen() const;

END Protected

Return Value

Returns the size, in bytes, of the reserve area.

See Also

streambuf::base, streambuf::ebuf, streambuf::setb

streambuf::dbp

void dbp();

Remarks

Writes ASCII debugging information directly on **stdout**. Treat this function as part of the protected interface.

Example

```
STREAMBUF DEBUG INFO: this = 00E7:09DC
base()=00E7:0A0C, ebuf()=00E7:0C0C,  blen()=512
eback()=0000:0000, gptr()=0000:0000, egptr()=0000:0000
pbase()=00E7:0A0C, pptr()=00E7:0A22, epptr()=00E7:0C0C
```

streambuf::doallocate

Protected →

virtual int doallocate();

END Protected

Return Value

Called by **allocate** when space is needed. The **doallocate** function must allocate a reserve area, then call **setb** to attach the reserve area to the **streambuf** object. If the reserve area allocation fails, **doallocate** returns **EOF**.

Remarks

By default, this function attempts to allocate a reserve area using operator **new**.

See Also

streambuf::allocate, streambuf::setb

streambuf::eback

Protected →

char* eback() const;

END Protected

Return Value

Returns the lower bound of the get area. Space between the **eback** and **gptr** pointers is available for putting a character back into the stream.

See Also

streambuf::sputbackc, streambuf::gptr

streambuf::ebuf

Protected →

char* ebuf() const;

END Protected

Return Value

Returns a pointer to the byte after the last byte of the reserve area. The reserve area consists of space between the pointers returned by **base** and **ebuf**.

See Also

streambuf::base, streambuf::setb, streambuf::blen

streambuf::egptr

Protected →

char* egptr() const;

END Protected

Return Value

Returns a pointer to the byte after the last byte of the get area.

See Also

streambuf::setg, streambuf::eback, streambuf::gptr

streambuf::epptr

Protected →

char* epptr() const;

END Protected

Return Value

Returns a pointer to the byte after the last byte of the put area.

See Also

streambuf::setp, streambuf::pbase, streambuf::pptr

streambuf::gbump

Protected →

void gbump(int nCount);

END Protected

Parameter

Count

The number of bytes to increment the get pointer. May be positive or negative.

Remarks

Increments the get pointer. No bounds checks are made on the result.

See Also

streambuf::pbump

streambuf::gptr

Protected →

char* gptr() const;

END Protected

Return Value

Returns a pointer to the next character to be fetched from the **streambuf** buffer. This pointer is known as the get pointer.

See Also

streambuf::setg, streambuf::eback, streambuf::egptr

streambuf::in_avail

int in_avail() const;

Return Value

Returns the number of characters in the get area that are available for fetching. These characters are between the **gptr** and **egptr** pointers and may be fetched with a guarantee of no errors.

streambuf::out_waiting

int out_waiting() const;

Return Value

Returns the number of characters in the put area that have not been sent to the final output destination. These characters are between the **pbase** and **pptr** pointers.

streambuf::overflow

virtual int overflow(int *nCh* = EOF) = 0;

Return Value

EOF to indicate an error.

Parameter

nCh
    EOF or the character to output.

Remarks

The virtual **overflow** function, together with the **sync** and **underflow** functions, defines the characteristics of the **streambuf**-derived class. Each derived class might implement **overflow** differently, but the interface with the calling stream class is the same.

The **overflow** function is most frequently called by public **streambuf** functions like **sputc** and **sputn** when the put area is full, but other classes, including the stream classes, can call **overflow** anytime.

The function "consumes" the characters in the put area between the **pbase** and **pptr** pointers and then reinitializes the put area. The **overflow** function must also consume *nCh* (if *nCh* is not **EOF**), or it might choose to put that character in the new put area so that it will be consumed on the next call.

The definition of "consume" varies among derived classes. For example, the **filebuf** class writes its characters to a file, while the **strsteambuf** class keeps them in its buffer and (if the buffer is designated as dynamic) expands the buffer in response to a call to **overflow**. This expansion is achieved by freeing the old buffer and replacing it with a new, larger one. The pointers are adjusted as necessary.

Default Implementation

No default implementation. Derived classes must define this function.

See Also

streambuf::pbase, streambuf::pptr, streambuf::setp, streambuf::sync, streambuf::underflow

streambuf::pbackfail

virtual int pbackfail(int nCh);

Return Value

The *nCh* parameter if successful; otherwise **EOF**.

Parameter

nCh

   The character used in a previous **sputbackc** call.

Remarks

This function is called by **sputbackc** if it fails, usually because the **eback** pointer equals the **gptr** pointer. The **pbackfail** function should deal with the situation, if possible, by such means as repositioning the external file pointer.

Default implementation

Returns EOF.

See Also

streambuf::sputbackc

streambuf::pbase

Protected →

char* pbase() const;

END Protected

Return Value

Returns a pointer to the start of the put area. Characters between the **pbase** pointer and the **pptr** pointer have been stored in the buffer but not flushed to the final output destination.

See Also

streambuf::pptr, streambuf::setp, streambuf::out_waiting

streambuf::pbump

Protected →

void pbump(int nCount);

END Protected

Parameter

nCount

   The number of bytes to increment the put pointer. May be positive or negative.

Remarks

Increments the put pointer. No bounds checks are made on the result.

See Also

streambuf::gbump, streambuf::setp

streambuf::pptr

Protected →

char* pptr() const;

END Protected

Return Value

Returns a pointer to the first byte of the put area. This pointer is known as the put pointer and is the destination for the next character(s) sent to the **streambuf** object.

See Also

streambuf::epptr, streambuf::pbase, streambuf::setp

streambuf::sbumpc

int sbumpc();

Return Value

Returns the current character, then advances the get pointer. Returns **EOF** if the get pointer is currently at the end of the sequence (equal to the **egptr** pointer).

See Also

streambuf::epptr, streambuf::gbump

streambuf::seekoff

virtual streampos seekoff(streamoff *off*, **ios::seek_dir** *dir*, **int** *nMode* = **ios::in** | **ios::out**);

Return Value

The new position value. This is the byte offset from the start of the file (or string). If both **ios::in** and **ios::out** are specified, the function returns the output position. If the derived class does not support positioning, the function returns **EOF**.

Parameters

off

   The new offset value; **streamoff** is a **typedef** equivalent to **long**.

dir

   One of the following seek directions specified by the enumerated type **seek_dir:**

   - **ios::beg**   Seek from the beginning of the stream.

   - **ios::cur**   Seek from the current position in the stream.

   - **ios::end**   Seek from the end of the stream.

nMode

> An integer that contains a bitwise OR (|) combination of the enumerators **ios::in** and **ios::out**.

Remarks

Changes the position for the **streambuf** object. Not all derived classes of **streambuf** need to support positioning; however, the **filebuf, strstreambuf**, and **stdiobuf** classes do support positioning.

Classes derived from **streambuf** often support independent input and output position values. The *nMode* parameter determines which value(s) is set.

Default Implementation

Returns EOF.

See Also

streambuf::seekpos

streambuf::seekpos

virtual streampos seekpos(streampos *pos*, **int** *nMode* = **ios::in | ios::out);**

Return Value

The new position value. If both **ios::in** and **ios::out** are specified, the function returns the output position. If the derived class does not support positioning, the function returns **EOF**.

Parameters

pos

> The new position value; **streampos** is a **typedef** equivalent to **long**.

nMode

> An integer that contains mode bits defined as **ios** enumerators that can be combined with the OR (|) operator. See "**ofstream::ofstream**" for a listing of the enumerators.

Remarks

Changes the position, relative to the beginning of the stream, for the **streambuf** object. Not all derived classes of streambuf need to support positioning; however, the **filebuf, strstreambuf,** and **stdiobuf** classes do support positioning.

Classes derived from **streambuf** often support independent input and output position values. The *nMode* parameter determines which value(s) is set.

Default Implementation

Calls **seekoff((streamoff)** *pos*, **ios::beg,** *nMode* **).** Thus, to define seeking in a derived class, it is usually necessary to redefine only **seekoff**.

See Also

streambuf::seekoff

streambuf::setb

Protected →

void setb(char* pb, char* peb, int nDelete = 0);

END Protected

Parameters

pb

> The new value for the base pointer.

peb

> The new value for the ebuf pointer.

nDelete

> Flag that controls automatic deletion. If *nDelete* is not 0, the reserve area will be deleted when: (1) the base pointer is changed by another **setb** call, or (2) the **streambuf** destructor is called.

Remarks

Sets the values of the reserve area pointers. If both *pb* and *peb* are **NULL**, there is no reserve area. If *pb* is not **NULL** and *peb* is **NULL**, the reserve area has a length of 0.

See Also

streambuf::base, streambuf::ebuf

streambuf::setbuf

virtual streambuf* setbuf(char* *pr*, int *nLength*);

Return Value

A **streambuf** pointer if the buffer is accepted; otherwise **NULL**.

Parameters

pr

> A pointer to a previously allocated reserve area of length *nLength*. A **NULL** value indicates an unbuffered stream.

nLength

> The length (in bytes) of the reserve area. A length of 0 indicates an unbuffered stream.

Remarks

Attaches the specified reserve area to the **streambuf** object. Derived classes may or may not use this area.

Default Implementation

Accepts the request if there is not a reserved area already.

streambuf::setg

Protected →

void setg(char* peb, char* pg, char* peg);

END Protected

Parameters

peb
   The new value for the **eback** pointer.

pg
   The new value for the **gptr** pointer.

peg
   The new value for the **egptr** pointer.

Remarks

Sets the values for the get area pointers.

See Also

streambuf::eback, streambuf::gptr, streambuf::egptr

streambuf::setp

Protected →

void setp(char* *pp*, char* *pep*);

END Protected

Parameters

pp
   The new value for the **pbase** and **pptr** pointers.

pep
   The new value for the **epptr** pointer.

Remarks

Sets the values for the put area pointers.

See Also

streambuf::pptr, streambuf::pbase, streambuf::epptr

streambuf::sgetc

int sgetc();

Remarks

Returns the character at the get pointer. The **sgetc** function does not move the get pointer. Returns **EOF** if there is no character available.

See Also

streambuf::sbumpc, streambuf::sgetn, streambuf::snextc, streambuf::stossc

streambuf::sgetn

int sgetn(char* *pch*, **int** *nCount* **);**

Return Value

The number of characters fetched.

Parameters

pch
> A pointer to a buffer that will receive characters from the **streambuf** object.

nCount
> The number of characters to get.

Remarks

Gets the *nCount* characters that follow the get pointer and stores them in the area starting at *pch*. When fewer than *nCount* characters remain in the **streambuf** object, **sgetn** fetches whatever characters remain. The function repositions the get pointer to follow the fetched characters.

See Also

streambuf::sbumpc, streambuf::sgetc, streambuf::snextc, streambuf::stossc

streambuf::snextc

int snextc();

Return Value

First tests the get pointer, then returns EOF if it is already at the end of the get area. Otherwise, it moves the get pointer forward one character and returns the character that follows the new position. It returns EOF if the pointer has been moved to the end of the get area.

See Also

streambuf::sbumpc, streambuf::sgetc, streambuf::sgetn, streambuf::stossc

streambuf::sputbackc

int sputbackc(char *ch*);

Return Value

EOF on failure.

Parameter

ch

> The character to be put back to the **streambuf** object.

Remarks

Moves the get pointer back one character. The *ch* character must match the character just before the get pointer.

See Also

streambuf::sbumpc, streambuf::pbackfail

streambuf::sputc

int sputc(int *nCh*);

Return Value

The number of characters successfully stored; **EOF** on error.

Parameter

nCh

> The character to store in the **streambuf** object.

Remarks

Stores a character in the put area and advances the put pointer.

This public function is available to code outside the class, including the classes derived from **ios**. A derived **streambuf** class can gain access to its buffer directly by using protected member functions.

See Also

streambuf::sputn

streambuf::sputn

int sputn(const char* *pch***, int** *nCount* **);**

Return Value

The number of characters stored. This number is usually *nCount* but could be less if an error occurs.

Parameters

pch
> A pointer to a buffer that contains data to be copied to the **streambuf** object.

nCount
> The number of characters in the buffer.

Remarks

Copies *nCount* characters from *pch* to the **streambuf** buffer following the put pointer. The function repositions the put pointer to follow the stored characters.

See Also

streambuf::sputc

streambuf::stossc

void stossc();

Remarks

Moves the get pointer forward one character. If the pointer is already at the end of the get area, the function has no effect.

See Also

streambuf::sbumpc, streambuf::sgetn, streambuf::snextc, streambuf::sgetc

streambuf::streambuf

Protected →

streambuf();
streambuf(char* *pr***, int** *nLength* **);**

END Protected

Parameters

pr
> A pointer to a previously allocated reserve area of length *nLength*. A **NULL** value indicates an unbuffered stream.

nLength

> The length (in bytes) of the reserve area. A length of 0 indicates an unbuffered stream.

Remarks

The first constructor makes an uninitialized **streambuf** object. This object is not suitable for use until a **setbuf** call is made. A derived class constructor usually calls **setbuf** or uses the second constructor.

The second constructor initializes the **streambuf** object with the specified reserve area or marks it as unbuffered.

See Also

streambuf::setbuf

streambuf::~streambuf

Protected →

virtual ~streambuf();

END Protected

Remarks

The **streambuf** destructor flushes the buffer if the stream is being used for output.

streambuf::sync

virtual int sync();

Return Value

EOF if an error occurs.

Remarks

The virtual **sync** function, with the **overflow** and **underflow** functions, defines the characteristics of the **streambuf**-derived class. Each derived class might implement **sync** differently, but the interface with the calling stream class is the same.

The **sync** function flushes the put area. It also empties the get area and, in the process, sends any unprocessed characters back to the source, if necessary.

Default Implementation

Returns 0 if the get area is empty and there are no more characters to output; otherwise, it returns **EOF**.

See Also

streambuf::overflow

streambuf::unbuffered

Protected →

void unbuffered(int *nState* **);**
int unbuffered() const;

END Protected

Parameter

nState
>   The value of the buffering state variable; 0 = buffered, nonzero = unbuffered.

Remarks

The first overloaded **unbuffered** function sets the value of the **streambuf** object's buffering state. This variable's primary purpose is to control whether the **allocate** function automatically allocates a reserve area.

The second function returns the current buffering state variable.

See Also

streambuf::allocate, streambuf::doallocate

streambuf::underflow

mfvirtual int underflow() = 0;

Remarks

The virtual **underflow** function, with the **sync** and **overflow** functions, defines the characteristics of the **streambuf**-derived class. Each derived class might implement **underflow** differently, but the interface with the calling stream class is the same.

The **underflow** function is most frequently called by public **streambuf** functions like **sgetc** and **sgetn** when the get area is empty, but other classes, including the stream classes, can call **underflow** anytime.

The **underflow** function supplies the get area with characters from the input source. If the get area contains characters, **underflow** returns the first character. If the get area is empty, it fills the get area and returns the next character (which it leaves in the get area). If there are no more characters available, then **underflow** returns **EOF** and leaves the get area empty.

In the **strstreambuf** class, **underflow** adjusts the **egptr** pointer to access storage that was dynamically allocated by a call to overflow.

Default Implementation

No default implementation. Derived classes must define this function.

class strstream

#include <strstrea.h>

The **strstream** class supports I/O streams that have character arrays as a source and destination. You can allocate a character array prior to construction, or the constructor can internally allocate a dynamic array. You can then use all the input and output stream operators and functions to fill the array.

Be aware that a put pointer and a get pointer are working independently behind the scenes in the attached **strstreambuf** class. The put pointer advances as you insert fields into the stream's array, and the get pointer advances as you extract fields. The **ostream::seekp** function moves the put pointer, and the **istream::seekg** function moves the get pointer. If either pointer reaches the end of the string (and sets the **ios::eof** flag), you must call **clear** before seeking.

Construction/Destruction — Public Members

strstream
Constructs a **strstream** object.

~strstream
Destroys a **strstream** object.

Other Functions — Public Members

pcount
Returns the number of bytes that have been stored in the stream's buffer.

rdbuf
Returns a pointer to the stream's associated **strstreambuf** object.

str
Returns a pointer to the string stream's character buffer and freezes it.

See Also

strstreambuf, streambuf, istrstream, ostrstream

Member Functions

strstream::pcount

int pcount() const;

Return Value

Returns the number of bytes stored in the buffer. This information is especially useful when you have stored binary data in the object.

strstream::rdbuf

strstreambuf* rdbuf() const;

Return Value

Returns a pointer to the **strstreambuf** buffer object that is associated with this stream. This is not the character buffer; the **strstreambuf** object contains a pointer to the character area.

See Also

strstream::str

strstream::str

char* str();

Return Value

Returns a pointer to the internal character array. If the stream was built with the **void**-argument constructor, then **str** freezes the array. You must not send characters to a frozen stream, and you are responsible for deleting the array. You can unfreeze the stream by calling **rdbuf->freeze(0)**.

If the stream was built with the constructor that specified the buffer, the pointer contains the same address as the array used to construct the **ostrstream** object.

See Also

strstreambuf::freeze, strstream::rdbuf

strstream::strstream

strstream();
strstream(char* *pch***, int** *nLength***, int** *nMode* **);**

Parameters

pch

A character array that is large enough to accommodate future output stream activity.

nLength

The size (in characters) of *pch*. If 0, *pch* is assumed to point to a null-terminated array; if less than 0, the array is assumed to have infinite length.

nMode

The stream creation mode, which must be one of the following enumerators as defined in class **ios**:

- **ios::in**   Retrieval begins at the beginning of the array.

- **ios::out**   By default, storing begins at *pch*.

- **ios::ate**   The *pch* parameter is assumed to be a null-terminated array; storing begins at the **NULL** character.

- **ios::app**   Same as **ios::ate**.

The use of the **ios::in** and **ios::out** flags is optional for this class; both input and output are implied.

Remarks

The first constructor makes an **strstream** object that uses an internal, dynamic buffer that is initially empty.

The second constructor makes an **strstream** object out of the first *nLength* characters of the *psc* buffer. The stream will not accept characters once the length reaches *nLength*.

strstream::~strstream

~strstream();

Remarks

Destroys a **strstream** object and its associated **strstreambuf** object, thus releasing all internally allocated memory. If you used the **void**-argument constructor, the internally allocated character buffer is released; otherwise, you must release it.

An internally allocated character buffer will not be released if it was previously frozen by calling **rdbuf–>freeze(0)**.

See Also

strstream::rdbuf

class strstreambuf

#include <strstrea.h>

The **strstreambuf** class is a derived class of **streambuf** that manages an in-memory character array.

The file stream classes, **ostrstream**, **istrstream**, and **strstream**, use **strstreambuf** member functions to fetch and store characters. Some of these member functions are virtual functions defined for the **streambuf** class.

The reserve area, put area, and get area were introduced in the **streambuf** class description. For **strsteambuf** objects, the put area is the same as the get area, but the **get** pointer and the **put** pointer move independently.

Construction/Destruction — Public Members

strstreambuf
> Constructs a **strstreambuf** object.

~strstreambuf
> Destroys a strstreambuf object.

Other Functions — Public Members

freeze
> Freezes a stream.

str
> Returns a pointer to the string.

See Also

istrstream, ostrstream, filebuf, stdiobuf

Member Functions

strstreambuf::freeze

void freeze(int n = 1);

Parameter

n
> A 0 value permits automatic deletion of the current array and its automatic growth (if it is dynamic); a nonzero value prevents deletion.

Remarks

If a **strstreambuf** object has a dynamic array, memory is usually deleted on destruction and size adjustment. The **freeze** function provides a way to prevent that automatic deletion.

Once an array is frozen, no further input or output is permitted. The results of such operations are undefined.

The **freeze** function can also unfreeze a frozen buffer.

See Also

strstreambuf::str

strstreambuf::str

char* str();

Return Value

Returns a pointer to the object's internal character array. If the **strstreambuf** object was constructed with a user-supplied buffer, that buffer address is returned. If the object has a dynamic array, **str** freezes the array. You must not send characters to a frozen **strstreambuf** object, and you are responsible for deleting the array. If a dynamic array is empty, then **str** returns **NULL**.

Use the **freeze** function with a 0 parameter to unfreeze a **strstreambuf** object.

See Also

strstreambuf::freeze

strstreambuf::strstreambuf

strstreambuf();
strstreambuf(int *nBytes*);
strstreambuf(char* *pch*, int *n*, char* *pstart* = **0**);
strstreambuf(unsigned char* *puch*, int **n**, unsigned char* *pustart* = **0**);
strstreambuf(signed char* *psch*, int *n*, signed char* *psstart* = **0**);
strstreambuf(void* (*falloc)(long), void (*ffree)(void*));

Parameters

nBytes
    The initial length of a dynamic stream buffer.

pch, puch, psch
    A pointer to a character buffer that will be attached to the object. The **get** pointer is initialized to this value.

n

    One of the following integer parameters:

    • positive   *n* bytes, starting at *pch*, is used as a fixed-length stream buffer.

- 0   The *pch* parameter points to the start of a null-terminated string that constitutes the stream buffer (terminator excluded).

- negative   The *pch* parameter points to a stream buffer that continues indefinitely.

pstart, pustart, psstart
: The initial value of the **put** pointer.

falloc
: A memory-allocation function with the prototype **void* falloc(long)**. The default is **new**.

ffree
: A function that frees allocated memory with the prototype **void ffree(void*)**. The default is **delete**.

Remarks

The four **streambuf** constructors are described as follows:

Constructor	Description
strstreambuf()	Constructs an empty **strstreambuf** object with dynamic buffering. The buffer is allocated internally by the class and grows as needed, unless it is frozen.
strstreambuf(int)	Constructs an empty **strstreambuf** object with a dynamic buffer *n* bytes long to start with. The buffer is allocated internally by the class and grows as needed, unless it is frozen.
strstreambuf(char*, int, char*)	Constructs a **strstreambuf** object from already-allocated memory as specified by the arguments. There are constructor variations for both unsigned and signed character arrays.
strstreambuf(void*(*), void(*))	Constructs an empty **strstreambuf** object with dynamic buffering. The *falloc* function is called for allocation. The **long** parameter specifies the buffer length and the function returns the buffer address. If the *falloc* pointer is **NULL**, operator **new** is used. The *ffree* function frees memory allocated by *falloc*. If the *ffree* pointer is **NULL**, the operator **delete** is used.

strstreambuf::~strstreambuf

~strstreambuf();

Remarks

Destroys a **strstreambuf** object and releases internally allocated dynamic memory unless the object is frozen. The destructor does not release user-allocated memory.

Index

Microsoft®
Visual
C++® 6.0
Run-Time
Library
Reference

Contents

Introduction

The Microsoft run-time library provides routines for programming for the Microsoft Windows NT and Windows 95 operating systems. These routines automate many common programming tasks that are not provided by the C and C++ languages.

C Run-Time Libraries

The following table lists the release versions of the C run-time library files, along with their associated compiler options and environment variables. Prior to Visual C++ 4.2, the C run-time libraries contained the iostream library functions. In Visual C++ 4.2 and later, the old iostream library functions have been removed from LIBC.LIB, LIBCMT.LIB, and MSVCRT.LIB. (This change was made because the Standard C++ library has been added to Visual C++, and it contains a new set of iostream libraries. Thus, two sets of iostream functions are now included in Visual C++.) The old iostream functions now exist in their own libraries: LIBCI.LIB, LIBCIMT.LIB, and MSVCIRT.LIB. The new iostream functions, as well as many other new functions, exist in the Standard C++ libraries: LIBCP.LIB, LIBCPMT.LIB, and MSVCPRT.LIB.

The Standard C++ library and the old iostream library are incompatible, and only one of them can be linked with your project. See "Port to the Standard C++ Library" and the "Standard C++ Library Overview" for details.

When you build a release version of your project, one of the basic C run-time libraries (LIBC.LIB, LIBCMT.LIB, and MSVCRT.LIB) is linked by default, depending on the compiler option you choose (single-threaded, multithreaded, or DLL). Depending on the headers you use in your code, a library from the Standard C++ libraries or one from the old iostream libraries may also be linked:

- If you include a "Standard C++ library header" in your code, a Standard C++ library will be linked in automatically by Visual C++ at compile time. For example:

  ```
  #include <ios>
  ```

- If you include an "old iostream library header," an old iostream library will be linked in automatically by Visual C++ at compile time. For example:

  ```
  #include <ios.h>
  ```

Note that headers from the Standard C++ library and the old iostream library cannot be mixed.

Headers determine whether a Standard C++ library, an old iostream library, or neither will be linked. Compiler options determine which of the libraries to be linked is the default (single-threaded, multithreaded, or DLL). When a specific library compiler option is defined, that library is considered to be the default and its environment variables are automatically defined.

C Run-Time Library (without iostream)	Characteristics	Option	Defined
LIBC.LIB	Single threaded, static link	/ML	
LIBCMT.LIB	Multithreaded, static link	/MT	_MT
MSVCRT.LIB	Multithreaded, dynamic link (import library for MSVCRT.DLL)	/MD	_MT, _DLL

Standard C++ Library	Characteristics	Option	Defined
LIBCP.LIB	Single threaded, static link	/ML	
LIBCPMT.LIB	Multithreaded, static link	/MT	_MT
MSVCPRT.LIB	Multithreaded, dynamic link (import library for MSVCRT.DLL)	/MD	_MT, _DLL

Old Iostream Library	Characteristics	Option	Defined
LIBCI.LIB	Single threaded, static link	/ML	
LIBCIMT.LIB	Multithreaded, static link	/MT	_MT
MSVCIRT.LIB	Multithreaded, dynamic link (import library for MSVCIRT.DLL)	/MD	_MT, _DLL

To build a debug version of your application, the _DEBUG flag must be defined and the application must be linked with a debug version of one of these libraries. For more information about using the debug versions of the library files, see Chapter 4, "Debug Version of the Run-Time Library."

Building the Run-Time Libraries

There are two batch files provided for building the C run-time libraries from the source code included with Visual C++:

- \Microsoft Visual Studio\VC98\CRT\SRC\BLDWIN95.BAT, used when building on Windows 95

- \Microsoft Visual Studio\VC98\CRT\SRC\BLDNT.CMD, used when building on Windows NT

When using either BLDNT.CMD or BLDWIN95.BAT, set the V5TOOLS environment variable to the root of the Visual C++ installation (such as C:\Microsoft Visual Studio\ VC98\Bin). If this environment variable is not set, an error message will be displayed and the batch file will exit.

Compatibility

The Microsoft run-time library supports American National Standards Institute (ANSI) C and UNIX C. In this book, references to UNIX include XENIX, other UNIX-like systems, and the POSIX subsystem in Windows NT and Windows 95. The description of each run-time library routine in this book includes a compatibility section for these targets: ANSI, Windows 95 (listed as Win 95), and Windows NT (Win NT). All run-time library routines included with this product are compatible with the Win32 API.

ANSI C Compliance

The naming convention for all Microsoft-specific identifiers in the run-time system (such as functions, macros, constants, variables, and type definitions) is ANSI-compliant. In this book, any run-time function that follows the ANSI/ISO C standards is noted as being ANSI compatible. ANSI-compliant applications should only use these ANSI compatible functions.

The names of Microsoft-specific functions and global variables begin with a single underscore. These names can be overridden only locally, within the scope of your code. For example, when you include Microsoft run-time header files, you can still locally override the Microsoft-specific function named **_open** by declaring a local variable of the same name. However, you cannot use this name for your own global function or global variable.

The names of Microsoft-specific macros and manifest constants begin with two underscores, or with a single leading underscore immediately followed by an uppercase letter. The scope of these identifiers is absolute. For example, you cannot use the Microsoft-specific identifier **_UPPER** for this reason.

UNIX

If you plan to transport your programs to UNIX, follow these guidelines:

- Do not remove header files from the SYS subdirectory. You can place the SYS header files elsewhere only if you do not plan to transport your programs to UNIX.

- Use the UNIX-compatible path delimiter in routines that take strings representing paths and filenames as arguments. UNIX supports only the forward slash (/) for this purpose, whereas Win32 operating systems support both the backslash (\) and the forward slash (/). Thus this book uses UNIX-compatible forward slashes as path delimiters in **#include** statements, for example. (However, the Windows NT and Windows 95 command shell, CMD.EXE, does not support the forward slash in commands entered at the command prompt.)

- Use paths and filenames that work correctly in UNIX, which is case sensitive. The file allocation table (FAT) file system in Win32 operating systems is not case sensitive; the installable Windows NT file system (NTFS) of Windows NT preserves case for directory listings but ignores case in file searches and other system operations.

  Note In this version of Visual C++, UNIX compatibility information has been removed from the function descriptions.

Win32 Platforms

The C run-time libraries support Windows 95 and Windows NT, but not Win32s. Windows 95 and Windows NT support the Win32 Application Programming Interface (API), but only Windows NT provides full Unicode support. In addition, any Win32 application can use a multibyte character set (MBCS).

Backward Compatibility

The compiler views a structure that has both an old name and a new name as two different types. You cannot copy from an old structure type to a new structure type. Old prototypes that take **struct** pointers use the old **struct** names in the prototype.

For compatibility with Microsoft C professional development system version 6.0 and earlier Microsoft C versions, the library OLDNAMES.LIB maps old names to new names. For instance, **open** maps to **_open**. You must explicitly link with OLDNAMES.LIB only when you compile with the following combinations of command-line options:

- /Zl (omit default library name from object file) and /Ze (the default — use Microsoft extensions)

- /link (linker-control), /NOD (no default-library search), and /Ze

For more information about compiler command-line options, see "Compiler Reference" in the *Visual C++ Programmer's Guide* online.

Required and Optional Header Files

The description of each run-time routine in this book includes a list of the required and optional include, or header (.H), files for that routine. Required header files need to be included to obtain the function declaration for the routine or a definition used by another routine called internally. Optional header files are usually included to take advantage of predefined constants, type definitions, or inline macros. The following table lists some examples of optional header file contents:

Definition	Example
Macro definition	If a library routine is implemented as a macro, the macro definition may be in a header file other than the header file for the original routine. For instance, the **toupper** macro is defined in the header file CTYPE.H, while the function **toupper** is declared in STDLIB.H.
Manifest constant	Many library routines refer to constants that are defined in header files. For instance, the _**open** routine uses constants such as _**O_CREAT**, which is defined in the header file FCNTL.H.
Type definition	Some library routines return a structure or take a structure as an argument. For example, stream input/output routines use a structure of type **FILE**, which is defined in STDIO.H.

The run-time library header files provide function declarations in the ANSI/ISO C standard recommended style. The compiler performs "type checking" on any routine reference that occurs after its associated function declaration. Function declarations are especially important for routines that return a value of some type other than **int**, which is the default. Routines that do not specify their appropriate return value in their declaration will be considered by the compiler to return an **int**, which can cause unexpected results. See "Type Checking," later in this Introduction, for more information.

Choosing Between Functions and Macros

Most Microsoft run-time library routines are compiled or assembled functions, but some routines are implemented as macros. When a header file declares both a function and a macro version of a routine, the macro definition takes precedence, because it always appears after the function declaration. When you invoke a routine that is implemented as both a function and a macro, you can force the compiler to use the function version in two ways:

- Enclose the routine name in parentheses.

```
#include <ctype.h>
a = toupper(a);     //use macro version of toupper
a = (toupper)(a);   //force compiler to use function version of toupper
```

- "Undefine" the macro definition with the **#undef** directive:

```
#include <ctype.h>
#undef toupper
```

If you need to choose between a function and a macro implementation of a library routine, consider the following trade-offs:

- Speed versus size. The main benefit of using macros is faster execution time. During preprocessing, a macro is expanded (replaced by its definition) inline each time it is used. A function definition occurs only once regardless of how many times it is called. Macros may increase code size but do not have the overhead associated with function calls.

- Function evaluation. A function evaluates to an address; a macro does not. Thus you cannot use a macro name in contexts requiring a pointer. For instance, you can declare a pointer to a function, but not a pointer to a macro.

- Macro side effects. A macro may treat arguments incorrectly when the macro evaluates its arguments more than once. For instance, the **toupper** macro is defined as:

```
#define toupper(c) ( (islower(c)) ? _toupper(c) :  (c) )
```

In the following example, the **toupper** macro produces a side effect:

```
#include <ctype.h>

int a = 'm';
a = toupper(a++);
```

The example code increments a when passing it to **toupper**. The macro evaluates the argument a++ twice, once to check case and again for the result, therefore increasing a by 2 instead of 1. As a result, the value operated on by **islower** differs from the value operated on by **toupper**.

- Type-checking. When you declare a function, the compiler can check the argument types. Because you cannot declare a macro, the compiler cannot check macro argument types, although it can check the number of arguments you pass to a macro.

Type Checking

The compiler performs limited type checking on functions that can take a variable number of arguments, as follows:

Function Call	Type-Checked Arguments
_cprintf, _cscanf, printf, scanf	First argument (format string)
fprintf, fscanf, sprintf, sscanf	First two arguments (file or buffer and format string)
_snprintf	First three arguments (file or buffer, count, and format string)
_open	First two arguments (path and **_open** flag)
_sopen	First three arguments (path, **_open** flag, and sharing mode)
_execl, _execle, _execlp, _execlpe	First two arguments (path and first argument pointer)
_spawnl, _spawnle, _spawnlp, _spawnlpe	First three arguments (mode flag, path, and first argument pointer)

The compiler performs the same limited type checking on the wide-character counterparts of these functions.

CHAPTER 1

Run-Time Routines by Category

This chapter lists and describes Microsoft run-time library routines by category. For reference convenience, some routines are listed in more than one category. Multibyte-character routines and wide-character routines are grouped with single-byte-character counterparts, where they exist.

The main categories of Microsoft run-time library routines are:

Argument access	Floating-point support
Buffer manipulation	Input and output
Byte classification	Internationalization
Character classification	Memory allocation
Data conversion	Process and environment control
Debug	Searching and sorting
Directory control	String manipulation
Error handling	System calls
Exception handling	Time management
File handling	

Argument Access

The **va_arg**, **va_end**, and **va_start** macros provide access to function arguments when the number of arguments is variable. These macros are defined in STDARG.H for ANSI C compatibility, and in VARARGS.H for compatibility with UNIX System V.

Argument-Access Macros

Macro	Use
va_arg	Retrieve argument from list
va_end	Reset pointer
va_start	Set pointer to beginning of argument list

Buffer Manipulation

Use these routines to work with areas of memory on a byte-by-byte basis.

Buffer-Manipulation Routines

Routine	Use
_memccpy	Copy characters from one buffer to another until given character or given number of characters has been copied
memchr	Return pointer to first occurrence, within specified number of characters, of given character in buffer
memcmp	Compare specified number of characters from two buffers
memcpy	Copy specified number of characters from one buffer to another
_memicmp	Compare specified number of characters from two buffers without regard to case
memmove	Copy specified number of characters from one buffer to another
memset	Use given character to initialize specified number of bytes in the buffer
_swab	Swap bytes of data and store them at specified location

When the source and target areas overlap, only **memmove** is guaranteed to copy the full source properly.

Byte Classification

Each of these routines tests a specified byte of a multibyte character for satisfaction of a condition. Except where specified otherwise, the test result depends on the multibyte code page currently in use.

> **Note** By definition, the ASCII character set is a subset of all multibyte-character sets. For example, the Japanese katakana character set includes ASCII as well as non-ASCII characters.

The manifest constants in the following table are defined in CTYPE.H:

Multibyte-Character Byte-Classification Routines

Routine	Byte Test Condition
isleadbyte	Lead byte; test result depends on **LC_CTYPE** category setting of current locale
_ismbbalnum	**isalnum ‖ _ismbbkalnum**
_ismbbalpha	**isalpha ‖ _ismbbkalnum**

Multibyte-Character Byte-Classification Routines   *(continued)*

Routine	Byte Test Condition
_ismbbgraph	Same as **_ismbbprint**, but **_ismbbgraph** does not include the space character (0x20).
_ismbbkalnum	Non-ASCII text symbol other than punctuation. For example, in code page 932 only, **_ismbbkalnum** tests for katakana alphanumeric.
_ismbbkana	Katakana (0xA1–0xDF), code page 932 only.
_ismbbkprint	Non-ASCII text or non-ASCII punctuation symbol. For example, in code page 932 only, **_ismbbkprint** tests for katakana alphanumeric or katakana punctuation (range: 0xA1– 0xDF).
_ismbbkpunct	Non-ASCII punctuation. For example, in code page 932 only, **_ismbbkpunct** tests for katakana punctuation.
_ismbblead	First byte of multibyte character. For example, in code page 932 only, valid ranges are 0x81–0x9F, 0xE0–0xFC.
_ismbbprint	**isprint ‖ _ismbbkprint. ismbbprint** includes the space character (0x20).
_ismbbpunct	**ispunct ‖ _ismbbkpunct**
_ismbbtrail	Second byte of multibyte character. For example, in code page 932 only, valid ranges are 0x40–0x7E, 0x80–0xEC.
_ismbslead	Lead byte (in string context)
_ismbstrail	Trail byte (in string context)
_mbbtype	Return byte type based on previous byte
_mbsbtype	Return type of byte within string

The **MB_LEN_MAX** macro, defined in LIMITS.H, expands to the maximum length in bytes that any multibyte character can have. **MB_CUR_MAX**, defined in STDLIB.H, expands to the maximum length in bytes of any multibyte character in the current locale.

Character Classification

Each of these routines tests a specified single-byte character, wide character, or multibyte character for satisfaction of a condition. (By definition, the ASCII character set is a subset of all multibyte-character sets. For example, Japanese katakana includes ASCII as well as non-ASCII characters.) Generally these routines execute faster than tests you might write. For example, the following code executes slower than a call to **isalpha**(*c*):

```
if ((c >= 'A') && (c <= 'Z')) || ((c >= 'a') && (c <= 'z'))
    return TRUE;
```

Character-Classification Routines

Routine	Character Test Condition
isalnum, iswalnum, _ismbcalnum	Alphanumeric
isalpha, iswalpha, _ismbcalpha	Alphabetic
__isascii, iswascii	ASCII
iscntrl, iswcntrl	Control
__iscsym	Letter, underscore, or digit
__iscsymf	Letter or underscore
isdigit, iswdigit, _ismbcdigit	Decimal digit
isgraph, iswgraph, _ismbcgraph	Printable other than space
islower, iswlower, _ismbclower	Lowercase
_ismbchira	Hiragana
_ismbckata	Katakana
_ismbclegal	Legal multibyte character
_ismbcl0	Japan-level 0 multibyte character
_ismbcl1	Japan-level 1 multibyte character
_ismbcl2	Japan-level 2 multibyte character
_ismbcsymbol	Non-alphanumeric multibyte character
isprint, iswprint, _ismbcprint	Printable
ispunct, iswpunct, _ismbcpunct	Punctuation
isspace, iswspace, _ismbcspace	White-space
isupper, iswupper, _ismbcupper	Uppercase
iswctype	Property specified by *desc* argument
isxdigit, iswxdigit	Hexadecimal digit
mblen	Return length of valid multibyte character; result depends on **LC_CTYPE** category setting of current locale

Data Conversion

These routines convert data from one form to another. Generally these routines execute faster than conversions you might write. Each routine that begins with a **to** prefix is implemented as a function and as a macro. See "Choosing Between Functions and Macros" in the Introduction for information about choosing an implementation.

Data-Conversion Routines

Routine	Use
abs	Find absolute value of integer
atof	Convert string to **float**
atoi, _atoi64	Convert string to **int**
atol	Convert string to **long**
_ecvt	Convert **double** to string of specified length
_fcvt	Convert **double** to string with specified number of digits following decimal point
_gcvt	Convert **double** number to string; store string in buffer
_itoa, _i64toa, _itow, _i64tow	Convert **int** to string
labs	Find absolute value of **long** integer
_ltoa, _ltow	Convert **long** to string
_mbbtombc	Convert 1-byte multibyte character to corresponding 2-byte multibyte character
_mbcjistojms	Convert Japan Industry Standard (JIS) character to Japan Microsoft (JMS) character
_mbcjmstojis	Convert JMS character to JIS character
_mbctohira	Convert multibyte character to 1-byte hiragana code
_mbctokata	Convert multibyte character to 1-byte katakana code
_mbctombb	Convert 2-byte multibyte character to corresponding 1-byte multibyte character
mbstowcs	Convert sequence of multibyte characters to corresponding sequence of wide characters
mbtowc	Convert multibyte character to corresponding wide character

(continued)

Data-Conversion Routines *(continued)*

Routine	Use
strtod, wcstod	Convert string to **double**
strtol, wcstol	Convert string to **long** integer
strtoul, wcstoul	Convert string to **unsigned long** integer
strxfrm, wcsxfrm	Transform string into collated form based on locale-specific information
__toascii	Convert character to ASCII code
tolower, towlower, _mbctolower	Test character and convert to lowercase if currently uppercase
_tolower	Convert character to lowercase unconditionally
toupper, towupper, _mbctoupper	Test character and convert to uppercase if currently lowercase
_toupper	Convert character to uppercase unconditionally
_ultoa, _ultow	Convert **unsigned long** to string
wcstombs	Convert sequence of wide characters to corresponding sequence of multibyte characters
wctomb	Convert wide character to corresponding multibyte character
_wtoi	Convert wide-character string to **int**
_wtol	Convert wide-character string to **long**

Debug Routines

With this version, Visual C++ introduces debug support for the C run-time library. The new debug version of the library supplies many diagnostic services that make debugging programs easier and allow developers to:

- Step directly into run-time functions during debugging
- Resolve assertions, errors, and exceptions
- Trace heap allocations and prevent memory leaks
- Report debug messages to the user

To use these routines, the _DEBUG flag must be defined. All of these routines do nothing in a retail build of an application. For more information on how to use the new debug routines, see "Using C Run-Time Library Debugging Support" in the *Visual C++ Programmer's Guide* online.

Chapter 1 Run-Time Routines by Category

Debug Versions of the C Run-time Library Routines

Routine	Use
_ASSERT	Evaluate an expression and generates a debug report when the result is FALSE
_ASSERTE	Similar to **_ASSERT**, but includes the failed expression in the generated report
_CrtCheckMemory	Confirm the integrity of the memory blocks allocated on the debug heap
_CrtDbgReport	Generate a debug report with a user message and send the report to three possible destinations
_CrtDoForAllClientObjects	Call an application-supplied function for all **_CLIENT_BLOCK** types on the heap
_CrtDumpMemoryLeaks	Dump all of the memory blocks on the debug heap when a significant memory leak has occurred
_CrtIsValidHeapPointer	Verify that a specified pointer is in the local heap
_CrtIsMemoryBlock	Verify that a specified memory block is located within the local heap and that it has a valid debug heap block type identifier
_CrtIsValidPointer	Verify that a specified memory range is valid for reading and writing
_CrtMemCheckpoint	Obtain the current state of the debug heap and store it in an application-supplied **_CrtMemState** structure
_CrtMemDifference	Compare two memory states for significant differences and return the results
_CrtMemDumpAllObjectsSince	Dump information about objects on the heap since a specified checkpoint was taken or from the start of program execution
_CrtMemDumpStatistics	Dump the debug header information for a specified memory state in a user-readable form
_CrtSetAllocHook	Install a client-defined allocation function by hooking it into the C run-time debug memory allocation process
_CrtSetBreakAlloc	Set a breakpoint on a specified object allocation order number
_CrtSetDbgFlag	Retrieve or modify the state of the **_crtDbgFlag** flag to control the allocation behavior of the debug heap manager

(continued)

Run-Time Library Reference **7**

Debug Versions of the C Run-time Library Routines *(continued)*

Routine	Use
_CrtSetDumpClient	Install an application-defined function that is called every time a debug dump function is called to dump **_CLIENT_BLOCK** type memory blocks
_CrtSetReportFile	Identify the file or stream to be used as a destination for a specific report type by **_CrtDbgReport**
_CrtSetReportHook	Install a client-defined reporting function by hooking it into the C run-time debug reporting process
_CrtSetReportMode	Specify the general destination(s) for a specific report type generated by **_CrtDbgReport**
_RPT[0,1,2,3,4]	Track the application's progress by generating a debug report by calling **_CrtDbgReport** with a format string and a variable number of arguments. Provides no source file and line number information.
_RPTF[0,1,2,3,4]	Similar to the **_RPTn** macros, but provides the source file name and line number where the report request originated
_calloc_dbg	Allocate a specified number of memory blocks on the heap with additional space for a debugging header and overwrite buffers
_expand_dbg	Resize a specified block of memory on the heap by expanding or contracting the block
_free_dbg	Free a block of memory on the heap
_malloc_dbg	Allocate a block of memory on the heap with additional space for a debugging header and overwrite buffers
_msize_dbg	Calculate the size of a block of memory on the heap
_realloc_dbg	Reallocate a specified block of memory on the heap by moving and/or resizing the block

The debug routines can be used to step through the source code for most of the other C run-time routines during the debugging process. However, Microsoft considers some technology to be proprietary and, therefore, does not provide the source code for these routines. Most of these routines belong to either the exception handling or floating-point processing groups, but a few others are included as well. The following table lists these routines.

C Run-time Routines That Are Not Available in Source Code Form

acos	_fpclass	_nextafter
asin	_fpieee_flt	pow
atan, atan2	_fpreset	printf, wprintf*
_cabs	frexp	_scalb
ceil	_hypot	scanf, wscanf*
_chgsign	_isnan	setjmp
_clear87, _clearfp	_j0	sin
_control87, _controlfp	_j1	sinh
_copysign	_jn	sqrt
cos	ldexp	_status87, _statusfp
cosh	log	tan
exp	log10	tanh
fabs	_logb	_y0
_finite	longjmp	_y1
floor	_matherr	_yn
fmod	modf	

* Although source code is available for most of this routine, it makes an internal call to another routine for which source code is not provided.

Some C run-time functions and C++ operators behave differently when called from a debug build of an application. (Note that a debug build of an application can be done by either defining the _DEBUG flag or by linking with a debug version of the C run-time library.) The behavioral differences usually consist of extra features or information provided by the routine to support the debugging process. The following table lists these routines.

Routines That Behave Differently in a Debug Build of an Application

C abort routine	C++ delete operator
C assert routine	C++ new operator

For more information about using the debug versions of the C++ operators in the preceding table, see "Using the Debug Heap from C++" in the *Visual C++ Programmer's Guide* online.

Directory Control

These routines access, modify, and obtain information about the directory structure.

Directory-Control Routines

Routine	Use
_chdir, _wchdir	Change current working directory.
_chdrive	Change current drive.
_getcwd, _wgetcwd	Get current working directory for default drive.
_getdcwd, _wgetdcwd	Get current working directory for specified drive.
_getdrive	Get current (default) drive.
_mkdir, _wmkdir	Make new directory.
_rmdir, _wrmdir	Remove directory.
_searchenv, _wsearchenv	Search for given file on specified paths.

Error Handling

Use these routines to handle program errors.

Error-Handling Routines

Routine	Use
assert macro	Test for programming logic errors; available in both the release and debug versions of the run-time library
_ASSERT, _ASSERTE macros	Similar to **assert**, but only available in the debug versions of the run-time library
clearerr	Reset error indicator. Calling **rewind** or closing a stream also resets the error indicator.
_eof	Check for end of file in low-level I/O
feof	Test for end of file. End of file is also indicated when **_read** returns 0.
ferror	Test for stream I/O errors
_RPT, _RPTF macros	Generate a report similar to **printf**, but only available in the debug versions of the run-time library

Exception Handling Routines

Use the C++ exception-handling functions to recover from unexpected events during program execution.

Exception-Handling Functions

Function	Use
_set_se_translator	Handle Win32 exceptions (C structured exceptions) as C++ typed exceptions
set_terminate	Install your own termination routine to be called by **terminate**
set_unexpected	Install your own termination function to be called by **unexpected**
terminate	Called automatically under certain circumstances after exception is thrown. The **terminate** function calls **abort** or a function you specify using **set_terminate**
unexpected	Calls **terminate** or a function you specify using **set_unexpected**. The **unexpected** function is not used in current Microsoft C++ exception-handling implementation

File Handling

Use these routines to create, delete, and manipulate files and to set and check file-access permissions.

The C run-time libraries have a preset limit for the number of files that can be open at any one time. The limit for applications that link with the single-thread static library (LIBC.LIB) is 64 file handles or 20 file streams. Applications that link with either the static or dynamic multithread library (LIBCMT.LIB or MSVCRT.LIB and MSVCRT.DLL), have a limit of 256 file handles or 40 file streams. Attempting to open more than the maximum number of file handles or file streams causes program failure.

The following routines operate on files designated by a file handle:

File-Handling Routines (File Handle)

Routine	Use
_chsize	Change file size
_filelength	Get file length
_fstat, _fstati64	Get file-status information on handle
_isatty	Check for character device
_locking	Lock areas of file
_setmode	Set file-translation mode

The following routines operate on files specified by a path or filename:

File-Handling Routines (Path or Filename)

Routine	Use
_access, _waccess	Check file-permission setting
_chmod, _wchmod	Change file-permission setting
_fullpath, _wfullpath	Expand a relative path to its absolute path name
_get_osfhandle	Return operating-system file handle associated with existing stream **FILE** pointer
_makepath, _wmakepath	Merge path components into single, full path
_mktemp, _wmktemp	Create unique filename
_open_osfhandle	Associate C run-time file handle with existing operating-system file handle
remove, _wremove	Delete file
rename, _wrename	Rename file
_splitpath, _wsplitpath	Parse path into components
_stat, _stati64, _wstat, _wstati64	Get file-status information on named file
_umask	Set default permission mask for new files created by program
_unlink, _wunlink	Delete file

Floating-Point Support

Many Microsoft run-time library functions require floating-point support from a math coprocessor or from the floating-point libraries that accompany the compiler. Floating-point support functions are loaded only if required.

When you use a floating-point type specifier in the format string of a call to a function in the **printf** or **scanf** family, you must specify a floating-point value or a pointer to a floating-point value in the argument list to tell the compiler that floating-point support is required. The math functions in the Microsoft run-time library handle exceptions the same way that the UNIX V math functions do.

The Microsoft run-time library sets the default internal precision of the math coprocessor (or emulator) to 64 bits. This default applies only to the internal precision at which all intermediate calculations are performed; it does not apply to the size of arguments, return values, or variables. You can override this default and set the chip (or emulator) back to 80-bit precision by linking your program with LIB/FP10.OBJ. On the linker command line, FP10.OBJ must appear before LIBC.LIB, LIBCMT.LIB, or MSVCRT.LIB.

Floating-Point Functions

Routine	Use
abs	Return absolute value of **int**
acos	Calculate arccosine
asin	Calculate arcsine
atan, atan2	Calculate arctangent
atof	Convert character string to double-precision floating-point value
Bessel functions	Calculate Bessel functions **_j0**, **_j1**, **_jn**, **_y0**, **_y1**, **_yn**
_cabs	Find absolute value of complex number
ceil	Find integer ceiling
_chgsign	Reverse sign of double-precision floating-point argument
_clear87, _clearfp	Get and clear floating-point status word
_control87, _controlfp	Get old floating-point control word and set new control-word value
_copysign	Return one value with sign of another
cos	Calculate cosine
cosh	Calculate hyperbolic cosine
difftime	Compute difference between two specified time values
div	Divide one integer by another, returning quotient and remainder
_ecvt	Convert **double** to character string of specified length
exp	Calculate exponential function
fabs	Find absolute value
_fcvt	Convert **double** to string with specified number of digits following decimal point
_finite	Determine whether given double-precision floating-point value is finite
floor	Find largest integer less than or equal to argument
fmod	Find floating-point remainder
_fpclass	Return status word containing information on floating-point class
_fpieee_flt	Invoke user-defined trap handler for IEEE floating-point exceptions
_fpreset	Reinitialize floating-point math package
frexp	Calculate exponential value
_gcvt	Convert floating-point value to character string

(continued)

Floating-Point Functions *(continued)*

Routine	Use
_hypot	Calculate hypotenuse of right triangle
_isnan	Check given double-precision floating-point value for not a number (NaN)
labs	Return absolute value of **long**
ldexp	Calculate product of argument and 2 to specified power
ldiv	Divide one **long** integer by another, returning quotient and remainder
log	Calculate natural logarithm
log10	Calculate base-10 logarithm
_logb	Extract exponential value of double-precision floating-point argument
_lrotl, _lrotr	Shift **unsigned long int** left (**_lrotl**) or right (**_lrotr**)
_matherr	Handle math errors
__max	Return larger of two values
__min	Return smaller of two values
modf	Split argument into integer and fractional parts
_nextafter	Return next representable neighbor
pow	Calculate value raised to a power
printf, wprintf	Write data to **stdout** according to specified format
rand	Get pseudorandom number
_rotl, _rotr	Shift **unsigned int** left (**_rotl**) or right (**_rotr**)
_scalb	Scale argument by power of 2
scanf, wscanf	Read data from **stdin** according to specified format and write data to specified location
sin	Calculate sine
sinh	Calculate hyperbolic sine
sqrt	Find square root
srand	Initialize pseudorandom series
_status87, _statusfp	Get floating-point status word
strtod	Convert character string to double-precision value
tan	Calculate tangent
tanh	Calculate hyperbolic tangent

Long Double

Previous 16-bit versions of Microsoft C/C++ and Microsoft Visual C++ supported the **long double**, 80-bit precision data type. In Win32 programming, however, the **long double** data type maps to the **double**, 64-bit precision data type. The Microsoft run-time library provides **long double** versions of the math functions only for backward compatibility. The **long double** function prototypes are identical to the prototypes for their **double** counterparts, except that the **long double** data type replaces the **double** data type. The **long double** versions of these functions should not be used in new code.

Double Functions and Their Long Double Counterparts

Function	Long Double Counterpart	Function	Long Double Counterpart
acos	**acosl**	frexp	**frexpl**
asin	**asinl**	_hypot	**_hypotl**
atan	**atanl**	ldexp	**ldexpl**
atan2	**atan2l**	log	**logl**
atof	**_atold**	log10	**log10l**
Bessel functions j0, j1, jn	**j0l, j1l, jnl**	_matherr	**_matherrl**
Bessel functions y0, y1, yn	**y0l, y1l, ynl**	modf	**modfl**
_cabs	**_cabsl**	pow	**powl**
ceil	**ceill**	sin	**sinl**
cos	**cosl**	sinh	**sinhl**
cosh	**coshl**	sqrt	**sqrtl**
exp	**expl**	strtod	**_strtold**
fabs	**fabsl**	tan	**tanl**
floor	**floorl**	tanh	**tanhl**
fmod	**fmodl**		

Input and Output

The I/O functions read and write data to and from files and devices. File I/O operations take place in text mode or binary mode. The Microsoft run-time library has three types of I/O functions:

- Stream I/O functions treat data as a stream of individual characters.

- Low-level I/O functions invoke the operating system directly for lower-level operation than that provided by stream I/O.

- Console and port I/O functions read or write directly to a console (keyboard and screen) or an I/O port (such as a printer port).

  Warning Because stream functions are buffered and low-level functions are not, these two types of functions are generally incompatible. For processing a particular file, use either stream or low-level functions exclusively.

Text and Binary Mode File I/O

File I/O operations take place in one of two translation modes, text or binary, depending on the mode in which the file is opened. Data files are usually processed in text mode. To control the file translation mode, you can:

- Retain the current default setting and specify the alternative mode only when you open selected files.

- Change the default translation mode directly by setting the global variable _fmode in your program. The initial default setting of **_fmode** is **_O_TEXT**, for text mode.

When you call a file-open function such as _open, fopen, freopen, or _fsopen, you can override the current default setting of **_fmode** by specifying the appropriate argument to the function. The **stdin**, **stdout**, and **stderr** streams always open in text mode by default; you can also override this default when opening any of these files. Use _setmode to change the translation mode using the file handle after the file is open.

Unicode Stream I/O in Text and Binary Modes

When a Unicode stream I/O routine (such as **fwprintf**, **fwscanf**, **fgetwc**, **fputwc**, **fgetws**, or **fputws**) operates on a file that is open in text mode (the default), two kinds of character conversions take place:

- Unicode-to-MBCS or MBCS-to-Unicode conversion. When a Unicode stream-I/O function operates in text mode, the source or destination stream is assumed to be a sequence of multibyte characters. Therefore, the Unicode stream-input functions convert multibyte characters to wide characters (as if by a call to the **mbtowc** function). For the same reason, the Unicode stream-output functions convert wide characters to multibyte characters (as if by a call to the **wctomb** function).

- Carriage return-linefeed (CR-LF) translation. This translation occurs before the MBCS–Unicode conversion (for Unicode stream input functions) and after the Unicode–MBCS conversion (for Unicode stream output functions). During input, each carriage return-linefeed combination is translated into a single linefeed character. During output, each linefeed character is translated into a carriage return-linefeed combination.

However, when a Unicode stream-I/O function operates in binary mode, the file is assumed to be Unicode, and no CR-LF translation or character conversion occurs during input or output.

Stream I/O

These functions process data in different sizes and formats, from single characters to large data structures. They also provide buffering, which can improve performance. The default size of a stream buffer is 4K. These routines affect only buffers created by the run-time library routines, and have no effect on buffers created by the operating system.

Stream I/O Routines

Routine	Use
clearerr	Clear error indicator for stream
fclose	Close stream
_fcloseall	Close all open streams except **stdin**, **stdout**, and **stderr**
_fdopen, wfdopen	Associate stream with handle to open file
feof	Test for end of file on stream
ferror	Test for error on stream
fflush	Flush stream to buffer or storage device
fgetc, fgetwc	Read character from stream (function versions of **getc** and **getwc**)
_fgetchar, _fgetwchar	Read character from **stdin** (function versions of **getchar** and **getwchar**)
fgetpos	Get position indicator of stream
fgets, fgetws	Read string from stream
_fileno	Get file handle associated with stream
_flushall	Flush all streams to buffer or storage device
fopen, _wfopen	Open stream
fprintf, fwprintf	Write formatted data to stream
fputc, fputwc	Write a character to a stream (function versions of **putc** and **putwc**)

(continued)

Stream I/O Routines *(continued)*

Routine	Use
_fputchar, _fputwchar	Write character to **stdout** (function versions of **putchar** and **putwchar**)
fputs, fputws	Write string to stream
fread	Read unformatted data from stream
freopen, _wfreopen	Reassign **FILE** stream pointer to new file or device
fscanf, fwscanf	Read formatted data from stream
fseek	Move file position to given location
fsetpos	Set position indicator of stream
_fsopen, _wfsopen	Open stream with file sharing
ftell	Get current file position
fwrite	Write unformatted data items to stream
getc, getwc	Read character from stream (macro versions of **fgetc** and **fgetwc**)
getchar, getwchar	Read character from **stdin** (macro versions of **fgetchar** and **fgetwchar**)
gets, getws	Read line from **stdin**
_getw	Read binary **int** from stream
printf, wprintf	Write formatted data to **stdout**
putc, putwc	Write character to a stream (macro versions of **fputc** and **fputwc**)
putchar, putwchar	Write character to **stdout** (macro versions of **fputchar** and **fputwchar**)
puts, _putws	Write line to stream
_putw	Write binary **int** to stream
rewind	Move file position to beginning of stream
_rmtmp	Remove temporary files created by **tmpfile**
scanf, wscanf	Read formatted data from **stdin**
setbuf	Control stream buffering
_setmaxstdio	Set a maximum for the number of simultaneously open files at the stream I/O level.
setvbuf	Control stream buffering and buffer size
_snprintf, _snwprintf	Write formatted data of specified length to string
sprintf, swprintf	Write formatted data to string

Stream I/O Routines   *(continued)*

Routine	Use
sscanf, swscanf	Read formatted data from string
_tempnam, _wtempnam	Generate temporary filename in given directory
tmpfile	Create temporary file
tmpnam, _wtmpnam	Generate temporary filename
ungetc, ungetwc	Push character back onto stream
vfprintf, vfwprintf	Write formatted data to stream
vprintf, vwprintf	Write formatted data to **stdout**
_vsnprintf, _vsnwprintf	Write formatted data of specified length to buffer
vsprintf, vswprintf	Write formatted data to buffer

When a program begins execution, the startup code automatically opens several streams: standard input (pointed to by **stdin**), standard output (pointed to by **stdout**), and standard error (pointed to by **stderr**). These streams are directed to the console (keyboard and screen) by default. Use **freopen** to redirect **stdin**, **stdout**, or **stderr** to a disk file or a device.

Files opened using the stream routines are buffered by default. The **stdout** and **stderr** functions are flushed whenever they are full or, if you are writing to a character device, after each library call. If a program terminates abnormally, output buffers may not be flushed, resulting in loss of data. Use **fflush** or **_flushall** to ensure that the buffer associated with a specified file or all open buffers are flushed to the operating system, which can cache data before writing it to disk. The commit-to-disk feature ensures that the flushed buffer contents are not lost in the event of a system failure.

There are two ways to commit buffer contents to disk:

- Link with the file COMMODE.OBJ to set a global commit flag. The default setting of the global flag is **n**, for "no-commit."

- Set the mode flag to **c** with **fopen** or **_fdopen**.

Any file specifically opened with either the **c** or the **n** flag behaves according to the flag, regardless of the state of the global commit/no-commit flag.

If your program does not explicitly close a stream, the stream is automatically closed when the program terminates. However, you should close a stream when your program finishes with it, as the number of streams that can be open at one time is limited. See "_setmaxstdio" in the alphabetic reference for information on this limit.

Input can follow output directly only with an intervening call to **fflush** or to a file-positioning function (**fseek**, **fsetpos**, or **rewind**). Output can follow input without an intervening call to a file-positioning function if the input operation encounters the end of the file.

Low-level I/O

These functions invoke the operating system directly for lower-level operation than that provided by stream I/O. Low-level input and output calls do not buffer or format data.

Low-level routines can access the standard streams opened at program startup using the following predefined handles:

Stream	Handle
Stdin	0
Stdout	1
Stderr	2

Low-level I/O routines set the errno global variable when an error occurs. You must include STDIO.H when you use low-level functions only if your program requires a constant that is defined in STDIO.H, such as the end-of-file indicator (**EOF**).

Low-Level I/O Functions

Function	Use
_close	Close file
_commit	Flush file to disk
_creat, _wcreat	Create file
_dup	Return next available file handle for given file
_dup2	Create second handle for given file
_eof	Test for end of file
_lseek, _lseeki64	Reposition file pointer to given location
_open, _wopen	Open file
_read	Read data from file
_sopen, _wsopen	Open file for file sharing
_tell, _telli64	Get current file-pointer position
_umask	Set file-permission mask
_write	Write data to file

_dup and **_dup2** are typically used to associate the predefined file handles with different files.

Console and Port I/O

These routines read and write on your console or on the specified port. The console I/O routines are not compatible with stream I/O or low-level I/O library routines. The console or port does not have to be opened or closed before I/O is performed, so there are no open or close routines in this category. In Windows NT and Windows 95, the output from these functions is always directed to the console and cannot be redirected.

Console and Port I/O Routines

Routine	Use
_cgets	Read string from console
_cprintf	Write formatted data to console
_cputs	Write string to console
_cscanf	Read formatted data from console
_getch	Read character from console
_getche	Read character from console and echo it
_inp	Read one byte from specified I/O port
_inpd	Read double word from specified I/O port
_inpw	Read 2-byte word from specified I/O port
_kbhit	Check for keystroke at console; use before attempting to read from console
_outp	Write one byte to specified I/O port
_outpd	Write double word to specified I/O port
_outpw	Write word to specified I/O port
_putch	Write character to console
_ungetch	"Unget" last character read from console so it becomes next character read

Internationalization

The Microsoft run-time library provides many routines that are useful for creating different versions of a program for international markets. This includes locale-related routines, wide-character routines, multibyte-character routines, and generic-text routines. For convenience, most locale-related routines are also categorized in this reference according to the operations they perform. In this chapter and in this book's alphabetic reference, multibyte-character routines and wide-character routines are described with single-byte-character counterparts, where they exist.

Locale

Use the setlocale function to change or query some or all of the current program locale information. "Locale" refers to the locality (the country and language) for which you can customize certain aspects of your program. Some locale-dependent categories include the formatting of dates and the display format for monetary values. For more information, see "Locale Categories" in Chapter 3, "Global Constants."

Locale-Dependent Routines

Routine	Use	setlocale Category Setting Dependence
atof, atoi, atol	Convert character to floating-point, integer, or long integer value, respectively	**LC_NUMERIC**
is Routines	Test given integer for particular condition.	**LC_CTYPE**
isleadbyte	Test for lead byte ()	**LC_CTYPE**
localeconv	Read appropriate values for formatting numeric quantities	**LC_MONETARY, LC_NUMERIC**
MB_CUR_MAX	Maximum length in bytes of any multibyte character in current locale (macro defined in STDLIB.H)	**LC_CTYPE**
_mbccpy	Copy one multibyte character	**LC_CTYPE**
_mbclen	Return length, in bytes, of given multibyte character	**LC_CTYPE**
mblen	Validate and return number of bytes in multibyte character	**LC_CTYPE**
_mbstrlen	For multibyte-character strings: validate each character in string; return string length	**LC_CTYPE**
mbstowcs	Convert sequence of multibyte characters to corresponding sequence of wide characters	**LC_CTYPE**
mbtowc	Convert multibyte character to corresponding wide character	**LC_CTYPE**
printf functions	Write formatted output	**LC_NUMERIC** (determines radix character output)
scanf functions	Read formatted input	**LC_NUMERIC** (determines radix character recognition)

Locale-Dependent Routines *(continued)*

Routine	Use	setlocale Category Setting Dependence
setlocale, _wsetlocale	Select locale for program	Not applicable
strcoll, wcscoll	Compare characters of two strings	**LC_COLLATE**
_stricoll, _wcsicoll	Compare characters of two strings (case insensitive)	**LC_COLLATE**
_strncoll, _wcsncoll	Compare first *n* characters of two strings	**LC_COLLATE**
_strnicoll, _wcsnicoll	Compare first *n* characters of two strings (case insensitive)	**LC_COLLATE**
strftime, wcsftime	Format date and time value according to supplied *format* argument	**LC_TIME**
_strlwr	Convert, in place, each uppercase letter in given string to lowercase	**LC_CTYPE**
strtod, wcstod, strtol, wcstol, strtoul, wcstoul	Convert character string to double, long, or unsigned long value	**LC_NUMERIC** (determines radix character recognition)
_strupr	Convert, in place, each lowercase letter in string to uppercase	**LC_CTYPE**
strxfrm, wcsxfrm	Transform string into collated form according to locale	**LC_COLLATE**
tolower, towlower	Convert given character to corresponding lowercase character	**LC_CTYPE**
toupper, towupper	Convert given character to corresponding uppercase letter	**LC_CTYPE**
wcstombs	Convert sequence of wide characters to corresponding sequence of multibyte characters	**LC_CTYPE**
wctomb	Convert wide character to corresponding multibyte character	**LC_CTYPE**
_wtoi, _wtol	Convert wide-character string to **int** or **long**	**LC_NUMERIC**

Code Pages

A *code page* is a character set, which can include numbers, punctuation marks, and other glyphs. Different languages and locales may use different code pages. For example, ANSI code page 1252 is used for American English and most European languages; OEM code page 932 is used for Japanese Kanji.

A code page can be represented in a table as a mapping of characters to single-byte values or multibyte values. Many code pages share the ASCII character set for characters in the range 0x00–0x7F.

The Microsoft run-time library uses the following types of code pages:

- System-default ANSI code page. By default, at startup the run-time system automatically sets the multibyte code page to the system-default ANSI code page, which is obtained from the operating system. The call

```
setlocale ( LC_ALL, "" );
```

  also sets the locale to the system-default ANSI code page.

- Locale code page. The behavior of a number of run-time routines is dependent on the current locale setting, which includes the locale code page. (For more information, see Locale-Dependent Routines.on the previous page) By default, all locale-dependent routines in the Microsoft run-time library use the code page that corresponds to the "C" locale. At run-time you can change or query the locale code page in use with a call to setlocale.

- Multibyte code page. The behavior of most of the multibyte-character routines in the run-time library depends on the current multibyte code page setting. By default, these routines use the system-default ANSI code page. At run-time you can query and change the multibyte code page with _getmbcp and _setmbcp, respectively.

- The "C" locale is defined by ANSI to correspond to the locale in which C programs have traditionally executed. The code page for the "C" locale ("C" code page) corresponds to the ASCII character set. For example, in the "C" locale, **islower** returns true for the values 0x61–0x7A only. In another locale, **islower** may return true for these as well as other values, as defined by that locale.

Interpretation of Multibyte Character Sequences

Most multibyte-character routines in the Microsoft run-time library recognize multibyte-character sequences according to the current multibyte code page setting. The following multibyte-character routines depend instead on the locale code page (specifically, on the **LC_CTYPE** category setting of the current locale):

Locale-Dependent Multibyte Routines

Routine	Use
mblen	Validate and return number of bytes in multibyte character
_mbstrlen	For multibyte-character strings: validate each character in string; return string length
mbstowcs	Convert sequence of multibyte characters to corresponding sequence of wide characters
mbtowc	Convert multibyte character to corresponding wide character
wcstombs	Convert sequence of wide characters to corresponding sequence of multibyte characters
wctomb	Convert wide character to corresponding multibyte character

Single-Byte and Multibyte Character Sets

The ASCII character set defines characters in the range 0x00–0x7F. There are a number of other character sets, primarily European, that define the characters within the range 0x00–0x7F identically to the ASCII character set and also define an extended character set from 0x80–0xFF. Thus an 8-bit, single-byte-character set (SBCS) is sufficient to represent the ASCII character set as well as the character sets for many European languages. However, some non-European character sets, such as Japanese Kanji, include many more characters than can be represented in a single-byte coding scheme, and therefore require multibyte-character set (MBCS) encoding.

> **Note** Many SBCS routines in the Microsoft run-time library handle multibyte bytes, characters, and strings as appropriate. Many multibyte-character sets define the ASCII character set as a subset. In many multibyte character sets, each character in the range 0x00–0x7F is identical to the character that has the same value in the ASCII character set. For example, in both ASCII and MBCS character strings, the one-byte **NULL** character ('\0') has value 0x00 and indicates the terminating null character.

A multibyte character set may consist of both one-byte and two-byte characters. Thus multibyte-character string may contain a mixture of single-byte and double-byte characters. A two-byte multibyte character has a lead byte and a trail byte. In a particular multibyte-character set, the lead bytes fall within a certain range, as do the trail bytes. When these ranges overlap, it may be necessary to evaluate the context to determine whether a given byte is functioning as a lead byte or a trail byte.

SBCS and MBCS Data Types

Any Microsoft MBCS run-time library routine that handles only one multibyte character or one byte of a multibyte character expects an unsigned **int** argument (where 0x00 <= character value <= 0xFFFF and 0x00 <= byte value <= 0xFF). An MBCS routine that handles multibyte bytes or characters in a string context expects a multibyte-character string to be represented as an unsigned **char** pointer.

> **Caution** Each byte of a multibyte character can be represented in an 8-bit **char**. However, an SBCS or MBCS single-byte character of type **char** with a value greater than 0x7F is negative. When such a character is converted directly to an **int** or a **long**, the result is sign-extended by the compiler and can therefore yield unexpected results.

Therefore it is best to represent a byte of a multibyte character as an 8-bit **unsigned char**. Or, to avoid a negative result, simply convert a single-byte character of type **char** to an **unsigned char** before converting it to an **int** or a **long**.

Because some SBCS string-handling functions take (signed) **char*** parameters, a type mismatch compiler warning will result when **_MBCS** is defined. There are three ways to avoid this warning, listed in order of efficiency:

1. Use the "type-safe" inline function thunks in TCHAR.H. This is the default behavior.

2. Use the "direct" macros in TCHAR.H by defining **_MB_MAP_DIRECT** on the command line. If you do this, you must manually match types. This is the fastest method, but is not type-safe.

3. Use the "type-safe" statically linked library function thunks in TCHAR.H. To do so, define the constant **_NO_INLINING** on the command line. This is the slowest method, but the most type-safe.

Unicode: The Wide-Character Set

A wide character is a 2-byte multilingual character code. Any character in use in modern computing worldwide, including technical symbols and special publishing characters, can be represented according to the Unicode specification as a wide character. Developed and maintained by a large consortium that includes Microsoft, the Unicode standard is now widely accepted. Because every wide character is always represented in a fixed size of 16 bits, using wide characters simplifies programming with international character sets.

A wide character is of type **wchar_t**. A wide-character string is represented as a **wchar_t[]** array and is pointed to by a **wchar_t*** pointer. You can represent any ASCII character as a wide character by prefixing the letter L to the character. For example, L'\0' is the terminating wide (16-bit) **NULL** character. Similarly, you can represent any ASCII string literal as a wide-character string literal simply by prefixing the letter L to the ASCII literal (L"Hello").

Generally, wide characters take up more space in memory than multibyte characters but are faster to process. In addition, only one locale can be represented at a time in multibyte encoding, whereas all character sets in the world are represented simultaneously by the Unicode representation.

Using Generic-Text Mappings

Microsoft Specific →

To simplify code development for various international markets, the Microsoft run-time library provides Microsoft-specific "generic-text" mappings for many data types, routines, and other objects. These mappings are defined in TCHAR.H. You can use these name mappings to write generic code that can be compiled for any of the three kinds of character sets: ASCII (SBCS), MBCS, or Unicode, depending on a manifest constant you define using a **#define** statement. Generic-text mappings are Microsoft extensions that are not ANSI compatible.

Preprocessor Directives for Generic-Text Mappings

#define	Compiled Version	Example
_UNICODE	Unicode (wide-character)	**_tcsrev** maps to **_wcsrev**
_MBCS	Multibyte-character	**_tcsrev** maps to **_mbsrev**
None (the default: neither **_UNICODE** nor **_MBCS** defined)	SBCS (ASCII)	**_tcsrev** maps to **strrev**

For example, the generic-text function **_tcsrev**, defined in TCHAR.H, maps to **mbsrev** if **MBCS** has been defined in your program, or to **_wcsrev** if **_UNICODE** has been defined. Otherwise **_tcsrev** maps to **strrev**.

The generic-text data type **_TCHAR**, also defined in TCHAR.H, maps to type **char** if **_MBCS** is defined, to type **wchar_t** if **_UNICODE** is defined, and to type **char** if neither constant is defined. Other data type mappings are provided in TCHAR.H for programming convenience, but **_TCHAR** is the type that is most useful.

Generic-Text Data Type Mappings

Generic-Text Data Type Name	SBCS (_UNICODE, _MBCS Not Defined)	_MBCS Defined	_UNICODE Defined
_TCHAR	char	char	wchar_t
_TINT	int	int	wint_t
_TSCHAR	signed char	signed char	wchar_t
_TUCHAR	unsigned char	unsigned char	wchar_t
_TXCHAR	char	unsigned char	wchar_t
_T or **_TEXT**	No effect (removed by preprocessor)	No effect (removed by preprocessor)	**L** (converts following character or string to its Unicode counterpart)

For a complete list of generic-text mappings of routines, variables, and other objects, see Appendix B, "Generic-Text Mappings."

The following code fragments illustrate the use of **_TCHAR** and **_tcsrev** for mapping to the MBCS, Unicode, and SBCS models.

```
_TCHAR *RetVal, *szString;
RetVal = _tcsrev(szString);
```

If **MBCS** has been defined, the preprocessor maps the preceding fragment to the following code:

```
char *RetVal, *szString;
RetVal = _mbsrev(szString);
```

If **_UNICODE** has been defined, the preprocessor maps the same fragment to the following code:

```
wchar_t *RetVal, *szString;
RetVal = _wcsrev(szString);
```

If neither **_MBCS** nor **_UNICODE** has been defined, the preprocessor maps the fragment to single-byte ASCII code, as follows:

```
char *RetVal, *szString;
RetVal = strrev(szString);
```

Thus you can write, maintain, and compile a single source code file to run with routines that are specific to any of the three kinds of character sets.

See Also

Generic-text mappings, Data type mappings, Constants and global variable mappings, Routine mappings, A sample generic-text program

END Microsoft Specific

A Sample Generic-Text Program

Microsoft Specific →

The following program, GENTEXT.C, provides a more detailed illustration of the use of generic-text mappings defined in TCHAR.H:

```
/*
 * GENTEXT.C: use of generic-text mappings defined in TCHAR.H
 *            Generic-Text-Mapping example program
 */
```

```
#include <stdio.h>
#include <stdlib.h>
#include <string.h>
#include <direct.h>
#include <errno.h>
#include <tchar.h>

int __cdecl _tmain(int argc, _TCHAR **argv, _TCHAR **envp)
{
    _TCHAR buff[_MAX_PATH];
    _TCHAR *str = _T("Astring");
    char *amsg = "Reversed";
    wchar_t *wmsg = L"Is";

#ifdef _UNICODE
    printf("Unicode version\n");
#else /* _UNICODE */
#ifdef _MBCS
    printf("MBCS version\n");
#else
    printf("SBCS version\n");
#endif
#endif /* _UNICODE */

    if (_tgetcwd(buff, _MAX_PATH) == NULL)
        printf("Can't Get Current Directory - errno=%d\n", errno);
    else
        _tprintf(_T("Current Directory is '%s'\n"), buff);
    _tprintf(_T("'%s' %hs %ls:\n"), str, amsg, wmsg);
    _tprintf(_T("'%s'\n"), _tcsrev(str));
    return 0;
}
```

If **_MBCS** has been defined, GENTEXT.C maps to the following MBCS program:

```
/*
 * MBCSGTXT.C: use of generic-text mappings defined in TCHAR.H
 *             Generic-Text-Mapping example program
 *             MBCS version of GENTEXT.C
 */

#include <stdlib.h>
#include <direct.h>
```

```
int __cdecl main(int argc, char **argv, char **envp)
{
    char buff[_MAX_PATH];
    char *str = "Astring";
    char *amsg = "Reversed";
    wchar_t *wmsg = L"Is";

    printf("MBCS version\n");

    if (_getcwd(buff, _MAX_PATH) == NULL) {
        printf("Can't Get Current Directory - errno=%d\n", errno);
    }
    else {
        printf("Current Directory is '%s'\n", buff);
    }

    printf("'%s' %hs %ls:\n", str, amsg, wmsg);
    printf("'%s'\n", _mbsrev(str));
    return 0;
}
```

If **_UNICODE** has been defined, GENTEXT.C maps to the following Unicode version of the program. For more information about using **wmain** in Unicode programs as a replacement for **main**, see "Using wmain" in the *C Language Reference* section of the *Microsoft Visual C++ 6.0 Language Reference* volume of the *Microsoft Visual C++ 6.0 Reference Library*.

```
/*
 * UNICGTXT.C: use of generic-text mappings defined in TCHAR.H
 *             Generic-Text-Mapping example program
 *             Unicode version of GENTEXT.C
 */

#include <stdlib.h>
#include <direct.h>

int __cdecl wmain(int argc, wchar_t **argv, wchar_t **envp)
{
    wchar_t buff[_MAX_PATH];
    wchar_t *str = L"Astring";
    char *amsg = "Reversed";
    wchar_t *wmsg = L"Is";

    printf("Unicode version\n");

    if (_wgetcwd(buff, _MAX_PATH) == NULL) {
        printf("Can't Get Current Directory - errno=%d\n", errno);
    }
```

```
else {
    wprintf(L"Current Directory is '%s'\n", buff);
}
wprintf(L"'%s' %hs %ls:\n", str, amsg, wmsg);
wprintf(L"'%s'\n", wcsrev(str));
return 0;
}
```

If neither **_MBCS** nor **_UNICODE** has been defined, GENTEXT.C maps to single-byte
ASCII code, as follows:

```
/*
 * SBCSGTXT.C: use of generic-text mappings defined in TCHAR.H
 *             Generic-Text-Mapping example program
 *             Single-byte (SBCS) Ascii version of GENTEXT.C
 */


#include <stdlib.h>
#include <direct.h>

int __cdecl main(int argc, char **argv, char **envp)
{
    char buff[_MAX_PATH];
    char *str = "Astring";
    char *amsg = "Reversed";
    wchar_t *wmsg = L"Is";

    printf("SBCS version\n");

    if (_getcwd(buff, _MAX_PATH) == NULL) {
        printf("Can't Get Current Directory - errno=%d\n", errno);
    }
    else {
        printf("Current Directory is '%s'\n", buff);
    }

    printf("'%s' %hs %ls:\n", str, amsg, wmsg);
    printf("'%s'\n", strrev(str));
    return 0;
}
```

See Also

Generic-text mappings, Data type mappings, Constants and global variable mappings,
Routine mappings, Using generic-text mappings

END Microsoft Specific

Using TCHAR.H Data Types with _MBCS

Microsoft Specific →

As the table of generic-text routine mappings indicates (see Appendix B, Generic-Text Mappings), when the manifest constant **_MBCS** is defined, a given generic-text routine maps to one of the following kinds of routines:

- An SBCS routine that handles multibyte bytes, characters, and strings appropriately. In this case, the string arguments are expected to be of type **char***. For example, **_tprintf** maps to **printf**; the string arguments to **printf** are of type **char***. If you use the **_TCHAR** generic-text data type for your string types, the formal and actual parameter types for **printf** match because **_TCHAR*** maps to **char***.

- An MBCS-specific routine. In this case, the string arguments are expected to be of type **unsigned char***. For example, **_tcsrev** maps to **_mbsrev**, which expects and returns a string of type **unsigned char***. Again, if you use the **_TCHAR** generic-text data type for your string types, there is a potential type conflict because **_TCHAR** maps to type **char**.

Following are three solutions for preventing this type conflict (and the C compiler warnings or C++ compiler errors that would result):

- Use the default behavior. TCHAR.H provides generic-text routine prototypes for routines in the run-time libraries, as in the following example.

  ```
  char *_tcsrev(char *);
  ```

  In the default case, the prototype for **_tcsrev** maps to **_mbsrev** through a thunk in LIBC.LIB. This changes the types of the **_mbsrev** incoming parameters and outgoing return value from **_TCHAR** * (i.e., **char** *) to **unsigned char** *. This method ensures type matching when you are using **_TCHAR**, but it is relatively slow because of the function call overhead.

- Use function inlining by incorporating the following preprocessor statement in your code.

  ```
  #define _USE_INLINING
  ```

  This method causes an inline function thunk, provided in TCHAR.H, to map the generic-text routine directly to the appropriate MBCS routine. The following code excerpt from TCHAR.H provides an example of how this is done.

  ```
  __inline char *_tcsrev(char *_s1)
  {return (char *)_mbsrev((unsigned char *)_s1);}
  ```

  If you can use inlining, this is the best solution, because it guarantees type matching and has no additional time cost.

- Use "direct mapping" by incorporating the following preprocessor statement in your code.

```
#define _MB_MAP_DIRECT
```

This approach provides a fast alternative if you do not want to use the default behavior or cannot use inlining. It causes the generic-text routine to be mapped by a macro directly to the MBCS version of the routine, as in the following example from TCHAR.H.

```
#define _tcschr _mbschr
```

When you take this approach, you must be careful to ensure that appropriate data types are used for string arguments and string return values. You can use type casting to ensure proper type matching or you can use the **_TXCHAR** generic-text data type. **_TXCHAR** maps to type **char** in SBCS code but maps to type **unsigned char** in MBCS code. For more information about generic-text macros, see Appendix B, "Generic-Text Mappings."

END Microsoft Specific

Memory Allocation

Use these routines to allocate, free, and reallocate memory.

Memory-Allocation Routines

Routine	Use
_alloca	Allocate memory from stack
calloc	Allocate storage for array, initializing every byte in allocated block to 0
_calloc_dbg	Debug version of **calloc**; only available in the debug versions of the run-time libraries
_expand	Expand or shrink block of memory without moving it
_expand_dbg	Debug version of **_expand**; only available in the debug versions of the run-time libraries
free	Free allocated block
_free_dbg	Debug version of **free**; only available in the debug versions of the run-time libraries
_get_sbh_threshold	Return the upper limit for the size of a memory allocation that will be supported by the small-block heap
_heapadd	Add memory to heap
_heapchk	Check heap for consistency
_heapmin	Release unused memory in heap *(continued)*

Memory-Allocation Routines *(continued)*

Routine	Use
_heapset	Fill free heap entries with specified value
_heapwalk	Return information about each entry in heap
malloc	Allocate block of memory from heap
_malloc_dbg	Debug version of **malloc**; only available in the debug versions of the run-time libraries
_msize	Return size of allocated block
_msize_dbg	Debug version of **_msize**; only available in the debug versions of the run-time libraries
_query_new_handler	Return address of current new handler routine as set by **_set_new_handler**
_query_new_mode	Return integer indicating new handler mode set by **_set_new_mode** for **malloc**
realloc	Reallocate block to new size
_realloc_dbg	Debug version of **realloc**; only available in the debug versions of the run-time libraries
_set_new_handler	Enable error-handling mechanism when **new** operator fails (to allocate memory) and enable compilation of Standard Template Libraries (STL)
_set_new_mode	Set new handler mode for **malloc**
_set_sbh_threshold	Set the upper limit for the size of a memory allocation that will be supported by the small-block heap

Process and Environment Control

Use the process-control routines to start, stop, and manage processes from within a program. Use the environment-control routines to get and change information about the operating-system environment.

Process and Environment Control Functions

Routine	Use
abort	Abort process without flushing buffers or calling functions registered by **atexit** and **_onexit**
assert	Test for logic error
_ASSERT, _ASSERTE macros	Similar to **assert**, but only available in the debug versions of the run-time libraries

Process and Environment Control Functions   *(continued)*

Routine	Use
atexit	Schedule routines for execution at program termination
_beginthread, _beginthreadex	Create a new thread on a Windows NT or Windows 95 process
_cexit	Perform **exit** termination procedures (such as flushing buffers), then return control to calling program without terminating process
_c_exit	Perform **_exit** termination procedures, then return control to calling program without terminating process
_cwait	Wait until another process terminates
_endthread, _endthreadex	Terminate a Windows NT or Windows 95 thread
_execl, _wexecl	Execute new process with argument list
_execle, _wexecle	Execute new process with argument list and given environment
_execlp, _wexeclp	Execute new process using **PATH** variable and argument list
_execlpe, _wexeclpe	Execute new process using **PATH** variable, given environment, and argument list
_execv, _wexecv	Execute new process with argument array
_execve, _wexecve	Execute new process with argument array and given environment
_execvp, _wexecvp	Execute new process using **PATH** variable and argument array
_execvpe, _wexecvpe	Execute new process using **PATH** variable, given environment, and argument array
exit	Call functions registered by **atexit** and **_onexit**, flush all buffers, close all open files, and terminate process
_exit	Terminate process immediately without calling **atexit** or **_onexit** or flushing buffers
getenv, _wgetenv	Get value of environment variable
_getpid	Get process ID number
longjmp	Restore saved stack environment; use it to execute a nonlocal **goto**
_onexit	Schedule routines for execution at program termination; use for compatibility with Microsoft C/C++ version 7.0 and earlier
_pclose	Wait for new command processor and close stream on associated pipe
perror, _wperror	Print error message

(continued)

Process and Environment Control Functions *(continued)*

Routine	Use
_pipe	Create pipe for reading and writing
_popen, _wpopen	Create pipe and execute command
_putenv, _wputenv	Add or change value of environment variable
raise	Send signal to calling process
setjmp	Save stack environment; use to execute nonlocal **goto**
signal	Handle interrupt signal
_spawnl, _wspawnl	Create and execute new process with specified argument list
_spawnle, _wspawnle	Create and execute new process with specified argument list and environment
_spawnlp, _wspawnlp	Create and execute new process using **PATH** variable and specified argument list
_spawnlpe, _wspawnlpe	Create and execute new process using **PATH** variable, specified environment, and argument list
_spawnv, _wspawnv	Create and execute new process with specified argument array
_spawnve, _wspawnve	Create and execute new process with specified environment and argument array
_spawnvp, _wspawnvp	Create and execute new process using **PATH** variable and specified argument array
_spawnvpe, _wspawnvpe	Create and execute new process using **PATH** variable, specified environment, and argument array
System, _wsystem	Execute operating-system command

In Windows NT and Windows 95, the spawned process is equivalent to the spawning process. Therefore, the OS/2 **wait** function, which allows a parent process to wait for its children to terminate, is not available. Instead, any process can use **_cwait** to wait for any other process for which the process ID is known.

The difference between the **_exec** and **_spawn** families is that a **_spawn** function can return control from the new process to the calling process. In a **_spawn** function, both the calling process and the new process are present in memory unless **_P_OVERLAY** is specified. In an **_exec** function, the new process overlays the calling process, so control cannot return to the calling process unless an error occurs in the attempt to start execution of the new process.

The differences among the functions in the **_exec** family, as well as among those in the **_spawn** family, involve the method of locating the file to be executed as the new process, the form in which arguments are passed to the new process, and the method of setting the environment, as shown in the following table. Use a function that passes an argument list when the number of arguments is constant or is known at compile time. Use a function that passes a pointer to an array containing the arguments when the number of arguments is to be determined at run time. The information in the following table also applies to the wide-character counterparts of the **_spawn** and **_exec** functions.

_spawn and _exec Function Families

Functions	Use PATH Variable to Locate File	Argument-Passing Convention	Environment Settings
_execl, _spawnl	No	List	Inherited from calling process
_execle, _spawnle	No	List	Pointer to environment table for new process passed as last argument
_execlp, _spawnlp	Yes	List	Inherited from calling process
_execlpe, _spawnlpe	Yes	List	Pointer to environment table for new process passed as last argument
_execv, _spawnv	No	Array	Inherited from calling process
_execve, _spawnve	No	Array	Pointer to environment table for new process passed as last argument
_execvp, _spawnvp	Yes	Array	Inherited from calling process
_execvpe, _spawnvpe	Yes	Array	Pointer to environment table for new process passed as last argument

Searching and Sorting

Use the following functions for searching and sorting:

Searching and Sorting Functions

Function	Search or Sort
bsearch	Binary search
_lfind	Linear search for given value
_lsearch	Linear search for given value, which is added to array if not found
qsort	Quick sort

String Manipulation

These routines operate on null-terminated single-byte character, wide-character, and multibyte-character strings. Use the buffer-manipulation routines, described in Buffer Manipulation, to work with character arrays that do not end with a null character.

String-Manipulation Routines

Routine	Use
_mbscoll, _mbsicoll, _mbsncoll, _mbsnicoll	Compare two multibyte-character strings using multibyte code page information (**_mbsicoll** and **_mbsnicoll** are case-insensitive)
_mbsdec, _strdec, _wcsdec	Move string pointer back one character
_mbsinc, _strinc, _wcsinc	Advance string pointer by one character
_mbslen	Get number of multibyte characters in multibyte-character string; dependent upon OEM code page
_mbsnbcat	Append, at most, first *n* bytes of one multibyte-character string to another
_mbsnbcmp	Compare first *n* bytes of two multibyte-character strings
_mbsnbcnt	Return number of multibyte-character bytes within supplied character count
_mbsnbcpy	Copy *n* bytes of string
_mbsnbicmp	Compare *n* bytes of two multibyte-character strings, ignoring case
_mbsnbset	Set first *n* bytes of multibyte-character string to specified character
_mbsnccnt	Return number of multibyte characters within supplied byte count
_mbsnextc, _strnextc, _wcsnextc	Find next character in string
_mbsninc. _strninc, _wcsninc	Advance string pointer by *n* characters
_mbsspnp, _strspnp, _wcsspnp	Return pointer to first character in given string that is not in another given string
_mbstrlen	Get number of multibyte characters in multibyte-character string; locale-dependent
sprintf, _stprintf	Write formatted data to a string
strcat, wcscat, _mbscat	Append one string to another
strchr, wcschr, _mbschr	Find first occurrence of specified character in string
strcmp, wcscmp, _mbscmp	Compare two strings

String-Manipulation Routines   *(continued)*

Routine	Use
strcoll, wcscoll, _stricoll, _wcsicoll, _strncoll, _wcsncoll, _strnicoll, _wcsnicoll	Compare two strings using current locale code page information (**_stricoll**, **_wcsicoll**, **_strnicoll**, and **_wcsnicoll** are case-insensitive)
strcpy, wcscpy, _mbscpy	Copy one string to another
strcspn, wcscspn, _mbscspn,	Find first occurrence of character from specified character set in string
_strdup, _wcsdup, _mbsdup	Duplicate string
strerror	Map error number to message string
_strerror	Map user-defined error message to string
strftime, wcsftime	Format date-and-time string
_stricmp, _wcsicmp, _mbsicmp	Compare two strings without regard to case
strlen, wcslen, _mbslen, _mbstrlen	Find length of string
_strlwr, _wcslwr, _mbslwr	Convert string to lowercase
strncat, wcsncat, _mbsncat	Append characters of string
strncmp, wcsncmp, _mbsncmp	Compare characters of two strings
strncpy, wcsncpy, _mbsncpy	Copy characters of one string to another
_strnicmp, _wcsnicmp, _mbsnicmp	Compare characters of two strings without regard to case
_strnset, _wcsnset, _mbsnset	Set first *n* characters of string to specified character
strpbrk, wcspbrk, _mbspbrk	Find first occurrence of character from one string in another string
strrchr, wcsrchr,_mbsrchr	Find last occurrence of given character in string
_strrev, _wcsrev,_mbsrev	Reverse string
_strset, _wcsset, _mbsset	Set all characters of string to specified character
strspn, wcsspn, _mbsspn	Find first substring from one string in another string
strstr, wcsstr, _mbsstr	Find first occurrence of specified string in another string
strtok, wcstok, _mbstok	Find next token in string
_strupr, _wcsupr, _mbsupr	Convert string to uppercase
strxfrm, wcsxfrm	Transform string into collated form based on locale-specific information
vsprintf, _vstprint	Write formatted output using a pointer to a list of arguments

System Calls

The following functions are Windows NT and Windows 95 operating-system calls:

System Call Functions

Function	Use
_findclose	Release resources from previous find operations
_findfirst, _findfirsti64, _wfindfirst, _wfindfirsti64	Find file with specified attributes
_findnext, _findnexti64, _wfindnext, _wfindnexti64	Find next file with specified attributes

Time Management

Use these functions to get the current time and convert, adjust, and store it as necessary. The current time is the system time.

The **_ftime** and **localtime** routines use the **TZ** environment variable. If **TZ** is not set, the run-time library attempts to use the time-zone information specified by the operating system. If this information is unavailable, these functions use the default value of PST8PDT. For more information on **TZ**, see "_tzset"; also see "_daylight, _timezone, and _tzname" in Chapter 2, "Global Variables and Standard Types."

Time Routines

Function	Use
asctime, _wasctime	Convert time from type **struct tm** to character string
clock	Return elapsed CPU time for process
ctime, _wctime	Convert time from type **time_t** to character string
difftime	Compute difference between two times
_ftime	Store current system time in variable of type **struct _timeb**
_futime	Set modification time on open file
gmtime	Convert time from type **time_t** to **struct tm**
localtime	Convert time from type **time_t** to **struct tm** with local correction
mktime	Convert time to calendar value
_strdate, _wstrdate	Return current system date as string

Time Routines *(continued)*

Function	Use
strftime, wcsftime	Format date-and-time string for international use
_strtime, _wstrtime	Return current system time as string
time	Get current system time as type **time_t**
_tzset	Set external time variables from environment time variable **TZ**
_utime, _wutime	Set modification time for specified file using either current time or time value stored in structure

Note In all versions of Microsoft C/C++ except Microsoft C/C++ version 7.0, and in all versions of Microsoft Visual C++, the **time** function returns the current time as the number of seconds elapsed since midnight on January 1, 1970. In Microsoft C/C++ version 7.0, **time** returned the current time as the number of seconds elapsed since midnight on December 31, 1899.

CHAPTER 2

Global Variables and Standard Types

The Microsoft run-time library contains definitions for global variables, control flags, and standard types used by library routines. Access these variables, flags, and types by declaring them in your program or by including the appropriate header files.

Global Variables

The Microsoft run-time library provides the following global variables.

Variable	Description
_amblksiz	Controls memory heap granularity
_daylight, _timezone, _tzname	Adjust for local time; used in some date and time functions
_doserrno, errno, _sys_errlist, _sys_nerr	Store error codes and related information
_environ, _wenviron	Pointers to arrays of pointers to strings that constitute process environment
_fileinfo	Specifies whether information regarding open files of a process is passed to new processes
_fmode	Sets default file-translation mode
_osver, _winmajor, _winminor, _winver	Store build and version numbers of operating system
_pgmptr, _wpgmptr	Initialized at program startup to value such as program name, filename, relative path, or full path

_amblksiz

_amblksiz controls memory heap granularity. It is declared in MALLOC.H as

extern unsigned int _amblksiz;

The value of **_amblksiz** specifies the size of blocks allocated by the operating system for the heap. The initial requested size for a segment of heap memory is just enough to satisfy the current allocation request (for example, a call to **malloc**) plus memory required for heap manager overhead. The value of **_amblksiz** should represent a trade-off between the number of times the operating system is to be called to increase the heap to required size and the amount of memory potentially wasted (available but not used) at the end of the heap.

The default value of **_amblksiz** is 8K. You can change this value by direct assignment in your program. For example:

```
_amblksiz = 2045;
```

If you assign a value to **_amblksiz,** the actual value used internally by the heap manager is the assigned value rounded up to the nearest whole power of 2. Thus, in the previous example, the heap manager would reset the value of **_amblksize** to 2048.

_daylight, _timezone, and _tzname

_daylight, **_timezone**, and **_tzname** are used in some time and date routines to make local-time adjustments. They are declared in TIME.H as

extern int _daylight;
extern long _timezone;
extern char *_tzname[2];

On a call to **_ftime**, **localtime**, or **_tzset**, the values of **_daylight**, **_timezone**, and **_tzname** are determined from the value of the **TZ** environment variable. If you do not explicitly set the value of **TZ**, **_tzname[0]** and **_tzname[1]** contain empty strings, but the time-manipulation functions (_tzset, _ftime, and localtime) attempt to set the values of **_daylight** and **_timezone** by querying the operating system for the default value of each variable. The time-zone global variable values are as follows.

Variable	Value
_daylight	Nonzero if daylight-saving-time zone (DST) is specified in **TZ**; otherwise, 0. Default value is 1.
_timezone	Difference in seconds between coordinated universal time and local time. Default value is 28,800.
_tzname[0]	Time-zone name derived from **TZ** environment variable.
_tzname[1]	DST zone name derived from **TZ** environment variable. Default value is PDT (Pacific daylight time). If DST zone is omitted from **TZ**, **_tzname[1]** is empty string.

_doserrno, errno, _sys_errlist, and _sys_nerr

These global variables hold error codes used by the perror and strerror functions for printing error messages. Manifest constants for these variables are declared in STDLIB.H as follows:

extern int _doserrno;
extern int errno;
extern char *_sys_errlist[ ];
extern int _sys_nerr;

errno is set on an error in a system-level call. Because **errno** holds the value for the last call that set it, this value may be changed by succeeding calls. Always check **errno** immediately before and after a call that may set it. All **errno** values, defined as manifest constants in ERRNO.H, are UNIX-compatible. The values valid for 32-bit Windows applications are a subset of these UNIX values.

On an error, **errno** is not necessarily set to the same value as the error code returned by a system call. For I/O operations only, use **_doserrno** to access the operating-system error-code equivalents of **errno** codes. For other operations the value of **_doserrno** is undefined.

Each **errno** value is associated with an error message that can be printed using **perror** or stored in a string using **strerror**. **perror** and **strerror** use the **_sys_errlist** array and **_sys_nerr**, the number of elements in **_sys_errlist**, to process error information.

Library math routines set **errno** by calling _matherr. To handle math errors differently, write your own routine according to the **_matherr** reference description and name it **_matherr**.

The following **errno** values are compatible with 32-bit Windows applications. Only **ERANGE** and **EDOM** are specified in the ANSI standard.

Constant	System Error Message	Value
E2BIG	Argument list too long	7
EACCES	Permission denied	13
EAGAIN	No more processes or not enough memory or maximum nesting level reached	11
EBADF	Bad file number	9
ECHILD	No spawned processes	10
EDEADLOCK	Resource deadlock would occur	36

(continued)

(continued)

Constant	System Error Message	Value
EDOM	Math argument	33
EEXIST	File exists	17
EINVAL	Invalid argument	22
EMFILE	Too many open files	24
ENOENT	No such file or directory	2
ENOEXEC	Exec format error	8
ENOMEM	Not enough memory	12
ENOSPC	No space left on device	28
ERANGE	Result too large	34
EXDEV	Cross-device link	18

_environ, _wenviron

The **_environ** variable is a pointer to an array of pointers to the multibyte-character strings that constitute the process environment. **_environ** is declared in STDLIB.H as

extern char **_environ;

In a program that uses the **main** function, **_environ** is initialized at program startup according to settings taken from the operating-system environment. The environment consists of one or more entries of the form

ENVVARNAME=*string*

getenv and _putenv use the **_environ** variable to access and modify the environment table. When **_putenv** is called to add or delete environment settings, the environment table changes size. Its location in memory may also change, depending on the program's memory requirements. The value of **_environ** is automatically adjusted accordingly.

The _wenviron variable, declared in STDLIB.H as **extern wchar_t **_wenviron;**, is a wide-character version of **_environ**. In a program that uses the **wmain** function, **_wenviron** is initialized at program startup according to settings taken from the operating-system environment.

In a program that uses **main**, **_wenviron** is initially **NULL**, because the environment is composed of multibyte-character strings. On the first call to **_wgetenv** or **_wputenv**, a corresponding wide-character string environment is created and is pointed to by **_wenviron**.

Similarly, in a program that uses **wmain**, **_environ** is initially **NULL** because the environment is composed of wide-character strings. On the first call to **_getenv** or **_putenv**, a corresponding wide-character string environment is created and is pointed to by **_environ**.

When two copies of the environment (MBCS and Unicode) exist simultaneously in a program, the run-time system must maintain both copies, resulting in slower execution time. For example, whenever you call **_putenv**, a call to **_wputenv** is also executed automatically, so that the two environment strings correspond.

> **Caution** In rare instances, when the run-time system is maintaining both a Unicode version and a multibyte version of the environment, these two environment versions may not correspond exactly. This is because, although any unique multibyte-character string maps to a unique Unicode string, the mapping from a unique Unicode string to a multibyte-character string is not necessarily unique. Therefore, two distinct Unicode strings may map to the same multibyte string.

The following pseudocode illustrates how this can happen.

```
int i, j;
i = _wputenv( "env_var_x=string1" ); // results in the implicit call:
                                      // putenv ("env_var_z=string1")
j = _wputenv( "env_var_y=string2" ); // also results in implicit call:
                                      // putenv("env_var_z=string2")
```

In the notation used for this example, the character strings are not C string literals; rather, they are placeholders that represent Unicode environment string literals in the **_wputenv** call and multibyte environment strings in the **putenv** call. The character-placeholders 'x' and 'y' in the two distinct Unicode environment strings do not map uniquely to characters in the current MBCS. Instead, both map to some MBCS character 'z' that is the default result of the attempt to convert the strings.

Thus in the multibyte environment the value of "*env_var_z*" after the first implicit call to **putenv** would be "*string1*," but this value would be overwritten on the second implicit call to **putenv**, when the value of "*env_var_z*" is set to "*string2*." The Unicode environment (in **_wenviron**) and the multibyte environment (in **_environ**) would therefore differ following this series of calls.

_fileinfo

The **_fileinfo** variable determines whether information about the open files of a process is passed to new processes by functions such as _spawn. **_fileinfo** is declared in STDLIB.H as

extern int _fileinfo;

If **_fileinfo** is 0 (the default), information about open files is not passed to new processes; otherwise the information is passed. You can modify the default value of **_fileinfo** by setting the **_fileinfo** variable to a nonzero value in your program.

_fmode

The **_fmode** variable sets the default file-translation mode for text or binary translation. It is declared in STDLIB.H as

extern int _fmode;

The default setting of **_fmode** is **_O_TEXT** for text-mode translation. **_O_BINARY** is the setting for binary mode.

You can change the value of **_fmode** in either of two ways:

- Link with BINMODE.OBJ. This changes the initial setting of **_fmode** to **_O_BINARY**, causing all files except **stdin**, **stdout**, and **stderr** to be opened in binary mode.

- Change the value of **_fmode** directly by setting it in your program.

_osver, _winmajor, _winminor, _winver

These variables store build and version numbers of the 32-bit Windows operating systems. Declarations for these variables in STDLIB.H are as follows:

extern unsigned int _osver;
extern unsigned int _winmajor;
extern unsigned int _winminor;
extern unsigned int _winver;

These variables are useful in programs that run in different versions of Windows NT or Windows 95.

Variable	Description
_osver	Current build number
_winmajor	Major version number
_winminor	Minor version number
_winver	Holds value of **_winmajor** in high byte and value of **_winminor** in low byte

_pgmptr, _wpgmptr

When a program is run from the command interpreter (CMD.EXE), **_pgmptr** is automatically initialized to the full path of the executable file. For example, if HELLO.EXE is in C:\BIN and C:\BIN is in the path, **_pgmptr** is set to C:\BIN\HELLO.EXE when you execute

```
C> hello
```

When a program is not run from the command line, **_pgmptr** may be initialized to the program name (the file's base name without the extension), or to a filename, a relative path, or a full path.

_wpgmptr is the wide-character counterpart of **_pgmptr** for use with programs that use **wmain**. **_pgmptr** and **_wpgmptr** are declared in STDLIB.H as

extern char *_pgmptr;
extern wchar_t *_pgmptr;

The following program demonstrates the use of **_pgmptr**.

```
/*
 * PGMPTR.C: The following program demonstrates the use of _pgmptr.
 */

#include <stdio.h>
#include <stdlib.h>
void main( void )
{
    printf("The full path of the executing program is : %Fs\n",_pgmptr);
}
```

Control Flags

The debug version of the Microsoft C run-time library uses the following flags to control the heap allocation and reporting process. For more information, see "Using C Run-Time Library Debugging Support" in the *Visual C++ Programmer's Guide* online.

Flag	Description
_CRTDBG_MAP_ALLOC	Maps the base heap functions to their debug version counterparts
_DEBUG	Enables the use of the debugging versions of the run-time functions
_crtDbgFlag	Controls how the debug heap manager tracks allocations

These flags can be defined with a /D command-line option or with a **#define** directive. When the flag is defined with **#define**, the directive must appear before the header file include statement for the routine declarations.

_CRTDBG_MAP_ALLOC

When the **_CRTDBG_MAP_ALLOC** flag is defined in the debug version of an application, the base version of the heap functions are directly mapped to their debug versions. This flag is declared in CRTDBG.H. This flag is only available when the _DEBUG flag has been defined in the application.

For more information about using the debug version versus the base version of a heap function, see "Using the Debug Version Versus the Base Version" in the *Visual C++ Programmer's Guide* online.

_DEBUG

The compiler defines **_DEBUG** when you specify the /MTd or /Mdd option. These options specify debug versions of the C run-time library.

For more information, see "Using C Run-Time Library Debugging Support" in the *Visual C++ Programmer's Guide* online.

_crtDbgFlag

The **_crtDbgFlag** flag consists of five bit fields that control how memory allocations on the debug version of the heap are tracked, verified, reported, and dumped. The bit fields of the flag are set using the _CrtSetDbgFlag function. This flag and its bit fields are declared in CRTDBG.H. This flag is only available when the _DEBUG flag has been defined in the application.

For more information about using this flag in conjunction with other debug functions, see "Heap State Reporting Functions" in the *Visual C++ Programmer's Guide* online.

Standard Types

The Microsoft run-time library defines the following standard types.

Type	Description	Declared In
clock_t structure	Stores time values; used by clock.	TIME.H
_complex structure	Stores real and imaginary parts of complex numbers; used by _cabs.	MATH.H
_dev_t short or unsigned integer	Represents device handles.	SYS\TYPES.H
div_t, ldiv_t structures	Store values returned by div and ldiv, respectively.	STDLIB.H
_exception structure	Stores error information for _matherr.	MATH.H
FILE structure	Stores information about current state of stream; used in all stream I/O operations.	STDIO.H
_finddata_t, _wfinddata_t, _wfinddatai64_t structures	**_finddata_t** stores file-attribute information returned by _findfirst and _findnext. **_wfinddata_t** stores file-attribute information returned by _wfindfirst and _wfindnext. **_wfinddatai64_t** stores file-attribute information returned by _wfindfirsti64 and _wfindnexti64.	**_finddata_t**: IO.H **_wfinddata_t**: IO.H, WCHAR.H **_wfinddatai64_t**: IO.H, WCHAR.H

(continued)

Type	Description	Declared In
_FPIEEE_RECORD structure	Contains information pertaining to IEEE floating-point exception; passed to user-defined trap handler by _fpieee_flt.	FPIEEE.H
fpos_t (long integer, __int64, or structure, depending on the target platform)	Used by fgetpos and fsetpos to record information for uniquely specifying every position within a file.	STDIO.H
_HEAPINFO structure	Contains information about next heap entry for _heapwalk.	MALLOC.H
jmp_buf array	Used by setjmp and longjmp to save and restore program environment.	SETJMP.H
lconv structure	Contains formatting rules for numeric values in different countries.	LOCALE.H
_off_t long integer	Represents file-offset value.	SYS\TYPES.H
_onexit_t pointer	Returned by _onexit.	STDLIB.H
_PNH pointer to function	Type of argument to _set_new_handler.	NEW.H
ptrdiff_t integer	Result of subtraction of two pointers.	STDDEF.H
sig_atomic_t integer	Type of object that can be modified as atomic entity, even in presence of asynchronous interrupts; used with signal.	SIGNAL.H
size_t unsigned integer	Result of **sizeof** operator.	STDDEF.H and other include files
_stat structure	Contains file-status information returned by _stat and _fstat.	SYS\STAT.H
time_t long integer	Represents time values in mktime and time.	TIME.H
_timeb structure	Used by _ftime to store current system time.	SYS\TIMEB.H
tm structure	Used by asctime, gmtime, localtime, mktime, and strftime to store and retrieve time information.	TIME.H
_utimbuf structure	Stores file access and modification times used by _utime to change file-modification dates.	SYS\UTIME.H

(continued)

(continued)

Type	Description	Declared In
va_list structure	Used to hold information needed by va_arg and va_end macros. Called function declares variable of type **va_list** that can be passed as argument to another function.	STDARG.H
wchar_t internal type of a wide character	Useful for writing portable programs for international markets.	STDDEF.H, STDLIB.H
wctrans_t integer	Represents locale-specific character mappings.	WCTYPE.H
wctype_t integer	Can represent all characters of any national character set.	WCHAR.H
wint_t integer	Type of data object that can hold any wide character or wide end-of-file value.	WCHAR.H

CHAPTER 3

Global Constants

The Microsoft run-time library contains definitions for global constants used by library routines. To use these constants, include the appropriate header files as indicated in the description for each constant. The global constants are listed in the following table.

BUFSIZ	**__LOCAL_SIZE**
CLOCKS_PER_SEC, CLK_TCK	Locale Categories
Commit-To-Disk Constants	**_locking** Constants
Data Type Constants	Math Error Constants
EOF, WEOF	**MB_CUR_MAX**
errno Constants	**NULL**
Exception-Handling Constants	Path Field Limits
EXIT_SUCCESS, EXIT_FAILURE	**RAND_MAX**
File Attribute Constants	**setvbuf** Constants
File Constants	Sharing Constants
File Permission Constants	**signal** Constants
File Read/Write Access Constants	**signal** Action Constants
File Translation Constants	**_spawn** Constants
FILENAME_MAX	**_stat** Structure **st_mode** Field Constants
FOPEN_MAX, _SYS_OPEN	**stdin, stdout, stderr**
_FREEENTRY, _USEDENTRY	**TMP_MAX, L_tmpnam**
fseek, _lseek Constants	Translation Mode Constants
Heap Constants	**_WAIT_CHILD, _WAIT_GRANDCHILD**
_HEAP_MAXREQ	32-bit Windows Time/Date Formats
HUGE_VAL	

BUFSIZ

#include <stdio.h>

Remarks

BUFSIZ is the required user-allocated buffer for the setvbuf routine.

CLOCKS_PER_SEC, CLK_TCK

#include <time.h>

Remarks

The time in seconds is the value returned by the **clock** function, divided by **CLOCKS_PER_SEC**. **CLK_TCK** is equivalent, but considered obsolete.

See Also

clock

Commit-To-Disk Constants

Microsoft Specific →

#include <stdio.h>

Remarks

These Microsoft-specific constants specify whether the buffer associated with the open file is flushed to operating system buffers or to disk. The mode is included in the string specifying the type of read/write access (**"r"**, **"w"**, **"a"**, **"r+"**, **"w+"**, **"a+"**).

The commit-to-disk modes are as follows:

c Writes the unwritten contents of the specified buffer to disk. This commit-to-disk functionality only occurs at explicit calls to either the fflush or the _flushall function. This mode is useful when dealing with sensitive data. For example, if your program terminates after a call to **fflush** or **_flushall**, you can be sure that your data reached the operating system's buffers. However, unless a file is opened with the **c** option, the data might never make it to disk if the operating system also terminates.

n Writes the unwritten contents of the specified buffer to the operating system's buffers. The operating system can cache data and then determine an optimal time to write to disk. Under many conditions, this behavior makes for efficient program behavior. However, if the retention of data is critical (such as bank transactions or airline ticket information) consider using the **c** option. The **n** mode is the default.

Note The **c** and **n** options are not part of the ANSI standard for **fopen**, but are Microsoft extensions and should not be used where ANSI portability is desired.

Using the Commit-to-Disk Feature with Existing Code

By default, calls to the fflush or _flushall library functions write data to buffers maintained by the operating system. The operating system determines the optimal time to actually write the data to disk. The commit-to-disk feature of the run-time library lets you ensure that critical data is written directly to disk rather than to the operating system's buffers. You can give this capability to an existing program without rewriting it by linking its object files with COMMODE.OBJ.

In the resulting executable file, calls to **fflush** write the contents of the buffer directly to disk, and calls to **_flushall** write the contents of all buffers to disk. These two functions are the only ones affected by COMMODE.OBJ.

END Microsoft Specific

See Also

_fdopen, **fopen**

Data Type Constants

Remarks

Data type constants are implementation-dependent ranges of values allowed for integral data types. The constants listed below give the ranges for the integral data types and are defined in LIMITS.H.

Note The /J compiler option changes the default **char** type to **unsigned**.

Constant	Value	Meaning
SCHAR_MAX	127	Maximum signed **char** value
SCHAR_MIN	–128	Minimum signed **char** value
UCHAR_MAX	255 (0xff)	Maximum **unsigned char** value
CHAR_BIT	8	Number of bits in a **char**
USHRT_MAX	65535 (0xffff)	Maximum **unsigned short** value
SHRT_MAX	32767	Maximum (signed) **short** value
SHRT_MIN	–32768	Minimum (signed) **short** value
UINT_MAX	4294967295 (0xffffffff)	Maximum **unsigned int** value
ULONG_MAX	4294967295 (0xffffffff)	Maximum **unsigned long** value

(continued)

(continued)

Constant	Value	Meaning
INT_MAX	2147483647	Maximum (signed) **int** value
INT_MIN	−2147483647−1	Minimum (signed) **int** value
LONG_MAX	2147483647	Maximum (signed) **long** value
LONG_MIN	−2147483647−1	Minimum (signed) **long** value
CHAR_MAX	127 (255 if /J option used)	Maximum **char** value
CHAR_MIN	−128 (0 if /J option used)	Minimum **char** value
MB_LEN_MAX	2	Maximum number of bytes in multibyte **char**

The following constants give the range and other characteristics of the **double** and **float** data types, and arc defined in FLOAT.H:

Constant	Value	Description
DBL_DIG	15	# of decimal digits of precision
DBL_EPSILON	2.2204460492503131e−016	Smallest such that 1.0+**DBL_EPSILON** !=1.0
DBL_MANT_DIG	53	# of bits in mantissa
DBL_MAX	1.7976931348623158e+308	Maximum value
DBL_MAX_10_EXP	308	Maximum decimal exponent
DBL_MAX_EXP	1024	Maximum binary exponent
DBL_MIN	2.2250738585072014e−308	Minimum positive value
DBL_MIN_10_EXP	(−307)	Minimum decimal exponent
DBL_MIN_EXP	(−1021)	Minimum binary exponent
_DBL_RADIX	2	Exponent radix
_DBL_ROUNDS	1	Addition rounding: near
FLT_DIG	6	Number of decimal digits of precision
FLT_EPSILON	1.192092896e−07F	Smallest such that 1.0+**FLT_EPSILON** !=1.0
FLT_MANT_DIG	24	Number of bits in mantissa
FLT_MAX	3.402823466e+38F	Maximum value
FLT_MAX_10_EXP	38	Maximum decimal exponent

(continued)

Constant	Value	Description
FLT_MAX_EXP	128	Maximum binary exponent
FLT_MIN	1.175494351e–38F	Minimum positive value
FLT_MIN_10_EXP	(–37)	Minimum decimal exponent
FLT_MIN_EXP	(–125)	Minimum binary exponent
FLT_RADIX	2	Exponent radix
FLT_ROUNDS	1	Addition rounding: near

EOF, WEOF

Remarks

EOF is returned by an I/O routine when the end-of-file (or in some cases, an error) is encountered.

WEOF yields the return value, of type **wint_t**, used to signal the end of a wide stream, or to report an error condition.

See Also

putc, ungetc, scanf, fflush, _fcloseall, _ungetch, _putch, __isascii

errno Constants

#include <errno.h>

Remarks

The **errno** values are constants assigned to errno in the event of various error conditions.

ERRNO.H contains the definitions of the **errno** values. However, not all the definitions given in ERRNO.H are used in 32-bit Windows operating systems. Some of the values in ERRNO.H are present to maintain compatibility with the UNIX family of operating systems.

The **errno** values in a 32-bit Windows operating system are a subset of the values for **errno** in XENIX systems. Thus, the **errno** value is not necessarily the same as the actual error code returned by a Windows NT or Windows 95 system call. To access the actual operating system error code, use the _doserrno variable, which contains this value.

The following **errno** values are supported:

ECHILD

No spawned processes.

EAGAIN

No more processes. An attempt to create a new process failed because there are no more process slots, or there is not enough memory, or the maximum nesting level has been reached.

E2BIG

Argument list too long.

EACCES

Permission denied. The file's permission setting does not allow the specified access. This error signifies that an attempt was made to access a file (or, in some cases, a directory) in a way that is incompatible with the file's attributes.

For example, the error can occur when an attempt is made to read from a file that is not open, to open an existing read-only file for writing, or to open a directory instead of a file. Under MS DOS operating system versions 3.0 and later, **EACCES** may also indicate a locking or sharing violation.

The error can also occur in an attempt to rename a file or directory or to remove an existing directory.

EBADF

Bad file number. There are two possible causes: 1) The specified file handle is not a valid file-handle value or does not refer to an open file. 2) An attempt was made to write to a file or device opened for read-only access.

EDEADLOCK

Resource deadlock would occur. The argument to a math function is not in the domain of the function.

EDOM

Math argument.

EEXIST

Files exist. An attempt has been made to create a file that already exists. For example, the **_O_CREAT** and **_O_EXCL** flags are specified in an **_open** call, but the named file already exists.

EINVAL

Invalid argument. An invalid value was given for one of the arguments to a function. For example, the value given for the origin when positioning a file pointer (by means of a call to **fseek**) is before the beginning of the file.

EMFILE

Too many open files. No more file handles are available, so no more files can be opened.

ENOENT

No such file or directory. The specified file or directory does not exist or cannot be found. This message can occur whenever a specified file does not exist or a component of a path does not specify an existing directory.

ENOEXEC

Exec format error. An attempt was made to execute a file that is not executable or that has an invalid executable-file format.

ENOMEM

Not enough core. Not enough memory is available for the attempted operator. For example, this message can occur when insufficient memory is available to execute a child process, or when the allocation request in a **_getcwd** call cannot be satisfied.

ENOSPC

No space left on device. No more space for writing is available on the device (for example, when the disk is full).

ERANGE

Result too large. An argument to a math function is too large, resulting in partial or total loss of significance in the result. This error can also occur in other functions when an argument is larger than expected (for example, when the *buffer* argument to **_getcwd** is longer than expected).

EXDEV

Cross-device link. An attempt was made to move a file to a different device (using the **rename** function).

Exception-Handling Constants

Remarks

The constant **EXCEPTION_CONTINUE_SEARCH**, **EXCEPTION_CONTINUE_EXECUTION**, or **EXCEPTION_EXECUTE_HANDLER** is returned when an exception occurs during execution of the guarded section of a **try-except** statement. The return value determines how the exception is handled. For more information, see "The Try-except Statement" in the *Language Quick Reference* online.

EXIT_SUCCESS, EXIT_FAILURE

#include <stdlib.h>

Remarks

These are arguments for the **exit** and **_exit** functions and the return values for the **atexit** and **_onexit** functions.

See Also

atexit, exit, _onexit

File Attribute Constants

#include <io.h>

Remarks

These constants specify the current attributes of the file or directory specified by the function.

The attributes are represented by the following manifest constants:

_A_ARCH
Archive. Set whenever the file is changed, and cleared by the BACKUP command. Value: 0x20

_A_HIDDEN
Hidden file. Not normally seen with the DIR command, unless the /AH option is used. Returns information about normal files as well as files with this attribute. Value: 0x02

_A_NORMAL
Normal. File can be read or written to without restriction. Value: 0x00

_A_RDONLY
Read-only. File cannot be opened for writing, and a file with the same name cannot be created. Value: 0x01

_A_SUBDIR
Subdirectory. Value: 0x10

_A_SYSTEM
System file. Not normally seen with the DIR command, unless the /AS option is used. Value: 0x04

Multiple constants can be combined with the OR operator (|).

See Also

_find Functions

File Constants

#include <fcntl.h>

Remarks

The integer expression formed from one or more of these constants determines the type of reading or writing operations permitted. It is formed by combining one or more constants with a translation-mode constant.

The file constants are as follows:

_O_APPEND
   Repositions the file pointer to the end of the file before every write operation.

_O_CREAT
   Creates and opens a new file for writing; this has no effect if the file specified by *filename* exists.

_O_EXCL
   Returns an error value if the file specified by *filename* exists. Only applies when used with **_O_CREAT**.

_O_RDONLY
   Opens file for reading only; if this flag is given, neither **_O_RDWR** nor **_O_WRONLY** can be given.

_O_RDWR
   Opens file for both reading and writing; if this flag is given, neither **_O_RDONLY** nor **_O_WRONLY** can be given.

_O_TRUNC
   Opens and truncates an existing file to zero length; the file must have write permission. The contents of the file are destroyed. If this flag is given, you cannot specify **_O_RDONLY**.

_O_WRONLY
   Opens file for writing only; if this flag is given, neither **_O_RDONLY** nor **_O_RDWR** can be given.

See Also

_open, _sopen

File Permission Constants

#include <sys/stat.h>

Remarks

One of these constants is required when **_O_CREAT** (**_open**, **_sopen**) is specified.

The *pmode* argument specifies the file's permission settings as follows.

Constant	Meaning
_S_IREAD	Reading permitted
_S_IWRITE	Writing permitted
_S_IREAD	_S_IWRITE	Reading and writing permitted

When used as the *pmode* argument for **_umask**, the manifest constant sets the permission setting, as follows.

Constant	Meaning
_S_IREAD	Writing not permitted (file is read-only)
_S_IWRITE	Reading not permitted (file is write-only)
_S_IREAD	_S_IWRITE	Neither reading nor writing permitted

See Also

_open, _sopen, _umask, _stat structure

File Read/Write Access Constants

#include <stdio.h>

Remarks

These constants specify the access type ("a", "r", or "w") requested for the file. Both the translation mode ("b" or "t") and the commit-to-disk mode ("c" or "n") can be specified with the type of access.

The access types are described below.

"a"

Opens for writing at the end of the file (appending); creates the file first if it does not exist. All write operations occur at the end of the file. Although the file pointer can be repositioned using **fseek** or **rewind**, it is always moved back to the end of the file before any write operation is carried out.

"a+"

Same as above, but also allows reading.

"r"

Opens for reading. If the file does not exist or cannot be found, the call to open the file will fail.

"r+"

Opens for both reading and writing. If the file does not exist or cannot be found, the call to open the file will fail.

"w"

Opens an empty file for writing. If the given file exists, its contents are destroyed.

"w+"

Opens an empty file for both reading and writing. If the given file exists, its contents are destroyed.

When the "r+", "w+", or "a+" type is specified, both reading and writing are allowed (the file is said to be open for "update"). However, when you switch between reading and writing, there must be an intervening **fflush**, **fsetpos**, **fseek**, or **rewind** operation. The current position can be specified for the **fsetpos** or **fseek** operation.

See Also

_fdopen, fopen, freopen, _fsopen, _popen

File Translation Constants

#include <stdio.h>

Remarks

These constants specify the mode of translation (**"b"** or **"t"**). The mode is included in the string specifying the type of access (**"r"**, **"w"**, **"a"**, **"r+"**, **"w+"**, **"a+"**).

The translation modes are as follows:

t

Opens in text (translated) mode. In this mode, carriage-return–linefeed (CR–LF) combinations are translated into single linefeeds (LF) on input, and LF characters are translated into CR–LF combinations on output. Also, CTRL+Z is interpreted as an end-of-file character on input. In files opened for reading or reading/writing, **fopen** checks for CTRL+Z at the end of the file and removes it, if possible. This is done because using the **fseek** and **ftell** functions to move within a file ending with CTRL+Z may cause **fseek** to behave improperly near the end of the file.

> **Note**   The **t** option is not part of the ANSI standard for **fopen** and **freopen**. It is a Microsoft extension and should not be used where ANSI portability is desired.

b

Opens in binary (untranslated) mode. The above translations are suppressed.

If **t** or **b** is not given in *mode*, the translation mode is defined by the default-mode variable _fmode. For more information about using text and binary modes, see "Text and Binary Mode File I/O" in Chapter 1, "Run-Time Routines by Categories."

See Also

_fdopen, fopen, freopen, _fsopen

FILENAME_MAX

#include <stdio.h>

Remarks

This is the maximum permissible length for *filename*.

See Also

Path Field Limits

FOPEN_MAX, _SYS_OPEN

#include <stdio.h>

Remarks

This is the maximum number of files that can be opened simultaneously. **FOPEN_MAX** is the ANSI-compatible name. **_SYS_OPEN** is provided for compatibility with existing code.

_FREEENTRY, _USEDENTRY

#include <malloc.h>

Remarks

These constants represent values assigned by the **_heapwalk** routines to the **_useflag** element of the **_HEAPINFO** structure. They indicate the status of the heap entry.

See Also

_heapwalk

fseek, _lseek Constants

#include <stdio.h>

Remarks

The *origin* argument specifies the initial position and can be one of the manifest constants shown below:

Constant	Meaning
SEEK_END	End of file
SEEK_CUR	Current position of file pointer
SEEK_SET	Beginning of file

See Also

fseek, _lseek, _lseeki64

Heap Constants

#include <malloc.h>

Remarks

These constants give the return value indicating status of the heap.

Constant	Meaning
_HEAPBADBEGIN	Initial header information was not found or was invalid.
_HEAPBADNODE	Bad node was found, or heap is damaged.
_HEAPBADPTR	**_pentry** field of **_HEAPINFO** structure does not contain valid pointer into heap (**_heapwalk** routine only).
_HEAPEMPTY	Heap has not been initialized.
_HEAPEND	End of heap was reached successfully (**_heapwalk** routine only).
_HEAPOK	Heap is consistent (**_heapset** and **_heapchk** routines only). No errors so far; **_HEAPINFO** structure contains information about next entry (**_heapwalk** routine only).

See Also

_heapchk, _heapset, _heapwalk

_HEAP_MAXREQ

#include <malloc.h>

Remarks

The maximum size of a user request for memory that can be granted.

See Also

malloc, calloc

HUGE_VAL

#include <math.h>

Remarks

HUGE_VAL is the largest representable double value. This value is returned by many run-time math functions when an error occurs. For some functions, –**HUGE_VAL** is returned.

__LOCAL_SIZE

Remarks

The compiler provides a symbol, __**LOCAL_SIZE**, for use in the inline assembler block of function prolog code. This symbol is used to allocate space for local variables on the stack frame in your custom prolog code.

The compiler determines the value of __**LOCAL_SIZE**. Its value is the total number of bytes of all user-defined locals as well as compiler-generated temporary variables. __**LOCAL_SIZE** can be used as an immediate operand; it cannot be used in an expression. You must not change or redefine the value of this symbol. For example:

```
mov      eax, __LOCAL_SIZE            ;Immediate operand
mov      eax, [ebp - __LOCAL_SIZE]    ;Expression
```

The following is a example of a naked function containing custom prolog and epilog sequences using the __**LOCAL_SIZE** symbol in the prolog sequence:

```
__declspec ( naked ) func()
{
   int i;
   int j;

   _asm        /* prolog */
     {
     push      ebp
     mov       ebp, esp
     sub       esp, __LOCAL_SIZE
     }

   /* Function body */

   __asm       /* epilog */
     {
     mov       esp, ebp
     pop       ebp
     ret
     }
}
```

For related information, see "naked" in the *Language Quick Reference* online.

Locale Categories

#include <locale.h>

Remarks

Locale categories are manifest constants used by the localization routines to specify which portion of a program's locale information will be used. The locale refers to the locality (or country) for which certain aspects of your program can be customized. Locale-dependent areas include, for example, the formatting of dates or the display format for monetary values.

Locale Category	Parts of Program Affected
LC_ALL	All locale-specific behavior (all categories)
LC_COLLATE	Behavior of **strcoll** and **strxfrm** functions
LC_CTYPE	Behavior of character-handling functions (except **isdigit**, **isxdigit**, **mbstowcs**, and **mbtowc**, which are unaffected)
LC_MAX	Same as **LC_TIME**
LC_MIN	Same as **LC_ALL**
LC_MONETARY	Monetary formatting information returned by the **localeconv** function
LC_NUMERIC	Decimal-point character for formatted output routines (for example, **printf**), data conversion routines, and nonmonetary formatting information returned by **localeconv** function
LC_TIME	Behavior of **strftime** function

See Also

localeconv, setlocale, strcoll Functions, strftime, strxfrm

_locking Constants

#include <sys/locking.h>

Remarks

The *mode* argument in the call to the **_locking** function specifies the locking action to be performed.

The *mode* argument must be one of the following manifest constants:

_LK_LOCK
> Locks the specified bytes. If the bytes cannot be locked, the function tries again after one second. If, after ten attempts, the bytes cannot be locked, the function returns an error.

_LK_RLCK

Same as **_LK_LOCK**.

_LK_NBLCK

Locks the specified bytes. If bytes cannot be locked, the function returns an error.

_LK_NBRLCK

Same as **_LK_NBLCK**.

_LK_UNLCK

Unlocks the specified bytes. (The bytes must have been previously locked.)

See Also

_locking

Math Error Constants

#include <math.h>

Remarks

The math routines of the run-time library can generate math error constants.

These errors, described as follows, correspond to the exception types defined in MATH.H and are returned by the **_matherr** function when a math error occurs.

Constant	Meaning
_DOMAIN	Argument to function is outside domain of function.
_OVERFLOW	Result is too large to be represented in function's return type.
_PLOSS	Partial loss of significance occurred.
_SING	Argument singularity: argument to function has illegal value. (For example, value 0 is passed to function that requires nonzero value.)
_TLOSS	Total loss of significance occurred.
_UNDERFLOW	Result is too small to be represented.

See Also

_matherr

MB_CUR_MAX

#include <stdlib.h>

Context: ANSI multibyte- and wide-character conversion functions

Remarks

The value of **MB_CUR_MAX** is the maximum number of bytes in a multibyte character for the current locale.

See Also

mblen, mbstowcs, mbtowc, wchar_t, wcstombs, wctomb, Data Type Constants

NULL

Remarks

NULL is the null-pointer value used with many pointer operations and functions.

Path Field Limits

#include <stdlib.h>

Remarks

These constants define the maximum length for the path and for the individual fields within the path.

Constant	Meaning
_MAX_DIR	Maximum length of directory component
_MAX_DRIVE	Maximum length of drive component
_MAX_EXT	Maximum length of extension component
_MAX_FNAME	Maximum length of filename component
_MAX_PATH	Maximum length of full path

The sum of the fields should not exceed **_MAX_PATH**.

RAND_MAX

#include <stdlib.h>

Remarks

The constant **RAND_MAX** is the maximum value that can be returned by the **rand** function. **RAND_MAX** is defined as the value 0x7fff.

See Also

rand

setvbuf Constants

#include <stdio.h>

Remarks

These constants represent the type of buffer for **setvbuf**.

The possible values are given by the following manifest constants:

Constant	Meaning
_IOFBF	Full buffering: Buffer specified in call to **setvbuf** is used and its size is as specified in **setvbuf** call. If buffer pointer is **NULL**, automatically allocated buffer of specified size is used.
_IOLBF	Same as **_IOFBF**.
_IONBF	No buffer is used, regardless of arguments in call to **setvbuf**.

See Also

setbuf

Sharing Constants

#include <share.h>

Remarks

The *shflag* argument determines the sharing mode, which consists of one or more manifest constants. These can be combined with the *oflag* arguments (see "File Constants" in this section).

The constants and their meanings are listed below:

Constant	Meaning
_SH_COMPAT	Sets compatibility mode
_SH_DENYRW	Denies read and write access to file
_SH_DENYWR	Denies write access to file
_SH_DENYRD	Denies read access to file
_SH_DENYNO	Permits read and write access

See Also

_sopen, _fsopen

signal Constants

#include <signal.h>

Remarks

The *sig* argument must be one of the manifest constants listed below (defined in SIGNAL.H).

SIGABRT
Abnormal termination. The default action terminates the calling program with exit code 3.

SIGFPE
Floating-point error, such as overflow, division by zero, or invalid operation. The default action terminates the calling program.

SIGILL
Illegal instruction. The default action terminates the calling program.

SIGINT
CTRL+C interrupt. The default action issues **INT 23H**.

SIGSEGV
Illegal storage access. The default action terminates the calling program.

SIGTERM
Termination request sent to the program. The default action terminates the calling program.

See Also

signal, **raise**

signal Action Constants

#include <signal.h>

Remarks

The action taken when the interrupt signal is received depends on the value of *func*.

The *func* argument must be either a function address or one of the manifest constants listed below and defined in SIGNAL.H.

SIG_DFL

Uses system-default response. If the calling program uses stream I/O, buffers created by the run-time library are not flushed.

SIG_IGN

Ignores interrupt signal. This value should never be given for **SIGFPE**, since the floating-point state of the process is left undefined.

See Also

signal

_spawn Constants

#include <process.h>

Remarks

The *mode* argument determines the action taken by the calling process before and during a spawn operation. The following values for *mode* are possible:

Constant	Meaning
_P_OVERLAY	Overlays calling process with new process, destroying calling process (same effect as **_exec** calls).
_P_WAIT	Suspends calling thread until execution of new process is complete (synchronous **_spawn**).
_P_NOWAIT or **_P_NOWAITO**	Continues to execute calling process concurrently with new process (asynchronous **_spawn**, valid only in 32-bit Windows applications).
_P_DETACH	Continues to execute calling process; new process is run in background with no access to console or keyboard. Calls to **_cwait** against new process will fail. This is an asynchronous **_spawn** and is valid only in 32-bit Windows applications.

See Also

_spawn Functions

_stat Structure st_mode Field Constants

#include <sys/stat.h>

Remarks

These constants are used to indicate file type in the **st_mode** field of the _stat structure.

The bit mask constants are described below:

Constant	Meaning
_S_IFMT	File type mask
_S_IFDIR	Directory
_S_IFCHR	Character special (indicates a device if set)
_S_IFREG	Regular
_S_IREAD	Read permission, owner
_S_IWRITE	Write permission, owner
_S_IEXEC	Execute/search permission, owner

See Also

_stat, **_fstat**, **Standard Types**

stdin, stdout, stderr

FILE *stdin;
FILE *stdout;
FILE *stderr;

#include <stdio.h>

Remarks

These are standard streams for input, output, and error output.

By default, standard input is read from the keyboard, while standard output and standard error are printed to the screen.

The following stream pointers are available to access the standard streams:

Pointer	Stream
stdin	Standard input
stdout	Standard output
stderr	Standard error

These pointers can be used as arguments to functions. Some functions, such as **getchar** and **putchar**, use **stdin** and **stdout** automatically.

These pointers are constants, and cannot be assigned new values. The **freopen** function can be used to redirect the streams to disk files or to other devices. The operating system allows you to redirect a program's standard input and output at the command level.

TMP_MAX, L_tmpnam

#include <stdio.h>

Remarks

TMP_MAX is the maximum number of unique filenames that the **tmpnam** function can generate. **L_tmpnam** is the length of temporary filenames generated by **tmpnam**.

Translation Mode Constants

#include <fcntl.h>

Remarks

The **_O_BINARY** and **_O_TEXT** manifest constants determine the translation mode for files (**_open** and **_sopen**) or the translation mode for streams (**_setmode**).

The allowed values are:

_O_TEXT
Opens file in text (translated) mode. Carriage return–linefeed (CR–LF) combinations are translated into a single linefeed (LF) on input. Linefeed characters are translated into CR–LF combinations on output. Also, CTRL+Z is interpreted as an end-of-file character on input. In files opened for reading and reading/writing, **fopen** checks for CTRL+Z at the end of the file and removes it, if possible. This is done because using the **fseek** and **ftell** functions to move within a file ending with CTRL+Z may cause **fseek** to behave improperly near the end of the file.

_O_BINARY
Opens file in binary (untranslated) mode. The above translations are suppressed.

_O_RAW
Same as **_O_BINARY**. Supported for C 2.0 compatibility.

For more information, see "Text and Binary Mode File I/O" in Chapter 1, "Run-Time Routines by Categories," and "File Translation Constants" in this chapter.

See Also

_open, _pipe, _sopen, _setmode

_WAIT_CHILD, _WAIT_GRANDCHILD

#include <process.h>

Remarks

The **_cwait** function can be used by any process to wait for any other process
(if the process ID is known). The action argument can be one of the following values:

Constant	Meaning
_WAIT_CHILD	Calling process waits until specified new process terminates.
_WAIT_GRANDCHILD	Calling process waits until specified new process, and all processes created by that new process, terminate.

See Also

_cwait

32-bit Windows Time/Date Formats

Remarks

The file time and the date are stored individually, using unsigned integers as bit fields.
File time and date are packed as follows:

Time

Bit Position:	0 1 2 3 4	5 6 7 8 9 A	B C D E F
Length:	5	6	5
Contents:	hours	minutes	2-second increments
Value Range:	0–23	0–59	0–29 in 2-second intervals

Date

Bit Position:	0 1 2 3 4 5 6	7 8 9 A	B C D E F
Length:	7	4	5
Contents:	year	month	day
Value Range:	0–119 (relative to 1980)	1–12	1–31

CHAPTER 4

Debug Version of the C Run-Time Library

Visual C++ has extensive debug support for the C run-time library, letting you step directly into run-time functions when debugging an application. The library also provides a variety of tools to keep track of heap allocations, locate memory leaks, and track down other memory-related problems. This chapter is an alphabetic reference of the debug functions and macros available for these purposes.

_ASSERT, _ASSERTE Macros

Evaluate an expression and generate a debug report when the result is FALSE (debug version only).

_ASSERT(*booleanExpression*);
_ASSERTE(*booleanExpression*);

Macro	Required Header	Compatibility
_ASSERT	<crtdbg.h>	Win NT, Win 95
_ASSERTE	<crtdbg.h>	Win NT, Win 95

For additional compatibility information, see "Compatibility" in the Introduction.

Libraries

LIBCD.LIB	Single thread static library, debug version
LIBCMTD.LIB	Multithread static library, debug version
MSVCRTD.LIB	Import library for MSVCRTD.DLL, debug version

Although **_ASSERT** and **_ASSERTE** are macros and are obtained by including CRTDBG.H, the application must link with one of the libraries listed above because these macros call other run-time functions.

Return Value

None

Parameter

booleanExpression
Expression (including pointers) that evaluates to nonzero or 0

Remarks

The **_ASSERT** and **_ASSERTE** macros provide an application with a clean and simple mechanism for checking assumptions during the debugging process. They are very flexible because they do not need to be enclosed in **#ifdef** statements to prevent them from being called in a retail build of an application. This flexibility is achieved by using the _DEBUG macro. **_ASSERT** and **_ASSERTE** are only available when **_DEBUG** is defined. When **_DEBUG** is not defined, calls to these macros are removed during preprocessing.

_ASSERT and **_ASSERTE** evaluate their *booleanExpression* argument and when the result is FALSE (0), they print a diagnostic message and call _CrtDbgReport to generate a debug report. The **_ASSERT** macro prints a simple diagnostic message, while **_ASSERTE** includes a string representation of the failed expression in the message. These macros do nothing when *booleanExpression* evaluates to nonzero.

Because the **_ASSERTE** macro specifies the failed expression in the generated report, it enables users to identify the problem without referring to the application source code. However, a disadvantage exists in that every expression evaluated by **_ASSERTE** must be included in the debug version of your application as a string constant. Therefore, if a large number of calls are made to **_ASSERTE**, these expressions can take up a significant amount of space.

_CrtDbgReport generates the debug report and determines its destination(s), based on the current report mode(s) and file defined for the **_CRT_ASSERT** report type. By default, assertion failures and errors are directed to a debug message window. The _CrtSetReportMode and _CrtSetReportFile functions are used to define the destination(s) for each report type.

When the destination is a debug message window and the user chooses the Retry button, **_CrtDbgReport** returns 1, causing the **_ASSERT** and **_ASSERTE** macros to start the debugger, provided that "just-in-time" (JIT) debugging is enabled. See "Debug Reporting Functions of the C Run-Time Library" in the *Visual C++ Programmer's Guide* online for an example of an assert message box under Windows NT.

For more information about the reporting process, see the "**_CrtDbgReport**" function and the section "Debug Reporting Functions of the C Run-Time Library" in the *Visual C++ Programmer's Guide* online. For more information about resolving assertion failures and using these macros as a debugging error handling mechanism, see "Using Macros for Verification and Reporting" in the *Visual C++ Programmer's Guide* online.

The _RPT, _RPTF debug macros are also available for generating a debug report, but they do not evaluate an expression. The **_RPT** macros generate a simple report and the **_RPTF** macros include the source file and line number where the report macro was called, in the generated report. In addition to the **_ASSERTE** macros, the ANSI assert routine can also be used to verify program logic. This routine is available in both the debug and release versions of the libraries.

Example

```
/*
 * DBGMACRO.C
 * In this program, calls are made to the _ASSERT and _ASSERTE
 * macros to test the condition 'string1 == string2'.  If the
 * condition fails, these macros print a diagnostic message.
 * The _RPTn and _RPTFn group of macros are also exercised in
 * this program, as an alternative to the printf function.
 */

#include <stdio.h>
#include <string.h>
#include <malloc.h>
#include <crtdbg.h>

int main()
{
    char *p1, *p2;

    /*
     * The Reporting Mode and File must be specified
     * before generating a debug report via an assert
     * or report macro.
     * This program sends all report types to STDOUT
     */
    _CrtSetReportMode(_CRT_WARN, _CRTDBG_MODE_FILE);
    _CrtSetReportFile(_CRT_WARN, _CRTDBG_FILE_STDOUT);
    _CrtSetReportMode(_CRT_ERROR, _CRTDBG_MODE_FILE);
    _CrtSetReportFile(_CRT_ERROR, _CRTDBG_FILE_STDOUT);
    _CrtSetReportMode(_CRT_ASSERT, _CRTDBG_MODE_FILE);
    _CrtSetReportFile(_CRT_ASSERT, _CRTDBG_FILE_STDOUT);

    /*
     * Allocate and assign the pointer variables
     */
    p1 = (char *)malloc(10);
    strcpy(p1, "I am p1");
    p2 = (char *)malloc(10);
    strcpy(p2, "I am p2");

    /*
     * Use the report macros as a debugging
     * warning mechanism, similar to printf.
     *
     * Use the assert macros to check if the
     * p1 and p2 variables are equivalent.
     *
```

```
* If the expression fails, _ASSERTE will
* include a string representation of the
* failed expression in the report.
* _ASSERT does not include the
* expression in the generated report.
*/
_RPT0(_CRT_WARN, "\n\n Use the assert macros to evaluate the expression p1 == p2.\n");
_RPTF2(_CRT_WARN, "\n Will _ASSERT find '%s' == '%s' ?\n", p1, p2);
_ASSERT(p1 == p2);

_RPTF2(_CRT_WARN, "\n\n Will _ASSERTE find '%s' == '%s' ?\n", p1, p2);
_ASSERTE(p1 == p2);

_RPT2(_CRT_ERROR, "\n \n '%s' != '%s'\n", p1, p2);

free(p2);
free(p1);

return 0;
}
```

Output

```
Use the assert macros to evaluate the expression p1 == p2.

dbgmacro.c(54) : Will _ASSERT find 'I am p1' == 'I am p2' ?
dbgmacro.c(55) : Assertion failed

dbgmacro.c(57) : Will _ASSERTE find 'I am p1' == 'I am p2' ?
dbgmacro.c(58) : Assertion failed: p1 == p2

'I am p1' != 'I am p2'
```

See Also

_RPT, _RPTF

_calloc_dbg

Allocates a number of memory blocks in the heap with additional space for a debugging header and overwrite buffers (debug version only).

void *_calloc_dbg(size_t *num*, **size_t** *size*, **int** *blockType*,
    const char *filename, **int** *linenumber* **);**

Routine	Required Header	Compatibility
_calloc_dbg	<crtdbg.h>	Win NT, Win 95

For additional compatibility information, see "Compatibility" in the Introduction.

Libraries

LIBCD.LIB	Single thread static library, debug version
LIBCMTD.LIB	Multithread static library, debug version
MSVCRTD.LIB	Import library for MSVCRTD.DLL, debug version

Return Value

Upon successful completion, this function either returns a pointer to the user portion of the last allocated memory block, calls the new handler function, or returns NULL. See the following "Remarks" section for a complete description of the return behavior. See the "**calloc**" function in the alphabetic reference for more information on how the new handler function is used.

Parameters

num
> Requested number of memory blocks

size
> Requested size of each memory block (bytes)

blockType
> Requested type of memory block: **_CLIENT_BLOCK** or **_NORMAL_BLOCK**

filename
> Pointer to name of source file that requested allocation operation or NULL

linenumber
> Line number in source file where allocation operation was requested or NULL

The *filename* and *linenumber* parameters are only available when **_calloc_dbg** has been called explicitly or the _CRTDBG_MAP_ALLOC preprocessor constant has been defined.

Remarks

_calloc_dbg is a debug version of the calloc function. When _DEBUG is not defined, calls to **_calloc_dbg** are removed during preprocessing. Both **calloc** and **_calloc_dbg** allocate *num* memory blocks in the base heap, but **_calloc_dbg** offers several debugging features: buffers on either side of the user portion of the block to test for leaks, a block type parameter to track specific allocation types, and *filename/linenumber* information to determine the origin of allocation requests.

_calloc_dbg allocates each memory block with slightly more space than the requested *size*. The additional space is used by the debug heap manager to link the debug memory blocks together and to provide the application with debug header information and overwrite buffers. When the block is allocated, the user portion of the block is filled with the value 0xCD and each of the overwrite buffers are filled with 0xFD.

For information about how memory blocks are allocated, initialized, and managed in the debug version of the base heap, see "Memory Management and the Debug Heap" in the *Visual C++ Programmer's Guide* online. For information about the allocation block types and how they are used, see "Types of Blocks on the Debug Heap" in the *Visual C++ Programmer's Guide* online. For information on the differences between calling a standard heap function versus its debug version in a debug build of an application, see "Using the Debug Version Versus the Base Version" in the *Visual C++ Programmer's Guide* online.

Example

```
/*
 * CALLOCD.C
 * This program uses _calloc_dbg to allocate space for
 * 40 long integers. It initializes each element to zero.
 */
#include <stdio.h>
#include <malloc.h>
#include <crtdbg.h>

void main( void )
{
     long *bufferN, *bufferC;

    /*
     * Call _calloc_dbg to include the filename and line number
     * of our allocation request in the header and also so we can
     * allocate CLIENT type blocks specifically
     */
    bufferN = (long *)_calloc_dbg( 40, sizeof(long), _NORMAL_BLOCK, __FILE__, __LINE__ );
    bufferC = (long *)_calloc_dbg( 40, sizeof(long), _CLIENT_BLOCK, __FILE__, __LINE__ );
    if( bufferN != NULL && bufferC != NULL )
        printf( "Allocated memory successfully\n" );
    else
        printf( "Problem allocating memory\n" );

    /*
     * _free_dbg must be called to free CLIENT type blocks
     */
    free( bufferN );
    _free_dbg( bufferC, _CLIENT_BLOCK );
}
```

Output

```
Allocated memory successfully
```

See Also

calloc, _malloc_dbg, _DEBUG

_CrtCheckMemory

Confirms the integrity of the memory blocks allocated in the debug heap (debug version only).

int _CrtCheckMemory(void);

Routine	Required Header	Compatibility
_CrtCheckMemory	<crtdbg.h>	Win NT, Win 95

For additional compatibility information, see "Compatibility" in the Introduction.

Libraries

LIBCD.LIB	Single thread static library, debug version
LIBCMTD.LIB	Multithread static library, debug version
MSVCRTD.LIB	Import library for MSVCRTD.DLL, debug version

Return Value

If successful, **_CrtCheckMemory** returns TRUE; otherwise, the function returns FALSE.

Remarks

The **_CrtCheckMemory** function validates memory allocated by the debug heap manager by verifying the underlying base heap and inspecting every memory block. If an error or memory inconsistency is encountered in the underlying base heap, the debug header information, or the overwrite buffers, **_CrtCheckMemory** generates a debug report with information describing the error condition. When _DEBUG is not defined, calls to **_CrtCheckMemory** are removed during preprocessing.

The behavior of **_CrtCheckMemory** can be controlled by setting the bit fields of the _crtDbgFlag flag using the _CrtSetDbgFlag function. Turning the **_CRTDBG_CHECK_ALWAYS_DF** bit field ON results in **_CrtCheckMemory** being called every time a memory allocation operation is requested. Although this method slows down execution, it is useful for catching errors quickly. Turning the **_CRTDBG_ALLOC_MEM_DF** bit field OFF causes **_CrtCheckMemory** to not verify the heap and immediately return TRUE.

Because this function returns TRUE or FALSE, it can be passed to one of the _ASSERT macros to create a simple debugging error handling mechanism. The following example will cause an assertion failure if corruption is detected in the heap:

```
_ASSERTE( _CrtCheckMemory( ) );
```

For more information about how **_CrtCheckMemory** can be used with other debug functions, see "Heap State Reporting Functions" in the *Visual C++ Programmer's Guide* online. For an overview of memory management and the debug heap, see "Memory Management and the Debug Heap" in the *Visual C++ Programmer's Guide* online.

Example

```
/*********************************************************************
 *   EXAMPLE  1                                                      *
 *   This simple program illustrates the basic debugging features    *
 *   of the C runtime libraries, and the kind of debug output        *
 *   that these features generate.                                   *
 *********************************************************************/

#include <stdio.h>
#include <string.h>
#include <malloc.h>
#include <crtdbg.h>

// This routine place comments at the head of a section of debug output
void OutputHeading( const char * explanation )
{
    _RPT1( _CRT_WARN, "\n\n%s:\n*************************************\
*********************************\n", explanation );
}

// The following macros set and clear, respectively, given bits
// of the C runtime library debug flag, as specified by a bitmask.
#ifdef   _DEBUG
#define  SET_CRT_DEBUG_FIELD(a) \
            _CrtSetDbgFlag((a) | _CrtSetDbgFlag(_CRTDBG_REPORT_FLAG))
#define  CLEAR_CRT_DEBUG_FIELD(a) \
            _CrtSetDbgFlag(~(a) & _CrtSetDbgFlag(_CRTDBG_REPORT_FLAG))
#else
#define  SET_CRT_DEBUG_FIELD(a)   ((void) 0)
#define  CLEAR_CRT_DEBUG_FIELD(a) ((void) 0)
#endif

void main( )
{
    char *p1, *p2;
    _CrtMemState s1, s2, s3;

    // Send all reports to STDOUT
    _CrtSetReportMode( _CRT_WARN, _CRTDBG_MODE_FILE );
    _CrtSetReportFile( _CRT_WARN, _CRTDBG_FILE_STDOUT );
    _CrtSetReportMode( _CRT_ERROR, _CRTDBG_MODE_FILE );
    _CrtSetReportFile( _CRT_ERROR, _CRTDBG_FILE_STDOUT );
    _CrtSetReportMode( _CRT_ASSERT, _CRTDBG_MODE_FILE );
    _CrtSetReportFile( _CRT_ASSERT, _CRTDBG_FILE_STDOUT );
```

```
// Allocate 2 memory blocks and store a string in each
p1 = malloc( 34 );
strcpy( p1, "This is the p1 string (34 bytes)." );

p2 = malloc( 34 );
strcpy( p2, "This is the p2 string (34 bytes)." );

OutputHeading(
    "Use _ASSERTE to check that the two strings are identical" );
_ASSERTE( strcmp( p1, p2 ) == 0 );

OutputHeading(
    "Use a _RPT macro to report the string contents as a warning" );
_RPT2( _CRT_WARN, "p1 points to '%s' and \np2 points to '%s'\n", p1, p2 );

OutputHeading(
    "Use _CRTMemDumpAllObjectsSince to check the p1 and p2 allocations" );
_CrtMemDumpAllObjectsSince( NULL );

free( p2 );

OutputHeading(
    "Having freed p2, dump allocation information about p1 only" );
_CrtMemDumpAllObjectsSince( NULL );

// Store a memory checkpoint in the s1 memory-state structure
_CrtMemCheckpoint( &s1 );

// Allocate another block, pointed to by p2
p2 = malloc( 38 );
strcpy( p2, "This new p2 string occupies 38 bytes.");

// Store a 2nd memory checkpoint in s2
_CrtMemCheckpoint( &s2 );

OutputHeading(
    "Dump the changes that occurred between two memory checkpoints" );
if ( _CrtMemDifference( &s3, &s1, &s2 ) )
    _CrtMemDumpStatistics( &s3 );

// Free p2 again and store a new memory checkpoint in s2
free( p2 );
_CrtMemCheckpoint( &s2 );

OutputHeading(
    "Now the memory state at the two checkpoints is the same" );
if ( _CrtMemDifference( &s3, &s1, &s2 ) )
    _CrtMemDumpStatistics( &s3 );
```

```
    strcpy( p1, "This new p1 string is over 34 bytes" );
    OutputHeading( "Free p1 after overwriting the end of the allocation" );
    free( p1 );

    // Set the debug-heap flag so that freed blocks are kept on the
    // linked list, to catch any inadvertent use of freed memory
    SET_CRT_DEBUG_FIELD( _CRTDBG_DELAY_FREE_MEM_DF );

    p1 = malloc( 10 );
    free( p1 );
    strcpy( p1, "Oops" );

    OutputHeading( "Perform a memory check after corrupting freed memory" );
    _CrtCheckMemory( );

    // Use explicit calls to _malloc_dbg to save file name and line number
    // information, and also to allocate Client type blocks for tracking
    p1 = _malloc_dbg( 40, _NORMAL_BLOCK, __FILE__, __LINE__ );
    p2 = _malloc_dbg( 40, _CLIENT_BLOCK, __FILE__, __LINE__ );
    strcpy( p1, "p1 points to a Normal allocation block" );
    strcpy( p2, "p2 points to a Client allocation block" );

    // You must use _free_dbg to free a Client block
    OutputHeading(
        "Using free( ) to free a Client block causes an assertion failure" );
    free( p1 );
    free( p2 );

    p1 = malloc( 10 );
    OutputHeading( "Examine outstanding allocations (dump memory leaks)" );
    _CrtDumpMemoryLeaks( );

    // Set the debug-heap flag so that memory leaks are reported when
    // the process terminates. Then, exit.
    OutputHeading( "Program exits without freeing a memory block" );
    SET_CRT_DEBUG_FIELD( _CRTDBG_LEAK_CHECK_DF );
}
```

Output

```
Use _ASSERTE to check that the two strings are identical:
***********************************************************************
C:\DEV\EXAMPLE1.C(56) : Assertion failed: strcmp( p1, p2 ) == 0

Use a _RPT macro to report the string contents as a warning:
***********************************************************************
p1 points to 'This is the p1 string (34 bytes).' and
p2 points to 'This is the p2 string (34 bytes).'
```

```
Use _CRTMemDumpAllObjectsSince to check the p1 and p2 allocations:
****************************************************************
Dumping objects ->
{13} normal block at 0x00660B5C, 34 bytes long
 Data: <This is the p2 s> 54 68 69 73 20 69 73 20 74 68 65 20 70 32 20 73
{12} normal block at 0x00660B10, 34 bytes long
 Data: <This is the p1 s> 54 68 69 73 20 69 73 20 74 68 65 20 70 31 20 73
Object dump complete.

Having freed p2, dump allocation information about p1 only:
****************************************************************
Dumping objects ->
{12} normal block at 0x00660B10, 34 bytes long
 Data: <This is the p1 s> 54 68 69 73 20 69 73 20 74 68 65 20 70 31 20 73
Object dump complete.

Dump the changes that occurred between two memory checkpoints:
****************************************************************
0 bytes in 0 Free Blocks.
38 bytes in 1 Normal Blocks.
0 bytes in 0 CRT Blocks.
0 bytes in 0 IgnoreClient Blocks.
0 bytes in 0 (null) Blocks.
Largest number used: 4 bytes.
Total allocations: 38 bytes.

Now the memory state at the two checkpoints is the same:
****************************************************************

Free p1 after overwriting the end of the allocation:
****************************************************************
memory check error at 0x00660B32 = 0x73, should be 0xFD.
memory check error at 0x00660B33 = 0x00, should be 0xFD.
DAMAGE: after Normal block (#12) at 0x00660B10.

Perform a memory check after corrupting freed memory:
****************************************************************
memory check error at 0x00660B10 = 0x4F, should be 0xDD.
memory check error at 0x00660B11 = 0x6F, should be 0xDD.
memory check error at 0x00660B12 = 0x70, should be 0xDD.
memory check error at 0x00660B13 = 0x73, should be 0xDD.
memory check error at 0x00660B14 = 0x00, should be 0xDD.
DAMAGE: on top of Free block at 0x00660B10.
DAMAGED located at 0x00660B10 is 10 bytes long.

Using free( ) to free a Client block causes an assertion failure:
****************************************************************
dbgheap.c(1039) : Assertion failed: pHead->nBlockUse == nBlockUse
```

```
Examine outstanding allocations (dump memory leaks):
***********************************************************************
Detected memory leaks!
Dumping objects ->
{18} normal block at 0x00660BE4, 10 bytes long
 Data: <            > CD CD CD CD CD CD CD CD CD CD
Object dump complete.

Program exits without freeing a memory block:
***********************************************************************
Detected memory leaks!
Dumping objects ->
{18} normal block at 0x00660BE4, 10 bytes long
 Data: <            > CD CD CD CD CD CD CD CD CD CD
Object dump complete.
```

See Also

_crtDbgFlag, _CrtSetDbgFlag

_CrtDbgReport

Generates a report with a debugging message and sends the report to three possible destinations (debug version only).

int _CrtDbgReport(int *reportType*, **const char** **filename*,
    int *linenumber*, **const char** **moduleName*, **const char** **format* [, *argument*] ... **);**

Routine	Required Header	Compatibility
_CrtDbgReport	<crtdbg.h>	Win NT, Win 95

For additional compatibility information, see "Compatibility" in the Introduction.

Libraries

LIBCD.LIB	Single thread static library, debug version
LIBCMTD.LIB	Multithread static library, debug version
MSVCRTD.LIB	Import library for MSVCRTD.DLL, debug version

Return Value

For all report destinations, **_CrtDbgReport** returns –1 if an error occurs and 0 if no errors are encountered. However, when the report destination is a debug message window and the user chooses the Retry button, **_CrtDbgReport** returns 1. If the user chooses the Abort button in the debug message window, **_CrtDbgReport** immediately aborts and does not return a value.

The _ASSERT[E] and _RPT, _RPTF debug macros call **_CrtDbgReport** to generate their debug report. When **_CrtDbgReport** returns 1, these macros start the debugger, provided that "just-in-time" (JIT) debugging is enabled.

Parameters

reportType
> Report type: **_CRT_WARN, _CRT_ERROR, _CRT_ASSERT**

filename
> Pointer to name of source file where assert/report occurred or NULL

linenumber
> Line number in source file where assert/report occured or NULL

moduleName
> Pointer to name of module (.EXE or .DLL) where assert/report occurred

format
> Pointer to format-control string used to create the user message

argument
> Optional substitution arguments used by *format*

Remarks

The **_CrtDbgReport** function is similar to the printf function, as it can be used to report warnings, errors, and assert information to the user during the debugging process. However, this function is more flexible than **printf** because it does not need to be enclosed in **#ifdef** statements to prevent it from being called in a retail build of an application. This is achieved by using the _DEBUG flag: When _DEBUG is not defined, calls to **_CrtDbgReport** are removed during preprocessing.

_CrtDbgReport can send the debug report to three different destinations: a debug report file, a debug monitor (the Visual C++ debugger), or a debug message window. Two configuration functions, _CrtSetReportMode and _CrtSetReportFile, are used to specify the destination(s) for each report type. These functions allow the reporting destination(s) for each report type to be separately controlled. For example, it is possible to specify that a *reportType* of **_CRT_WARN** only be sent to the debug monitor, while a *reportType* of **_CRT_ASSERT** be sent to a debug message window and a user-defined report file.

_CrtDbgReport creates the user message for the debug report by substituting the *argument*[*n*] arguments into the *format* string, using the same rules defined by the **printf** function. **_CrtDbgReport** then generates the debug report and determines the destination(s), based on the current report modes and file defined for *reportType*. When the report is sent to a debug message window, the *filename*, *lineNumber*, and *moduleName* are included in the information displayed in the window.

The following table lists the available choices for the report mode(s) and file and the resulting behavior of **_CrtDbgReport**. These options are defined as bit-flags in CRTDBG.H.

Report Mode	Report File	_CrtDbgReport Behavior
CRTDBG-MODE_DEBUG	Not applicable	Writes message to Windows OutputDebugString API.
CRTDBG-MODE_WNDW	Not applicable	Calls Windows MessageBox **API to** create message box to display the message along with Abort, Retry, and Ignore buttons. If user selects Abort, **_CrtDbgReport** immediately aborts. If user selects Retry, it returns 1. If user selects Ignore, execution continues and **_CrtDbgReport** returns 0. Note that choosing Ignore when an error condition exists often results in "undefined behavior."
CRTDBG-MODE_FILE	__HFILE	Writes message to user-supplied **HANDLE**, using the Windows WriteFile API, and does not verify validity of file handle; the application is responsible for opening the report file and passing a valid file handle.
CRTDBG-MODE_FILE	_CRTDBG_-FILE_STDERR	Writes message to **stderr**.
CRTDBG-MODE_FILE	_CRTDBG_-FILE_STDOUT	Writes message to **stdout**.

The report may be sent to one, two, or three destinations, or no destination at all.
For more information about specifying the report mode(s) and report file, see the
"**_CrtSetReportMode**" and "**_CrtSetReportFile**" functions. For more information about
using the debug macros and reporting functions, see "Using Macros for Verification
and Reporting" and "Debug Reporting Functions of the C Run-Time Library" in the
Visual C++ Programmer's Guide online.

If your application needs more flexibility than that provided by **_CrtDbgReport**, you
can write your own reporting function and hook it into the C run-time library reporting
mechanism by using the _CrtSetReportHook function.

Example

```
/*
 * REPORT.C:
 * In this program, calls are made to the _CrtSetReportMode,
 * _CrtSetReportFile, and _CrtSetReportHook functions.
 * The _ASSERT macros are called to evaluate their expression.
 * When the condition fails, these macros print a diagnostic message
 * and call _CrtDbgReport to generate a debug report and the
 * client-defined reporting function is called as well.
 * The _RPTn and _RPTFn group of macros are also exercised in
 * this program, as an alternative to the printf function.
 * When these macros are called, the client-defined reporting function
 * takes care of all the reporting - _CrtDbgReport won't be called.
 */
```

```c
#include <stdio.h>
#include <string.h>
#include <malloc.h>
#include <crtdbg.h>

#define FALSE 0
#define TRUE !FALSE

/*
 * Define our own reporting function.
 * We'll hook it into the debug reporting
 * process later using _CrtSetReportHook.
 *
 * Define a global int to keep track of
 * how many assertion failures occur.
 */
int gl_num_asserts=0;
int OurReportingFunction( int reportType, char *userMessage, int *retVal )
{
    /*
     * Tell the user our reporting function is being called.
     * In other words - verify that the hook routine worked.
     */
    fprintf(stdout, "Inside the client-defined reporting function.\n");
    fflush(stdout);

    /*
     * When the report type is for an ASSERT,
     * we'll report some information, but we also
     * want _CrtDbgReport to get called -
     * so we'll return TRUE.
     *
     * When the report type is a WARNing or ERROR,
     * we'll take care of all of the reporting. We don't
     * want _CrtDbgReport to get called -
     * so we'll return FALSE.
     */
    if (reportType == _CRT_ASSERT)
    {
        gl_num_asserts++;
        fprintf(stdout, "This is the number of Assertion failures
        ⮑ that have occurred: %d \n", gl_num_asserts);
        fflush(stdout);
        fprintf(stdout, "Returning TRUE from the client-defined reporting function.\n");
        fflush(stdout);
        return(TRUE);
```

```
    } else {
        fprintf(stdout, "This is the debug user message: %s \n", userMessage);
        fflush(stdout);
        fprintf(stdout, "Returning FALSE from the client-defined reporting function.\n");
        fflush(stdout);
        return(FALSE);
    }

    /*
     * By setting retVal to zero, we are instructing _CrtDbgReport
     * to continue with normal execution after generating the report.
     * If we wanted _CrtDbgReport to start the debugger, we would set
     * retVal to one.
     */
    retVal = 0;
}

int main()
{
    char *p1, *p2;

    /*
     * Hook in our client-defined reporting function.
     * Every time a _CrtDbgReport is called to generate
     * a debug report, our function will get called first.
     */
    _CrtSetReportHook( OurReportingFunction );

    /*
     * Define the report destination(s) for each type of report
     * we are going to generate.  In this case, we are going to
     * generate a report for every report type: _CRT_WARN,
     * _CRT_ERROR, and _CRT_ASSERT.
     * The destination(s) is defined by specifying the report mode(s)
     * and report file for each report type.
     * This program sends all report types to stdout.
     */
    _CrtSetReportMode(_CRT_WARN, _CRTDBG_MODE_FILE);
    _CrtSetReportFile(_CRT_WARN, _CRTDBG_FILE_STDOUT);
    _CrtSetReportMode(_CRT_ERROR, _CRTDBG_MODE_FILE);
    _CrtSetReportFile(_CRT_ERROR, _CRTDBG_FILE_STDOUT);
    _CrtSetReportMode(_CRT_ASSERT, _CRTDBG_MODE_FILE);
    _CrtSetReportFile(_CRT_ASSERT, _CRTDBG_FILE_STDOUT);

    /*
     * Allocate and assign the pointer variables
     */
```

```
p1 = malloc(10);
strcpy(p1, "I am p1");
p2 = malloc(10);
strcpy(p2, "I am p2");

/*
 * Use the report macros as a debugging
 * warning mechanism, similar to printf.
 *
 * Use the assert macros to check if the
 * p1 and p2 variables are equivalent.
 *
 * If the expression fails, _ASSERTE will
 * include a string representation of the
 * failed expression in the report.
 *
 *  _ASSERT does not include the
 * expression in the generated report.
 */
_RPT0(_CRT_WARN, "\n\n Use the assert macros to evaluate the expression p1 == p2.\n");
_RPTF2(_CRT_WARN, "\n Will _ASSERT find '%s' == '%s' ?\n", p1, p2);
_ASSERT(p1 == p2);

_RPTF2(_CRT_WARN, "\n\n Will _ASSERTE find '%s' == '%s' ?\n", p1, p2);
_ASSERTE(p1 == p2);

_RPT2(_CRT_ERROR, "\n \n '%s' != '%s'\n", p1, p2);

free(p2);
free(p1);

return 0;
}
```

Output

```
Inside the client-defined reporting function.
This is the debug user message: Use the assert macros to evaluate the expression p1 == p2
Returning FALSE from the client-defined reporting function.
Inside the client-defined reporting function.
This is the debug user message: dbgmacro.c(54) : Will _ASSERT find 'I am p1' == 'I am p2' ?
Returning FALSE from the client-defined reporting function.
Inside the client-defined reporting function.
This is the number of Assertion failures that have occurred: 1
Returning TRUE from the client-defined reporting function.
dbgmacro.c(55) : Assertion failed
Inside the client-defined reporting function.
```

```
This is the debug user message: dbgmacro.c(57) : Will _ASSERTE find 'I am p1' == 'I am p2' ?
Returning FALSE from the client-defined reporting function.
Inside the client-defined reporting function.
This is the number of Assertion failures that have occurred: 2
Returning TRUE from the client-defined reporting function.
dbgmacro.c(58) : Assertion failed: p1 == p2
Inside the client-defined reporting function.
This is the debug user message: 'I am p1' != 'I am p2'
Returning FALSE from the client-defined reporting function.
```

See Also

_CrtSetReportMode, _CrtSetReportFile, printf, _DEBUG

_CrtDoForAllClientObjects

Calls an application-supplied function for all **_CLIENT_BLOCK** types in the heap (debug version only).

void _CrtDoForAllClientObjects(void (*pfn)(void *, void *), void *context);

Routine	Required Header	Compatibility
_CrtDoForAllClientObjects	<crtdbg.h>	Win NT, Win 95

For additional compatibility information, see "Compatibility" in the Introduction.

Libraries

LIBCD.LIB	Single thread static library, debug version
LIBCMTD.LIB	Multithread static library, debug version
MSVCRTD.LIB	Import library for MSVCRTD.DLL, debug version

Return Value

None

Parameters

*void (*pfn)(void *, void *)*
    Pointer to the application-supplied function to call

context
    Pointer to the application-supplied context to pass to the application-supplied function

Remarks

The **_CrtDoForAllClientObjects** function searches the heap's linked list for memory blocks with the **_CLIENT_BLOCK** type and calls the application-supplied function when a block of this type is found. The found block and the *context* parameter are passed as arguments to the application-supplied function. During debugging, an application can track a specific group of allocations by explicitly calling the debug heap functions to allocate the memory and specifying that the blocks be assigned the **_CLIENT_BLOCK** block type. These blocks can then be tracked separately and reported on differently during leak detection and memory state reporting.

If the **_CRTDBG_ALLOC_MEM_DF** bit field of the _crtDbgFlag flag is not turned on, **_CrtDoForAllClientObjects** immediately returns. When _DEBUG is not defined, calls to **_CrtDoForAllClientObjects** are removed during preprocessing.

For more information about the **_CLIENT_BLOCK** type and how it can be used by other debug functions, see "Types of Blocks on the Debug Heap" in the *Visual C++ Programmer's Guide* online. For information about how memory blocks are allocated, initialized, and managed in the debug version of the base heap, see "Memory Management and the Debug Heap" in the *Visual C++ Programmer's Guide* online.

Example

```
/*
 * DFACOBJS.C
 * This program allocates some CLIENT type blocks of memory
 * and then calls _CrtDoForAllClientObjects to print out the contents
 * of each client block found on the heap.
 */

#include <crtdbg.h>
#include <stdio.h>
#include <malloc.h>
#include <stdlib.h>

/*
 * My Memory Block linked-list data structure
 */
typedef struct MyMemoryBlockStruct
{
    struct MyMemoryBlockStruct *NextPtr;
    int blockType;
    int allocNum;
} aMemoryBlock;
aMemoryBlock *HeadPtr;
aMemoryBlock *TailPtr;

/*
 * CreateMemoryBlock
 * allocates a block of memory, fills in the data structure
 * and adds the new block to the linked list
 * Returns 1 if successful, otherwise 0
 */
int CreateMemoryBlock(
    int allocNum,
    int blockType
    )
```

```
{
    aMemoryBlock *blockPtr;
    size_t size;

    size = sizeof( struct MyMemoryBlockStruct );
    if ( blockType == _CLIENT_BLOCK )
        blockPtr = (aMemoryBlock *) _malloc_dbg( size, _CLIENT_BLOCK, __FILE__, __LINE__ );
    else
        blockPtr = (aMemoryBlock *) _malloc_dbg( size, _NORMAL_BLOCK, __FILE__, __LINE__ );

    if ( blockPtr == NULL )
        return(0);

    blockPtr->allocNum = allocNum;
    blockPtr->blockType = blockType;

    blockPtr->NextPtr = NULL;
    if ( HeadPtr == NULL )
        HeadPtr = blockPtr;
    else
        TailPtr->NextPtr = blockPtr;
    TailPtr = blockPtr;
    return(1);
}


/*
 * RestoreMemoryToHeap
 * restores all of the memory that we allocated on the heap
 */
void RestoreMemoryToHeap( )
{
    aMemoryBlock *blockPtr;

    if (!HeadPtr)
        return;

    while ( HeadPtr->NextPtr != NULL )
    {
        blockPtr = HeadPtr->NextPtr;
        if ( HeadPtr->blockType == _CLIENT_BLOCK )
            _free_dbg( HeadPtr, _CLIENT_BLOCK );
        else
            _free_dbg( HeadPtr, _NORMAL_BLOCK );

        HeadPtr = blockPtr;
    }
}
```

```
/*
 * MyClientObjectHook
 * A hook function for performing some action on all
 * client blocks found on the heap - In this case, print
 * out the value stored at each memory address.
 */
void __cdecl MyClientObjectHook(
    void * pUserData,
    void * ignored
    )
{
    aMemoryBlock *blockPtr;
    long allocReqNum;
    int success;

    blockPtr = (aMemoryBlock *) pUserData;

    /*
     * Let's retrieve the actual object allocation order request number
     * and see if it's different from the allocation number we stored in
     * in our data structure.
     */
    success = _CrtIsMemoryBlock((const void *) blockPtr,
            (unsigned int) sizeof( struct MyMemoryBlockStruct ), &allocReqNum,
            NULL, NULL );
    if ( success )
    printf( "Block #%d \t Type: %d \t Allocation Number: %d\n", blockPtr->allocNum,
            blockPtr->blockType, allocReqNum);
    else
    {
            printf("ERROR: not a valid memory block.\n");
            exit( 1 );
    }
}

void main( void )
{
    div_t div_result;
    int i, success, tmpFlag;

    /*
     * Set the _crtDbgFlag to turn debug type allocations.
     * This will enable us to specify that blocks of type
     * _CLIENT_BLOCK can be allocated and tracked separately.
     * Turn off checking for internal CRT blocks.
     */
    tmpFlag = _CrtSetDbgFlag( _CRTDBG_REPORT_FLAG );
    tmpFlag |= _CRTDBG_ALLOC_MEM_DF;
    tmpFlag &= _CRTDBG_CHECK_CRT_DF;
    _CrtSetDbgFlag( tmpFlag );
```

```
    /*
     * We're going to allocate 22 blocks and every other block is
     * going to be of type _CLIENT_BLOCK.
     * Blocks numbered 2, 4, 6, 8, 10, 12, 14, 16, 18, 20, and 22
     * should all be _CLIENT_BLOCKS.
     */
    HeadPtr = NULL;
    printf("Allocating the memory ");
    for (i=1; i < 23; i++)
    {
            div_result = div( i, 2);
    if ( div_result.rem > 0 )
       success = CreateMemoryBlock( i, _NORMAL_BLOCK );
    else
       success = CreateMemoryBlock( i, _CLIENT_BLOCK );

    if ( !success )
    {
        printf(" ERROR.\n");
            exit( 1 );
    }
    else
       printf(".");
    }
    printf(" done.\n");

    /*
     * We're going to call _CrtDoForAllClientObjects to make sure
     * that only blocks numbered 2, 4, 6, 8, 10, 12, 14, 16, 18, 20, and 22
     * got allocated as _CLIENT_BLOCKS.
     */
    _CrtDoForAllClientObjects( MyClientObjectHook, NULL );

    /*
     * Restore the memory to the heap
     */
    RestoreMemoryToHeap();
    exit( 0 );
}
```

Output

```
The instruction at "0x00401153" referenced memory at "0x00000004".
↳ The memory could not be "read".
```

See Also

_CrtSetDbgFlag, Heap State Reporting Functions

_CrtDumpMemoryLeaks

Dumps all of the memory blocks in the debug heap when a memory leak has occurred (debug version only).

int _CrtDumpMemoryLeaks(void);

Routine	Required Header	Compatibility
_CrtDumpMemoryLeaks	<crtdbg.h>	Win NT, Win 95

For additional compatibility information, see "Compatibility" in the Introduction.

Libraries

LIBCD.LIB	Single thread static library, debug version
LIBCMTD.LIB	Multithread static library, debug version
MSVCRTD.LIB	Import library for MSVCRTD.DLL, debug version

Return Value

_CrtDumpMemoryLeaks returns TRUE if a memory leak is found; otherwise, the function returns FALSE.

Remarks

The **_CrtDumpMemoryLeaks** function determines whether a memory leak has occurred since the start of program execution. When a leak is found, the debug header information for all of the objects in the heap is dumped in a user-readable form. When _DEBUG is not defined, calls to **_CrtDumpMemoryLeaks** are removed during preprocessing.

_CrtDumpMemoryLeaks is frequently called at the end of program execution to verify that all memory allocated by the application has been freed. The function can be called automatically at program termination by turning on the **_CRTDBG_LEAK_CHECK_DF** bit field of the _crtDbgFlag flag using the _CrtSetDbgFlag function.

_CrtDumpMemoryLeaks calls _CrtMemCheckpoint to obtain the current state of the heap and then scans the state for blocks that have not been freed. When an unfreed block is encountered, **_CrtDumpMemoryLeaks** calls _CrtMemDumpAllObjectsSince to dump information for all of the objects allocated in the heap from the start of program execution.

By default, internal C run-time blocks (**_CRT_BLOCK**) are not included in memory dump operations. The _CrtSetDbgFlag function can be used to turn on the **_CRTDBG_CHECK_CRT_DF** bit of **_crtDbgFlag** to include these blocks in the leak detection process.

For more information about heap state functions and the **_CrtMemState** structure, see the "Heap State Reporting Functions" in the *Visual C++ Programmer's Guide* online. For information about how memory blocks are allocated, initialized, and managed in the debug version of the base heap, see "Memory Management and the Debug Heap" in the *Visual C++ Programmer's Guide* online.

Example

See Example 1 on page 84.

_CrtIsMemoryBlock

Verifies that a specified memory block is in the local heap and that it has a valid debug heap block type identifier (debug version only).

int _CrtIsMemoryBlock(const void *userData*, **unsigned int** *size*, **long** **requestNumber*, **char** ***filename*, **int** **linenumber* **);**

Routine	Required Header	Compatibility
_CrtIsMemoryBlock	<crtdbg.h>	Win NT, Win 95

For additional compatibility information, see "Compatibility" in the Introduction.

Libraries

LIBCD.LIB	Single thread static library, debug version
LIBCMTD.LIB	Multithread static library, debug version
MSVCRTD.LIB	Import library for MSVCRTD.DLL, debug version

Return Value

_CrtIsMemoryBlock returns TRUE if the specified memory block is located within the local heap and has a valid debug heap block type identifier; otherwise, the function returns FALSE.

Parameter

userData
Pointer to the beginning of the memory block to verify

size
Size of the specified block (bytes)

requestNumber
Pointer to the allocation number of the block or NULL

filename
Pointer to name of source file that requested the block or NULL

linenumber
Pointer to the line number in the source file or NULL

Remarks

The **_CrtIsMemoryBlock** function verifies that a specified memory block is located within the application's local heap and that it has a valid block type identifier. This function can also be used to obtain the object allocation order number and source file name/line number where the memory block allocation was originally requested. Passing non-NULL values for the *requestNumber*, *filename*, and/or *linenumber* parameters causes **_CrtIsMemoryBlock** to set these parameters to the values in the memory block's debug header, if it finds the block in the local heap. When _DEBUG is not defined, calls to **_CrtIsMemoryBlock** are removed during preprocessing.

Because this function returns TRUE or FALSE, it can be passed to one of the _ASSERT macros to create a simple debugging error handling mechanism. The following example will cause an assertion failure if the specified address is not located within the local heap:

```
_ASSERTE( _CrtIsMemoryBlock( userData, size, &requestNumber, &filename, &linenumber ) );
```

For more information about how **_CrtIsMemoryBlock** can be used with other debug functions and macros, see "Using Macros for Verification and Reporting" in the *Visual C++ Programmer's Guide* online. For information about how memory blocks are allocated, initialized, and managed in the debug version of the base heap, see "Memory Management and the Debug Heap" in the *Visual C++ Programmer's Guide* online.

Example

```
/*
 * ISVALID.C
 * This program allocates a block of memory using _malloc_dbg
 * and then tests the validity of this memory by calling _CrtIsMemoryBlock,
 * _CrtIsValidPointer, and _CrtIsValidHeapPointer.
 */

#include <stdio.h>
#include <string.h>
#include <malloc.h>
#include <crtdbg.h>

#define  TRUE   1
#define  FALSE  0

void main( void )
{
        char *my_pointer;
        /*
         * Call _malloc_dbg to include the filename and line number
         * of our allocation request in the header information
         */
        my_pointer = (char *)_malloc_dbg( sizeof(char) *
        ➜ 10, _NORMAL_BLOCK, __FILE__, __LINE__ );
```

```
        /*
         * Ensure that the memory got allocated correctly
         */
        _CrtIsMemoryBlock((const void *)my_pointer, sizeof(char) * 10, NULL, NULL, NULL );

        /*
         * Test for read/write accessibility
         */
        if (_CrtIsValidPointer((const void *)my_pointer, sizeof(char) * 10, TRUE))
                printf("my_pointer has read and write accessibility.\n");
        else
                printf("my_pointer only has read access.\n");

        /*
         * Make sure my_pointer is within the local heap
         */
        if (_CrtIsValidHeapPointer((const void *)my_pointer))
                printf("my_pointer is within the local heap.\n");
        else
                printf("my_pointer is not located within the local heap.\n");

        free(my_pointer);
}
```

Output

```
my_pointer has read and write accessibility.
my_pointer is within the local heap.
```

_CrtIsValidHeapPointer

Verifies that a specified pointer is in the local heap (debug version only).

int _CrtIsValidHeapPointer(const void *userData* **);**

Routine	Required Header	Compatibility
_CrtIsValidHeapPointer	<crtdbg.h>	Win NT, Win 95

For additional compatibility information, see "Compatibility" in the Introduction.

Libraries

LIBCD.LIB	Single thread static library, debug version
LIBCMTD.LIB	Multithread static library, debug version
MSVCRTD.LIB	Import library for MSVCRTD.DLL, debug version

Return Value

_CrtIsValidHeapPointer returns TRUE if the specified pointer is in the local heap; otherwise, the function returns FALSE.

Parameter

userData
  Pointer to the beginning of an allocated memory block

Remarks

The **_CrtIsValidHeapPointer** function is used to ensure that a specific memory address is within the local heap. The "local" heap refers to the heap created and managed by a particular instance of the C run-time library. If a dynamically linked library (DLL) contains a static link to the run-time library, then it has its own instance of the run-time heap, and therefore its own heap, independent of the application's local heap. When _DEBUG is not defined, calls to **_CrtIsValidHeapPointer** are removed during preprocessing.

Because this function returns TRUE or FALSE, it can be passed to one of the _ASSERT macros to create a simple debugging error handling mechanism. The following example will cause an assertion failure if the specified address is not located within the local heap:

```
_ASSERTE( _CrtIsValidHeapPointer( userData ) );
```

For more information about how **_CrtIsValidHeapPointer** can be used with other debug functions and macros, see "Using Macros for Verification and Reporting" in the *Visual C++ Programmer's Guide* online. For information about how memory blocks are allocated, initialized, and managed in the debug version of the base heap, see "Memory Management and the Debug Heap" in the *Visual C++ Programmer's Guide* online.

Example

```
/*
 * ISVALID.C
 * This program allocates a block of memory using _malloc_dbg
 * and then tests the validity of this memory by calling _CrtIsMemoryBlock,
 * _CrtIsValidPointer, and _CrtIsValidHeapPointer.
 */

#include <stdio.h>
#include <string.h>
#include <malloc.h>
#include <crtdbg.h>

#define  TRUE    1
#define  FALSE   0

void main( void )
{
        char *my_pointer;
```

```
    /*
     * Call _malloc_dbg to include the filename and line number
     * of our allocation request in the header information
     */
    my_pointer = (char *)_malloc_dbg( sizeof(char) *
    ↪ 10, _NORMAL_BLOCK, __FILE__, __LINE__ );

    /*
     * Ensure that the memory got allocated correctly
     */
    _CrtIsMemoryBlock((const void *)my_pointer, sizeof(char) * 10, NULL, NULL, NULL );

    /*
     * Test for read/write accessibility
     */
    if (_CrtIsValidPointer((const void *)my_pointer, sizeof(char) * 10, TRUE))
            printf("my_pointer has read and write accessibility.\n");
    else
            printf("my_pointer only has read access.\n");
    /*
     * Make sure my_pointer is within the local heap
     */
    if (_CrtIsValidHeapPointer((const void *)my_pointer))
            printf("my_pointer is within the local heap.\n");
    else
            printf("my_pointer is not located within the local heap.\n");

    free(my_pointer);
}
```

Output

```
my_pointer has read and write accessibility.
my_pointer is within the local heap.
```

_CrtIsValidPointer

Verifies that a specified memory range is valid for reading and writing
(debug version only).

int _CrtIsValidPointer(const void * address **, unsigned int** size **, int** access **);**

Routine	Required Header	Compatibility
_CrtIsValidPointer	<crtdbg.h>	Win NT, Win 95

For additional compatibility information, see "Compatibility" in the Introduction.

Libraries

LIBCD.LIB	Single thread static library, debug version
LIBCMTD.LIB	Multithread static library, debug version
MSVCRTD.LIB	Import library for MSVCRTD.DLL, debug version

Return Value

_CrtIsValidPointer returns TRUE if the specified memory range is valid for the specified operation(s); otherwise, the function returns FALSE.

Parameter

address
    Points to the beginning of the memory range to test for validity

size
    Size of the specified memory range (bytes)

access
    Read/Write accessibility to determine for the memory range

Remarks

The **_CrtIsValidPointer** function verifies that the memory range beginning at *address* and extending for *size* bytes, is valid for the specified accessibility operation(s). When *access* is set to TRUE, the memory range is verified for both reading and writing. When *address* is FALSE, the memory range is only validated for reading. When _DEBUG is not defined, calls to **_CrtIsValidPointer** are removed during preprocessing.

Because this function returns TRUE or FALSE, it can be passed to one of the _ASSERT macros to create a simple debugging error handling mechanism. The following example will cause an assertion failure if the memory range is not valid for both reading and writing operations:

```
_ASSERTE( _CrtIsValidPointer( address, size, TRUE ) );
```

For more information about how **_CrtIsValidPointer** can be used with other debug functions and macros, see "Using Macros for Verification and Reporting" in the *Visual C++ Programmer's Guide* online. For information about how memory blocks are allocated, initialized, and managed in the debug version of the base heap, see "Memory Management and the Debug Heap" in the *Visual C++ Programmer's Guide* online.

Example

```
/*
 * ISVALID.C
 * This program allocates a block of memory using _malloc_dbg
 * and then tests the validity of this memory by calling _CrtIsMemoryBlock,
 * _CrtIsValidPointer, and _CrtIsValidHeapPointer.
 */
```

```
#include <stdio.h>
#include <string.h>
#include <malloc.h>
#include <crtdbg.h>

#define  TRUE   1
#define  FALSE  0

void main( void )
{
        char *my_pointer;

        /*
         * Call _malloc_dbg to include the filename and line number
         * of our allocation request in the header information
         */
        my_pointer = (char *)_malloc_dbg( sizeof(char) *
        → 10, _NORMAL_BLOCK, __FILE__, __LINE__ );

        /*
         * Ensure that the memory got allocated correctly
         */
        _CrtIsMemoryBlock((const void *)my_pointer, sizeof(char) * 10, NULL, NULL, NULL );

        /*
         * Test for read/write accessibility
         */
        if (_CrtIsValidPointer((const void *)my_pointer, sizeof(char) * 10, TRUE))
                printf("my_pointer has read and write accessibility.\n");
        else
                printf("my_pointer only has read access.\n");

        /*
         * Make sure my_pointer is within the local heap
         */
        if (_CrtIsValidHeapPointer((const void *)my_pointer))
                printf("my_pointer is within the local heap.\n");
        else
                printf("my_pointer is not located within the local heap.\n");

        free(my_pointer);
}
```

Output

```
my_pointer has read and write accessibility.
my_pointer is within the local heap.
```

_CrtMemCheckpoint

Obtains the current state of the debug heap and stores in an application-supplied **_CrtMemState** structure (debug version only).

void _CrtMemCheckpoint(_CrtMemState *state* **);**

Routine	Required Header	Compatibility
_CrtMemCheckpoint	<crtdbg.h>	Win NT, Win 95

For additional compatibility information, see "Compatibility" in the Introduction.

Libraries

LIBCD.LIB	Single thread static library, debug version
LIBCMTD.LIB	Multithread static library, debug version
MSVCRTD.LIB	Import library for MSVCRTD.DLL, debug version

Return Value

None

Parameter

state
    Pointer to **_CrtMemState** structure to fill with the memory checkpoint

Remarks

The **_CrtMemCheckpoint** function creates a snapshot of the current state of the debug heap at any given moment, which can be used by other heap state functions to help detect memory leaks and other problems. When _DEBUG is not defined, calls to **_CrtMemState** are removed during preprocessing.

The application must pass a pointer to a previously allocated instance of the **_CrtMemState** structure, defined in CRTDBG.H, in the *state* parameter. If **_CrtMemCheckpoint** encounters an error during the checkpoint creation, the function generates a **_CRT_WARN** debug report describing the problem.

For more information about heap state functions and the **_CrtMemState** structure, see "Heap State Reporting Functions" in the *Visual C++ Programmer's Guide* online. For information about how memory blocks are allocated, initialized, and managed in the debug version of the base heap, see "Memory Management and the Debug Heap" in the *Visual C++ Programmer's Guide* online.

Example

See Example 1 on page 84.

_CrtMemDifference

Compares two memory states and returns their differences (debug version only).

int _CrtMemDifference(_CrtMemState **stateDiff*,
    const _CrtMemState **oldState*, **const _CrtMemState** **newState* **);**

Routine	Required Header	Compatibility
_CrtMemDifference	<crtdbg.h>	Win NT, Win 95

For additional compatibility information, see "Compatibility" in the Introduction.

Libraries

LIBCD.LIB	Single thread static library, debug version
LIBCMTD.LIB	Multithread static library, debug version
MSVCRTD.LIB	Import library for MSVCRTD.DLL, debug version

Return Value

If the memory states are significantly different, **_CrtMemDifference** returns TRUE; otherwise, the function returns FALSE.

Parameters

stateDiff
    Pointer to a **_CrtMemState** structure that will be used to store the differences between the two memory states (returned)

oldState
    Pointer to an earlier memory state (**_CrtMemState** structure)

newState
    Pointer to a later memory state (**_CrtMemState** structure)

Remarks

The **_CrtMemDifference** function compares *oldState* and *newState* and stores their differences in *stateDiff*, which can then be used by the application to detect memory leaks and other memory problems. When _DEBUG is not defined, calls to **_CrtMemDifference** are removed during preprocessing.

newState and *oldState* must each be a valid pointer to a **_CrtMemState** structure, defined in CRTDBG.H, that has been filled in by _CrtMemCheckpoint before calling **_CrtMemDifference**. *stateDiff* must be a pointer to a previously allocated instance of the **_CrtMemState** structure.

_CrtMemDifference compares the **_CrtMemState** field values of the blocks in *oldState* to those in *newState* and stores the result in *stateDiff*. When the number of allocated block types or total number of allocated blocks for each type differs between the two memory states, the states are said to be significantly different. The difference between the two states' high water count and total allocations is also stored in *stateDiff*.

By default, internal C run-time blocks (**_CRT_BLOCK**) are not included in memory state operations. The _CrtSetDbgFlag function can be used to turn on the **_CRTDBG_CHECK_CRT_DF** bit of **_crtDbgFlag** to include these blocks in leak detection and other memory state operations. Freed memory blocks (**_FREE_BLOCK**) do not cause **_CrtMemDifference** to return TRUE.

For more information about heap state functions and the **_CrtMemState** structure, see "Heap State Reporting Functions" in the *Visual C++ Programmer's Guide* online. For information about how memory blocks are allocated, initialized, and managed in the debug version of the base heap, see "Memory Management and the Debug Heap" in the *Visual C++ Programmer's Guide* online.

Example

See Example 1 on page 84.

See Also

_crtDbgFlag

_CrtMemDumpAllObjectsSince

Dumps information about objects in the heap from the start of program execution or from a specified heap state (debug version only).

void _CrtMemDumpAllObjectsSince(const _CrtMemState *state* **);**

Routine	Required Header	Compatibility
_CrtMemDumpAllObjectsSince	<crtdbg.h>	Win NT, Win 95

For additional compatibility information, see "Compatibility" in the Introduction.

Libraries

LIBCD.LIB	Single thread static library, debug version
LIBCMTD.LIB	Multithread static library, debug version
MSVCRTD.LIB	Import library for MSVCRTD.DLL, debug version

Return Value

None

Parameter

state
> Pointer to the heap state to begin dumping from or NULL

Remarks

The **_CrtMemDumpAllObjectsSince** function dumps the debug header information of objects allocated in the heap in a user-readable form. The dump information can be used by the application to track allocations and detect memory problems. When _DEBUG is not defined, calls to **_CrtMemDumpAllObjectsSince** are removed during preprocessing.

_CrtMemDumpAllObjectsSince uses the value of the *state* parameter to determine where to initiate the dump operation. To begin dumping from a specified heap state, the *state* parameter must be a pointer to a **_CrtMemState** structure that has been filled in by _CrtMemCheckpoint before **_CrtMemDumpAllObjectsSince** was called. When *state* is NULL, the function begins the dump from the start of program execution.

If the application has installed a dump hook function by calling _CrtSetDumpClient, then every time **_CrtMemDumpAllObjectsSince** dumps information about a **_CLIENT_BLOCK** type of block, it calls the application-supplied dump function as well. By default, internal C run-time blocks (**_CRT_BLOCK**) are not included in memory dump operations. The _CrtSetDbgFlag function can be used to turn on the **_CRTDBG_CHECK_CRT_DF** bit of **_crtDbgFlag** to include these blocks. In addition, blocks marked as freed or ignored (**_FREE_BLOCK**, **_IGNORE_BLOCK**) are not included in the memory dump.

For more information about heap state functions and the **_CrtMemState** structure, see "Heap State Reporting Functions" in the *Visual C++ Programmer's Guide* online. For information about how memory blocks are allocated, initialized, and managed in the debug version of the base heap, see "Memory Management and the Debug Heap" in the *Visual C++ Programmer's Guide* online.

Example

```
/************************************************************
 *   EXAMPLE  2                                             *
 *   ----------                                             *
 *   This program illustrates several ways to use debugging hook *
 *   functions with the new debug versions of the C runtime *
 *   libraries. To add some realism, it has a few elements of an *
 *   actual application, including two bugs.                *
 *                                                          *
 *   The program stores birthdate information in a linked list *
 *   of Client blocks. A Client-dump hook function validates the *
 *   birthday data and reports the contents of the Client blocks. *
 *   An allocation hook function logs heap operations to a text *
 *   file, and the report hook function logs reports to the same *
 *   text file.                                             *
 *                                                          *
```

```
*   NOTE: The allocation hook function explicitly excludes CRT      *
*         blocks (the memory allocated internally by the C          *
*         runtime library) from its log. It is important to         *
*         understand why! The hook function uses fprintf( ) to      *
*         write to the log file, and fprintf( ) allocates a CRT     *
*         block. If CRT blocks were not excluded in this case,      *
*         an endless loop would be created in which fprintf( )      *
*         would cause the hook function to be called, and the       *
*         hook would in turn call fprintf( ), which would cause     *
*         the hook to be called again, and so on. The moral is:     *
*                                                                   *
*   -->   IF YOUR ALLOCATION HOOK USES ANY C RUNTIME FUNCTION       *
*         THAT ALLOCATES MEMORY, THE HOOK MUST IGNORE CRT-TYPE      *
*         ALLOCATION OPERATIONS!                                    *
*                                                                   *
*   HINT: If you want to be able to report CRT-type blocks in       *
*         your allocation hook, use Windows API functions for       *
*         formatting and output, instead of C runtime functions.    *
*         Since the Windows APIs do not use the CRT heap, they      *
*         will not trap your hook in an endless loop.               *
*                                                                   *
*   BUGS: There are two bugs in the program below, which the        *
*         debug heap features identify in several ways. One bug     *
*         is that the birthDay.Name field is not large enough       *
*         to hold several of the test names. The field should       *
*         be larger, and strncpy( ) should be used in place of      *
*         strcpy( ). The second bug is that the while( ) loop       *
*         in the printRecords( ) function should not end until      *
*         HeadPtr itself == NULL. This bug results not only in      *
*         an incomplete display of birthdays, but also in a         *
*         memory leak. In addition to these two bugs, Gauss'        *
*         birthday data is out of range (April 30, not 32).         *
*                                                                   *
********************************************************************/

#include <stdio.h>
#include <stdlib.h>
#include <string.h>
#include <malloc.h>
#include <time.h>
#include <crtdbg.h>

/*******************************************************************
 *   DATA DECLARATIONS AND DEFINES                                 *
 *******************************************************************/

// The following arrays provide test data for the example program:
const char * Names[] =
```

```
    {
        "George Washington",
        "Thomas Jefferson",
        "Carl Friedrich Gauss",
        "Ludwig van Beethoven",
        "Thomas Carlyle"
    } ;

    const int Dates[] =
    {
        1732,  2, 11,
        1743,  4, 13,
        1777,  4, 32,
        1795, 12,  4,
        1770, 12, 16
    } ;

#define  TEST_RECS          5
// A generic sort of linked-list data structure, in this case for birthdays:
typedef struct BirthdayStruct
    {
        struct BirthdayStruct * NextRec;
        int   Year;
        int   Month;
        int   Day;
        char  Name[20];
    } birthDay;

birthDay * HeadPtr;
birthDay * TailPtr;

#define  FILE_IO_ERROR      0
#define  OUT_OF_MEMORY      1

#define  TRUE               7
#define  FALSE              0

// Macros for setting or clearing bits in the CRT debug flag
#ifdef _DEBUG
#define  SET_CRT_DEBUG_FIELD(a)    _CrtSetDbgFlag((a) |
↳_CrtSetDbgFlag(_CRTDBG_REPORT_FLAG))
#define  CLEAR_CRT_DEBUG_FIELD(a) _CrtSetDbgFlag(~(a) &
↳_CrtSetDbgFlag(_CRTDBG_REPORT_FLAG))
#else
#define  SET_CRT_DEBUG_FIELD(a)    ((void) 0)
#define  CLEAR_CRT_DEBUG_FIELD(a) ((void) 0)
#endif
```

```
/*******************************************************************
 *   SPECIAL-PURPOSE ROUTINES                                      *
 *******************************************************************/

/* ERROR HANDLER
   -------------
   Handling serious errors gracefully is a real test of craftsmanship.
   This function is just a stub; it doesn't really handle errors.
*/
void FatalError( int ErrType )
{
    exit( 1 );
}

/* MEMORY ALLOCATION FUNCTION
   --------------------------
   The createRecord function allocates memory for a new birthday record,
   fills in the structure members, and then adds the record to a linked list.
   In debug builds, it makes these allocations in Client blocks. If memory
   is not available, it calls the error handler.
*/
void createRecord(
    const int     Year,
    const int     Month,
    const int     Day,
    const char * Name
#ifdef _DEBUG
,   const unsigned char * szFileName, int nLine
#endif
    )
{
    birthDay * ptr;
    size_t n;

    n = sizeof( struct BirthdayStruct );
    ptr = (birthDay *) _malloc_dbg( n, _CLIENT_BLOCK, szFileName, nLine );
    if( ptr == NULL )
        FatalError( OUT_OF_MEMORY );
    ptr->Year = Year;
    ptr->Month = Month;
    ptr->Day = Day;
    strcpy( ptr->Name, Name );

    ptr->NextRec = NULL;
    if ( HeadPtr == NULL )    // If this is the first record in the linked list
        HeadPtr = ptr;
    else
        TailPtr->NextRec = ptr;
    TailPtr = ptr;
}
```

```
/* BIRTHDAY DISPLAY FUNCTION
   -------------------------
   This function traverses the linked list, displays the birthday data,
   and then frees the memory blocks used to store the birthdays.
*/
void printRecords( )
{
    birthDay * ptr;
    char *months[] = {
        "", "January", "February", "March", "April", "May", "June", "July",
        "August", "September", "October", "November", "December" };

    if ( HeadPtr == NULL )          // Do nothing if list is empty
        return;

    printf( "\n\nThis is the birthday list:\n" );
    while ( HeadPtr->NextRec != NULL )
    {
        printf( "    %s was born on %s %d, %d.\n",
                HeadPtr->Name, months[HeadPtr->Month], HeadPtr->Day, HeadPtr->Year );
        ptr = HeadPtr->NextRec;
        _free_dbg( HeadPtr, _CLIENT_BLOCK );
        HeadPtr = ptr;
    }
}


/*******************************************************************
 *   DEBUG C RUNTIME LIBRARY HOOK FUNCTIONS AND DEFINES            *
 *******************************************************************/
#ifdef _DEBUG
#define  createRecord(a, b, c, d) \
         createRecord(a, b, c, d, __FILE__, __LINE__ )
FILE *logFile;                   // Used to log allocation information
const char lineStr[] = { "---------------------------------------\
------------------------------------\n"  };


/* CLIENT DUMP HOOK FUNCTION
   -------------------------
   A hook function for dumping a Client block usually reports some
   or all of the contents of the block in question.  The function
   below also checks the data in several ways, and reports corruption
   or inconsistency as an assertion failure.
*/
void __cdecl MyDumpClientHook(
    void * pUserData,
    size_t nBytes
    )
```

```
{
    birthDay * bday;

    bday = (birthDay *) pUserData;

    _RPT4( _CRT_WARN, "   The birthday of %s is %d/%d/%d.\n",
            bday->Name, bday->Month, bday->Day, bday->Year );
    _ASSERTE( ( bday->Day > 0 ) && ( bday->Day < 32 ) );
    _ASSERTE( ( bday->Month > 0 ) && ( bday->Month < 13 ) );
    _ASSERTE( ( bday->Year > 0 ) && ( bday->Year < 1996 ) );
}


/* ALLOCATION HOOK FUNCTION
   ------------------------
   An allocation hook function can have many, many different
   uses. This one simply logs each allocation operation in a file.
*/
int __cdecl MyAllocHook(
    int       nAllocType,
    void    * pvData,
    size_t    nSize,
    int       nBlockUse,
    long      lRequest,
    const unsigned char * szFileName,
    int       nLine
    )
{
    char *operation[] = { "", "allocating", "re-allocating", "freeing" };
    char *blockType[] = { "Free", "Normal", "CRT", "Ignore", "Client" };

    if ( nBlockUse == _CRT_BLOCK )   // Ignore internal C runtime library allocations
        return( TRUE );

    _ASSERT( ( nAllocType > 0 ) && ( nAllocType < 4 ) );
    _ASSERT( ( nBlockUse >= 0 ) && ( nBlockUse < 5 ) );

    fprintf( logFile,
            "Memory operation in %s, line %d: %s a %d-byte '%s' block (# %ld)\n",
            szFileName, nLine, operation[nAllocType], nSize,
            blockType[nBlockUse], lRequest );
    if ( pvData != NULL )
        fprintf( logFile, " at %X", pvData );

    return( TRUE );           // Allow the memory operation to proceed
}
```

```
    /* REPORT HOOK FUNCTION
       --------------------
       Again, report hook functions can serve a very wide variety of purposes.
       This one logs error and assertion failure debug reports in the
       log file, along with 'Damage' reports about overwritten memory.

       By setting the retVal parameter to zero, we are instructing _CrtDbgReport
       to return zero, which causes execution to continue. If we want the function
       to start the debugger, we should have _CrtDbgReport return one.
    */
    int MyReportHook(
        int    nRptType,
        char *szMsg,
        int    *retVal
        )
    {
        char *RptTypes[] = { "Warning", "Error", "Assert" };

        if ( ( nRptType > 0 ) || ( strstr( szMsg, "DAMAGE" ) ) )
            fprintf( logFile, "%s: %s", RptTypes[nRptType], szMsg );

        retVal = 0;

        return( TRUE );          // Allow the report to be made as usual

    }
    #endif                       // End of #ifdef _DEBUG


    /******************************************************************
     *   MAIN FUNCTION                                               *
     ******************************************************************/
    void main( )
    {
        int i, j;

    #ifdef _DEBUG
        _CrtMemState checkPt1;
        char timeStr[10], dateStr[10];          // Used to set up log file

        // Send all reports to STDOUT, since this example is a console app
        _CrtSetReportMode(_CRT_WARN, _CRTDBG_MODE_FILE);
        _CrtSetReportFile(_CRT_WARN, _CRTDBG_FILE_STDOUT);
        _CrtSetReportMode(_CRT_ERROR, _CRTDBG_MODE_FILE);
        _CrtSetReportFile(_CRT_ERROR, _CRTDBG_FILE_STDOUT);
        _CrtSetReportMode(_CRT_ASSERT, _CRTDBG_MODE_FILE);
        _CrtSetReportFile(_CRT_ASSERT, _CRTDBG_FILE_STDOUT);
```

```
// Set the debug heap to report memory leaks when the process terminates,
// and to keep freed blocks in the linked list.
SET_CRT_DEBUG_FIELD( _CRTDBG_LEAK_CHECK_DF | _CRTDBG_DELAY_FREE_MEM_DF );

// Open a log file for the hook functions to use
logFile = fopen( "MEM-LOG.TXT", "w" );
if ( logFile == NULL )
   FatalError( FILE_IO_ERROR );
_strtime( timeStr );
_strdate( dateStr );
fprintf( logFile,
         "Memory Allocation Log File for Example Program, run at %s on %s.\n",
         timeStr, dateStr );
fputs( lineStr, logFile );

// Install the hook functions
_CrtSetDumpClient( MyDumpClientHook );
_CrtSetAllocHook( MyAllocHook );
_CrtSetReportHook( MyReportHook );

#endif                      // End of #ifdef _DEBUG

HeadPtr = NULL;

// Create a trial birthday record.
createRecord( 1749, 3, 23, "Pierre de Laplace" );

// Check the debug heap, and dump the new birthday record. --Note that
// debug C runtime library functions such as _CrtCheckMemory( ) and
// _CrtMemDumpAllObjectsSince( ) automatically disappear in a release build.
_CrtMemDumpAllObjectsSince( NULL );
_CrtCheckMemory( );
_CrtMemCheckpoint( &checkPt1 );

// Since everything has worked so far, create more records
for ( i = 0, j = 0; i < TEST_RECS; i++, j+=3 )
   createRecord( Dates[j], Dates[j+1], Dates[j+2], Names[i] );

// Examine the results
_CrtMemDumpAllObjectsSince( &checkPt1 );
_CrtMemCheckpoint( &checkPt1 );
_CrtMemDumpStatistics( &checkPt1 );
_CrtCheckMemory( );

// This fflush needs to be removed...
fflush( logFile );

// Now try displaying the records, which frees the memory being used
printRecords( );
```

```
    // OK, time to go. Did I forget to turn out any lights? I could check
    // explicitly using _CrtDumpMemoryLeaks( ), but I have set
    // _CRTDBG_LEAK_CHECK_DF, so the C runtime library debug heap will
    // automatically alert me at exit of any memory leaks.

#ifdef _DEBUG
    fclose( logFile );
#endif
}
```

Output

Screen output:

```
Dumping objects ->
C:\DEV\EXAMPLE2.C(327) : {13} client block at 0x00661B38, subtype 0, 36 bytes long:
    The birthday of Pierre de Laplace is 3/23/1749.
Object dump complete.
Dumping objects ->
C:\DEV\EXAMPLE2.C(338) : {18} client block at 0x00661CB4, subtype 0, 36 bytes long:
    The birthday of Thomas Carlyle is 12/16/1770.
C:\DEV\EXAMPLE2.C(338) : {17} client block at 0x00661C68, subtype 0, 36 bytes long:
    The birthday of Ludwig van Beethoven is 12/4/1795.
C:\DEV\EXAMPLE2.C(338) : {16} client block at 0x00661C1C, subtype 0, 36 bytes long:
    The birthday of Carl Friedrich Gauss is 4/32/1777.
C:\DEV\EXAMPLE2.C(219) : Assertion failed: ( bday->Day > 0 ) && ( bday->Day < 32 )
C:\DEV\EXAMPLE2.C(338) : {15} client block at 0x00661BD0, subtype 0, 36 bytes long:
    The birthday of Thomas Jefferson is 4/13/1743.
C:\DEV\EXAMPLE2.C(338) : {14} client block at 0x00661B84, subtype 0, 36 bytes long:
    The birthday of George Washington is 2/11/1732.
Object dump complete.
0 bytes in 0 Free Blocks.
0 bytes in 0 Normal Blocks.
6442 bytes in 12 CRT Blocks.
0 bytes in 0 IgnoreClient Blocks.
216 bytes in 6 (null) Blocks.
Largest number used: 6658 bytes.
Total allocations: 6658 bytes.
memory check error at 0x00661C8C = 0x00, should be 0xFD.
DAMAGE: after (null) block (#17) at 0x00661C68.
(null) allocated at file C:\DEV\EXAMPLE2.C(338).
(null) located at 0x00661C68 is 36 bytes long.
memory check error at 0x00661C40 = 0x00, should be 0xFD.
DAMAGE: after (null) block (#16) at 0x00661C1C.
(null) allocated at file C:\DEV\EXAMPLE2.C(338).
(null) located at 0x00661C1C is 36 bytes long.
memory check error at 0x00661C40 = 0x00, should be 0xFD.
DAMAGE: after (null) block (#16) at 0x00661C1C.
memory check error at 0x00661C8C = 0x00, should be 0xFD.
DAMAGE: after (null) block (#17) at 0x00661C68.
```

```
This is the birthday list:
    Pierre de Laplace was born on March 23, 1749.
    George Washington was born on February 11, 1732.
    Thomas Jefferson was born on April 13, 1743.
    Carl Friedrich Gauss was born on April 32, 1777.
    Ludwig van Beethoven was born on December 4, 1795.
Detected memory leaks!
Dumping objects ->
C:\DEV\EXAMPLE2.C(338) : {18} client block at 0x00661CB4, subtype 0, 36 bytes long:
    The birthday of Thomas Carlyle is 12/16/1770.
Object dump complete.
```

Log file output:

```
Memory Allocation Log File for Example Program, run at 14:11:01 on 04/28/95.
---------------------------------------------------------------------------
Memory operation in C:\DEV\EXAMPLE2.C, line 327:
                              allocating a 36-byte 'Client' block (# 13)
Memory operation in C:\DEV\EXAMPLE2.C, line 338:
                              allocating a 36-byte 'Client' block (# 14)
Memory operation in C:\DEV\EXAMPLE2.C, line 338:
                              allocating a 36-byte 'Client' block (# 15)
Memory operation in C:\DEV\EXAMPLE2.C, line 338:
                              allocating a 36-byte 'Client' block (# 16)
Memory operation in C:\DEV\EXAMPLE2.C, line 338:
                              allocating a 36-byte 'Client' block (# 17)
Memory operation in C:\DEV\EXAMPLE2.C, line 338:
                              allocating a 36-byte 'Client' block (# 18)
Assert: C:\DEV\EXAMPLE2.C(219) : Assertion failed:
                              ( bday->Day > 0 ) && ( bday->Day < 32 )
Warning: DAMAGE: after (null) block (#17) at 0x00661C68.
Warning: DAMAGE: after (null) block (#16) at 0x00661C1C.
Memory operation in (null), line 0: freeing a 0-byte 'Client' block (# 0)
   at 661B38Memory operation in (null), line 0:
                              freeing a 0-byte 'Client' block (# 0)
   at 661B84Memory operation in (null), line 0:
                              freeing a 0-byte 'Client' block (# 0)
   at 661BD0Memory operation in (null), line 0:
                              freeing a 0-byte 'Client' block (# 0)
   at 661C1CError: DAMAGE: after (null) block (#16) at 0x00661C1C.
Memory operation in (null), line 0: freeing a 0-byte 'Client' block (# 0)
   at 661C68Error: DAMAGE: after (null) block (#17) at 0x00661C68.
```

See Also

_crtDbgFlag

_CrtMemDumpStatistics

Dumps the debug header information for a specified heap state in a user-readable form (debug version only).

void _CrtMemDumpStatistics(const _CrtMemState *state* **);**

Routine	Required Header	Compatibility
_CrtMemDumpStatistics	<crtdbg.h>	Win NT, Win 95

For additional compatibility information, see "Compatibility" in the Introduction.

Libraries

LIBCD.LIB	Single thread static library, debug version
LIBCMTD.LIB	Multithread static library, debug version
MSVCRTD.LIB	Import library for MSVCRTD.DLL, debug version

Return Value

None

Parameter

state
    Pointer to the heap state to dump

Remarks

The **_CrtMemDumpStatistics** function dumps the debug header information for a specified state of the heap in a user-readable form. The dump statistics can be used by the application to track allocations and detect memory problems. The memory state may contain a specific heap state, or the difference between two states. When _DEBUG is not defined, calls to **_CrtMemDumpStatistics** are removed during preprocessing.

The *state* parameter must be a pointer to a **_CrtMemState** structure that has been filled in by _CrtMemCheckpoint or returned by _CrtMemDifference before **_CrtMemDumpStatistics** is called.

For more information about heap state functions and the **_CrtMemState** structure, see "Heap State Reporting Functions" in the *Visual C++ Programmer's Guide* online. For information about how memory blocks are allocated, initialized, and managed in the debug version of the base heap, see "Memory Management and the Debug Heap" in the *Visual C++ Programmer's Guide* online.

Example

See Example 1 on page 84.

_CrtSetAllocHook

Installs a client-defined allocation function by hooking it into the C run-time debug memory allocation process (debug version only).

_CRT_ALLOC_HOOK _CrtSetAllocHook(_CRT_ALLOC_HOOK *allocHook* **);**

Routine	Required Header	Compatibility
_CrtSetAllocHook	<crtdbg.h>	Win NT, Win 95

For additional compatibility information, see "Compatibility" in the Introduction.

Libraries

LIBCD.LIB	Single thread static library, debug version
LIBCMTD.LIB	Multithread static library, debug version
MSVCRTD.LIB	Import library for MSVCRTD.DLL, debug version

Return Value

_CrtSetAllocHook returns the previously defined allocation hook function.

Parameter

allocHook
New client-defined allocation function to hook into the C run-time debug memory allocation process

Remarks

_CrtSetAllocHook allows an application to hook its own allocation function into the C run-time debug library memory allocation process. As a result, every call to a debug allocation function to allocate, reallocate, or free a memory block triggers a call to the application's hook function. **_CrtSetAllocHook** provides an application with an easy method for testing how the application handles insufficient memory situations, the ability to examine allocation patterns, and the opportunity to log allocation information for later analysis. When _DEBUG is not defined, calls to **_CrtSetAllocHook** are removed during preprocessing.

The **_CrtSetAllocHook** function installs the new client-defined allocation function specified in *allocHook* and returns the previously defined hook function. The following example demonstrates how a client-defined allocation hook should be prototyped:

```
int YourAllocHook( int allocType, void *userData, size_t size, int blockType,
   long requestNumber, const unsigned char *filename, int lineNumber);
```

The allocType argument specifies the type of allocation operation (**_HOOK_ALLOC**, **_HOOK_REALLOC**, **_HOOK_FREE**) that triggered the call to the allocation's hook function. When the triggering allocation type is **_HOOK_FREE**, userData is a pointer to the user data section of the memory block about to be freed. However, when the triggering allocation type is **_HOOK_ALLOC** or **_HOOK_REALLOC**, userData is NULL because the memory block has not been allocated yet.

size specifies the size of the memory block in bytes, blockType indicates the type of the memory block, requestNumber is the object allocation order number of the memory block, and if available, filename and lineNumber specify the source file name and line number where the triggering allocation operation was initiated.

After the hook function has finished processing, it must return a Boolean value, which tells the main C run-time allocation process how to continue. When the hook function wants the main allocation process to continue as if the hook function had never been called, then the hook function should return TRUE. This causes the original triggering allocation operation to be executed. Using this implementation, the hook function can gather and save allocation information for later analysis, without interfering with the current allocation operation or state of the debug heap.

When the hook function wants the main allocation process to continue as if the triggering allocation operation was called and it failed, then the hook function should return FALSE. Using this implementation, the hook function can simulate a wide range of memory conditions and debug heap states to test how the application handles each situation.

For more information about how **_CrtSetAllocHook** can be used with other memory management functions or how to write your own client-defined hook functions, see "Writing Your Own Debugging Hook Functions" in the *Visual C++ Programmer's Guide* online.

Example

See Example 2 on page 110.

_CrtSetBreakAlloc

Sets a breakpoint on a specified object allocation order number (debug version only).

long _CrtSetBreakAlloc(long *lBreakAlloc* **);**

Routine	Required Header	Compatibility
_CrtSetBreakAlloc	<crtdbg.h>	Win NT, Win 95

For additional compatibility information, see "Compatibility" in the Introduction.

Libraries

LIBCD.LIB	Single thread static library, debug version
LIBCMTD.LIB	Multithread static library, debug version
MSVCRTD.LIB	Import library for MSVCRTD.DLL, debug version

Return Value

_CrtSetBreakAlloc returns the previous object allocation order number that had a breakpoint set.

Parameter

lBreakAlloc
   Allocation order number, for which to set the breakpoint

Remarks

_CrtSetBreakAlloc allows an application to perform memory leak detection by breaking at a specific point of memory allocation and tracing back to the origin of the request. The function uses the sequential object allocation order number assigned to the memory block when it was allocated in the heap. When _DEBUG is not defined, calls to **_CrtSetBreakAlloc** are removed during preprocessing.

The object allocation order number is stored in the *lRequest* field of the **_CrtMemBlockHeader** structure, defined in CRTDBG.H. When information about a memory block is reported by one of the debug dump functions, this number is enclosed in curly brackets; for example, {36}.

For more information about how **_CrtSetBreakAlloc** can be used with other memory management functions, see "Tracking Heap Allocation Requests" in the *Visual C++ Programmer's Guide* online.

Example

```
/*
 * SETBRKAL.C
 * In this program, a call is made to the _CrtSetBreakAlloc routine
 * to verify that the debugger halts program execution when it reaches
 * a specified allocation number.
 */

#include <malloc.h>
#include <crtdbg.h>

void main( )
{
        long allocReqNum;
        char *my_pointer;
```

```
        /*
         * Allocate "my_pointer" for the first
         * time and ensure that it gets allocated correctly
         */
        my_pointer = malloc(10);
        _CrtIsMemoryBlock(my_pointer, 10, &allocReqNum, NULL, NULL);

        /*
         * Set a breakpoint on the allocation request
         * number for "my_pointer"
         */
        _CrtSetBreakAlloc(allocReqNum+2);
        _crtBreakAlloc = allocReqNum+2;

        /*
         * Alternate freeing and reallocating "my_pointer"
         * to verify that the debugger halts program execution
         * when it reaches the allocation request
         */
        free(my_pointer);
        my_pointer = malloc(10);
        free(my_pointer);
        my_pointer = malloc(10);
        free(my_pointer);
}
```

Output

```
The exception Breakpoint
A breakpoint has been reached.
(0x0000003) occurred in the application at location 0x00401255.
```

_CrtSetDbgFlag

Retrieves and/or modifies the state of the **_crtDbgFlag** flag to control the allocation behavior of the debug heap manager (debug version only).

int _CrtSetDbgFlag(int *newFlag* **);**

Routine	Required Header	Compatibility
_CrtSetDbgFlag	<crtdbg.h>	Win NT, Win 95

For additional compatibility information, see "Compatibility" in the Introduction.

Libraries

LIBCD.LIB	Single thread static library, debug version
LIBCMTD.LIB	Multithread static library, debug version
MSVCRTD.LIB	Import library for MSVCRTD.DLL, debug version

_CrtSetDbgFlag returns the previous state of **_crtDbgFlag**.

Parameter

newFlag
   New state for the **_crtDbgFlag**

Remarks

The **_CrtSetDbgFlag** function allows the application to control how the debug heap
manager tracks memory allocations by modifying the bit fields of the **_crtDbgFlag** flag.
By setting the bits (turning on), the application can instruct the debug heap manager to
perform special debugging operations, including checking for memory leaks when the
application exits and reporting if any are found, simulating low memory conditions
by specifying that freed memory blocks should remain in the heap's linked list, and
verifying the integrity of the heap by inspecting each memory block at every allocation
request. When _DEBUG is not defined, calls to **_CrtSetDbgFlag** are removed during
preprocessing.

The following table lists the bit fields for **_crtDbgFlag** and describes their behavior.
Because setting the bits results in increased diagnostic output and reduced program
execution speed, most of the bits are not set (turned off) by default. For more information
about these bit fields, see "Using the Debug Heap" in the *Visual C++ Programmer's
Guide* online.

Bit field	Default	Description
_CRTDBG_ALLOC_MEM_DF	ON	ON: Enable debug heap allocations and use of memory block type identifiers, such as **_CLIENT_BLOCK**. OFF: Add new allocations to heap's linked list, but set block type to **IGNORE_BLOCK**.
_CRTDBG_CHECK_ALWAYS_DF	OFF	ON: Call _CrtCheckMemory at every allocation and deallocation request. OFF: **_CrtCheckMemory** must be called explicitly.
_CRTDBG_CHECK_CRT_DF	OFF	ON: Include **_CRT_BLOCK** types in leak detection and memory state difference operations. OFF: Memory used internally by the run-time library is ignored by these operations.

(continued)

(continued)

Bit field	Default	Description
_CRTDBG_DELAY_FREE_MEM_DF	OFF	ON: Keep freed memory blocks in the heap's linked list, assign them the **_FREE_BLOCK** type, and fill them with the byte value 0xDD. OFF: Do not keep freed blocks in the heap's linked list.
_CRTDBG_LEAK_CHECK_DF	OFF	ON: Perform automatic leak checking at program exit via a call to _CrtDumpMemoryLeaks and generate an error report if the application failed to free all the memory it allocated. OFF: Do not automatically perform leak checking at program exit.

newFlag is the new state to apply to the **_crtDbgFlag** and is a combination of the values for each of the bit fields. To change one or more of these bit fields and create a new state for the flag, follow these steps:

1. Call **_CrtSetDbgFlag** with *newFlag* equal to **_CRTDBG_REPORT_FLAG** to obtain the current **_crtDbgFlag** state and store the returned value in a temporary variable.

2. Turn on any bits by OR-ing the temporary variable with the corresponding bitmasks (represented in the application code by manifest constants).

3. Turn off the other bits by AND-ing the variable with a bitwise NOT of the appropriate bitmasks.

4. Call **_CrtSetDbgFlag** with *newFlag* equal to the value stored in the temporary variable to set the new state for **_crtDbgFlag**.

The following lines of code demonstrate how to simulate low memory conditions by keeping freed memory blocks in the heap's linked list and prevent **_CrtCheckMemory** from being called at every allocation request:

```
// Get the current state of the flag
// and store it in a temporary variable
int tmpFlag = _CrtSetDbgFlag( _CRTDBG_REPORT_FLAG );

// Turn On (OR) - Keep freed memory blocks in the
// heap's linked list and mark them as freed
tmpFlag |= _CRTDBG_DELAY_FREE_MEM_DF;

// Turn Off (AND) - prevent _CrtCheckMemory from
// being called at every allocation request
tmpFlag &= ~_CRTDBG_CHECK_ALWAYS_DF;

// Set the new state for the flag
_CrtSetDbgFlag( tmpFlag );
```

For an overview of memory management and the debug heap, see "Memory Management and the Debug Heap" in the *Visual C++ Programmer's Guide* online.

To disable a flag with the **_CrtSetDbgFlag** function, you should AND the variable with the bitwise NOT of the bitmask.

Example

```
/*
 * SETDFLAG.C
 * This program concentrates on allocating and freeing memory
 * blocks to test the functionality of the _crtDbgFlag flag..
 */

#include <string.h>
#include <malloc.h>
#include <crtdbg.h>

void main( )
{
        char *p1, *p2;
        int tmpDbgFlag;

        /*
         * Set the debug-heap flag to keep freed blocks in the
         * heap's linked list - This will allow us to catch any
         * inadvertent use of freed memory
         */
        tmpDbgFlag = _CrtSetDbgFlag(_CRTDBG_REPORT_FLAG);
        tmpDbgFlag |= _CRTDBG_DELAY_FREE_MEM_DF;
        tmpDbgFlag |= _CRTDBG_LEAK_CHECK_DF;
        _CrtSetDbgFlag(tmpDbgFlag);

        /*
         * Allocate 2 memory blocks and store a string in each
         */
        p1 = malloc( 34 );
        p2 = malloc( 38 );
        strcpy( p1, "p1 points to a Normal allocation block" );
        strcpy( p2, "p2 points to a Client allocation block" );

        /*
         * Free both memory blocks
         */
        free( p2 );
        free( p1 );
```

```
        /*
         * Set the debug-heap flag to no longer keep freed blocks in the
         * heap's linked list and turn on Debug type allocations (CLIENT)
         */
        tmpDbgFlag = _CrtSetDbgFlag(_CRTDBG_REPORT_FLAG);
        tmpDbgFlag |= _CRTDBG_ALLOC_MEM_DF;
        tmpDbgFlag &= ~_CRTDBG_DELAY_FREE_MEM_DF;
        _CrtSetDbgFlag(tmpDbgFlag);

        /*
         * Explicitly call _malloc_dbg to obtain the filename and line number
         * of our allocation request and also so we can allocate CLIENT type
         * blocks specifically for tracking
         */
        p1 = _malloc_dbg( 40, _NORMAL_BLOCK, __FILE__, __LINE__ );
        p2 = _malloc_dbg( 40, _CLIENT_BLOCK, __FILE__, __LINE__ );
        strcpy( p1, "p1 points to a Normal allocation block" );
        strcpy( p2, "p2 points to a Client allocation block" );

        /*
         * _free_dbg must be called to free the CLIENT block
         */
        _free_dbg( p2, _CLIENT_BLOCK );
        free( p1 );

        /*
         * Allocate p1 again and then exit - this will leave unfreed
         * memory on the heap
         */
        p1 = malloc( 10 );
}
```

Output

```
Debug Error!
Program: C:\code\setdflag.exe
DAMAGE: after Normal block (#31) at 0x002D06A8.
Press Retry to debug the application.
```

See Also

_crtDbgFlag, _CrtCheckMemory, Heap State Reporting Functions

_CrtSetDumpClient

Installs an application-defined function to dump **_CLIENT_BLOCK** type memory blocks
(debug version only).

_CRT_DUMP_CLIENT _CrtSetDumpClient(_CRT_DUMP_CLIENT *dumpClient* **);**

Routine	Required Header	Compatibility
_CrtSetDumpClient	<crtdbg.h>	Win NT, Win 95

For additional compatibility information, see "Compatibility" in the Introduction.

Libraries

LIBCD.LIB	Single thread static library, debug version
LIBCMTD.LIB	Multithread static library, debug version
MSVCRTD.LIB	Import library for MSVCRTD.DLL, debug version

Return Value

_CrtSetDumpClient returns the previously defined client block dump function.

Parameter

dumpClient
    New client-defined memory dump function to hook into the C run-time debug
    memory dump process

Remarks

The **_CrtSetDumpClient** function allows the application to hook its own function
to dump objects stored in **_CLIENT_BLOCK** memory blocks into the C run-time
debug memory dump process. As a result, every time a debug dump function
such as _CrtMemDumpAllObjectsSince or _CrtDumpMemoryLeaks dumps a
_CLIENT_BLOCK memory block, the application's dump function will be called
as well. **_CrtSetDumpClient** provides an application with an easy method for

detecting memory leaks in and validating or reporting the contents of data stored in
_CLIENT_BLOCK blocks. When _DEBUG is not defined, calls to **_CrtSetDumpClient**
are removed during preprocessing.

The **_CrtSetDumpClient** function installs the new application-defined dump function
specified in *dumpClient* and returns the previously defined dump function. An example
of a client block dump function is as follows:

```
void DumpClientFunction( void *userPortion, size_t blockSize );
```

The userPortion argument is a pointer to the beginning of the user data portion of the memory block and blockSize specifies the size of the allocated memory block in bytes. The client block dump function must return **void**. The pointer to the client dump function that is passed to **_CrtSetDumpClient** is of type **_CRT_DUMP_CLIENT**, as defined in CRTDBG.H:

```
typedef void (__cdecl *_CRT_DUMP_CLIENT)( void *, size_t );
```

For an example of how to implement an application-defined dump function, see "Sample: Hook Function C Run-Time Application" in the *Visual C++ Programmer's Guide* online. For more information about functions that operate on **_CLIENT_BLOCK** type memory blocks, see "Client Block Hook Functions" in the *Visual C++ Programmer's Guide* online.

Example

See Example 2 on page 110.

_CrtSetReportFile

Identifies the file or stream to be used by **_CrtDbgReport** as a destination for a specific report type (debug version only).

_HFILE _CrtSetReportFile(int *reportType***, _HFILE** *reportFile* **);**

Routine	Required Header	Compatibility
_CrtSetReportFile	<crtdbg.h>	Win NT, Win 95

For additional compatibility information, see "Compatibility" in the Introduction.

Libraries

LIBCD.LIB	Single thread static library, debug version
LIBCMTD.LIB	Multithread static library, debug version
MSVCRTD.LIB	Import library for MSVCRTD.DLL, debug version

Return Value

Upon successful completion, **_CrtSetReportFile** returns the previous report file defined for the report type specified in *reportType*. If an error occurs, the report file for *reportType* is not modified and **_CrtSetReportFile** returns **_CRTDBG_HFILE_ERROR**.

Parameters

reportType
    Report type: **_CRT_WARN, _CRT_ERROR, _CRT_ASSERT**

reportFile
    New report file for *reportType*, see the following table

Remarks

_CrtSetReportFile is used in conjunction with the _CrtSetReportMode function to define the destination(s) for a specific report type generated by **_CrtDbgReport**. When **_CrtSetReportMode** has been called to assign the **_CRTDBG_MODE_FILE** reporting mode for a specific report type, **_CrtSetReportFile** should then be called to define the specific file or stream to use as the destination. When _DEBUG is not defined, calls to **_CrtSetReportFile** are removed during preprocessing.

The **_CrtSetReportFile** function assigns the new report file specified in *reportFile* to the report type specified in *reportType* and returns the previously defined report file for *reportType*. The following table lists the available choices for *reportFile* and the resulting behavior of **_CrtDbgReport**. These options are defined as bit-flags in CRTDBG.H.

Report File	_CrtDbgReport Behavior
_HFILE	**_CrtDbgReport** writes the message to a user-supplied **HANDLE** and does not verify the validity of the file handle. The application is responsible for opening and closing the report file and passing a valid file handle.
_CRTDBG_FILE_STDERR	**_CrtDbgReport** writes message to **stderr**.
_CRTDBG_FILE_STDOUT	**_CrtDbgReport** writes message to **stdout**.
_CRTDBG_REPORT_FILE	**_CrtDbgReport** is not called and the report file for *reportType* is not modified. **_CrtSetReportFile** simply returns the current report file for *reportType*.

When the report destination is a file, **_CrtSetReportMode** is called to set the file bit-flag and **_CrtSetReportFile** is called to define the specific file to use. The following code fragment demonstrates this configuration:

```
_CrtSetReportMode( _CRT_ASSERT, _CRTDBG_MODE_FILE );
_CrtSetReportFile( _CRT_ASSERT, _CRTDBG_FILE_STDERR );
```

The report file used by each report type can be separately controlled. For example, it is possible to specify that a *reportType* of **_CRT_ERROR** be reported to **stderr**, while a *reportType* of **_CRT_ASSERT** be reported to a user-defined file handle or stream.

For more information about defining the report mode(s) and file for a specific report type, see "**_CrtDbgReport**," "**_CrtSetReportMode**" and the section "Debug Reporting Functions of the C Run-Time Library" in the *Visual C++ Programmer's Guide* online.

Example

```
/*
 * REPORT.C:
 * In this program, calls are made to the _CrtSetReportMode,
 * _CrtSetReportFile, and _CrtSetReportHook functions.
 * The _ASSERT macros are called to evaluate their expression.
 * When the condition fails, these macros print a diagnostic message
 * and call _CrtDbgReport to generate a debug report and the
 * client-defined reporting function is called as well.
 * The _RPTn and _RPTFn group of macros are also exercised in
 * this program, as an alternative to the printf function.
 * When these macros are called, the client-defined reporting function
 * takes care of all the reporting - _CrtDbgReport won't be called.
 */


#include <stdio.h>
#include <string.h>
#include <malloc.h>
#include <crtdbg.h>


/*
 * Define our own reporting function.
 * We'll hook it into the debug reporting
 * process later using _CrtSetReportHook.
 *
 * Define a global int to keep track of
 * how many assertion failures occur.
 */
int gl_num_asserts=0;
int OurReportingFunction( int reportType, char *userMessage, int *retVal )
{
    /*
     * Tell the user our reporting function is being called.
     * In other words - verify that the hook routine worked.
     */
    fprintf("Inside the client-defined reporting function.\n", STDOUT);
    fflush(STDOUT);

    /*
     * When the report type is for an ASSERT, we'll report
     * some information, but we also want _CrtDbgReport to
     * get called - so we'll return TRUE.
     *
     * When the report type is a WARNing or ERROR,
     * we'll take care of all of the reporting. We don't
     * want _CrtDbgReport to get called -
     * so we'll return FALSE.
     */
```

```
   if (reportType == _CRT_ASSERT)
   {
      gl_num_asserts++;
      fprintf("This is the number of Assertion failures that have
      ↵ occurred: %d \n", gl_num_asserts, STDOUT);
      fflush(STDOUT);
      fprintf("Returning TRUE from the client-defined reporting function.\n", STDOUT);
      fflush(STDOUT);
      return(TRUE);
   } else {
      fprintf("This is the debug user message: %s \n", userMessage, STDOUT);
      fflush(STDOUT);
      fprintf("Returning FALSE from the client-defined reporting function.\n", STDOUT);
      fflush(STDOUT);
      return(FALSE);
   }

   /*
    * By setting retVal to zero, we are instructing _CrtDbgReport
    * to continue with normal execution after generating the report.
    * If we wanted _CrtDbgReport to start the debugger, we would set
    * retVal to one.
    */
   retVal = 0;
}

int main()
{
      char *p1, *p2;

   /*
    * Hook in our client-defined reporting function.
    * Every time a _CrtDbgReport is called to generate
    * a debug report, our function will get called first.
    */
   _CrtSetReportHook( OurReportingFunction );

   /*
    * Define the report destination(s) for each type of report
    * we are going to generate.  In this case, we are going to
    * generate a report for every report type: _CRT_WARN,
    * _CRT_ERROR, and _CRT_ASSERT.
    * The destination(s) is defined by specifying the report mode(s)
    * and report file for each report type.
    * This program sends all report types to STDOUT.
    */
```

```
_CrtSetReportMode(_CRT_WARN, _CRTDBG_MODE_FILE);
_CrtSetReportFile(_CRT_WARN, _CRTDBG_FILE_STDOUT);
_CrtSetReportMode(_CRT_ERROR, _CRTDBG_MODE_FILE);
_CrtSetReportFile(_CRT_ERROR, _CRTDBG_FILE_STDOUT);
_CrtSetReportMode(_CRT_ASSERT, _CRTDBG_MODE_FILE);
_CrtSetReportFile(_CRT_ASSERT, _CRTDBG_FILE_STDOUT);

/*
 * Allocate and assign the pointer variables
 */
p1 = malloc(10);
strcpy(p1, "I am p1");
p2 = malloc(10);
strcpy(p2, "I am p2");

/*
 * Use the report macros as a debugging
 * warning mechanism, similar to printf.
 *
 * Use the assert macros to check if the
 * p1 and p2 variables are equivalent.
 *
 * If the expression fails, _ASSERTE will
 * include a string representation of the
 * failed expression in the report.
 *
 *  _ASSERT does not include the
 * expression in the generated report.
 */
_RPT0(_CRT_WARN, "\n\n Use the assert macros to evaluate the expression p1 == p2.\n");
_RPTF2(_CRT_WARN, "\n Will _ASSERT find '%s' == '%s' ?\n", p1, p2);
_ASSERT(p1 == p2);

_RPTF2(_CRT_WARN, "\n\n Will _ASSERTE find '%s' == '%s' ?\n", p1, p2);
_ASSERTE(p1 == p2);

_RPT2(_CRT_ERROR, "\n \n '%s' != '%s'\n", p1, p2);

free(p2);
free(p1);

return 0;
}
```

Output

```
Inside the client-defined reporting function.
This is the debug user message: Use the assert macros to evaluate the expression p1 == p2
Returning FALSE from the client-defined reporting function.
Inside the client-defined reporting function.
This is the debug user message: dbgmacro.c(54) : Will _ASSERT find 'I am p1' == 'I am p2' ?
Returning FALSE from the client-defined reporting function.
Inside the client-defined reporting function.
This is the number of Assertion failures that have occurred: 1
Returning TRUE from the client-defined reporting function.
dbgmacro.c(55) : Assertion failed
Inside the client-defined reporting function.
This is the debug user message: dbgmacro.c(57) : Will _ASSERTE find 'I am p1' == 'I am p2' ?
Returning FALSE from the client-defined reporting function.
Inside the client-defined reporting function.
This is the number of Assertion failures that have occurred: 2
Returning TRUE from the client-defined reporting function.
dbgmacro.c(58) : Assertion failed: p1 == p2
Inside the client-defined reporting function.
This is the debug user message: 'I am p1' != 'I am p2'
Returning FALSE from the client-defined reporting function.
```

See Also

_CrtDbgReport

_CrtSetReportHook

Installs a client-defined reporting function by hooking it into the C run-time debug reporting process (debug version only).

_CRT_REPORT_HOOK _CrtSetReportHook(_CRT_REPORT_HOOK *reportHook* **);**

Routine	Required Header	Compatibility
_CrtSetReportHook	<crtdbg.h>	Win NT, Win 95

For additional compatibility information, see "Compatibility" in the Introduction.

Libraries

LIBCD.LIB	Single thread static library, debug version
LIBCMTD.LIB	Multithread static library, debug version
MSVCRTD.LIB	Import library for MSVCRTD.DLL, debug version

Return Value

_CrtSetReportHook returns the previous client-defined reporting function.

Parameter

reportHook
> New client-defined reporting function to hook into the C run-time debug reporting process

Remarks

_CrtSetReportHook allows an application to use its own reporting function into the C run-time debug library reporting process. As a result, whenever _CrtDbgReport is called to generate a debug report, the application's reporting function is called first. This functionality enables an application to perform operations such as filtering debug reports so it can focus on specific allocation types or send a report to destinations not available by using **_CrtDbgReport**. When _DEBUG is not defined, calls to **_CrtSetReportHook** are removed during preprocessing.

The **_CrtSetReportHook** function installs the new client-defined reporting function specified in *reportHook* and returns the previous client-defined hook. The following example demonstrates how a client-defined report hook should be prototyped:

```
int YourReportHook( int reportType, char *message, int *returnValue );
```

where reportType is the debug report type (**_CRT_WARN**, **_CRT_ERROR**, **_CRT_ASSERT**), message is the fully assembled debug user message to be contained in the report, and returnValue is the value specified by the client-defined reporting function that should be returned by **_CrtDbgReport**. See the "_CrtSetReportMode" function for a complete description of the available report types.

If the client-defined reporting function completely handles the debug message such that no further reporting is required, then the function should return **TRUE**. When the function returns **FALSE**, **_CrtDbgReport** will be called to generate the debug report using the current settings for the report type, mode, and file. In addition, by specifying the **_CrtDbgReport** return value in returnValue, the application can also control whether a debug break occurs. See "**_CrtSetReportMode**," "_CrtSetReportFile," and "**_CrtDbgReport**" for a complete description of how the debug report is configured and generated.

For more information about other hook-capable run-time functions and writing your own client-defined hook functions, see "Writing Your Own Debug Hook Functions" in the *Visual C++ Programmer's Guide* online.

Example

```
/*
 * REPORT.C:
 * In this program, calls are made to the _CrtSetReportMode,
 * _CrtSetReportFile, and _CrtSetReportHook functions.
 * The _ASSERT macros are called to evaluate their expression.
 * When the condition fails, these macros print a diagnostic message
 * and call _CrtDbgReport to generate a debug report and the
 * client-defined reporting function is called as well.
```

```
 * The _RPTn and _RPTFn group of macros are also exercised in
 * this program, as an alternative to the printf function.
 * When these macros are called, the client-defined reporting function
 * takes care of all the reporting - _CrtDbgReport won't be called.
 */

#include <stdio.h>
#include <string.h>
#include <malloc.h>
#include <crtdbg.h>

/*
 * Define our own reporting function.
 * We'll hook it into the debug reporting
 * process later using _CrtSetReportHook.
 *
 * Define a global int to keep track of
 * how many assertion failures occur.
 */
int gl_num_asserts=0;
int OurReportingFunction( int reportType, char *userMessage, int *retVal )
{
    /*
     * Tell the user our reporting function is being called.
     * In other words - verify that the hook routine worked.
     */
    fprintf("Inside the client-defined reporting function.\n", STDOUT);
    fflush(STDOUT);
    /*
     * When the report type is for an ASSERT,
     * we'll report some information, but we also
     * want _CrtDbgReport to get called -
     * so we'll return TRUE.
     *
     * When the report type is a WARNing or ERROR,
     * we'll take care of all of the reporting. We don't
     * want _CrtDbgReport to get called -
     * so we'll return FALSE.
     */
    if (reportType == _CRT_ASSERT)
    {
        gl_num_asserts++;
        fprintf("This is the number of Assertion failures that have
        ↪ occurred: %d \n", gl_num_asserts, STDOUT);
        fflush(STDOUT);
        fprintf("Returning TRUE from the client-defined reporting function.\n", STDOUT);
        fflush(STDOUT);
        return(TRUE);
```

```
    } else {
        fprintf("This is the debug user message: %s \n", userMessage, STDOUT);
        fflush(STDOUT);
        fprintf("Returning FALSE from the client-defined reporting function.\n", STDOUT);
        fflush(STDOUT);
        return(FALSE);
    }

    /*
     * By setting retVal to zero, we are instructing _CrtDbgReport
     * to continue with normal execution after generating the report.
     * If we wanted _CrtDbgReport to start the debugger, we would set
     * retVal to one.
     */
    retVal = 0;
}


int main()
{
    char *p1, *p2;

    /*
     * Hook in our client-defined reporting function.
     * Every time a _CrtDbgReport is called to generate
     * a debug report, our function will get called first.
     */
    _CrtSetReportHook( OurReportingFunction );

    /*
     * Define the report destination(s) for each type of report
     * we are going to generate.  In this case, we are going to
     * generate a report for every report type: _CRT_WARN,
     * _CRT_ERROR, and _CRT_ASSERT.
     * The destination(s) is defined by specifying the report mode(s)
     * and report file for each report type.
     * This program sends all report types to STDOUT.
     */
    _CrtSetReportMode(_CRT_WARN, _CRTDBG_MODE_FILE);
    _CrtSetReportFile(_CRT_WARN, _CRTDBG_FILE_STDOUT);
    _CrtSetReportMode(_CRT_ERROR, _CRTDBG_MODE_FILE);
    _CrtSetReportFile(_CRT_ERROR, _CRTDBG_FILE_STDOUT);
    _CrtSetReportMode(_CRT_ASSERT, _CRTDBG_MODE_FILE);
    _CrtSetReportFile(_CRT_ASSERT, _CRTDBG_FILE_STDOUT);

    /*
     * Allocate and assign the pointer variables
     */
```

```
    p1 = malloc(10);
    strcpy(p1, "I am p1");
    p2 = malloc(10);
    strcpy(p2, "I am p2");


    /*
     * Use the report macros as a debugging
     * warning mechanism, similar to printf.
     *
     * Use the assert macros to check if the
     * p1 and p2 variables are equivalent.
     *
     * If the expression fails, _ASSERTE will
     * include a string representation of the
     * failed expression in the report.
     *
     *  _ASSERT does not include the
     * expression in the generated report.
     */
    _RPT0(_CRT_WARN, "\n\n Use the assert macros to evaluate the expression p1 == p2.\n");
    _RPTF2(_CRT_WARN, "\n Will _ASSERT find '%s' == '%s' ?\n", p1, p2);
    _ASSERT(p1 == p2);

    _RPTF2(_CRT_WARN, "\n\n Will _ASSERTE find '%s' == '%s' ?\n", p1, p2);
    _ASSERTE(p1 == p2);

    _RPT2(_CRT_ERROR, "\n \n '%s' != '%s'\n", p1, p2);

    free(p2);
    free(p1);

    return 0;
}
```

Output

```
Inside the client-defined reporting function.
This is the debug user message: Use the assert macros to evaluate the expression p1 == p2
Returning FALSE from the client-defined reporting function.
Inside the client-defined reporting function.
This is the debug user message: dbgmacro.c(54) : Will _ASSERT find 'I am p1' == 'I am p2' ?
Returning FALSE from the client-defined reporting function.
Inside the client-defined reporting function.
This is the number of Assertion failures that have occurred: 1
Returning TRUE from the client-defined reporting function.
dbgmacro.c(55) : Assertion failed
Inside the client-defined reporting function.
This is the debug user message: dbgmacro.c(57) : Will _ASSERTE find 'I am p1' == 'I am p2' ?
Returning FALSE from the client-defined reporting function.
```

```
Inside the client-defined reporting function.
This is the number of Assertion failures that have occurred: 2
Returning TRUE from the client-defined reporting function.
dbgmacro.c(58) : Assertion failed: p1 == p2
Inside the client-defined reporting function.
This is the debug user message: 'I am p1' != 'I am p2'
Returning FALSE from the client-defined reporting function.
```

_CrtSetReportMode

Specifies the general destination(s) for a specific report type generated by **_CrtDbgReport** (debug version only).

int _CrtSetReportMode(int *reportType*, **int** *reportMode*);

Routine	Required Header	Compatibility
_CrtSetReportMode	<crtdbg.h>	Win NT, Win 95

For additional compatibility information, see "Compatibility" in the Introduction.

Libraries

LIBCD.LIB	Single thread static library, debug version
LIBCMTD.LIB	Multithread static library, debug version
MSVCRTD.LIB	Import library for MSVCRTD.DLL, debug version

Return Value

Upon successful completion, **_CrtSetReportMode** returns the previous report mode(s) for the report type specified in *reportType*. If an error occurs, the report mode(s) for *reportType* are not modified and **_CrtSetReportMode** returns –1.

Parameters

reportType
> Report type: **_CRT_WARN, _CRT_ERROR, _CRT_ASSERT**

reportMode
> New report mode(s) for *reportType*, see the table in the "Remarks" section

Remarks

_CrtSetReportMode is used in conjunction with the _CrtSetReportFile function to define the destination(s) for a specific report type generated by _CrtDbgReport. If **_CrtSetReportMode** and **_CrtSetReportFile** are not called to define the reporting method(s) for a specific report type, then **_CrtDbgReport** generates the report type using default destinations: Assertion failures and errors are directed to a debug message window, warnings from Windows applications are sent to the debugger, and warnings from console applications are directed to **stderr**. When _DEBUG is not defined, calls to **_CrtSetReportMode** are removed during preprocessing.

The following table lists the report types defined in CRTDBG.H.

Report Type	Description
_CRT_WARN	Warnings, messages, and information that does not need immediate attention.
_CRT_ERROR	Errors, unrecoverable problems, and issues that require immediate attention.
_CRT_ASSERT	Assertion failures (asserted expressions that evaluate to FALSE).

The **_CrtSetReportMode** function assigns the new report mode specified in *reportMode* to the report type specified in *reportType* and returns the previously defined report mode for *reportType*. The following table lists the available choices for *reportMode* and the resulting behavior of **_CrtDbgReport**. These options are defined as bit-flags in CRTDBG.H.

Report Mode	_CrtDbgReport Behavior
_CRTDBG_MODE_DEBUG	Writes the message to an output debug string.
_CRTDBG_MODE_FILE	Writes the message to a user-supplied file handle. **_CrtSetReportFile** should be called to define the specific file or stream to use as the destination.
_CRTDBG_MODE_WNDW	Creates a message box to display the message along with the Abort, Retry, and Ignore buttons.
_CRTDBG_REPORT_MODE	It is not called, and the report mode for *reportType* is not modified. **_CrtSetReportMode** simply returns the current report mode for *reportType*.

Each report type may be reported using one, two, or three modes, or no mode at all. Therefore, it is possible to have more than one destination defined for a single report type. For example, the following code fragment causes assertion failures to be sent to both a debug message window and to **stderr**:

```
_CrtSetReportMode( _CRT_ASSERT, _CRTDBG_MODE_FILE | _CRTDBG_MODE_WNDW );
_CrtSetReportFile( _CRT_ASSERT, _CRTDBG_FILE_STDERR );
```

In addition, the reporting mode(s) for each report type can be separately controlled. For example, it is possible to specify that a *reportType* of **_CRT_WARN** be sent to an output debug string, while **_CRT_ASSERT** be displayed using a a debug message window and sent to **stderr**, as illustrated above.

For more information about defining the report mode(s) and file for a specific report type, see "**_CrtDbgReport**," "**_CrtSetReportFile**" and the section "Debug Reporting Functions of the C Run-Time Library" in the *Visual C++ Programmer's Guide* online.

Example

```
/*
 * REPORT.C:
 * In this program, calls are made to the _CrtSetReportMode,
 * _CrtSetReportFile, and _CrtSetReportHook functions.
 * The _ASSERT macros are called to evaluate their expression.
 * When the condition fails, these macros print a diagnostic message
 * and call _CrtDbgReport to generate a debug report and the
 * client-defined reporting function is called as well.
 * The _RPTn and _RPTFn group of macros are also exercised in
 * this program, as an alternative to the printf function.
 * When these macros are called, the client-defined reporting function
 * takes care of all the reporting - _CrtDbgReport won't be called.
 */

#include <stdio.h>
#include <string.h>
#include <malloc.h>
#include <crtdbg.h>

/*
 * Define our own reporting function.
 * We'll hook it into the debug reporting
 * process later using _CrtSetReportHook.
 *
 * Define a global int to keep track of
 * how many assertion failures occur.
 */
int gl_num_asserts=0;
int OurReportingFunction( int reportType, char *userMessage, int *retVal )
{
    /*
     * Tell the user our reporting function is being called.
     * In other words - verify that the hook routine worked.
     */
    fprintf("Inside the client-defined reporting function.\n", STDOUT);
    fflush(STDOUT);

    /*
     * When the report type is for an ASSERT,
     * we'll report some information, but we also
     * want _CrtDbgReport to get called -
     * so we'll return TRUE.
     *
     * When the report type is a WARNing or ERROR,
     * we'll take care of all of the reporting. We don't
     * want _CrtDbgReport to get called -
     * so we'll return FALSE.
     */
```

```
   if (reportType == _CRT_ASSERT)
   {
      gl_num_asserts++;
      fprintf("This is the number of Assertion failures that have occurred:
      ↳ %d \n", gl_num_asserts, STDOUT);
      fflush(STDOUT);
      fprintf("Returning TRUE from the client-defined reporting function.\n", STDOUT);
      fflush(STDOUT);
      return(TRUE);
   } else {
      fprintf("This is the debug user message: %s \n", userMessage, STDOUT);
      fflush(STDOUT);
      fprintf("Returning FALSE from the client-defined reporting function.\n", STDOUT);
      fflush(STDOUT);
      return(FALSE);
   }


   /*
    * By setting retVal to zero, we are instructing _CrtDbgReport
    * to continue with normal execution after generating the report.
    * If we wanted _CrtDbgReport to start the debugger, we would set
    * retVal to one.
    */
   retVal = 0;
}


int main()
{
      char *p1, *p2;

   /*
    * Hook in our client-defined reporting function.
    * Every time a _CrtDbgReport is called to generate
    * a debug report, our function will get called first.
    */
   _CrtSetReportHook( OurReportingFunction );

   /*
    * Define the report destination(s) for each type of report
    * we are going to generate.  In this case, we are going to
    * generate a report for every report type: _CRT_WARN,
    * _CRT_ERROR, and _CRT_ASSERT.
    * The destination(s) is defined by specifying the report mode(s)
    * and report file for each report type.
    * This program sends all report types to STDOUT.
    */
```

```
_CrtSetReportMode(_CRT_WARN, _CRTDBG_MODE_FILE);
_CrtSetReportFile(_CRT_WARN, _CRTDBG_FILE_STDOUT);
_CrtSetReportMode(_CRT_ERROR, _CRTDBG_MODE_FILE);
_CrtSetReportFile(_CRT_ERROR, _CRTDBG_FILE_STDOUT);
_CrtSetReportMode(_CRT_ASSERT, _CRTDBG_MODE_FILE);
_CrtSetReportFile(_CRT_ASSERT, _CRTDBG_FILE_STDOUT);

/*
 * Allocate and assign the pointer variables
 */
p1 = malloc(10);
strcpy(p1, "I am p1");
p2 = malloc(10);
strcpy(p2, "I am p2");

/*
 * Use the report macros as a debugging
 * warning mechanism, similar to printf.
 *
 * Use the assert macros to check if the
 * p1 and p2 variables are equivalent.
 *
 * If the expression fails, _ASSERTE will
 * include a string representation of the
 * failed expression in the report.
 *
 *   _ASSERT does not include the
 * expression in the generated report.
 */
_RPT0(_CRT_WARN, "\n\n Use the assert macros to evaluate the expression p1 == p2.\n");
_RPTF2(_CRT_WARN, "\n Will _ASSERT find '%s' == '%s' ?\n", p1, p2);
_ASSERT(p1 == p2);

_RPTF2(_CRT_WARN, "\n\n Will _ASSERTE find '%s' == '%s' ?\n", p1, p2);
_ASSERTE(p1 == p2);

_RPT2(_CRT_ERROR, "\n \n '%s' != '%s'\n", p1, p2);

free(p2);
free(p1);

return 0;
}
```

144 Run-Time Library Reference

Output

```
Inside the client-defined reporting function.
This is the debug user message: Use the assert macros to evaluate the expression p1 == p2
Returning FALSE from the client-defined reporting function.
Inside the client-defined reporting function.
This is the debug user message: dbgmacro.c(54) : Will _ASSERT find 'I am p1' == 'I am p2' ?
Returning FALSE from the client-defined reporting function.
Inside the client-defined reporting function.
This is the number of Assertion failures that have occurred: 1
Returning TRUE from the client-defined reporting function.
dbgmacro.c(55) : Assertion failed
Inside the client-defined reporting function.
This is the debug user message: dbgmacro.c(57) : Will _ASSERTE find 'I am p1' == 'I am p2' ?
Returning FALSE from the client-defined reporting function.
Inside the client-defined reporting function.
This is the number of Assertion failures that have occurred: 2
Returning TRUE from the client-defined reporting function.
dbgmacro.c(58) : Assertion failed: p1 == p2
Inside the client-defined reporting function.
This is the debug user message: 'I am p1' != 'I am p2'
Returning FALSE from the client-defined reporting function.
```

_expand_dbg

Resizes a specified block of memory in the heap by expanding or contracting the block (debug version only).

void *_expand_dbg(void *userData**, size_t** newSize**, int** blockType**,
const char** *filename**, int** linenumber **);**

Routine	Required Header	Compatibility
_expand_dbg	<crtdbg.h>	Win NT, Win 95

For additional compatibility information, see "Compatibility" in the Introduction.

Libraries

LIBCD.LIB	Single thread static library, debug version
LIBCMTD.LIB	Multithread static library, debug version
MSVCRTD.LIB	Import library for MSVCRTD.DLL, debug version

Return Value

Upon successful completion, **_expand_dbg** returns a pointer to the resized memory block, otherwise it returns NULL.

Parameters

userData
> Pointer to the previously allocated memory block

newSize
> Requested new size for block (bytes)

blockType
> Requested type for resized block: **_CLIENT_BLOCK** or **_NORMAL_BLOCK**

filename
> Pointer to name of source file that requested expand operation or NULL

linenumber
> Line number in source file where expand operation was requested or NULL

The *filename* and *linenumber* parameters are only available when **_expand_dbg** has been called explicitly or the _CRTDBG_MAP_ALLOC preprocessor constant has been defined.

Remarks

The **_expand_dbg** function is a debug version of the _expand function. When _DEBUG is not defined, calls to **_expand_dbg** are removed during preprocessing. Both **_expand** and **_expand_dbg** resize a memory block in the base heap, but **_expand_dbg** accommodates several debugging features: buffers on either side of the user portion of the block to test for leaks, a block type parameter to track specific allocation types, and *filename/linenumber* information to determine the origin of allocation requests.

_expand_dbg resizes the specified memory block with slightly more space than the requested *newSize*. *newSize* may be greater or less than the size of the originally allocated memory block. The additional space is used by the debug heap manager to link the debug memory blocks together and to provide the application with debug header information and overwrite buffers. The resize is accomplished by either expanding or contracting the original memory block. **_expand_dbg** does *not* move the memory block, as does the _realloc_dbg function.

When *newSize* is greater than the original block size, the memory block is expanded. During an expansion, if the memory block cannot be expanded to accommodate the requested size, the block is expanded as much as possible. When *newSize* is less than the original block size, the memory block is contracted until the new size is obtained.

For information about how memory blocks are allocated, initialized, and managed in the debug version of the base heap, see "Memory Management and the Debug Heap" in the *Visual C++ Programmer's Guide* online. For information about the allocation block types and how they are used, see "Types of Blocks on the Debug Heap" in the *Visual C++ Programmer's Guide* online. For information on the differences between calling a standard heap function versus its debug version in a debug build of an application, see "Using the Debug Version Versus the Base Version" in the *Visual C++ Programmer's Guide* online.

Example

```
/*
 * EXPANDD.C
 * This program allocates a block of memory using _malloc_dbg
 * and then calls _msize_dbg to display the size of that block.
 * Next, it uses _expand_dbg to expand the amount of
 * memory used by the buffer and then calls _msize_dbg again to
 * display the new amount of memory allocated to the buffer.
 */

#include <stdio.h>
#include <malloc.h>
#include <stdlib.h>
#include <crtdbg.h>

void main( void )
{
        long *buffer;
        size_t size;

        /*
         * Call _malloc_dbg to include the filename and line number
         * of our allocation request in the header
         */
        buffer = (long *)_malloc_dbg( 40 * sizeof(long),
        ↪ _NORMAL_BLOCK, __FILE__, __LINE__ );
        if( buffer == NULL )
                exit( 1 );

        /*
         * Get the size of the buffer by calling _msize_dbg
         */
        size = _msize_dbg( buffer, _NORMAL_BLOCK );
        printf( "Size of block after _malloc_dbg of 40 longs: %u\n", size );

        /*
         * Expand the buffer using _expand_dbg and show the new size
         */
        buffer = _expand_dbg( buffer, size + (40 * sizeof(long)),
        ↪ _NORMAL_BLOCK, __FILE__, __LINE__ );
        if( buffer == NULL )
                exit( 1 );
        size = _msize_dbg( buffer, _NORMAL_BLOCK );
        printf( "Size of block after _expand_dbg of 40 more longs: %u\n", size );

        free( buffer );
        exit( 0 );
}
```

Output

```
Size of block after _malloc_dbg of 40 longs: 160
Size of block after _expand_dbg of 40 more longs: 320
```

See Also

_malloc_dbg

_free_dbg

Frees a block of memory in the heap (debug version only).

void _free_dbg(void *userData*, **int** *blockType* **);**

Routine	Required Header	Compatibility
_free_dbg	<crtdbg.h>	Win NT, Win 95

For additional compatibility information, see "Compatibility" in the Introduction.

Libraries

LIBCD.LIB	Single thread static library, debug version
LIBCMTD.LIB	Multithread static library, debug version
MSVCRTD.LIB	Import library for MSVCRTD.DLL, debug version

Return Value

None

Parameters

userData
    Pointer to the allocated memory block to be freed

blockType
    Type of allocated memory block to be freed: **_CLIENT_BLOCK**,
    _NORMAL_BLOCK, or **_IGNORE_BLOCK**

Remarks

The **_free_dbg** function is a debug version of the free function. When _DEBUG is not defined, calls to **_free_dbg** are removed during preprocessing. Both **free** and **_free_dbg** free a memory block in the base heap, but **_free_dbg** accomodates two debugging features: the ability to keep freed blocks in the heap's linked list to simulate low memory conditions and a block type parameter to free specific allocation types.

_free_dbg performs a validity check on all specified files and block locations before performing the free operation?the application is not expected to provide this information. When a memory block is freed, the debug heap manager automatically checks the integrity of the buffers on either side of the user portion and issues an error report if overwriting has occurred. If the **_CRTDBG_DELAY_FREE_MEM_DF** bit field of the _crtDbgFlag flag is set, the freed block is filled with the value 0xDD, assigned the **_FREE_BLOCK** block type, and kept in the heap's linked list of memory blocks.

For information about how memory blocks are allocated, initialized, and managed in the debug version of the base heap, see "Memory Management and the Debug Heap" in the *Visual C++ Programmer's Guide* online. For information about the allocation block types and how they are used, see "Types of Blocks on the Debug Heap" in the *Visual C++ Programmer's Guide* online. For information on the differences between calling a standard heap function versus its debug version in a debug build of an application, see "Using the Debug Version Versus the Base Version" in the *Visual C++ Programmer's Guide* online.

Example

See Example 2 on page 110.

See Also

_malloc_dbg

_malloc_dbg

Allocates a block of memory in the heap with additional space for a debugging header and overwrite buffers (debug version only).

void *_malloc_dbg(size_t *size*, **int** *blockType*, **const char** **filename*, **int** *linenumber* **);**

Routine	Required Header	Compatibility
_malloc_dbg	<crtdbg.h>	Win NT, Win 95

For additional compatibility information, see "Compatibility" in the Introduction.

Libraries

LIBCD.LIB	Single thread static library, debug version
LIBCMTD.LIB	Multithread static library, debug version
MSVCRTD.LIB	Import library for MSVCRTD.DLL, debug version

Return Value

Upon successful completion, this function either returns a pointer to the user portion of the allocated memory block, calls the new handler function, or returns NULL. See the following "Remarks" section for a complete description of the return behavior. See the **"malloc"** function for more information on how the new handler function is used.

Parameters

size
> Requested size of memory block (bytes)

blockType
> Requested type of memory block: **_CLIENT_BLOCK** or **_NORMAL_BLOCK**

filename
> Pointer to name of source file that requested allocation operation or NULL

linenumber
> Line number in source file where allocation operation was requested or NULL

The *filename* and *linenumber* parameters are only available when **_malloc_dbg** has been called explicitly or the _CRTDBG_MAP_ALLOC preprocessor constant has been defined.

Remarks

_malloc_dbg is a debug version of the **malloc** function. When _DEBUG is not defined, calls to **_malloc_dbg** are removed during preprocessing. Both **malloc** and **_malloc_dbg** allocate a block of memory in the base heap, but **_malloc_dbg** offers several debugging features: buffers on either side of the user portion of the block to test for leaks, a block type parameter to track specific allocation types, and *filename/linenumber* information to determine the origin of allocation requests.

_malloc_dbg allocates the memory block with slightly more space than the requested *size*. The additional space is used by the debug heap manager to link the debug memory blocks together and to provide the application with debug header information and overwrite buffers. When the block is allocated, the user portion of the block is filled with the value 0xCD and each of the overwrite buffers are filled with 0xFD.

For information about how memory blocks are allocated, initialized, and managed in the debug version of the base heap, see "Memory Management and the Debug Heap" in the *Visual C++ Programmer's Guide* online. For information about the allocation block types and how they are used, see "Types of Blocks on the Debug Heap" in the *Visual C++ Programmer's Guide* online. For information on the differences between calling a standard heap function versus its debug version in a debug build of an application, see "Using the Debug Version Versus the Base Version" in the *Visual C++ Programmer's Guide* online.

Example

See Example 1 on page 84.

_msize_dbg

Calculates the size of a block of memory in the heap (debug version only).

size_t _msize_dbg(void *userData*, **int** *blockType* **);**

Routine	Required Header	Compatibility
_msize_dbg	<crtdbg.h>	Win NT, Win 95

For additional compatibility information, see "Compatibility" in the Introduction.

Libraries

LIBCD.LIB	Single thread static library, debug version
LIBCMTD.LIB	Multithread static library, debug version
MSVCRTD.LIB	Import library for MSVCRTD.DLL, debug version

Return Value

Upon successful completion, **_msize_dbg** returns the size (bytes) of the specified memory block, otherwise it returns NULL.

Parameters

userData
    Pointer to the memory block for which to determine the size

blockType
    Type of the specified memory block: **_CLIENT_BLOCK** or **_NORMAL_BLOCK**

Remarks

_msize_dbg is a debug version of the _msize function. When _DEBUG is not defined, calls to **_msize_dbg** are removed during preprocessing. Both **_msize** and **_msize_dbg** calculate the size of a memory block in the base heap, but **_msize_dbg** adds two debugging features: It includes the buffers on either side of the user portion of the memory block in the returned size, and it allows size calculations for specific block types.

For information about how memory blocks are allocated, initialized, and managed in the debug version of the base heap, see "Memory Management and the Debug Heap" in the *Visual C++ Programmer's Guide* online. For information about the allocation block types and how they are used, see "Types of Blocks on the Debug Heap" in the *Visual C++ Programmer's Guide* online. For information on the differences between calling a standard heap function versus its debug version in a debug build of an application, see "Using the Debug Version Versus the Base Version" in the *Visual C++ Programmer's Guide* online.

Example

```
/*
 * REALLOCD.C
 * This program allocates a block of memory using _malloc_dbg
 * and then calls _msize_dbg to display the size of that block.
 * Next, it uses _realloc_dbg to expand the amount of
 * memory used by the buffer and then calls _msize_dbg again to
 * display the new amount of memory allocated to the buffer.
 */

#include <stdio.h>
#include <malloc.h>
#include <stdlib.h>
#include <crtdbg.h>

void main( void )
{
        long *buffer;
        size_t size;

        /*
         * Call _malloc_dbg to include the filename and line number
         * of our allocation request in the header
         */
        buffer = (long *)_malloc_dbg( 40 * sizeof(long),
        ↪ _NORMAL_BLOCK, __FILE__, __LINE__ );
        if( buffer == NULL )
                exit( 1 );

        /*
         * Get the size of the buffer by calling _msize_dbg
         */
        size = _msize_dbg( buffer, _NORMAL_BLOCK );
        printf( "Size of block after _malloc_dbg of 40 longs: %u\n", size );

        /*
         * Reallocate the buffer using _realloc_dbg and show the new size
         */
        buffer = _realloc_dbg( buffer, size + (40 * sizeof(long)),
        ↪ _NORMAL_BLOCK, __FILE__, __LINE__ );
        if( buffer == NULL )
                exit( 1 );
        size = _msize_dbg( buffer, _NORMAL_BLOCK );
        printf( "Size of block after _realloc_dbg of 40 more longs: %u\n", size );

        free( buffer );
        exit( 0 );
}
```

Output

```
Size of block after _malloc_dbg of 40 longs: 160
Size of block after _realloc_dbg of 40 more longs: 320
```

See Also

_malloc_dbg

_realloc_dbg

Reallocates a specified block of memory in the heap by moving and/or resizing the block (debug version only).

void *_realloc_dbg(void *userData, **size_t** newSize, **int** blockType,
  const char *filename, **int** linenumber **);**

Routine	Required Header	Compatibility
_realloc_dbg	<crtdbg.h>	Win NT, Win 95

For additional compatibility information, see "Compatibility" in the Introduction.

Libraries

LIBCD.LIB	Single thread static library, debug version
LIBCMTD.LIB	Multithread static library, debug version
MSVCRTD.LIB	Import library for MSVCRTD.DLL, debug version

Return Value

Upon successful completion, this function either returns a pointer to the user portion of the reallocated memory block, calls the new handler function, or returns NULL. See the following "Remarks" section for a complete description of the return behavior. See the "realloc" function for more information on how the new handler function is used.

Parameters

userData
  Pointer to the previously allocated memory block

newSize
  Requested size for reallocated block (bytes)

blockType
  Requested type for reallocated block: **_CLIENT_BLOCK** or **_NORMAL_BLOCK**

filename

>   Pointer to name of source file that requested **realloc** operation or NULL

linenumber

>   Line number in source file where **realloc** operation was requested or NULL

The *filename* and *linenumber* parameters are only available when **_realloc_dbg** has been called explicitly or the _CRTDBG_MAP_ALLOC preprocessor constant has been defined.

Remarks

_realloc_dbg is a debug version of the realloc function. When _DEBUG is not defined, calls to **_realloc_dbg** are removed during preprocessing. Both **realloc** and **_realloc_dbg** reallocate a memory block in the base heap, but **_realloc_dbg** accommodates several debugging features: buffers on either side of the user portion of the block to test for leaks, a block type parameter to track specific allocation types, and *filename/linenumber* information to determine the origin of allocation requests.

_realloc_dbg reallocates the specified memory block with slightly more space than the requested *newSize*. *newSize* may be greater or less than the size of the originally allocated memory block. The additional space is used by the debug heap manager to link the debug memory blocks together and to provide the application with debug header information and overwrite buffers. The reallocation may result in moving the original memory block to a different location in the heap, as well as changing the size of the memory block. If the memory block is moved, the contents of the original block are copied over.

For information about how memory blocks are allocated, initialized, and managed in the debug version of the base heap, see "Memory Management and the Debug Heap" in the *Visual C++ Programmer's Guide* online. For information about the allocation block types and how they are used, see "Types of Blocks on the Debug Heap" in the *Visual C++ Programmer's Guide* online. For information on the differences between calling a standard heap function versus its debug version in a debug build of an application, see "Using the Debug Version Versus the Base Version" in the *Visual C++ Programmer's Guide* online.

Example

```
/*
 * REALLOCD.C
 * This program allocates a block of memory using _malloc_dbg
 * and then calls _msize_dbg to display the size of that block.
 * Next, it uses _realloc_dbg to expand the amount of
 * memory used by the buffer and then calls _msize_dbg again to
 * display the new amount of memory allocated to the buffer.
 */

#include <stdio.h>
#include <malloc.h>
#include <stdlib.h>
#include <crtdbg.h>
```

```c
void main( void )
{
        long *buffer;
        size_t size;

        /*
         * Call _malloc_dbg to include the filename and line number
         * of our allocation request in the header
         */
        buffer = (long *)_malloc_dbg( 40 * sizeof(long),
        ↪ _NORMAL_BLOCK, __FILE__, __LINE__ );
        if( buffer == NULL )
                exit( 1 );

        /*
         * Get the size of the buffer by calling _msize_dbg
         */
        size = _msize_dbg( buffer, _NORMAL_BLOCK );
        printf( "Size of block after _malloc_dbg of 40 longs: %u\n", size );

        /*
         * Reallocate the buffer using _realloc_dbg and show the new size
         */
        buffer = _realloc_dbg( buffer, size + (40 * sizeof(long)),
        ↪ _NORMAL_BLOCK, __FILE__, __LINE__ );
        if( buffer == NULL )
                exit( 1 );
        size = _msize_dbg( buffer, _NORMAL_BLOCK );
        printf( "Size of block after _realloc_dbg of 40 more longs: %u\n", size );

        free( buffer );
        exit( 0 );
}
```

Output

```
Size of block after _malloc_dbg of 40 longs: 160
Size of block after _realloc_dbg of 40 more longs: 320
```

See Also

_malloc_dbg

_RPT, _RPTF Macros

Track an application's progress by generating a debug report (debug version only).

_RPT0(*reportType, format*);
_RPT1(*reportType, format, arg1*);
_RPT2(*reportType, format, arg1, arg2*);
_RPT3(*reportType, format, arg1, arg2, arg3*);
_RPT4(*reportType, format, arg1, arg2, arg3, arg4*);
_RPTF0(*reportType, format*);
_RPTF1(*reportType, format, arg1*);
_RPTF2(*reportType, format, arg1, arg2*);
_RPTF3(*reportType, format, arg1, arg2, arg3*);
_RPTF4(*reportType, format, arg1, arg2, arg3, arg4*);

Macro	Required Header	Compatibility
_RPT macros	<crtdbg.h>	Win NT, Win 95
_RPTF macros	<crtdbg.h>	Win NT, Win 95

For additional compatibility information, see "Compatibility" in the Introduction.

Libraries

LIBCD.LIB	Single thread static library, debug version
LIBCMTD.LIB	Multithread static library, debug version
MSVCRTD.LIB	Import library for MSVCRTD.DLL, debug version

Although these are macros and are obtained by including CRTDBG.H, the application must link with one of the libraries listed above because these macros call other run-time functions.

Return Value

None

Parameters

reportType
   Report type: **_CRT_WARN, _CRT_ERROR, _CRT_ASSERT**

format
   Format-control string used to create the user message

arg1
  Name of first substitution argument used by *format*

arg2
  Name of second substitution argument used by *format*

arg3
  Name of third substitution argument used by *format*

arg4
  Name of fourth substitution argument used by *format*

All of these macros take the *reportType* and *format* parameters. In addition, they might also take *arg1* through *arg4*, signified by the number appended to the macro name. For example, **_RPT0** and **_RPTF0** take no additional arguments, **_RPT1** and **_RPTF1** take *arg1*, **_RPT2** and **_RPTF2** take *arg1* and *arg2*, and so on.

Remarks

The **_RPT** and **_RPTF** macros are similar to the printf function, as they can be used to track an application's progress during the debugging process. However, these macros are more flexible than **printf** because they do not need to be enclosed in **#ifdef** statements to prevent them from being called in a retail build of an application. This flexibility is achieved by using the _DEBUG macro. The **_RPT** and **_RPTF** macros are only available when the **_DEBUG** flag is defined. When **_DEBUG** is not defined, calls to these macros are removed during preprocessing.

The **_RPT** macros call the _CrtDbgReport function to generate a debug report with a user message. The **_RPTF** macros create a debug report with the source file and line number where the report macro was called, in addition to the user message. The user message is created by substituting the *arg[n]* arguments into the *format* string, using the same rules defined by the printf function.

_CrtDbgReport generates the debug report and determines its destination(s), based on the current report modes and file defined for *reportType*. The _CrtSetReportMode and _CrtSetReportFile functions are used to define the destination(s) for each report type.

When the destination is a debug message window and the user chooses the Retry button, **_CrtDbgReport** returns 1, causing these macros to start the debugger, provided that "just-in-time" (JIT) debugging is enabled. For more information about using these macros as a debugging error handling mechanism, see "Using Macros for Verification and Reporting" in the *Visual C++ Programmer's Guide* online.

Two other macros exist that generate a debug report. The _ASSERT macro generates a report, but only when its expression argument evaluates to FALSE. _ASSERTE is exactly like **_ASSERT**, but includes the failed expression in the generated report.

Example

```
/*
 * DBGMACRO.C
 * In this program, calls are made to the _ASSERT and _ASSERTE
 * macros to test the condition 'string1 == string2'.  If the
 * condition fails, these macros print a diagnostic message.
 * The _RPTn and _RPTFn group of macros are also exercised in
 * this program, as an alternative to the printf function.
 */

#include <stdio.h>
#include <string.h>
#include <malloc.h>
#include <crtdbg.h>

int main()
{
    char *p1, *p2;

    /*
     * The Reporting Mode and File must be specified
     * before generating a debug report via an assert
     * or report macro.
     * This program sends all report types to STDOUT
     */
    _CrtSetReportMode(_CRT_WARN, _CRTDBG_MODE_FILE);
    _CrtSetReportFile(_CRT_WARN, _CRTDBG_FILE_STDOUT);
    _CrtSetReportMode(_CRT_ERROR, _CRTDBG_MODE_FILE);
    _CrtSetReportFile(_CRT_ERROR, _CRTDBG_FILE_STDOUT);
    _CrtSetReportMode(_CRT_ASSERT, _CRTDBG_MODE_FILE);
    _CrtSetReportFile(_CRT_ASSERT, _CRTDBG_FILE_STDOUT);

    /*
     * Allocate and assign the pointer variables
     */
    p1 = malloc(10);
    strcpy(p1, "I am p1");
    p2 = malloc(10);
    strcpy(p2, "I am p2");

    /*
     * Use the report macros as a debugging
     * warning mechanism, similar to printf.
     *
     * Use the assert macros to check if the
     * p1 and p2 variables are equivalent.
     *
```

```
 * If the expression fails, _ASSERTE will
 * include a string representation of the
 * failed expression in the report.
 * _ASSERT does not include the
 * expression in the generated report.
 */
_RPT0(_CRT_WARN, "\n\n Use the assert macros to evaluate the expression p1 == p2.\n");
_RPTF2(_CRT_WARN, "\n Will _ASSERT find '%s' == '%s' ?\n", p1, p2);
_ASSERT(p1 == p2);

_RPTF2(_CRT_WARN, "\n\n Will _ASSERTE find '%s' == '%s' ?\n", p1, p2);
_ASSERTE(p1 == p2);

_RPT2(_CRT_ERROR, "\n \n '%s' != '%s'\n", p1, p2);

free(p2);
free(p1);

return 0;
}
```

Output

```
Use the assert macros to evaluate the expression p1 == p2.

dbgmacro.c(54) : Will _ASSERT find 'I am p1' == 'I am p2' ?
dbgmacro.c(55) : Assertion failed

dbgmacro.c(57) : Will _ASSERTE find 'I am p1' == 'I am p2' ?
dbgmacro.c(58) : Assertion failed: p1 == p2

'I am p1' != 'I am p2'
```

_set_error_mode

_set_error_mode modifies **__error_mode** to determine a non-default location where the C runtime writes an error message for an error that will, possibly, end the program.

int _set_error_mode(int *modeval* **);**

Macro	Required Header	Compatibility
_set_error_mode	<stdlib.h>	ANSI, Win 95, Win NT

Libraries

LIBCD.LIB	Single thread static library, debug version
LIBC.LIB	Single thread static library, retail version
LIBCMTD.LIB	Multithread static library, debug version
LIBCMT.LIB	Multithread static library, retail version
MSVCRTD.LIB	Import library for MSVCRTD.DLL, debug version
MSVCRT.LIB	Import library for MSVCRT.DLL, retail version

Return Value

Returns old setting or –1 if an error occurs.

Parameter

modeval
    destination of error messages

Remarks

Control the error output sink by setting the value of __**error_mode**. Explicit controls are to direct output to standard error or to use the MessageBox API.

The *modeval* parameter can be set to one of the follow:

Parameter	Description
_OUT_TO_DEFAULT	error sink is determined by __app_type
_OUT_TO_STDERR	error sink is standard error
_OUT_TO_MSGBOX	error sink is a message box
_REPORT_ERRMODE	report the current __error_mode value

When used with an **_ASSERT**, **_set_errror_mode** will display the failed statement in the dialog box and give you the option of selecting **Ignore**, which allows you to continue executing the program.

Example

```
#include <stdlib.h>
#include <assert.h>

main()
{
_set_error_mode(_OUT_TO_MSGBOX);
    assert(!"this is a test");
}
```

CHAPTER 5

Microsoft Alphabetic Run-Time Library Reference

The following topics describe, in alphabetical order, the functions and macros in the Microsoft run-time library. In some cases, related routines are clustered in the same description. For example, the standard, wide-character, and multibyte versions of **strchr** are discussed in the same place, as are the various forms of the exec functions. Differences are noted where appropriate. To locate any function that does not appear in the expected position within the alphabetic reference, choose Search from the Help menu and type the name of the function you are looking for.

abort

Aborts the current process and returns an error code.

void abort(void);

Routine	Required Header	Compatibility
abort	<process.h> or <stdlib.h>	ANSI, Win 95, Win NT

For additional compatibility information, see "Compatibility" in the Introduction.

Libraries

LIBC.LIB	Single thread static library, retail version
LIBCMT.LIB	Multithread static library, retail version
MSVCRT.LIB	Import library for MSVCRT.DLL, retail version

Return Value

abort does not return control to the calling process. By default, it terminates the current process and returns an exit code of 3.

Remarks

The **abort** routine prints the message "`abnormal program termination`" and then calls **raise(SIGABRT)**. The action taken in response to the **SIGABRT** signal depends on what action has been defined for that signal in a prior call to the **signal** function. The default **SIGABRT** action is for the calling process to terminate with exit code 3, returning control to the calling process or operating system. **abort** does not flush stream buffers or do **atexit/_onexit** processing.

abort determines the destination of the message based on the type of application that called the routine. Console applications always receive the message via **stderr**. In a single or multithreaded Windows application, **abort** calls the Windows MessageBox **API to** create a message box to display the message along with an **OK** button. When the user selects **OK**, the program aborts immediately.

When the application is linked with a debug version of the run-time libraries, **abort** creates a message box with three buttons: **Abort, Retry**, and **Ignore**. If the user selects **Abort**, the program aborts immediately. If the user selects **Retry**, the debugger is called and the user can debug the program if Just-In-Time (JIT) debugging is enabled. If the user selects **Ignore**, **abort** continues with its normal execution: creating the message box with the **OK** button. For more information, see "Using C Run-Time Library Debugging Support," in the *Visual C++ Programmer's Guide* online.

Example

```
/* ABORT.C:  This program tries to open a
 * file and aborts if the attempt fails.
 */

#include  <stdio.h>
#include  <stdlib.h>

void main( void )
{
   FILE *stream;

   if( (stream = fopen( "NOSUCHF.ILE", "r" )) == NULL )

   {
      perror( "Couldn't open file" );
      abort();
   }
   else
      fclose( stream );
}
```

Output

```
Couldn't open file: No such file or directory

abnormal program termination
```

See Also

_exec Function Overview, exit, raise, signal, _spawn Function Overview, _DEBUG

abs

Calculates the absolute value.

int abs(int *n*);

Routine	Required Header	Compatibility
abs	<stdlib.h> or <math.h>	ANSI, Win 95, Win NT

For additional compatibility information, see "Compatibility" in the Introduction.

Libraries

LIBC.LIB	Single thread static library, retail version
LIBCMT.LIB	Multithread static library, retail version
MSVCRT.LIB	Import library for MSVCRT.DLL, retail version

Return Value

The **abs** function returns the absolute value of its parameter. There is no error return.

Parameter

n

    Integer value

Example

```
/* ABS.C: This program computes and displays
 * the absolute values of several numbers.
 */

#include  <stdio.h>
#include  <math.h>
#include  <stdlib.h>

void main( void )
{
    int   ix = -4, iy;
    long     lx = -41567L, ly;
    double dx = -3.141593, dy;
```

```
    iy = abs( ix );
    printf( "The absolute value of %d is %d\n", ix, iy);

    ly = labs( lx );
    printf( "The absolute value of %ld is %ld\n", lx, ly);

    dy = fabs( dx );
    printf( "The absolute value of %f is %f\n", dx, dy );
}
```

Output

```
The absolute value of -4 is 4
The absolute value of -41567 is 41567
The absolute value of -3.141593 is 3.141593
```

See Also

_cabs, **fabs**, **labs**

_access, _waccess

Determine file-access permission.

int _access(const char * *path* **, int** *mode* **);**
int _waccess(const wchar_t * *path* **, int** *mode* **);**

Routine	Required Header	Optional Headers	Compatibility
_access	<io.h>	<errno.h>	Win 95, Win NT
_waccess	<wchar.h> or <io.h>	<errno.h>	Win NT

For additional compatibility information, see "Compatibility" in the Introduction.

Libraries

LIBC.LIB	Single thread static library, retail version
LIBCMT.LIB	Multithread static library, retail version
MSVCRT.LIB	Import library for MSVCRT.DLL, retail version

Return Value

Each of these functions returns 0 if the file has the given mode. The function returns –1 if the named file does not exist or is not accessible in the given mode; in this case, **errno** is set as follows:

EACCES
    Access denied: file's permission setting does not allow specified access.

ENOENT
    Filename or path not found.

Parameters

path
  File or directory path

mode
  Permission setting

Remarks

When used with files, the **_access** function determines whether the specified file exists and can be accessed as specified by the value of *mode*. When used with directories, **_access** determines only whether the specified directory exists; in Windows NT, all directories have read and write access.

mode Value	Checks File For
00	Existence only
02	Write permission
04	Read permission
06	Read and write permission

_waccess is a wide-character version of **_access**; the *path* argument to **_waccess** is a wide-character string. **_waccess** and **_access** behave identically otherwise.

Generic-Text Routine Mappings

TCHAR.H Routine	_UNICODE & _MBCS Not Defined	_MBCS Defined	_UNICODE Defined
_taccess	_access	_access	_waccess

Example

```
/* ACCESS.C: This example uses _access to check the
 * file named "ACCESS.C" to see if it exists and if
 * writing is allowed.
 */

#include <io.h>
#include <stdio.h>
#include <stdlib.h>
```

```
void main( void )
{
   /* Check for existence */
   if( (_access( "ACCESS.C", 0 )) != -1 )
   {
      printf( "File ACCESS.C exists\n" );
      /* Check for write permission */
      if( (_access( "ACCESS.C", 2 )) != -1 )
         printf( "File ACCESS.C has write permission\n" );
   }
}
```

Output

```
File ACCESS.C exists
File ACCESS.C has write permission
```

See Also

_chmod, _fstat, _open, _stat

acos

Calculates the arccosine.

double acos(double *x*);

Routine	Required Header	Optional Headers	Compatibility
acos	<math.h>	<errno.h>	ANSI, Win 95, Win NT

For additional compatibility information, see "Compatibility" in the Introduction.

Libraries

LIBC.LIB	Single thread static library, retail version
LIBCMT.LIB	Multithread static library, retail version
MSVCRT.LIB	Import library for MSVCRT.DLL, retail version

Return Value

The **acos** function returns the arccosine of x in the range 0 to π radians. If x is less than -1 or greater than 1, **acos** returns an indefinite (same as a quiet NaN). You can modify error handling with the **_matherr** routine.

Parameter

x

Value between -1 and 1 whose arccosine is to be calculated

Example

```
/* ASINCOS.C: This program prompts for a value in the range
 * -1 to 1. Input values outside this range will produce
 * _DOMAIN error messages.If a valid value is entered, the
 * program prints the arcsine and the arccosine of that value.
 */

#include <math.h>
#include <stdio.h>
#include <stdlib.h>
#include <errno.h>

void main( void )
{
   double x, y;

   printf( "Enter a real number between -1 and 1: " );
   scanf( "%lf", &x );
   y = asin( x );
   printf( "Arcsine of %f = %f\n", x, y );
   y = acos( x );
   printf( "Arccosine of %f = %f\n", x, y );
}
```

Output

```
Enter a real number between -1 and 1: .32696
Arcsine of 0.326960 = 0.333085
Arccosine of 0.326960 = 1.237711
```

See Also

asin, atan, cos, _matherr, sin, tan

_alloca

Allocates memory on the stack.

void *_alloca(size_t *size* **);**

Routine	Required Header	Compatibility
_alloca	<malloc.h>	Win 95, Win NT

For additional compatibility information, see "Compatibility" the Introduction.

Libraries

LIBC.LIB	Single thread static library, retail version
LIBCMT.LIB	Multithread static library, retail version
MSVCRT.LIB	Import library for MSVCRT.DLL, retail version

Return Value

The **_alloca** routine returns a **void** pointer to the allocated space, which is guaranteed to be suitably aligned for storage of any type of object. To get a pointer to a type other than **char**, use a type cast on the return value. A stack overflow exception is generated if the space cannot be allocated.

Parameter

size

Bytes to be allocated from stack

Remarks

_alloca allocates *size* bytes from the program stack. The allocated space is automatically freed when the calling function exits. Therefore, do not pass the pointer value returned by **_alloca** as an argument to free.

There are restrictions to explicitly calling **_alloca** in an exception handler (EH). EH routines that run on x86-class processors operate in their own memory "frame": They perform their tasks in memory space that is not based on the current location of the stack pointer of the enclosing function. The most common implementations include Windows NT structured exception handling (SEH) and C++ catch clause expressions. Therefore, explicitly calling **_alloca** in any of the following scenarios results in program failure during the return to the calling EH routine:

- Windows NT SEH exception filter expression: **__except (alloca())**

- Windows NT SEH final exception handler: **__finally { alloca() }**

- C++ EH catch clause expression

However, **_alloca** can be called directly from within an EH routine or from an application-supplied callback that gets invoked by one of the EH scenarios listed above.

See Also

calloc, malloc, realloc

asctime, _wasctime

Converts a **tm** time structure to a character string.

char *asctime(const struct tm *timeptr **);**
wchar_t *_wasctime(const struct tm *timeptr **);**

Routine	Required Header	Compatibility
asctime	<time.h>	ANSI, Win 95, Win NT
_wasctime	<time.h> or <wchar.h>	Win 95, Win NT

For additional compatibility information, see "Compatibility" in the Introduction.

Libraries

LIBC.LIB	Single thread static library, retail version
LIBCMT.LIB	Multithread static library, retail version
MSVCRT.LIB	Import library for MSVCRT.DLL, retail version

Return Value

asctime returns a pointer to the character string result; **_wasctime** returns a pointer to the wide-character string result. There is no error return value.

Parameter

timeptr
   Time/date structure

Remarks

The **asctime** function converts a time stored as a structure to a character string. The *timeptr* value is usually obtained from a call to **gmtime** or **localtime**, which both return a pointer to a **tm** structure, defined in TIME.H.

timeptr Field	Value
tm_hour	Hours since midnight (0–23)
tm_isdst	Positive if daylight saving time is in effect; 0 if daylight saving time is not in effect; negative if status of daylight saving time is unknown. The C run-time library assumes the United States's rules for implementing the calculation of Daylight Saving Time (DST).
tm_mday	Day of month (1–31)
tm_min	Minutes after hour (0–59)
tm_mon	Month (0–11; January = 0)
tm_sec	Seconds after minute (0–59)
tm_wday	Day of week (0–6; Sunday = 0)
tm_yday	Day of year (0–365; January 1 = 0)
tm_year	Year (current year minus 1900)

The converted character string is also adjusted according to the local time zone settings. See the time, _ftime, and localtime functions for information on configuring the local time and the _tzset function for details about defining the time zone environment and global variables.

The string result produced by **asctime** contains exactly 26 characters and has the form `Wed Jan 02 02:03:55 1980\n\0`. A 24-hour clock is used. All fields have a constant width. The newline character and the null character occupy the last two positions of the string. **asctime** uses a single, statically allocated buffer to hold the return string. Each call to this function destroys the result of the previous call.

_wasctime is a wide-character version of **asctime**. **_wasctime** and **asctime** behave identically otherwise.

Generic-Text Routine Mapping:

TCHAR.H Routine	_UNICODE & _MBCS Not Defined	_MBCS Defined	_UNICODE Defined
_tasctime	asctime	asctime	_wasctime

Example

```
/* ASCTIME.C: This program places the system time
 * in the long integer aclock, translates it into the
 * structure newtime and then converts it to string
 * form for output, using the asctime function.
 */

#include <time.h>
#include <stdio.h>

struct tm *newtime;
time_t aclock;

void main( void )
{
    time( &aclock );                /* Get time in seconds */

    newtime = localtime( &aclock ); /* Convert time to struct */
                                    /* tm form */

    /* Print local time as a string */
    printf( "The current date and time are: %s", asctime( newtime ) );
}
```

Output

```
The current date and time are: Sun May 01 20:27:01 1994
```

See Also

ctime, _ftime, gmtime, localtime, time, _tzset

asin

Calculates the arcsine.

double asin(double *x* **);**

Routine	Required Header	Compatibility
asin	<math.h>	ANSI, Win 95, Win NT

For additional compatibility information, see "Compatibility" in the Introduction.

Libraries

LIBC.LIB	Single thread static library, retail version
LIBCMT.LIB	Multithread static library, retail version
MSVCRT.LIB	Import library for MSVCRT.DLL, retail version

Return Value

The **asin** function returns the arcsine of *x* in the range $-\pi/2$ to $\pi/2$ radians. If *x* is less than -1 or greater than 1, **asin** returns an indefinite (same as a quiet NaN). You can modify error handling with the **_matherr** routine.

Parameter

x

　　Value whose arcsine is to be calculated

Example

```
/* ASINCOS.C: This program prompts for a value in the range
 * -1 to 1. Input values outside this range will produce
 * _DOMAIN error messages.If a valid value is entered, the
 * program prints the arcsine and the arccosine of that value.
 */

#include <math.h>
#include <stdio.h>
#include <stdlib.h>
#include <errno.h>

void main( void )
{
    double x, y;

    printf( "Enter a real number between -1 and 1: " );
    scanf( "%lf", &x );
    y = asin( x );
    printf( "Arcsine of %f = %f\n", x, y );
    y = acos( x );
    printf( "Arccosine of %f = %f\n", x, y );
}
```

```
Enter a real number between -1 and 1: .32696
Arcsine of 0.326960 = 0.333085
Arccosine of 0.326960 = 1.237711
```

See Also

acos, **atan**, **cos**, **_matherr**, **sin**, **tan**

assert

Evaluates an expression and when the result is FALSE, prints a diagnostic message and aborts the program.

void assert(int *expression* **);**

Routine	Required Header	Compatibility
assert	<assert.h>	ANSI, Win 95, Win NT

For additional compatibility information, see "Compatibility" in the Introduction.

Libraries

LIBC.LIB	Single thread static library, retail version
LIBCMT.LIB	Multithread static library, retail version
MSVCRT.LIB	Import library for MSVCRT.DLL, retail version

Return Value

None

Parameter

expression
   Expression (including pointers) that evaluates to nonzero or 0

Remarks

The ANSI **assert** macro is typically used to identify logic errors during program development, by implementing the *expression* argument to evaluate to false only when the program is operating incorrectly. After debugging is complete, assertion checking can be turned off without modifying the source file by defining the identifier **NDEBUG**. **NDEBUG** can be defined with a /D command-line option or with a **#define** directive. If **NDEBUG** is defined with **#define**, the directive must appear before ASSERT.H is included.

assert prints a diagnostic message when *expression* evaluates to false (0) and calls abort to terminate program execution. No action is taken if *expression* is true (nonzero). The diagnostic message includes the failed expression and the name of the source file and line number where the assertion failed.

The destination of the diagnostic message depends on the type of application that called the routine. Console applications always receive the message via **stderr**. In a single- or multithreaded Windows application, **assert** calls the Windows MessageBox **API to** create a message box to display the message along with an **OK** button. When the user chooses **OK**, the program aborts immediately.

When the application is linked with a debug version of the run-time libraries, **assert** creates a message box with three buttons: **Abort, Retry, and Ignore**. If the user selects **Abort**, the program aborts immediately. If the user selects **Retry**, the debugger is called and the user can debug the program if Just-In-Time (JIT) debugging is enabled. If the user selects **Ignore**, **assert** continues with its normal execution: creating the message box with the **OK** button. Note that choosing **Ignore** when an error condition exists can result in "undefined behavior." For more information, see "Using C Run-Time Library Debugging Support," in the *Visual C++ Programmer's Guide* online. The **assert** routine is available in both the release and debug versions of the C run-time libraries. Two other assertion macros, _ASSERT and _ASSERTE, are also available, but they only evaluate the expressions passed to them when the _DEBUG flag has been defined.

Example

```
/* ASSERT.C: In this program, the analyze_string function uses
 * the assert function to test several conditions related to
 * string and length. If any of the conditions fails, the program
 * prints a message indicating what caused the failure.
 */

#include <stdio.h>
#include <assert.h>
#include <string.h>

void analyze_string( char *string );   /* Prototype */

void main( void )
{
    char  test1[] = "abc", *test2 = NULL, test3[] = "";

    printf ( "Analyzing string '%s'\n", test1 );
    analyze_string( test1 );
    printf ( "Analyzing string '%s'\n", test2 );
    analyze_string( test2 );
    printf ( "Analyzing string '%s'\n", test3 );
    analyze_string( test3 );
}
```

```
/* Tests a string to see if it is NULL, */
/*   empty, or longer than 0 characters */
void analyze_string( char * string )
{
   assert( string != NULL );        /* Cannot be NULL */
   assert( *string != '\0' );       /* Cannot be empty */
   assert( strlen( string ) > 2 );  /* Length must exceed 2 */
}
```

Output

```
Analyzing string 'abc'
Analyzing string '(null)'
Assertion failed: string != NULL, file assert.c, line 24

abnormal program termination
```

See Also

abort, **raise**, **signal**, **_ASSERT**, **_ASSERTE**, **_DEBUG**

atan, atan2

Calculates the arctangent of *x* (**atan**) or the arctangent of *y/x* (**atan2**).

double atan(double *x* **);**
double atan2(double *y*, **double** *x* **);**

Routine	Required Header	Compatibility
atan	<math.h>	ANSI, Win 95, Win NT
atan2	<math.h>	ANSI, Win 95, Win NT

For additional compatibility information, see "Compatibility" in the Introduction.

Libraries

LIBC.LIB	Single thread static library, retail version
LIBCMT.LIB	Multithread static library, retail version
MSVCRT.LIB	Import library for MSVCRT.DLL, retail version

Return Value

atan returns the arctangent of *x*. **atan2** returns the arctangent of *y/x*. If *x* is 0, **atan** returns 0. If both parameters of **atan2** are 0, the function returns 0. You can modify error handling by using the **_matherr** routine. **atan** returns a value in the range $-\pi/2$ to $\pi/2$ radians; **atan2** returns a value in the range $-\pi$ to π radians, using the signs of both parameters to determine the quadrant of the return value.

Parameters

x, y
    Any numbers

Remarks

The **atan** function calculates the arctangent of *x*. **atan2** calculates the arctangent of *y/x*.
atan2 is well defined for every point other than the origin, even if *x* equals 0 and *y* does
not equal 0.

Example

```
/* ATAN.C: This program calculates
 * the arctangent of 1 and -1.
 */

#include <math.h>
#include <stdio.h>
#include <errno.h>

void main( void )
{
    double x1, x2, y;

    printf( "Enter a real number: " );
    scanf( "%lf", &x1 );
    y = atan( x1 );
    printf( "Arctangent of %f: %f\n", x1, y );
    printf( "Enter a second real number: " );
    scanf( "%lf", &x2 );
    y = atan2( x1, x2 );
    printf( "Arctangent of %f / %f: %f\n", x1, x2, y );
}
```

Output

```
Enter a real number: -862.42
Arctangent of -862.420000: -1.569637
Enter a second real number: 78.5149
Arctangent of -862.420000 / 78.514900: -1.480006
```

See Also

acos, asin, cos, _matherr, sin, tan

atexit

Processes the specified function at exit.

int atexit(void (__cdecl *func **)(void));**

Routine	Required Header	Compatibility
atexit	<stdlib.h>	ANSI, Win 95, Win NT

For additional compatibility information, see "Compatibility" in the Introduction.

Libraries

LIBC.LIB	Single thread static library, retail version
LIBCMT.LIB	Multithread static library, retail version
MSVCRT.LIB	Import library for MSVCRT.DLL, retail version

To generate an ANSI-compliant application, use the ANSI-standard **atexit** function (rather than the similar **_onexit** function).

Return Value

atexit returns 0 if successful, or a nonzero value if an error occurs.

Parameter

func
    Function to be called

Remarks

The **atexit** function is passed the address of a function (*func*) to be called when the program terminates normally. Successive calls to **atexit** create a register of functions that are executed in LIFO (last-in-first-out) order. The functions passed to **atexit** cannot take parameters. **atexit** and **_onexit** use the heap to hold the register of functions. Thus, the number of functions that can be registered is limited only by heap memory.

Example

```
/* ATEXIT.C: This program pushes four functions onto
 * the stack of functions to be executed when atexit
 * is called. When the program exits, these programs
 * are executed on a "last in, first out" basis.
 */

#include <stdlib.h>
#include <stdio.h>

void fn1( void ), fn2( void ), fn3( void ), fn4( void );

void main( void )
{
   atexit( fn1 );
   atexit( fn2 );
   atexit( fn3 );
   atexit( fn4 );
   printf( "This is executed first.\n" );
}
```

```
void fn1()
{
   printf( "next.\n" );
}

void fn2()
{
   printf( "executed " );
}

void fn3()
{
   printf( "is " );
}

void fn4()
{
   printf( "This " );
}

Output
This is executed first.
This is executed next.
```

See Also

abort, exit, _onexit

atof, atoi, _atoi64, atol

Convert strings to double (**atof**), integer (**atoi, _atoi64**), or long (**atol**).

double atof(const char *string **);**
int atoi(const char *string **);**
__int64 _atoi64(const char *string **);**
long atol(const char *string **);**

Routine	Required Header	Compatibility
atof	\<math.h\> and \<stdlib.h\>	ANSI, Win 95, Win NT
atoi	\<stdlib.h\>	ANSI, Win 95, Win NT
_atoi64	\<stdlib.h\>	Win 95, Win NT
atol	\<stdlib.h\>	ANSI, Win 95, Win NT

For additional compatibility information, see "Compatibility" in the Introduction.

Libraries

LIBC.LIB	Single thread static library, retail version
LIBCMT.LIB	Multithread static library, retail version
MSVCRT.LIB	Import library for MSVCRT.DLL, retail version

Return Value

Each function returns the **double**, **int**, **__int64** or **long** value produced by interpreting the input characters as a number. The return value is 0 (for **atoi** and **_atoi64**), 0L (for **atol**), or 0.0 (for **atof**) if the input cannot be converted to a value of that type. The return value is undefined in case of overflow.

Parameter

string
> String to be converted

Remarks

These functions convert a character string to a double-precision floating-point value (**atof**), an integer value (**atoi** and **_atoi64**), or a long integer value (**atol**). The input string is a sequence of characters that can be interpreted as a numerical value of the specified type. The output value is affected by the setting of the **LC_NUMERIC** category in the current locale. For more information on the **LC_NUMERIC** category, see setlocale. The longest string size that **atof** can handle is 100 characters. The function stops reading the input string at the first character that it cannot recognize as part of a number. This character may be the null character ('\0') terminating the string.

The *string* argument to **atof** has the following form:

[*whitespace*] [*sign*] [*digits*] [*.digits*] [{**d** | **D** | **e** | **E** }[*sign*]*digits*]

A *whitespace* consists of space and/or tab characters, which are ignored; *sign* is either plus (+) or minus (–); and *digits* are one or more decimal digits. If no digits appear before the decimal point, at least one must appear after the decimal point. The decimal digits may be followed by an exponent, which consists of an introductory letter (**d**, **D**, **e**, or **E**) and an optionally signed decimal integer.

atoi, **_atoi64**, and **atol** do not recognize decimal points or exponents. The *string* argument for these functions has the form:

[*whitespace*] [*sign*]*digits*

where *whitespace*, *sign*, and *digits* are exactly as described above for **atof**.

Generic-Text Routine Mappings

TCHAR.H Routine	_UNICODE & _MBCS Not Defined	_MBCS Defined	_UNICODE Defined
_ttoi	atoi	atoi	_wtoi
_ttol	atol	atol	_wtol

Example

```
/* ATOF.C: This program shows how numbers stored
 * as strings can be converted to numeric values
 * using the atof, atoi, and atol functions.
 */

#include <stdlib.h>
#include <stdio.h>

void main( void )
{
    char *s; double x; int i; long l;

    s = "  -2309.12E-15";    /* Test of atof */
    x = atof( s );
    printf( "atof test: ASCII string: %s\tfloat:  %e\n", s, x );

    s = "7.8912654773d210";  /* Test of atof */
    x = atof( s );
    printf( "atof test: ASCII string: %s\tfloat:  %e\n", s, x );

    s = "  -9885 pigs";      /* Test of atoi */
    i = atoi( s );
    printf( "atoi test: ASCII string: %s\t\tinteger: %d\n", s, i );

    s = "98854 dollars";     /* Test of atol */
    l = atol( s );
    printf( "atol test: ASCII string: %s\t\tlong: %ld\n", s, l );
}
```

Output

```
atof test: ASCII string:      -2309.12E-15  float:   -2.309120e-012
atof test: ASCII string: 7.8912654773d210  float:    7.891265e+210
atoi test: ASCII string:   -9885 pigs       integer: -9885
atol test: ASCII string: 98854 dollars     long:     98854
```

See Also

_ecvt, _fcvt, _gcvt, setlocale, strtod, wcstol, strtoul

_beginthread, _beginthreadex

Create a thread.

unsigned long _beginthread(void(__cdecl *start_address)(void *), unsigned *stack_size,* **void** **arglist* **);**
unsigned long _beginthreadex(void **security,* **unsigned** *stack_size,* **unsigned (__stdcall** **start_address* **)**
   (void *), void **arglist,* **unsigned** *initflag,* **unsigned** **thrdaddr* **);**

Routine	Required Header	Compatibility
_beginthread	<process.h>	Win 95, Win NT
_beginthreadex	<process.h>	Win 95, Win NT

For additional compatibility information, see "Compatibility" in the Introduction.

Libraries

LIBCMT.LIB	Multithread static library, retail version
MSVCRT.LIB	Import library for MSVCRT.DLL, retail version

To use **_beginthread** or **_beginthreadex**, the application must link with one of the multithreaded C run-time libraries.

Return Value

If successful, each of these functions returns a handle to the newly created thread.
_beginthread returns –1 on an error, in which case **errno** is set to **EAGAIN** if there are too many threads, or to **EINVAL** if the argument is invalid or the stack size is incorrect.
_beginthreadex returns 0 on an error, in which case **errno** and **doserrno** are set.

Parameters

start_address
   Start address of routine that begins execution of new thread

stack_size
   Stack size for new thread or 0

arglist
   Argument list to be passed to new thread or NULL

security
   Security descriptor for new thread; must be NULL for Windows 95 applications

initflag
   Initial state of new thread (**0** for running or **CREATE_SUSPEND** for suspended)

thrdaddr
   Address of new function

Remarks

The **_beginthread** function creates a thread that begins execution of a routine at *start_address*. The routine at *start_address* must use the __**cdecl** calling convention and should have no return value. When the thread returns from that routine, it is terminated automatically.

_beginthreadex resembles the Win32 CreateThread API more closely than does **_beginthread**. **_beginthreadex** differs from **_beginthread** in the following ways:

- **_beginthreadex** has three additional parameters: *initflag, security, threadaddr*. The new thread can be created in a suspended state, with a specified security (Windows NT only), and can be accessed using *thrdaddr*, which is the thread identifier.

- The routine at *start_address* passed to **_beginthreadex** must use the __**stdcall** calling convention and must return a thread exit code.

- **_beginthreadex** returns 0 on failure, rather than –1.

- A thread created with **_beginthreadex** is terminated by a call to **_endthreadex.**

You can call _endthread or _endthreadex explicitly to terminate a thread; however, **_endthread** or **_endthreadex** is called automatically when the thread returns from the routine passed as a parameter. Terminating a thread with a call to **endthread** or **_endthreadex** helps to ensure proper recovery of resources allocated for the thread.

_endthread automatically closes the thread handle (whereas **_endthreadex** does not). Therefore, when using **_beginthread** and **_endthread**, do not explicitly close the thread handle by calling the Win32 CloseHandle API. This behavior differs from the Win32 ExitThread API.

> **Note** For an executable file linked with LIBCMT.LIB, do not call the Win32 **ExitThread** API; this prevents the run-time system from reclaiming allocated resources. **_endthread** and **_endthreadex** reclaim allocated thread resources and then call **ExitThread**.

The operating system handles the allocation of the stack when either **_beginthread** or **_beginthreadex** is called; you do not need to pass the address of the thread stack to either of these functions. In addition, the *stack_size* argument can be 0, in which case the operating system uses the same value as the stack specified for the main thread.

arglist is a parameter to be passed to the newly created thread. Typically it is the address of a data item, such as a character string. *arglist* may be NULL if it is not needed, but **_beginthread** and **_beginthreadex** must be provided with some value to pass to the new thread. All threads are terminated if any thread calls **abort, exit, _exit**, or **ExitProcess**.

Example

```
/* BEGTHRD.C illustrates multiple threads using functions:
 *
 *      _beginthread            _endthread
 *
 *
 * This program requires the multithreaded library. For example,
 * compile with the following command line:
 *      CL /MT /D "_X86_" BEGTHRD.C
 *
 * If you are using the Visual C++ development environment, select the
 * Multi-Threaded runtime library in the compiler Project Settings
 * dialog box.
 *
 */

#include <windows.h>
#include <process.h>      /* _beginthread, _endthread */
#include <stddef.h>
#include <stdlib.h>
#include <conio.h>

void Bounce( void *ch );
void CheckKey( void *dummy );

/* GetRandom returns a random integer between min and max. */
#define GetRandom( min, max ) ((rand() % (int)(((max) + 1) - (min))) + (min))

BOOL repeat = TRUE;      /* Global repeat flag and video variable */
HANDLE hStdOut;          /* Handle for console window */
CONSOLE_SCREEN_BUFFER_INFO csbi;    /* Console information structure */

void main()
{
    CHAR    ch = 'A';

    hStdOut = GetStdHandle( STD_OUTPUT_HANDLE );

    /* Get display screen's text row and column information. */
    GetConsoleScreenBufferInfo( hStdOut, &csbi );

    /* Launch CheckKey thread to check for terminating keystroke. */
    _beginthread( CheckKey, 0, NULL );

    /* Loop until CheckKey terminates program. */
    while( repeat )
```

```
    {
        /* On first loops, launch character threads. */
        _beginthread( Bounce, 0, (void *) (ch++)  );

        /* Wait one second between loops. */
        Sleep( 1000L );
    }
}


/* CheckKey - Thread to wait for a keystroke, then clear repeat flag. */
void CheckKey( void *dummy )
{
    _getch();
    repeat = 0;      /* _endthread implied */
}


/* Bounce - Thread to create and and control a colored letter that moves
 * around on the screen.
 *
 * Params: ch - the letter to be moved
 */
void Bounce( void *ch )
{
    /* Generate letter and color attribute from thread argument. */
    char    blankcell = 0x20;
    char    blockcell = (char) ch;
    BOOL    first = TRUE;
    COORD   oldcoord, newcoord;
    DWORD   result;

    /* Seed random number generator and get initial location. */
    srand( _threadid );
    newcoord.X = GetRandom( 0, csbi.dwSize.X - 1 );
    newcoord.Y = GetRandom( 0, csbi.dwSize.Y - 1 );
    while( repeat )
    {
    /* Pause between loops. */
        Sleep( 100L );

        /* Blank out our old position on the screen, and draw new letter. */
        if( first )
            first = FALSE;
        else
            WriteConsoleOutputCharacter( hStdOut, &blankcell, 1, oldcoord, &result );
            WriteConsoleOutputCharacter( hStdOut, &blockcell, 1, newcoord, &result );
```

```
       /* Increment the coordinate for next placement of the block. */
       oldcoord.X = newcoord.X;
       oldcoord.Y = newcoord.Y;
       newcoord.X += GetRandom( -1, 1 );
       newcoord.Y += GetRandom( -1, 1 );

       /* Correct placement (and beep) if about to go off the screen. */
       if( newcoord.X < 0 )
           newcoord.X = 1;
       else if( newcoord.X == csbi.dwSize.X )
           newcoord.X = csbi.dwSize.X - 2;
       else if( newcoord.Y < 0 )
           newcoord.Y = 1;
       else if( newcoord.Y == csbi.dwSize.Y )
           newcoord.Y = csbi.dwSize.Y - 2;

       /* If not at a screen border, continue, otherwise beep. */
       else
           continue;
       Beep( ((char) ch - 'A') * 100, 175 );
   }
   /* _endthread given to terminate */
   _endthread();
}
```

See Also

_endthread, abort, exit

Bessel Functions

The Bessel functions are commonly used in the mathematics of electromagnetic wave theory.

_j0, _j1, _jn
   These routines return Bessel functions of the first kind: orders 0, 1, and n, respectively.

_y0, _y1, _yn
   These routines return Bessel functions of the second kind: orders 0, 1, and n, respectively.

Example

```
/* BESSEL.C: This program illustrates Bessel functions,
 * including:    _j0   _j1   _jn   _y0   _y1   _yn
 */

#include <math.h>
#include <stdio.h>
```

```
void main( void )
{
   double x = 2.387;
   int n = 3, c;

   printf( "Bessel functions for x = %f:\n", x );
   printf( " Kind\t\tOrder\tFunction\tResult\n\n" );
   printf( " First\t\t0\t_j0( x )\t%f\n", _j0( x ) );
   printf( " First\t\t1\t_j1( x )\t%f\n", _j1( x ) );
   for( c = 2; c < 5; c++ )
      printf( " First\t\t%d\t_jn( n, x )\t%f\n", c, _jn( c, x ) );
   printf( " Second\t0\t_y0( x )\t%f\n", _y0( x ) );
   printf( " Second\t1\t_y1( x )\t%f\n", _y1( x ) );
   for( c = 2; c < 5; c++ )
      printf( " Second\t%d\t_yn( n, x )\t%f\n", c, _yn( c, x ) );
}
```

Output

```
Bessel functions for x = 2.387000:
   Kind     Order   Function     Result

   First      0     _j0( x )      0.009288
   First      1     _j1( x )      0.522941
   First      2     _jn( n, x )   0.428870
   First      3     _jn( n, x )   0.195734
   First      4     _jn( n, x )   0.063131
   Second     0     _y0( x )      0.511681
   Second     1     _y1( x )      0.094374
   Second     2     _yn( n, x )  -0.432608
   Second     3     _yn( n, x )  -0.819314
   Second     4     _yn( n, x )  -1.626833
```

See Also

_matherr

Bessel Functions: _j0, _j1, _jn

Compute the Bessel function.

double _j0(double x);
double _j1(double x);
double _jn(int n, double x);

Routine	Required Header	Compatibility
_j0	<math.h>	Win 95, Win NT
_j1	<math.h>	Win 95, Win NT
_jn	<math.h>	Win 95, Win NT

For additional compatibility information, see "Compatibility" in the Introduction.

Libraries

LIBC.LIB	Single thread static library, retail version
LIBCMT.LIB	Multithread static library, retail version
MSVCRT.LIB	Import library for MSVCRT.DLL, retail version

Return Value

Each of these routines returns a Bessel function of x. You can modify error handling by using **_matherr**.

Parameters

x

Floating-point value

n

Integer order of Bessel function

Remarks

The **_j0**, **_j1**, and **_jn** routines return Bessel functions of the first kind: orders 0, 1, and n, respectively.

Example

```
/* BESSEL.C: This program illustrates Bessel functions,
 * including:    _j0    _j1    _jn    _y0    _y1    _yn
 */

#include <math.h>
#include <stdio.h>

void main( void )
{
   double x = 2.387;
   int n = 3, c;

   printf( "Bessel functions for x = %f:\n", x );
   printf( " Kind\t\tOrder\tFunction\tResult\n\n" );
   printf( " First\t\t0\t_j0( x )\t%f\n", _j0( x ) );
   printf( " First\t\t1\t_j1( x )\t%f\n", _j1( x ) );
   for( c = 2; c < 5; c++ )
      printf( " First\t%d\t_jn( n, x )\t%f\n", c, _jn( c, x ) );
   printf( " Second\t0\t_y0( x )\t%f\n", _y0( x ) );
   printf( " Second\t1\t_y1( x )\t%f\n", _y1( x ) );
   for( c = 2; c < 5; c++ )
      printf( " Second\t%d\t_yn( n, x )\t%f\n", c, _yn( c, x ) );
}
```

Output

```
Bessel functions for x = 2.387000:
   Kind     Order    Function      Result

   First      0      _j0( x )      0.009288
   First      1      _j1( x )      0.522941
   First      2      _jn( n, x )   0.428870
   First      3      _jn( n, x )   0.195734
   First      4      _jn( n, x )   0.063131
   Second     0      _y0( x )      0.511681
   Second     1      _y1( x )      0.094374
   Second     2      _yn( n, x )  -0.432608
   Second     3      _yn( n, x )  -0.819314
   Second     4      _yn( n, x )  -1.626833
```

See Also

_matherr

Bessel Functions: _y0, _y1, _yn

Compute the Bessel function.

double _y0(double *x*);
double _y1(double *x*);
double _yn(int *n*, double *x*);

Routine	Required Header	Compatibility
_y0	<math.h>	Win 95, Win NT
_y1	<math.h>	Win 95, Win NT
_yn	<math.h>	Win 95, Win NT

For additional compatibility information, see "Compatibility" in the Introduction.

Libraries

LIBC.LIB	Single thread static library, retail version
LIBCMT.LIB	Multithread static library, retail version
MSVCRT.LIB	Import library for MSVCRT.DLL, retail version

Return Value

Each of these routines returns a Bessel function of *x*. If *x* is negative, the routine sets **errno** to **EDOM**, prints a **_DOMAIN** error message to **stderr**, and returns **_HUGE_VAL**. You can modify error handling by using **_matherr**.

Parameters

x

> Floating-point value

n

> Integer order of Bessel function

Remarks

The **_y0**, **_y1**, and **_yn** routines return Bessel functions of the second kind: orders 0, 1, and n, respectively.

Example

```
/* BESSEL.C: This program illustrates Bessel functions,
 * including:   _j0   _j1   _jn   _y0   _y1   _yn
 */

#include <math.h>
#include <stdio.h>

void main( void )
{
   double x = 2.387;
   int n = 3, c;

   printf( "Bessel functions for x = %f:\n", x );
   printf( " Kind\t\tOrder\tFunction\tResult\n\n" );
   printf( " First\t\t0\t_j0( x )\t%f\n", _j0( x ) );
   printf( " First\t\t1\t_j1( x )\t%f\n", _j1( x ) );
   for( c = 2; c < 5; c++ )
      printf( " First\t\t%d\t_jn( n, x )\t%f\n", c, _jn( c, x ) );
   printf( " Second\t0\t_y0( x )\t%f\n", _y0( x ) );
   printf( " Second\t1\t_y1( x )\t%f\n", _y1( x ) );
   for( c = 2; c < 5; c++ )
      printf( " Second\t%d\t_yn( n, x )\t%f\n", c, _yn( c, x ) );
}
```

Output

```
Bessel functions for x = 2.387000:
   Kind      Order    Function      Result

   First       0     _j0( x )       0.009288
   First       1     _j1( x )       0.522941
   First       2     _jn( n, x )    0.428870
   First       3     _jn( n, x )    0.195734
   First       4     _jn( n, x )    0.063131
   Second      0     _y0( x )       0.511681
   Second      1     _y1( x )       0.094374
```

```
Second    2    _yn( n, x )    -0.432608
Second    3    _yn( n, x )    -0.819314
Second    4    _yn( n, x )    -1.626833
```

See Also

_matherr

bsearch

Performs a binary search of a sorted array.

void *bsearch(const void *key**, const void ***base**, size_t** num**, size_t** width**,**
 int (__cdecl *compare **) (const void ***elem1**, const void ***elem2 **));**

Routine	Required Header	Compatibility
bsearch	<stdlib.h> and <search.h>	ANSI, Win 95, Win NT

For additional compatibility information, see "Compatibility" in the Introduction.

Libraries

LIBC.LIB	Single thread static library, retail version
LIBCMT.LIB	Multithread static library, retail version
MSVCRT.LIB	Import library for MSVCRT.DLL, retail version

Return Value

bsearch returns a pointer to an occurrence of *key* in the array pointed to by *base*. If *key*
is not found, the function returns **NULL**. If the array is not in ascending sort order or
contains duplicate records with identical keys, the result is unpredictable.

Parameters

key
 Object to search for

base
 Pointer to base of search data

num
 Number of elements

width
 Width of elements

compare
 Function that compares two elements: *elem1* and *elem2*

elem1
>   Pointer to the key for the search

elem2
>   Pointer to the array element to be compared with the key

Remarks

The **bsearch** function performs a binary search of a sorted array of *num* elements, each of *width* bytes in size. The *base* value is a pointer to the base of the array to be searched, and *key* is the value being sought. The *compare* parameter is a pointer to a user-supplied routine that compares two array elements and returns a value specifying their relationship. **bsearch** calls the *compare* routine one or more times during the search, passing pointers to two array elements on each call. The *compare* routine compares the elements, then returns one of the following values:

Value Returned by *compare* Routine	Description
< 0	*elem1* less than *elem2*
0	*elem1* equal to *elem2*
> 0	*elem1* greater than *elem2*

Example

```c
/* BSEARCH.C: This program reads the command-line
 * parameters, sorting them with qsort, and then
 * uses bsearch to find the word "cat."
 */

#include <search.h>
#include <string.h>
#include <stdio.h>

int compare( char **arg1, char **arg2 ); /* Declare a function for compare */

void main( int argc, char **argv )
{
    char **result;
    char *key = "cat";
    int i;

    /* Sort using Quicksort algorithm: */
    qsort( (void *)argv, (size_t)argc, sizeof( char * ),
    ⬏ (int (*)(const void*, const void*))compare );

    for( i = 0; i < argc; ++i )     /* Output sorted list */
        printf( "%s ", argv[i] );
```

```
   /* Find the word "cat" using a binary search algorithm: */
   result = (char **)bsearch( (char *) &key, (char *)argv, argc,
   ↪ sizeof( char * ), (int (*)(const void*, const void*))compare );
   if( result )
       printf( "\n%s found at %Fp\n", *result, result );
   else
       printf( "\nCat not found!\n" );
}

int compare( char **arg1, char **arg2 )
{
   /* Compare all of both strings: */
   return _strcmpi( *arg1, *arg2 );
}
```

Output

```
[C:\work]bsearch dog pig horse cat human rat cow goat
bsearch cat cow dog goat horse human pig rat
cat found at 002D0008
```

See Also

_lfind, **_lsearch**, **qsort**

_cabs

Calculates the absolute value of a complex number.

double _cabs(struct _complex *z* **);**

Routine	Required Header	Compatibility
_cabs	<math.h>	Win 95, Win NT

For additional compatibility information, see "Compatibility" in the Introduction.

Libraries

LIBC.LIB	Single thread static library, retail version
LIBCMT.LIB	Multithread static library, retail version
MSVCRT.LIB	Import library for MSVCRT.DLL, retail version

Return Value

_cabs returns the absolute value of its argument if successful. On overflow **_cabs** returns **HUGE_VAL** and sets **errno** to **ERANGE**. You can change error handling with _matherr.

Parameter

z

> Complex number

Remarks

The **_cabs** function calculates the absolute value of a complex number, which must be a structure of type _complex. The structure *z* is composed of a real component *x* and an imaginary component *y*. A call to **_cabs** produces a value equivalent to that of the expression **sqrt**($z.x*z.x + z.y*z.y$).

Example

```
/* CABS.C: Using _cabs, this program calculates
 * the absolute value of a complex number.
 */
#include <math.h>
#include <stdio.h>

void main( void )
{
   struct _complex number = { 3.0, 4.0 };
   double d;

   d = _cabs( number );
   printf( "The absolute value of %f + %fi is %f\n",
       number.x, number.y, d );
}

Output
The absolute value of 3.000000 + 4.000000i is 5.000000
```

See Also

abs, **fabs**, **labs**

calloc

Allocates an array in memory with elements initialized to 0.

void *calloc(size_t *num*, **size_t** *size* **);**

Routine	Required Header	Compatibility
calloc	<stdlib.h> and <malloc.h>	ANSI, Win 95, Win NT

For additional compatibility information, see "Compatibility" in the Introduction.

Libraries

LIBC.LIB	Single thread static library, retail version
LIBCMT.LIB	Multithread static library, retail version
MSVCRT.LIB	Import library for MSVCRT.DLL, retail version

Return Value

calloc returns a pointer to the allocated space. The storage space pointed to by the return value is guaranteed to be suitably aligned for storage of any type of object. To get a pointer to a type other than **void**, use a type cast on the return value.

Parameters

num
   Number of elements

size
   Length in bytes of each element

Remarks

The calloc function allocates storage space for an array of *num* elements, each of length *size* bytes. Each element is initialized to 0.

calloc calls **malloc** in order to use the C++ _set_new_mode function to set the new handler mode. The new handler mode indicates whether, on failure, **malloc** is to call the new handler routine as set by _set_new_handler. By default, **malloc** does not call the new handler routine on failure to allocate memory. You can override this default behavior so that, when **calloc** fails to allocate memory, **malloc** calls the new handler routine in the same way that the **new** operator does when it fails for the same reason. To override the default, call

```
_set_new_mode(1)
```

early in your program, or link with NEWMODE.OBJ.

When the application is linked with a debug version of the C run-time libraries, **calloc** resolves to _calloc_dbg. For more information about how the heap is managed during the debugging process, see "Using C Run-Time Library Debugging Support," in the *Visual C++ Programmer's Guide* online.

Example

```
/* CALLOC.C: This program uses calloc to allocate space for
 * 40 long integers. It initializes each element to zero.
 */
#include <stdio.h>
#include <malloc.h>

void main( void )
{
    long *buffer;
```

```
    buffer = (long *)calloc( 40, sizeof( long ) );
    if( buffer != NULL )
        printf( "Allocated 40 long integers\n" );
    else
        printf( "Can't allocate memory\n" );
    free( buffer );
}
```

```
Output
Allocated 40 long integers
```

See Also

free, malloc, realloc

ceil

Calculates the ceiling of a value.

double ceil(double *x*);

Routine	Required Header	Compatibility
ceil	<math.h>	ANSI, Win 95, Win NT

For additional compatibility information, see "Compatibility" in the Introduction.

Libraries

LIBC.LIB	Single thread static library, retail version
LIBCMT.LIB	Multithread static library, retail version
MSVCRT.LIB	Import library for MSVCRT.DLL, retail version

Return Value

The **ceil** function returns a **double** value representing the smallest integer that is greater than or equal to x. There is no error return.

Parameter

x

Floating-point value

Example

```
/* FLOOR.C: This example displays the largest integers
 * less than or equal to the floating-point values 2.8
 * and -2.8. It then shows the smallest integers greater
 * than or equal to 2.8 and -2.8.
 */
```

```
#include <math.h>
#include <stdio.h>

void main( void )
{
   double y;

   y = floor( 2.8 );
   printf( "The floor of 2.8 is %f\n", y );
   y = floor( -2.8 );
   printf( "The floor of -2.8 is %f\n", y );

   y = ceil( 2.8 );
   printf( "The ceil of 2.8 is %f\n", y );
   y = ceil( -2.8 );
   printf( "The ceil of -2.8 is %f\n", y );
}
```

Output

```
The floor of 2.8 is 2.000000
The floor of -2.8 is -3.000000
The ceil of 2.8 is 3.000000
The ceil of -2.8 is -2.000000
```

See Also

floor, fmod

_cexit, _c_exit

Perform cleanup operations and return without terminating the process.

void _cexit(void);
void _c_exit(void);

Routine	Required Header	Compatibility
_cexit	<process.h>	Win 95, Win NT
_c_exit	<process.h>	Win 95, Win NT

For additional compatibility information, see "Compatibility" in the Introduction.

Libraries

LIBC.LIB	Single thread static library, retail version
LIBCMT.LIB	Multithread static library, retail version
MSVCRT.LIB	Import library for MSVCRT.DLL, retail version

Return Value

None

Remarks

The **_cexit** function calls, in last-in-first-out (LIFO) order, the functions registered by **atexit** and **_onexit**. Then **_cexit** flushes all I/O buffers and closes all open streams before returning. **_c_exit** is the same as **_exit** but returns to the calling process without processing **atexit** or **_onexit** or flushing stream buffers. The behavior of **exit**, **_exit**, **_cexit**, and **_c_exit** is as follows:

Function	Behavior
exit	Performs complete C library termination procedures, terminates process, and exits with supplied status code
_exit	Performs "quick" C library termination procedures, terminates process, and exits with supplied status code
_cexit	Performs complete C library termination procedures and returns to caller, but does not terminate process
_c_exit	Performs "quick" C library termination procedures and returns to caller, but does not terminate process

See Also

abort, **atexit**, **_exec Functions**, **exit**, **_onexit**, **_spawn Functions**, **system**

_cgets

Gets a character string from the console.

char *_cgets(char *buffer**);**

Routine	Required Header	Compatibility
_cgets	<conio.h>	Win 95, Win NT

For additional compatibility information, see "Compatibility" in the Introduction.

Libraries

LIBC.LIB	Single thread static library, retail version
LIBCMT.LIB	Multithread static library, retail version
MSVCRT.LIB	Import library for MSVCRT.DLL, retail version

Return Value

_cgets returns a pointer to the start of the string, at buffer[2]. There is no error return.

Parameter

buffer

    Storage location for data

Remarks

The **_cgets** function reads a string of characters from the console and stores the string and its length in the location pointed to by *buffer*. The *buffer* parameter must be a pointer to a character array. The first element of the array, *buffer*[0], must contain the maximum length (in characters) of the string to be read. The array must contain enough elements to hold the string, a terminating null character ('\0'), and two additional bytes. The function reads characters until a carriage-return – linefeed (CR-LF) combination or the specified number of characters is read. The string is stored starting at *buffer*[2]. If the function reads a CR-LF, it stores the null character ('\0'). **_cgets** then stores the actual length of the string in the second array element, *buffer* [1]. Because all editing keys are active when **_cgets** is called, pressing F3 repeats the last entry.

Example

```
/* CGETS.C: This program creates a buffer and initializes
 * the first byte to the size of the buffer: 2. Next, the
 * program accepts an input string using _cgets and displays
 * the size and text of that string.
 */

#include <conio.h>
#include <stdio.h>

void main( void )
{
    char buffer[82] = { 80 };  /* Maximum characters in 1st byte */
    char *result;

    printf( "Input line of text, followed by carriage return:\n");
    result = _cgets( buffer );  /* Input a line of text */
    printf( "\nLine length = %d\nText = %s\n", buffer[1], result );
}
```

Output

```
Input line of text, followed by carriage return:
This is a line of text

Line length = 22
Text = This is a line of text.
```

See Also

_getch

_chdir, _wchdir

Change the current working directory.

int _chdir(const char *dirname* **);**
int _wchdir(const wchar_t *dirname* **);**

Routine	Required Header	Optional Headers	Compatibility
_chdir	<direct.h>	<errno.h>	Win 95, Win NT
_wchdir	<direct.h> or <wchar.h>	<errno.h>	Win NT

For additional compatibility information, see "Compatibility" in the Introduction.

Libraries

LIBC.LIB	Single thread static library, retail version
LIBCMT.LIB	Multithread static library, retail version
MSVCRT.LIB	Import library for MSVCRT.DLL, retail version

Return Value

Each of these functions returns a value of 0 if successful. A return value of −1 indicates that the specified path could not be found, in which case **errno** is set to **ENOENT**.

Parameter

dirname
　　Path of new working directory

Remarks

The **_chdir** function changes the current working directory to the directory specified by *dirname*. The *dirname* parameter must refer to an existing directory. This function can change the current working directory on any drive and if a new drive letter is specified in *dirname*, the default drive letter will be changed as well. For example, if A is the default drive letter and \BIN is the current working directory, the following call changes the current working directory for drive C and establishes C as the new default drive:

```
_chdir("c:\\temp");
```

When you use the optional backslash character (\) in paths, you must place two backslashes (\\) in a C string literal to represent a single backslash (\).

_wchdir is a wide-character version of **_chdir**; the dirname argument to **_wchdir** is a wide-character string. **_wchdir** and **_chdir** behave identically otherwise.

Generic-Text Routine Mapping:

TCHAR.H Routine	_UNICODE & _MBCS Not Defined	_MBCS Defined	_UNICODE Defined
_tchdir	_chdir	_chdir	_wchdir

Example

```
/* CHGDIR.C: This program uses the _chdir function to verify
 * that a given directory exists.
 */

#include <direct.h>
#include <stdio.h>
#include <stdlib.h>

void main( int argc, char *argv[] )
{
   if( _chdir( argv[1] )   )
      printf( "Unable to locate the directory: %s\n", argv[1] );
   else
      system( "dir *.wri");
}
```

Output

```
Volume in drive C is CDRIVE
Volume Serial Number is 0E17-1702

Directory of C:\write

04/21/95  01:06p                3,200 ERRATA.WRI
04/21/95  01:06p                2,816 README.WRI
              2 File(s)         6,016 bytes
                           71,432,116 bytes free
```

See Also

_mkdir, _rmdir, system

_chdrive

Changes the current working drive.

int _chdrive(int *drive* **);**

Routine	Required Header	Compatibility
_chdrive	<direct.h>	Win 95, Win NT

For additional compatibility information, see "Compatibility" in the Introduction.

Libraries

LIBC.LIB	Single thread static library, retail version
LIBCMT.LIB	Multithread static library, retail version
MSVCRT.LIB	Import library for MSVCRT.DLL, retail version

Return Value

_chdrive returns a value of 0 if the working drive is successfully changed. A return value of –1 indicates an error.

Parameter

drive
  Number of new working drive

Remarks

The **_chdrive** function changes the current working drive to the drive specified by *drive*. The *drive* parameter uses an integer to specify the new working drive (1=A, 2=B, and so forth). This function changes only the working drive; **_chdir** changes the working directory.

Example

```
/* GETDRIVE.C illustrates drive functions including:
 *      _getdrive       _chdrive        _getdcwd
 */

#include <stdio.h>
#include <conio.h>
#include <direct.h>
#include <stdlib.h>
#include <ctype.h>

void main( void )
{
    int ch, drive, curdrive;
    static char path[_MAX_PATH];

    /* Save current drive. */
    curdrive = _getdrive();

    printf( "Available drives are: \n" );

    /* If we can switch to the drive, it exists. */
    for( drive = 1; drive <= 26; drive++ )
        if( !_chdrive( drive ) )
            printf( "%c: ", drive + 'A' - 1 );
```

```
    while( 1 )
    {
        printf( "\nType drive letter to check or ESC to quit: " );
        ch = _getch();
        if( ch == 27 )
            break;
        if( isalpha( ch ) )
            _putch( ch );
        if( _getdcwd( toupper( ch ) - 'A' + 1, path, _MAX_PATH ) != NULL )
            printf( "\nCurrent directory on that drive is %s\n", path );
    }

    /* Restore original drive.*/
    _chdrive( curdrive );
    printf( "\n" );
}
```

Output

```
Available drives are:
A: B: C: L: M: O: U: V:
Type drive letter to check or ESC to quit: c
Current directory on that drive is C:\CODE

Type drive letter to check or ESC to quit: m
Current directory on that drive is M:\

Type drive letter to check or ESC to quit:
```

See Also

_chdir, **_fullpath**, **_getcwd**, **_getdrive**, **_mkdir**, **_rmdir**, **system**

_chgsign

Reverses the sign of a double-precision floating-point argument.

double _chgsign(double *x* **);**

Routine	Required Header	Compatibility
_chgsign	<float.h>	Win 95, Win NT

For additional compatibility information, see "Compatibility" in the Introduction.

Libraries

LIBC.LIB	Single thread static library, retail version
LIBCMT.LIB	Multithread static library, retail version
MSVCRT.LIB	Import library for MSVCRT.DLL, retail version

Return Value

_chgsign returns a value equal to its double-precision floating-point argument *x*, but with its sign reversed. There is no error return.

Parameter

x

Double-precision floating-point value to be changed

See Also

fabs, _copysign

_chmod, _wchmod

Change the file-permission settings.

int _chmod(const char **filename*, **int** *pmode* **);**
int _wchmod(const wchar_t **filename*, **int** *pmode* **);**

Routine	Required Header	Optional Headers	Compatibility
_chmod	<io.h>	<sys/types.h>, <sys/stat.h>, <errno.h>	Win 95, Win NT
_wchmod	<io.h> or <wchar.h>	<sys/types.h>, <sys/stat.h>, <errno.h>	Win NT

For additional compatibility information, see "Compatibility" in the Introduction.

Libraries

LIBC.LIB	Single thread static library, retail version
LIBCMT.LIB	Multithread static library, retail version
MSVCRT.LIB	Import library for MSVCRT.DLL, retail version

Return Value

Each of these functions returns 0 if the permission setting is successfully changed. A return value of –1 indicates that the specified file could not be found, in which case **errno** is set to **ENOENT**.

Parameters

filename

Name of existing file

pmode

Permission setting for file

Remarks

The **_chmod** function changes the permission setting of the file specified by *filename*. The permission setting controls read and write access to the file. The integer expression *pmode* contains one or both of the following manifest constants, defined in SYS\STAT.H:

_S_IWRITE
Writing permitted

_S_IREAD
Reading permitted

_S_IREAD | _S_IWRITE
Reading and writing permitted

Any other values for *pmode* are ignored. When both constants are given, they are joined with the bitwise-OR operator (|). If write permission is not given, the file is read-only. Note that all files are always readable; it is not possible to give write-only permission. Thus the modes **_S_IWRITE** and **_S_IREAD | _S_IWRITE** are equivalent.

_wchmod is a wide-character version of **_chmod**; the *filename* argument to **_wchmod** is a wide-character string. **_wchmod** and **_chmod** behave identically otherwise.

Generic-Text Routine Mappings

TCHAR.H Routine	_UNICODE & _MBCS Not Defined	_MBCS Defined	_UNICODE Defined
_tchmod	_chmod	_chmod	_wchmod

Example

```
/* CHMOD.C: This program uses _chmod to
 * change the mode of a file to read-only.
 * It then attempts to modify the file.
 */

#include <sys/types.h>
#include <sys/stat.h>
#include <io.h>
#include <stdio.h>
#include <stdlib.h>

void main( void )
{
    /* Make file read-only: */
    if( _chmod( "CHMOD.C", _S_IREAD ) == -1 )
        perror( "File not found\n" );
    else
        printf( "Mode changed to read-only\n" );
    system( "echo /* End of file */ >> CHMOD.C" );
```

```
    /* Change back to read/write: */
    if( _chmod( "CHMOD.C", _S_IWRITE ) == -1 )
       perror( "File not found\n" );
    else
       printf( "Mode changed to read/write\n" );
    system( "echo /* End of file */ >> CHMOD.C" );
}
```

Output

```
Mode changed to read-only
Access is denied
Mode changed to read/write
```

See Also

_access, _creat, _fstat, _open, _stat

_chsize

Changes the file size.

int _chsize(int *handle*, **long** *size* **);**

Routine	Required Header	Optional Headers	Compatibility
_chsize	<io.h>	<errno.h>	Win 95, Win NT

For additional compatibility information, see "Compatibility" in the Introduction.

Libraries

LIBC.LIB	Single thread static library, retail version
LIBCMT.LIB	Multithread static library, retail version
MSVCRT.LIB	Import library for MSVCRT.DLL, retail version

Return Value

_chsize returns the value 0 if the file size is successfully changed. A return value of –1 indicates an error: **errno** is set to **EACCES** if the specified file is locked against access, to **EBADF** if the specified file is read-only or the handle is invalid, or to **ENOSPC** if no space is left on the device.

Parameters

handle
   Handle referring to open file

size
   New length of file in bytes

Remarks

The **_chsize** function extends or truncates the file associated with *handle* to the length specified by *size*. The file must be open in a mode that permits writing. Null characters ('\0') are appended if the file is extended. If the file is truncated, all data from the end of the shortened file to the original length of the file is lost.

Example

```
/* CHSIZE.C: This program uses _filelength to report the size
 * of a file before and after modifying it with _chsize.
 */

#include <io.h>
#include <fcntl.h>
#include <sys/types.h>
#include <sys/stat.h>
#include <stdio.h>

void main( void )
{
    int fh, result;
    unsigned int nbytes = BUFSIZ;

    /* Open a file */
    if( (fh = _open( "data", _O_RDWR | _O_CREAT, _S_IREAD
                    | _S_IWRITE ))  != -1 )
    {
        printf( "File length before: %ld\n", _filelength( fh ) );
        if( ( result = _chsize( fh, 329678 ) ) == 0 )
            printf( "Size successfully changed\n" );
        else
            printf( "Problem in changing the size\n" );
        printf( "File length after:  %ld\n", _filelength( fh ) );
        _close( fh );
    }
}
```

Output

```
File length before: 0
Size successfully changed
File length after:  329678
```

See Also

_close, **_creat**, **_open**

_clear87, _clearfp

Get and clear the floating-point status word.

unsigned int _clear87(void);
unsigned int _clearfp(void);

Routine	Required Header	Compatibility
_clear87	<float.h>	Win 95, Win NT
_clearfp	<float.h>	Win 95, Win NT

For additional compatibility information, see "Compatibility" in the Introduction.

Libraries

LIBC.LIB	Single thread static library, retail version
LIBCMT.LIB	Multithread static library, retail version
MSVCRT.LIB	Import library for MSVCRT.DLL, retail version

Return Value

The bits in the value returned indicate the floating-point status before the call to **_clear87** or **_clearfp**. See FLOAT.H for a complete definition of the bits returned by **_clear87**. Many of the math library functions modify the 8087/80287 status word, with unpredictable results. Return values from **_clear87** and **_status87** become more reliable as fewer floating-point operations are performed between known states of the floating-point status word.

Remarks

The **_clear87** function clears the exception flags in the floating-point status word, sets the busy bit to 0, and returns the status word. The floating-point status word is a combination of the 8087/80287 status word and other conditions detected by the 8087/80287 exception handler, such as floating-point stack overflow and underflow.

_clearfp is a platform-independent, portable version of the **_clear87** routine. It is identical to **_clear87** on Intel (x86) platforms and is also supported by the MIPS and ALPHA platforms. To ensure that your floating-point code is portable to MIPS or ALPHA, use **_clearfp**. If you are only targeting x86 platforms, you can use either **_clear87** or **_clearfp**.

Example

```
/* CLEAR87.C: This program creates various floating-point
 * problems, then uses _clear87 to report on these problems.
 * Compile this program with Optimizations disabled (/Od).
 * Otherwise the optimizer will remove the code associated with
 * the unused floating-point values.
 */
```

```
#include <stdio.h>
#include <float.h>

void main( void )
{
    double a = 1e-40, b;
    float x, y;

    printf( "Status: %.4x - clear\n", _clear87()  );

    /* Store into y is inexact and underflows: */
    y = a;
    printf( "Status: %.4x - inexact, underflow\n", _clear87() );

    /* y is denormal: */
    b = y;
    printf( "Status: %.4x - denormal\n", _clear87() );
}
```

Output

```
Status: 0000 - clear
Status: 0003 - inexact, underflow
Status: 80000 - denormal
```

See Also

_control87, _status87

clearerr

Resets the error indicator for a stream.

void clearerr(FILE *stream);

Routine	Required Header	Compatibility
clearerr	<stdio.h>	ANSI, Win 95, Win NT

For additional compatibility information, see "Compatibility" in the Introduction.

Libraries

LIBC.LIB	Single thread static library, retail version
LIBCMT.LIB	Multithread static library, retail version
MSVCRT.LIB	Import library for MSVCRT.DLL, retail version

Return Value

None

Parameter

stream
> Pointer to **FILE** structure

Remarks

The **clearerr** function resets the error indicator and end-of-file indicator for *stream*. Error indicators are not automatically cleared; once the error indicator for a specified stream is set, operations on that stream continue to return an error value until **clearerr**, **fseek**, **fsetpos**, or **rewind** is called.

Example

```
/* CLEARERR.C: This program creates an error
 * on the standard input stream, then clears
 * it so that future reads won't fail.
 */

#include <stdio.h>

void main( void )
{
   int c;
   /* Create an error by writing to standard input. */
   putc( 'c', stdin );
   if( ferror( stdin ) )
   {
      perror( "Write error" );
      clearerr( stdin );
   }

   /* See if read causes an error. */
   printf( "Will input cause an error? " );
   c = getc( stdin );
   if( ferror( stdin ) )
   {
      perror( "Read error" );
      clearerr( stdin );
   }
}
```

Output

```
Write error: No error
Will input cause an error? n
```

See Also

_eof, feof, ferror, perror

clock

Calculates the processor time used by the calling process.

clock_t clock(void);

Routine	Required Header	Compatibility
clock	<time.h>	ANSI, Win 95, Win NT

For additional compatibility information, see "Compatibility" in the Introduction.

Libraries

LIBC.LIB	Single thread static library, retail version
LIBCMT.LIB	Multithread static library, retail version
MSVCRT.LIB	Import library for MSVCRT.DLL, retail version

Return Value

clock returns the number of clock ticks of elapsed processor time. The returned value is the product of the amount of time that has elapsed since the start of a process and the value of the **CLOCKS_PER_SEC** constant. If the amount of elapsed time is unavailable, the function returns –1, cast as a **clock_t**.

Remarks

The **clock** function tells how much processor time the calling process has used. The time in seconds is approximated by dividing the clock return value by the value of the constant. In other words, **clock** returns the number of processor timer ticks that have elapsed. A timer tick is approximately equal to 1/**CLOCKS_PER_SEC** second. In versions of Microsoft C before 6.0, the **CLOCKS_PER_SEC** constant was called **CLK_TCK**.

Example

```
/* CLOCK.C: This example prompts for how long
 * the program is to run and then continuously
 * displays the elapsed time for that period.
 */

#include <stdio.h>
#include <stdlib.h>
#include <time.h>

void sleep( clock_t wait );
```

```
void main( void )
{
    long    i = 600000L;
    clock_t start, finish;
    double  duration;

    /* Delay for a specified time. */
    printf( "Delay for three seconds\n" );
    sleep( (clock_t)3 * CLOCKS_PER_SEC );
    printf( "Done!\n" );

    /* Measure the duration of an event. */
    printf( "Time to do %ld empty loops is ", i );
    start = clock();
    while( i-- )
        ;
    finish = clock();
    duration = (double)(finish - start) / CLOCKS_PER_SEC;
    printf( "%2.1f seconds\n", duration );
}

/* Pauses for a specified number of milliseconds. */
void sleep( clock_t wait )
{
    clock_t goal;
    goal = wait + clock();
    while( goal > clock() )
        ;
}
```

Output

```
Delay for three seconds
Done!
Time to do 600000 empty loops is 0.1 seconds
```

See Also

difftime, time

_close

Closes a file.

int _close(int *handle* **);**

Routine	Required Header	Optional Headers	Compatibility
_close	<io.h>	<errno.h>	Win 95, Win NT

For additional compatibility information, see "Compatibility" in the Introduction.

Libraries

LIBC.LIB	Single thread static library, retail version
LIBCMT.LIB	Multithread static library, retail version
MSVCRT.LIB	Import library for MSVCRT.DLL, retail version

Return Value

_close returns 0 if the file was successfully closed. A return value of −1 indicates an error, in which case **errno** is set to **EBADF**, indicating an invalid file-handle parameter.

Parameter

handle
    Handle referring to open file

Remarks

The **_close** function closes the file associated with handle.

Example

```
/* OPEN.C: This program uses _open to open a file
 * named OPEN.C for input and a file named OPEN.OUT
 * for output. The files are then closed.
 */

#include <fcntl.h>
#include <sys/types.h>
#include <sys/stat.h>
#include <io.h>
#include <stdio.h>

void main( void )
{
   int fh1, fh2;

   fh1 = _open( "OPEN.C", _O_RDONLY );
   if( fh1 == -1 )
      perror( "open failed on input file" );
   else
   {
      printf( "open succeeded on input file\n" );
      _close( fh1 );
   }
```

```
        fh2 = _open( "OPEN.OUT", _O_WRONLY | _O_CREAT, _S_IREAD |
                                 _S_IWRITE );
        if( fh2 == -1 )
           perror( "Open failed on output file" );
        else
        {
           printf( "Open succeeded on output file\n" );
           _close( fh2 );
        }
   }
```

Output

```
Open succeeded on input file
Open succeeded on output file
```

See Also

_chsize, _creat, _dup, _open, _unlink

_commit

Flushes a file directly to disk.

int _commit(int *handle* **);**

Routine	Required Header	Optional Headers	Compatibility
_commit	<io.h>	<errno.h>	Win 95, Win NT

For additional compatibility information, see "Compatibility" in the Introduction.

Libraries

LIBC.LIB	Single thread static library, retail version
LIBCMT.LIB	Multithread static library, retail version
MSVCRT.LIB	Import library for MSVCRT.DLL, retail version

Return Value

_commit returns 0 if the file was successfully flushed to disk. A return value of –1
indicates an error, and **errno** is set to **EBADF**, indicating an invalid file-handle parameter.

Parameter

handle
    Handle referring to open file

Remarks

The **_commit** function forces the operating system to write the file associated with *handle* to disk. This call ensures that the specified file is flushed immediately, not at the operating system's discretion.

Example

```
/* COMMIT.C illustrates low-level file I/O functions including:
 *
 *      _close    _commit    memset    _open    _write
 *
 * This is example code; to keep the code simple and readable
 * return values are not checked.
 */

#include <io.h>
#include <stdio.h>
#include <fcntl.h>
#include <memory.h>
#include <errno.h>

#define MAXBUF 32

int log_receivable( int );

void main( void )
{
    int fhandle;
    fhandle = _open( "TRANSACT.LOG", _O_APPEND | _O_CREAT |
                                     _O_BINARY | _O_RDWR );
    log_receivable( fhandle );
    _close( fhandle );
}

int log_receivable( int fhandle )
{
/* The log_receivable function prompts for a name and a monetary
 * amount and places both values into a buffer (buf). The _write
 * function writes the values to the operating system and the
 * _commit function ensures that they are written to a disk file.
 */

    int i;
    char  buf[MAXBUF];

    memset( buf, '\0', MAXBUF );
    /* Begin Transaction. */
    printf( "Enter name: " );
    gets( buf );
```

```
for( i = 1; buf[i] != '\0'; i++ );
/* Write the value as a '\0' terminated string. */
_write( fhandle, buf, i+1 );
printf( "\n" );

memset( buf, '\0', MAXBUF );
printf( "Enter amount: $" );
gets( buf );
for( i = 1; buf[i] != '\0'; i++ );
/* Write the value as a '\0' terminated string. */
_write( fhandle, buf, i+1 );
printf( "\n" );

/* The _commit function ensures that two important pieces of
 * data are safely written to disk. The return value of the
 * _commit function is returned to the calling function.
 */
return _commit( fhandle );
}
```

See Also

_creat, _open, _read, _write

_control87, _controlfp

Get and set the floating-point control word.

unsigned int _control87(unsigned int *new*, **unsigned int** *mask* **);**
unsigned int _controlfp(unsigned int *new*, **unsigned int** *mask* **);**

Routine	Required Header	Compatibility
_control87	<float.h>	Win 95, Win NT
_controlfp	<float.h>	Win 95, Win NT

For additional compatibility information, see "Compatibility" in the Introduction.

Libraries

LIBC.LIB	Single thread static library, retail version
LIBCMT.LIB	Multithread static library, retail version
MSVCRT.LIB	Import library for MSVCRT.DLL, retail version

Return Value

The bits in the value returned indicate the floating-point control state. See FLOAT.H for a complete definition of the bits returned by **_control87**.

Parameters

new

New control-word bit values

mask

Mask for new control-word bits to set

Remarks

The **_control87** function gets and sets the floating-point control word. The floating-point control word allows the program to change the precision, rounding, and infinity modes in the floating-point math package. You can also mask or unmask floating-point exceptions using **_control87**. If the value for *mask* is equal to 0, **_control87** gets the floating-point control word. If *mask* is nonzero, a new value for the control word is set: For any bit that is on (equal to 1) in *mask*, the corresponding bit in *new* is used to update the control word. In other words, *fpcntrl* = ((*fpcntrl* **&** **~mask**) | (**new & mask**)) where *fpcntrl* is the floating-point control word.

Note The run-time libraries mask all floating-point exceptions by default.

_controlfp is a platform-independent, portable version of **_control87**. It is nearly identical to the **_control87** function on Intel (x86) platforms and is also supported by the MIPS and ALPHA platforms. To ensure that your floating-point code is portable to MIPS or ALPHA, use **_controlfp**. If you are targeting x86 platforms, use either **_control87** or **_controlfp**.

The difference between **_control87** and **_controlfp** is the way these two functions treat DENORMAL values. For Intel (x86) platforms, **_control87** can set and clear the DENORMAL OPERAND exception mask. ALPHA platforms do not support this exception, and **_controlfp** does not modify the DENORMAL OPERAND exception mask. The following example demonstrates the difference:

```
_control87( _EM_INVALID, _MCW_EM ); // DENORMAL is unmasked by this call
_controlfp( _EM_INVALID, _MCW_EM ); // DENORMAL exception mask remains unchanged
```

The possible values for the mask constant (mask) and new control values (new) are shown in Table R.1. Use the portable constants listed below (**_MCW_EM**, **_EM_INVALID**, and so forth) as arguments to these functions, rather than supplying the hexadecimal values explicitly.

ALPHA platforms support the DENORMAL input and output values in software. The default behavior of Windows NT on these platforms is to flush the DENORMAL input and output values to zero. **_controlfp** provides a new mask to preserve and flush the input and output DENORMAL values.

Intel (x86) platforms support the DENORMAL input and output values in hardware. The behavior is to preserve DENORMAL values. **_control87** does not provide a mask to change this behavior. The following example demonstrates this difference:

```
controlfp( _DN_SAVE, _MCW_DN); // Denormal values preserved by software on ALPHA.
                               // NOP on x86
controlfp( _DN_FLUSH, _MCW_DN);// Denormal values flushed to zero by hardware on Alpha.
                               // Ignored on x86
```

Table R.1 Hexadecimal Values

Mask	Hex Value	Constant	Hex Value
_MCW_DN (Denormal control)	0x03000000		
		_DN_SAVE	0x00000000
		_DN_FLUSH	0x01000000
_MCW_EM (Interrupt exception)	0x0008001F		
		_EM_INVALID	0x00000010
		_EM_DENORMAL	0x00080000
		_EM_ZERODIVIDE	0x00000008
		_EM_OVERFLOW	0x00000004
		_EM_UNDERFLOW	0x00000002
		_EM_INEXACT	0x00000001
_MCW_IC (Infinity control)	0x00040000		
		_IC_AFFINE	0x00040000
		_IC_PROJECTIVE	0x00000000
_MCW_RC (Rounding control)	0x00000300		
		_RC_CHOP	0x00000300
		_RC_UP	0x00000200
		_RC_DOWN	0x00000100
		_RC_NEAR	0x00000000
_MCW_PC (Precision control)	0x00030000		
		_PC_24 (24 bits)	0x00020000
		_PC_53 (53 bits)	0x00010000
		_PC_64 (64 bits)	0x00000000

Example

```
/* CNTRL87.C: This program uses _control87 to output the control
 * word, set the precision to 24 bits, and reset the status to
 * the default.
 */

#include <stdio.h>
#include <float.h>

void main( void )
{
    double a = 0.1;

    /* Show original control word and do calculation. */
    printf( "Original: 0x%.4x\n", _control87( 0, 0 ) );
    printf( "%1.1f * %1.1f = %.15e\n", a, a, a * a );

    /* Set precision to 24 bits and recalculate. */
    printf( "24-bit:   0x%.4x\n", _control87( _PC_24, MCW_PC ) );
    printf( "%1.1f * %1.1f = %.15e\n", a, a, a * a );

    /* Restore to default and recalculate. */
    printf( "Default:  0x%.4x\n",
            _control87( _CW_DEFAULT, 0xfffff ) );
    printf( "%1.1f * %1.1f = %.15e\n", a, a, a * a );
}
```

Output

```
Original: 0x9001f
0.1 * 0.1 = 1.000000000000000e-002
24-bit:   0xa001f
0.1 * 0.1 = 9.999999776482582e-003
Default:  0x001f
0.1 * 0.1 = 1.000000000000000e-002
```

See Also

_clear87, _status87

_copysign

Return one value with the sign of another.

double _copysign(double *x*, **double** *y* **);**

Routine	Required Header	Compatibility
_copysign	<float.h>	Win 95, Win NT

For additional compatibility information, see "Compatibility" in the Introduction.

Libraries

LIBC.LIB	Single thread static library, retail version
LIBCMT.LIB	Multithread static library, retail version
MSVCRT.LIB	Import library for MSVCRT.DLL, retail version

Return Value

_copysign returns its double-precision floating point argument x with the same sign as its double-precision floating-point argument y. There is no error return.

Parameters

x

    Double-precision floating-point value to be changed

y

    Double-precision floating-point value

See Also

fabs, **_chgsign**

cos, cosh

Calculate the cosine (**cos**) or hyperbolic cosine (**cosh**).

double cos(double *x* **);**
double cosh(double *x* **);**

Routine	Required Header	Compatibility
cos	<math.h>	ANSI, Win 95, Win NT
cosh	<math.h>	ANSI, Win 95, Win NT

For additional compatibility information, see "Compatibility" in the Introduction.

Libraries

LIBC.LIB	Single thread static library, retail version
LIBCMT.LIB	Multithread static library, retail version
MSVCRT.LIB	Import library for MSVCRT.DLL, retail version

Return Value

The **cos** and **cosh** functions return the cosine and hyperbolic cosine, respectively, of *x*.
If *x* is greater than or equal to 263, or less than or equal to –263, a loss of significance in
the result of a call to **cos** occurs, in which case the function generates a **_TLOSS** error and
returns an indefinite (same as a quiet NaN).

If the result is too large in a **cosh** call, the function returns **HUGE_VAL** and sets **errno** to
ERANGE. You can modify error handling with **_matherr**.

Parameter

x

Angle in radians

Example

```
/* SINCOS.C: This program displays the sine, hyperbolic
 * sine, cosine, and hyperbolic cosine of pi / 2.
 */

#include <math.h>
#include <stdio.h>

void main( void )
{
    double pi = 3.1415926535;
    double x, y;

    x = pi / 2;
    y = sin( x );
    printf( "sin( %f ) = %f\n", x, y );
    y = sinh( x );
    printf( "sinh( %f ) = %f\n",x, y );
    y = cos( x );
    printf( "cos( %f ) = %f\n", x, y );
    y = cosh( x );
    printf( "cosh( %f ) = %f\n",x, y );
}
```

Output

```
sin( 1.570796 ) = 1.000000
sinh( 1.570796 ) = 2.301299
cos( 1.570796 ) = 0.000000
cosh( 1.570796 ) = 2.509178
```

See Also

acos, **asin**, **atan**, **_matherr**, **sin**, **tan**

_cprintf

Formats and prints to the console.

int _cprintf(const char **format* [, *argument*] ... **);**

Routine	Required Header	Compatibility
_cprintf	<conio.h>	Win 95, Win NT

For additional compatibility information, see "Compatibility" in the Introduction.

Libraries

LIBC.LIB	Single thread static library, retail version
LIBCMT.LIB	Multithread static library, retail version
MSVCRT.LIB	Import library for MSVCRT.DLL, retail version

Return Value

_cprintf returns the number of characters printed.

Parameters

format
    Format-control string

argument
    Optional parameters

Remarks

The **_cprintf** function formats and prints a series of characters and values directly to the console, using the **_putch** function to output characters. Each *argument* (if any) is converted and output according to the corresponding format specification in *format*. The *format* has the same form and function as the *format* parameter for the printf function. Unlike the **fprintf**, **printf**, and **sprintf** functions, **_cprintf** does not translate linefeed characters into carriage return–linefeed (CR-LF) combinations on output.

Example

```
/* CPRINTF.C: This program displays
 * some variables to the console.
 */

#include <conio.h>

void main( void )
{
    int      i = -16, h = 29;
    unsigned u = 62511;
    char     c = 'A';
    char     s[] = "Test";

    /* Note that console output does not translate \n as
     * standard output does. Use \r\n instead.
     */
    _cprintf( "%d  %.4x  %u  %c %s\r\n", i, h, u, c, s );
}
```

Output

```
-16  001d  62511  A Test
```

See Also

_cscanf, fprintf, printf, sprintf, vfprintf

_cputs

Puts a string to the console.

int _cputs(const char *string* **);**

Routine	Required Header	Compatibility
_cputs	<conio.h>	Win 95, Win NT

For additional compatibility information, see "Compatibility" in the Introduction.

Libraries

LIBC.LIB	Single thread static library, retail version
LIBCMT.LIB	Multithread static library, retail version
MSVCRT.LIB	Import library for MSVCRT.DLL, retail version

Return Value

If successful, **_cputs** returns a 0. If the function fails, it returns a nonzero value.

Parameter

string

   Output string

Remarks

The **_cputs** function writes the null-terminated string pointed to by *string* directly to the console. A carriage return–linefeed (CR-LF) combination is not automatically appended to the string.

Example

```
/* CPUTS.C: This program first displays
 * a string to the console.
 */

#include <conio.h>

void main( void )
{
   /* String to print at console.
   * Note the \r (return) character.
   */
   char *buffer = "Hello world (courtesy of _cputs)!\r\n";

   _cputs( buffer );
}
```

Output

```
Hello world (courtesy of _cputs)!
```

See Also

_putch

_creat, _wcreat

Creates a new file.

int _creat(const char **filename*, **int** *pmode* **);**
int _wcreat(const wchar_t **filename*, **int** *pmode* **);**

Routine	Required Header	Optional Headers	Compatibility
_creat	<io.h>	<sys/types.h>, <sys/stat.h>, <errno.h>	Win 95, Win NT
_wcreat	<io.h> or <wchar.h>	<sys/types.h>, <sys/stat.h>, <errno.h>	Win NT

For additional compatibility information, see "Compatibility" in the Introduction.

Libraries

LIBC.LIB	Single thread static library, retail version
LIBCMT.LIB	Multithread static library, retail version
MSVCRT.LIB	Import library for MSVCRT.DLL, retail version

Return Value

Each of these functions, if successful, returns a handle to the created file. Otherwise the function returns –1 and sets **errno** as follows.

errno Setting	Description
EACCES	Filename specifies an existing read-only file or specifies a directory instead of a file
EMFILE	No more file handles are available
ENOENT	The specified file could not be found

Parameters

filename
   Name of new file

pmode
   Permission setting

Remarks

The **_creat** function creates a new file or opens and truncates an existing one. **_wcreat** is a wide-character version of **_creat**; the *filename* argument to **_wcreat** is a wide-character string. **_wcreat** and **_creat** behave identically otherwise.

Generic-Text Routine Mappings

TCHAR.H Routine	_UNICODE & _MBCS Not Defined	_MBCS Defined	_UNICODE Defined
_tcreat	_creat	_creat	_wcreat

If the file specified by *filename* does not exist, a new file is created with the given permission setting and is opened for writing. If the file already exists and its permission setting allows writing, **_creat** truncates the file to length 0, destroying the previous contents, and opens it for writing. The permission setting, *pmode*, applies to newly created files only. The new file receives the specified permission setting after it is closed for the first time. The integer expression pmode contains one or both of the manifest constants **_S_IWRITE** and **_S_IREAD**, defined in SYS\STAT.H. When both constants are given, they are joined with the bitwise-OR operator (|). The *pmode* parameter is set to one of the following values:

_S_IWRITE
   Writing permitted

_S_IREAD

Reading permitted

_S_IREAD | _S_IWRITE

Reading and writing permitted

If write permission is not given, the file is read-only. All files are always readable; it is impossible to give write-only permission. Thus the modes **_S_IWRITE** and **_S_IREAD | _S_IWRITE** are equivalent. Files opened using **_creat** are always opened in compatibility mode (see _sopen) with **_SH_DENYNO**.

_creat applies the current file-permission mask to *pmode* before setting the permissions (see _umask). **_creat** is provided primarily for compatibility with previous libraries. A call to **_open** with **_O_CREAT** and **_O_TRUNC** in the *oflag* parameter is equivalent to **_creat** and is preferable for new code.

Example

```
/* CREAT.C: This program uses _creat to create
 * the file (or truncate the existing file)
 * named data and open it for writing.
 */

#include <sys/types.h>
#include <sys/stat.h>
#include <io.h>
#include <stdio.h>
#include <stdlib.h>

void main( void )
{
   int fh;

   fh = _creat( "data", _S_IREAD | _S_IWRITE );
   if( fh == -1 )
      perror( "Couldn't create data file" );
   else
   {
      printf( "Created data file.\n" );
      _close( fh );
   }
}
```

Output

```
Created data file.
```

See Also

_chmod, _chsize, _close, _dup, _open, _sopen, _umask

_cscanf

Reads formatted data from the console.

int _cscanf(const char **format* [, *argument*] ... **);**

Routine	Required Header	Compatibility
_cscanf	<conio.h>	Win 95, Win NT

For additional compatibility information, see "Compatibility" in the Introduction.

Libraries

LIBC.LIB	Single thread static library, retail version
LIBCMT.LIB	Multithread static library, retail version
MSVCRT.LIB	Import library for MSVCRT.DLL, retail version

Return Value

_cscanf returns the number of fields that were successfully converted and assigned. The return value does not include fields that were read but not assigned. The return value is **EOF** for an attempt to read at end of file. This can occur when keyboard input is redirected at the operating-system command-line level. A return value of 0 means that no fields were assigned.

Parameters

format
    Format-control string

argument
    Optional parameters

Remarks

The **_cscanf** function reads data directly from the console into the locations given by *argument*. The _getche function is used to read characters. Each optional parameter must be a pointer to a variable with a type that corresponds to a type specifier in *format*. The format controls the interpretation of the input fields and has the same form and function as the *format* parameter for the scanf function. While **_cscanf** normally echoes the input character, it does not do so if the last call was to **_ungetch**.

Example

```
/* CSCANF.C: This program prompts for a string
 * and uses _cscanf to read in the response.
 * Then _cscanf returns the number of items
 * matched, and the program displays that number.
 */
```

```
#include <stdio.h>
#include <conio.h>

void main( void )
{
   int   result, i[3];

   _cprintf( "Enter three integers: " );
   result = _cscanf( "%i %i %i", &i[0], &i[1], &i[2] );
   _cprintf( "\r\nYou entered " );
   while( result-- )
      _cprintf( "%i ", i[result] );
   _cprintf( "\r\n" );
}
```

Output

```
Enter three integers: 1  2  3
You entered 3 2 1
```

See Also

_cprintf, fscanf, scanf, sscanf

ctime, _wctime

Convert a time value to a string and adjust for local time zone settings.

char *ctime(const time_t *timer **);**
wchar_t *_wctime(const time_t *timer **);**

Routine	Required Header	Compatibility
ctime	<time.h>	ANSI, Win 95, Win NT
_wctime	<time.h> or <wchar.h>	Win 95, Win NT

For additional compatibility information, see "Compatibility" in the Introduction.

Libraries

LIBC.LIB	Single thread static library, retail version
LIBCMT.LIB	Multithread static library, retail version
MSVCRT.LIB	Import library for MSVCRT.DLL, retail version

Return Value

Each of these functions returns a pointer to the character string result. If time represents a date before midnight, January 1, 1970, UTC, the function returns **NULL**.

Parameter

timer
    Pointer to stored time

Remarks

The **ctime** function converts a time value stored as a time_t structure into a character string. The *timer* value is usually obtained from a call to time, which returns the number of seconds elapsed since midnight (00:00:00), January 1, 1970, coordinated universal time (UTC). The string result produced by **ctime** contains exactly 26 characters and has the form:

```
Wed Jan 02 02:03:55 1980\n\0
```

A 24-hour clock is used. All fields have a constant width. The newline character (`'\n'`) and the null character (`'\0'`) occupy the last two positions of the string.

The converted character string is also adjusted according to the local time zone settings. See the time, _ftime, and localtime functions for information on configuring the local time and the _tzset function for details about defining the time zone environment and global variables.

A call to **ctime** modifies the single statically allocated buffer used by the **gmtime** and **localtime** functions. Each call to one of these routines destroys the result of the previous call. **ctime** shares a static buffer with the **asctime** function. Thus, a call to **ctime** destroys the results of any previous call to **asctime**, **localtime**, or **gmtime**.

_wctime is a wide-character version of **ctime**; **_wctime** returns a pointer to a wide-character string. **_wctbime** and **ctime** behave identically otherwise.

Generic-Text Routine Mappings

TCHAR.H Routine	_UNICODE & _MBCS Not Defined	_MBCS Defined	_UNICODE Defined
_tctime	ctime	ctime	_wctime

Example

```c
/* CTIME.C: This program gets the current
 * time in time_t form, then uses ctime to
 * display the time in string form.
 */

#include <time.h>
#include <stdio.h>

void main( void )
{
    time_t ltime;

    time( &ltime );
    printf( "The time is %s\n", ctime( &ltime ) );
}
```

Output

```
The time is Fri Apr 29 12:25:12 1994
```

See Also

asctime, _ftime, gmtime, localtime, time

_cwait

Waits until another process terminates.

int _cwait(int *_termstat_, int _procHandle_, int _action_);

Routine	Required Header	Optional Headers	Compatibility
_cwait	<process.h>	<errno.h>	Win 95, Win NT

For additional compatibility information, see "Compatibility" in the Introduction.

Libraries

LIBC.LIB	Single thread static library, retail version
LIBCMT.LIB	Multithread static library, retail version
MSVCRT.LIB	Import library for MSVCRT.DLL, retail version

Return Value

When the specified process has "successfully" completed, **_cwait** returns the handle of the specified process and sets _termstat_ to the result code returned by the specified process. Otherwise, **_cwait** returns –1 and sets _errno_ as follows.

Value	Description
ECHILD	No specified process exists, procHandle is invalid, or the call to the GetExitCodeProcess or WaitForSingleObject API failed
EINVAL	action is invalid

Parameters

termstat
  Pointer to a buffer where the result code of the specified process will be stored, or NULL

procHandle
  Handle to the current process or thread

action
  NULL: Ignored by Windows NT and Windows 95 applications; for other applications: action code to perform on _procHandle_

Remarks

The **_cwait** function waits for the termination of the process ID of the specified process that is provided by *procHandle*. The value of *procHandle* passed to **_cwait** should be the value returned by the call to the _spawn function that created the specified process. If the process ID terminates before **_cwait** is called, **_cwait** returns immediately. **_cwait** can be used by any process to wait for any other known process for which a valid handle (*procHandle*) exists.

termstat points to a buffer where the return code of the specified process will be stored. The value of *termstat* indicates whether the specified process terminated "normally" by calling the Windows NT **ExitProcess** API. ExitProcess is called internally if the specified process calls **exit** or **_exit**, returns from **main**, or reaches the end of **main**. See **GetExitCodeProcess** for more information regarding the value passed back through *termstat*. If **_cwait** is called with a NULL value for *termstat*, the return code of the specified process will not be stored.

The *action* parameter is ignored by Windows NT and Windows 95 because parent-child relationships are not implemented in these environments. Therefore, the OS/2 **wait** function, which allows a parent process to wait for any of its immediate children to terminate, is not available.

Example

```
/* CWAIT.C: This program launches several processes and waits
 * for a specified process to finish.
 */

#include <windows.h>
#include <process.h>
#include <stdlib.h>
#include <stdio.h>
#include <time.h>

/* Macro to get a random integer within a specified range */
#define getrandom( min, max ) (( rand() % (int)((( max ) + 1 ) - ( min ))) + ( min ))

struct PROCESS
{

    int     nPid;
    char    name[40];

} process[4] = { { 0, "Ann" }, { 0, "Beth" }, { 0, "Carl" }, { 0, "Dave" } };
```

```
void main( int argc, char *argv[] )
{
    int termstat, c;

    srand( (unsigned)time( NULL ) );     /* Seed randomizer */
    /* If no arguments, this is the calling process */
    if( argc == 1 )
    {

        /* Spawn processes in numeric order */
        for( c = 0; c < 4; c++ ){
            _flushall();
            process[c].nPid = spawnl( _P_NOWAIT, argv[0], argv[0],
                             process[c].name, NULL );
        }

        /* Wait for randomly specified process, and respond when done */
        c = getrandom( 0, 3 );
        printf( "Come here, %s.\n", process[c].name );
        _cwait( &termstat, process[c].nPid, _WAIT_CHILD );
        printf( "Thank you, %s.\n", process[c].name );
    }

    /* If there are arguments, this must be a spawned process */
    else
    {
        /* Delay for a period determined by process number */
        Sleep( (argv[1][0] - 'A' + 1) * 1000L );
        printf( "Hi, Dad. It's %s.\n", argv[1] );
    }
}
```

Output

```
Hi, Dad. It's Ann.
Come here, Ann.
Thank you, Ann.
Hi, Dad. It's Beth.
Hi, Dad. It's Carl.
Hi, Dad. It's Dave.
```

See Also

_spawn Functions

difftime

Finds the difference between two times.

double difftime(time_t *timer1***, time_t** *timer0* **);**

Routine	Required Header	Compatibility
difftime	<time.h>	ANSI, Win 95, Win NT

For additional compatibility information, see "Compatibility" in the Introduction.

Libraries

LIBC.LIB	Single thread static library, retail version
LIBCMT.LIB	Multithread static library, retail version
MSVCRT.LIB	Import library for MSVCRT.DLL, retail version

Return Value

difftime returns the elapsed time in seconds, from *timer0* to *timer1*. The value returned is a double-precision floating-point number.

Parameters

timer1
  Ending time

timer0
  Beginning time

Remarks

The **difftime** function computes the difference between the two supplied time values *timer0* and *timer1*.

Example

```
/* DIFFTIME.C: This program calculates the amount of time
 * needed to do a floating-point multiply 10 million times.
 */

#include <stdio.h>
#include <stdlib.h>
#include <time.h>
```

```
void main( void )
{
    time_t    start, finish;
    long loop;
    double    result, elapsed_time;

    printf( "Multiplying 2 floating point numbers 10 million times...\n" );
    time( &start );
    for( loop = 0; loop < 10000000; loop++ )
        result = 3.63 * 5.27;
    time( &finish );
    elapsed_time = difftime( finish, start );
    printf( "\nProgram takes %6.0f seconds.\n", elapsed_time );
}
```

Output

```
Multiplying 2 floats 10 million times...
Program takes      2 seconds.
```

See Also

time

div

Computes the quotient and the remainder of two integer values.

div_t div(int *numer*, **int** *denom* **);**

Routine	Required Header	Compatibility
div	<stdlib.h>	ANSI, Win 95, Win NT

For additional compatibility information, see "Compatibility" in the Introduction.

Libraries

LIBC.LIB	Single thread static library, retail version
LIBCMT.LIB	Multithread static library, retail version
MSVCRT.LIB	Import library for MSVCRT.DLL, retail version

Return Value

div returns a structure of type **div_t**, comprising the quotient and the remainder.
The structure is defined in STDLIB.H.

Parameters

numer
    Numerator

denom
    Denominator

Remarks

The **div** function divides *numer* by *denom*, computing the quotient and the remainder. The div_t structure contains **int quot**, the quotient, and **int rem**, the remainder. The sign of the quotient is the same as that of the mathematical quotient. Its absolute value is the largest integer that is less than the absolute value of the mathematical quotient. If the denominator is 0, the program terminates with an error message.

Example

```
/* DIV.C: This example takes two integers as command-line
 * arguments and displays the results of the integer
 * division. This program accepts two arguments on the
 * command line following the program name, then calls
 * div to divide the first argument by the second.
 * Finally, it prints the structure members quot and rem.
 */

#include <stdlib.h>
#include <stdio.h>
#include <math.h>

void main( int argc, char *argv[] )
{
    int x,y;
    div_t div_result;

    x = atoi( argv[1] );
    y = atoi( argv[2] );

    printf( "x is %d, y is %d\n", x, y );
    div_result = div( x, y );
    printf( "The quotient is %d, and the remainder is %d\n",
            div_result.quot, div_result.rem );
}
```

Output

```
x is 876, y is 13
The quotient is 67, and the remainder is 5
```

See Also

ldiv

_dup, _dup2

Create a second handle for an open file (**_dup**), or reassign a file handle (**_dup2**).

int_dup(int *handle* **);**
int _dup2(int *handle1***, int** *handle2* **);**

Routine	Required Header	Compatibility
_dup	<io.h>	Win 95, Win NT
_dup2	<io.h>	Win 95, Win NT

For additional compatibility information, see "Compatibility" in the Introduction.

Libraries

LIBC.LIB	Single thread static library, retail version
LIBCMT.LIB	Multithread static library, retail version
MSVCRT.LIB	Import library for MSVCRT.DLL, retail version

Return Value

_dup returns a new file handle. **_dup2** returns 0 to indicate success. If an error occurs, each function returns –1 and sets **errno** to **EBADF** if the file handle is invalid, or to **EMFILE** if no more file handles are available.

Parameters

handle, handle1
    Handles referring to open file

handle2
    Any handle value

Remarks

The **_dup** and **_dup2** functions associate a second file handle with a currently open file. These functions can be used to associate a predefined file handle, such as that for **stdout**, with a different file. Operations on the file can be carried out using either file handle. The type of access allowed for the file is unaffected by the creation of a new handle. **_dup** returns the next available file handle for the given file. **_dup2** forces *handle2* to refer to the same file as *handle1*. If *handle2* is associated with an open file at the time of the call, that file is closed.

Both **_dup** and **_dup2** accept file handles as parameters. To pass a stream (**FILE ***) to either of these functions, use _fileno. The **fileno** routine returns the file handle currently associated with the given stream. The following example shows how to associate **stderr** (defined as **FILE *** in STDIO.H) with a handle:

```
cstderr = _dup( _fileno( stderr ));
```

Example

```
/* DUP.C: This program uses the variable old to save
 * the original stdout. It then opens a new file named
 * new and forces stdout to refer to it. Finally, it
 * restores stdout to its original state.
 */

#include <io.h>
#include <stdlib.h>
#include <stdio.h>

void main( void )
{
   int old;
   FILE *new;

   old = _dup( 1 );    /* "old" now refers to "stdout" */
                       /* Note:  file handle 1 == "stdout" */
   if( old == -1 )
   {
      perror( "_dup( 1 ) failure" );
      exit( 1 );
   }
   write( old, "This goes to stdout first\r\n", 27 );
   if( ( new = fopen( "data", "w" ) ) == NULL )
   {
      puts( "Can't open file 'data'\n" );
      exit( 1 );
   }

   /* stdout now refers to file "data" */
   if( -1 == _dup2( _fileno( new ), 1 ) )
   {
      perror( "Can't _dup2 stdout" );
      exit( 1 );
   }
   puts( "This goes to file 'data'\r\n" );
   /* Flush stdout stream buffer so it goes to correct file */
   fflush( stdout ); fclose( new );
   /* Restore original stdout */
   _dup2( old, 1 );
   puts( "This goes to stdout\n" );
   puts( "The file 'data' contains:" );
   system( "type data" );
}
```

Output

```
This goes to stdout first
This goes to file 'data'

This goes to stdout
The file 'data' contains:
This goes to file 'data'
```
See Also

_close, _creat, _open

_ecvt

Converts a double number to a string.

char *_ecvt(double *value*, **int** *count*, **int** *dec, **int** *sign **);**

Function	Required Header	Compatibility
_ecvt	<stdlib.h>	Win 95, Win NT

For additional compatibility information, see "Compatibility" in the Introduction.

Libraries

LIBC.LIB	Single thread static library, retail version
LIBCMT.LIB	Multithread static library, retail version
MSVCRT.LIB	Import library for MSVCRT.DLL, retail version

Return Value

_ecvt returns a pointer to the string of digits. There is no error return.

Parameters

value
Number to be converted

count
Number of digits stored

dec
Stored decimal-point position

sign
Sign of converted number

Remarks

The **_ecvt** function converts a floating-point number to a character string. The *value* parameter is the floating-point number to be converted. This function stores up to *count* digits of value as a string and appends a null character ('\0'). If the number of digits in *value* exceeds *count*, the low-order digit is rounded. If there are fewer than *count* digits, the string is padded with zeros.

Only digits are stored in the string. The position of the decimal point and the sign of *value* can be obtained from *dec* and *sign* after the call. The *dec* parameter points to an integer value giving the position of the decimal point with respect to the beginning of the string. A 0 or negative integer value indicates that the decimal point lies to the left of the first digit. The *sign* parameter points to an integer that indicates the sign of the converted number. If the integer value is 0, the number is positive. Otherwise, the number is negative.

_ecvt and **_fcvt** use a single statically allocated buffer for the conversion. Each call to one of these routines destroys the result of the previous call.

Example

```
/* ECVT.C: This program uses _ecvt to convert a
 * floating-point number to a character string.
 */

#include <stdlib.h>
#include <stdio.h>

void main( void )
{
    int     decimal,  sign;
    char    *buffer;
    int     precision = 10;
    double  source = 3.1415926535;

    buffer = _ecvt( source, precision, &decimal, &sign );
    printf( "source: %2.10f    buffer: '%s'   decimal: %d   sign: %d\n",
            source, buffer, decimal, sign );
}
```

Output

```
source: 3.1415926535    buffer: '3141592654'   decimal: 1    sign: 0
```

See Also

atof, _fcvt, _gcvt

_endthread, _endthreadex

void _endthread(void);
void _endthreadex(unsigned *retval* **);**

Function	Required Header	Compatibility
_endthread	<process.h>	Win 95, Win NT
_endthreadex	<process.h>	Win 95, Win NT

For additional compatibility information, see "Compatibility" in the Introduction.

Libraries

LIBCMT.LIB	Multithread static library, retail version
MSVCRT.LIB	Import library for MSVCRT.DLL, retail version

Return Value

None

Parameter

retval
    Thread exit code

Remarks

The **_endthread** and **_endthreadex** functions terminate a thread created by **_beginthread** or **_beginthreadex**, respectively. You can call **_endthread** or **_endthreadex** explicitly to terminate a thread; however, **_endthread** or **_endthreadex** is called automatically when the thread returns from the routine passed as a parameter to **_beginthread** or **_beginthreadex**. Terminating a thread with a call to **endthread** or **_endthreadex** helps to ensure proper recovery of resources allocated for the thread.

> **Note** For an executable file linked with LIBCMT.LIB, do not call the Win32 **ExitThread** API; this prevents the run-time system from reclaiming allocated resources. **_endthread** and **_endthreadex** reclaim allocated thread resources and then call **ExitThread**.

_endthread automatically closes the thread handle. (This behavior differs from the Win32 ExitThread API.) Therefore, when you use **_beginthread** and **_endthread**, do not explicitly close the thread handle by calling the Win32 **CloseHandle** API.

Like the Win32 **ExitThread** API, **_endthreadex** does not close the thread handle. Therefore, when you use **_beginthreadex** and **_endthreadex**, you must close the thread handle by calling the Win32 **CloseHandle** API.

Example

```
/* BEGTHRD.C illustrates multiple threads using functions:
 *
 *      _beginthread            _endthread
 *
 *
 * This program requires the multithreaded library. For example,
 * compile with the following command line:
 *     CL /MT /D "_X86_" BEGTHRD.C
 *
 * If you are using the Visual C++ development environment, select the
 * Multi-Threaded runtime library in the compiler Project Options dialog
 * box.
 *
 */

#include <windows.h>
#include <process.h>    /* _beginthread, _endthread */
#include <stddef.h>
#include <stdlib.h>
#include <conio.h>

void Bounce( void *ch );
void CheckKey( void *dummy );

/* GetRandom returns a random integer between min and max. */
#define GetRandom( min, max ) ((rand() % (int)(((max) + 1) - (min))) + (min))

BOOL repeat = TRUE;       /* Global repeat flag and video variable */
HANDLE hStdOut;           /* Handle for console window */
CONSOLE_SCREEN_BUFFER_INFO csbi;    /* Console information structure */

void main()
{
    CHAR    ch = 'A';

    hStdOut = GetStdHandle( STD_OUTPUT_HANDLE );

    /* Get display screen's text row and column information. */
    GetConsoleScreenBufferInfo( hStdOut, &csbi );

    /* Launch CheckKey thread to check for terminating keystroke. */
    _beginthread( CheckKey, 0, NULL );
```

```
        /* Loop until CheckKey terminates program. */
        while( repeat )
        {
                /* On first loops, launch character threads. */
                _beginthread( Bounce, 0, (void *) (ch++)  );

                /* Wait one second between loops. */
                Sleep( 1000L );
        }
}


/* CheckKey - Thread to wait for a keystroke, then clear repeat flag. */
void CheckKey( void *dummy )
{
    _getch();
    repeat = 0;     /* _endthread implied */

}

/* Bounce - Thread to create and and control a colored letter that moves
 * around on the screen.
 *
 * Params: ch - the letter to be moved
 */
void Bounce( void *ch )
{
    /* Generate letter and color attribute from thread argument. */
    char    blankcell = 0x20;
    char    blockcell = (char) ch;
    BOOL    first = TRUE;
    COORD   oldcoord, newcoord;
    DWORD   result;


    /* Seed random number generator and get initial location. */
    srand( _threadid );
    newcoord.X = GetRandom( 0, csbi.dwSize.X - 1 );
    newcoord.Y = GetRandom( 0, csbi.dwSize.Y - 1 );
    while( repeat )
    {
            /* Pause between loops. */
            Sleep( 100L );

            /* Blank out our old position on the screen, and draw new letter. */
            if( first )
                first = FALSE;
        else
            WriteConsoleOutputCharacter( hStdOut, &blankcell, 1, oldcoord, &result );
            WriteConsoleOutputCharacter( hStdOut, &blockcell, 1, newcoord, &result );
```

```
      /* Increment the coordinate for next placement of the block. */
      oldcoord.X = newcoord.X;
      oldcoord.Y = newcoord.Y;
      newcoord.X += GetRandom( -1, 1 );
      newcoord.Y += GetRandom( -1, 1 );

      /* Correct placement (and beep) if about to go off the screen. */
      if( newcoord.X < 0 )
         newcoord.X = 1;
   else if( newcoord.X == csbi.dwSize.X )
         newcoord.X = csbi.dwSize.X - 2;
   else if( newcoord.Y < 0 )
         newcoord.Y = 1;
   else if( newcoord.Y == csbi.dwSize.Y )
         newcoord.Y = csbi.dwSize.Y - 2;

   /* If not at a screen border, continue, otherwise beep. */
      else
         continue;
      Beep( ((char) ch - 'A') * 100, 175 );
   }
   /* _endthread given to terminate */
   _endthread();
}
```

See Also

_beginthread

_eof

Tests for end-of-file.

int _eof(int *handle* **);**

Function	Required Header	Optional Headers	Compatibility
_eof	<io.h>	<errno.h>	Win 95, Win NT

For additional compatibility information, see "Compatibility" in the Introduction.

Libraries

LIBC.LIB	Single thread static library, retail version
LIBCMT.LIB	Multithread static library, retail version
MSVCRT.LIB	Import library for MSVCRT.DLL, retail version

Return Value

_eof returns 1 if the current position is end of file, or 0 if it is not. A return value of −1 indicates an error; in this case, **errno** is set to **EBADF**, which indicates an invalid file handle.

Parameter

handle

   Handle referring to open file

Remarks

The **_eof** function determines whether the end of the file associated with **handle** has been reached.

Example

```
/* EOF.C: This program reads data from a file
 * ten bytes at a time until the end of the
 * file is reached or an error is encountered.
 */
#include <io.h>
#include <fcntl.h>
#include <stdio.h>
#include <stdlib.h>
void main( void )
{
    int   fh, count, total = 0;
    char buf[10];
    if( (fh = _open( "eof.c", _O_RDONLY )) == - 1 )
    {
        perror( "Open failed");
        exit( 1 );
    }
    /* Cycle until end of file reached: */
    while( !_eof( fh ) )
    {
        /* Attempt to read in 10 bytes: */
        if( (count = _read( fh, buf, 10 )) == -1 )
        {
            perror( "Read error" );
            break;
        }
        /* Total actual bytes read */
        total += count;
    }
    printf( "Number of bytes read = %d\n", total );
    _close( fh );
}
```

```
Number of bytes read = 754
```

See Also

clearerr, feof, ferror, perror

_exec, _wexec Functions

Each of the functions in this family loads and executes a new process.

_execl, _wexecl	_execv, _wexecv
_execle, _wexecle	_execve, _wexecve
_execlp, _wexeclp	_execvp, _wexecvp
_execlpe, _wexeclpe	_execvpe, _wexecvpe

The letter(s) at the end of the function name determine the variation.

_exec Function Suffix	Description
e	*envp*, array of pointers to environment settings, is passed to new process.
l	Command-line arguments are passed individually to **_exec** function. Typically used when number of parameters to new process is known in advance.
p	**PATH** environment variable is used to find file to execute.
v	*argv*, array of pointers to command-line arguments, is passed to **_exec**. Typically used when number of parameters to new process is variable.

Remarks

Each of the **_exec** functions loads and execute a new process. All **_exec** functions use the same operating-system function. The **_exec** functions automatically handle multibyte-character string arguments as appropriate, recognizing multibyte-character sequences according to the multibyte code page currently in use. The **_wexec** functions are wide-character versions of the **_exec** functions. The **_wexec** functions behave identically to their **_exec** family counterparts except that they do not handle multibyte-character strings.

Generic-Text Routine Mappings:

TCHAR.H Routine	_UNICODE & _MBCS Not Defined	_MBCS Defined	_UNICODE Defined
_texecl	_execl	_execl	_wexecl
_texecle	_execle	_execle	_wexecle
_texeclp	_execlp	_execlp	_wexeclp
_texeclpe	_execlpe	_execlpe	_wexeclpe
_texecv	_execv	_execv	_wexecv
_texecve	_execve	_execve	_wexecve
_texecvp	_execvp	_execvp	_wexecvp
_texecvpe	_execvpe	_execvpe	_wexecvpe

When a call to an **_exec** function is successful, the new process is placed in the memory previously occupied by the calling process. Sufficient memory must be available for loading and executing the new process.

The *cmdname* parameter specifies the file to be executed as the new process. It can specify a full path (from the root), a partial path (from the current working directory), or a filename. If *cmdname* does not have a filename extension or does not end with a period (.), the **_exec** function searches for the named file. If the search is unsuccessful, it tries the same base name with the .COM extension and then with the .EXE, .BAT, and .CMD extensions. If *cmdname* has an extension, only that extension is used in the search. If *cmdname* ends with a period, the **_exec** function searches for *cmdname* with no extension. **_execlp**, **_execlpe**, **_execvp**, and **_execvpe** search for *cmdname* (using the same procedures) in the directories specified by the PATH environment variable. If *cmdname* contains a drive specifier or any slashes (that is, if it is a relative path), the **_exec** call searches only for the specified file; the path is not searched.

Parameters are passed to the new process by giving one or more pointers to character strings as parameters in the **_exec** call. These character strings form the parameter list for the new process. The combined length of the inherited environment settings and the strings forming the parameter list for the new process must not exceed 32K bytes. The terminating null character ('\0') for each string is not included in the count, but space characters (inserted automatically to separate the parameters) are counted.

The argument pointers can be passed as separate parameters (in **_execl**, **_execle**, **_execlp**, and **_execlpe**) or as an array of pointers (in **_execv**, **_execve**, **_execvp**, and **_execvpe**). At least one parameter, *arg0*, must be passed to the new process; this parameter is *argv*[0] of the new process. Usually, this parameter is a copy of *cmdname*. (A different value does not produce an error.)

The **_execl**, **_execle**, **_execlp**, and **_execlpe** calls are typically used when the number of parameters is known in advance. The parameter *arg0* is usually a pointer to *cmdname*. The parameters *arg1* through *argn* point to the character strings forming the new parameter list. A null pointer must follow *argn* to mark the end of the parameter list.

The **_execv**, **_execve**, **_execvp**, and **_execvpe** calls are useful when the number of parameters to the new process is variable. Pointers to the parameters are passed as an array, *argv*. The parameter *argv*[0] is usually a pointer to *cmdname*. The parameters *argv*[1] through *argv*[n] point to the character strings forming the new parameter list. The parameter *argv*[n+1] must be a **NULL** pointer to mark the end of the parameter list.

Files that are open when an **_exec** call is made remain open in the new process. In **_execl**, **_execlp**, **_execv**, and **_execvp** calls, the new process inherits the environment of the calling process. **_execle**, **_execlpe**, **_execve**, and **_execvpe** calls alter the environment for the new process by passing a list of environment settings through the *envp* parameter. *envp* is an array of character pointers, each element of which (except for the final element) points to a null-terminated string defining an environment variable. Such a string usually has the form NAME=value where NAME is the name of an environment variable and value is the string value to which that variable is set. (Note that value is not enclosed in double quotation marks.) The final element of the *envp* array should be **NULL**. When *envp* itself is **NULL**, the new process inherits the environment settings of the calling process.

A program executed with one of the **_exec** functions is always loaded into memory as if the "maximum allocation" field in the program's .EXE file header were set to the default value of 0xFFFFH. You can use the EXEHDR utility to change the maximum allocation field of a program; however, such a program invoked with one of the **_exec** functions may behave differently from a program invoked directly from the operating-system command line or with one of the **_spawn** functions.

The **_exec** calls do not preserve the translation modes of open files. If the new process must use files inherited from the calling process, use the _setmode routine to set the translation mode of these files to the desired mode. You must explicitly flush (using **fflush** or **_flushall**) or close any stream before the **_exec** function call. Signal settings are not preserved in new processes that are created by calls to **_exec** routines. The signal settings are reset to the default in the new process.

Example

```
/* EXEC.C illustrates the different versions of exec including:
 *      _execl          _execle         _execlp         _execlpe
 *      _execv          _execve         _execvp         _execvpe
 *
 * Although EXEC.C can exec any program, you can verify how
 * different versions handle arguments and environment by
 * compiling and specifying the sample program ARGS.C. See
 * SPAWN.C for examples of the similar spawn functions.
 */
```

```
#include <stdio.h>
#include <conio.h>
#include <process.h>

char *my_env[] =                /* Environment for exec?e */
{
   "THIS=environment will be",
   "PASSED=to new process by",
   "the EXEC=functions",
   NULL
};

void main()
{
   char *args[4], prog[80];
   int ch;

   printf( "Enter name of program to exec: " );
   gets( prog );
   printf( " 1. _execl  2. _execle  3. _execlp  4. _execlpe\n" );
   printf( " 5. _execv  6. _execve  7. _execvp  8. _execvpe\n" );
   printf( "Type a number from 1 to 8 (or 0 to quit): " );
   ch = _getche();
   if( (ch < '1') || (ch > '8') )
      exit( 1 );
   printf( "\n\n" );

   /* Arguments for _execv? */
   args[0] = prog;
   args[1] = "exec??";
   args[2] = "two";
   args[3] = NULL;

   switch( ch )
   {
   case '1':
      _execl( prog, prog, "_execl", "two", NULL );
      break;
   case '2':
      _execle( prog, prog, "_execle", "two", NULL, my_env );
      break;
   case '3':
      _execlp( prog, prog, "_execlp", "two", NULL );
      break;
   case '4':
      _execlpe( prog, prog, "_execlpe", "two", NULL, my_env );
      break;
```

```
  case '5':
    _execv( prog, args );
    break;
  case '6':
    _execve( prog, args, my_env );
    break;
  case '7':
    _execvp( prog, args );
    break;
  case '8':
    _execvpe( prog, args, my_env );
    break;
  default:
    break;
  }

  /* This point is reached only if exec fails. */
  printf( "\nProcess was not execed." );
  exit( 0 );
}
```

See Also

abort, atexit, exit, _onexit, _spawn Function Overview, system

_execl, _wexecl

Load and execute new child processes.

int _execl(const char *cmdname*, **const char** *arg0*, **... const char** *argn*, **NULL**);
int _wexecl(const wchar_t *cmdname*, **const wchar_t** *arg0*, **... const wchar_t** *argn*, **NULL**);

Function	Required Header	Optional Headers	Compatibility
_execl	<process.h>	<errno.h>	Win 95, Win NT
_wexecl	<process.h> or <wchar.h>	<errno.h>	Win NT

For additional compatibility information, see "Compatibility" in the Introduction.

Libraries

LIBC.LIB	Single thread static library, retail version
LIBCMT.LIB	Multithread static library, retail version
MSVCRT.LIB	Import library for MSVCRT.DLL, retail version

Return Value

If successful, these functions do not return to the calling process. A return value of −1 indicates an error, in which case the **errno** global variable is set.

errno Value	Description
E2BIG	The space required for the arguments and environment settings exceeds 32K.
EACCES	The specified file has a locking or sharing violation.
EMFILE	Too many files open (the specified file must be opened to determine whether it is executable).
ENOENT	File or path not found.
ENOEXEC	The specified file is not executable or has an invalid executable-file format.
ENOMEM	Not enough memory is available to execute the new process; or the available memory has been corrupted; or an invalid block exists, indicating that the calling process was not allocated properly.

Parameters

cmdname
   Path of file to be executed

arg0, ... argn
   List of pointers to parameters

Remarks

Each of these functions loads and executes a new process, passing each command-line argument as a separate parameter.

Example

```
/* EXEC.C illustrates the different versions of exec including:
 *      _execl          _execle         _execlp         _execlpe
 *      _execv          _execve         _execvp         _execvpe
 *
 * Although EXEC.C can exec any program, you can verify how
 * different versions handle arguments and environment by
 * compiling and specifying the sample program ARGS.C. See
 * SPAWN.C for examples of the similar spawn functions.
 */

#include <stdio.h>
#include <conio.h>
#include <process.h>
```

```c
char *my_env[] =                 /* Environment for exec?e */
{
    "THIS=environment will be",
    "PASSED=to new process by",
    "the EXEC=functions",
    NULL
};

void main()
{
    char *args[4], prog[80];
    int ch;

    printf( "Enter name of program to exec: " );
    gets( prog );
    printf( " 1. _execl  2. _execle  3. _execlp  4. _execlpe\n" );
    printf( " 5. _execv  6. _execve  7. _execvp  8. _execvpe\n" );
    printf( "Type a number from 1 to 8 (or 0 to quit): " );
    ch = _getche();
    if( (ch < '1') || (ch > '8') )
        exit( 1 );
    printf( "\n\n" );

    /* Arguments for _execv? */
    args[0] = prog;
    args[1] = "exec??";
    args[2] = "two";
    args[3] = NULL;

    switch( ch )
    {
    case '1':
        _execl( prog, prog, "_execl", "two", NULL );
        break;
    case '2':
        _execle( prog, prog, "_execle", "two", NULL, my_env );
        break;
    case '3':
        _execlp( prog, prog, "_execlp", "two", NULL );
        break;
    case '4':
        _execlpe( prog, prog, "_execlpe", "two", NULL, my_env );
        break;
    case '5':
        _execv( prog, args );
        break;
    case '6':
        _execve( prog, args, my_env );
        break;
```

```
    case '7':
       _execvp( prog, args );
       break;
    case '8':
       _execvpe( prog, args, my_env );
       break;
    default:
       break;
    }

    /* This point is reached only if exec fails. */
    printf( "\nProcess was not execed." );
    exit( 0 );
}
```

See Also

abort, atexit, exit, _onexit, _spawn Function Overview, system

_execle, _wexecle

Load and execute new child processes.

int **_execle**(**const char** *cmdname, **const char** *arg0, ... **const char** *argn,
    NULL, const char *const *envp);
int **_wexecle**(**const wchar_t** *cmdname, **const wchar_t** *arg0, ... **const wchar_t** *argn,
    NULL, const char *const *envp);

Function	Required Header	Optional Headers	Compatibility
_execle	<process.h>	<errno.h>	Win 95, Win NT
_wexecle	<process.h> or <wchar.h>	<errno.h>	Win NT

For additional compatibility information, see "Compatibility" in the Introduction.

Libraries

LIBC.LIB	Single thread static library, retail version
LIBCMT.LIB	Multithread static library, retail version
MSVCRT.LIB	Import library for MSVCRT.DLL, retail version

Return Value

If successful, these functions do not return to the calling process. A return value of –1
indicates an error, in which case the **errno** global variable is set.

errno Value	Description
E2BIG	The space required for the arguments and environment settings exceeds 32K.
EACCES	The specified file has a locking or sharing violation.
EMFILE	Too many files open (the specified file must be opened to determine whether it is executable).
ENOENT	File or path not found.
ENOEXEC	The specified file is not executable or has an invalid executable-file format.
ENOMEM	Not enough memory is available to execute the new process; or the available memory has been corrupted; or an invalid block exists, indicating that the calling process was not allocated properly.

Parameters

cmdname
Path of file to execute

arg0, ... argn
List of pointers to parameters

envp
Array of pointers to environment settings

Remarks

Each of these functions loads and executes a new process, passing each command-line argument as a separate parameter and also passing an array of pointers to environment settings.

Example

```
/* EXEC.C illustrates the different versions of exec including:
 *      _execl          _execle         _execlp         _execlpe
 *      _execv          _execve         _execvp         _execvpe
 *
 * Although EXEC.C can exec any program, you can verify how
 * different versions handle arguments and environment by
 * compiling and specifying the sample program ARGS.C. See
 * SPAWN.C for examples of the similar spawn functions.
 */

#include <stdio.h>
#include <conio.h>
#include <process.h>
```

```
char *my_env[] =                    /* Environment for exec?e */
{
    "THIS=environment will be",
    "PASSED=to new process by",
    "the EXEC=functions",
    NULL
};

void main()
{
    char *args[4], prog[80];
    int ch;

    printf( "Enter name of program to exec: " );
    gets( prog );
    printf( " 1. _execl  2. _execle  3. _execlp  4. _execlpe\n" );
    printf( " 5. _execv  6. _execve  7. _execvp  8. _execvpe\n" );
    printf( "Type a number from 1 to 8 (or 0 to quit): " );
    ch = _getche();
    if( (ch < '1') || (ch > '8') )
        exit( 1 );
    printf( "\n\n" );

    /* Arguments for _execv? */
    args[0] = prog;
    args[1] = "exec??";
    args[2] = "two";
    args[3] = NULL;

    switch( ch )
    {
    case '1':
        _execl( prog, prog, "_execl", "two", NULL );
        break;
    case '2':
        _execle( prog, prog, "_execle", "two", NULL, my_env );
        break;
    case '3':
        _execlp( prog, prog, "_execlp", "two", NULL );
        break;
    case '4':
        _execlpe( prog, prog, "_execlpe", "two", NULL, my_env );
        break;
    case '5':
        _execv( prog, args );
        break;
    case '6':
        _execve( prog, args, my_env );
        break;
```

```
case '7':
  _execvp( prog, args );
  break;
case '8':
  _execvpe( prog, args, my_env );
  break;
default:
  break;
}

/* This point is reached only if exec fails. */
printf( "\nProcess was not execed." );
exit( 0 );
}
```

See Also

abort, atexit, exit, _onexit, _spawn Function Overview, system

_execlp, _wexeclp

Load and execute new child processes.

int _execlp(const char *cmdname*, **const char** *arg0*, ... **const char** *argn*, **NULL**);
int _wexeclp(const wchar_t *cmdname*, **const wchar_t** *arg0*, ... **const wchar_t** *argn*, **NULL**);

Function	Required Header	Optional Headers	Compatibility
_execlp	<process.h>	<errno.h>	Win 95, Win NT
_wexeclp	<process.h> or <wchar.h>	<errno.h>	Win NT

For additional compatibility information, see "Compatibility" in the Introduction.

Libraries

LIBC.LIB	Single thread static library, retail version
LIBCMT.LIB	Multithread static library, retail version
MSVCRT.LIB	Import library for MSVCRT.DLL, retail version

Return Value

If successful, these functions do not return to the calling process. A return value of −1 indicates an error, in which case the **errno** global variable is set.

errno Value	Description
E2BIG	The space required for the arguments and environment settings exceeds 32K.
EACCES	The specified file has a locking or sharing violation.
EMFILE	Too many files open (the specified file must be opened to determine whether it is executable).
ENOENT	File or path not found.
ENOEXEC	The specified file is not executable or has an invalid executable-file format.
ENOMEM	Not enough memory is available to execute the new process; or the available memory has been corrupted; or an invalid block exists, indicating that the calling process was not allocated properly.

Parameters

cmdname
  Path of file to execute

arg0, ... argn
  List of pointers to parameters

Remarks

Each of these functions loads and executes a new process, passing each command-line argument as a separate parameter and using the **PATH** environment variable to find the file to execute.

Example

```
/* EXEC.C illustrates the different versions of exec including:
 *      _execl        _execle        _execlp        _execlpe
 *      _execv        _execve        _execvp        _execvpe
 *
 * Although EXEC.C can exec any program, you can verify how
 * different versions handle arguments and environment by
 * compiling and specifying the sample program ARGS.C. See
 * SPAWN.C for examples of the similar spawn functions.
 */

#include <stdio.h>
#include <conio.h>
#include <process.h>

char *my_env[] =                  /* Environment for exec?e */
{
   "THIS=environment will be",
   "PASSED=to new process by",
   "the EXEC=functions",
   NULL
};
```

```
void main()
{
   char *args[4], prog[80];
   int ch;

   printf( "Enter name of program to exec: " );
   gets( prog );
   printf( " 1. _execl  2. _execle  3. _execlp  4. _execlpe\n" );
   printf( " 5. _execv  6. _execve  7. _execvp  8. _execvpe\n" );
   printf( "Type a number from 1 to 8 (or 0 to quit): " );
   ch = _getche();
   if( (ch < '1') || (ch > '8') )
      exit( 1 );
   printf( "\n\n" );

   /* Arguments for _execv? */
   args[0] = prog;
   args[1] = "exec??";
   args[2] = "two";
   args[3] = NULL;

   switch( ch )
   {
   case '1':
      _execl( prog, prog, "_execl", "two", NULL );
      break;
   case '2':
      _execle( prog, prog, "_execle", "two", NULL, my_env );
      break;
   case '3':
      _execlp( prog, prog, "_execlp", "two", NULL );
      break;
   case '4':
      _execlpe( prog, prog, "_execlpe", "two", NULL, my_env );
      break;
   case '5':
      _execv( prog, args );
      break;
   case '6':
      _execve( prog, args, my_env );
      break;
   case '7':
      _execvp( prog, args );
      break;
   case '8':
      _execvpe( prog, args, my_env );
      break;
   default:
      break;
   }
```

```
    /* This point is reached only if exec fails. */
    printf( "\nProcess was not execed." );
    exit( 0 );
}
```

See Also

abort, atexit, exit, _onexit, _spawn Function Overview, system

_execlpe, _wexeclpe

Load and execute new child processes.

int _execlpe(const char *cmdname*, **const char** *arg0*, ... **const char** *argn*,
  NULL, const char *const *envp* **);**
int _wexeclpe(const wchar_t *cmdname*, **const wchar_t** *arg0*, ... **const wchar_t** *argn*,
  NULL, const wchar_t *const *envp* **);**

Function	Required Header	Optional Headers	Compatibility
_execlpe	<process.h>	<errno.h>	Win 95, Win NT
_wexeclpe	<process.h> or <wchar.h>	<errno.h>	Win NT

For additional compatibility information, see "Compatibility" in the Introduction.

Libraries

LIBC.LIB	Single thread static library, retail version
LIBCMT.LIB	Multithread static library, retail version
MSVCRT.LIB	Import library for MSVCRT.DLL, retail version

Return Value

If successful, these functions do not return to the calling process. A return value of –1
indicates an error, in which case the **errno** global variable is set.

errno Value	Description
E2BIG	The space required for the arguments and environment settings exceeds 32K.
EACCES	The specified file has a locking or sharing violation.
EMFILE	Too many files open (the specified file must be opened to determine whether it is executable).
ENOENT	File or path not found.
ENOEXEC	The specified file is not executable or has an invalid executable-file format.
ENOMEM	Not enough memory is available to execute the new process; or the available memory has been corrupted; or an invalid block exists, indicating that the calling process was not allocated properly.

Parameters

cmdname
Path of file to execute

arg0, ... argn
List of pointers to parameters

envp
Array of pointers to environment settings

Remarks

Each of these functions loads and executes a new process, passing each command-line argument as a separate parameter and also passing an array of pointers to environment settings. These functions use the **PATH** environment variable to find the file to execute.

Example

```
/* EXEC.C illustrates the different versions of exec including:
 *       _execl         _execle        _execlp        _execlpe
 *       _execv         _execve        _execvp        _execvpe
 *
 * Although EXEC.C can exec any program, you can verify how
 * different versions handle arguments and environment by
 * compiling and specifying the sample program ARGS.C. See
 * SPAWN.C for examples of the similar spawn functions.
 */

#include <stdio.h>
#include <conio.h>
#include <process.h>

char *my_env[] =                 /* Environment for exec?e */
{
    "THIS=environment will be",
    "PASSED=to new process by",
    "the EXEC=functions",
    NULL
};

void main()
{
    char *args[4], prog[80];
    int ch;

    printf( "Enter name of program to exec: " );
    gets( prog );
    printf( " 1. _execl  2. _execle  3. _execlp  4. _execlpe\n" );
    printf( " 5. _execv  6. _execve  7. _execvp  8. _execvpe\n" );
    printf( "Type a number from 1 to 8 (or 0 to quit): " );
```

```
        ch = _getche();
        if( (ch < '1') || (ch > '8') )
            exit( 1 );
        printf( "\n\n" );

        /* Arguments for _execv? */
        args[0] = prog;
        args[1] = "exec??";
        args[2] = "two";
        args[3] = NULL;

        switch( ch )
        {
        case '1':
            _execl( prog, prog, "_execl", "two", NULL );
            break;
        case '2':
            _execle( prog, prog, "_execle", "two", NULL, my_env );
            break;
        case '3':
            _execlp( prog, prog, "_execlp", "two", NULL );
            break;
        case '4':
            _execlpe( prog, prog, "_execlpe", "two", NULL, my_env );
            break;
        case '5':
            _execv( prog, args );
            break;
        case '6':
            _execve( prog, args, my_env );
            break;
        case '7':
            _execvp( prog, args );
            break;
        case '8':
            _execvpe( prog, args, my_env );
            break;
        default:
            break;
        }

        /* This point is reached only if exec fails. */
        printf( "\nProcess was not execed." );
        exit( 0 );
    }
```

See Also

abort, atexit, exit, _onexit, _spawn Function Overview, system

_execv, _wexecv

Load and execute new child processes.

int _execv(const char *cmdname*, **const char *const** *argv* **);**
int _wexecv(const wchar_t *cmdname*, **const wchar_t *const** *argv* **);**

Function	Required Header	Optional Headers	Compatibility
_execv	<process.h>	<errno.h>	Win 95, Win NT
_wexecv	<process.h> or <wchar.h>	<errno.h>	Win NT

For additional compatibility information, see "Compatibility" in the Introduction.

Libraries

LIBC.LIB	Single thread static library, retail version
LIBCMT.LIB	Multithread static library, retail version
MSVCRT.LIB	Import library for MSVCRT.DLL, retail version

Return Value

If successful, these functions do not return to the calling process. A return value of –1 indicates an error, in which case the **errno** global variable is set.

errno Value	Description
E2BIG	The space required for the arguments and environment settings exceeds 32K.
EACCES	The specified file has a locking or sharing violation.
EMFILE	Too many files open (the specified file must be opened to determine whether it is executable).
ENOENT	File or path not found.
ENOEXEC	The specified file is not executable or has an invalid executable-file format.
ENOMEM	Not enough memory is available to execute the new process; or the available memory has been corrupted; or an invalid block exists, indicating that the calling process was not allocated properly.

Parameters

cmdname
Path of file to execute

argv
Array of pointers to parameters

Remarks

Each of these functions loads and executes a new process, passing an array of pointers to command-line arguments.

Example

```
/* EXEC.C illustrates the different versions of exec including:
 *      _execl          _execle         _execlp         _execlpe
 *      _execv          _execve         _execvp         _execvpe
 *
 * Although EXEC.C can exec any program, you can verify how
 * different versions handle arguments and environment by
 * compiling and specifying the sample program ARGS.C. See
 * SPAWN.C for examples of the similar spawn functions.
 */

#include <stdio.h>
#include <conio.h>
#include <process.h>

char *my_env[] =                /* Environment for exec?e */
{
    "THIS=environment will be",
    "PASSED=to new process by",
    "the EXEC=functions",
    NULL
};

void main()
{
    char *args[4], prog[80];
    int ch;

    printf( "Enter name of program to exec: " );
    gets( prog );
    printf( " 1. _execl   2. _execle  3. _execlp  4. _execlpe\n" );
    printf( " 5. _execv   6. _execve  7. _execvp  8. _execvpe\n" );
    printf( "Type a number from 1 to 8 (or 0 to quit): " );
    ch = _getche();
    if( (ch < '1') || (ch > '8') )
        exit( 1 );
    printf( "\n\n" );

    /* Arguments for _execv? */
    args[0] = prog;
    args[1] = "exec??";
    args[2] = "two";
    args[3] = NULL;
```

```
switch( ch )
{
case '1':
   _execl( prog, prog, "_execl", "two", NULL );
   break;
case '2':
   _execle( prog, prog, "_execle", "two", NULL, my_env );
   break;
case '3':
   _execlp( prog, prog, "_execlp", "two", NULL );
   break;
case '4':
   _execlpe( prog, prog, "_execlpe", "two", NULL, my_env );
   break;
case '5':
   _execv( prog, args );
   break;
case '6':
   _execve( prog, args, my_env );
   break;
case '7':
   _execvp( prog, args );
   break;
case '8':
   _execvpe( prog, args, my_env );
   break;
default:
   break;
}

/* This point is reached only if exec fails. */
printf( "\nProcess was not execed." );
exit( 0 );
}
```

See Also

abort, atexit, exit, _onexit, _spawn Function Overview, system

_execve, _wexecve

Load and execute new child processes.

int _execve(const char *cmdname,* **const char *const** **argv,* **const char *const** **envp* **);**
int _wexecve(const wchar_t **cmdname,* **const wchar_t *const** **argv,*
   const wchar_t *const **envp* **);**

Function	Required Header	Optional Headers	Compatibility
_execve	<process.h>	<errno.h>	Win 95, Win NT
_wexecve	<process.h> or <wchar.h>	<errno.h>	Win NT

For additional compatibility information, see "Compatibility" in the Introduction.

Libraries

LIBC.LIB	Single thread static library, retail version
LIBCMT.LIB	Multithread static library, retail version
MSVCRT.LIB	Import library for MSVCRT.DLL, retail version

Return Value

If successful, these functions do not return to the calling process. A return value of –1 indicates an error, in which case the **errno** global variable is set.

errno Value	Description
E2BIG	The space required for the arguments and environment settings exceeds 32K.
EACCES	The specified file has a locking or sharing violation.
EMFILE	Too many files open (the specified file must be opened to determine whether it is executable).
ENOENT	File or path not found.
ENOEXEC	The specified file is not executable or has an invalid executable-file format.
ENOMEM	Not enough memory is available to execute the new process; or the available memory has been corrupted; or an invalid block exists, indicating that the calling process was not allocated properly.

Parameters

cmdname
  Path of file to execute

argv
  Array of pointers to parameters

envp
  Array of pointers to environment settings

Remarks

Each of these functions loads and executes a new process, passing an array of pointers to command-line arguments and an array of pointers to environment settings.

Example

```
/* EXEC.C illustrates the different versions of exec including:
 *      _execl          _execle         _execlp         _execlpe
 *      _execv          _execve         _execvp         _execvpe
 *
 * Although EXEC.C can exec any program, you can verify how
 * different versions handle arguments and environment by
 * compiling and specifying the sample program ARGS.C. See
 * SPAWN.C for examples of the similar spawn functions.
 */

#include <stdio.h>
#include <conio.h>
#include <process.h>

char *my_env[] =                   /* Environment for exec?e */
{
    "THIS=environment will be",
    "PASSED=to new process by",
    "the EXEC=functions",
    NULL
};

void main()
{
    char *args[4], prog[80];
    int ch;

    printf( "Enter name of program to exec: " );
    gets( prog );
    printf( " 1. _execl  2. _execle  3. _execlp  4. _execlpe\n" );
    printf( " 5. _execv  6. _execve  7. _execvp  8. _execvpe\n" );
    printf( "Type a number from 1 to 8 (or 0 to quit): " );
    ch = _getche();
    if( (ch < '1') || (ch > '8') )
        exit( 1 );
    printf( "\n\n" );

    /* Arguments for _execv? */
    args[0] = prog;
    args[1] = "exec??";
    args[2] = "two";
    args[3] = NULL;
```

```
        switch( ch )
        {
        case '1':
           _execl( prog, prog, "_execl", "two", NULL );
           break;
        case '2':
           _execle( prog, prog, "_execle", "two", NULL, my_env );
           break;
        case '3':
           _execlp( prog, prog, "_execlp", "two", NULL );
           break;
        case '4':
           _execlpe( prog, prog, "_execlpe", "two", NULL, my_env );
           break;
        case '5':
           _execv( prog, args );
           break;
        case '6':
           _execve( prog, args, my_env );
           break;
        case '7':
           _execvp( prog, args );
           break;
        case '8':
           _execvpe( prog, args, my_env );
           break;
        default:
           break;
        }

        /* This point is reached only if exec fails. */
        printf( "\nProcess was not execed." );
        exit( 0 );
   }
```

See Also

abort, atexit, exit, _onexit, _spawn Function Overview, system

_execvp, _wexecvp

Load and execute new child processes.

int _execvp(const char *cmdname*, **const char** *const **argv*);
int _wexecvp(const wchar_t *cmdname*, **const wchar_t** *const **argv*);

Function	Required Header	Optional Headers	Compatibility
_execvp	<process.h>	<errno.h>	Win 95, Win NT
_wexecvp	<process.h> or <wchar.h>	<errno.h>	Win NT

For additional compatibility information, see "Compatibility" in the Introduction.

Libraries

LIBC.LIB	Single thread static library, retail version
LIBCMT.LIB	Multithread static library, retail version
MSVCRT.LIB	Import library for MSVCRT.DLL, retail version

Return Value

If successful, these functions do not return to the calling process. A return value of –1 indicates an error, in which case the **errno** global variable is set.

errno Value	Description
E2BIG	The space required for the arguments and environment settings exceeds 32K.
EACCES	The specified file has a locking or sharing violation.
EMFILE	Too many files open (the specified file must be opened to determine whether it is executable).
ENOENT	File or path not found.
ENOEXEC	The specified file is not executable or has an invalid executable-file format.
ENOMEM	Not enough memory is available to execute the new process; or the available memory has been corrupted; or an invalid block exists, indicating that the calling process was not allocated properly.

Parameters

cmdname
    Path of file to execute

argv
    Array of pointers to parameters

Remarks

Each of these functions loads and executes a new process, passing an array of pointers to command-line arguments and using the **PATH** environment variable to find the file to execute.

Example

```
/* EXEC.C illustrates the different versions of exec including:
 *        _execl          _execle          _execlp          _execlpe
 *        _execv          _execve          _execvp          _execvpe
 *
 * Although EXEC.C can exec any program, you can verify how
 * different versions handle arguments and environment by
 * compiling and specifying the sample program ARGS.C. See
 * SPAWN.C for examples of the similar spawn functions.
 */

#include <stdio.h>
#include <conio.h>
#include <process.h>

char *my_env[] =                    /* Environment for exec?e */
{
    "THIS=environment will be",
    "PASSED=to new process by",
    "the EXEC=functions",
    NULL
};

void main()
{
    char *args[4], prog[80];
    int ch;

    printf( "Enter name of program to exec: " );
    gets( prog );
    printf( " 1. _execl  2. _execle  3. _execlp  4. _execlpe\n" );
    printf( " 5. _execv  6. _execve  7. _execvp  8. _execvpe\n" );
    printf( "Type a number from 1 to 8 (or 0 to quit): " );
    ch = _getche();
    if( (ch < '1') || (ch > '8') )
       exit( 1 );
    printf( "\n\n" );

    /* Arguments for _execv? */
    args[0] = prog;
    args[1] = "exec??";
    args[2] = "two";
    args[3] = NULL;
```

```
switch( ch )
{
case '1':
   _execl( prog, prog, "_execl", "two", NULL );
   break;
case '2':
   _execle( prog, prog, "_execle", "two", NULL, my_env );
   break;
case '3':
   _execlp( prog, prog, "_execlp", "two", NULL );
   break;
case '4':
   _execlpe( prog, prog, "_execlpe", "two", NULL, my_env );
   break;
case '5':
   _execv( prog, args );
   break;
case '6':
   _execve( prog, args, my_env );
   break;
case '7':
   _execvp( prog, args );
   break;
case '8':
   _execvpe( prog, args, my_env );
   break;
default:
   break;
}

/* This point is reached only if exec fails. */
printf( "\nProcess was not execed." );
exit( 0 );
}
```

See Also

abort, atexit, exit, _onexit, _spawn Function Overview, system

_execvpe, _wexecvpe

Load and execute new child processes.

int _execvpe(const char *cmdname*, **const char *const** *argv*, **const char *const** *envp* **);**
int _wexecvpe(const wchar_t *cmdname*, **const wchar_t *const** *argv*,
    const wchar_t *const *envp* **);**

Function	Required Header	Optional Headers	Compatibility
_execvpe	<process.h>	<errno.h>	Win 95, Win NT
_wexecvpe	<process.h> or <wchar.h>	<errno.h>	Win NT

For additional compatibility information, see "Compatibility" in the Introduction.

Libraries

LIBC.LIB	Single thread static library, retail version
LIBCMT.LIB	Multithread static library, retail version
MSVCRT.LIB	Import library for MSVCRT.DLL, retail version

Return Value

If successful, these functions do not return to the calling process. A return value of −1 indicates an error, in which case the **errno** global variable is set.

errno Value	Description
E2BIG	The space required for the arguments and environment settings exceeds 32K.
EACCES	The specified file has a locking or sharing violation.
EMFILE	Too many files open (the specified file must be opened to determine whether it is executable).
ENOENT	File or path not found.
ENOEXEC	The specified file is not executable or has an invalid executable-file format.
ENOMEM	Not enough memory is available to execute the new process; or the available memory has been corrupted; or an invalid block exists, indicating that the calling process was not allocated properly.

Parameters

cmdname
    Path of file to execute

argv
    Array of pointers to parameters

envp
    Array of pointers to environment settings

Remarks

Each of these functions loads and executes a new process, passing an array of pointers to command-line arguments and an array of pointers to environment settings. These functions use the **PATH** environment variable to find the file to execute.

Example

```
/* EXEC.C illustrates the different versions of exec including:
 *      _execl          _execle          _execlp          _execlpe
 *      _execv          _execve          _execvp          _execvpe
 *
 * Although EXEC.C can exec any program, you can verify how
 * different versions handle arguments and environment by
 * compiling and specifying the sample program ARGS.C. See
 * SPAWN.C for examples of the similar spawn functions.
 */

#include <stdio.h>
#include <conio.h>
#include <process.h>

char *my_env[] =                 /* Environment for exec?e */
{
    "THIS=environment will be",
    "PASSED=to new process by",
    "the EXEC=functions",
    NULL
};

void main()
{
    char *args[4], prog[80];
    int ch;

    printf( "Enter name of program to exec: " );
    gets( prog );
    printf( " 1. _execl  2. _execle  3. _execlp  4. _execlpe\n" );
    printf( " 5. _execv  6. _execve  7. _execvp  8. _execvpe\n" );
    printf( "Type a number from 1 to 8 (or 0 to quit): " );
    ch = _getche();
    if( (ch < '1') || (ch > '8') )
        exit( 1 );
    printf( "\n\n" );

    /* Arguments for _execv? */
    args[0] = prog;
    args[1] = "exec??";
    args[2] = "two";
    args[3] = NULL;
```

```
        switch( ch )
        {
        case '1':
           _execl( prog, prog, "_execl", "two", NULL );
           break;
        case '2':
           _execle( prog, prog, "_execle", "two", NULL, my_env );
           break;
        case '3':
           _execlp( prog, prog, "_execlp", "two", NULL );
           break;
        case '4':
           _execlpe( prog, prog, "_execlpe", "two", NULL, my_env );
           break;
        case '5':
           _execv( prog, args );
           break;
        case '6':
           _execve( prog, args, my_env );
           break;
        case '7':
           _execvp( prog, args );
           break;
        case '8':
           _execvpe( prog, args, my_env );
           break;
        default:
        break;
        }

        /* This point is reached only if exec fails. */
        printf( "\nProcess was not execed." );
        exit( 0 );
}
```

See Also

abort, **atexit**, **exit**, **_onexit**, **_spawn Function Overview**, **system**

exit, _exit

Terminate the calling process after cleanup (**exit**) or immediately (**_exit**).

void exit(int *status* **);**
void _exit(int *status* **);**

Function	Required Header	Compatibility
exit	<process.h> or <stdlib.h>	ANSI, Win 95, Win NT
_exit	<process.h> or <stdlib.h>	Win 95, Win NT

For additional compatibility information, see "Compatibility" in the Introduction.

Libraries

LIBC.LIB	Single thread static library, retail version
LIBCMT.LIB	Multithread static library, retail version
MSVCRT.LIB	Import library for MSVCRT.DLL, retail version

Return Value

None

Parameter

status
    Exit status

Remarks

The **exit** and **_exit** functions terminate the calling process. **exit** calls, in last-in-first-out (LIFO) order, the functions registered by **atexit** and **_onexit**, then flushes all file buffers before terminating the process. **_exit** terminates the process without processing **atexit** or **_onexit** or flushing stream buffers. The *status* value is typically set to 0 to indicate a normal exit and set to some other value to indicate an error.

Although the **exit** and **_exit** calls do not return a value, the low-order byte of *status* is made available to the waiting calling process, if one exists, after the calling process exits. The *status* value is available to the operating-system batch command **ERRORLEVEL** and is represented by one of two constants: **EXIT_SUCCESS**, which represents a value of 0, or **EXIT_FAILURE**, which represents a value of 1. The behavior of **exit, _exit, _cexit,** and **_c_exit** is as follows.

Function	Description
exit	Performs complete C library termination procedures, terminates the process, and exits with the supplied status code.
_exit	Performs "quick" C library termination procedures, terminates the process, and exits with the supplied status code.
_cexit	Performs complete C library termination procedures and returns to the caller, but does not terminate the process.
_c_exit	Performs "quick" C library termination procedures and returns to the caller, but does not terminate the process.

Example

```
/* EXITER.C: This program prompts the user for a yes
 * or no and returns an exit code of 1 if the
 * user answers Y or y; otherwise it returns 0. The
 * error code could be tested in a batch file.
 */

#include <conio.h>
#include <stdlib.h>

void main( void )
{
   int ch;

   _cputs( "Yes or no? " );
   ch = _getch();
   _cputs( "\r\n" );
   if( toupper( ch ) == 'Y' )
      exit( 1 );
   else
      exit( 0 );
}
```

See Also

**abort, atexit, _cexit, _exec Function Overview, _onexit, _spawn Function Overview,
system**

exp

Calculates the exponential.

double exp(double x **);**

Function	Required Header	Compatibility
exp	<math.h>	ANSI, Win 95, Win NT

For additional compatibility information, see "Compatibility" in the Introduction.

Libraries

LIBC.LIB	Single thread static library, retail version
LIBCMT.LIB	Multithread static library, retail version
MSVCRT.LIB	Import library for MSVCRT.DLL, retail version

Return Value

The **exp** function returns the exponential value of the floating-point parameter, x, if successful. On overflow, the function returns INF (infinite) and on underflow, **exp** returns 0.

Parameter

x

    Floating-point value

Example

```
/* EXP.C */

#include <math.h>
#include <stdio.h>

void main( void )
{
   double x = 2.302585093, y;

   y = exp( x );
   printf( "exp( %f ) = %f\n", x, y );
}
```

Output

```
exp( 2.302585 ) = 10.000000
```

See Also

log

_expand

Changes the size of a memory block.

void *_expand(void *memblock*, **size_t** *size* **);**

Function	Required Header	Compatibility
_expand	<malloc.h>	Win 95, Win NT

For additional compatibility information, see "Compatibility" in the Introduction.

Libraries

LIBC.LIB	Single thread static library, retail version
LIBCMT.LIB	Multithread static library, retail version
MSVCRT.LIB	Import library for MSVCRT.DLL, retail version

Return Value

_expand returns a void pointer to the reallocated memory block. **_expand**, unlike **realloc**, cannot move a block to change its size. Thus, if there is sufficient memory available to expand the block without moving it, the *memblock* parameter to **_expand** is the same as the return value.

_expand returns **NULL** when an error is detected during its operation. For example, if **_expand** is used to shrink a memory block, it might detect a corruption in the small block heap or an invalid block pointer and return **NULL**.

if there is insufficient memory available to expand the block to the given size without moving it. The item pointed to by *memblock* is expanded as much as possible in its current location.

The return value points to a storage space that is guaranteed to be suitably aligned for storage of any type of object. To check the new size of the item, use **_msize**. To get a pointer to a type other than **void**, use a type cast on the return value.

Parameters

memblock
    Pointer to previously allocated memory block

size
    New size in bytes

Remarks

The **_expand** function changes the size of a previously allocated memory block by trying to expand or contract the block without moving its location in the heap. The *memblock* parameter points to the beginning of the block. The *size* parameter gives the new size of the block, in bytes. The contents of the block are unchanged up to the shorter of the new and old sizes. *memblock* can also point to a block that has been freed, as long as there has been no intervening call to **calloc**, **_expand**, **malloc**, or **realloc**. If *memblock* points to a freed block, the block remains free after a call to **_expand**.

When the application is linked with a debug version of the C run-time libraries, **_expand** resolves to _expand_dbg. For more information about how the heap is managed during the debugging process, see "Using C Run-Time Library Debugging Support," in the *Visual C++ Programmer's Guide* online.

Example

```
/* EXPAND.C */

#include <stdio.h>
#include <malloc.h>
#include <stdlib.h>
```

```
void main( void )
{
   char *bufchar;
   printf( "Allocate a 512 element buffer\n" );
   if( (bufchar = (char *)calloc( 512, sizeof( char ) )) == NULL )
      exit( 1 );
   printf( "Allocated %d bytes at %Fp\n",
         _msize( bufchar ), (void *)bufchar );
   if( (bufchar = (char *)_expand( bufchar, 1024 )) == NULL )
      printf( "Can't expand" );
   else
      printf( "Expanded block to %d bytes at %Fp\n",
            _msize( bufchar ), (void *)bufchar );
   /* Free memory */
   free( bufchar );
   exit( 0 );
}
```

Output

```
Allocate a 512 element buffer
Allocated 512 bytes at 002C12BC
Expanded block to 1024 bytes at 002C12BC
```

See Also

calloc, free, malloc, _msize, realloc

fabs

Calculates the absolute value of the floating-point argument.

double fabs(double *x* **);**

Function	Required Header	Compatibility
fabs	<math.h>	ANSI, Win 95, Win NT

For additional compatibility information, see "Compatibility" in the Introduction.

Libraries

LIBC.LIB	Single thread static library, retail version
LIBCMT.LIB	Multithread static library, retail version
MSVCRT.LIB	Import library for MSVCRT.DLL, retail version

Return Value

fabs returns the absolute value of its argument. There is no error return.

Parameter

x

> Floating-point value

Example

```
/* ABS.C: This program computes and displays
 * the absolute values of several numbers.
 */

#include  <stdio.h>
#include  <math.h>
#include  <stdlib.h>

void main( void )
{
    int    ix = -4, iy;
    long   lx = -41567L, ly;
    double dx = -3.141593, dy;

    iy = abs( ix );
    printf( "The absolute value of %d is %d\n", ix, iy);

    ly = labs( lx );
    printf( "The absolute value of %ld is %ld\n", lx, ly);

    dy = fabs( dx );
    printf( "The absolute value of %f is %f\n", dx, dy );
}
```

Output

```
The absolute value of -4 is 4
The absolute value of -41567 is 41567
The absolute value of -3.141593 is 3.141593
```

See Also

abs, _cabs, labs

fclose, _fcloseall

Closes a stream (**fclose**) or closes all open streams (**_fcloseall**).

int fclose(FILE *stream);
int _fcloseall(void);

Function	Required Header	Compatibility
fclose	<stdio.h>	ANSI, Win 95, Win NT
_fcloseall	<stdio.h>	ANSI, Win 95, Win NT

For additional compatibility information, see "Compatibility" in the Introduction.

Libraries

LIBC.LIB	Single thread static library, retail version
LIBCMT.LIB	Multithread static library, retail version
MSVCRT.LIB	Import library for MSVCRT.DLL, retail version

Return Value

fclose returns 0 if the stream is successfully closed. **_fcloseall** returns the total number of streams closed. Both functions return **EOF** to indicate an error.

Parameter

stream
    Pointer to **FILE** structure

Remarks

The **fclose** function closes *stream*. **_fcloseall** closes all open streams except **stdin**, **stdout**, **stderr** (and, in MS-DOS, **_stdaux** and **_stdprn**). It also closes and deletes any temporary files created by **tmpfile**. In both functions, all buffers associated with the stream are flushed prior to closing. System-allocated buffers are released when the stream is closed. Buffers assigned by the user with **setbuf** and **setvbuf** are not automatically released.

Example

```
/* FOPEN.C: This program opens files named "data"
 * and "data2".It  uses fclose to close "data" and
 * _fcloseall to close all remaining files.
 */

#include <stdio.h>

FILE *stream, *stream2;

void main( void )
{
   int numclosed;

   /* Open for read (will fail if file "data" does not exist) */
   if( (stream  = fopen( "data", "r" )) == NULL )
      printf( "The file 'data' was not opened\n" );
   else
      printf( "The file 'data' was opened\n" );
```

```
    /* Open for write */
    if( (stream2 = fopen( "data2", "w+" )) == NULL )
       printf( "The file 'data2' was not opened\n" );
    else
       printf( "The file 'data2' was opened\n" );

    /* Close stream */
    if( fclose( stream ) )
       printf( "The file 'data' was not closed\n" );

    /* All other files are closed: */
    numclosed = _fcloseall( );
    printf( "Number of files closed by _fcloseall: %u\n", numclosed );
}
```

Output

```
The file 'data' was opened
The file 'data2' was opened
Number of files closed by _fcloseall: 1
```

See Also

_close, _fdopen, fflush, fopen, freopen

_fcvt

Converts a floating-point number to a string.

char *_fcvt(double *value*, **int** *count*, **int ****dec*, **int ****sign* **);**

Function	Required Header	Compatibility
_fcvt	<stdlib.h>	Win 95, Win NT

For additional compatibility information, see "Compatibility" in the Introduction.

Libraries

LIBC.LIB	Single thread static library, retail version
LIBCMT.LIB	Multithread static library, retail version
MSVCRT.LIB	Import library for MSVCRT.DLL, retail version

Return Value

_fcvt returns a pointer to the string of digits. There is no error return.

Parameters

value
  Number to be converted

count
  Number of digits after decimal point

dec
  Pointer to stored decimal-point position

sign
  Pointer to stored sign indicator

Remarks

The **_fcvt** function converts a floating-point number to a null-terminated character string. The *value* parameter is the floating-point number to be converted. **_fcvt** stores the digits of *value* as a string and appends a null character ('\0'). The *count* parameter specifies the number of digits to be stored after the decimal point. Excess digits are rounded off to *count* places. If there are fewer than *count* digits of precision, the string is padded with zeros.

Only digits are stored in the string. The position of the decimal point and the sign of *value* can be obtained from *dec* and *sign* after the call. The *dec* parameter points to an integer value; this integer value gives the position of the decimal point with respect to the beginning of the string. A zero or negative integer value indicates that the decimal point lies to the left of the first digit. The parameter *sign* points to an integer indicating the sign of *value*. The integer is set to 0 if *value* is positive and is set to a nonzero number if *value* is negative.

_ecvt and **_fcvt** use a single statically allocated buffer for the conversion. Each call to one of these routines destroys the results of the previous call.

Example

```
/* FCVT.C: This program converts the constant
 * 3.1415926535 to a string and sets the pointer
 * *buffer to point to that string.
 */

#include <stdlib.h>
#include <stdio.h>

void main( void )
{
    int   decimal, sign;
    char *buffer;
    double source = 3.1415926535;

    buffer = _fcvt( source, 7, &decimal, &sign );
    printf( "source: %2.10f   buffer: '%s'   decimal: %d   sign: %d\n",
     ↪ source, buffer, decimal, sign );
}
```

Output

```
source: 3.1415926535   buffer: '31415927'   decimal: 1   sign: 0
```

See Also

atof, _ecvt, _gcvt

_fdopen, _wfdopen

Associate a stream with a file that was previously opened for low-level I/O.

FILE *_fdopen(int *handle***, const char ****mode* **);**
FILE *_wfdopen(int *handle***, const wchar_t ****mode* **);**

Function	Required Header	Compatibility
_fdopen	<stdio.h>	Win 95, Win NT
_wfdopen	<stdio.h> or <wchar.h>	Win 95, Win NT

For additional compatibility information, see "Compatibility" in the Introduction.

Libraries

LIBC.LIB	Single thread static library, retail version
LIBCMT.LIB	Multithread static library, retail version
MSVCRT.LIB	Import library for MSVCRT.DLL, retail version

Return Value

Each of these functions returns a pointer to the open stream. A null pointer value indicates an error.

Parameters

handle
   Handle to open file

mode
   Type of file access

Remarks

The **_fdopen** function associates an I/O stream with the file identified by *handle*, thus allowing a file opened for low-level I/O to be buffered and formatted. **_wfdopen** is a wide-character version of **_fdopen**; the *mode* argument to **_wfdopen** is a wide-character string. **_wfdopen** and **_fdopen** behave identically otherwise.

Generic-Text Routine Mappings

TCHAR.H Routine	_UNICODE & _MBCS Not Defined	_MBCS Defined	_UNICODE Defined
_tfdopen	_fdopen	_fdopen	_wfdopen

The *mode* character string specifies the type of file and file access.

The character string *mode* specifies the type of access requested for the file, as follows:

"r"
Opens for reading. If the file does not exist or cannot be found, the **fopen** call fails.

"w"
Opens an empty file for writing. If the given file exists, its contents are destroyed.

"a"
Opens for writing at the end of the file (appending); creates the file first if it doesn't exist.

"r+"
Opens for both reading and writing. (The file must exist.)

"w+"
Opens an empty file for both reading and writing. If the given file exists, its contents are destroyed.

"a+"
Opens for reading and appending; creates the file first if it doesn't exist.

When a file is opened with the **"a"** or **"a+"** access type, all write operations occur at the end of the file. The file pointer can be repositioned using **fseek** or **rewind**, but is always moved back to the end of the file before any write operation is carried out. Thus, existing data cannot be overwritten. When the **"r+"**, **"w+"**, or **"a+"** access type is specified, both reading and writing are allowed (the file is said to be open for "update"). However, when you switch between reading and writing, there must be an intervening **fflush**, **fsetpos**, **fseek**, or **rewind** operation. The current position can be specified for the **fsetpos** or **fseek** operation, if desired.

In addition to the above values, the following characters can be included in *mode* to specify the translation mode for newline characters:

t
Open in text (translated) mode. In this mode, carriage-return–linefeed (CR–LF) combinations are translated into single linefeeds (LF) on input, and LF characters are translated to CR–LF combinations on output. Also, CTRL+Z is interpreted as an end-of-file character on input. In files opened for reading/writing, **fopen** checks for a CTRL+Z at the end of the file and removes it, if possible. This is done because using the **fseek** and **ftell** functions to move within a file that ends with a CTRL+Z may cause **fseek** to behave improperly near the end of the file.

b

> Open in binary (untranslated) mode; the above translations are suppressed.

c

> Enable the commit flag for the associated *filename* so that the contents of the file buffer are written directly to disk if either **fflush** or **_flushall** is called.

n

> Reset the commit flag for the associated *filename* to "no-commit." This is the default. It also overrides the global commit flag if you link your program with COMMODE.OBJ. The global commit flag default is "no-commit" unless you explicitly link your program with COMMODE.OBJ.

The **t**, **c**, and **n** *mode* options are Microsoft extensions for **fopen** and **_fdopen** and should not be used where ANSI portability is desired.

If **t** or **b** is not given in *mode*, the default translation mode is defined by the global variable _fmode. If **t** or **b** is prefixed to the argument, the function fails and returns **NULL**. For a discussion of text and binary modes, see "Text and Binary Mode File I/O" in Chapter 1, "Run-Time Routines by Category."

Valid characters for the *mode* string used in **fopen** and **_fdopen** correspond to *oflag* arguments used in _open and _sopen, as follows.

Characters in *mode* String	Equivalent *oflag* Value for _open/_sopen
a	**_O_WRONLY	_O_APPEND** (usually **_O_WRONLY | _O_CREAT | _O_APPEND**)
a+	**_O_RDWR	_O_APPEND** (usually **_O_RDWR | _O_APPEND | _O_CREAT**)
r	**_O_RDONLY**
r+	**_O_RDWR**
w	**_O_WRONLY** (usually **_O_WRONLY | _O_CREAT | _O_TRUNC**)
w+	**_O_RDWR** (usually **_O_RDWR | _O_CREAT | _O_TRUNC**)
b	**_O_BINARY**
t	**_O_TEXT**
c	None
n	None

Example

```
/* _FDOPEN.C: This program opens a file using low-
 * level I/O, then uses _fdopen to switch to stream
 * access. It counts the lines in the file.
 */
```

```
#include <stdlib.h>
#include <stdio.h>
#include <fcntl.h>
#include <io.h>

void main( void )
{
   FILE *stream;
   int  fh, count = 0;
   char inbuf[128];

   /* Open a file handle. */
   if( (fh = _open( "_fdopen.c", _O_RDONLY )) == -1 )
      exit( 1 );

   /* Change handle access to stream access. */
   if( (stream = _fdopen( fh, "r" )) == NULL )
      exit( 1 );

   while( fgets( inbuf, 128, stream ) != NULL )
      count++;

   /* After _fdopen, close with fclose, not _close. */
   fclose( stream );
   printf( "Lines in file: %d\n", count );
}
```

Output

```
Lines in file: 32
```

See Also

_dup, fclose, fopen, freopen, _open

feof

Tests for end-of-file on a stream.

int feof(FILE *stream);

Function	Required Header	Compatibility
feof	<stdio.h>	ANSI, Win 95, Win NT

For additional compatibility information, see "Compatibility" in the Introduction.

Libraries

LIBC.LIB	Single thread static library, retail version
LIBCMT.LIB	Multithread static library, retail version
MSVCRT.LIB	Import library for MSVCRT.DLL, retail version

Return Value

The **feof** function returns a nonzero value after the first read operation that attempts to read past the end of the file. It returns 0 if the current position is not end of file. There is no error return.

Parameter

stream
   Pointer to **FILE** structure

Remarks

The **feof** routine (implemented both as a function and as a macro) determines whether the end of *stream* has been reached. When end of file is reached, read operations return an end-of-file indicator until the stream is closed or until **rewind**, **fsetpos**, **fseek**, or **clearerr** is called against it.

Example

```
/* FEOF.C: This program uses feof to indicate when
 * it reaches the end of the file FEOF.C. It also
 * checks for errors with ferror.
 */

#include <stdio.h>
#include <stdlib.h>

void main( void )
{
    int  count, total = 0;
    char buffer[100];
    FILE *stream;

    if( (stream = fopen( "feof.c", "r" )) == NULL )
        exit( 1 );

    /* Cycle until end of file reached: */
    while( !feof( stream ) )
    {
        /* Attempt to read in 10 bytes: */
        count = fread( buffer, sizeof( char ), 100, stream );
```

```
    if( ferror( stream ) )      {
       perror( "Read error" );
       break;
    }

    /* Total up actual bytes read */
    total += count;
  }
  printf( "Number of bytes read = %d\n", total );
  fclose( stream );
}
```

Output

```
Number of bytes read = 745
```

See Also

clearerr, **_eof**, **ferror**, **perror**

ferror

Tests for an error on a stream.

int ferror(FILE *_stream_);

Function	Required Header	Compatibility
ferror	<stdio.h>	ANSI, Win 95, Win NT

For additional compatibility information, see "Compatibility" in the Introduction.

Libraries

LIBC.LIB	Single thread static library, retail version
LIBCMT.LIB	Multithread static library, retail version
MSVCRT.LIB	Import library for MSVCRT.DLL, retail version

Return Value

If no error has occurred on _stream_, **ferror** returns 0. Otherwise, it returns a nonzero value.

Parameter

stream
    Pointer to **FILE** structure

Remarks

The **ferror** routine (implemented both as a function and as a macro) tests for a reading or writing error on the file associated with *stream*. If an error has occurred, the error indicator for the stream remains set until the stream is closed or rewound, or until **clearerr** is called against it.

Example

```
/* FEOF.C: This program uses feof to indicate when
 * it reaches the end of the file FEOF.C. It also
 * checks for errors with ferror.
 */

#include <stdio.h>
#include <stdlib.h>

void main( void )
{
    int  count, total = 0;
    char buffer[100];
    FILE *stream;

    if( (stream = fopen( "feof.c", "r" )) == NULL )
        exit( 1 );

    /* Cycle until end of file reached: */
    while( !feof( stream ) )
    {
        /* Attempt to read in 10 bytes: */
        count = fread( buffer, sizeof( char ), 100, stream );
        if( ferror( stream ) )          {
            perror( "Read error" );
            break;
        }

        /* Total up actual bytes read */
        total += count;
    }
    printf( "Number of bytes read = %d\n", total );
    fclose( stream );
}
```

Output

```
Number of bytes read = 745
```

See Also

clearerr, _eof, feof, fopen, perror

fflush

Flushes a stream.

int fflush(FILE *stream* **);**

Function	Required Header	Compatibility
fflush	<stdio.h>	ANSI, Win 95, Win NT

For additional compatibility information, see "Compatibility" in the Introduction.

Libraries

LIBC.LIB	Single thread static library, retail version
LIBCMT.LIB	Multithread static library, retail version
MSVCRT.LIB	Import library for MSVCRT.DLL, retail version

Return Value

fflush returns 0 if the buffer was successfully flushed. The value 0 is also returned in cases in which the specified stream has no buffer or is open for reading only. A return value of **EOF** indicates an error.

> **Note** If **fflush** returns **EOF**, data may have been lost due to a write failure. When setting up a critical error handler, it is safest to turn buffering off with the **setvbuf** function or to use low-level I/O routines such as **_open**, **_close**, and **_write** instead of the stream I/O functions.

Parameter

stream
Pointer to **FILE** structure

Remarks

The **fflush** function flushes a stream. If the file associated with *stream* is open for output, **fflush** writes to that file the contents of the buffer associated with the stream. If the stream is open for input, **fflush** clears the contents of the buffer. **fflush** negates the effect of any prior call to **ungetc** against *stream*. Also, **fflush(NULL)** flushes all streams opened for output. The stream remains open after the call. **fflush** has no effect on an unbuffered stream.

Buffers are normally maintained by the operating system, which determines the optimal time to write the data automatically to disk: when a buffer is full, when a stream is closed, or when a program terminates normally without closing the stream. The commit-to-disk feature of the run-time library lets you ensure that critical data is written directly to disk rather than to the operating-system buffers. Without rewriting an existing program, you can enable this feature by linking the program's object files with COMMODE.OBJ. In the resulting executable file, calls to **_flushall** write the contents of all buffers to disk. Only **_flushall** and **fflush** are affected by COMMODE.OBJ.

For information about controlling the commit-to-disk feature, see **fopen**, **_fdopen,** and "Stream I/O" in Chapter 1, "Run-Time Routines by Category."

Example

```
/* FFLUSH.C */

#include <stdio.h>
#include <conio.h>

void main( void )
{
    int integer;
    char string[81];

    /* Read each word as a string. */
    printf( "Enter a sentence of four words with scanf: " );
    for( integer = 0; integer < 4; integer++ )
    {
        scanf( "%s", string );
        printf( "%s\n", string );
    }

    /* You must flush the input buffer before using gets. */
    fflush( stdin );
    printf( "Enter the same sentence with gets: " );
    gets( string );
    printf( "%s\n", string );
}
```

Output

```
Enter a sentence of four words with scanf: This is a test
This
is
a
test
Enter the same sentence with gets: This is a test
This is a test
```

See Also

fclose, _flushall, setvbuf

fgetc, fgetwc, _fgetchar, _fgetwchar

Read a character from a stream (**fgetc**, **fgetwc**) or **stdin** (**_fgetchar**, **_fgetwchar**).

int fgetc(FILE *stream **);**
wint_t fgetwc(FILE *stream **);**
int _fgetchar(void);
wint_t _fgetwchar(void);

Function	Required Header	Compatibility
fgetc	<stdio.h>	ANSI, Win 95, Win NT
fgetwc	<stdio.h> or <wchar.h>	ANSI, Win 95, Win NT
_fgetchar	<stdio.h>	Win 95, Win NT
_fgetwchar	<stdio.h> or <wchar.h>	Win 95, Win NT

For additional compatibility information, see "Compatibility" in the Introduction.

Libraries

LIBC.LIB	Single thread static library, retail version
LIBCMT.LIB	Multithread static library, retail version
MSVCRT.LIB	Import library for MSVCRT.DLL, retail version

Return Value

fgetc and **_fgetchar** return the character read as an **int** or return **EOF** to indicate an error or end of file. **fgetwc** and **_fgetwchar** return, as a wint_t, the wide character that corresponds to the character read or return **WEOF** to indicate an error or end of file. For all four functions, use **feof** or **ferror** to distinguish between an error and an end-of-file condition. For **fgetc** and **fgetwc**, if a read error occurs, the error indicator for the stream is set.

Parameter

stream
    Pointer to **FILE** structure

Remarks

Each of these functions reads a single character from the current position of a file; in the case of **fgetc** and **fgetwc**, this is the file associated with *stream*. The function then increments the associated file pointer (if defined) to point to the next character. If the stream is at end of file, the end-of-file indicator for the stream is set. Routine-specific remarks follow.

Routine	Remarks
fgetc	Equivalent to **getc**, but implemented only as a function, rather than as a function and a macro.
fgetwc	Wide-character version of **fgetc**. Reads *c* as a multibyte character or a wide character according to whether *stream* is opened in text mode or binary mode.
_fgetchar	Equivalent to **fgetc(stdin)**. Also equivalent to **getchar**, but implemented only as a function, rather than as a function and a macro. Microsoft-specific; not ANSI-compatible.
_fgetwchar	Wide-character version of **_fgetchar**. Reads *c* as a multibyte character or a wide character according to whether *stream* is opened in text mode or binary mode. Microsoft-specific; not ANSI-compatible.

For more information about processing wide characters and multibyte characters in text and binary modes, see "Unicode Stream I/O in Text and Binary Modes," in Chapter 1, "Run-Time Routines by Category."

Generic-Text Routine Mappings

TCHAR.H Routine	_UNICODE & _MBCS Not Defined	_MBCS Defined	_UNICODE Defined
_fgettc	fgetc	fgetc	fgetwc
_fgettchar	fgetchar	fgetchar	_fgetwchar

Example

```
/* FGETC.C: This program uses getc to read the first
 * 80 input characters (or until the end of input)
 * and place them into a string named buffer.
 */

#include <stdio.h>
#include <stdlib.h>

void main( void )
{
   FILE *stream;
   char buffer[81];
   int  i, ch;

   /* Open file to read line from: */
   if( (stream = fopen( "fgetc.c", "r" )) == NULL )
      exit( 0 );

   /* Read in first 80 characters and place them in "buffer": */
   ch = fgetc( stream );
   for( i=0; (i < 80 ) && ( feof( stream ) == 0 ); i++ )
```

```
    {
        buffer[i] = (char)ch;
        ch = fgetc( stream );
    }

    /* Add null to end string */
    buffer[i] = '\0';
    printf( "%s\n", buffer );
    fclose( stream );
}
```

Output

```
/* FGETC.C: This program uses getc to read the first
 * 80 input characters (or
```

See Also

fputc, **getc**

fgetpos

Gets a stream's file-position indicator.

int fgetpos(FILE *__stream__, fpos_t *__pos__);

Function	Required Header	Compatibility
fgetpos	<stdio.h>	ANSI, Win 95, Win NT

For additional compatibility information, see "Compatibility" in the Introduction.

Libraries

LIBC.LIB	Single thread static library, retail version
LIBCMT.LIB	Multithread static library, retail version
MSVCRT.LIB	Import library for MSVCRT.DLL, retail version

Return Value

If successful, **fgetpos** returns 0. On failure, it returns a nonzero value and sets **errno** to one of the following manifest constants (defined in STDIO.H): **EBADF**, which means the specified stream is not a valid file handle or is not accessible, or **EINVAL**, which means the *stream* value is invalid.

Parameters

stream

Target stream

pos

Position-indicator storage

Remarks

The **fgetpos** function gets the current value of the *stream* argument's file-position indicator and stores it in the object pointed to by *pos*. The **fsetpos** function can later use information stored in *pos* to reset the *stream* argument's pointer to its position at the time **fgetpos** was called. The *pos* value is stored in an internal format and is intended for use only by **fgetpos** and **fsetpos**.

Example

```
/* FGETPOS.C: This program opens a file and reads
 * bytes at several different locations.
 */

#include <stdio.h>

void main( void )
{
    FILE    *stream;
    fpos_t  pos;
    char    buffer[20];

    if( (stream = fopen( "fgetpos.c", "rb" )) == NULL )
        printf( "Trouble opening file\n" );
    else
    {
        /* Read some data and then check the position. */
        fread( buffer, sizeof( char ), 10, stream );
        if( fgetpos( stream, &pos ) != 0 )
        perror( "fgetpos error" );
        else
        {
        fread( buffer, sizeof( char ), 10, stream );
        printf( "10 bytes at byte %ld: %.10s\n", pos, buffer );
        }

    /* Set a new position and read more data */
    pos = 140;
    if( fsetpos( stream, &pos ) != 0 )
        perror( "fsetpos error" );
```

```
fread( buffer, sizeof( char ), 10, stream );
printf( "10 bytes at byte %ld: %.10s\n", pos, buffer );
fclose( stream );
}
}
```

Output

```
10 bytes at byte 10: .C: This p
10 bytes at byte 140:
{
    FIL
```

See Also

fsetpos

fgets, fgetws

Get a string from a stream.

char *fgets(char **string***, int *****n***, FILE ****stream* **);**
wchar_t *fgetws(wchar_t **string***, int *****n***, FILE ****stream* **);**

Function	Required Header	Compatibility
fgets	<stdio.h>	ANSI, Win 95, Win NT
fgetws	<stdio.h> or <wchar.h>	ANSI, Win 95, Win NT

For additional compatibility information, see "Compatibility" in the Introduction.

Libraries

LIBC.LIB	Single thread static library, retail version
LIBCMT.LIB	Multithread static library, retail version
MSVCRT.LIB	Import library for MSVCRT.DLL, retail version

Return Value

Each of these functions returns *string*. **NULL** is returned to indicate an error or an end-of-file condition. Use **feof** or **ferror** to determine whether an error occurred.

Parameters

string
    Storage location for data

n
    Maximum number of characters to read

stream
    Pointer to **FILE** structure

Remarks

The **fgets** function reads a string from the input *stream* argument and stores it in *string*. **fgets** reads characters from the current stream position to and including the first newline character, to the end of the stream, or until the number of characters read is equal to $n - 1$, whichever comes first. The result stored in *string* is appended with a null character. The newline character, if read, is included in the string.

fgets is similar to the **gets** function; however, **gets** replaces the newline character with **NULL**. **fgetws** is a wide-character version of **fgets**.

fgetws reads the wide-character argument *string* as a multibyte-character string or a wide-character string according to whether *stream* is opened in text mode or binary mode, respectively. For more information about using text and binary modes in Unicode and multibyte stream-I/O, see "Text and Binary Mode File I/O" and "Unicode Stream I/O in Text and Binary Modes," in Chapter 1, "Run-Time Routines by Category."

Generic-Text Routine Mappings

TCHAR.H Routine	_UNICODE & _MBCS Not Defined	_MBCS Defined	_UNICODE Defined
_fgetts	fgets	fgets	fgetws

Example

```
/* FGETS.C: This program uses fgets to display
 * a line from a file on the screen.
 */

#include <stdio.h>

void main( void )
{
    FILE *stream;
    char line[100];

    if( (stream = fopen( "fgets.c", "r" )) != NULL )
    {
        if( fgets( line, 100, stream ) == NULL)
            printf( "fgets error\n" );
        else
            printf( "%s", line);
        fclose( stream );
    }
}
```

Output

```
/* FGETS.C: This program uses fgets to display
```

See Also

fputs, gets, puts

_filelength, _filelengthi64

Get the length of a file.

long _filelength(int *handle* **);**
__int64 _filelengthi64(int *handle* **);**

Function	Required Header	Compatibility
_filelength	<io.h>	Win 95, Win NT
_filelengthi64	<io.h>	Win 95, Win NT

For additional compatibility information, see "Compatibility" in the Introduction.

Libraries

LIBC.LIB	Single thread static library, retail version
LIBCMT.LIB	Multithread static library, retail version
MSVCRT.LIB	Import library for MSVCRT.DLL, retail version

Return Value

Both **_filelength** and **_filelengthi64** return the file length, in bytes, of the target file associated with *handle*. Both functions return a value of –1L to indicate an error, and an invalid handle sets **errno** to **EBADF**.

Parameter

handle
    Target file handle

Example

```
/* CHSIZE.C: This program uses _filelength to report the size
 * of a file before and after modifying it with _chsize.
 */

#include <io.h>
#include <fcntl.h>
#include <sys/types.h>
#include <sys/stat.h>
#include <stdio.h>
```

```
void main( void )
{
    int fh, result;
    unsigned int nbytes = BUFSIZ;

    /* Open a file */
    if( (fh = _open( "data", _O_RDWR | _O_CREAT, _S_IREAD |
    ↪ _S_IWRITE ))  != -1 )
    {
        printf( "File length before: %ld\n", _filelength( fh ) );
        if( ( result = _chsize( fh, 329678 ) ) == 0 )
            printf( "Size successfully changed\n" );
        else
            printf( "Problem in changing the size\n" );
    printf( "File length after:  %ld\n", _filelength( fh ) );
        _close( fh );
    }
}
```

Output

```
File length before: 0
Size successfully changed
File length after:  329678
```

See Also

_chsize, _fileno, _fstat, _fstati64, _stat, _stati64

_fileno

Gets the file handle associated with a stream.

int _fileno(FILE *stream);

Function	Required Header	Compatibility
_fileno	\<stdio.h\>	Win 95, Win NT

For additional compatibility information, see "Compatibility" in the Introduction.

Libraries

LIBC.LIB	Single thread static library, retail version
LIBCMT.LIB	Multithread static library, retail version
MSVCRT.LIB	Import library for MSVCRT.DLL, retail version

Return Value

_fileno returns the file handle. There is no error return. The result is undefined if *stream* does not specify an open file.

Parameter

stream
    Pointer to **FILE** structure

Remarks

The **_fileno** routine returns the file handle currently associated with *stream*. This routine is implemented both as a function and as a macro. For details on choosing either implementation, see "Choosing Between Functions and Macros," in the Introduction.

Example

```
/* FILENO.C: This program uses _fileno to obtain
 * the file handle for some standard C streams.
 */

#include <stdio.h>

void main( void )
{
    printf( "The file handle for stdin is %d\n", _fileno( stdin ) );
    printf( "The file handle for stdout is %d\n", _fileno( stdout ) );
    printf( "The file handle for stderr is %d\n", _fileno( stderr ) );
}
```

Output

```
The file handle for stdin is 0
The file handle for stdout is 1
The file handle for stderr is 2
```

See Also

_fdopen, _filelength, fopen, freopen

_find, _wfind Functions

These functions search for and close searches for specified filenames.

- _findclose
- _findnext, _findnexti64, _wfindnext, _wfindnexti64
- _findfirst, _findfirsti64, _wfindfirst, _wfindfirsti64

Remarks

The **_findfirst** function provides information about the first instance of a filename that matches the file specified in the *filespec* argument. Any wildcard combination supported by the host operating system can be used in *filespec*. File information is returned in a **_finddata_t** structure, defined in IO.H. The **_finddata_t** structure includes the following elements:

unsigned attrib
File attribute

time_t time_create
Time of file creation (−1L for FAT file systems)

time_t time_access
Time of last file access (−1L for FAT file systems)

time_t time_write
Time of last write to file

_fsize_t size
Length of file in bytes

char name[_MAX_FNAME]
Null-terminated name of matched file/directory, without the path

In file systems that do not support the creation and last access times of a file, such as the FAT system, the **time_create** and **time_access** fields are always −1L.

_MAX_FNAME is defined in STDLIB.H as 256 bytes.

You cannot specify target attributes (such as **_A_RDONLY**) by which to limit the find operation. This attribute is returned in the **attrib** field of the **_finddata_t** structure and can have the following values (defined in IO.H).

_A_ARCH
Archive. Set whenever the file is changed, and cleared by the BACKUP command. Value: 0x20

_A_HIDDEN
Hidden file. Not normally seen with the DIR command, unless the /AH option is used. Returns information about normal files as well as files with this attribute. Value: 0x02

_A_NORMAL
Normal. File can be read or written to without restriction. Value: 0x00

_A_RDONLY
Read-only. File cannot be opened for writing, and a file with the same name cannot be created. Value: 0x01

_A_SUBDIR
Subdirectory. Value: 0x10

_A_SYSTEM

System file. Not normally seen with the DIR command, unless the /A or /A:S option is used. Value: 0x04

_findnext finds the next name, if any, that matches the *filespec* argument specified in a prior call to **_findfirst**. The *fileinfo* argument should point to a structure initialized by a previous call to **_findfirst**. If a match is found, the *fileinfo* structure contents are altered as described above. **_findclose** closes the specified search handle and releases all associated resources for both **_findfirst** and **_findnext**. The handle returned by either **_findfirst** or **_findnext** must first be passed to **_findclose**, before modification operations, such as deleting, can be performed on the directories that form the paths passed to them.

The **_find** functions allow nested calls. For example, if the file found by a call to **_findfirst** or **_findnext** is a subdirectory, a new search can be initiated with another call to **_findfirst** or **_findnext**.

_wfindfirst and **_wfindnext** are wide-character versions of **_findfirst** and **_findnext**. The structure argument of the wide-character versions has the **_wfinddata_t** data type, which is defined in IO.H and in WCHAR.H. The fields of this data type are the same as those of the **_finddata_t** data type, except that in **_wfinddata_t** the name field is of type **wchar_t** rather than type **char**. Otherwise **_wfindfirst** and **_wfindnext** behave identically to **_findfirst** and **_findnext**. Functions **_findfirsti64**, **_findnexti64**, **_wfindfirsti64**, and **_wfindnexti64** also behave identically except they use and return 64-bit file lengths.

Example

```
/* FFIND.C: This program uses the 32-bit _find functions to print
 * a list of all files (and their attributes) with a .C extension
 * in the current directory.
 */

#include <stdio.h>
#include <io.h>
#include <time.h>

void main( void )
{
    struct _finddata_t c_file;
    long hFile;

    /* Find first .c file in current directory */
    if( (hFile = _findfirst( "*.c", &c_file )) == -1L )
        printf( "No *.c files in current directory!\n" );
    else
    {
        printf( "Listing of .c files\n\n" );
        printf( "\nRDO HID SYS ARC  FILE          DATE %25c SIZE\n", ' ' );
        printf( "--- --- --- ---  ----          ---- %25c ----\n", ' ' );
        printf( ( c_file.attrib & _A_RDONLY ) ? " Y  " : " N  " );
```

```
        printf( ( c_file.attrib & _A_SYSTEM ) ? " Y  " : " N  " );
        printf( ( c_file.attrib & _A_HIDDEN ) ? " Y  " : " N  " );
        printf( ( c_file.attrib & _A_ARCH )   ? " Y  " : " N  " );
        printf( " %-12s %.24s  %9ld\n",
        ↪ c_file.name, ctime( &( c_file.time_write ) ), c_file.size );

        /* Find the rest of the .c files */
        while( _findnext( hFile, &c_file ) == 0 )
        {
            printf( ( c_file.attrib & _A_RDONLY ) ? " Y  " : " N  " );
            printf( ( c_file.attrib & _A_SYSTEM ) ? " Y  " : " N  " );
            printf( ( c_file.attrib & _A_HIDDEN ) ? " Y  " : " N  " );
            printf( ( c_file.attrib & _A_ARCH )   ? " Y  " : " N  " );
            printf( " %-12s %.24s  %9ld\n",
            ↪ c_file.name, ctime( &( c_file.time_write ) ), c_file.size );
        }

        _findclose( hFile );
    }
}
```

Output

```
Listing of .c files

RDO HID SYS ARC  FILE          DATE                        SIZE
--- --- --- ---  ----          ----                        ----
 N   N   N   Y   CWAIT.C       Tue Jun 01 04:07:26 1993    1611
 N   N   N   Y   SPRINTF.C     Thu May 27 04:59:18 1993     617
 N   N   N   Y   CABS.C        Thu May 27 04:58:46 1993     359
 N   N   N   Y   BEGTHRD.C     Tue Jun 01 04:00:48 1993    3726
```

_findclose

Closes the specified search handle and releases associated resources.

int _findclose(long *handle* **);**

Function	Required Header	Compatibility
_findclose	<io.h>	Win 95, Win NT

For additional compatibility information, see "Compatibility" in the Introduction.

Libraries

LIBC.LIB	Single thread static library, retail version
LIBCMT.LIB	Multithread static library, retail version
MSVCRT.LIB	Import library for MSVCRT.DLL, retail version

Return Value

If successful, **_findclose** returns 0. Otherwise, it returns –1 and sets **errno** to **ENOENT**, indicating that no more matching files could be found.

Parameter

handle
   Search handle returned by a previous call to **_findfirst**

_findfirst, _findfirsti64, _wfindfirst, _wfindfirsti64

Provides information about the first instance of a filename that matches the file specified in the *filespec* argument.

long _findfirst(char **filespec*, **struct _finddata_t** **fileinfo*);
__int64 _findfirsti64(char **filespec*, **struct _finddata_t** **fileinfo*);
long _wfindfirst(wchar_t **filespec*, **struct _wfinddata_t** **fileinfo*);
__int64 _wfindfirsti64(wchar_t **filespec*, **struct _wfinddata_t** **fileinfo*);

Function	Required Header	Compatibility
_findfirst	<io.h>	Win 95, Win NT
_findfirsti64	<io.h>	Win 95, Win NT
_wfindfirst	<io.h> or <wchar.h>	Win NT
_wfindfirsti64	<io.h> or <wchar.h>	Win NT

For additional compatibility information, see "Compatibility" in the Introduction.

Libraries

LIBC.LIB	Single thread static library, retail version
LIBCMT.LIB	Multithread static library, retail version
MSVCRT.LIB	Import library for MSVCRT.DLL, retail version

Return Value

If successful, **_findfirst** and **_wfindfirst** return a unique search handle identifying the file or group of files matching the *filespec* specification, which can be used in a subsequent call to **_findnext** or **_wfindnext**, respectively, or to **_findclose**. Otherwise, **_findfirst** and **_wfindfirst** return –1 and set **errno** to one of the following values:

ENOENT
   File specification that could not be matched

EINVAL
   Invalid filename specification

Parameters

filespec
   Target file specification (may include wildcards)

fileinfo
   File information buffer

Generic-Text Routine Mappings

TCHAR.H Routine	_UNICODE & _MBCS Not Defined	_MBCS Defined	_UNICODE Defined
_tfindfirst	_findfirst	_findfirst	_wfindfirst
_tfindfirsti64	_findfirsti64	_findfirsti64	_wfindfirsti64

_findnext, _findnexti64, _wfindnext, _wfindnexti64

Find the next name, if any, that matches the *filespec* argument in a previous call to **_findfirst**, and then alters the *fileinfo* structure contents accordingly.

int _findnext(long *handle***, struct _finddata_t ****fileinfo* **);**
__int64 _findnexti64(long *handle***, struct _finddata_t ****fileinfo* **);**
int _wfindnext(long *handle***, struct _wfinddata_t ****fileinfo* **);**
__int64 _wfindnexti64(long *handle***, struct _wfinddata_t ****fileinfo* **);**

Function	Required Header	Compatibility
_findnext	<io.h>	Win 95, Win NT
_findnexti64	<io.h>	Win 95, Win NT
_wfindnext	<io.h> or <wchar.h>	Win NT
_wfindnexti64	<io.h> or <wchar.h>	Win NT

For additional compatibility information, see "Compatibility" in the Introduction.

Libraries

LIBC.LIB	Single thread static library, retail version
LIBCMT.LIB	Multithread static library, retail version
MSVCRT.LIB	Import library for MSVCRT.DLL, retail version

Return Value

If successful, **_findnext** and **_wfindnext** return 0. Otherwise, they return –1 and set **errno** to **ENOENT**, indicating that no more matching files could be found.

Parameters

handle
Search handle returned by a previous call to **_findfirst**

fileinfo
File information buffer

Generic-Text Routine Mappings

TCHAR.H Routine	_UNICODE & _MBCS Not Defined	_MBCS Defined	_UNICODE Defined
_tfindnext	_findnext	_findnext	_wfindnext
_tfindnexti64	_findnexti64	_findnexti64	_wfindnexti64

_finite

Determines whether given double-precision floating point value is finite.

int _finite(double *x*);

Function	Required Header	Compatibility
_finite	<float.h>	Win 95, Win NT

For additional compatibility information, see "Compatibility" in the Introduction.

Libraries

LIBC.LIB	Single thread static library, retail version
LIBCMT.LIB	Multithread static library, retail version
MSVCRT.LIB	Import library for MSVCRT.DLL, retail version

Return Value

_finite returns a nonzero value (TRUE) if its argument *x* is not infinite, that is, if $-INF < x < +INF$. It returns 0 (FALSE) if the argument is infinite or a NaN.

Parameter

x
Double-precision floating-point value

See Also

_isnan, **_fpclass**

floor

Calculates the floor of a value.

double floor(double *x* **);**

Function	Required Header	Compatibility
floor	<math.h>	ANSI, Win 95, Win NT

For additional compatibility information, see "Compatibility" in the Introduction.

Libraries

LIBC.LIB	Single thread static library, retail version
LIBCMT.LIB	Multithread static library, retail version
MSVCRT.LIB	Import library for MSVCRT.DLL, retail version

Return Value

The **floor** function returns a floating-point value representing the largest integer that is less than or equal to *x*. There is no error return.

Parameter

x

    Floating-point value

Example

```
/* FLOOR.C: This example displays the largest integers
 * less than or equal to the floating-point values 2.8
 * and -2.8. It then shows the smallest integers greater
 * than or equal to 2.8 and -2.8.
 */

#include <math.h>
#include <stdio.h>

void main( void )
{
   double y;

   y = floor( 2.8 );
   printf( "The floor of 2.8 is %f\n", y );
   y = floor( -2.8 );
   printf( "The floor of -2.8 is %f\n", y );
```

```
    y = ceil( 2.8 );
    printf( "The ceil of 2.8 is %f\n", y );
    y = ceil( -2.8 );
    printf( "The ceil of -2.8 is %f\n", y );
}
```

Output

```
The floor of 2.8 is 2.000000
The floor of -2.8 is -3.000000
The ceil of 2.8 is 3.000000
The ceil of -2.8 is -2.000000
```

See Also

ceil, fmod

_flushall

Flushes all streams; clears all buffers.

int _flushall(void);

Function	Required Header	Compatibility
_flushall	<stdio.h>	Win 95, Win NT

For additional compatibility information, see "Compatibility" in the Introduction.

Libraries

LIBC.LIB	Single thread static library, retail version
LIBCMT.LIB	Multithread static library, retail version
MSVCRT.LIB	Import library for MSVCRT.DLL, retail version

Return Value

_flushall returns the number of open streams (input and output). There is no error return.

Remarks

By default, the **_flushall** function writes to appropriate files the contents of all buffers associated with open output streams. All buffers associated with open input streams are cleared of their current contents. (These buffers are normally maintained by the operating system, which determines the optimal time to write the data automatically to disk: when a buffer is full, when a stream is closed, or when a program terminates normally without closing streams.)

If a read follows a call to **_flushall**, new data is read from the input files into the buffers. All streams remain open after the call to **_flushall**.

The commit-to-disk feature of the run-time library lets you ensure that critical data is written directly to disk rather than to the operating system buffers. Without rewriting an existing program, you can enable this feature by linking the program's object files with COMMODE.OBJ. In the resulting executable file, calls to **_flushall** write the contents of all buffers to disk. Only **_flushall** and **fflush** are affected by COMMODE.OBJ.

For information about controlling the commit-to-disk feature, see **fopen**, **_fdopen** and, "Stream I/O" in Chapter 1, "Run-Time Routines by Category."

Example

```
/* FLUSHALL.C: This program uses _flushall
 * to flush all open buffers.
 */

#include <stdio.h>

void main( void )
{
    int numflushed;

    numflushed = _flushall();
    printf( "There were %d streams flushed\n", numflushed );
}
```

Output

```
There were 3 streams flushed
```

See Also

_commit, **fclose**, **fflush**, **_flushall**, **setvbuf**

fmod

Calculates the floating-point remainder.

double fmod(double *x*, double *y*);

Function	Required Header	Compatibility
fmod	<math.h>	ANSI, Win 95, Win NT

For additional compatibility information, see "Compatibility" in the Introduction.

Libraries

LIBC.LIB	Single thread static library, retail version
LIBCMT.LIB	Multithread static library, retail version
MSVCRT.LIB	Import library for MSVCRT.DLL, retail version

Return Value

fmod returns the floating-point remainder of x / y. If the value of y is 0.0, **fmod** returns a quiet NaN. For information about representation of a quiet NaN by the **printf** family, see **printf**.

Parameters

x, y

Floating-point values

Remarks

The **fmod** function calculates the floating-point remainder f of x / y such that $x = i * y + f$, where i is an integer, f has the same sign as x, and the absolute value of f is less than the absolute value of y.

Example

```
/* FMOD.C: This program displays a
 * floating-point remainder.
 */

#include <math.h>
#include <stdio.h>

void main( void )
{
    double w = -10.0, x = 3.0, y = 0.0, z;

    z = fmod( x, y );
    printf( "The remainder of %.2f / %.2f is %f\n", w, x, z );
    printf( "The remainder of %.2f / %.2f is %f\n", x, y, z );

}
```

Output

```
The remainder of -10.00 / 3.00 is -1.000000
```

See Also

ceil, **fabs**, **floor**

fopen, _wfopen

Open a file.

FILE *fopen(const char *_filename_, const char *_mode_);
FILE *_wfopen(const wchar_t *_filename_, const wchar_t *_mode_);

Function	Required Header	Compatibility
fopen	<stdio.h>	ANSI, Win 95, Win NT
_wfopen	<stdio.h> or <wchar.h>	Win NT

For additional compatibility information, see "Compatibility" in the Introduction.

Libraries

LIBC.LIB	Single thread static library, retail version
LIBCMT.LIB	Multithread static library, retail version
MSVCRT.LIB	Import library for MSVCRT.DLL, retail version

The **c**, **n**, and **t** _mode_ options are Microsoft extensions for **fopen** and **_fdopen** and should not be used where ANSI portability is desired.

Return Value

Each of these functions returns a pointer to the open file. A null pointer value indicates an error.

Parameters

filename
   Filename

mode
   Type of access permitted

Remarks

The **fopen** function opens the file specified by _filename_. **_wfopen** is a wide-character version of **fopen**; the arguments to **_wfopen** are wide-character strings. **_wfopen** and **fopen** behave identically otherwise.

Generic-Text Routine Mappings

TCHAR.H Routine	_UNICODE & _MBCS Not Defined	_MBCS Defined	_UNICODE Defined
_tfopen	fopen	fopen	_wfopen

The character string _mode_ specifies the type of access requested for the file, as follows:

"r"

Opens for reading. If the file does not exist or cannot be found, the **fopen** call fails.

"w"

Opens an empty file for writing. If the given file exists, its contents are destroyed.

"a"

Opens for writing at the end of the file (appending) without removing the EOF marker before writing new data to the file; creates the file first if it doesn't exist.

"r+"

Opens for both reading and writing. (The file must exist.)

"w+"

Opens an empty file for both reading and writing. If the given file exists, its contents are destroyed.

"a+"

Opens for reading and appending; the appending operation includes the removal of the EOF marker before new data is written to the file and the EOF marker is restored after writing is complete; creates the file first if it doesn't exist.

When a file is opened with the **"a"** or **"a+"** access type, all write operations occur at the end of the file. The file pointer can be repositioned using **fseek** or **rewind**, but is always moved back to the end of the file before any write operation is carried out. Thus, existing data cannot be overwritten.

The **"a"** mode does not remove the EOF marker before appending to the file. After appending has occurred, the MS-DOS TYPE command only shows data up to the original EOF marker and not any data appended to the file. The **"a+"** mode does remove the EOF marker before appending to the file. After appending, the MS-DOS TYPE command shows all data in the file. The **"a+"** mode is required for appending to a stream file that is terminated with the CTRL+Z EOF marker.

When the **"r+"**, **"w+"**, or **"a+"** access type is specified, both reading and writing are allowed (the file is said to be open for "update"). However, when you switch between reading and writing, there must be an intervening **fflush**, **fsetpos**, **fseek**, or **rewind** operation. The current position can be specified for the **fsetpos** or **fseek** operation, if desired.

In addition to the above values, the following characters can be included in *mode* to specify the translation mode for newline characters:

t

Open in text (translated) mode. In this mode, CTRL+Z is interpreted as an end-of-file character on input. In files opened for reading/writing with **"a+"**, **fopen** checks for a CTRL+Z at the end of the file and removes it, if possible. This is done because using **fseek** and **ftell** to move within a file that ends with a CTRL+Z, may cause **fseek** to behave improperly near the end of the file.

Also, in text mode, carriage return–linefeed combinations are translated into single linefeeds on input, and linefeed characters are translated to carriage return–linefeed combinations on output. When a Unicode stream-I/O function operates in text mode (the default), the source or destination stream is assumed to be a sequence of multibyte characters. Therefore, the Unicode stream-input functions convert multibyte characters to wide characters (as if by a call to the **mbtowc** function). For the same reason, the Unicode stream-output functions convert wide characters to multibyte characters (as if by a call to the **wctomb** function).

b

> Open in binary (untranslated) mode; translations involving carriage-return and linefeed characters are suppressed.

If **t** or **b** is not given in *mode*, the default translation mode is defined by the global variable _fmode. If **t** or **b** is prefixed to the argument, the function fails and returns **NULL**.

For more information about using text and binary modes in Unicode and multibyte stream-I/O, see "Text and Binary Mode File I/O" and "Unicode Stream I/O in Text and Binary Modes" in Chapter 1, "Run-Time Routines by Category."

c

> Enable the commit flag for the associated *filename* so that the contents of the file buffer are written directly to disk if either **fflush** or **_flushall** is called.

n

> Reset the commit flag for the associated *filename* to "no-commit." This is the default. It also overrides the global commit flag if you link your program with COMMODE.OBJ. The global commit flag default is "no-commit" unless you explicitly link your program with COMMODE.OBJ.

Valid characters for the *mode* string used in **fopen** and **_fdopen** correspond to *oflag* arguments used in _open and _sopen, as follows.

Characters in *mode* String	Equivalent *oflag* Value for _open/_sopen
a	**_O_WRONLY	_O_APPEND** (usually **_O_WRONLY | _O_CREAT | _O_APPEND**)
a+	**_O_RDWR	_O_APPEND** (usually **_O_RDWR | _O_APPEND | _O_CREAT**)
r	**_O_RDONLY**
r+	**_O_RDWR**
w	**_O_WRONLY** (usually **_O_WRONLY | _O_CREAT | _O_TRUNC**)
w+	**_O_RDWR** (usually **_O_RDWR | _O_CREAT | _O_TRUNC**)
b	**_O_BINARY**
t	**_O_TEXT**
c	None
n	None

Example

```
/* FOPEN.C: This program opens files named "data"
 * and "data2".It  uses fclose to close "data" and
 * _fcloseall to close all remaining files.
 */

#include <stdio.h>

FILE *stream, *stream2;

void main( void )
{
    int numclosed;

    /* Open for read (will fail if file "data" does not exist) */
    if( (stream  = fopen( "data", "r" )) == NULL )
       printf( "The file 'data' was not opened\n" );
    else
       printf( "The file 'data' was opened\n" );

    /* Open for write */
    if( (stream2 = fopen( "data2", "w+" )) == NULL )
       printf( "The file 'data2' was not opened\n" );
    else
       printf( "The file 'data2' was opened\n" );

    /* Close stream */
    if( fclose( stream ) )
       printf( "The file 'data' was not closed\n" );

    /* All other files are closed: */
    numclosed = _fcloseall( );
    printf( "Number of files closed by _fcloseall: %u\n", numclosed );
}
```

Output

```
The file 'data' was opened
The file 'data2' was opened
Number of files closed by _fcloseall: 1
```

See Also

fclose, _fdopen, ferror, _fileno, freopen, _open, _setmode

_fpclass

Returns status word containing information on floating-point class.

int _fpclass(double *x* **);**

Function	Required Header	Compatibility
_fpclass	<float.h>	Win 95, Win NT

For additional compatibility information, see "Compatibility" in the Introduction.

Libraries

LIBC.LIB	Single thread static library, retail version
LIBCMT.LIB	Multithread static library, retail version
MSVCRT.LIB	Import library for MSVCRT.DLL, retail version

Return Value

_fpclass returns an integer value that indicates the floating-point class of its argument *x*. The status word may have one of the following values, defined in FLOAT.H.

Value	Meaning
_FPCLASS_SNAN	Signaling NaN
_FPCLASS_QNAN	Quiet NaN
_FPCLASS_NINF	Negative infinity (–INF)
_FPCLASS_NN	Negative normalized non-zero
_FPCLASS_ND	Negative denormalized
_FPCLASS_NZ	Negative zero (–0)
_FPCLASS_PZ	Positive 0 (+0)
_FPCLASS_PD	Positive denormalized
_FPCLASS_PN	Positive normalized non-zero
_FPCLASS_PINF	Positive infinity (+INF)

Parameter

x

Double-precision floating-point value

See Also

_isnan

_fpieee_flt

Invokes user-defined trap handler for IEEE floating-point exceptions.

int _fpieee_flt(unsigned long *exc_code*, **struct _EXCEPTION_POINTERS** **exc_info*,
 int *handler*(**_FPIEEE_RECORD ***) **);**

Function	Required Header	Compatibility
_fpieee_flt	<fpieee.h>	Win 95, Win NT

For additional compatibility information, see "Compatibility" in the Introduction.

Libraries

LIBC.LIB	Single thread static library, retail version
LIBCMT.LIB	Multithread static library, retail version
MSVCRT.LIB	Import library for MSVCRT.DLL, retail version

Return Value

The return value of **_fpieee_flt** is the value returned by *handler.* As such, the IEEE filter routine may be used in the except clause of a structured exception-handling (SEH) mechanism.

Parameters

exc_code
 Exception code

exc_info
 Pointer to the Windows NT exception information structure

handler
 Pointer to user's IEEE trap-handler routine

Remarks

The **_fpieee_flt** function invokes a user-defined trap handler for IEEE floating-point exceptions and provides it with all relevant information. This routine serves as an exception filter in the SEH mechanism, which invokes your own IEEE exception handler when necessary.

The **_FPIEEE_RECORD** structure, defined in FPIEEE.H, contains information pertaining to an IEEE floating-point exception. This structure is passed to the user-defined trap handler by **_fpieee_flt**.

_FPIEEE_RECORD Field	Description
unsigned int **RoundingMode**, unsigned int **Precision**	These fields contain information on the floating-point environment at the time the exception occurred.
unsigned int **Operation**	Indicates the type of operation that caused the trap. If the type is a comparison (**_FpCodeCompare**), you can supply one of the special **_FPIEEE_COMPARE_RESULT** values (as defined in FPIEEE.H) in the **Result.Value** field. The conversion type (**_FpCodeConvert**) indicates that the trap occurred during a floating-point conversion operation. You can look at the **Operand1** and **Result** types to determine the type of conversion being attempted.
_FPIEEE_VALUE Operand1, **_FPIEEE_VALUE Operand2**, **_FPIEEE_VALUE Result**	These structures indicate the types and values of the proposed result and operands: **OperandValid** Flag indicating whether the responding value is valid. **Format** Data type of the corresponding value. The format type may be returned even if the corresponding value is not valid. **Value** Result or operand data value.

Example

```
/* FPIEEE.C: This program demonstrates the implementation of
 * a user-defined floating-point exception handler using the
 * _fpieee_flt function.
 */

#include <fpieee.h>
#include <excpt.h>
#include <float.h>

int fpiee_handler( _FPIEEE_RECORD * );

int fpieee_handler( _FPIEEE_RECORD *pieee )
{
    // user-defined ieee trap handler routine:
    // there is one handler for all
    // IEEE exceptions

    // Assume the user wants all invalid
    // operations to return 0.

    if ((pieee->Cause.InvalidOperation) &&
        (pieee->Result.Format == _FpFormatFp32))
    {
        pieee->Result.Value.Fp32Value = 0.0F;

        return EXCEPTION_CONTINUE_EXECUTION;
    }
```

```
    else
        return EXCEPTION_EXECUTE_HANDLER;
}

#define _EXC_MASK   \
    _EM_UNDERFLOW  + \
    _EM_OVERFLOW   + \
    _EM_ZERODIVIDE + \
    _EM_INEXACT

void main( void )
{
    // ...

    __try {
        // unmask invalid operation exception
        _controlfp(_EXC_MASK, _MCW_EM);

        // code that may generate
        // fp exceptions goes here
    }
    __except ( _fpieee_flt( GetExceptionCode(),
                GetExceptionInformation(),
                fpieee_handler ) ){

        // code that gets control

        // if fpieee_handler returns
        // EXCEPTION_EXECUTE_HANDLER goes here
    }

    // ...
}
```

See Also

_control87

_fpreset

Resets the floating-point package.

void _fpreset(void);

Function	Required Header	Compatibility
_fpreset	<float.h>	Win 95, Win NT

For additional compatibility information, see "Compatibility" in the Introduction.

Libraries

LIBC.LIB	Single thread static library, retail version
LIBCMT.LIB	Multithread static library, retail version
MSVCRT.LIB	Import library for MSVCRT.DLL, retail version

Return Value

None

Remarks

The **_fpreset** function reinitializes the floating-point math package. **_fpreset** is usually used with **signal**, **system**, or the **_exec** or **_spawn** functions. If a program traps floating-point error signals (**SIGFPE**) with **signal**, it can safely recover from floating-point errors by invoking **_fpreset** and using **longjmp**.

Example

```
/* FPRESET.C: This program uses signal to set up a
 * routine for handling floating-point errors.
 */

#include <stdio.h>
#include <signal.h>
#include <setjmp.h>
#include <stdlib.h>
#include <float.h>
#include <math.h>
#include <string.h>

#pragma warning(disable : 4113) /* C4113 warning expected */

jmp_buf mark;            /* Address for long jump to jump to */
int     fperr;           /* Global error number */

void __cdecl fphandler( int sig, int num );   /* Prototypes */
void fpcheck( void );

void main( void )
{
    double n1, n2, r;
    int jmpret;
    /* Unmask all floating-point exceptions. */
    _control87( 0, _MCW_EM );
    /* Set up floating-point error handler. The compiler
     * will generate a warning because it expects
     * signal-handling functions to take only one argument.
     */
    if( signal( SIGFPE, fphandler ) == SIG_ERR )
```

```
   {
      fprintf( stderr, "Couldn't set SIGFPE\n" );
      abort();    }

   /* Save stack environment for return in case of error. First
    * time through, jmpret is 0, so true conditional is executed.
    * If an error occurs, jmpret will be set to -1 and false
    * conditional will be executed.
    */
   jmpret = setjmp( mark );
   if( jmpret == 0 )
   {
      printf( "Test for invalid operation - " );
      printf( "enter two numbers: " );
      scanf( "%lf %lf", &n1, &n2 );
      r = n1 / n2;
      /* This won't be reached if error occurs. */
      printf( "\n\n%4.3g / %4.3g = %4.3g\n", n1, n2, r );

      r = n1 * n2;
      /* This won't be reached if error occurs. */
      printf( "\n\n%4.3g * %4.3g = %4.3g\n", n1, n2, r );
   }
   else
      fpcheck();
}
/* fphandler handles SIGFPE (floating-point error) interrupt. Note
 * that this prototype accepts two arguments and that the
 * prototype for signal in the run-time library expects a signal
 * handler to have only one argument.
 *
 * The second argument in this signal handler allows processing of
 * _FPE_INVALID, _FPE_OVERFLOW, _FPE_UNDERFLOW, and
 * _FPE_ZERODIVIDE, all of which are Microsoft-specific symbols
 * that augment the information provided by SIGFPE. The compiler
 * will generate a warning, which is harmless and expected.

 */
void fphandler( int sig, int num )
{
   /* Set global for outside check since we don't want
    * to do I/O in the handler.
    */
   fperr = num;
   /* Initialize floating-point package. */
   _fpreset();
   /* Restore calling environment and jump back to setjmp. Return
    * -1 so that setjmp will return false for conditional test.
    */
```

```
    longjmp( mark, -1 );
}
void fpcheck( void )
{
    char fpstr[30];
    switch( fperr )
    {
    case _FPE_INVALID:
        strcpy( fpstr, "Invalid number" );
        break;
    case _FPE_OVERFLOW:
        strcpy( fpstr, "Overflow" );

        break;
    case _FPE_UNDERFLOW:
        strcpy( fpstr, "Underflow" );
        break;
    case _FPE_ZERODIVIDE:
        strcpy( fpstr, "Divide by zero" );
        break;
    default:
        strcpy( fpstr, "Other floating point error" );
        break;
    }
    printf( "Error %d: %s\n", fperr, fpstr );
}
```

Output

```
Test for invalid operation - enter two numbers: 5 0
Error 131: Divide by zero
```

See Also

_exec Function Overview, **signal**, **_spawn Function Overview**, **system**

fprintf, fwprintf

Print formatted data to a stream.

int fprintf(FILE **stream*, **const char** **format* [, *argument*]...**);**
int fwprintf(FILE **stream*, **const wchar_t** **format* [, *argument*]...**);**

Function	Required Header	Compatibility
fprintf	<stdio.h>	ANSI, Win 95, Win NT
fwprintf	<stdio.h> or <wchar.h>	ANSI, Win 95, Win NT

For additional compatibility information, see "Compatibility" in the Introduction.

Libraries

LIBC.LIB	Single thread static library, retail version
LIBCMT.LIB	Multithread static library, retail version
MSVCRT.LIB	Import library for MSVCRT.DLL, retail version

Return Value

fprintf returns the number of bytes written. **fwprintf** returns the number of wide characters written. Each of these functions returns a negative value instead when an output error occurs.

Parameters

stream
   Pointer to **FILE** structure

format
   Format-control string

argument
   Optional arguments

Remarks

fprintf formats and prints a series of characters and values to the output *stream*. Each function *argument* (if any) is converted and output according to the corresponding format specification in *format*. For **fprintf**, the *format* argument has the same syntax and use that it has in **printf**.

fwprintf is a wide-character version of **fprintf**; in **fwprintf**, *format* is a wide-character string. These functions behave identically otherwise.

Generic-Text Routine Mappings

TCHAR.H Routine	_UNICODE & _MBCS Not Defined	_MBCS Defined	_UNICODE Defined
_ftprintf	fprintf	fprintf	fwprintf

For more information, see "Format Specification Fields" on page 543.

Example

```
/* FPRINTF.C: This program uses fprintf to format various
 * data and print it to the file named FPRINTF.OUT. It
 * then displays FPRINTF.OUT on the screen using the system
 * function to invoke the operating-system TYPE command.
 */
```

```
#include <stdio.h>
#include <process.h>

FILE *stream;

void main( void )
{
    int    i = 10;
    double fp = 1.5;
    char   s[] = "this is a string";
    char   c = '\n';

    stream = fopen( "fprintf.out", "w" );
    fprintf( stream, "%s%c", s, c );
    fprintf( stream, "%d\n", i );
    fprintf( stream, "%f\n", fp );
    fclose( stream );
    system( "type fprintf.out" );
}
```

Output

```
this is a string
10
1.500000
```

See Also

_cprintf, **fscanf**, **sprintf**

fputc, fputwc, _fputchar, _fputwchar

Writes a character to a stream (**fputc**, **fputwc**) or to **stdout** (**_fputchar**, **_fputwchar**).

int fputc(int c, **FILE ****stream* **);**
wint_t fputwc(wint_t c, **FILE ****stream* **);**
int _fputchar(int c **);**
wint_t _fputwchar(wint_t c **);**

Function	Required Header	Compatibility
fputc	<stdio.h>	ANSI, Win 95, Win NT
fputwc	<stdio.h> or <wchar.h>	ANSI, Win 95, Win NT
_fputchar	<stdio.h>	Win 95, Win NT
_fputwchar	<stdio.h> or <wchar.h>	Win 95, Win NT

For additional compatibility information, see "Compatibility" in the Introduction.

Libraries

LIBC.LIB	Single thread static library, retail version
LIBCMT.LIB	Multithread static library, retail version
MSVCRT.LIB	Import library for MSVCRT.DLL, retail version

Return Value

Each of these functions returns the character written. For **fputc** and **_fputchar**, a return value of **EOF** indicates an error. For **fputwc** and **_fputwchar**, a return value of **WEOF** indicates an error.

Parameters

c
Character to be written

stream
Pointer to **FILE** structure

Remarks

Each of these functions writes the single character *c* to a file at the position indicated by the associated file position indicator (if defined) and advances the indicator as appropriate. In the case of **fputc** and **fputwc**, the file is associated with *stream*. If the file cannot support positioning requests or was opened in append mode, the character is appended to the end of the stream. Routine-specific remarks follow.

Routine	Remarks
fputc	Equivalent to **putc**, but implemented only as a function, rather than as a function and a macro.
fputwc	Wide-character version of **fputc**. Writes *c* as a multibyte character or a wide character according to whether *stream* is opened in text mode or binary mode.
_fputchar	Equivalent to **fputc(stdout)**. Also equivalent to **putchar**, but implemented only as a function, rather than as a function and a macro. Microsoft-specific; not ANSI-compatible.
_fputwchar	Wide-character version of **_fputchar**. Writes *c* as a multibyte character or a wide character according to whether *stream* is opened in text mode or binary mode. Microsoft-specific; not ANSI-compatible.

Generic-Text Routine Mappings

TCHAR.H Routine	_UNICODE & _MBCS Not Defined	_MBCS Defined	_UNICODE Defined
_fputtc	fputc	fputc	fputwc
_fputtchar	_fputchar	_fputchar	_fputwchar

Example

```
/* FPUTC.C: This program uses fputc and _fputchar
 * to send a character array to stdout.
 */

#include <stdio.h>

void main( void )
{
    char strptr1[] = "This is a test of fputc!!\n";
    char strptr2[] = "This is a test of _fputchar!!\n";
    char *p;

    /* Print line to stream using fputc. */
    p = strptr1;
    while( (*p != '\0') && fputc( *(p++), stdout ) != EOF ) ;

    /* Print line to stream using _fputchar. */
    p = strptr2;
    while( (*p != '\0') && _fputchar( *(p++) ) != EOF )
        ;
}
```

See Also

fgetc, **putc**

fputs, fputws

Write a string to a stream.

int fputs(const char *string***, FILE** *stream* **);**
int fputws(const wchar_t *string***, FILE** *stream* **);**

Function	Required Header	Compatibility
fputs	<stdio.h>	ANSI, Win 95, Win NT
fputws	<stdio.h> or <wchar.h>	ANSI, Win 95, Win NT

For additional compatibility information, see "Compatibility" in the Introduction.

Libraries

LIBC.LIB	Single thread static library, retail version
LIBCMT.LIB	Multithread static library, retail version
MSVCRT.LIB	Import library for MSVCRT.DLL, retail version

Return Value

Each of these functions returns a nonnegative value if it is successful. On an error, **fputs** returns **EOF**, and **fputws** returns **WEOF**.

Parameters

string
   Output string

stream
   Pointer to **FILE** structure

Remarks

Each of these functions copies *string* to the output *stream* at the current position. **fputws** copies the wide-character argument *string* to *stream* as a multibyte-character string or a wide-character string according to whether *stream* is opened in text mode or binary mode, respectively. Neither function copies the terminating null character.

Generic-Text Routine Mappings

TCHAR.H Routine	_UNICODE & _MBCS Not Defined	_MBCS Defined	_UNICODE Defined
_fputts	fputs	fputs	fputws

Example

```
/* FPUTS.C: This program uses fputs to write
 * a single line to the stdout stream.
 */

#include <stdio.h>

void main( void )
{
    fputs( "Hello world from fputs.\n", stdout );
}
```

Output

```
Hello world from fputs.
```

See Also

fgets, gets, puts, _putws

fread

Reads data from a stream.

size_t fread(void *buffer***, size_t** *size***, size_t** *count***, FILE** **stream* **);**

Function	Required Header	Compatibility
fread	<stdio.h>	ANSI, Win 95, Win NT

For additional compatibility information, see "Compatibility" in the Introduction.

Libraries

LIBC.LIB	Single thread static library, retail version
LIBCMT.LIB	Multithread static library, retail version
MSVCRT.LIB	Import library for MSVCRT.DLL, retail version

Return Value

fread returns the number of full items actually read, which may be less than *count* if an error occurs or if the end of the file is encountered before reaching *count.* Use the **feof** or **ferror** function to distinguish a read error from an end-of-file condition. If *size* or *count* is 0, **fread** returns 0 and the buffer contents are unchanged.

Parameters

buffer
    Storage location for data

size
    Item size in bytes

count
    Maximum number of items to be read

stream
    Pointer to **FILE** structure

Remarks

The **fread** function reads up to *count* items of *size* bytes from the input *stream* and stores them in *buffer.* The file pointer associated with *stream* (if there is one) is increased by the number of bytes actually read. If the given stream is opened in text mode, carriage return–linefeed pairs are replaced with single linefeed characters. The replacement has no effect on the file pointer or the return value. The file-pointer position is indeterminate if an error occurs. The value of a partially read item cannot be determined.

Example

```
/* FREAD.C: This program opens a file named FREAD.OUT and
 * writes 25 characters to the file. It then tries to open
 * FREAD.OUT and read in 25 characters. If the attempt succeeds,
 * the program displays the number of actual items read.
 */

#include <stdio.h>

void main( void )
{
   FILE *stream;
   char list[30];
   int  i, numread, numwritten;

   /* Open file in text mode: */
   if( (stream = fopen( "fread.out", "w+t" )) != NULL )
   {
      for ( i = 0; i < 25; i++ )
         list[i] = (char)('z' - i);
      /* Write 25 characters to stream */
      numwritten = fwrite( list, sizeof( char ), 25, stream );
      printf( "Wrote %d items\n", numwritten );
      fclose( stream );
   }
   else
      printf( "Problem opening the file\n" );

   if( (stream = fopen( "fread.out", "r+t" )) != NULL )
   {
      /* Attempt to read in 25 characters */
      numread = fread( list, sizeof( char ), 25, stream );
      printf( "Number of items read = %d\n", numread );
      printf( "Contents of buffer = %.25s\n", list );
      fclose( stream );
   }
   else
      printf( "File could not be opened\n" );
}
```

Output

```
Wrote 25 items
Number of items read = 25
Contents of buffer = zyxwvutsrqponmlkjihgfedcb
```

See Also

fwrite, **_read**

free

Deallocates or frees a memory block.

void free(void *memblock* **);**

Function	Required Header	Compatibility
free	<stdlib.h> and <malloc.h>	ANSI, Win 95, Win NT

For additional compatibility information, see "Compatibility" in the Introduction.

Libraries

LIBC.LIB	Single thread static library, retail version
LIBCMT.LIB	Multithread static library, retail version
MSVCRT.LIB	Import library for MSVCRT.DLL, retail version

Return Value

None

Parameter

memblock
    Previously allocated memory block to be freed

Remarks

The **free** function deallocates a memory block (*memblock*) that was previously allocated by a call to **calloc**, **malloc**, or **realloc**. The number of freed bytes is equivalent to the number of bytes requested when the block was allocated (or reallocated, in the case of **realloc**). If *memblock* is **NULL**, the pointer is ignored and **free** immediately returns. Attempting to free an invalid pointer (a pointer to a memory block that was not allocated by **calloc**, **malloc**, or **realloc**) may affect subsequent allocation requests and cause errors.

After a memory block has been freed, _heapmin minimizes the amount of free memory on the heap by coalescing the unused regions and releasing them back to the operating system. Freed memory that is not released to the operating system is restored to the free pool and is available for allocation again.

When the application is linked with a debug version of the C run-time libraries, **free** resolves to _free_dbg. For more information about how the heap is managed during the debugging process, see "Using C Run-Time Library Debugging Support" in the *Visual C++ Programmer's Guide* online.

Example

```
/* MALLOC.C: This program allocates memory with
 * malloc, then frees the memory with free.
 */
```

```
#include <stdlib.h>          /* For _MAX_PATH definition */
#include <stdio.h>
#include <malloc.h>

void main( void )
{
   char *string;

   /* Allocate space for a path name */
   string = malloc( _MAX_PATH );
   if( string == NULL )
      printf( "Insufficient memory available\n" );
   else
   {
      printf( "Memory space allocated for path name\n" );
      free( string );
      printf( "Memory freed\n" );
   }
}
```

Output

```
Memory space allocated for path name
Memory freed
```

See Also

_alloca, calloc, malloc, realloc, _free_dbg, _heapmin

freopen, _wfreopen

Reassign a file pointer.

FILE *freopen(const char **path***, const char ****mode***, FILE ****stream* **);**
FILE *_wfreopen(const wchar_t **path***, const wchar_t ****mode***, FILE ****stream* **);**

Function	Required Header	Compatibility
freopen	<stdio.h>	ANSI, Win 95, Win NT
_wfreopen	<stdio.h> or <wchar.h>	Win NT

For additional compatibility information, see "Compatibility" in the Introduction.

Libraries

LIBC.LIB	Single thread static library, retail version
LIBCMT.LIB	Multithread static library, retail version
MSVCRT.LIB	Import library for MSVCRT.DLL, retail version

Return Value

Each of these functions returns a pointer to the newly opened file. If an error occurs, the original file is closed and the function returns a **NULL** pointer value.

Parameters

path
>Path of new file

mode
>Type of access permitted

stream
>Pointer to **FILE** structure

Remarks

The **freopen** function closes the file currently associated with *stream* and reassigns *stream* to the file specified by *path*. **_wfreopen** is a wide-character version of **_freopen**; the *path* and *mode* arguments to **_wfreopen** are wide-character strings. **_wfreopen** and **_freopen** behave identically otherwise.

Generic-Text Routine Mappings

TCHAR.H Routine	_UNICODE & _MBCS Not Defined	_MBCS Defined	_UNICODE Defined
_tfreopen	freopen	freopen	_wfreopen

freopen is typically used to redirect the pre-opened files **stdin**, **stdout**, and **stderr** to files specified by the user. The new file associated with *stream* is opened with *mode,* which is a character string specifying the type of access requested for the file, as follows:

"r"
>Opens for reading. If the file does not exist or cannot be found, the **freopen** call fails.

"w"
>Opens an empty file for writing. If the given file exists, its contents are destroyed.

"a"
>Opens for writing at the end of the file (appending) without removing the EOF marker before writing new data to the file; creates the file first if it does not exist.

"r+"
>Opens for both reading and writing. (The file must exist.)

"w+"
>Opens an empty file for both reading and writing. If the given file exists, its contents are destroyed.

"a+"

Opens for reading and appending; the appending operation includes the removal of the EOF marker before new data is written to the file and the EOF marker is restored after writing is complete; creates the file first if it does not exist.

Use the **"w"** and **"w+"** types with care, as they can destroy existing files.

When a file is opened with the **"a"** or **"a+"** access type, all write operations take place at the end of the file. Although the file pointer can be repositioned using **fseek** or **rewind**, the file pointer is always moved back to the end of the file before any write operation is carried out. Thus, existing data cannot be overwritten.

The **"a"** mode does not remove the EOF marker before appending to the file. After appending has occurred, the MS-DOS TYPE command only shows data up to the original EOF marker and not any data appended to the file. The **"a+"** mode does remove the EOF marker before appending to the file. After appending, the MS-DOS TYPE command shows all data in the file. The **"a+"** mode is required for appending to a stream file that is terminated with the CTRL+Z EOF marker.

When the **"r+"**, **"w+"**, or **"a+"** access type is specified, both reading and writing are allowed (the file is said to be open for "update"). However, when you switch between reading and writing, there must be an intervening fsetpos, fseek, or rewind operation. The current position can be specified for the **fsetpos** or **fseek** operation, if desired. In addition to the above values, one of the following characters may be included in the *mode* string to specify the translation mode for new lines.

t

Open in text (translated) mode; carriage-return–linefeed (CR–LF) combinations are translated into single linefeed (LF) characters on input; LF characters are translated to CR–LF combinations on output. Also, CTRL+Z is interpreted as an end-of-file character on input. In files opened for reading or for writing and reading with **"a+"**, the run-time library checks for a CTRL+Z at the end of the file and removes it, if possible. This is done because using **fseek** and **ftell** to move within a file may cause **fseek** to behave improperly near the end of the file. The **t** option is a Microsoft extension that should not be used where ANSI portability is desired.

b

Open in binary (untranslated) mode; the above translations are suppressed.

If **t** or **b** is not given in the *mode* string, the translation mode is defined by the default mode variable **_fmode**.

For a discussion of text and binary modes, see "Text and Binary Mode File I/O" in Chapter 1, "Run-Time Routines by Category."

Example

```
/* FREOPEN.C: This program reassigns stderr to the file
 * named FREOPEN.OUT and writes a line to that file.
 */
```

```
#include <stdio.h>
#include <stdlib.h>

FILE *stream;

void main( void )
{
   /* Reassign "stderr" to "freopen.out": */
   stream = freopen( "freopen.out", "w", stderr );

   if( stream == NULL )
      fprintf( stdout, "error on freopen\n" );
   else
   {
      fprintf( stream, "This will go to the file 'freopen.out'\n" );
      fprintf( stdout, "successfully reassigned\n" );
      fclose( stream );
   }
   system( "type freopen.out" );
}
```

Output

```
successfully reassigned
This will go to the file 'freopen.out'
```

See Also

fclose, **_fdopen**, **_fileno**, **fopen**, **_open**, **_setmode**

frexp

Gets the mantissa and exponent of a floating-point number.

double frexp(double *x*, **int** ***expptr**);

Function	Required Header	Compatibility
frexp	<math.h>	ANSI, Win 95, Win NT

For additional compatibility information, see "Compatibility" in the Introduction.

Libraries

LIBC.LIB	Single thread static library, retail version
LIBCMT.LIB	Multithread static library, retail version
MSVCRT.LIB	Import library for MSVCRT.DLL, retail version

Return Value

frexp returns the mantissa. If x is 0, the function returns 0 for both the mantissa and the exponent. There is no error return.

Parameters

x

Floating-point value

expptr

Pointer to stored integer exponent

Remarks

The **frexp** function breaks down the floating-point value (x) into a mantissa (m) and an exponent (n), such that the absolute value of m is greater than or equal to 0.5 and less than 1.0, and $x = m*2^n$. The integer exponent n is stored at the location pointed to by *expptr*.

Example

```
/* FREXP.C: This program calculates frexp( 16.4, &n )
 * then displays y and n.
 */

#include <math.h>
#include <stdio.h>

void main( void )
{
   double x, y;
   int n;

   x = 16.4;
   y = frexp( x, &n );
   printf( "frexp( %f, &n ) = %f, n = %d\n", x, y, n );
}
```

Output

```
frexp( 16.400000, &n ) = 0.512500, n = 5
```

See Also

ldexp, modf

fscanf, fwscanf

Read formatted data from a stream.

int fscanf(FILE **stream*, **const char** **format* [, *argument*]... **);**
int fwscanf(FILE **stream*, **const wchar_t** **format* [, *argument*]... **);**

Function	Required Header	Compatibility
fscanf	<stdio.h>	ANSI, Win 95, Win NT
fwscanf	<stdio.h> or <wchar.h>	ANSI, Win 95, Win NT

For additional compatibility information, see "Compatibility" in the Introduction.

Libraries

LIBC.LIB	Single thread static library, retail version
LIBCMT.LIB	Multithread static library, retail version
MSVCRT.LIB	Import library for MSVCRT.DLL, retail version

Return Value

Each of these functions returns the number of fields successfully converted and assigned; the return value does not include fields that were read but not assigned. A return value of 0 indicates that no fields were assigned. If an error occurs, or if the end of the file stream is reached before the first conversion, the return value is **EOF** for fscanf or **WEOF** for **fwscanf**.

Parameters

stream
    Pointer to **FILE** structure

format
    Format-control string

argument
    Optional arguments

Remarks

The **fscanf** function reads data from the current position of *stream* into the locations given by *argument* (if any). Each *argument* must be a pointer to a variable of a type that corresponds to a type specifier in *format*. *format* controls the interpretation of the input fields and has the same form and function as the *format* argument for **scanf**; see **scanf** for a description of *format*. If copying takes place between strings that overlap, the behavior is undefined.

fwscanf is a wide-character version of **fscanf**; the format argument to **fwscanf** is a wide-character string. These functions behave identically otherwise.

Generic-Text Routine Mappings

TCHAR.H Routine	_UNICODE & _MBCS Not Defined	_MBCS Defined	_UNICODE Defined
_ftscanf	fscanf	fscanf	fwscanf

For more information, see "Format Specification Fields — scanf functions and wscanf Functions" on page 543.

Example

```
/* FSCANF.C: This program writes formatted
 * data to a file. It then uses fscanf to
 * read the various data back from the file.
 */

#include <stdio.h>

FILE *stream;

void main( void )
{
   long l;
   float fp;
   char s[81];
   char c;

   stream = fopen( "fscanf.out", "w+" );
   if( stream == NULL )
      printf( "The file fscanf.out was not opened\n" );
   else
   {
      fprintf( stream, "%s %ld %f%c", "a-string",
      65000, 3.14159, 'x' );

      /* Set pointer to beginning of file: */
      fseek( stream, 0L, SEEK_SET );

      /* Read data back from file: */
      fscanf( stream, "%s", s );
      fscanf( stream, "%ld", &l );

      fscanf( stream, "%f", &fp );
      fscanf( stream, "%c", &c );
```

```
        /* Output data read: */
        printf( "%s\n", s );
        printf( "%ld\n", l );
        printf( "%f\n", fp );
        printf( "%c\n", c );

        fclose( stream );
    }
}
```

Output

```
a-string
65000
3.141590
x
```

See Also

_cscanf, fprintf, scanf, sscanf

fseek

Moves the file pointer to a specified location.

int fseek(FILE **stream*, **long** *offset*, **int** *origin* **);**

Function	Required Header	Compatibility
fseek	<stdio.h>	ANSI, Win 95, Win NT

For additional compatibility information, see "Compatibility" in the Introduction.

Libraries

LIBC.LIB	Single thread static library, retail version
LIBCMT.LIB	Multithread static library, retail version
MSVCRT.LIB	Import library for MSVCRT.DLL, retail version

Return Value

If successful, **fseek** returns 0. Otherwise, it returns a nonzero value. On devices incapable of seeking, the return value is undefined.

Parameters

stream
    Pointer to **FILE** structure

offset

   Number of bytes from *origin*

origin

   Initial position

Remarks

The **fseek** function moves the file pointer (if any) associated with *stream* to a new location that is *offset* bytes from *origin*. The next operation on the stream takes place at the new location. On a stream open for update, the next operation can be either a read or a write. The argument origin must be one of the following constants, defined in STDIO.H:

SEEK_CUR

   Current position of file pointer

SEEK_END

   End of file

SEEK_SET

   Beginning of file

You can use **fseek** to reposition the pointer anywhere in a file. The pointer can also be positioned beyond the end of the file. **fseek** clears the end-of-file indicator and negates the effect of any prior **ungetc** calls against *stream*.

When a file is opened for appending data, the current file position is determined by the last I/O operation, not by where the next write would occur. If no I/O operation has yet occurred on a file opened for appending, the file position is the start of the file.

For streams opened in text mode, **fseek** has limited use, because carriage return–linefeed translations can cause **fseek** to produce unexpected results. The only **fseek** operations guaranteed to work on streams opened in text mode are:

- Seeking with an offset of 0 relative to any of the origin values.

- Seeking from the beginning of the file with an offset value returned from a call to **ftell**.

Also in text mode, CTRL+Z is interpreted as an end-of-file character on input. In files opened for reading/writing, **fopen** and all related routines check for a CTRL+Z at the end of the file and remove it if possible. This is done because using **fseek** and **ftell** to move within a file that ends with a CTRL+Z may cause **fseek** to behave improperly near the end of the file.

Example

```
/* FSEEK.C: This program opens the file FSEEK.OUT and
 * moves the pointer to the file's beginning.
 */

#include <stdio.h>
```

```
void main( void )
{
    FILE *stream;
    char line[81];
    int  result;

    stream = fopen( "fseek.out", "w+" );
    if( stream == NULL )
        printf( "The file fseek.out was not opened\n" );
    else
    {
        fprintf( stream, "The fseek begins here: "
        ↵    "This is the file 'fseek.out'.\n" );
        result = fseek( stream, 23L, SEEK_SET);
        if( result )
            perror( "Fseek failed" );
        else
        {
            printf( "File pointer is set to middle of first line.\n" );
            fgets( line, 80, stream );
            printf( "%s", line );
        }
        fclose( stream );
    }
}
```

Output

```
File pointer is set to middle of first line.
This is the file 'fseek.out'.
```

See Also

ftell, **_lseek**, **rewind**

fsetpos

Sets the stream-position indicator.

int fsetpos(FILE *_stream_, const fpos_t *_pos_);

Function	Required Header	Compatibility
fsetpos	<stdio.h>	ANSI, Win 95, Win NT

For additional compatibility information, see "Compatibility" in the Introduction.

Libraries

LIBC.LIB	Single thread static library, retail version
LIBCMT.LIB	Multithread static library, retail version
MSVCRT.LIB	Import library for MSVCRT.DLL, retail version

Return Value

If successful, **fsetpos** returns 0. On failure, the function returns a nonzero value and sets **errno** to one of the following manifest constants (defined in ERRNO.H): **EBADF**, which means the file is not accessible or the object that *stream* points to is not a valid file handle; or **EINVAL**, which means an invalid stream value was passed.

Parameters

stream
    Pointer to **FILE** structure

pos
    Position-indicator storage

Remarks

The **fsetpos** function sets the file-position indicator for *stream* to the value of *pos,* which is obtained in a prior call to **fgetpos** against *stream*. The function clears the end-of-file indicator and undoes any effects of ungetc on *stream*. After calling **fsetpos**, the next operation on *stream* may be either input or output.

Example

```
/* FGETPOS.C: This program opens a file and reads
 * bytes at several different locations.
 */

#include <stdio.h>

void main( void )
{
    FILE   *stream;
    fpos_t pos;
    char   buffer[20];

    if( (stream = fopen( "fgetpos.c", "rb" )) == NULL )
        printf( "Trouble opening file\n" );
    else
    {
        /* Read some data and then check the position. */
        fread( buffer, sizeof( char ), 10, stream );
        if( fgetpos( stream, &pos ) != 0 )
            perror( "fgetpos error" );
```

```
        else
        {
            fread( buffer, sizeof( char ), 10, stream );
            printf( "10 bytes at byte %ld: %.10s\n", pos, buffer );
        }

    /* Set a new position and read more data */
    pos = 140;
    if( fsetpos( stream, &pos ) != 0 )
        perror( "fsetpos error" );

    fread( buffer, sizeof( char ), 10, stream );
    printf( "10 bytes at byte %ld: %.10s\n", pos, buffer );
    fclose( stream );
    }
}
```

Output

```
10 bytes at byte 10: .C: This p
10 bytes at byte 140:
{
    FIL
```

See Also

fgetpos

_fsopen, _wfsopen

Open a stream with file sharing.

FILE *_fsopen(const char **filename***, const char ****mode***, int** *shflag* **);**
FILE *_wfsopen(const wchar_t **filename***, const wchar_t ****mode***, int** *shflag* **);**

Function	Required Header	Optional Headers	Compatibility
_fsopen	<stdio.h>	<share.h>*	Win 95, Win NT
_wfsopen	<stdio.h> or <wchar.h>	<share.h>*	Win NT

* For manifest constant for *shflag* parameter.

For additional compatibility information, see "Compatibility" in the Introduction.

Libraries

LIBC.LIB	Single thread static library, retail version
LIBCMT.LIB	Multithread static library, retail version
MSVCRT.LIB	Import library for MSVCRT.DLL, retail version

Return Value

Each of these functions returns a pointer to the stream. A **NULL** pointer value indicates an error.

Parameters

filename
    Name of file to open

mode
    Type of access permitted

shflag
    Type of sharing allowed

Remarks

The **_fsopen** function opens the file specified by *filename* as a stream and prepares the file for subsequent shared reading or writing, as defined by the mode and *shflag* arguments. **_wfsopen** is a wide-character version of **_fsopen**; the *filename* and *mode* arguments to **_wfsopen** are wide-character strings. **_wfsopen** and **_fsopen** behave identically otherwise.

Generic-Text Routine Mappings

TCHAR.H Routine	_UNICODE & _MBCS Not Defined	_MBCS Defined	_UNICODE Defined
_tfsopen	_fsopen	_fsopen	_wfsopen

The character string *mode* specifies the type of access requested for the file, as follows:

"r"
    Opens for reading. If the file does not exist or cannot be found, the **_fsopen** call fails.

"w"
    Opens an empty file for writing. If the given file exists, its contents are destroyed.

"a"
    Opens for writing at the end of the file (appending); creates the file first if it does not exist.

"r+"
    Opens for both reading and writing. (The file must exist.)

"w+"
    Opens an empty file for both reading and writing. If the given file exists, its contents are destroyed.

"a+"
    Opens for reading and appending; creates the file first if it does not exist.

Use the **"w"** and **"w+"** types with care, as they can destroy existing files.

When a file is opened with the **"a"** or **"a+"** access type, all write operations occur at the end of the file. The file pointer can be repositioned using **fseek** or **rewind**, but is always moved back to the end of the file before any write operation is carried out. Thus existing data cannot be overwritten. When the **"r+"**, **"w+"**, or **"a+"** access type is specified, both reading and writing are allowed (the file is said to be open for "update"). However, when switching between reading and writing, there must be an intervening fsetpos, fseek, or rewind operation. The current position can be specified for the **fsetpos** or **fseek** operation, if desired. In addition to the above values, one of the following characters can be included in *mode* to specify the translation mode for new lines:

t

Opens a file in text (translated) mode. In this mode, carriage return–linefeed (CR–LF) combinations are translated into single linefeeds (LF) on input and LF characters are translated to CR–LF combinations on output. Also, CTRL+Z is interpreted as an end-of-file character on input. In files opened for reading or reading/writing, **_fsopen** checks for a CTRL+Z at the end of the file and removes it, if possible. This is done because using **fseek** and **ftell** to move within a file that ends with a CTRL+Z may cause **fseek** to behave improperly near the end of the file.

b

Opens a file in binary (untranslated) mode; the above translations are suppressed.

If **t** or **b** is not given in *mode,* the translation mode is defined by the default-mode variable **_fmode**. If **t** or **b** is prefixed to the argument, the function fails and returns **NULL**. For a discussion of text and binary modes, see "Text and Binary Mode File I/O" in Chapter 1, "Run-Time Routines by Category."

The argument *shflag* is a constant expression consisting of one of the following manifest constants, defined in SHARE.H:

_SH_COMPAT

Sets Compatibility mode for 16-bit applications

_SH_DENYNO

Permits read and write access

_SH_DENYRD

Denies read access to file

_SH_DENYRW

Denies read and write access to file

_SH_DENYWR

Denies write access to file

Example

```
/* FSOPEN.C:
 */

#include <stdio.h>
#include <stdlib.h>
#include <share.h>

void main( void )
{
    FILE *stream;

    /* Open output file for writing. Using _fsopen allows us to
     * ensure that no one else writes to the file while we are
     * writing to it.
     */
    if( (stream = _fsopen( "outfile", "wt", _SH_DENYWR )) != NULL )
    {
        fprintf( stream, "No one else in the network can write "
        ↳ "to this file until we are done.\n" );
        fclose( stream );
    }
    /* Now others can write to the file while we read it. */
    system( "type outfile" );
}
```

Output

```
No one else in the network can write to this file until we are done.
```

See Also

fclose, _fdopen, ferror, _fileno, fopen, freopen, _open, _setmode, _sopen

_fstat, _fstati64

Get information about an open file.

int _fstat(int *handle***, struct _stat ***buffer* **);**
__int64 _fstati64(int *handle***, struct _stat ***buffer* **);**

Function	Required Header	Compatibility
_fstat	<sys/stat.h> and <sys/types.h>	Win 95, Win NT
_fstati64	<sys/stat.h> and <sys/types.h>	Win 95, Win NT

For additional compatibility information, see "Compatibility" in the Introduction.

Libraries

LIBC.LIB	Single thread static library, retail version
LIBCMT.LIB	Multithread static library, retail version
MSVCRT.LIB	Import library for MSVCRT.DLL, retail version

Return Value

_fstat and **_fstati64** return 0 if the file-status information is obtained. A return value of –1 indicates an error, in which case **errno** is set to **EBADF**, indicating an invalid file handle.

Parameters

handle
>   Handle of open file

buffer
>   Pointer to structure to store results

Remarks

The **_fstat** function obtains information about the open file associated with *handle* and stores it in the structure pointed to by *buffer*. The **_stat** structure, defined in SYS\STAT.H, contains the following fields:

st_atime
>   Time of last file access.

st_ctime
>   Time of creation of file.

st_dev
>   If a device, *handle*; otherwise 0.

st_mode
>   Bit mask for file-mode information. The **_S_IFCHR** bit is set if *handle* refers to a device. The **_S_IFREG** bit is set if *handle* refers to an ordinary file. The read/write bits are set according to the file's permission mode. **_S_IFCHR** and other constants are defined in SYS\STAT.H.

st_mtime
>   Time of last modification of file.

st_nlink
>   Always 1 on non-NTFS file systems.

st_rdev
>   If a device, *handle*; otherwise 0.

st_size
>   Size of the file in bytes.

If *handle* refers to a device, the **st_atime**, **st_ctime**, and **st_mtime** and **st_size** fields are not meaningful.

Because STAT.H uses the _dev_t type, which is defined in TYPES.H, you must include TYPES.H before STAT.H in your code.

Example

```
/* FSTAT.C: This program uses _fstat to report
 * the size of a file named F_STAT.OUT.
 */

#include <io.h>
#include <fcntl.h>
#include <time.h>
#include <sys/types.h>
#include <sys/stat.h>
#include <stdio.h>
#include <stdlib.h>
#include <string.h>

void main( void )
{
    struct _stat buf;
    int fh, result;
    char buffer[] = "A line to output";

    if( (fh = _open( "f_stat.out", _O_CREAT | _O_WRONLY |
    ↳ _O_TRUNC )) == -1 )
    _write( fh, buffer, strlen( buffer ) );

    /* Get data associated with "fh": */
    result = _fstat( fh, &buf );

    /* Check if statistics are valid: */
    if( result != 0 )
        printf( "Bad file handle\n" );
    else
    {
        printf( "File size     : %ld\n", buf.st_size );

        printf( "Time modified : %s", ctime( &buf.st_ctime ) );
    }
    _close( fh );
}
```

Output

```
File size     : 0
Time modified : Tue Mar 21 15:23:08 1995
```

See Also

_access, **_chmod**, **_filelength**, **_stat**

ftell

Gets the current position of a file pointer.

long ftell(FILE *_stream_);

Function	Required Header	Optional Headers	Compatibility
ftell	<stdio.h>	<errno.h>	ANSI, Win 95, Win NT

For additional compatibility information, see "Compatibility" in the Introduction.

Libraries

LIBC.LIB	Single thread static library, retail version
LIBCMT.LIB	Multithread static library, retail version
MSVCRT.LIB	Import library for MSVCRT.DLL, retail version

Return Value

ftell returns the current file position. The value returned by **ftell** may not reflect the physical byte offset for streams opened in text mode, because text mode causes carriage return–linefeed translation. Use **ftell** with **fseek** to return to file locations correctly. On error, **ftell** returns –1L and **errno** is set to one of two constants, defined in ERRNO.H. The **EBADF** constant means the _stream_ argument is not a valid file-handle value or does not refer to an open file. **EINVAL** means an invalid _stream_ argument was passed to the function. On devices incapable of seeking (such as terminals and printers), or when _stream_ does not refer to an open file, the return value is undefined.

Parameter

stream
 Target **FILE** structure

Remarks

The **ftell** function gets the current position of the file pointer (if any) associated with _stream_. The position is expressed as an offset relative to the beginning of the stream.

Note that when a file is opened for appending data, the current file position is determined by the last I/O operation, not by where the next write would occur. For example, if a file is opened for an append and the last operation was a read, the file position is the point where the next read operation would start, not where the next write would start. (When a file is opened for appending, the file position is moved to end of file before any write operation.) If no I/O operation has yet occurred on a file opened for appending, the file position is the beginning of the file.

In text mode, CTRL+Z is interpreted as an end-of-file character on input. In files opened for reading/writing, **fopen** and all related routines check for a CTRL+Z at the end of the file and remove it if possible. This is done because using **ftell** and **fseek** to move within a file that ends with a CTRL+Z may cause **ftell** to behave improperly near the end of the file.

Example

```c
/* FTELL.C: This program opens a file named FTELL.C
 * for reading and tries to read 100 characters. It
 * then uses ftell to determine the position of the
 * file pointer and displays this position.
 */

#include <stdio.h>

FILE *stream;

void main( void )
{
    long position;
    char list[100];
    if( (stream = fopen( "ftell.c", "rb" )) != NULL )
    {
        /* Move the pointer by reading data: */
        fread( list, sizeof( char ), 100, stream );
        /* Get position after read: */
        position = ftell( stream );
        printf( "Position after trying to read 100 bytes: %ld\n", position );
        fclose( stream );
    }
}
```

Output

```
Position after trying to read 100 bytes: 100
```

See Also

fgetpos, fseek, _lseek, _tell

_ftime

Gets the current time.

void _ftime(struct _timeb *_timeptr_);

Function	Required Header	Compatibility
_ftime	<sys/types.h> and <sys/timeb.h>	Win 95, Win NT

For additional compatibility information, see "Compatibility" in the Introduction.

Libraries

LIBC.LIB	Single thread static library, retail version
LIBCMT.LIB	Multithread static library, retail version
MSVCRT.LIB	Import library for MSVCRT.DLL, retail version

Return Value

_ftime does not return a value, but fills in the fields of the structure pointed to by _timeptr_.

Parameter

timeptr
    Pointer to **_timeb** structure

Remarks

The **_ftime** function gets the current local time and stores it in the structure pointed to by _timeptr_. The **_timeb** structure is defined in SYS\TIMEB.H. It contains four fields:

dstflag
    Nonzero if daylight savings time is currently in effect for the local time zone. (See **_tzset** for an explanation of how daylight savings time is determined.)

millitm
    Fraction of a second in milliseconds.

time
    Time in seconds since midnight (00:00:00), January 1, 1970, coordinated universal time (UTC).

timezone
    Difference in minutes, moving westward, between UTC and local time. The value of _timezone_ is set from the value of the global variable **_timezone** (see **_tzset**).

Example

```
/* FTIME.C: This program uses _ftime to obtain the current
 * time and then stores this time in timebuffer.
 */

#include <stdio.h>
#include <sys/timeb.h>
#include <time.h>

void main( void )
{
   struct _timeb timebuffer;
   char *timeline;

   _ftime( &timebuffer );
   timeline = ctime( & ( timebuffer.time ) );

   printf( "The time is %.19s.%hu %s", timeline, timebuffer.millitm, &timeline[20] );
}
```

Output

```
The time is Tue Mar 21 15:26:41.341 1995
```

See Also

asctime, **ctime**, **gmtime**, **localtime**, **time**

_fullpath, _wfullpath

Create an absolute or full path name for the specified relative path name.

char *_fullpath(char **absPath***, const char ****relPath***, size_t** *maxLength* **);**
wchar_t *_wfullpath(wchar_t **absPath***, const wchar_t ****relPath***, size_t** *maxLength* **);**

Function	Required Header	Compatibility
_fullpath	<stdlib.h>	Win 95, Win NT
_wfullpath	<stdlib.h> or <wchar.h>	Win NT

For additional compatibility information, see "Compatibility" in the Introduction.

Libraries

LIBC.LIB	Single thread static library, retail version
LIBCMT.LIB	Multithread static library, retail version
MSVCRT.LIB	Import library for MSVCRT.DLL, retail version

Return Value

Each of these functions returns a pointer to a buffer containing the absolute path name (*absPath*). If there is an error (for example, if the value passed in *relPath* includes a drive letter that is not valid or cannot be found, or if the length of the created absolute path name (*absPath*) is greater than *maxLength*) the function returns **NULL**.

Parameters

absPath

Pointer to a buffer containing the absolute or full path name

relPath

Relative path name

maxLength

Maximum length of the absolute path name buffer (*absPath*). This length is in bytes for **_fullpath** but in wide characters (**wchar_t**) for **_wfullpath**.

Remarks

The **_fullpath** function expands the relative path name in *relPath* to its fully qualified or "absolute" path, and stores this name in *absPath*. A relative path name specifies a path to another location from the current location (such as the current working directory: "."). An absolute path name is the expansion of a relative path name that states the entire path required to reach the desired location from the root of the filesystem. Unlike **_makepath**, **_fullpath** can be used to obtain the absolute path name for relative paths (*relPath*) that include "./" or "../" in their names.

For example, to use C run-time routines, the application must include the header files that contain the declarations for the routines. Each header file include statement references the location of the file in a relative manner (from the application's working directory):

```
#include <stdlib.h>
```

when the absolute path (actual file system location) of the file may be:

```
\\machine\shareName\msvcSrc\crt\headerFiles\stdlib.h
```

_fullpath automatically handles multibyte-character string arguments as appropriate, recognizing multibyte-character sequences according to the multibyte code page currently in use. **_wfullpath** is a wide-character version of **_fullpath**; the string arguments to **_wfullpath** are wide-character strings. **_wfullpath** and **_fullpath** behave identically except that **_wfullpath** does not handle multibyte-character strings.

Generic-Text Routine Mappings

TCHAR.H Routine	_UNICODE & _MBCS Not Defined	_MBCS Defined	_UNICODE Defined
_tfullpath	_fullpath	_fullpath	_wfullpath

If the *absPath* buffer is **NULL**, **_fullpath** calls malloc to allocate a buffer of size **_MAX_PATH** and ignores the *maxLength* argument. It is the caller's responsibility to deallocate this buffer (using free) as appropriate. If the *relPath* argument specifies a disk drive, the current directory of this drive is combined with the path.

Example

```
/* FULLPATH.C: This program demonstrates how _fullpath
 * creates a full path from a partial path.
 */

#include <stdio.h>
#include <conio.h>
#include <stdlib.h>
#include <direct.h>

char full[_MAX_PATH], part[_MAX_PATH];

void main( void )
{
   while( 1 )
   {
      printf( "Enter partial path or ENTER to quit: " );
      gets( part );
      if( part[0] == 0 )
         break;

      if( _fullpath( full, part, _MAX_PATH ) != NULL )
         printf( "Full path is: %s\n", full );
      else
         printf( "Invalid path\n" );
   }
}
```

See Also

_getcwd, **_getdcwd**, **_makepath**, **_splitpath**

_futime

Sets modification time on an open file.

int _futime(int *handle*, **struct _utimbuf** **filetime* **);**

Function	Required Header	Optional Headers	Compatibility
_futime	<sys/utime.h>	<errno.h>	Win 95, Win NT

For additional compatibility information, see "Compatibility" in the Introduction.

Libraries

LIBC.LIB	Single thread static library, retail version
LIBCMT.LIB	Multithread static library, retail version
MSVCRT.LIB	Import library for MSVCRT.DLL, retail version

Return Value

_futime returns 0 if successful. If an error occurs, this function returns –1 and **errno** is set to **EBADF**, indicating an invalid file handle.

Parameters

handle
 Handle to open file

filetime
 Pointer to structure containing new modification date

Remarks

The **_futime** routine sets the modification date and the access time on the open file associated with *handle*. **_futime** is identical to _utime, except that its argument is the handle to an open file, rather than the name of a file or a path to a file. The **_utimbuf** structure contains fields for the new modification date and access time. Both fields must contain valid values.

Example

```
/* FUTIME.C: This program uses _futime to set the
 * file-modification time to the current time.
 */

#include <stdio.h>
#include <stdlib.h>
#include <fcntl.h>
#include <io.h>
#include <sys/types.h>
#include <sys/stat.h>
#include <sys/utime.h>

void main( void )
{

    int hFile;

    /* Show file time before and after. */
    system( "dir futime.c" );

    hFile = _open("futime.c", _O_RDWR);
```

```
   if( _futime( hFile, NULL ) == -1 )
      perror( "_futime failed\n" );
   else
      printf( "File time modified\n" );

   close (hFile);

   system( "dir futime.c" );
}
```

Output

```
Volume in drive C is CDRIVE
Volume Serial Number is 1D37-7A7A

Directory of C:\code

05/03/95  01:30p                 601 futime.c
             1 File(s)           601 bytes
                        16,269,312 bytes free
Volume in drive C is CDRIVE
Volume Serial Number is 1D37-7A7A

Directory of C:\code

05/03/95  01:36p                 601 futime.c
             1 File(s)           601 bytes
                        16,269,312 bytes free
File time modified
```

fwrite

Writes data to a stream.

size_t fwrite(const void *buffer*, **size_t** *size*, **size_t** *count*, **FILE** *stream* **);**

Function	Required Header	Compatibility
fwrite	<stdio.h>	ANSI, Win 95, Win NT

For additional compatibility information, see "Compatibility" in the Introduction.

Libraries

LIBC.LIB	Single thread static library, retail version
LIBCMT.LIB	Multithread static library, retail version
MSVCRT.LIB	Import library for MSVCRT.DLL, retail version

Return Value

fwrite returns the number of full items actually written, which may be less than *count* if an error occurs. Also, if an error occurs, the file-position indicator cannot be determined.

Parameters

buffer
> Pointer to data to be written

size
> Item size in bytes

count
> Maximum number of items to be written

stream
> Pointer to **FILE** structure

Remarks

The **fwrite** function writes up to *count* items, of *size* length each, from *buffer* to the output *stream.* The file pointer associated with *stream* (if there is one) is incremented by the number of bytes actually written. If *stream* is opened in text mode, each carriage return is replaced with a carriage return–linefeed pair. The replacement has no effect on the return value.

Example

```
/* FREAD.C: This program opens a file named FREAD.OUT and
 * writes 25 characters to the file. It then tries to open
 * FREAD.OUT and read in 25 characters. If the attempt succeeds,
 * the program displays the number of actual items read.
 */

#include <stdio.h>

void main( void )
{
    FILE *stream;
    char list[30];
    int  i, numread, numwritten;

    /* Open file in text mode: */
    if( (stream = fopen( "fread.out", "w+t" )) != NULL )
    {
        for ( i = 0; i < 25; i++ )
            list[i] = (char)('z' - i);
        /* Write 25 characters to stream */
        numwritten = fwrite( list, sizeof( char ), 25, stream );
        printf( "Wrote %d items\n", numwritten );
```

```
      fclose( stream );
   }
   else
      printf( "Problem opening the file\n" );

   if( (stream = fopen( "fread.out", "r+t" )) != NULL )
   {
      /* Attempt to read in 25 characters */
      numread = fread( list, sizeof( char ), 25, stream );
      printf( "Number of items read = %d\n", numread );
      printf( "Contents of buffer = %.25s\n", list );
      fclose( stream );
   }
   else
      printf( "File could not be opened\n" );
}
```

Output

```
Wrote 25 items
Number of items read = 25
Contents of buffer = zyxwvutsrqponmlkjihgfedcb
```

See Also

fread, **_write**

_gcvt

Converts a floating-point value to a string, which it stores in a buffer.

char *_gcvt(double *value*, **int** *digits*, **char** *buffer **);**

Routine	Required Header	Compatibility
_gcvt	<stdlib.h>	Win 95, Win NT

For additional compatibility information, see "Compatibility" in the Introduction.

Libraries

LIBC.LIB	Single thread static library, retail version
LIBCMT.LIB	Multithread static library, retail version
MSVCRT.LIB	Import library for MSVCRT.DLL, retail version

Return Value

_gcvt returns a pointer to the string of digits. There is no error return.

Parameters

value
> Value to be converted

digits
> Number of significant digits stored

buffer
> Storage location for result

Remarks

The **_gcvt** function converts a floating-point *value* to a character string (which includes a decimal point and a possible sign byte) and stores the string in *buffer*. The *buffer* should be large enough to accommodate the converted value plus a terminating null character, which is appended automatically. If a buffer size of *digits* + 1 is used, the function overwrites the end of the buffer. This is because the converted string includes a decimal point and can contain sign and exponent information. There is no provision for overflow. **_gcvt** attempts to produce *digits* digits in decimal format. If it cannot, it produces *digits* digits in exponential format. Trailing zeros may be suppressed in the conversion.

Example

```
/* _GCVT.C: This program converts -3.1415e5
 * to its string representation.
 */

#include <stdlib.h>
#include <stdio.h>

void main( void )
{
   char buffer[50];
   double source = -3.1415e5;
   _gcvt( source, 7, buffer );
   printf( "source: %f  buffer: '%s'\n", source, buffer );
   _gcvt( source, 7, buffer );
   printf( "source: %e  buffer: '%s'\n", source, buffer );
}
```

Output

```
source: -314150.000000  buffer: '-314150.'
source: -3.141500e+005  buffer: '-314150.'
```

See Also

atof, _ecvt, _fcvt

getc, getwc, getchar, getwchar

Read a character from a stream (**getc**, **getwc**), or get a character from stdin
(**getchar**, **getwchar**).

int getc(FILE **stream* **);**
wint_t getwc(FILE **stream* **);**
int getchar(void);
wint_t getwchar(void);

Routine	Required Header	Compatibility
getc	<stdio.h>	ANSI, Win 95, Win NT
getwc	<stdio.h> or <wchar.h>	ANSI, Win 95, Win NT
getchar	<stdio.h>	ANSI, Win 95, Win NT
getwchar	<stdio.h> or <wchar.h>	ANSI, Win 95, Win NT

For additional compatibility information, see "Compatibility" in the Introduction.

Libraries

LIBC.LIB	Single thread static library, retail version
LIBCMT.LIB	Multithread static library, retail version
MSVCRT.LIB	Import library for MSVCRT.DLL, retail version

Return Value

Each of these functions returns the character read. To indicate an read error or end-of-file
condition, **getc** and **getchar** return **EOF**, and **getwc** and **getwchar** return **WEOF**. For **getc**
and **getchar**, use **ferror** or **feof** to check for an error or for end of file.

Parameter

stream
   Input stream

Remarks

Each of these routines reads a single character from a file at the current position and
increments the associated file pointer (if defined) to point to the next character. In the case
of **getc** and **getwc**, the file is associated with *stream* (see "Choosing Between Functions
and Macros" in the Introduction). Routine-specific remarks follow.

Routine	Remarks
getc	Same as **fgetc**, but implemented as a function and as a macro.
getwc	Wide-character version of **getc**. Reads a multibyte character or a wide character according to whether *stream* is opened in text mode or binary mode.
getchar	Same as **_fgetchar**, but implemented as a function and as a macro.
getwchar	Wide-character version of **getchar**. Reads a multibyte character or a wide character according to whether *stream* is opened in text mode or binary mode.

Generic-Text Routine Mappings

TCHAR.H Routine	_UNICODE & _MBCS Not Defined	_MBCS Defined	_UNICODE Defined
_gettc	getc	getc	getwc
_gettchar	getchar	getchar	getwchar

Example

```
/* GETC.C: This program uses getchar to read a single line
 * of input from stdin, places this input in buffer, then
 * terminates the string before printing it to the screen.
 */

#include <stdio.h>

void main( void )
{
   char buffer[81];
   int i, ch;

   printf( "Enter a line: " );

   /* Read in single line from "stdin": */
   for( i = 0; (i < 80) && ((ch = getchar()) != EOF)
                     && (ch != '\n'); i++ )
      buffer[i] = (char)ch;

   /* Terminate string with null character: */
   buffer[i] = '\0';
   printf( "%s\n", buffer );
}
```

Output

```
Enter a line: This is a test
This is a test
```

See Also

fgetc, **_getch**, **putc**, **ungetc**

_getch, _getche

Get a character from the console without echo (_getch) or with echo (_getche).

int _getch(void);
int _getche(void);

Routine	Required Header	Compatibility
_getch	<conio.h>	Win 95, Win NT
_getche	<conio.h>	Win 95, Win NT

For additional compatibility information, see "Compatibility" in the Introduction.

Libraries

LIBC.LIB	Single thread static library, retail version
LIBCMT.LIB	Multithread static library, retail version
MSVCRT.LIB	Import library for MSVCRT.DLL, retail version

Return Value

Both **_getch** and **_getche** return the character read. There is no error return.

Remarks

The **_getch** function reads a single character from the console without echoing. **_getche** reads a single character from the console and echoes the character read. Neither function can be used to read CTRL+C. When reading a function key or an arrow key, **_getch** and **_getche** must be called twice; the first call returns 0 or 0xE0, and the second call returns the actual key code.

Example

```
/* GETCH.C: This program reads characters from
 * the keyboard until it receives a 'Y' or 'y'.
 */

#include <conio.h>
#include <ctype.h>

void main( void )
{
   int ch;

   _cputs( "Type 'Y' when finished typing keys: " );
   do
```

```
    {
        ch = _getch();
        ch = toupper( ch );
    } while( ch != 'Y' );

    _putch( ch );
    _putch( '\r' );    /* Carriage return */
    _putch( '\n' );    /* Line feed       */
}
```

Output

```
Type 'Y' when finished typing keys: Y
```

See Also

_cgets, getc, _ungetch

_getcwd, _wgetcwd

Get the current working directory.

char *_getcwd(char *buffer*, **int** *maxlen* **);**
wchar_t *_wgetcwd(wchar_t *buffer*, **int** *maxlen* **);**

Routine	Required Header	Compatibility
_getcwd	<direct.h>	Win 95, Win NT
_wgetcwd	<direct.h> or <wchar.h>	Win NT

For additional compatibility information, see "Compatibility" in the Introduction.

Libraries

LIBC.LIB	Single thread static library, retail version
LIBCMT.LIB	Multithread static library, retail version
MSVCRT.LIB	Import library for MSVCRT.DLL, retail version

Return Value

Each of these functions returns a pointer to *buffer*. A **NULL** return value indicates an error, and **errno** is set either to **ENOMEM**, indicating that there is insufficient memory to allocate *maxlen* bytes (when a **NULL** argument is given as *buffer*), or to **ERANGE**, indicating that the path is longer than *maxlen* characters.

Parameters

buffer
Storage location for path

maxlen
Maximum length of path in characters: **char** for **_getcwd** and wchar_t for **_wgetcwd**

Remarks

The **_getcwd** function **gets** the full path of the current working directory for the default drive and stores it at *buffer*. The integer argument *maxlen* specifies the maximum length for the path. An error occurs if the length of the path (including the terminating null character) exceeds *maxlen*. The buffer argument can be **NULL**; a buffer of at least size *maxlen* (more only if necessary) will automatically be allocated, using **malloc**, to store the path. This buffer can later be freed by calling **free** and passing it the **_getcwd** return value (a pointer to the allocated buffer).

_getcwd returns a string that represents the path of the current working directory. If the current working directory is the root, the string ends with a backslash (\ ). If the current working directory is a directory other than the root, the string ends with the directory name and not with a backslash.

_wgetcwd is a wide-character version of **_getcwd**; the *buffer* argument and return value of **_wgetcwd** are wide-character strings. **_wgetcwd** and **_getcwd** behave identically otherwise.

Generic-Text Routine Mappings

TCHAR.H Routine	_UNICODE & _MBCS Not Defined	_MBCS Defined	_UNICODE Defined
_tgetcwd	_getcwd	_getcwd	_wgetcwd

Example

```
// GETCWD.C
/* This program places the name of the current directory in the
 * buffer array, then displays the name of the current directory
 * on the screen. Specifying a length of _MAX_PATH leaves room
 * for the longest legal path name.
 */

#include <direct.h>
#include <stdlib.h>
#include <stdio.h>

void main( void )
{
    char buffer[_MAX_PATH];
```

```
      /* Get the current working directory: */
      if( _getcwd( buffer, _MAX_PATH ) == NULL )
         perror( "_getcwd error" );
      else
         printf( "%s\n", buffer );
   }
```

Output

```
C:\code
```

See Also

_chdir, _mkdir, _rmdir

_getdcwd, _wgetdcwd

Get full path name of current working directory on the specified drive.

char *_getdcwd(int *drive*, **char** *buffer, **int** *maxlen* **);**
wchar_t *_wgetdcwd(int *drive*, **wchar_t** *buffer, **int** *maxlen* **);**

Routine	Required Header	Compatibility
_getdcwd	<direct.h>	Win 95, Win NT
_wgetdcwd	<direct.h> or <wchar.h>	Win NT

For additional compatibility information, see "Compatibility" in the Introduction.

Libraries

LIBC.LIB	Single thread static library, retail version
LIBCMT.LIB	Multithread static library, retail version
MSVCRT.LIB	Import library for MSVCRT.DLL, retail version

Return Value

Each of these functions returns *buffer*. A **NULL** return value indicates an error, and **errno** is set either to **ENOMEM**, indicating that there is insufficient memory to allocate *maxlen* bytes (when a **NULL** argument is given as *buffer*), or to **ERANGE**, indicating that the path is longer than *maxlen* characters.

Parameters

drive
   Disk drive

buffer
   Storage location for path

maxlen
   Maximum length of path

Remarks

The **_getdcwd** function **gets** the full path of the current working directory on the specified drive and stores it at *buffer*. An error occurs if the length of the path (including the terminating null character) exceeds *maxlen*. The *drive* argument specifies the drive (0 = default drive, 1 = A, 2 = B, and so on). The *buffer* argument can be **NULL**; a buffer of at least size *maxlen* (more only if necessary) will automatically be allocated, using **malloc**, to store the path. This buffer can later be freed by calling **free** and passing it the **_getdcwd** return value (a pointer to the allocated buffer).

_getdcwd returns a string that represents the path of the current working directory. If the current working directory is set to the root, the string ends with a backslash (\ ). If the current working directory is set to a directory other than the root, the string ends with the name of the directory and not with a backslash.

_wgetdcwd is a wide-character version of **_getdcwd**; the *buffer* argument and return value of **_wgetdcwd** are wide-character strings. **_wgetdcwd** and **_getdcwd** behave identically otherwise.

Generic-Text Routine Mappings

TCHAR.H Routine	_UNICODE & _MBCS Not Defined	_MBCS Defined	_UNICODE Defined
_tgetdcwd	_getdcwd	_getdcwd	_wgetdcwd

Example

```
/* GETDRIVE.C illustrates drive functions including:
 *     _getdrive      _chdrive      _getdcwd
 */

#include <stdio.h>
#include <conio.h>
#include <direct.h>
#include <stdlib.h>
#include <ctype.h>

void main( void )
{
    int ch, drive, curdrive;
    static char path[_MAX_PATH];

    /* Save current drive. */
    curdrive = _getdrive();

    printf( "Available drives are: \n" );
```

```
        /* If we can switch to the drive, it exists. */
        for( drive = 1; drive <= 26; drive++ )
            if( !_chdrive( drive ) )
                printf( "%c: ", drive + 'A' - 1 );

        while( 1 )
        {
            printf( "\nType drive letter to check or ESC to quit: " );
            ch = _getch();
            if( ch == 27 )
                break;
            if( isalpha( ch ) )
                _putch( ch );
            if( _getdcwd( toupper( ch ) - 'A' + 1, path, _MAX_PATH ) != NULL )
                printf( "\nCurrent directory on that drive is %s\n", path );
        }

        /* Restore original drive.*/
        _chdrive( curdrive );
        printf( "\n" );
}
```

Output

```
Available drives are:
A: B: C: L: M: O: U: V:
Type drive letter to check or ESC to quit: c
Current directory on that drive is C:\CODE

Type drive letter to check or ESC to quit: m
Current directory on that drive is M:\

Type drive letter to check or ESC to quit:
```

See Also

_chdir, **_getcwd**, **_getdrive**, **_mkdir**, **_rmdir**

_getdrive

Gets the current disk drive.

int _getdrive(void);

Routine	Required Header	Compatibility
_getdrive	<direct.h>	Win 95, Win NT

For additional compatibility information, see "Compatibility" in the Introduction.

Libraries

LIBC.LIB	Single thread static library, retail version
LIBCMT.LIB	Multithread static library, retail version
MSVCRT.LIB	Import library for MSVCRT.DLL, retail version

Return Value

_getdrive returns the current (default) drive (1=A, 2=B, and so on). There is no error return.

Example

```
/* GETDRIVE.C illustrates drive functions including:
 *      _getdrive       _chdrive        _getdcwd
 */

#include <stdio.h>
#include <conio.h>
#include <direct.h>
#include <stdlib.h>
#include <ctype.h>

void main( void )
{
   int ch, drive, curdrive;
   static char path[_MAX_PATH];

   /* Save current drive. */
   curdrive = _getdrive();

   printf( "Available drives are: \n" );

   /* If we can switch to the drive, it exists. */
   for( drive = 1; drive <= 26; drive++ )
      if( !_chdrive( drive ) )
         printf( "%c: ", drive + 'A' - 1 );

   while( 1 )
   {
      printf( "\nType drive letter to check or ESC to quit: " );
      ch = _getch();
      if( ch == 27 )
         break;
      if( isalpha( ch ) )
         _putch( ch );
      if( _getdcwd( toupper( ch ) - 'A' + 1, path, _MAX_PATH ) != NULL )
         printf( "\nCurrent directory on that drive is %s\n", path );
   }
```

```
    /* Restore original drive.*/
    _chdrive( curdrive );
    printf( "\n" );
}
```

Output

```
Available drives are:
A: B: C: L: M: O: U: V:
Type drive letter to check or ESC to quit: c
Current directory on that drive is C:\CODE

Type drive letter to check or ESC to quit: m
Current directory on that drive is M:\

Type drive letter to check or ESC to quit:
```

See Also

_chdrive, _getcwd, _getdcwd

getenv, _wgetenv

Get a value from the current environment.

char *getenv(const char *varname**);**
wchar_t *_wgetenv(const wchar_t *varname**);**

Routine	Required Header	Compatibility
getenv	<stdlib.h>	ANSI, Win 95, Win NT
_wgetenv	<stdlib.h> or <wchar.h>	Win 95, Win NT

For additional compatibility information, see "Compatibility" in the Introduction.

Libraries

LIBC.LIB	Single thread static library, retail version
LIBCMT.LIB	Multithread static library, retail version
MSVCRT.LIB	Import library for MSVCRT.DLL, retail version

Return Value

Each of these functions returns a pointer to the environment table entry containing *varname*. It is not safe to modify the value of the environment variable using the returned pointer. Use the **_putenv** function to modify the value of an environment variable. The return value is **NULL** if *varname* is not found in the environment table.

Parameter

varname
    Environment variable name

Remarks

The **getenv** function searches the list of environment variables for *varname*. **getenv** is not case sensitive in Windows NT and Windows 95. **getenv** and _putenv use the copy of the environment pointed to by the global variable **_environ** to access the environment. **getenv** operates only on the data structures accessible to the run-time library and not on the environment "segment" created for the process by the operating system. Therefore, programs that use the *envp* argument to main or wmain may retrieve invalid information.

_wgetenv is a wide-character version of **getenv**; the argument and return value of **_wgetenv** are wide-character strings. The **_wenviron** global variable is a wide-character version of **_environ**.

In an MBCS program (for example, in an SBCS ASCII program), **_wenviron** is initially **NULL** because the environment is composed of multibyte-character strings. Then, on the first call to **_wputenv**, or on the first call to **_wgetenv** if an (MBCS) environment already exists, a corresponding wide-character string environment is created and is then pointed to by **_wenviron**.

Similarly in a Unicode (**_wmain**) program, **_environ** is initially **NULL** because the environment is composed of wide-character strings. Then, on the first call to **_putenv**, or on the first call to **getenv** if a (Unicode) environment already exists, a corresponding MBCS environment is created and is then pointed to by **_environ**.

When two copies of the environment (MBCS and Unicode) exist simultaneously in a program, the run-time system must maintain both copies, resulting in slower execution time. For example, whenever you call **_putenv**, a call to **_wputenv** is also executed automatically, so that the two environment strings correspond.

> **Caution** In rare instances, when the run-time system is maintaining both a Unicode version and a multibyte version of the environment, these two environment versions may not correspond exactly. This is because, although any unique multibyte-character string maps to a unique Unicode string, the mapping from a unique Unicode string to a multibyte-character string is not necessarily unique. For more information, see **_environ**, **_wenviron**.

Generic-Text Routine Mappings

TCHAR.H Routine	_UNICODE & _MBCS Not Defined	_MBCS Defined	_UNICODE Defined
_tgetenv	getenv	getenv	_wgetenv

To check or change the value of the **TZ** environment variable, use **getenv**, **_putenv** and **_tzset** as necessary. For more information about **TZ**, see **_tzset** and see "_daylight, _timezone, and _tzname" in Chapter 2, "Global Variables and Standard Types."

Example

```
/* GETENV.C: This program uses getenv to retrieve
 * the LIB environment variable and then uses
 * _putenv to change it to a new value.
 */

#include <stdlib.h>
#include <stdio.h>

void main( void )
{
   char *libvar;

   /* Get the value of the LIB environment variable. */
   libvar = getenv( "LIB" );

   if( libvar != NULL )
      printf( "Original LIB variable is: %s\n", libvar );

   /* Attempt to change path. Note that this only affects the environment
    * variable of the current process. The command processor's environment
    * is not changed.
    */
   _putenv( "LIB=c:\\mylib;c:\\yourlib" );

   /* Get new value. */
   libvar = getenv( "LIB" );

   if( libvar != NULL )
      printf( "New LIB variable is: %s\n", libvar );
}
```

Output

```
Original LIB variable is: C:\progra~1\devstu~1\vc\lib
New LIB variable is: c:\mylib;c:\yourlib
```

See Also

_putenv

_getmbcp

int _getmbcp(void);

Routine	Required Header	Compatibility
_getmbcp	<mbctype.h>	Win 95, Win NT

For additional compatibility information, see "Compatibility" in the Introduction.

Libraries

LIBC.LIB	Single thread static library, retail version
LIBCMT.LIB	Multithread static library, retail version
MSVCRT.LIB	Import library for MSVCRT.DLL, retail version

Return Value

_getmbcp returns the current multibyte code page. A return value of 0 indicates that a single byte code page is in use.

See Also

_setmbcp

_get_osfhandle

Gets operating-system file handle associated with existing stream **FILE** pointer.

long _get_osfhandle(int *filehandle* **);**

Routine	Required Header	Compatibility
_get_osfhandle	<io.h>	Win 95, Win NT

For additional compatibility information, see "Compatibility" in the Introduction.

Libraries

LIBC.LIB	Single thread static library, retail version
LIBCMT.LIB	Multithread static library, retail version
MSVCRT.LIB	Import library for MSVCRT.DLL, retail version

Return Value

If successful, **_get_osfhandle** returns an operating-system file handle corresponding to *filehandle*. Otherwise, it returns –1 and sets **errno** to **EBADF**, indicating an invalid file handle.

Parameter

filehandle
    User file handle

Remarks

The **_get_osfhandle** function returns *filehandle* if it is in range and if it is internally marked as free.

See Also

_close, **_creat**, **_dup**, **_open**

_getpid

Gets the process identification.

int _getpid(void);

Routine	Required Header	Compatibility
_getpid	<process.h>	Win 95, Win NT

For additional compatibility information, see "Compatibility" in the Introduction.

Libraries

LIBC.LIB	Single thread static library, retail version
LIBCMT.LIB	Multithread static library, retail version
MSVCRT.LIB	Import library for MSVCRT.DLL, retail version

Return Value

_getpid returns the process ID obtained from the system. There is no error return.

Remarks

The **_getpid** function obtains the process ID from the system. The process ID uniquely identifies the calling process.

Example

```
/* GETPID.C: This program uses _getpid to obtain
 * the process ID and then prints the ID.
 */

#include <stdio.h>
#include <process.h>

void main( void )
{
    /* If run from command line, shows different ID for
    * command line than for operating system shell.
    */
    printf( "\nProcess id: %d\n", _getpid() );
}
```

Output

```
Process id: 193
```

See Also

_mktemp

_get_sbh_threshold

Returns the upper limit for the size of a memory allocation that will be supported by the small-block heap.

size_t _get_sbh_threshold(void);

Routine	Required Header	Compatibility
_get_sbh_threshold	<malloc.h>	Win 95, Win NT

For additional compatibility information, see "Compatibility" in the Introduction.

Libraries

LIBC.LIB	Single thread static library, retail version
LIBCMT.LIB	Multithread static library, retail version
MSVCRT.LIB	Import library for MSVCRT.DLL, retail version

Return Value

This function returns the upper limit for the size of a memory allocation that will be supported by the small-block heap.

Remarks

Call this function to get the current threshold value for the small-block heap. The default threshold size is 480 bytes for Windows 95 and all Windows NT platforms except the DEC Alpha platforms, and 896 bytes for DEC Alpha Platforms.

See Also

_set_sbh_threshold

gets, _getws

Get a line from the **stdin** stream.

char *gets(char *_buffer_);
wchar_t *_getws(wchar_t *_buffer_);

Routine	Required Header	Compatibility
gets	<stdio.h>	ANSI, Win 95, Win NT
_getws	<stdio.h> or <wchar.h>	ANSI, Win 95, Win NT

For additional compatibility information, see "Compatibility" in the Introduction.

Libraries

LIBC.LIB	Single thread static library, retail version
LIBCMT.LIB	Multithread static library, retail version
MSVCRT.LIB	Import library for MSVCRT.DLL, retail version

Return Value

Each of these functions returns its argument if successful. A **NULL** pointer indicates an error or end-of-file condition. Use ferror or feof to determine which one has occurred.

Parameter

buffer
    Storage location for input string

Remarks

The **gets** function reads a line from the standard input stream **stdin** and stores it in *buffer*. The line consists of all characters up to and including the first newline character ('\n'). **gets** then replaces the newline character with a null character ('\0') before returning the line. In contrast, the **fgets** function retains the newline character. **_getws** is a wide-character version of **gets**; its argument and return value are wide-character strings.

Generic-Text Routine Mappings

TCHAR.H Routine	_UNICODE & _MBCS Not Defined	_MBCS Defined	_UNICODE Defined
_getts	gets	gets	_getws

Example

```
/* GETS.C */

#include <stdio.h>

void main( void )
{
   char line[81];

   printf( "Input a string: " );
   gets( line );
   printf( "The line entered was: %s\n", line );
}
```

Output

```
Input a string: Hello!
The line entered was: Hello!
```

See Also

fgets, fputs, puts

_getw

Gets an integer from a stream.

int _getw(FILE *_stream_);

Routine	Required Header	Compatibility
_getw	<stdio.h>	Win 95, Win NT

For additional compatibility information, see "Compatibility" in the Introduction.

Libraries

LIBC.LIB	Single thread static library, retail version
LIBCMT.LIB	Multithread static library, retail version
MSVCRT.LIB	Import library for MSVCRT.DLL, retail version

Return Value

_getw returns the integer value read. A return value of **EOF** indicates either an error or end of file. However, because the **EOF** value is also a legitimate integer value, use **feof** or **ferror** to verify an end-of-file or error condition.

Parameter

stream
    Pointer to **FILE** structure

Remarks

The **_getw** function reads the next binary value of type **int** from the file associated with _stream_ and increments the associated file pointer (if there is one) to point to the next unread character. **_getw** does not assume any special alignment of items in the stream. Problems with porting may occur with **_getw** because the size of the **int** type and the ordering of bytes within the **int** type differ across systems.

Example

```
/* GETW.C: This program uses _getw to read a word
 * from a stream, then performs an error check.
 */

#include <stdio.h>
#include <stdlib.h>

void main( void )
{
    FILE *stream;
    int i;

    if( (stream = fopen( "getw.c", "rb" )) == NULL )
        printf( "Couldn't open file\n" );
    else
    {
        /* Read a word from the stream: */
        i = _getw( stream );

        /* If there is an error... */
        if( ferror( stream ) )
        {
            printf( "_getw failed\n" );
            clearerr( stream );
        }
        else
            printf( "First data word in file: 0x%.4x\n", i );
        fclose( stream );
    }
}
```

Output

```
First data word in file: 0x47202a2f
```

See Also

_putw

gmtime

Converts a time value to a structure.

struct tm *gmtime(const time_t *timer**);**

Routine	Required Header	Compatibility
gmtime	<time.h>	ANSI, Win 95, Win NT

For additional compatibility information, see "Compatibility" in the Introduction.

Libraries

LIBC.LIB	Single thread static library, retail version
LIBCMT.LIB	Multithread static library, retail version
MSVCRT.LIB	Import library for MSVCRT.DLL, retail version

Return Value

gmtime returns a pointer to a structure of type tm. The fields of the returned structure hold the evaluated value of the *timer* argument in UTC rather than in local time. Each of the structure fields is of type **int**, as follows:

tm_sec
Seconds after minute (0–59)

tm_min
Minutes after hour (0–59)

tm_hour
Hours since midnight (0–23)

tm_mday
Day of month (1–31)

tm_mon
Month (0–11; January = 0)

tm_year
Year (current year minus 1900)

tm_wday
Day of week (0–6; Sunday = 0)

tm_yday
Day of year (0–365; January 1 = 0)

tm_isdst
Always 0 for **gmtime**

The **gmtime**, **mktime**, and **localtime** functions use the same single, statically allocated structure to hold their results. Each call to one of these functions destroys the result of any previous call. If *timer* represents a date before midnight, January 1, 1970, **gmtime** returns **NULL**. There is no error return.

Parameter

timer
Pointer to stored time. The time is represented as seconds elapsed since midnight (00:00:00), January 1, 1970, coordinated universal time (UTC).

Remarks

The **gmtime** function breaks down the *timer* value and stores it in a statically allocated structure of type **tm**, defined in TIME.H. The value of *timer* is usually obtained from a call to the **time** function.

> **Note** The target environment should try to determine whether daylight savings time is in effect. The C run-time library assumes the United States's rules for implementing the calculation of Daylight Saving Time (DST).

Example

```
/* GMTIME.C: This program uses gmtime to convert a long-
 * integer representation of coordinated universal time
 * to a structure named newtime, then uses asctime to
 * convert this structure to an output string.
 */

#include <time.h>
#include <stdio.h>

void main( void )
{
    struct tm *newtime;
    long ltime;

    time( &ltime );

    /* Obtain coordinated universal time: */
    newtime = gmtime( &ltime );
    printf( "Coordinated universal time is %s\n",
                            asctime( newtime ) );
}
```

Output

```
Coordinated universal time is Tue Mar 23 02:00:56 1993
```

See Also

asctime, **ctime**, **_ftime**, **localtime**, **mktime**, **time**

_heapadd

Adds memory to the heap.

int _heapadd(void *memblock**, size_t** *size* **);**

Routine	Required Header	Optional Headers	Compatibility
_heapadd	<malloc.h>	<errno.h>	None

For additional compatibility information, see "Compatibility" in the Introduction.

Libraries

LIBC.LIB	Single thread static library, retail version
LIBCMT.LIB	Multithread static library, retail version
MSVCRT.LIB	Import library for MSVCRT.DLL, retail version

Return Value

If successful, **_heapadd** returns 0; otherwise, the function returns –1 and sets **errno** to **ENOSYS**.

Parameters

memblock
Pointer to heap memory

size
Size in bytes of memory to add

Remarks

Beginning with Visual C++ Version 4.0, the underlying heap structure was moved to the C run-time libraries to support the new debugging features. As a result, **_heapadd** is no longer supported on any Win32 platform and will immediately return –1 when called from an application of this type.

See Also

free, **_heapchk**, **_heapmin**, **_heapset**, **_heapwalk**, **malloc**, **realloc**

_heapchk

Runs consistency checks on the heap.

int _heapchk(void);

Routine	Required Header	Optional Headers	Compatibility
_heapchk	<malloc.h>	<errno.h>	Win NT

For additional compatibility information, see "Compatibility" in the Introduction.

Libraries

LIBC.LIB	Single thread static library, retail version
LIBCMT.LIB	Multithread static library, retail version
MSVCRT.LIB	Import library for MSVCRT.DLL, retail version

Return Value

_heapchk returns one of the following integer manifest constants defined in MALLOC.H:

_HEAPBADBEGIN
Initial header information is bad or cannot be found

_HEAPBADNODE
Bad node has been found or heap is damaged

_HEAPBADPTR
Pointer into heap is not valid

_HEAPEMPTY
Heap has not been initialized

_HEAPOK
Heap appears to be consistent

In addition, if an error occurs, **_heapchk** sets **errno** to **ENOSYS**.

Remarks

The **_heapchk** function helps debug heap-related problems by checking for minimal consistency of the heap.

Example

```
/* HEAPCHK.C: This program checks the heap for
 * consistency and prints an appropriate message.
 */

#include <malloc.h>
#include <stdio.h>

void main( void )
{
   int  heapstatus;
   char *buffer;

   /* Allocate and deallocate some memory */
   if( (buffer = (char *)malloc( 100 )) != NULL )
      free( buffer );

   /* Check heap status */
   heapstatus = _heapchk();
   switch( heapstatus )
   {
   case _HEAPOK:
      printf(" OK - heap is fine\n" );
      break;
```

```
   case _HEAPEMPTY:
      printf(" OK - heap is empty\n" );
      break;
   case _HEAPBADBEGIN:
      printf( "ERROR - bad start of heap\n" );
      break;
   case _HEAPBADNODE:
      printf( "ERROR - bad node in heap\n" );
      break;
   }
}
```

Output

```
OK - heap is fine
```

See Also

_heapadd, _heapmin, _heapset, _heapwalk

_heapmin

Releases unused heap memory to the operating system.

int _heapmin(void);

Routine	Required Header	Optional Headers	Compatibility
_heapmin	<malloc.h>	<errno.h>	Win NT

For additional compatibility information, see "Compatibility" in the Introduction.

Libraries

LIBC.LIB	Single thread static library, retail version
LIBCMT.LIB	Multithread static library, retail version
MSVCRT.LIB	Import library for MSVCRT.DLL, retail version

Return Value

If successful, **_heapmin** returns 0; otherwise, the function returns −1 and sets **errno** to **ENOSYS**.

Remarks

The **_heapmin** function minimizes the heap by releasing unused heap memory to the operating system.

Note In Visual C++ Version 4.0, the underlying heap structure was moved to the C run-time libraries to support the new debugging features. As a result, the only Win32 platform that is supported by **_heapmin** is Windows NT. The function returns −1 and sets **errno** to **ENOSYS**, when it is called by any other Win32 platform.

See Also

free, **_heapadd**, **_heapchk**, **_heapset**, **_heapwalk**, **malloc**

_heapset

Checks heaps for minimal consistency and sets the free entries to a specified value.

int _heapset(unsigned int *fill* **);**

Routine	Required Header	Optional Headers	Compatibility
_heapset	<malloc.h>	<errno.h>	Win NT

For additional compatibility information, see "Compatibility" in the Introduction.

Libraries

LIBC.LIB	Single thread static library, retail version
LIBCMT.LIB	Multithread static library, retail version
MSVCRT.LIB	Import library for MSVCRT.DLL, retail version

Return Value

_heapset returns one of the following integer manifest constants defined in MALLOC.H:

_HEAPBADBEGIN
   Initial header information invalid or not found

_HEAPBADNODE
   Heap damaged or bad node found

_HEAPEMPTY
   Heap not initialized

_HEAPOK
   Heap appears to be consistent

In addition, if an error occurs, **_heapset** sets **errno** to **ENOSYS**.

Parameter

fill
   Fill character

Remarks

The **_heapset** function shows free memory locations or nodes that have been unintentionally overwritten.

_heapset checks for minimal consistency on the heap, then sets each byte of the heap's free entries to the *fill* value. This known value shows which memory locations of the heap contain free nodes and which contain data that were unintentionally written to freed memory.

> **Note** In Visual C++ Version 4.0, the underlying heap structure was moved to the C run-time libraries to support the new debugging features. As a result, the only Win32 platform that is supported by **_heapset** is Windows NT. The function returns **_HEAPOK** and sets **errno** to **ENOSYS**, when it is called by any other Win32 platform.

Example

```c
/* HEAPSET.C: This program checks the heap and
 * fills in free entries with the character 'Z'.
 */

#include <malloc.h>
#include <stdio.h>
#include <stdlib.h>

void main( void )
{
   int heapstatus;
   char *buffer;

   if( (buffer = malloc( 1 )) == NULL ) /* Make sure heap is */
      exit( 0 );                        /*    initialized    */
   heapstatus = _heapset( 'Z' );        /* Fill in free entries */
   switch( heapstatus )
   {
   case _HEAPOK:
      printf( "OK - heap is fine\n" );
      break;
   case _HEAPEMPTY:
      printf( "OK - heap is empty\n" );
      break;
   case _HEAPBADBEGIN:
      printf( "ERROR - bad start of heap\n" );
      break;
   case _HEAPBADNODE:
      printf( "ERROR - bad node in heap\n" );
      break;
   }
   free( buffer );
}
```

Output

```
OK - heap is fine
```

See Also

_heapadd, _heapchk, _heapmin, _heapwalk

_heapwalk

Traverses the heap and returns information about the next entry.

int _heapwalk(_HEAPINFO *_entryinfo_);

Routine	Required Header	Optional Headers	Compatibility
_heapwalk	<malloc.h>	<errno.h>	Win NT

For additional compatibility information, see "Compatibility" in the Introduction.

Libraries

LIBC.LIB	Single thread static library, retail version
LIBCMT.LIB	Multithread static library, retail version
MSVCRT.LIB	Import library for MSVCRT.DLL, retail version

Return Value

_heapwalk returns one of the following integer manifest constants defined in MALLOC.H:

_HEAPBADBEGIN
Initial header information invalid or not found

_HEAPBADNODE
Heap damaged or bad node found

_HEAPBADPTR
_pentry field of **_HEAPINFO** structure does not contain valid pointer into heap

_HEAPEND
End of heap reached successfully

_HEAPEMPTY
Heap not initialized

_HEAPOK
No errors so far; **_HEAPINFO** structure contains information about next entry.

In addition, if an error occurs, **_heapwalk** sets **errno** to **ENOSYS**.

Parameter

entryinfo
Buffer to contain heap information

Remarks

The **_heapwalk** function helps debug heap-related problems in programs. The function walks through the heap, traversing one entry per call, and returns a pointer to a structure of type **_HEAPINFO** that contains information about the next heap entry. The **_HEAPINFO** type, defined in MALLOC.H, contains the following elements:

int *_pentry
Heap entry pointer

size_t _size
Size of heap entry

int _useflag
Flag that indicates whether heap entry is in use

A call to **_heapwalk** that returns **_HEAPOK** stores the size of the entry in the **_size** field and sets the **_useflag** field to either **_FREEENTRY** or **_USEDENTRY** (both are constants defined in MALLOC.H). To obtain this information about the first entry in the heap, pass **_heapwalk** a pointer to a **_HEAPINFO** structure whose **_pentry** member is **NULL**.

> **Note** Beginning with Visual C++ Version 4.0, the underlying heap structure was moved to the C run-time libraries to support the new debugging features. As a result, the only Win32 platform that is supported by **_heapwalk** is Windows NT. When it is called by any other Win32 platform, **_heapwalk** returns **_HEAPEND** and sets **errno** to **ENOSYS**.

Example

```
/* HEAPWALK.C: This program "walks" the heap, starting
 * at the beginning (_pentry = NULL). It prints out each
 * heap entry's use, location, and size. It also prints
 * out information about the overall state of the heap as
 * soon as _heapwalk returns a value other than _HEAPOK.
 */

#include <stdio.h>
#include <malloc.h>

void heapdump( void );

void main( void )
{
    char *buffer;
```

```
      heapdump();
      if( (buffer = malloc( 59 )) != NULL )
      {
          heapdump();
          free( buffer );
      }
      heapdump();
}

void heapdump( void )
{
    _HEAPINFO hinfo;
    int heapstatus;
    hinfo._pentry = NULL;
    while( ( heapstatus = _heapwalk( &hinfo ) ) == _HEAPOK )
    { printf( "%6s block at %Fp of size %4.4X\n",
          ( hinfo._useflag == _USEDENTRY ? "USED" : "FREE" ),
            hinfo._pentry, hinfo._size );
    }

    switch( heapstatus )
    {
    case _HEAPEMPTY:
       printf( "OK - empty heap\n" );
       break;
    case _HEAPEND:
       printf( "OK - end of heap\n" );
       break;
    case _HEAPBADPTR:
       printf( "ERROR - bad pointer to heap\n" );
       break;
    case _HEAPBADBEGIN:
       printf( "ERROR - bad start of heap\n" );
       break;
    case _HEAPBADNODE:
       printf( "ERROR - bad node in heap\n" );
       break;
    }
}
```

Output

```
USED block at 002C0004 of size 0014
USED block at 002C001C of size 0054
USED block at 002C0074 of size 0024
USED block at 002C009C of size 0010
USED block at 002C00B0 of size 0018
USED block at 002C00CC of size 000C
USED block at 002C00DC of size 001C
```

```
     USED block at 002C00FC of size 0010
     USED block at 002C0110 of size 0014
     USED block at 002C0128 of size 0010
     USED block at 002C013C of size 0028
     USED block at 002C0168 of size 0088
     USED block at 002C01F4 of size 001C
     USED block at 002C0214 of size 0014
     USED block at 002C022C of size 0010
     USED block at 002C0240 of size 0014
     USED block at 002C0258 of size 0010
     USED block at 002C026C of size 000C
     USED block at 002C027C of size 0010
     USED block at 002C0290 of size 0014
     USED block at 002C02A8 of size 0010
     USED block at 002C02BC of size 0010
     USED block at 002C02D0 of size 1000
     FREE block at 002C12D4 of size ED2C
OK - end of heap
```

See Also

_heapadd, **_heapchk**, **_heapmin**, **_heapset**

_hypot

Calculates the hypotenuse.

double _hypot(double *x*, double *y*);

Routine	Required Header	Compatibility
_hypot	<math.h>	Win 95, Win NT

For additional compatibility information, see "Compatibility" in the Introduction.

Libraries

LIBC.LIB	Single thread static library, retail version
LIBCMT.LIB	Multithread static library, retail version
MSVCRT.LIB	Import library for MSVCRT.DLL, retail version

Return Value

_hypot returns the length of the hypotenuse if successful or INF (infinity) on overflow.
The **errno** variable is set to **ERANGE** on overflow. You can modify error handling
with **_matherr**.

Parameters

x, y

> Floating-point values

Remarks

The **_hypot** function calculates the length of the hypotenuse of a right triangle, given the length of the two sides *x* and *y*. A call to **_hypot** is equivalent to the square root of $x^2 + y^2$.

Example

```
/* HYPOT.C: This program prints the
 * hypotenuse of a right triangle.
 */

#include <math.h>
#include <stdio.h>

void main( void )
{
   double x = 3.0, y = 4.0;

   printf( "If a right triangle has sides %2.1f and %2.1f, "
           "its hypotenuse is %2.1f\n", x, y, _hypot( x, y ) );
}
```

Output

```
If a right triangle has sides 3.0 and 4.0, its hypotenuse is 5.0
```

See Also

_cabs, **_matherr**

_inp, _inpw, _inpd

Input a byte (**_inp**), a word (**_inpw**), or a double word (**_inpd**) from a port.

int _inp(unsigned short *port* **);**
unsigned short _inpw(unsigned short *port* **);**
unsigned long _inpd(unsigned short *port* **);**

Routine	Required Header	Compatibility
_inp	<conio.h>	Win 95
_inpw	<conio.h>	Win 95
_inpd	<conio.h>	Win 95

For additional compatibility information, see "Compatibility" in the Introduction.

Libraries

LIBC.LIB	Single thread static library, retail version
LIBCMT.LIB	Multithread static library, retail version
MSVCRT.LIB	Import library for MSVCRT.DLL, retail version

Return Value

The functions return the byte, word, or double word read from *port*. There is no error return.

Parameter

port
    Port number

Remarks

The **_inp**, **_inpw**, and **_inpd** functions read a byte, a word, and a double word, respectively, from the specified input port. The input value can be any unsigned short integer in the range 0–65,535.

See Also

_outp

is, isw Routines

isalnum, iswalnum	islower, iswlower
isalpha, iswalpha	isprint, iswprint
__isascii, iswascii	ispunct, iswpunct
iscntrl, iswcntrl	isspace, iswspace
__iscsym, __iscsymf	isupper, iswupper
isdigit, iswdigit	iswctype
isgraph, iswgraph	isxdigit, iswxdigit

Remarks

These routines test characters for specified conditions.

The **is** routines produce meaningful results for any integer argument from –1 (**EOF**) to **UCHAR_MAX** (0xFF), inclusive. The expected argument type is **int**.

Warning For the **is** routines, passing an argument of type **char** may yield unpredictable results. An SBCS or MBCS single-byte character of type **char** with a value greater than 0x7F is negative. If a **char** is passed, the compiler may convert the value to a signed **int** or a signed **long**. This value may be sign-extended by the compiler, with unexpected results.

The **isw** routines produce meaningful results for any integer value from –1 (**WEOF**) to 0xFFFF, inclusive. The **wint_t** data type is defined in WCHAR.H as an **unsigned short**; it can hold any wide character or the wide-character end-of-file (**WEOF**) value.

For each of the **is** routines, the result of the test for the specified condition depends on the **LC_CTYPE** category setting of the current locale; see setlocale for more information. In the "C" locale, the test conditions for the **is** routines are as follows:

isalnum
> Alphanumeric (A–Z, a–z, or 0–9)

isalpha
> Alphabetic (A–Z or a–z)

__isascii
> ASCII character (0x00–0x7F)

iscntrl
> Control character (0x00–0x1F or 0x7F)

__iscsym
> Letter, underscore, or digit

__iscsymf
> Letter or underscore

isdigit
> Decimal digit (0–9)

isgraph
> Printable character except space ( )

islower
> Lowercase letter (a–z)

isprint
> Printable character including space (0x20–0x7E)

ispunct
> Punctuation character

isspace
> White-space character (0x09–0x0D or 0x20)

isupper
> Uppercase letter (A–Z)

isxdigit
> Hexadecimal digit (A–F, a–f, or 0–9)

For the **isw** routines, the result of the test for the specified condition is independent of locale. The test conditions for the **isw** functions are as follows:

iswalnum
>   **iswalpha** or **iswdigit**

iswalpha
>   Any wide character that is one of an implementation-defined set for which none of **iswcntrl**, **iswdigit**, **iswpunct**, or **iswspace** is true. **iswalpha** returns true only for wide characters for which **iswupper** or **iswlower** is true.

iswascii
>   Wide-character representation of ASCII character (0x0000–0x007F).

iswcntrl
>   Control wide character.

iswctype
>   Character has property specified by the *desc* argument. For each valid value of the *desc* argument of **iswctype**, there is an equivalent wide-character classification routine, as shown in the following table:

Equivalence of iswctype(*c, desc*) to Other isw Testing Routines

Value of *desc* Argument	iswctype(*c, desc*) Equivalent
_ALPHA	**iswalpha(** *c* **)**
**_ALPHA	_DIGIT**	**iswalnum(** *c* **)**
_CONTROL	**iswcntrl(** *c* **)**
_DIGIT	**iswdigit(** *c* **)**
**_ALPHA	_DIGIT	_PUNCT**	**iswgraph(** *c* **)**
_LOWER	**iswlower(** *c* **)**
**_ALPHA	_BLANK	_DIGIT	_PUNCT**	**iswprint(** *c* **)**
_PUNCT	**iswpunct(** *c* **)**
_SPACE	**iswspace(** *c* **)**
_UPPER	**iswupper(** *c* **)**
_HEX	**iswxdigit(** *c* **)**

iswdigit
>   Wide character corresponding to a decimal-digit character.

iswgraph
>   Printable wide character except space wide character (L' ').

iswlower

Lowercase letter, or one of implementation-defined set of wide characters for which none of **iswcntrl**, **iswdigit**, **iswpunct**, or **iswspace** is true. **iswlower** returns true only for wide characters that correspond to lowercase letters.

iswprint

Printable wide character, including space wide character (L' ').

iswpunct

Printable wide character that is neither space wide character (L' ') nor wide character for which **iswalnum** is true.

iswspace

Wide character that corresponds to standard white-space character or is one of implementation-defined set of wide characters for which **iswalnum** is false. Standard white-space characters are: space (L' '), formfeed (L'\f'), newline (L'\n'), carriage return (L'\r'), horizontal tab (L'\t'), and vertical tab (L'\v').

iswupper

Wide character that is uppercase or is one of an implementation-defined set of wide characters for which none of **iswcntrl**, **iswdigit**, **iswpunct**, or **iswspace** is true. **iswupper** returns true only for wide characters that correspond to uppercase characters.

iswxdigit

Wide character that corresponds to a hexadecimal-digit character.

Example

```
/* ISFAM.C: This program tests all characters between 0x0
 * and 0x7F, then displays each character with abbreviations
 * for the character-type codes that apply.

 * Editor's note: the following output is significantly
 * shortened with the use of ellipses. This full output
 * is too long and repetitive.
 */

#include <stdio.h>
#include <ctype.h>

void main( void )
{
    int ch;
    for( ch = 0; ch <= 0x7F; ch++ )
    {
        printf( "%.2x  ", ch );
        printf( " %c", isprint( ch )  ? ch   : '\0' );
        printf( "%4s", isalnum( ch )  ? "AN" : "" );
```

```
        printf( "%3s", isalpha( ch )  ? "A"  : "" );
        printf( "%3s", __isascii( ch )  ? "AS" : "" );
        printf( "%3s", iscntrl( ch )  ? "C"  : "" );
        printf( "%3s", __iscsym( ch )  ? "CS " : "" );
        printf( "%3s", __iscsymf( ch )  ? "CSF" : "" );
        printf( "%3s", isdigit( ch )  ? "D"  : "" );
        printf( "%3s", isgraph( ch )  ? "G"  : "" );
        printf( "%3s", islower( ch )  ? "L"  : "" );
        printf( "%3s", ispunct( ch )  ? "PU" : "" );
        printf( "%3s", isspace( ch )  ? "S"  : "" );
        printf( "%3s", isprint( ch )  ? "PR" : "" );
        printf( "%3s", isupper( ch )  ? "U"  : "" );
        printf( "%3s", isxdigit( ch ) ? "X"  : "" );
        printf( "\n" );
    }
}
```

Output

```
00
01
02
03
04
05
06
07
08
09
0a
0b
0c
0d
0e
0f
10
11
12
13
14
15
16
17
18
19
1a
1b
1c
1d
```

		AN	A	AS	CS	CSF	D	G	PU	S	PR	U	X
1e													
1f													
20				AS						S	PR		
21	!			AS				G	PU		PR		
22	"			AS				G	PU		PR		
23	#			AS				G	PU		PR		
24	$			AS				G	PU		PR		
25	%			AS				G	PU		PR		
26	&			AS				G	PU		PR		
27	'			AS				G	PU		PR		
28	(			AS				G	PU		PR		
29	)			AS				G	PU		PR		
2a	*			AS				G	PU		PR		
2b	+			AS				G	PU		PR		
2c	,			AS				G	PU		PR		
2d	-			AS				G	PU		PR		
2e	.			AS				G	PU		PR		
2f	/			AS				G	PU		PR		
30	0	AN		AS	CS		D	G			PR		X
31	1	AN		AS	CS		D	G			PR		X
32	2	AN		AS	CS		D	G			PR		X
33	3	AN		AS	CS		D	G			PR		X
34	4	AN		AS	CS		D	G			PR		X
35	5	AN		AS	CS		D	G			PR		X
36	6	AN		AS	CS		D	G			PR		X
37	7	AN		AS	CS		D	G			PR		X
38	8	AN		AS	CS		D	G			PR		X
.													
.													
.													
39	9	AN		AS	CS		D	G			PR		X
3a	:			AS				G	PU		PR		
3b	;			AS				G	PU		PR		
3c	<			AS				G	PU		PR		
3d	=			AS				G	PU		PR		
.													
.													
.													
3e	>			AS				G	PU		PR		
3f	?			AS				G	PU		PR		
40	@			AS				G	PU		PR		
41	A	AN	A	AS	CS	CSF		G			PR	U	X
42	B	AN	A	AS	CS	CSF		G			PR	U	X
43	C	AN	A	AS	CS	CSF		G			PR	U	X
44	D	AN	A	AS	CS	CSF		G			PR	U	X
45	E	AN	A	AS	CS	CSF		G			PR	U	X
46	F	AN	A	AS	CS	CSF		G			PR	U	X
47	G	AN	A	AS	CS	CSF		G			PR	U	
48	H	AN	A	AS	CS	CSF		G			PR	U	

		AN	A	AS	CS	CSF	G	L/PU	PR	U/X
49	I	AN	A	AS	CS	CSF	G		PR	U
4a	J	AN	A	AS	CS	CSF	G		PR	U
4b	K	AN	A	AS	CS	CSF	G		PR	U
4c	L	AN	A	AS	CS	CSF	G		PR	U
4d	M	AN	A	AS	CS	CSF	G		PR	U
4e	N	AN	A	AS	CS	CSF	G		PR	U
4f	O	AN	A	AS	CS	CSF	G		PR	U
50	P	AN	A	AS	CS	CSF	G		PR	U
51	Q	AN	A	AS	CS	CSF	G		PR	U
52	R	AN	A	AS	CS	CSF	G		PR	U
53	S	AN	A	AS	CS	CSF	G		PR	U
54	T	AN	A	AS	CS	CSF	G		PR	U
55	U	AN	A	AS	CS	CSF	G		PR	U
56	V	AN	A	AS	CS	CSF	G		PR	U
57	W	AN	A	AS	CS	CSF	G		PR	U
58	X	AN	A	AS	CS	CSF	G		PR	U
59	Y	AN	A	AS	CS	CSF	G		PR	U
5a	Z	AN	A	AS	CS	CSF	G		PR	U
5b	[			AS			G	PU	PR	
5c	\			AS			G	PU	PR	
5d	]			AS			G	PU	PR	
5e	^			AS			G	PU	PR	
5f	_			AS	CS	CSF	G	PU	PR	
60	`			AS			G	PU	PR	
61	a	AN	A	AS	CS	CSF	G	L	PR	X
62	b	AN	A	AS	CS	CSF	G	L	PR	X
63	c	AN	A	AS	CS	CSF	G	L	PR	X
64	d	AN	A	AS	CS	CSF	G	L	PR	X
65	e	AN	A	AS	CS	CSF	G	L	PR	X
66	f	AN	A	AS	CS	CSF	G	L	PR	X
67	g	AN	A	AS	CS	CSF	G	L	PR	
68	h	AN	A	AS	CS	CSF	G	L	PR	
69	i	AN	A	AS	CS	CSF	G	L	PR	
6a	j	AN	A	AS	CS	CSF	G	L	PR	
6b	k	AN	A	AS	CS	CSF	G	L	PR	
6c	l	AN	A	AS	CS	CSF	G	L	PR	
6d	m	AN	A	AS	CS	CSF	G	L	PR	
6e	n	AN	A	AS	CS	CSF	G	L	PR	
6f	o	AN	A	AS	CS	CSF	G	L	PR	
70	p	AN	A	AS	CS	CSF	G	L	PR	
71	q	AN	A	AS	CS	CSF	G	L	PR	
72	r	AN	A	AS	CS	CSF	G	L	PR	
73	s	AN	A	AS	CS	CSF	G	L	PR	
74	t	AN	A	AS	CS	CSF	G	L	PR	
75	u	AN	A	AS	CS	CSF	G	L	PR	
76	v	AN	A	AS	CS	CSF	G	L	PR	
77	w	AN	A	AS	CS	CSF	G	L	PR	
78	x	AN	A	AS	CS	CSF	G	L	PR	
79	y	AN	A	AS	CS	CSF	G	L	PR	

```
7a   z   AN   A  AS     CS CSF     G   L           PR
7b   {        AS                   G       PU      PR
7c   |        AS                   G       PU      PR
7d   }        AS                   G       PU      PR
7e   ~        AS                   G       PU      PR
7f
```

See Also

setlocale, to Function Overview

isalnum, iswalnum

int isalnum(int c **);**
int iswalnum(wint_t c **);**

Each of these routines returns true if c is a particular representation of an alphanumeric character.

Routine	Required Header	Compatibility
isalnum	<ctype.h>	ANSI, Win 95, Win NT
iswalnum	<ctype.h> or <wchar.h>	ANSI, Win 95, Win NT

For additional compatibility information, see "Compatibility" in the Introduction.

Libraries

LIBC.LIB	Single thread static library, retail version
LIBCMT.LIB	Multithread static library, retail version
MSVCRT.LIB	Import library for MSVCRT.DLL, retail version

Return Value

isalnum returns a non-zero value if either **isalpha** or **isdigit** is true for c, that is, if c is within the ranges A–Z, a–z, or 0–9. iswal**num** returns a non-zero value if either **iswalpha** or **iswdigit** is true for c. Each of these routines returns 0 if c does not satisfy the test condition.

The result of the test condition for the **isalnum** function depends on the **LC_CTYPE** category setting of the current locale; see setlocale for more information. For **iswalnum**, the result of the test condition is independent of locale.

Parameter

c
    Integer to test

Generic-Text Routine Mappings

TCHAR.H Routine	_UNICODE & _MBCS Not Defined	_MBCS Defined	_UNICODE Defined
_istalnum	isalnum	_ismbcalnum	iswalnum

isalpha, iswalpha

int isalpha(int *c* **);**
int iswalpha(wint_t *c* **);**

Each of these routines returns true if *c* is a particular representation of an alphabetic character.

Routine	Required Header	Compatibility
isalpha	<ctype.h>	ANSI, Win 95, Win NT
iswalpha	<ctype.h> or <wchar.h>	ANSI, Win 95, Win NT

For additional compatibility information, see "Compatibility" in the Introduction.

Libraries

LIBC.LIB	Single thread static library, retail version
LIBCMT.LIB	Multithread static library, retail version
MSVCRT.LIB	Import library for MSVCRT.DLL, retail version

Return Value

isalpha returns a non-zero value if *c* is within the ranges A–Z or a–z. iswalpha returns a non-zero value only for wide characters for which **iswupper** or **iswlower** is true, that is, for any wide character that is one of an implementation-defined set for which none of **iswcntrl**, **iswdigit**, **iswpunct**, or **iswspace** is true. Each of these routines returns 0 if *c* does not satisfy the test condition.

The result of the test condition for the **isalpha** function depends on the **LC_CTYPE** category setting of the current locale; see setlocale for more information. For **iswalpha**, the result of the test condition is independent of locale.

Parameter

c

   Integer to test

Generic-Text Routine Mappings

TCHAR.H Routine	_UNICODE & _MBCS Not Defined	_MBCS Defined	_UNICODE Defined
_istalpha	isalpha	_ismbcalpha	iswalpha

__isascii, iswascii

int __isascii(int *c* **);**
int iswascii(wint_t *c* **);**

Each of these routines returns true if *c* is a particular representation of an ASCII character.

Routine	Required Header	Compatibility
__isascii	<ctype.h>	Win 95, Win NT
iswascii	<ctype.h> or <wchar.h>	ANSI, Win 95, Win NT

For additional compatibility information, see "Compatibility" in the Introduction.

Libraries

LIBC.LIB	Single thread static library, retail version
LIBCMT.LIB	Multithread static library, retail version
MSVCRT.LIB	Import library for MSVCRT.DLL, retail version

Return Value

__isascii returns a non-zero value if *c* is an ASCII character (in the range 0x00–0x7F).
iswascii returns a non-zero value if *c* is a wide-character representation of an ASCII
character. Each of these routines returns 0 if *c* does not satisfy the test condition.

The result of the test condition for the **__isascii** function depends on the **LC_CTYPE**
category setting of the current locale; see setlocale for more information. For **iswascii**,
the result of the test condition is independent of locale.

Parameter

c
    Integer to test

Generic-Text Routine Mappings

TCHAR.H Routine	_UNICODE & _MBCS Not Defined	_MBCS Defined	_UNICODE Defined
_istascii	__isascii	__isascii	iswascii

iscntrl, iswcntrl

int iscntrl(int *c* **);**
int iswcntrl(wint_t *c* **);**

Each of these routines returns true if *c* is a particular representation of a control character.

Routine	Required Header	Compatibility
iscntrl	<ctype.h>	ANSI, Win 95, Win NT
iswcntrl	<ctype.h> or <wchar.h>	ANSI, Win 95, Win NT

For additional compatibility information, see "Compatibility" in the Introduction.

Libraries

LIBC.LIB	Single thread static library, retail version
LIBCMT.LIB	Multithread static library, retail version
MSVCRT.LIB	Import library for MSVCRT.DLL, retail version

Return Value

iscntrl returns a non-zero value if c is a control character (0x00–0x1F or 0x7F). **iswcntrl** returns a non-zero value if c is a control wide character. Each of these routines returns 0 if c does not satisfy the test condition.

The result of the test condition for the **iscntrl** function depends on the **LC_CTYPE** category setting of the current locale; see setlocale for more information. For **iswcntrl**, the result of the test condition is independent of locale.

Parameter

c
    Integer to test

Generic-Text Routine Mappings

TCHAR.H Routine	_UNICODE & _MBCS Not Defined	_MBCS Defined	_UNICODE Defined
_istcntrl	iscntrl	Iscntrl	iswcntrl

__iscsym, __iscsymf

int __iscsym(int *c* **);**
int __iscsymf(int *c* **);**

Routine	Required Header	Compatibility
__iscsym	<ctype.h>	Win 95, Win NT
__iscsymf	<ctype.h>	Win 95, Win NT

For additional compatibility information, see "Compatibility" in the Introduction.

Libraries

LIBC.LIB	Single thread static library, retail version
LIBCMT.LIB	Multithread static library, retail version
MSVCRT.LIB	Import library for MSVCRT.DLL, retail version

Return Value

__iscsym returns a non-zero value if *c* is a letter, underscore, or digit. **__iscsymf** returns a non-zero value if *c* is a letter or an underscore. Each of these routines returns 0 if *c* does not satisfy the test condition.

The result of the test condition for the **__iscsym** function depends on the **LC_CTYPE** category setting of the current locale; see setlocale for more information. For **__iscsymf**, the result of the test condition is independent of locale.

Parameter

c
> Integer to test

isdigit, iswdigit

int isdigit(int *c* **);**
int iswdigit(wint_t *c* **);**

Each of these routines returns true if *c* is a particular representation of a decimal-digit character.

Routine	Required Header	Compatibility
isdigit	<ctype.h>	ANSI, Win 95, Win NT
iswdigit	<ctype.h> or <wchar.h>	ANSI, Win 95, Win NT

For additional compatibility information, see "Compatibility" in the Introduction.

Libraries

LIBC.LIB	Single thread static library, retail version
LIBCMT.LIB	Multithread static library, retail version
MSVCRT.LIB	Import library for MSVCRT.DLL, retail version

Return Value

isdigit returns a non-zero value if *c* is a decimal digit (0–9). **iswdigit** returns a non-zero value if *c* is a wide character corresponding to a decimal-digit character. Each of these routines returns 0 if *c* does not satisfy the test condition.

The result of the test condition for the **isdigit** function depends on the **LC_CTYPE** category setting of the current locale; see setlocale for more information. For **iswdigit**, the result of the test condition is independent of locale.

Parameter

c

Integer to test

Generic-Text Routine Mappings

TCHAR.H Routine	_UNICODE & _MBCS Not Defined	_MBCS Defined	_UNICODE Defined
_istdigit	isdigit	_ismbcdigit	iswdigit

isgraph, iswgraph

int isgraph(int *c*);
int iswgraph(wint_t *c*);

Each of these routines returns true if *c* is a particular representation of a printable character other than a space.

Routine	Required Header	Compatibility
isgraph	<ctype.h>	ANSI, Win 95, Win NT
iswgraph	<ctype.h> or <wchar.h>	ANSI, Win 95, Win NT

For additional compatibility information, see "Compatibility" in the Introduction.

Libraries

LIBC.LIB	Single thread static library, retail version
LIBCMT.LIB	Multithread static library, retail version
MSVCRT.LIB	Import library for MSVCRT.DLL, retail version

Return Value

isgraph returns a non-zero value if *c* is a printable character other than a space. **iswgraph** returns a non-zero value if *c* is a printable wide character other than a wide-character space. Each of these routines returns 0 if *c* does not satisfy the test condition.

The result of the test condition for the **isgraph** function depends on the **LC_CTYPE** category setting of the current locale; see setlocale for more information. For **iswgraph**, the result of the test condition is independent of locale.

Parameter

c

Integer to test

Generic-Text Routine Mappings

TCHAR.H Routine	_UNICODE & _MBCS Not Defined	_MBCS Defined	_UNICODE Defined
_istgraph	isgraph	_ismbcgraph	iswgraph

islower, iswlower

int islower(int *c* **);**
int iswlower(wint_t *c* **);**

Each of these routines returns true if *c* is a particular representation of a lowercase character.

Routine	Required Header	Compatibility
islower	<ctype.h>	ANSI, Win 95, Win NT
iswlower	<ctype.h> or <wchar.h>	ANSI, Win 95, Win NT

For additional compatibility information, see "Compatibility" in the Introduction.

Libraries

LIBC.LIB	Single thread static library, retail version
LIBCMT.LIB	Multithread static library, retail version
MSVCRT.LIB	Import library for MSVCRT.DLL, retail version

Return Value

islower returns a non-zero value if *c* is a lowercase character (a–z). **iswlower** returns a non-zero value if *c* is a wide character that corresponds to a lowercase letter, or if *c* is one of an implementation-defined set of wide characters for which none of **iswcntrl**, **iswdigit**, **iswpunct**, or **iswspace** is true. Each of these routines returns 0 if *c* does not satisfy the test condition.

The result of the test condition for the **islower** function depends on the **LC_CTYPE** category setting of the current locale; see setlocale for more information. For **iswlower**, the result of the test condition is independent of locale.

Parameter

c
   Integer to test

Generic-Text Routine Mappings

TCHAR.H Routine	_UNICODE & _MBCS Not Defined	_MBCS Defined	_UNICODE Defined
_istlower	islower	_ismbclower	iswlower

isprint, iswprint

int isprint(int c **);**
int iswprint(wint_t c **);**

Each of these routines returns true if c is a particular representation of a printable character.

Routine	Required Header	Compatibility
isprint	<ctype.h>	ANSI, Win 95, Win NT
iswprint	<ctype.h> or <wchar.h>	ANSI, Win 95, Win NT

For additional compatibility information, see "Compatibility" in the Introduction.

Libraries

LIBC.LIB	Single thread static library, retail version
LIBCMT.LIB	Multithread static library, retail version
MSVCRT.LIB	Import library for MSVCRT.DLL, retail version

Return Value

isprint returns a nonzero value if c is a printable character, including the space character (0x20–0x7E). **iswprint** returns a nonzero value if c is a printable wide character, including the space wide character. Each of these routines returns 0 if c does not satisfy the test condition.

The result of the test condition for the **isprint** function depends on the **LC_CTYPE** category setting of the current locale; see setlocale for more information. For **iswprint**, the result of the test condition is independent of locale.

Parameter

c
Integer to test

Generic-Text Routine Mappings

TCHAR.H Routine	_UNICODE & _MBCS Not Defined	_MBCS Defined	_UNICODE Defined
_istprint	isprint	_ismbcprint	iswprint

ispunct, iswpunct

int ispunct(int c **);**
int iswpunct(wint_t c **);**

Each of these routines returns true if c is a particular representation of a punctuation character.

Routine	Required Header	Compatibility
ispunct	<ctype.h>	ANSI, Win 95, Win NT
iswpunct	<ctype.h> or <wchar.h>	ANSI, Win 95, Win NT

For additional compatibility information, see "Compatibility" in the Introduction.

Libraries

LIBC.LIB	Single thread static library, retail version
LIBCMT.LIB	Multithread static library, retail version
MSVCRT.LIB	Import library for MSVCRT.DLL, retail version

Return Value

ispunct returns a non-zero value for any printable character that is not a space character or a character for which **isalnum** is true. **iswpunct** returns a non-zero value for any printable wide character that is neither the space wide character nor a wide character for which **iswalnum** is true. Each of these routines returns 0 if c does not satisfy the test condition.

The result of the test condition for the **ispunct** function depends on the **LC_CTYPE** category setting of the current locale; see setlocale for more information. For **iswpunct**, the result of the test condition is independent of locale.

Parameter

c
    Integer to test

Generic-Text Routine Mappings

TCHAR.H Routine	_UNICODE & _MBCS Not Defined	_MBCS Defined	_UNICODE Defined
_istpunct	ispunct	_ismbcpunct	iswpunct

isspace, iswspace

int isspace(int *c*);
int iswspace(wint_t *c*);

Each of these routines returns true if c is a particular representation of a space character.

Routine	Required Header	Compatibility
isspace	<ctype.h>	ANSI, Win 95, Win NT
iswspace	<ctype.h> or <wchar.h>	ANSI, Win 95, Win NT

For additional compatibility information, see "Compatibility" in the Introduction.

Libraries

LIBC.LIB	Single thread static library, retail version
LIBCMT.LIB	Multithread static library, retail version
MSVCRT.LIB	Import library for MSVCRT.DLL, retail version

Return Value

isspace returns a non-zero value if c is a white-space character (0x09–0x0D or 0x20). **iswspace** returns a non-zero value if c is a wide character that corresponds to a standard white-space character or is one of an implementation-defined set of wide characters for which **iswalnum** is false. Each of these routines returns 0 if c does not satisfy the test condition.

The result of the test condition for the **isspace** function depends on the **LC_CTYPE** category setting of the current locale; see setlocale for more information. For **iswspace**, the result of the test condition is independent of locale.

Parameter

c
> Integer to test

Generic-Text Routine Mappings

TCHAR.H Routine	_UNICODE & _MBCS Not Defined	_MBCS Defined	_UNICODE Defined
_istspace	Isspace	_ismbcspace	Iswspace

isupper, iswupper

int isupper(int *c* **);**
int iswupper(wint_t *c* **);**

Each of these routines returns true if c is a particular representation of an uppercase letter.

Routine	Required Header	Compatibility
isupper	<ctype.h>	ANSI, Win 95, Win NT
iswupper	<ctype.h> or <wchar.h>	ANSI, Win 95, Win NT

For additional compatibility information, see "Compatibility" in the Introduction.

Libraries

LIBC.LIB	Single thread static library, retail version
LIBCMT.LIB	Multithread static library, retail version
MSVCRT.LIB	Import library for MSVCRT.DLL, retail version

Return Value

isupper returns a non-zero value if *c* is an uppercase character (a–z). **iswupper** returns a non-zero value if *c* is a wide character that corresponds to an uppercase letter, or if *c* is one of an implementation-defined set of wide characters for which none of **iswcntrl**, **iswdigit**, **iswpunct**, or **iswspace** is true. Each of these routines returns 0 if *c* does not satisfy the test condition.

The result of the test condition for the **isupper** function depends on the **LC_CTYPE** category setting of the current locale; see setlocale for more information. For **iswupper**, the result of the test condition is independent of locale.

Parameter

c
  Integer to test

Generic-Text Routine Mappings

TCHAR.H Routine	_UNICODE & _MBCS Not Defined	_MBCS Defined	_UNICODE Defined
_istupper	isupper	_ismbcupper	Iswupper

iswctype

int iswctype(wint_t *c*, wctype_t *desc*);

iswctype tests *c* for the property specified by the *desc* argument. For each valid value of *desc*, there is an equivalent wide-character classification routine.

Routine	Required Header	Compatibility
iswctype	<ctype.h> or <wchar.h>	ANSI, Win 95, Win NT

For additional compatibility information, see "Compatibility" in the Introduction.

Libraries

LIBC.LIB	Single thread static library, retail version
LIBCMT.LIB	Multithread static library, retail version
MSVCRT.LIB	Import library for MSVCRT.DLL, retail version

Return Value

iswctype returns a nonzero value if *c* has the property specified by *desc*, or 0 if it does not. The result of the test condition is independent of locale.

Parameters

c
>Integer to test

desc
>Property to test for

isxdigit, iswxdigit

int isxdigit(int *c* **);**
int iswxdigit(wint_t *c* **);**

Each of these routines returns true if *c* is a particular representation of a hexadecimal digit.

Routine	Required Header	Compatibility
isxdigit	<ctype.h>	ANSI, Win 95, Win NT
iswxdigit	<ctype.h> or <wchar.h>	ANSI, Win 95, Win NT

For additional compatibility information, see "Compatibility" in the Introduction.

Libraries

LIBC.LIB	Single thread static library, retail version
LIBCMT.LIB	Multithread static library, retail version
MSVCRT.LIB	Import library for MSVCRT.DLL, retail version

Return Value

isxdigit returns a non-zero value if *c* is a hexadecimal digit (A–F, a–f, or 0–9). **iswxdigit** returns a non-zero value if *c* is a wide character that corresponds to a hexadecimal digit character. Each of these routines returns 0 if *c* does not satisfy the test condition.

The result of the test condition for the **isxdigit** function depends on the **LC_CTYPE** category setting of the current locale; see setlocale for more information. For the "C" locale, the **iswxdigit** function does not provide support for Unicode fullwidth hexadecimal characters. The result of the test condition for **iswxdigit** is independent of any other locale.

Parameter

c
>Integer to test

Generic-Text Routine Mappings

TCHAR.H Routine	_UNICODE & _MBCS Not Defined	_MBCS Defined	_UNICODE Defined
_istxdigit	isxdigit	isxdigit	iswxdigit

_isatty

int _isatty(int *handle* **);**

Routine	Required Header	Compatibility
_isatty	<io.h>	Win 95, Win NT

For additional compatibility information, see "Compatibility" in the Introduction.

Libraries

LIBC.LIB	Single thread static library, retail version
LIBCMT.LIB	Multithread static library, retail version
MSVCRT.LIB	Import library for MSVCRT.DLL, retail version

Return Value

_isatty returns a nonzero value handle is associated with a character device. Otherwise, **_isatty** returns 0.

Parameter

handle
    Handle referring to device to be tested

Remarks

The **_isatty** function determines whether *handle* is associated with a character device (a terminal, console, printer, or serial port).

Example

```
/* ISATTY.C: This program checks to see whether
 * stdout has been redirected to a file.
 */

#include <stdio.h>
#include <io.h>

void main( void )
{
   if( _isatty( _fileno( stdout ) ) )
      printf( "stdout has not been redirected to a file\n" );
   else
      printf( "stdout has been redirected to a file\n");
}
```

Output

```
stdout has been redirected to a file
```

isleadbyte

int isleadbyte(int *c* **);**

Routine	Required Header	Compatibility
isleadbyte	<ctype.h>	ANSI, Win 95, Win NT

For additional compatibility information, see "Compatibility" in the Introduction.

Libraries

LIBC.LIB	Single thread static library, retail version
LIBCMT.LIB	Multithread static library, retail version
MSVCRT.LIB	Import library for MSVCRT.DLL, retail version

Return Value

isleadbyte returns a nonzero value if the argument satisfies the test condition or 0 if it does not. In the "C" locale and in single-byte-character set (SBCS) locales, **isleadbyte** always returns 0.

Parameter

c

Integer to test

Remarks

The **isleadbyte** macro returns a nonzero value if its argument is the first byte of a multibyte character. **isleadbyte** produces a meaningful result for any integer argument from –1 (**EOF**) to **UCHAR_MAX** (0xFF), inclusive. The result of the test depends upon the **LC_CTYPE** category setting of the current locale; see setlocale for more information.

The expected argument type of **isleadbyte** is **int**; if a signed character is passed, the compiler may convert it to an integer by sign extension, yielding unpredictable results.

Generic-Text Routine Mappings

TCHAR.H Routine	_UNICODE & _MBCS Not Defined	_MBCS Defined	_UNICODE Defined
_istleadbyte	Always returns false	_isleadbyte	Always returns false

See Also

_ismbb Routine Overview

_ismbb Routines

Each routine in the **_ismbb** family tests the given integer value *c* for a particular condition.

_ismbbalnum	_ismbbkana	_ismbbprint
_ismbbalpha	_ismbbkprint	_ismbbpunct
_ismbbgraph	_ismbbkpunct	_ismbbtrail
_ismbbkalnum	_ismbblead	

Remarks

Each routine in the **_ismbb** family tests the given integer value *c* for a particular condition. The test result depends on the multibyte code page in effect. By default, the multibyte code page is set to the system-default ANSI code page obtained from the operating system at program startup. You can query or change the multibyte code page in use with _getmbcp or _setmbcp, respectively.

The routines in the **_ismbb** family test the given integer *c* as follows.

Routine	Byte Test Condition
_ismbbalnum	**isalnum ‖ _ismbbkalnum**
_ismbbalpha	**isalpha ‖ _ismbbkalnum**
_ismbbgraph	Same as **_ismbbprint**, but _ismbbgraph does not include the space character (0x20).
_ismbbkalnum	Non-ASCII text symbol other than punctuation. For example, in code page 932 only, **_ismbbkalnum** tests for katakana alphanumeric.
_ismbbkana	Katakana (0xA1–0xDF). Specific to code page 932.
_ismbbkprint	Non-ASCII text or non-ASCII punctuation symbol. For example, in code page 932 only, **_ismbbkprint** tests for katakana alphanumeric or katakana punctuation (range: 0xA1–0xDF).
_ismbbkpunct	Non-ASCII punctuation. For example, in code page 932 only, **_ismbbkpunct** tests for katakana punctuation.
_ismbblead	First byte of multibyte character. For example, in code page 932 only, valid ranges are 0x81–0x9F, 0xE0–0xFC.
_ismbbprint	**isprint ‖ _ismbbkprint. ismbbprint** includes the space character (0x20).
_ismbbpunct	**ispunct ‖ _ismbbkpunct**
_ismbbtrail	Second byte of multibyte character. For example, in code page 932 only, valid ranges are 0x40–0x7E, 0x80–0xEC.

The following table shows the ORed values that compose the test conditions for these routines. The manifest constants **_BLANK**, **_DIGIT**, **_LOWER**, **_PUNCT**, and **_UPPER** are defined in CTYPE.H.

Routine	_BLANK	_DIGIT	LOWER	_PUNCT	UPPER	Non-ASCII Text	Non-ASCII Punct
_ismbbalnum	—	X	X	—	X	X	—
_ismbbalpha	—	—	X	—	X	X	—
_ismbbgraph	—	X	X	X	X	X	X
_ismbbkalnum	—	—	—	—	—	X	—
_ismbbkprint	—	—	—	—	—	X	X
_ismbbkpunct	—	—	—	—	—	—	X
_ismbbprint	X	X	X	X	X	X	X
_ismbbpunct	—	—	—	X	—	—	X

The **_ismbb** routines are implemented both as functions and as macros. For details on choosing either implementation, see "Choosing Between Functions and Macros" in the Introduction.

See Also

_mbbtombc, _mbctombb

_ismbbalnum

int _ismbbalnum(unsigned int *c*);

Routine	Required Header	Compatibility
_ismbbalnum	<mbctype.h>	Win 95, Win NT

For additional compatibility information, see "Compatibility" in the Introduction.

Libraries

LIBC.LIB	Single thread static library, retail version
LIBCMT.LIB	Multithread static library, retail version
MSVCRT.LIB	Import library for MSVCRT.DLL, retail version

Return Value

_ismbbalnum returns a nonzero value if the expression

```
isalnum || _ismbbkalnum
```

is true of *c*, or 0 if it is not.

Parameter

c

    Integer to be tested

_ismbbalpha

int _ismbbalpha(unsigned int *c*);

Routine	Required Header	Compatibility
_ismbbalpha	<mbctype.h>	Win 95, Win NT

For additional compatibility information, see "Compatibility" in the Introduction.

Libraries

LIBC.LIB	Single thread static library, retail version
LIBCMT.LIB	Multithread static library, retail version
MSVCRT.LIB	Import library for MSVCRT.DLL, retail version

Return Value

_ismbbalpha returns a nonzero value if the expression

```
isalpha || _ismbbkalnum
```

is true of *c*, or 0 if it is not.

Parameter

c

    Integer to be tested

_ismbbgraph

int _ismbbgraph (unsigned int *c*);

Routine	Required Header	Compatibility
_ismbbgraph	<mbctype.h>	Win 95, Win NT

For additional compatibility information, see "Compatibility" in the Introduction.

Libraries

LIBC.LIB	Single thread static library, retail version
LIBCMT.LIB	Multithread static library, retail version
MSVCRT.LIB	Import library for MSVCRT.DLL, retail version

Return Value

_ismbbgraph returns a nonzero value if the expression

`( _PUNCT | _UPPER | _LOWER | _DIGIT ) || _ismbbkprint`

is true of *c*, or 0 if it is not.

Parameter

c

   Integer to be tested

_ismbbkalnum

int _ismbbkalnum(unsigned int *c*);

Routine	Required Header	Compatibility
_ismbbkalnum	<mbctype.h>	Win 95, Win NT

For additional compatibility information, see "Compatibility" in the Introduction.

Libraries

LIBC.LIB	Single thread static library, retail version
LIBCMT.LIB	Multithread static library, retail version
MSVCRT.LIB	Import library for MSVCRT.DLL, retail version

Return Value

_ismbbkalnum returns a nonzero value if the integer *c* is a non-ASCII text symbol other than punctuation, or 0 if it is not.

Parameter

c

   Integer to be tested

_ismbbkana

int _ismbbkana(unsigned int *c*);

_ismbbkana tests for a katakana symbol and is specific to code page 932.

Routine	Required Header	Compatibility
_ismbbkana	<mbctype.h>	Win 95, Win NT

For additional compatibility information, see "Compatibility" in the Introduction.

Libraries

LIBC.LIB	Single thread static library, retail version
LIBCMT.LIB	Multithread static library, retail version
MSVCRT.LIB	Import library for MSVCRT.DLL, retail version

Return Value

_ismbbkana returns a nonzero value if the integer *c* is a katakana symbol, or 0 if it is not.

Parameter

c

    Integer to be tested

_ismbbkprint

int _ismbbkprint(unsigned int *c* **);**

Routine	Required Header	Compatibility
_ismbbkprint	<mbctype.h>	Win 95, Win NT

For additional compatibility information, see "Compatibility" in the Introduction.

Libraries

LIBC.LIB	Single thread static library, retail version
LIBCMT.LIB	Multithread static library, retail version
MSVCRT.LIB	Import library for MSVCRT.DLL, retail version

Return Value

_ismbbkprint returns a nonzero value if the integer *c* is a non-ASCII text or non-ASCII punctuation symbol, or 0 if it is not. For example, in code page 932 only, **_ismbbkprint** tests for katakana alphanumeric or katakana punctuation (range: 0xA1–0xDF).

Parameter

c

    Integer to be tested

_ismbbkpunct

int _ismbbkpunct(unsigned int *c* **);**

Routine	Required Header	Compatibility
_ismbbkpunct	<mbctype.h>	Win 95, Win NT

For additional compatibility information, see "Compatibility" in the Introduction.

Libraries

LIBC.LIB	Single thread static library, retail version
LIBCMT.LIB	Multithread static library, retail version
MSVCRT.LIB	Import library for MSVCRT.DLL, retail version

Return Value

_ismbbkpunct returns a nonzero value if the integer *c* is a non-ASCII punctuation symbol, or 0 if it is not. For example, in code page 932 only, **_ismbbkpunct** tests for katakana punctuation.

Parameter

c
   Integer to be tested

_ismbblead

int _ismbblead(unsigned int *c*);

Routine	Required Header	Optional Headers	Compatibility
_ismbblead	<mbctype.h> or <mbstring.h>	<ctype.h>,* <limits.h>, <stdlib.h>	Win 95, Win NT

* For manifest constants for the test conditions.

For additional compatibility information, see "Compatibility" in the Introduction.

Libraries

LIBC.LIB	Single thread static library, retail version
LIBCMT.LIB	Multithread static library, retail version
MSVCRT.LIB	Import library for MSVCRT.DLL, retail version

Return Value

_ismbblead returns a nonzero value if the integer *c* is the first byte of a multibyte character. For example, in code page 932 only, valid ranges are 0x81–0x9F and 0xE0–0xFC.

Parameter

c
   Integer to be tested

Generic-Text Routine Mappings

TCHAR.H Routine	_UNICODE & _MBCS Not Defined	_MBCS Defined	_UNICODE Defined
_istlead	Always returns false	_ismbblead	Always returns false

_ismbbprint

int _ismbbprint(unsigned int *c*);

Routine	Required Header	Compatibility
_ismbbprint	<mbctype.h>	Win 95, Win NT

For additional compatibility information, see "Compatibility" in the Introduction.

Libraries

LIBC.LIB	Single thread static library, retail version
LIBCMT.LIB	Multithread static library, retail version
MSVCRT.LIB	Import library for MSVCRT.DLL, retail version

Return Value

_ismbbprint returns a nonzero value if the expression

```
isprint || _ismbbkprint
```

is true of *c*, or 0 if it is not.

Parameter

c
    Integer to be tested

_ismbbpunct

int _ismbbpunct(unsigned int *c*);

Routine	Required Header	Compatibility
_ismbbpunct	<mbctype.h>	Win 95, Win NT

For additional compatibility information, see "Compatibility" in the Introduction.

Libraries

LIBC.LIB	Single thread static library, retail version
LIBCMT.LIB	Multithread static library, retail version
MSVCRT.LIB	Import library for MSVCRT.DLL, retail version

Return Value

_ismbbpunct returns a nonzero value if the integer *c* is a non-ASCII punctuation symbol.

Parameter

c

Integer to be tested

_ismbbtrail

int _ismbbtrail(unsigned int *c*);

Routine	Required Header	Optional Headers	Compatibility
_ismbbtrail	<mbctype.h> or <mbstring.h>	<ctype.h>,* <limits.h>, <stdlib.h>	Win 95, Win NT

* For manifest constants for the test conditions.

For additional compatibility information, see "Compatibility" in the Introduction.

Libraries

LIBC.LIB	Single thread static library, retail version
LIBCMT.LIB	Multithread static library, retail version
MSVCRT.LIB	Import library for MSVCRT.DLL, retail version

Return Value

_ismbbtrail returns a nonzero value if the integer *c* is the second byte of a multibyte character. For example, in code page 932 only, valid ranges are 0x40–0x7E and 0x80–0xEC.

Parameter

c

Integer to be tested

_ismbc Routines

Each of the **_ismbc** routines tests a given multibyte character *c* for a particular condition.

_ismbcalnum, _ismbcalpha, _ismbcdigit

_ismbcgraph, _ismbcprint, _ismbcpunct, _ismbcspace

_ismbchira, _ismbckata

_ismbcl0, _ismbcl1, _ismbcl2

_ismbclegal, _ismbcsymbol

_ismbclower, _ismbcupper

Remarks

The test result of each of the **_ismbc** routines depends on the multibyte code page in effect. Multibyte code pages have single byte alphabetic characters. By default, the multibyte code page is set to the system-default ANSI code page obtained from the operating system at program startup. You can query or change the multibyte code page in use with _getmbcp or _setmbcp, respectively.

Routine	Test Condition	Code Page 932 Example
_ismbcalnum	Alphanumeric	Returns true if and only if c is a single-byte representation of an ASCII English letter: See examples for **_ismbcdigit** and **_ismbcalpha**.
_ismbcalpha	Alphabetic	Returns true if and only if c is a single-byte representation of an ASCII English letter: See examples for **_ismbcupper** and **_ismbclower**; or a Katakana letter: $0xA6<=c<=0xDF$.
_ismbcdigit	Digit	Returns true if and only if c is a single-byte representation of an ASCII digit: $0x30<=c<=0x39$.
_ismbcgraph	Graphic	Returns true if and only if c is a single-byte representation of any ASCII or Katakana printable character except a white space ( ). See examples for **_ismbcdigit**, **_ismbcalpha**, and **_ismbcpunct**.
_ismbclegal	Valid multibyte character	Returns true if and only if the first byte of c is within ranges 0x81–0x9F or 0xE0–0xFC, while the second byte is within ranges 0x40–0x7E or 0x80-FC.
_ismbclower	Lowercase alphabetic	Returns true if and only if c is a single-byte representation of an ASCII lowercase English letter: $0x61<=c<=0x7A$.
_ismbcprint	Printable	Returns true if and only if c is a single-byte representation of any ASCII or Katakana printable character including a white space ( ): See examples for **_ismbcspace**, **_ismbcdigit**, **_ismbcalpha**, and **_ismbcpunct**.
_ismbcpunct	Punctuation	Returns true if and only if c is a single-byte representation of any ASCII or Katakana punctuation character.
_ismbcspace	Whitespace	Returns true if and only if c is a whitespace character: $c=0x20$ or $0x09<=c<=0x0D$.
_ismbcsymbol	Multibyte symbol	Returns true if and only if $0x8141<=c<=0x81AC$.
_ismbcupper	Uppercase alphabetic	Returns true if and only if c is a single-byte representation of an ASCII uppercase English letter: $0x41<=c<=0x5A$.

Code Page 932 Specific →

The following routines are specific to code page 932.

Routine	Test Condition (Code Page 932 Only)
_ismbchira	Double-byte Hiragana: $0x829F<=c<=0x82F1$.
_ismbckata	Double-byte Katakana: $0x8340<=c<=0x8396$.
_ismbcl0	JIS non-Kanji: $0x8140<=c<=0x889E$.
_ismbcl1	JIS level-1: $0x889F<=c<=0x9872$.
_ismbcl2	JIS level-2: $0x989F<=c<=0xEA9E$.

_ismbcl0, **_ismbcl1**, and **_ismbcl2** check that the specified value c matches the test conditions described in the preceding table, but do not check that c is a valid multibyte character. If the lower byte is in the ranges 0x00–0x3F, 0x7F, or 0xFD–0xFF, these functions return a nonzero value, indicating that the character satisfies the test condition. Use _ismbbtrail to test whether the multibyte character is defined.

END Code Page 932 Specific

See Also

is, isw Function Overview, **_ismbb** Function Overview

_ismbcl0, _ismbcl1, _ismbcl2

Code Page 932 Specific →

int _ismbcl0(unsigned int c);
int _ismbcl1(unsigned int c);
int _ismbcl2(unsigned int c);

Routine	Required Header	Compatibility
_ismbcl0	<mbstring.h>	Win 95, Win NT
_ismbcl1	<mbstring.h>	Win 95, Win NT
_ismbcl2	<mbstring.h>	Win 95, Win NT

For additional compatibility information, see "Compatibility" in the Introduction.

Libraries

LIBC.LIB	Single thread static library, retail version
LIBCMT.LIB	Multithread static library, retail version
MSVCRT.LIB	Import library for MSVCRT.DLL, retail version

Return Value

Each of these routines returns a nonzero value if the character satisfies the test condition or 0 if it does not. If $c <= 255$ and there is a corresponding **_ismbb** routine (for example, **_ismbcalnum** corresponds to **_ismbbalnum**), the result is the return value of the corresponding **_ismbb** routine.

Parameter

c

   Character to be tested

Remarks

Each of these functions tests a given multibyte character for a given condition.

Routine	Test Condition (Code Page 932 Only)
_ismbcl0	JIS non-Kanji: $0x8140 <= c <= 0x889E$.
_ismbcl1	JIS level-1: $0x889F <= c <= 0x9872$.
_ismbcl2	JIS level-2: $0x989F <= c <= 0xEA9E$.

_ismbcl0, **_ismbcl1**, and **_ismbcl2** check that the specified value *c* matches the test conditions described above, but do not check that *c* is a valid multibyte character. If the lower byte is in the ranges 0x00–0x3F, 0x7F, or 0xFD–0xFF, these functions return a nonzero value, indicating that the character satisfies the test condition. Use _ismbbtrail to test whether the multibyte character is defined.

End Code Page 932 Specific

See Also

is, **isw** Function Overview, **_ismbb** Function Overview

_ismbcalnum, _ismbcalpha, _ismbcdigit

int **_ismbcalnum**(unsigned int *c*);
int **_ismbcalpha**(unsigned int *c*);
int **_ismbcdigit**(unsigned int *c*);

Routine	Required Header	Compatibility
_ismbcalnum	<mbstring.h>	Win 95, Win NT
_ismbcalpha	<mbstring.h>	Win 95, Win NT
_ismbcdigit	<mbstring.h>	Win 95, Win NT

For additional compatibility information, see "Compatibility" in the Introduction.

Libraries

LIBC.LIB	Single thread static library, retail version
LIBCMT.LIB	Multithread static library, retail version
MSVCRT.LIB	Import library for MSVCRT.DLL, retail version

Return Value

Each of these routines returns a nonzero value if the character satisfies the test condition or 0 if it does not. If $c <= 255$ and there is a corresponding **_ismbb** routine (for example, **_ismbcalnum** corresponds to **_ismbbalnum**), the result is the return value of the corresponding **_ismbb** routine.

Parameter

c

   Character to be tested

Remarks

Each of these routines tests a given multibyte character for a given condition.

Routine	Test Condition	Code Page 932 Example
_ismbcalnum	Alphanumeric	Returns true if and only if *c* is a single-byte representation of an ASCII English letter: See examples for **_ismbcdigit** and **_ismbcalpha**.
_ismbcalpha	Alphabetic	Returns true if and only if *c* is a single-byte representation of an ASCII English letter: $0x41 <= c <= 0x5A$ or $0x61 <= c <= 0x7A$; or a Katakana letter: $0xA6 <= c <= 0xDF$.
_ismbcdigit	Digit	Returns true if and only if *c* is a single-byte representation of an ASCII digit: $0x30 <= c <= 0x39$.

See Also

is, **isw** Function Overview, **_ismbb** Function Overview

_ismbcgraph, _ismbcprint, _ismbcpunct, _ismbcspace

int _ismbcgraph(unsigned int *c* **);**
int _ismbcprint(unsigned int *c* **);**
int _ismbcpunct(unsigned int *c* **);**
int _ismbcspace(unsigned int *c* **);**

Routine	Required Header	Compatibility
_ismbcgraph	<mbstring.h>	Win 95, Win NT
_ismbcprint	<mbstring.h>	Win 95, Win NT
_ismbcpunct	<mbstring.h>	Win 95, Win NT
_ismbcspace	<mbstring.h>	Win 95, Win NT

For additional compatibility information, see "Compatibility" in the Introduction.

Libraries

LIBC.LIB	Single thread static library, retail version
LIBCMT.LIB	Multithread static library, retail version
MSVCRT.LIB	Import library for MSVCRT.DLL, retail version

Return Value

Each of these routines returns a nonzero value if the character satisfies the test condition or 0 if it does not. If $c <= 255$ and there is a corresponding **_ismbb** routine (for example, **_ismbcalnum** corresponds to **_ismbbalnum**), the result is the return value of the corresponding **_ismbb** routine.

Parameter

c

    Character to be tested

Remarks

Each of these functions tests a given multibyte character for a given condition.

Routine	Test Condition	Code Page 932 Example
_ismbcgraph	Graphic	Returns true if and only if *c* is a single-byte representation of any ASCII or Katakana printable character except a white space ( ).
_ismbcprint	Printable	Returns true if and only if *c* is a single-byte representation of any ASCII or Katakana printable character including a white space ( ).
_ismbcpunct	Punctuation	Returns true if and only if *c* is a single-byte representation of any ASCII or Katakana punctuation character.
_ismbcspace	Whitespace	Returns true if and only if *c* is a whitespace character: $c=0x20$ or $0x09 <= c <= 0x0D$.

See Also

is, **isw** Function Overview, **_ismbb** Function Overview

_ismbchira, _ismbckata

Code Page 932 Specific →

int _ismbchira(unsigned int *c*);
int _ismbckata(unsigned int *c*);

Routine	Required Header	Compatibility
_ismbchira	<mbstring.h>	Win 95, Win NT
_ismbckata	<mbstring.h>	Win 95, Win NT

For additional compatibility information, see "Compatibility" in the Introduction.

Libraries

LIBC.LIB	Single thread static library, retail version
LIBCMT.LIB	Multithread static library, retail version
MSVCRT.LIB	Import library for MSVCRT.DLL, retail version

Return Value

Each of these routines returns a nonzero value if the character satisfies the test condition or 0 if it does not. If *c*<= 255 and there is a corresponding **_ismbb** routine (for example, **_ismbcalnum** corresponds to **_ismbbalnum**), the result is the return value of the corresponding **_ismbb** routine.

Parameter

c

    Character to be tested

Remarks

Each of these functions tests a given multibyte character for a given condition.

Routine	Test Condition (Code Page 932 Only)
_ismbchira	Double-byte Hiragana: $0x829F<=c<=0x82F1$.
_ismbckata	Double-byte Katakana: $0x8340<=c<=0x8396$.

End Code Page 932 Specific

See Also

is, **isw** Function Overview, **_ismbb** Function Overview

_ismbclegal, _ismbcsymbol

int _ismbclegal(unsigned int *c* **);**
int _ismbcsymbol(unsigned int *c* **);**

Routine	Required Header	Compatibility
_ismbclegal	<mbstring.h>	Win 95, Win NT
_ismbcsymbol	<mbstring.h>	Win 95, Win NT

For additional compatibility information, see "Compatibility" in the Introduction.

Libraries

LIBC.LIB	Single thread static library, retail version
LIBCMT.LIB	Multithread static library, retail version
MSVCRT.LIB	Import library for MSVCRT.DLL, retail version

Return Value

Each of these routines returns a nonzero value if the character satisfies the test condition or 0 if it does not. If *c*<= 255 and there is a corresponding **_ismbb** routine (for example, **_ismbcalnum** corresponds to **_ismbbalnum**), the result is the return value of the corresponding **_ismbb** routine.

Parameter

c

    Character to be tested

Remarks

Each of these functions tests a given multibyte character for a given condition.

Routine	Test Condition	Code Page 932 Example
_ismbclegal	Valid multibyte	Returns true if and only if the first byte of *c* is within ranges 0x81–0x9F or 0xE0–xFC, while the second byte is within ranges 0x40-0x7E or 0x80-FC.
_ismbcsymbol	Multibyte symbol	Returns true if and only if $0x8141<=c<=0x81AC$.

Generic-Text Routine Mappings

TCHAR.H Routine	_UNICODE & _MBCS Not Defined	_MBCS Defined	_UNICODE Defined
_istlegal	Always returns false	_ismbclegal	Always returns false

See Also

is, isw Function Overview, **_ismbb** Function Overview

_ismbclower, _ismbcupper

int _ismbclower(unsigned int *c* **);**
int _ismbcupper(unsigned int *c* **);**

Routine	Required Header	Compatibility
_ismbclower	<mbstring.h>	Win 95, Win NT
_ismbcupper	<mbstring.h>	Win 95, Win NT

For additional compatibility information, see "Compatibility" in the Introduction.

Libraries

LIBC.LIB	Single thread static library, retail version
LIBCMT.LIB	Multithread static library, retail version
MSVCRT.LIB	Import library for MSVCRT.DLL, retail version

Return Value

Each of these routines returns a nonzero value if the character satisfies the test condition or 0 if it does not. If $c <= 255$ and there is a corresponding **_ismbb** routine (for example, **_ismbcalnum** corresponds to **_ismbbalnum**), the result is the return value of the corresponding **_ismbb** routine.

Parameter

c

   Character to be tested

Remarks

Each of these functions tests a given multibyte character for a given condition.

Routine	Test Condition	Code Page 932 Example
_ismbclower	Lowercase alphabetic	Returns true if and only if *c* is a single-byte representation of an ASCII lowercase English letter: $0x61 <= c <= 0x7A$.
_ismbcupper	Uppercase alphabetic	Returns true if and only if *c* is a single-byte representation of an ASCII uppercase English letter: $0x41 <= c <= 0x5A$.

See Also

is, isw Function Overview, **_ismbb** Function Overview

_ismbslead, _ismbstrail

int _ismbslead(const unsigned char *_string_, const unsigned char *_current_);
int _ismbstrail(const unsigned char *_string_, const unsigned char *_current_);

Routine	Required Header	Optional Headers	Compatibility
_ismbslead	<mbctype.h> or <mbstring.h>	<ctype.h>,[*] <limits.h>, <stdlib.h>	Win 95, Win NT
_ismbstrail	<mbctype.h> or <mbstring.h>	<ctype.h>,[*] <limits.h>, <stdlib.h>	Win 95, Win NT

* For manifest constants for the test conditions.

For additional compatibility information, see "Compatibility" in the Introduction.

Libraries

LIBC.LIB	Single thread static library, retail version
LIBCMT.LIB	Multithread static library, retail version
MSVCRT.LIB	Import library for MSVCRT.DLL, retail version

Return Value

_ismbslead and **_ismbstrail** return –1 if the character is a lead or trail byte, respectively. Otherwise they return zero.

Parameters

string
    Pointer to start of string or previous known lead byte

current
    Pointer to position in string to be tested

Remarks

The **_ismbslead** and **_ismbstrail** routines perform context-sensitive tests for multibyte-character string lead and trail bytes; they determine whether a given substring pointer points to a lead byte or a trail byte. **_ismbslead** and **_ismbstrail** are slower than their **_ismbblead** and **_ismbbtrail** counterparts because they take the string context into account.

See Also

is, **isw** Function Overview, **_ismbb** Function Overview

_isnan

Checks given double-precision floating-point value for not a number (NaN).

int _isnan(double *x* **);**

Routine	Required Header	Compatibility
_isnan	<float.h>	Win 95, Win NT

For additional compatibility information, see "Compatibility" in the Introduction.

Libraries

LIBC.LIB	Single thread static library, retail version
LIBCMT.LIB	Multithread static library, retail version
MSVCRT.LIB	Import library for MSVCRT.DLL, retail version

Return Value

_isnan returns a nonzero value (TRUE) if the argument *x* is a NaN; otherwise it returns 0 (FALSE).

Parameter

x

Double-precision floating-point value

Remarks

The **_isnan** function tests a given double-precision floating-point value *x*, returning a nonzero value if *x* is a NaN. A NaN is generated when the result of a floating-point operation cannot be represented in Institute of Electrical and Electronics Engineers (IEEE) format. For information about how a NaN is represented for output, see **printf**.

See Also

_finite, **_fpclass**

_itoa, _i64toa, _ui64toa, _itow, _i64tow, _ui64tow

Convert an integer to a string.

char *_itoa(int *value***, char ****string***, int** *radix* **);**
char *_i64toa(__int64 *value***, char ****string***, int** *radix* **);**
char * _ui64toa(unsigned _int64 *value***, char ****string***, int** *radix* **);**

wchar_t * _itow(int *value,* **wchar_t ****string,* **int** *radix* **);**
wchar_t * _i64tow(__int64 *value,* **wchar_t ****string,* **int** *radix* **);**
wchar_t * _ui64tow(unsigned __int64 *value,* **wchar_t ****string,* **int** *radix* **);**

Routine	Required Header	Compatibility
_itoa	<stdlib.h>	Win 95, Win NT
_i64toa	<stdlib.h>	Win 95, Win NT
_ui64toa	<stdlib.h>	Win 95, Win NT
_itow	<stdlib.h>	Win 95, Win NT
_i64tow	<stdlib.h>	Win 95, Win NT
_ui64tow	<stdlib.h>	Win 95, Win NT

For additional compatibility information, see "Compatibility" in the Introduction.

Libraries

LIBC.LIB	Single thread static library, retail version
LIBCMT.LIB	Multithread static library, retail version
MSVCRT.LIB	Import library for MSVCRT.DLL, retail version

Return Value

Each of these functions returns a pointer to *string*. There is no error return.

Parameters

value
    Number to be converted

string
    String result

radix
    Base of *value*; must be in the range 2–36

Remarks

The **_itoa**, **_i64toa**, and **_ui64toa** function convert the digits of the given *value* argument to a null-terminated character string and stores the result (up to 33 bytes) in *string*. If *radix* equals 10 and *value* is negative, the first character of the stored string is the minus sign (–). **_itow**, **_i64tow**, and **_ui64tow** are wide-character versions of **_itoa**, **_i64toa**, and **_ui64toa** respectively.

Generic-Text Routine Mappings

TCHAR.H Routine	_UNICODE & _MBCS Not Defined	_MBCS Defined	_UNICODE Defined
_itot	_itoa	_itoa	_itow

Example

```
/* ITOA.C: This program converts integers of various
 * sizes to strings in various radixes.
 */

#include <stdlib.h>
#include <stdio.h>

void main( void )
{
    char buffer[20];
    int  i = 3445;
    long l = -344115L;
    unsigned long ul = 1234567890UL;

    _itoa( i, buffer, 10 );
    printf( "String of integer %d (radix 10): %s\n", i, buffer );
    _itoa( i, buffer, 16 );
    printf( "String of integer %d (radix 16): 0x%s\n", i, buffer );
    _itoa( i, buffer, 2  );
    printf( "String of integer %d (radix 2): %s\n", i, buffer );

    _ltoa( l, buffer, 16 );
    printf( "String of long int %ld (radix 16): 0x%s\n", l,
                                              buffer );

    _ultoa( ul, buffer, 16 );
    printf( "String of unsigned long %lu (radix 16): 0x%s\n", ul,
                                              buffer );
}
```

Output

```
String of integer 3445 (radix 10): 3445
String of integer 3445 (radix 16): 0xd75
String of integer 3445 (radix 2): 110101110101
String of long int -344115 (radix 16): 0xfffabfcd
String of unsigned long 1234567890 (radix 16): 0x499602d2
```

See Also

_ltoa, _ultoa

_kbhit

Checks the console for keyboard input.

int _kbhit(void);

Routine	`Required Header	Compatibility
_kbhit	<conio.h>	Win 95, Win NT

For additional compatibility information, see "Compatibility" in the Introduction.

Libraries

LIBC.LIB	Single thread static library, retail version
LIBCMT.LIB	Multithread static library, retail version
MSVCRT.LIB	Import library for MSVCRT.DLL, retail version

Return Value

_kbhit returns a nonzero value if a key has been pressed. Otherwise, it returns 0.

Remarks

The **_kbhit** function checks the console for a recent keystroke. If the function returns a nonzero value, a keystroke is waiting in the buffer. The program can then call **_getch** or **_getche** to get the keystroke.

Example

```
/* KBHIT.C: This program loops until the user
 * presses a key. If _kbhit returns nonzero, a
 * keystroke is waiting in the buffer. The program
 * can call _getch or _getche to get the keystroke.
 */

#include <conio.h>
#include <stdio.h>

void main( void )
{
   /* Display message until key is pressed. */
   while( !_kbhit() )
      _cputs( "Hit me!! " );

   /* Use _getch to throw key away. */
   printf( "\nKey struck was '%c'\n", _getch() );
   _getch();
}
```

Output

```
Hit me!! Hit me!! Hit me!! Hit me!! Hit me!! Hit me!! Hit me!!
Key struck was 'q'
```

labs

Calculates the absolute value of a long integer.

long labs(long *n* **);**

Routine	Required Header	Compatibility
labs	<stdlib.h> and <math.h>	ANSI, Win 95, Win NT

For additional compatibility information, see "Compatibility" in the Introduction.

Libraries

LIBC.LIB	Single thread static library, retail version
LIBCMT.LIB	Multithread static library, retail version
MSVCRT.LIB	Import library for MSVCRT.DLL, retail version

Return Value

The **labs** function returns the absolute value of its argument. There is no error return.

Parameter

n

Long-integer value

Example

```
/* ABS.C: This program computes and displays
 * the absolute values of several numbers.
 */

#include  <stdio.h>
#include  <math.h>
#include  <stdlib.h>

void main( void )
{
    int    ix = -4, iy;
    long   lx = -41567L, ly;
    double dx = -3.141593, dy;
```

```
        iy = abs( ix );
        printf( "The absolute value of %d is %d\n", ix, iy);

        ly = labs( lx );
        printf( "The absolute value of %ld is %ld\n", lx, ly);

        dy = fabs( dx );
        printf( "The absolute value of %f is %f\n", dx, dy );
}
```

Output

```
The absolute value of -4 is 4
The absolute value of -41567 is 41567
The absolute value of -3.141593 is 3.141593
```

See Also

abs, **_cabs**, **fabs**

ldexp

Computes a real number from the mantissa and exponent.

double ldexp(double *x*, **int** *exp* **);**

Routine	Required Header	Compatibility
ldexp	<math.h>	ANSI, Win 95, Win NT

For additional compatibility information, see "Compatibility" in the Introduction.

Libraries

LIBC.LIB	Single thread static library, retail version
LIBCMT.LIB	Multithread static library, retail version
MSVCRT.LIB	Import library for MSVCRT.DLL, retail version

Return Value

The **ldexp** function returns the value of $x * 2^{exp}$ if successful. On overflow (depending on the sign of *x*), **ldexp** returns +/– **HUGE_VAL**; the **errno** variable is set to **ERANGE**.

Parameters

x
    Floating-point value

exp
    Integer exponent

Example

```
/* LDEXP.C */

#include <math.h>
#include <stdio.h>

void main( void )
{
    double x = 4.0, y;
    int p = 3;

    y = ldexp( x, p );
    printf( "%2.1f times two to the power of %d is %2.1f\n", x, p, y );
}
```

Output

```
4.0 times two to the power of 3 is 32.0
```

See Also

frexp, **modf**

ldiv

Computes the quotient and remainder of a long integer.

ldiv_t ldiv(long int *numer***, long int** *denom* **);**

Routine	Required Header	Compatibility
ldiv	<stdlib.h>	ANSI, Win 95, Win NT

For additional compatibility information, see "Compatibility" in the Introduction.

Libraries

LIBC.LIB	Single thread static library, retail version
LIBCMT.LIB	Multithread static library, retail version
MSVCRT.LIB	Import library for MSVCRT.DLL, retail version

Return Value

ldiv returns a structure of type **ldiv_t** that comprises both the quotient and the remainder.

Parameters

numer

Numerator

denom

Denominator

Remarks

The **ldiv** function divides *numer* by *denom*, computing the quotient and remainder. The sign of the quotient is the same as that of the mathematical quotient. The absolute value of the quotient is the largest integer that is less than the absolute value of the mathematical quotient. If the denominator is 0, the program terminates with an error message. **ldiv** is the same as **div**, except that the arguments of **ldiv** and the members of the returned structure are all of type **long int**.

The **ldiv_t** structure, defined in STDLIB.H, contains **long int quot**, the quotient, and **long int rem**, the remainder.

Example

```
/* LDIV.C: This program takes two long integers
 * as command-line arguments and displays the
 * results of the integer division.
 */

#include <stdlib.h>
#include <math.h>
#include <stdio.h>

void main( void )
{
    long x = 5149627, y = 234879;
    ldiv_t div_result;

    div_result = ldiv( x, y );
    printf( "For %ld / %ld, the quotient is ", x, y );
    printf( "%ld, and the remainder is %ld\n",
    ↪ div_result.quot, div_result.rem );
}
```

Output

```
For 5149627 / 234879, the quotient is 21, and the remainder is 217168
```

See Also

div

_lfind

Performs a linear search for the specified key.

void *_lfind(const void **key***, const void ****base***, unsigned int ****num***, unsigned int** *width***,**
  int (__cdecl **compare***)(const void ****elem1***, const void ****elem2***));**

Routine	Required Header	Compatibility
_lfind	<search.h>	Win 95, Win NT

For additional compatibility information, see "Compatibility" in the Introduction.

Libraries

LIBC.LIB	Single thread static library, retail version
LIBCMT.LIB	Multithread static library, retail version
MSVCRT.LIB	Import library for MSVCRT.DLL, retail version

Return Value

If the key is found, **_lfind** returns a pointer to the element of the array at *base* that matches *key*. If the key is not found, **_lfind** returns **NULL**.

Parameters

key
  Object to search for

base
  Pointer to base of search data

num
  Number of array elements

width
  Width of array elements

compare
  Pointer to comparison routine

elem1
  Pointer to key for search

elem2
  Pointer to array element to be compared with key

Remarks

The **_lfind** function performs a linear search for the value *key* in an array of *num* elements, each of *width* bytes in size. Unlike **bsearch**, **_lfind** does not require the array to be sorted. The *base* argument is a pointer to the base of the array to be searched. The *compare* argument is a pointer to a user-supplied routine that compares two array elements and then returns a value specifying their relationship. **_lfind** calls the *compare* routine one or more times during the search, passing pointers to two array elements on each call. The *compare* routine must compare the elements then return nonzero, meaning the elements are different, or 0, meaning the elements are identical.

Example

```
/* LFIND.C: This program uses _lfind to search for
 * the word "hello" in the command-line arguments.
 */

#include <search.h>
#include <string.h>
#include <stdio.h>

int compare( const void *arg1, const void *arg2 );

void main( unsigned int argc, char **argv )
{
   char **result;
   char *key = "hello";

   result = (char **)_lfind( &key, argv,
                    &argc, sizeof(char *), compare );
   if( result )
      printf( "%s found\n", *result );
   else
      printf( "hello not found!\n" );
}

int compare(const void *arg1, const void *arg2 )
{
   return( _stricmp( * (char**)arg1, * (char**)arg2 ) );
}
```

Output

```
[C:\code]lfind Hello
Hello found
```

See Also

bsearch, **_lsearch**, **qsort**

localeconv

Gets detailed information on locale settings.

struct lconv *localeconv(void);

Routine	Required Header	Compatibility
localeconv	<locale.h>	ANSI, Win 95, Win NT

For additional compatibility information, see "Compatibility" in the Introduction.

Libraries

LIBC.LIB	Single thread static library, retail version
LIBCMT.LIB	Multithread static library, retail version
MSVCRT.LIB	Import library for MSVCRT.DLL, retail version

Return Value

localeconv returns a pointer to a filled-in object of type struct lconv. The values contained in the object can be overwritten by subsequent calls to **localeconv** and do not directly modify the object. Calls to setlocale with *category* values of **LC_ALL**, **LC_MONETARY**, or **LC_NUMERIC** overwrite the contents of the structure.

Remarks

The **localeconv** function gets detailed information about numeric formatting for the current locale. This information is stored in a structure of type **lconv**. The **lconv** structure, defined in LOCALE.H, contains the following members:

char *decimal_point
Decimal-point character for nonmonetary quantities.

char *thousands_sep
Character that separates groups of digits to left of decimal point for nonmonetary quantities.

char *grouping
Size of each group of digits in nonmonetary quantities.

char *int_curr_symbol
International currency symbol for current locale. First three characters specify alphabetic international currency symbol as defined in the *ISO 4217 Codes for the Representation of Currency and Funds* standard. Fourth character (immediately preceding null character) separates international currency symbol from monetary quantity.

char *currency_symbol

Local currency symbol for current locale.

char *mon_decimal_point

Decimal-point character for monetary quantities.

char *mon_thousands_sep

Separator for groups of digits to left of decimal place in monetary quantities.

char *mon_grouping

Size of each group of digits in monetary quantities.

char *positive_sign

String denoting sign for nonnegative monetary quantities.

char *negative_sign

String denoting sign for negative monetary quantities.

char int_frac_digits

Number of digits to right of decimal point in internationally formatted monetary quantities.

char frac_digits

Number of digits to right of decimal point in formatted monetary quantities.

char p_cs_precedes

Set to 1 if currency symbol precedes value for nonnegative formatted monetary quantity. Set to 0 if symbol follows value.

char p_sep_by_space

Set to 1 if currency symbol is separated by space from value for nonnegative formatted monetary quantity. Set to 0 if there is no space separation.

char n_cs_precedes

Set to 1 if currency symbol precedes value for negative formatted monetary quantity. Set to 0 if symbol succeeds value.

char n_sep_by_space

Set to 1 if currency symbol is separated by space from value for negative formatted monetary quantity. Set to 0 if there is no space separation.

char p_sign_posn

Position of positive sign in nonnegative formatted monetary quantities.

char n_sign_posn

Position of positive sign in negative formatted monetary quantities.

The **char *** members of the structure are pointers to strings. Any of these (other than **char *decimal_point**) that equals "" is either of zero length or is not supported in the current locale. The **char** members of the structure are nonnegative numbers. Any of these that equals **CHAR_MAX** is not supported in the current locale.

The elements of **grouping** and **mon_grouping** are interpreted according to the following rules.

CHAR_MAX

Do not perform any further grouping.

0

Use previous element for each of remaining digits.

n

Number of digits that make up current group. Next element is examined to determine size of next group of digits before current group.

The values for **int_curr_symbol** are interpreted according to the following rules:

- The first three characters specify the alphabetic international currency symbol as defined in the *ISO 4217 Codes for the Representation of Currency and Funds* standard.

- The fourth character (immediately preceding the null character) separates the international currency symbol from the monetary quantity.

The values for **p_cs_precedes** and **n_cs_precedes** are interpreted according to the following rules (the **n_cs_precedes** rule is in parentheses):

0

Currency symbol follows value for nonnegative (negative) formatted monetary value.

1

Currency symbol precedes value for nonnegative (negative) formatted monetary value.

The values for **p_sep_by_space** and **n_sep_by_space** are interpreted according to the following rules (the **n_sep_by_space** rule is in parentheses):

0

Currency symbol is separated from value by space for nonnegative (negative) formatted monetary value.

1

There is no space separation between currency symbol and value for nonnegative (negative) formatted monetary value.

The values for **p_sign_posn** and **n_sign_posn** are interpreted according to the following rules:

0

Parentheses surround quantity and currency symbol

1

Sign string precedes quantity and currency symbol

2

Sign string follows quantity and currency symbol

3

Sign string immediately precedes currency symbol

4

Sign string immediately follows currency symbol

See Also

setlocale, **strcoll** Functions, **strftime**, **strxfrm**

localtime

Converts a time value and corrects for the local time zone.

struct tm *localtime(const time_t *timer **);**

Routine	Required Header	Compatibility
localtime	<time.h>	ANSI, Win 95, Win NT

For additional compatibility information, see "Compatibility" in the Introduction.

Libraries

LIBC.LIB	Single thread static library, retail version
LIBCMT.LIB	Multithread static library, retail version
MSVCRT.LIB	Import library for MSVCRT.DLL, retail version

Return Value

localtime returns a pointer to the structure result. If the value in *timer* represents a date before midnight, January 1, 1970, **localtime** returns **NULL**. The fields of the structure type tm store the following values, each of which is an **int**:

tm_sec
Seconds after minute (0–59)

tm_min
Minutes after hour (0–59)

tm_hour
Hours after midnight (0–23)

tm_mday
Day of month (1–31)

tm_mon
Month (0–11; January = 0)

tm_year

Year (current year minus 1900)

tm_wday

Day of week (0–6; Sunday = 0)

tm_yday

Day of year (0–365; January 1 = 0)

tm_isdst

Positive value if daylight saving time is in effect; 0 if daylight saving time is not in effect; negative value if status of daylight saving time is unknown. The C run-time library assumes the United States's rules for implementing the calculation of Daylight Saving Time (DST).

Parameter

timer

Pointer to stored time

Remarks

The **localtime** function converts a time stored as a time_t value and stores the result in a structure of type **tm**. The **long** value *timer* represents the seconds elapsed since midnight (00:00:00), January 1, 1970, coordinated universal time (UTC). This value is usually obtained from the **time** function.

gmtime, **mktime**, and **localtime** all use a single statically allocated **tm** structure for the conversion. Each call to one of these routines destroys the result of the previous call.

localtime corrects for the local time zone if the user first sets the global environment variable **TZ**. When **TZ** is set, three other environment variables (**_timezone**, **_daylight**, and **_tzname**) are automatically set as well. See **_tzset** for a description of these variables. **TZ** is a Microsoft extension and not part of the ANSI standard definition of **localtime**.

Note The target environment should try to determine whether daylight saving time is in effect.

Example

```
/* LOCALTIM.C: This program uses time to get the current time
 * and then uses localtime to convert this time to a structure
 * representing the local time. The program converts the result
 * from a 24-hour clock to a 12-hour clock and determines the
 * proper extension (AM or PM).
 */

#include <stdio.h>
#include <string.h>
#include <time.h>
```

```
void main( void )
{
    struct tm *newtime;
    char am_pm[] = "AM";
    time_t long_time;

    time( &long_time );                 /* Get time as long integer. */
    newtime = localtime( &long_time );  /* Convert to local time. */

    if( newtime->tm_hour > 12 )         /* Set up extension. */
        strcpy( am_pm, "PM" );
    if( newtime->tm_hour > 12 )         /* Convert from 24-hour */
        newtime->tm_hour -= 12;         /*   to 12-hour clock.  */
    if( newtime->tm_hour == 0 )         /*Set hour to 12 if midnight. */
        newtime->tm_hour = 12;

    printf( "%.19s %s\n", asctime( newtime ), am_pm );
}
```

Output

```
Tue Mar 23 11:28:17 AM
```

See Also

asctime, **ctime**, **_ftime**, **gmtime**, **time**, **_tzset**

_locking

Locks or unlocks bytes of a file.

int _locking(int *handle*, **int** *mode*, **long** *nbytes* **);**

Routine	Required Header	Optional Headers	Compatibility
_locking	<io.h> and <sys/locking.h>	<errno.h>	Win 95, Win NT

For additional compatibility information, see "Compatibility" in the Introduction.

Libraries

LIBC.LIB	Single thread static library, retail version
LIBCMT.LIB	Multithread static library, retail version
MSVCRT.LIB	Import library for MSVCRT.DLL, retail version

Return Value

_locking returns 0 if successful. A return value of –1 indicates failure, in which case errno is set to one of the following values:

EACCES

Locking violation (file already locked or unlocked).

EBADF

Invalid file handle.

EDEADLOCK

Locking violation. Returned when the **_LK_LOCK** or **_LK_RLCK** flag is specified and the file cannot be locked after 10 attempts.

EINVAL

An invalid argument was given to **_locking**.

Parameters

handle

File handle

mode

Locking action to perform

nbytes

Number of bytes to lock

Remarks

The **_locking** function locks or unlocks *nbytes* bytes of the file specified by *handle*. Locking bytes in a file prevents access to those bytes by other processes. All locking or unlocking begins at the current position of the file pointer and proceeds for the next *nbytes* bytes. It is possible to lock bytes past end of file.

mode must be one of the following manifest constants, which are defined in LOCKING.H:

_LK_LOCK

Locks the specified bytes. If the bytes cannot be locked, the program immediately tries again after 1 second. If, after 10 attempts, the bytes cannot be locked, the constant returns an error.

_LK_NBLCK

Locks the specified bytes. If the bytes cannot be locked, the constant returns an error.

_LK_NBRLCK

Same as **_LK_NBLCK**.

_LK_RLCK

Same as **_LK_LOCK**.

_LK_UNLCK

Unlocks the specified bytes, which must have been previously locked.

Multiple regions of a file that do not overlap can be locked. A region being unlocked must have been previously locked. **_locking** does not merge adjacent regions; if two locked regions are adjacent, each region must be unlocked separately. Regions should be locked only briefly and should be unlocked before closing a file or exiting the program.

Example

```
/* LOCKING.C: This program opens a file with sharing. It locks
 * some bytes before reading them, then unlocks them. Note that the
 * program works correctly only if the file exists.
 */

#include <io.h>
#include <sys/types.h>
#include <sys/stat.h>
#include <sys/locking.h>
#include <share.h>
#include <fcntl.h>
#include <stdio.h>
#include <stdlib.h>

void main( void )
{
    int  fh, numread;
    char buffer[40];

    /* Quit if can't open file or system doesn't
     * support sharing.
     */
    fh = _sopen( "locking.c", _O_RDWR, _SH_DENYNO,
                 _S_IREAD | _S_IWRITE );
    if( fh == -1 )
       exit( 1 );

    /* Lock some bytes and read them. Then unlock. */
    if( _locking( fh, LK_NBLCK, 30L ) != -1 )
    {
        printf( "No one can change these bytes while I'm reading them\n" );
        numread = _read( fh, buffer, 30 );
        printf( "%d bytes read: %.30s\n", numread, buffer );
        lseek( fh, 0L, SEEK_SET );
        _locking( fh, LK_UNLCK, 30L );
        printf( "Now I'm done. Do what you will with them\n" );
    }
    else
        perror( "Locking failed\n" );

    _close( fh );
}
```

Output

```
No one can change these bytes while I'm reading them
30 bytes read: /* LOCKING.C: This program ope
Now I'm done. Do what you will with them
```

See Also

_creat, _open

log, log10

Calculates logarithms.

double log(double *x* **);**
double log10(double *x* **);**

Routine	Required Header	Compatibility
log	<math.h>	ANSI, Win 95, Win NT
log10	<math.h>	ANSI, Win 95, Win NT

For additional compatibility information, see "Compatibility" in the Introduction.

Libraries

LIBC.LIB	Single thread static library, retail version
LIBCMT.LIB	Multithread static library, retail version
MSVCRT.LIB	Import library for MSVCRT.DLL, retail version

Return Value

The **log** functions return the logarithm of *x* if successful. If *x* is negative, these functions return an indefinite (same as a quiet NaN). If *x* is 0, they return INF (infinite). You can modify error handling by using the **_matherr** routine.

Parameter

x

Value whose logarithm is to be found

Example

```
/* LOG.C: This program uses log and log10
 * to calculate the natural logarithm and
 * the base-10 logarithm of 9,000.
 */

#include <math.h>
#include <stdio.h>

void main( void )
{
    double x = 9000.0;
    double y;
```

```
    y = log( x );
    printf( "log( %.2f ) = %f\n", x, y );
    y = log10( x );
    printf( "log10( %.2f ) = %f\n", x, y );
}
```

Output

```
log( 9000.00 ) = 9.104980
log10( 9000.00 ) = 3.954243
```

See Also

exp, _matherr, pow

_logb

Extracts exponential value of double-precision floating-point argument.

double _logb(double *x* **);**

Routine	Required Header	Compatibility
_logb	<float.h>	Win 95, Win NT

For additional compatibility information, see "Compatibility" in the Introduction.

Libraries

LIBC.LIB	Single thread static library, retail version
LIBCMT.LIB	Multithread static library, retail version
MSVCRT.LIB	Import library for MSVCRT.DLL, retail version

Return Value

_logb returns the unbiased exponential value of *x*.

Parameter

x

   Double-precision floating-point value

Remarks

The **_logb** function extracts the exponential value of its double-precision floating-point argument *x*, as though *x* were represented with infinite range. If the argument *x* is denormalized, it is treated as if it were normalized.

See Also

frexp

longjmp

Restores stack environment and execution locale.

void longjmp(jmp_buf *env***, int** *value* **);**

Routine	Required Header	Compatibility
longjmp	<setjmp.h>	ANSI, Win 95, Win NT

For additional compatibility information, see "Compatibility" in the Introduction.

Libraries

LIBC.LIB	Single thread static library, retail version
LIBCMT.LIB	Multithread static library, retail version
MSVCRT.LIB	Import library for MSVCRT.DLL, retail version

Return Value

None

Parameters

env
　　Variable in which environment is stored

value
　　Value to be returned to **setjmp** call

Remarks

The **longjmp** function restores a stack environment and execution locale previously saved in *env* by **setjmp**. **setjmp** and **longjmp** provide a way to execute a nonlocal **goto**; they are typically used to pass execution control to error-handling or recovery code in a previously called routine without using the normal call and return conventions.

A call to **setjmp** causes the current stack environment to be saved in *env*. A subsequent call to **longjmp** restores the saved environment and returns control to the point immediately following the corresponding **setjmp** call. Execution resumes as if *value* had just been returned by the **setjmp** call. The values of all variables (except register variables) that are accessible to the routine receiving control contain the values they had when **longjmp** was called. The values of register variables are unpredictable. The value returned by **setjmp** must be nonzero. If *value* is passed as 0, the value 1 is substituted in the actual return.

Call **longjmp** before the function that called **setjmp** returns; otherwise the results are unpredictable.

Observe the following restrictions when using **longjmp**:

- Do not assume that the values of the register variables will remain the same. The values of register variables in the routine calling **setjmp** may not be restored to the proper values after **longjmp** is executed.

- Do not use **longjmp** to transfer control out of an interrupt-handling routine unless the interrupt is caused by a floating-point exception. In this case, a program may return from an interrupt handler via **longjmp** if it first reinitializes the floating-point math package by calling **_fpreset**.

- Be careful when using **setjmp** and **longjmp** in C++ programs. Because these functions do not support C++ object semantics, it is safer to use the C++ exception-handling mechanism.

Example

```
/* FPRESET.C: This program uses signal to set up a
 * routine for handling floating-point errors.
 */

#include <stdio.h>
#include <signal.h>
#include <setjmp.h>
#include <stdlib.h>
#include <float.h>
#include <math.h>
#include <string.h>

jmp_buf mark;               /* Address for long jump to jump to */
int     fperr;              /* Global error number */

void __cdecl fphandler( int sig, int num );    /* Prototypes */
void fpcheck( void );

void main( void )
{
   double n1, n2, r;
   int jmpret;
   /* Unmask all floating-point exceptions. */
   _control87( 0, _MCW_EM );
   /* Set up floating-point error handler. The compiler
    * will generate a warning because it expects
    * signal-handling functions to take only one argument.
    */
   if( signal( SIGFPE, fphandler ) == SIG_ERR )

   {
      fprintf( stderr, "Couldn't set SIGFPE\n" );
      abort();
   }
```

```
    /* Save stack environment for return in case of error. First
     * time through, jmpret is 0, so true conditional is executed.
     * If an error occurs, jmpret will be set to -1 and false
     * conditional will be executed.
     */
    jmpret = setjmp( mark );
    if( jmpret == 0 )
    {
        printf( "Test for invalid operation - " );
        printf( "enter two numbers: " );
        scanf( "%lf %lf", &n1, &n2 );
        r = n1 / n2;
        /* This won't be reached if error occurs. */
        printf( "\n\n%4.3g / %4.3g = %4.3g\n", n1, n2, r );

        r = n1 * n2;
        /* This won't be reached if error occurs. */
        printf( "\n\n%4.3g * %4.3g = %4.3g\n", n1, n2, r );
    }
    else
        fpcheck();
}
/* fphandler handles SIGFPE (floating-point error) interrupt. Note
 * that this prototype accepts two arguments and that the
 * prototype for signal in the run-time library expects a signal
 * handler to have only one argument.
 *
 * The second argument in this signal handler allows processing of
 * _FPE_INVALID, _FPE_OVERFLOW, _FPE_UNDERFLOW, and
 * _FPE_ZERODIVIDE, all of which are Microsoft-specific symbols
 * that augment the information provided by SIGFPE. The compiler
 * will generate a warning, which is harmless and expected.
 */

void fphandler( int sig, int num )
{
    /* Set global for outside check since we don't want
     * to do I/O in the handler.
     */
    fperr = num;
    /* Initialize floating-point package. */
    _fpreset();
    /* Restore calling environment and jump back to setjmp. Return
     * -1 so that setjmp will return false for conditional test.
     */
    longjmp( mark, -1 );
}
```

```
void fpcheck( void )
{
    char fpstr[30];
    switch( fperr )
    {
    case _FPE_INVALID:
        strcpy( fpstr, "Invalid number" );
        break;
    case _FPE_OVERFLOW:
        strcpy( fpstr, "Overflow" );

        break;
    case _FPE_UNDERFLOW:
        strcpy( fpstr, "Underflow" );
        break;
    case _FPE_ZERODIVIDE:
        strcpy( fpstr, "Divide by zero" );
        break;
    default:
        strcpy( fpstr, "Other floating point error" );
        break;
    }
    printf( "Error %d: %s\n", fperr, fpstr );
}
```

Output

```
Test for invalid operation - enter two numbers: 5 0
Error 131: Divide by zero
```

See Also

setjmp

_lrotl, _lrotr

Rotate bits to the left (**_lrotl**) or right (**_lrotr**).

unsigned long _lrotl(unsigned long *value*, **int** *shift* **);**
unsigned long _lrotr(unsigned long *value*, **int** *shift* **);**

Routine	Required Header	Compatibility
_lrotl	<stdlib.h>	Win 95, Win NT
_lrotr	<stdlib.h>	Win 95, Win NT

For additional compatibility information, see "Compatibility" in the Introduction.

Libraries

LIBC.LIB	Single thread static library, retail version
LIBCMT.LIB	Multithread static library, retail version
MSVCRT.LIB	Import library for MSVCRT.DLL, retail version

Return Value

Both functions return the rotated value. There is no error return.

Parameters

value
   Value to be rotated

shift
   Number of bits to shift *value*

Remarks

The **_lrotl** and **_lrotr** functions rotate *value* by *shift* bits. **_lrotl** rotates the value left. **_lrotr** rotates the value right. Both functions "wrap" bits rotated off one end of *value* to the other end.

Example

```
/* LROT.C */

#include <stdlib.h>
#include <stdio.h>

void main( void )
{
    unsigned long val = 0x0fac35791;

    printf( "0x%8.8lx rotated left eight times is 0x%8.8lx\n",
    ↪val, _lrotl( val, 8 ) );
    printf( "0x%8.8lx rotated right four times is 0x%8.8lx\n",
    ↪val, _lrotr( val, 4 ) );
}
```

Output

```
0xfac35791 rotated left eight times is 0xc35791fa
0xfac35791 rotated right four times is 0x1fac3579
```

See Also

_rotl, _rotr

_lsearch

Performs a linear search for a value; adds to end of list if not found.

void *_lsearch(const void **key***, void ****base***, unsigned int ****num***, unsigned int** *width***,**
int (__ cdecl **compare***)(const void ****elem1***, const void ****elem2***));**

Routine	Required Header	Compatibility
_lsearch	<search.h>	Win 95, Win NT

For additional compatibility information, see "Compatibility" in the Introduction.

Libraries

LIBC.LIB	Single thread static library, retail version
LIBCMT.LIB	Multithread static library, retail version
MSVCRT.LIB	Import library for MSVCRT.DLL, retail version

Return Value

If the key is found, **_lsearch** returns a pointer to the element of the array at *base* that
matches *key*. If the key is not found, **_lsearch** returns a pointer to the newly added item
at the end of the array.

Parameters

key
　　Object to search for

base
　　Pointer to base of array to be searched

num
　　Number of elements

width
　　Width of each array element

compare
　　Pointer to comparison routine

elem1
　　Pointer to key for search

elem2
　　Pointer to array element to be compared with key

Remarks

The **_lsearch** function performs a linear search for the value *key* in an array of *num* elements, each of *width* bytes in size. Unlike **bsearch**, **_lsearch** does not require the array to be sorted. If *key* is not found, **_lsearch** adds it to the end of the array and increments *num*.

The *compare* argument is a pointer to a user-supplied routine that compares two array elements and returns a value specifying their relationship. **_lsearch** calls the *compare* routine one or more times during the search, passing pointers to two array elements on each call. *compare* must compare the elements, then return either nonzero, meaning the elements are different, or 0, meaning the elements are identical.

Example

```
/* LFIND.C: This program uses _lfind to search for
 * the word "hello" in the command-line arguments.
 */

#include <search.h>
#include <string.h>
#include <stdio.h>

int compare( const void *arg1, const void *arg2 );

void main( unsigned int argc, char **argv )
{
   char **result;
   char *key = "hello";

   result = (char **)_lfind( &key, argv,
   ↳ &argc, sizeof(char *), compare );
   if( result )
      printf( "%s found\n", *result );
   else
      printf( "hello not found!\n" );
}

int compare(const void *arg1, const void *arg2 )
{
   return( _stricmp( * (char**)arg1, * (char**)arg2 ) );
}
```

Output

```
[C:\code]lfind Hello
Hello found
```

See Also

bsearch, _lfind

_lseek, _lseeki64

Move a file pointer to the specified location.

long _lseek(int *handle***, long** *offset***, int** *origin* **);**
__int64 _lseeki64(int *handle***, __int64** *offset***, int** *origin* **);**

Routine	Required Header	Compatibility
_lseek	<io.h>	Win 95, Win NT
_lseeki64	<io.h>	Win 95, Win NT

For additional compatibility information, see "Compatibility" in the Introduction.

Libraries

LIBC.LIB	Single thread static library, retail version
LIBCMT.LIB	Multithread static library, retail version
MSVCRT.LIB	Import library for MSVCRT.DLL, retail version

Return Value

_lseek returns the offset, in bytes, of the new position from the beginning of the file. **_lseeki64** returns the offset in a 64-bit integer. The function returns –1L to indicate an error and sets errno either to **EBADF**, meaning the file handle is invalid, or to **EINVAL**, meaning the value for *origin* is invalid or the position specified by *offset* is before the beginning of the file. On devices incapable of seeking (such as terminals and printers), the return value is undefined.

Parameters

handle
    Handle referring to open file

offset
    Number of bytes from *origin*

origin
    Initial position

Remarks

The **_lseek** function moves the file pointer associated with *handle* to a new location that is *offset* bytes from *origin*. The next operation on the file occurs at the new location. The *origin* argument must be one of the following constants, which are defined in STDIO.H:

SEEK_SET

Beginning of file

SEEK_CUR

Current position of file pointer

SEEK_END

End of file

You can use **_lseek** to reposition the pointer anywhere in a file or beyond the end of the file.

Example

```
/* LSEEK.C: This program first opens a file named LSEEK.C.
 * It then uses _lseek to find the beginning of the file,
 * to find the current position in the file, and to find
 * the end of the file.
 */

#include <io.h>
#include <fcntl.h>
#include <stdlib.h>
#include <stdio.h>

void main( void )
{
    int fh;
    long pos;                   /* Position of file pointer */
    char buffer[10];

    fh = _open( "lseek.c", _O_RDONLY );

    /* Seek the beginning of the file: */
    pos = _lseek( fh, 0L, SEEK_SET );
    if( pos == -1L )
        perror( "_lseek to beginning failed" );
    else
        printf( "Position for beginning of file seek = %ld\n", pos );

    /* Move file pointer a little */
    _read( fh, buffer, 10 );

    /* Find current position: */
    pos = _lseek( fh, 0L, SEEK_CUR );
    if( pos == -1L )
        perror( "_lseek to current position failed" );
    else
        printf( "Position for current position seek = %ld\n", pos );
```

```
/* Set the end of the file: */
pos = _lseek( fh, 0L, SEEK_END );
if( pos == -1L )
   perror( "_lseek to end failed" );
else
   printf( "Position for end of file seek = %ld\n", pos );

_close( fh );
}
```

Output

```
Position for beginning of file seek = 0
Position for current position seek = 10
Position for end of file seek = 1207
```

See Also

fseek, _tell

_ltoa, _ltow

Convert a long integer to a string.

char *_ltoa(long *value*, **char** *string, **int** *radix* **);**
wchar_t *_ltow(long *value*, **wchar_t** *string, **int** *radix* **);**

Routine	Required Header	Compatibility
_ltoa	\<stdlib.h\>	Win 95, Win NT
_ltow	\<stdlib.h\>	Win 95, Win NT

For additional compatibility information, see "Compatibility" in the Introduction.

Libraries

LIBC.LIB	Single thread static library, retail version
LIBCMT.LIB	Multithread static library, retail version
MSVCRT.LIB	Import library for MSVCRT.DLL, retail version

Return Value

Each of these functions returns a pointer to *string*. There is no error return.

Parameters

value
   Number to be converted

string
> String result

radix
> Base of *value*

Remarks

The **_ltoa** function converts the digits of *value* to a null-terminated character string and stores the result (up to 33 bytes) in *string*. The *radix* argument specifies the base of *value*, which must be in the range 2–36. If *radix* equals 10 and *value* is negative, the first character of the stored string is the minus sign (–). **_ltow** is a wide-character version of **_ltoa**; the second argument and return value of **_ltow** are wide-character strings. Each of these functions is Microsoft-specific.

Generic-Text Routine Mappings

TCHAR.H Routine	_UNICODE & _MBCS Not Defined	_MBCS Defined	_UNICODE Defined
_ltot	_ltoa	_ltoa	_ltow

Example

```
/* ITOA.C: This program converts integers of various
 * sizes to strings in various radixes.
 */

#include <stdlib.h>
#include <stdio.h>

void main( void )
{
    char buffer[20];
    int  i = 3445;
    long l = -344115L;
    unsigned long ul = 1234567890UL;

    _itoa( i, buffer, 10 );
    printf( "String of integer %d (radix 10): %s\n", i, buffer );
    _itoa( i, buffer, 16 );
    printf( "String of integer %d (radix 16): 0x%s\n", i, buffer );
    _itoa( i, buffer, 2  );
    printf( "String of integer %d (radix 2): %s\n", i, buffer );

    _ltoa( l, buffer, 16 );
    printf( "String of long int %ld (radix 16): 0x%s\n", l, buffer );

    _ultoa( ul, buffer, 16 );
    printf( "String of unsigned long %lu (radix 16): 0x%s\n", ul, buffer );
}
```

Output

```
String of integer 3445 (radix 10): 3445
String of integer 3445 (radix 16): 0xd75
String of integer 3445 (radix 2): 110101110101
String of long int -344115 (radix 16): 0xfffabfcd
String of unsigned long 1234567890 (radix 16): 0x499602d2
```

See Also

_itoa, **_ultoa**

_makepath, _wmakepath

Create a path name from components.

void _makepath(char *path*, **const char** *drive*, **const char** *dir*,
   const char *fname*, **const char** *ext* **);**
void _wmakepath(wchar_t *path*, **const wchar_t** *drive*,
   const wchar_t *dir*, **const wchar_t** *fname*, **const wchar_t** *ext* **);**

Routine	Required Header	Compatibility
_makepath	<stdlib.h>	Win 95, Win NT
_wmakepath	<stdlib.h> or <wchar.h>	Win 95, Win NT

For additional compatibility information, see "Compatibility" in the Introduction.

Libraries

LIBC.LIB	Single thread static library, retail version
LIBCMT.LIB	Multithread static library, retail version
MSVCRT.LIB	Import library for MSVCRT.DLL, retail version

Return Value

None

Parameters

path
   Full path buffer

drive
   Drive letter

dir
   Directory path

fname
> Filename

ext
> File extension

Remarks

The **_makepath** function creates a single path and stores it in *path*. The path may include a drive letter, directory path, filename, and filename extension. **_wmakepath** is a wide-character version of **_makepath**; the arguments to **_wmakepath** are wide-character strings. **_wmakepath** and **_makepath** behave identically otherwise.

Generic-Text Routine Mappings

TCHAR.H Routine	_UNICODE & _MBCS Not Defined	_MBCS Defined	_UNICODE Defined
_tmakepath	_makepath	_makepath	_wmakepath

The following arguments point to buffers containing the path elements:

drive
> Contains a letter (A, B, and so on) corresponding to the desired drive and an optional trailing colon. **_makepath** inserts the colon automatically in the composite path if it is missing. If *drive* is a null character or an empty string, no drive letter and colon appear in the composite *path* string.

dir
> Contains the path of directories, not including the drive designator or the actual filename. The trailing slash is optional, and either a forward slash (/) or a backslash (\) or both may be used in a single *dir* argument. If a trailing slash (/ or \) is not specified, it is inserted automatically. If *dir* is a null character or an empty string, no slash is inserted in the composite *path* string.

fname
> Contains the base filename without any extensions. If *fname* is **NULL** or points to an empty string, no filename is inserted in the composite *path* string.

ext
> Contains the actual filename extension, with or without a leading period (**.**). **_makepath** inserts the period automatically if it does not appear in *ext*. If *ext* is a null character or an empty string, no period is inserted in the composite *path* string.

The *path* argument must point to an empty buffer large enough to hold the complete path. Although there are no size limits on any of the fields that constitute *path*, the composite *path* must be no larger than the **_MAX_PATH** constant, defined in STDLIB.H. **_MAX_PATH** may be larger than the current operating-system version will handle.

Example

```
/* MAKEPATH.C */
#include <stdlib.h>
#include <stdio.h>

void main( void )
{
   char path_buffer[_MAX_PATH];
   char drive[_MAX_DRIVE];
   char dir[_MAX_DIR];
   char fname[_MAX_FNAME];
   char ext[_MAX_EXT];

   _makepath( path_buffer, "c", "\\sample\\crt\\", "makepath", "c" );
   printf( "Path created with _makepath: %s\n\n", path_buffer );
   _splitpath( path_buffer, drive, dir, fname, ext );
   printf( "Path extracted with _splitpath:\n" );
   printf( "  Drive: %s\n", drive );
   printf( "  Dir: %s\n", dir );
   printf( "  Filename: %s\n", fname );
   printf( "  Ext: %s\n", ext );
}
```

Output

```
Path created with _makepath: c:\sample\crt\makepath.c

Path extracted with _splitpath:
   Drive: c:
   Dir: \sample\crt\
   Filename: makepath
   Ext: .c
```

See Also

_fullpath, _splitpath

malloc

Allocates memory blocks.

void *malloc(size_t *size* **);**

Routine	Required Header	Compatibility
malloc	<stdlib.h> and <malloc.h>	ANSI, Win 95, Win NT

For additional compatibility information, see "Compatibility" in the Introduction.

Libraries

LIBC.LIB	Single thread static library, retail version
LIBCMT.LIB	Multithread static library, retail version
MSVCRT.LIB	Import library for MSVCRT.DLL, retail version

Return Value

malloc returns a void pointer to the allocated space, or **NULL** if there is insufficient memory available. To return a pointer to a type other than **void**, use a type cast on the return value. The storage space pointed to by the return value is guaranteed to be suitably aligned for storage of any type of object. If size is 0, **malloc** allocates a zero-length item in the heap and returns a valid pointer to that item. Always check the return from **malloc**, even if the amount of memory requested is small.

Parameter

size
  Bytes to allocate

Remarks

The **malloc** function allocates a memory block of at least *size* bytes. The block may be larger than *size* bytes because of space required for alignment and maintenance information.

The startup code uses **malloc** to allocate storage for the **_environ**, **envp**, and **argv** variables. The following functions and their wide-character counterparts also call **malloc**:

calloc	**fscanf**	**_getw**	**setvbuf**
_exec functions	**fseek**	**_popen**	**_spawn** functions
fgetc	**fsetpos**	**printf**	**_strdup**
_fgetchar	**_fullpath**	**putc**	**system**
fgets	**fwrite**	**putchar**	**_tempnam**
fprintf	**getc**	**_putenv**	**ungetc**
fputc	**getchar**	**puts**	**vfprintf**
_fputchar	**_getcwd**	**_putw**	**vprintf**
fputs	**_getdcwd**	**scanf**	
fread	**gets**	**_searchenv**	

The C++ _set_new_mode function sets the new handler mode for **malloc**. The new handler mode indicates whether, on failure, **malloc** is to call the new handler routine as set by _set_new_handler. By default, **malloc** does not call the new handler routine on failure to allocate memory. You can override this default behavior so that, when **malloc** fails to allocate memory, **malloc** calls the new handler routine in the same way that the **new** operator does when it fails for the same reason. To override the default, call

```
setnew_mode(1)
```

early in your program, or link with NEWMODE.OBJ.

When the application is linked with a debug version of the C run-time libraries, **malloc** resolves to _malloc_dbg. For more information about how the heap is managed during the debugging process, see "Using C Run-Time Library Debugging Support" in the *Visual C++ Programmer's Guide* online.

Example

```
/* MALLOC.C: This program allocates memory with
 * malloc, then frees the memory with free.
 */

#include <stdlib.h>          /* For _MAX_PATH definition */
#include <stdio.h>
#include <malloc.h>

void main( void )
{
   char *string;
   /* Allocate space for a path name */
   string = malloc( _MAX_PATH );
   if( string == NULL )
      printf( "Insufficient memory available\n" );
   else
   {
      printf( "Memory space allocated for path name\n" );
      free( string );
      printf( "Memory freed\n" );
   }
}
```

Output

```
Memory space allocated for path name
Memory freed
```

See Also

calloc, **free**, **realloc**

_matherr

Handles math errors.

int _matherr(struct _exception *_except_);

Routine	Required Header	Compatibility
_matherr	<math.h>	Win 95, Win NT

For additional compatibility information, see "Compatibility" in the Introduction.

Libraries

LIBC.LIB	Single thread static library, retail version
LIBCMT.LIB	Multithread static library, retail version
MSVCRT.LIB	Import library for MSVCRT.DLL, retail version

Return Value

_matherr returns 0 to indicate an error or a non-zero value to indicate success. If **_matherr** returns 0, an error message can be displayed, and **errno** is set to an appropriate error value. If **_matherr** returns a nonzero value, no error message is displayed, and **errno** remains unchanged.

Parameter

except
    Pointer to structure containing error information

Remarks

The **_matherr** function processes errors generated by the floating-point functions of the math library. These functions call **_matherr** when an error is detected.

For special error handling, you can provide a different definition of **_matherr**. If you use the dynamically linked version of the C run-time library (MSVCRT.DLL), you can replace the default **_matherr** routine in a client executable with a user-defined version. However, you cannot replace the default **_matherr** routine in a DLL client of MSVCRT.DLL.

When an error occurs in a math routine, **_matherr** is called with a pointer to an **_exception** type structure (defined in MATH.H) as an argument. The **_exception** structure contains the following elements:

int type
    Exception type

char *name
    Name of function where error occurred

double arg1, arg2

First and second (if any) arguments to function

double retval

Value to be returned by function

The **type** specifies the type of math error. It is one of the following values, defined in MATH.H:

_DOMAIN

Argument domain error.

_SING

Argument singularity.

_OVERFLOW

Overflow range error.

_PLOSS

Partial loss of significance.

_TLOSS

Total loss of significance.

_UNDERFLOW

The result is too small to be represented. (This condition is not currently supported.)

The structure member **name** is a pointer to a null-terminated string containing the name of the function that caused the error. The structure members **arg1** and **arg2** specify the values that caused the error. (If only one argument is given, it is stored in **arg1**.)

The default return value for the given error is **retval**. If you change the return value, it must specify whether an error actually occurred.

Example

```
/* MATHERR.C illustrates writing an error routine for math
 * functions. The error function must be:
 * _matherr
 */

#include <math.h>
#include <string.h>
#include <stdio.h>

void main()
{
    /* Do several math operations that cause errors. The _matherr
     * routine handles _DOMAIN errors, but lets the system handle
     * other errors normally.
     */
```

```
      printf( "log( -2.0 ) = %e\n", log( -2.0 ) );
      printf( "log10( -5.0 ) = %e\n", log10( -5.0 ) );
      printf( "log( 0.0 ) = %e\n", log( 0.0 ) );
}


/* Handle several math errors caused by passing a negative argument
 * to log or log10 (_DOMAIN errors). When this happens, _matherr
 * returns the natural or base-10 logarithm of the absolute value
 * of the argument and suppresses the usual error message.
 */
int _matherr( struct _exception *except )
{
    /* Handle _DOMAIN errors for log or log10. */
    if( except->type == _DOMAIN )
    {
        if( strcmp( except->name, "log" ) == 0 )
        {
            except->retval = log( -(except->arg1) );
            printf( "Special: using absolute value: %s: _DOMAIN "
                    "error\n", except->name );
            return 1;
        }
        else if( strcmp( except->name, "log10" ) == 0 )
        {
            except->retval = log10( -(except->arg1) );
            printf( "Special: using absolute value: %s: _DOMAIN "
                    "error\n", except->name );
            return 1;
        }
    }
    else
    {
        printf( "Normal: " );
        return 0;     /* Else use the default actions */
     }
}
```

Output

```
Special: using absolute value: log: _DOMAIN error
log( -2.0 ) = 6.931472e-001
Special: using absolute value: log10: _DOMAIN error
log10( -5.0 ) = 6.989700e-001
Normal: log( 0.0 ) = -1.#INF00e+000
```

__max

Returns the larger of two values.

type __**max**(*type a*, *type b*);

Routine	Required Header	Compatibility
_max	<stdlib.h>	Win 95, Win NT

For additional compatibility information, see "Compatibility" in the Introduction.

Libraries

LIBC.LIB	Single thread static library, retail version
LIBCMT.LIB	Multithread static library, retail version
MSVCRT.LIB	Import library for MSVCRT.DLL, retail version

Return Value

__**max** returns the larger of its arguments.

Parameters

type
    Any numeric data type

a, b
    Values of any numeric type to be compared

Remarks

The __**max** macro compares two values and returns the value of the larger one. The arguments can be of any numeric data type, signed or unsigned. Both arguments and the return value must be of the same data type.

Example

```
/* MINMAX.C */
#include <stdlib.h>
#include <stdio.h>

void main( void )
{
    int a = 10;
    int b = 21;

    printf( "The larger of %d and %d is %d\n",  a, b, __max( a, b ) );
    printf( "The smaller of %d and %d is %d\n", a, b, __min( a, b ) );
}
```

Output

```
The larger of 10 and 21 is 21
The smaller of 10 and 21 is 10
```

See Also

__min

_mbbtombc

unsigned short **_mbbtombc**(unsigned short *c*);

Routine	Required Header	Compatibility
_mbbtombc	<mbstring.h>	Win 95, Win NT

For additional compatibility information, see "Compatibility" in the Introduction.

Libraries

LIBC.LIB	Single thread static library, retail version
LIBCMT.LIB	Multithread static library, retail version
MSVCRT.LIB	Import library for MSVCRT.DLL, retail version

Return Value

If **_mbbtombc** successfully converts *c*, it returns a multibyte character; otherwise it returns *c*.

Parameter

c

    Single-byte character to convert.

Remarks

The **_mbbtombc** function converts a given single-byte multibyte character to a corresponding double-byte multibyte character. Characters must be within the range 0x20–0x7E or 0xA1–0xDF to be converted.

In earlier versions, **_mbbtombc** was called **hantozen**. For new code, use **_mbbtombc** instead.

See Also

_mbctombb

_mbbtype

int _mbbtype(unsigned char *c*, **int** *type* **);**

Routine	Required Header	Optional Headers	Compatibility
_mbbtype	<mbstring.h>	<mbctype.h>[*]	Win 95, Win NT

* For definitions of manifest constants used as return values.

For additional compatibility information, see "Compatibility" in the Introduction.

Libraries

LIBC.LIB	Single thread static library, retail version
LIBCMT.LIB	Multithread static library, retail version
MSVCRT.LIB	Import library for MSVCRT.DLL, retail version

Return Value

_mbbtype returns the type of byte within a string. This decision is context-sensitive as specified by the value of *type*, which provides the control test condition. *type* is the type of the previous byte in the string.The manifest constants in the following table are defined in MBCTYPE.H.

Value of *type*	_mbbtype Tests For	Return Value	*c*
Any value except 1	Valid single byte or lead byte	**_MBC_SINGLE** (0)	Single byte (0x20–0x7E, 0xA1–0xDF)
Any value except 1	Valid single byte or lead byte	**_MBC_LEAD** (1)	Lead byte of multibyte character (0x81–0x9F, 0xE0–0xFC)
Any value except 1	Valid single-byte or lead byte	**_MBC_ILLEGAL** (–1)	Invalid character (any value except 0x20–0x7E, 0xA1–0xDF, 0x81–0x9F, 0xE0–0xFC
1	Valid trail byte	**_MBC_TRAIL** (2)	Trailing byte of multibyte character (0x40–0x7E, 0x80–0xFC)
1	Valid trail byte	**_MBC_ILLEGAL** (–1)	Invalid character (any value except 0x20–0x7E, 0xA1–0xDF, 0x81–0x9F, 0xE0–0xFC

Parameters

c
 Character to test

type
 Type of byte to test for

Remarks

The **_mbbtype** function determines the type of a byte in a multibyte character. If the value of *type* is any value except 1, **_mbbtype** tests for a valid single-byte or lead byte of a multibyte character. If the value of *type* is 1, **_mbbtype** tests for a valid trail byte of a multibyte character.

In earlier versions, **_mbbtype** was called **chkctype**. For new code, **_mbbtype** use instead.

_mbccpy

void _mbccpy(unsigned char *dest**, const unsigned char ***src **);**

Routine	Required Header	Compatibility
_mbccpy	<mbctype.h>	Win 95, Win NT

For additional compatibility information, see "Compatibility" in the Introduction.

Libraries

LIBC.LIB	Single thread static library, retail version
LIBCMT.LIB	Multithread static library, retail version
MSVCRT.LIB	Import library for MSVCRT.DLL, retail version

Return Value

None

Parameters

dest
    Copy destination

src
    Multibyte character to copy

Remarks

The **_mbccpy** function copies one multibyte character from *src* to *dest*. If *src* does not point to the lead byte of a multibyte character as determined by an implicit call to _ismbblead, no copy is performed.

Generic-Text Routine Mappings

TCHAR.H Routine	_UNICODE & _MBCS Not Defined	_MBCS Defined	_UNICODE Defined
_tccpy	Maps to macro or inline function	_mbccpy	Maps to macro or inline function

See Also

_mbclen

_mbcjistojms, _mbcjmstojis

unsigned int _mbcjistojms(unsigned int *c* **);**
unsigned int _mbcjmstojis(unsigned int *c* **);**

Routine	Required Header	Compatibility
_mbcjistojms	\<mbstring.h\>	Win 95, Win NT
_mbcjmstojis	\<mbstring.h\>	Win 95, Win NT

For additional compatibility information, see "Compatibility" in the Introduction.

Libraries

LIBC.LIB	Single thread static library, retail version
LIBCMT.LIB	Multithread static library, retail version
MSVCRT.LIB	Import library for MSVCRT.DLL, retail version

Return Value

_mbcjistojms and **_mbcjmstojis** return a converted character. Otherwise they return 0.

Parameter

c
    Character to convert

Remarks

The **_mbcjistojms** function converts a Japan Industry Standard (JIS) character to a Microsoft Kanji (Shift JIS) character. The character is converted only if the lead and trail bytes are in the range 0x21–0x7E.

The _mbcjmstojis function converts a Shift JIS character to a JIS character. The character is converted only if the lead byte is in the range 0x81–0x9F or 0xE0–0xFC, and the trail byte is in the range 0x40–0x7E or 0x80–0xFC.

The value *c* should be a 16-bit value whose upper eight bits represent the lead byte of the character to convert and whose lower eight bits represent the trail byte.

In earlier versions, **_mbcjistojms** and **_mbcjmstojis** were called **jistojms** and **jmstojis**, repectively. **_mbcjistojms** and **_mbcjmstojis** should be used instead.

See Also

_ismbb Routines

_mbclen, mblen

Get the length and determine the validity of a multibyte character.

size_t _mbclen(const unsigned char *c);
int mblen(const char *mbstr, size_t count);

Routine	Required Header	Compatibility
_mbclen	<mbstring.h>	Win 95, Win NT
mblen	<stdlib.h>	ANSI, Win 95, Win NT

For additional compatibility information, see "Compatibility" in the Introduction.

Libraries

LIBC.LIB	Single thread static library, retail version
LIBCMT.LIB	Multithread static library, retail version
MSVCRT.LIB	Import library for MSVCRT.DLL, retail version

Return Value

_mbclen returns 1 or 2, according to whether the multibyte character *c* is one or two bytes long. There is no error return for **_mbclen**. If *mbstr* is not **NULL**, **mblen** returns the length, in bytes, of the multibyte character. If *mbstr* is **NULL**, or if it points to the wide-character null character, **mblen** returns 0. If the object that *mbstr* points to does not form a valid multibyte character within the first *count* characters, **mblen** returns –1.

Parameters

c
   Multibyte character

mbstr
   Address of multibyte-character byte sequence

count
   Number of bytes to check

Remarks

The **_mbclen** function returns the length, in bytes, of the multibyte character *c*. If *c* does not point to the lead byte of a multibyte character as determined by an implicit call to **_ismbblead**, the result of **_mbclen** is unpredictable.

mblen returns the length in bytes of *mbstr* if it is a valid multibyte character. It examines *count* or fewer bytes contained in *mbstr*, but not more than **MB_CUR_MAX** bytes. **mblen** determines multibyte-character validity according to the **LC_CTYPE** category setting of the current locale. For more information on the **LC_CTYPE** category, see **setlocale**.

Generic-Text Routine Mappings

TCHAR.H Routine	_UNICODE & _MBCS Not Defined	_MBCS Defined	_UNICODE Defined
_tclen	Maps to macro or inline function	_mbclen	Maps to macro or inline function

Example

```
/* MBLEN.C illustrates the behavior of the mblen function
 */

#include <stdlib.h>
#include <stdio.h>

void main( void )
{
    int     i;
    char    *pmbc = (char *)malloc( sizeof( char ) );
    wchar_t wc   = L'a';

    printf( "Convert wide character to multibyte character:\n" );
    i = wctomb( pmbc, wc );
    printf( "\tCharacters converted: %u\n", i );
    printf( "\tMultibyte character: %x\n\n", pmbc );

    i = mblen( pmbc, MB_CUR_MAX );
    printf( "Length in bytes of multibyte character %x: %u\n", pmbc, i );

    pmbc = NULL;
    i = mblen( pmbc, MB_CUR_MAX );
    printf( "Length in bytes of NULL multibyte character %x: %u\n", pmbc, i );
}
```

Output

```
Convert wide character to multibyte character:
Characters converted: 1
Multibyte character: 2c02cc

Length in bytes of multibyte character 2c02cc: 1
Length in bytes of NULL multibyte character 0: 0
```

See Also

_mbccpy, _mbslen

_mbctohira, _mbctokata

unsigned int _mbctohira(unsigned int *c* **);**
unsigned int _mbctokata(unsigned int *c* **);**

Routine	Required Header	Compatibility
_mbctohira	<mbstring.h>	Win 95, Win NT
_mbctokata	<mbstring.h>	Win 95, Win NT

For additional compatibility information, see "Compatibility" in the Introduction.

Libraries

LIBC.LIB	Single thread static library, retail version
LIBCMT.LIB	Multithread static library, retail version
MSVCRT.LIB	Import library for MSVCRT.DLL, retail version

Return Value

Each of these functions returns the converted character *c*, if possible. Otherwise it returns the character *c* unchanged.

Parameter

c

  Multibyte character to convert

Remarks

The **_mbctohira** and **_mbctohira** functions test a character *c* and, if possible, apply one of the following conversions.

Routine	Converts
_mbctohira	Multibyte katakana to multibyte hiragana
_mbctokata	Multibyte hiragana to multibyte katakana

In previous versions, **_mbctohira** was called **jtohira** and **_mbctokata** was called **jtokata**. For new code, use the new names instead.

See Also

_mbcjistojms, _mbctolower, _mbctombb

_mbctolower, _mbctoupper

unsigned int _mbctolower(unsigned int *c* **);**
unsigned int _mbctoupper(unsigned int *c* **);**

Routine	Required Header	Compatibility
_mbctolower	<mbstring.h>	Win 95, Win NT
_mbctoupper	<mbstring.h>	Win 95, Win NT

For additional compatibility information, see "Compatibility" in the Introduction.

Libraries

LIBC.LIB	Single thread static library, retail version
LIBCMT.LIB	Multithread static library, retail version
MSVCRT.LIB	Import library for MSVCRT.DLL, retail version

Return Value

Each of these functions returns the converted character *c*, if possible. Otherwise it returns the character *c* unchanged.

Parameter

c

    Multibyte character to convert

Remarks

The **_mbctolower** and **_mbctoupper** functions test a character *c* and, if possible, apply one of the following conversions.

Routine	Converts
_mbctolower	Uppercase character to lowercase character
_mbctoupper	Lowercase character to uppercase character

In previous versions, **_mbctolower** was called **jtolower**, and **_mbctoupper** was called **jtoupper**. For new code, use the new names instead.

Generic-Text Routine Mappings

TCHAR.H Routine	_UNICODE & _MBCS Not Defined	_MBCS Defined	_UNICODE Defined
_totlower	tolower	_mbctolower	towlower
_totupper	toupper	_mbctoupper	towupper

See Also

_mbbtombc, _mbcjistojms, _mbctohira, _mbctombb

_mbctombb

unsigned int _mbctombb(unsigned int *c*);

Routine	Required Header	Compatibility
_mbctombb	<mbstring.h>	Win 95, Win NT

For additional compatibility information, see "Compatibility" in the Introduction.

Libraries

LIBC.LIB	Single thread static library, retail version
LIBCMT.LIB	Multithread static library, retail version
MSVCRT.LIB	Import library for MSVCRT.DLL, retail version

Return Value

If successful, **_mbctombb** returns the single-byte character that corresponds to *c*; otherwise it returns *c*.

Parameter

c

Multibyte character to convert.

Remarks

The **_mbctombb** function converts a given multibyte character to a corresponding single-byte multibyte character. Characters must correspond to single-byte characters within the range 0x20–0x7E or 0xA1–0xDF to be converted.

In previous versions, **_mbctombb** was called **zentohan**. Use **_mbctombb** instead.

See Also

_mbbtombc, _mbcjistojms, _mbctohira, _mbctolower

_mbsbtype

int _mbsbtype(const unsigned char **mbstr*, size_t *count*);

Routine	Required Header	Optional Headers	Compatibility
_mbsbtype	<mbstring.h>	<mbctype.h>*	Win 95, Win NT

* For manifest constants used as return values.

For additional compatibility information, see "Compatibility" in the Introduction.

Libraries

LIBC.LIB	Single thread static library, retail version
LIBCMT.LIB	Multithread static library, retail version
MSVCRT.LIB	Import library for MSVCRT.DLL, retail version

Return Value

_mbsbtype returns an integer value indicating the result of the test on the specified byte. The manifest constants in the following table are defined in MBCTYPE.H.

Return Value	Byte Type
_MBC_SINGLE (0)	Single-byte character. For example, in code page 932, _mbsbtype returns 0 if the specified byte is within the range 0x20–0x7E or 0xA1–0xDF.
_MBC_LEAD (1)	Lead byte of multibyte character. For example, in code page 932, _mbsbtype returns 1 if the specified byte is within the range 0x81–0x9F or 0xE0–0xFC.
_MBC_TRAIL (2)	Trailing byte of multibyte character. For example, in code page 932, _mbsbtype returns 2 if the specified byte is within the range 0x40–0x7E or 0x80–0xFC.
_MBC_ILLEGAL (–1)	Invalid character, or **NULL** byte found before the byte at offset *count* in *mbstr*.

Parameters

mbstr
    Address of a sequence of multibyte characters

count
    Byte offset from head of string

Remarks

The **_mbsbtype** function determines the type of a byte in a multibyte character string. The function examines only the byte at offset *count* in *mbstr*, ignoring invalid characters before the specified byte.

_mbsdec, _strdec, _wcsdec

unsigned char *_mbsdec(const unsigned char *start**,**
    const unsigned char *current**);**

Routine	Required Header	Optional Headers	Compatibility
_mbsdec	<mbstring.h>	<mbctype.h>	Win 95, Win NT
_strdec	<tchar.h>		Win 95, Win NT
_wcsdec	<tchar.h>		Win 95, Win NT

For additional compatibility information, see "Compatibility" in the Introduction.

Libraries

LIBC.LIB	Single thread static library, retail version
LIBCMT.LIB	Multithread static library, retail version
MSVCRT.LIB	Import library for MSVCRT.DLL, retail version

Return Value

_mbsdec, **_strdec** and **_wcsdec** each return a pointer to the character that immediately precedes *current*; **_mbsdec** returns **NULL** if the value of *start* is greater than or equal to that of *current*. **_tcsdec** maps to one of these functions and its return value depends on the mapping.

Parameters

start
Pointer to first byte of any multibyte character in the source string; *start* must precede *current* in the source string

current
Pointer to first byte of any multibyte character in the source string; *current* must follow *start* in the source string

Remarks

The **_mbsdec** function returns a pointer to the first byte of the multibyte-character that immediately precedes *current* in the string that contains *start*. **_mbsdec** recognizes multibyte-character sequences according to the multibyte code page currently in use.

The generic-text function **_tcsdec**, defined in TCHAR.H, maps to **_mbsdec** if the **_MBCS** preprocessor definition has been specified, or to **_wcsdec** if _UNICODE has been defined. **_tcsdec** when used with the appropriate preprocessor definition, lets you generate code that will work regardless of the width of character strings. Otherwise **_tcsdec** maps to **_strdec**. **_strdec** and **_wcsdec** are single-byte character and wide-character versions of **_mbsdec**. **_strdec** and **_wcsdec** are provided only for this mapping and should not be used otherwise. For more information, see "Using Generic-Text Mappings" in Chapter 1, "Run-Time Routines by Category," and see Appendix B, "Generic-Text Mappings."

Example

The following code snippet shows a use of **_tcsdec**.

```
const TCHAR *str = _T("some text");
const TCHAR *str2;
TCHAR *answer;
str2 = str;
str2++;
answer = _tcsdec( str, str2 );
```

The following code snippet shows a use of **_mbsdec**.

```
char *str = "some text";
char *str2;
unsigned char *answer;
str2 = str;
str2++;
answer = _mbsdec( reinterpret_cast<unsigned char *>( str ),
↪reinterpret_cast<unsigned char *>( str2 ));
```

See Also

_mbsinc, _mbsnextc, _mbsninc

_mbsinc, _strinc, _wcsinc

unsigned char *_mbsinc(const unsigned char *current**);**

Routine	Required Header	Compatibility
_mbsinc	<mbstring.h>	Win 95, Win NT
_strinc	<tchar.h>	Win 95, Win NT
_wcsinc	<tchar.h>	Win 95, Win NT

For additional compatibility information, see "Compatibility" in the Introduction.

Libraries

LIBC.LIB	Single thread static library, retail version
LIBCMT.LIB	Multithread static library, retail version
MSVCRT.LIB	Import library for MSVCRT.DLL, retail version

Return Value

Each of these routines returns a pointer to the character that immediately follows *current*.

Parameter

current
    Character pointer

Remarks

The **_mbsinc** function returns a pointer to the first byte of the multibyte character that immediately follows *current*. **_mbsinc** recognizes multibyte-character sequences according to the multibyte code page currently in use.

The generic-text function **_tcsinc**, defined in TCHAR.H, maps to **_mbsinc** if **_MBCS** has been defined, or to **_wcsinc** if **_UNICODE** has been defined. Otherwise **_tcsinc** maps to **_strinc**. **_strinc** and **_wcsinc** are single-byte character and wide-character versions of **_mbsinc**. **_strinc** and **_wcsinc** are provided only for this mapping and should not be used otherwise. For more information, see "Using Generic-Text Mappings" in Chapter 1, "Run-Time Routines by Category," and see Appendix B, "Generic-Text Mappings."

See Also

_mbsdec, _mbsnextc, _mbsninc

_mbsnbcat

unsigned char *_mbsnbcat(unsigned char *_dest_,
  const unsigned char *_src_, size_t _count_);

Routine	Required Header	Compatibility
_mbsnbcat	<mbstring.h>	Win 95, Win NT

For additional compatibility information, see "Compatibility" in the Introduction.

Libraries

LIBC.LIB	Single thread static library, retail version
LIBCMT.LIB	Multithread static library, retail version
MSVCRT.LIB	Import library for MSVCRT.DLL, retail version

Return Value

_mbsnbcat returns a pointer to the destination string. No return value is reserved to indicate an error.

Parameters

dest
  Null-terminated multibyte-character destination string

src
  Null-terminated multibyte-character source string

count
  Number of bytes from _src_ to append to _dest_

Remarks

The **_mbsnbcat** function appends, at most, the first _count_ bytes of _src_ to _dest_. If the byte immediately preceding the null character in _dest_ is a lead byte, the initial byte of _src_ overwrites this lead byte. Otherwise the initial byte of _src_ overwrites the terminating null character of _dest_. If a null byte appears in _src_ before _count_ bytes are appended, **_mbsnbcat** appends all bytes from _src_, up to the null character. If _count_ is greater than the length of _src_, the length of _src_ is used in place of _count_. The resulting string is terminated with a null character. If copying takes place between strings that overlap, the behavior is undefined.

Generic-Text Routine Mappings

TCHAR.H Routine	_UNICODE & _MBCS Not Defined	_MBCS Defined	_UNICODE Defined
_tcsncat	strncat	_mbsnbcat	wcsncat

See Also

_mbsnbcmp, _mbsnbcnt, _mbsnccnt, _mbsnbcpy, _mbsnbicmp, _mbsnbset, strncat

_mbsnbcmp

int **_mbsnbcmp**(const unsigned char *string1,
    const unsigned char string2, size_t count);

Routine	Required Header	Compatibility
_mbsnbcmp	<mbstring.h>	Win 95, Win NT

For additional compatibility information, see "Compatibility" in the Introduction.

Libraries

LIBC.LIB	Single thread static library, retail version
LIBCMT.LIB	Multithread static library, retail version
MSVCRT.LIB	Import library for MSVCRT.DLL, retail version

Return Value

The return value indicates the relation of the substrings of *string1* and *string*.

Return Value	Description
< 0	*string1* substring less than *string2* substring
0	*string1* substring identical to *string2* substring
> 0	*string1* substring greater than *string2* substring

On an error, **_mbsnbcmp** returns **_NLSCMPERROR**, which is defined in STRING.H and MBSTRING.H.

Parameters

string1, *string2*
    Strings to compare

count
    Number of bytes to compare

Remarks

The **_mbsnbcmp** function lexicographically compares, at most, the first *count* bytes in *string1* and *string2* and returns a value indicating the relationship between the substrings. **_mbsnbcmp** is a case-sensitive version of **_mbsnbicmp**. Unlike **strcoll**, **_mbsnbcmp** is not affected by locale. **_mbsnbcmp** recognizes multibyte-character sequences according to the current multibyte code page.

_mbsnbcmp is similar to **_mbsncmp**, except that **_mbsnbcmp** compares strings by characters rather than by bytes.

Generic-Text Routine Mappings

TCHAR.H Routine	_UNICODE & _MBCS Not Defined	_MBCS Defined	_UNICODE Defined
_tcsncmp	strncmp	_mbsnbcmp	wcsncmp

Example

```
/* STRNBCMP.C */
#include <mbstring.h>
#include <stdio.h>

char string1[] = "The quick brown dog jumps over the lazy fox";
char string2[] = "The QUICK brown fox jumps over the lazy dog";

void main( void )
{
   char tmp[20];
   int result;
   printf( "Compare strings:\n\t\t%s\n\t\t%s\n\n", string1, string2 );
   printf( "Function:\t_mbsnbcmp (first 10 characters only)\n" );
   result = _mbsncmp( string1, string2 , 10 );
   if( result > 0 )
     _mbscpy( tmp, "greater than" );
   else if( result < 0 )
     _mbscpy( tmp, "less than" );
   else
     _mbscpy( tmp, "equal to" );
   printf( "Result:\t\tString 1 is %s string 2\n\n", tmp );
   printf( "Function:\t_mbsnicmp _mbsnicmp (first 10 characters only)\n" );
   result = _mbsnicmp( string1, string2, 10 );
   if( result > 0 )
     _mbscpy( tmp, "greater than" );
   else if( result < 0 )
     _mbscpy( tmp, "less than" );
   else
     _mbscpy( tmp, "equal to" );
   printf( "Result:\t\tString 1 is %s string 2\n\n", tmp );
}
```

Output

```
Compare strings:
    The quick brown dog jumps over the lazy fox
    The QUICK brown fox jumps over the lazy dog

Function:_mbsnbcmp (first 10 characters only)
Result:   String 1 is greater than string 2

Function:_mbsnicmp (first 10 characters only)
Result:   String 1 is equal to string 2
```

See Also

_mbsnbcat, _mbsnbicmp, strncmp, _strnicmp

_mbsnbcnt, _mbsnccnt, _strncnt, _wcsncnt

Return number of characters or bytes within a supplied count

size_t _mbsnbcnt(const unsigned char *string***, size_t** *number* **);**
size_t _mbsnccnt(const unsigned char *string***, size_t** *number* **);**

Routine	Required Header	Compatibility
_mbsnbcnt	<mbstring.h>	Win 95, Win NT
_mbsnccnt	<mbstring.h>	Win 95, Win NT
_strncnt	<tchar.h>	Win 95, Win NT
_wcsncnt	<tchar.h>	Win 95, Win NT

For additional compatibility information, see "Compatibility" in the Introduction.

Libraries

LIBC.LIB	Single thread static library, retail version
LIBCMT.LIB	Multithread static library, retail version
MSVCRT.LIB	Import library for MSVCRT.DLL, retail version

Return Value

_mbsnbcnt returns the number of bytes found in the first *number* of multibyte characters of *string*. **_mbsnccnt** returns the number of characters found in the first *number* of bytes of *string*. If a NULL character is encountered before the examination of *string* has completed, they return the number of bytes or characters found before the NULL character. If *string* consists of fewer than *number* characters or bytes, they return the number of characters or bytes in the string. If *number* is less than zero, they return 0. In previous versions, these functions had a return value of type **int** rather than **size_t**.

_strncnt returns the number of characters in the first *number* bytes of the single-byte string *string*. **_wcsncnt** returns the number of bytes in the first *number* wide characters of the wide-character string *string*.

Parameters

string
> String to be examined

number
> Number of characters or bytes to be examined in *string*

Remarks

_mbsnbcnt counts the number of bytes found in the first *number* of multibyte characters of *string*. **_mbsnbcnt** replaces **mtob**, and should be used in place of **mtob**.

_mbsnccnt counts the number of characters found in the first *number* of bytes of *string*. If **_mbsnccnt** encounters a NULL in the second byte of a double-byte character, the first byte is also considered to be NULL and is not included in the returned count value. **_mbsnccnt** replaces **btom**, and should be used in place of **btom**.

If **_MBCS** is defined, **_mbsnbcnt** is mapped to **_tcsnbcnt** and **_mbsnbcnt** is mapped to **_tcsnccnt**. These two mapping routines provide generic-text support and are defined in TCHAR.H. If **_UNICODE** is defined, both **_mbsnbcnt** and **_mbsnccnt** are mapped to the **_wcsncnt** macro. When **_MBCS** and **_UNICODE** are not defined, both **_tcsnbcnt** and **_tcsnccnt** are mapped to the **_strncnt** macro. **_strncnt** is the single-byte-character string version and **_wcsncnt** is the wide-character-string version of these mapping routines. **_strncnt** and **_wcsncnt** are provided only for generic-text mapping and should not be used otherwise. For more information, see "Using Generic-Text Mappings" in Chapter 1, "Run-Time Routines by Category," and see Appendix B, "Generic-Text Mappings."

Example

```
/* MBSNBCNT.C */
#include <mbstring.h>
#include <stdio.h>

void main( void )
{
    unsigned char str[] = "This is a multibyte-character string.";
    unsigned int char_count, byte_count;
    char_count = _mbsnccnt( str, 10 );
    byte_count = _mbsnbcnt( str, 10 );
    if ( byte_count - char_count )
        printf( "The first 10 characters contain %s multibyte characters", char_count );
```

```
    else
        printf( "The first 10 characters are single-byte.");
}
```

Output

```
The first 10 characters are single-byte.
```

See Also

_mbsnbcat

_mbsnbcoll, _mbsnbicoll

int _mbsnbcoll(const unsigned char **string1**,**
const unsigned char *string2***, size_t** *count* **);**
int _mbsnbicoll(const unsigned char **string1**,**
const unsigned char *string2***, size_t** *count* **);**

Routine	Required Header	Compatibility
_mbsnbcoll	<mbstring.h>	Win 95, Win NT
_mbsnbicoll	<mbstring.h>	Win 95, Win NT

For additional compatibility information, see "Compatibility" in the Introduction.

Libraries

LIBC.LIB	Single thread static library, retail version
LIBCMT.LIB	Multithread static library, retail version
MSVCRT.LIB	Import library for MSVCRT.DLL, retail version

Return Value

The return value indicates the relation of the substrings of *string1* and *string2*.

Return Value	Description
< 0	*string1* substring less than *string2* substring
0	*string1* substring identical to *string2* substring
> 0	*string1* substring greater than *string2* substring

Each of these functions returns **_NLSCMPERROR** on an error. To use **_NLSCMPERROR**, include either STRING.H or MBSTRING.H.

Parameters

string1, *string2*
  Strings to compare

count
  Number of bytes to compare

Remarks

Each of these functions collates, at most, the first *count* bytes in *string1* and *string2* and returns a value indicating the relationship between the resulting substrings of *string1* and *string2*. If the final byte in the substring of *string1* or *string2* is a lead byte, it is not included in the comparison; these functions compare only complete characters in the substrings. **_mbsnbicoll** is a case-insensitive version of **_mbsnbcoll**. Like **_mbsnbcmp** and **_mbsnbicmp**, **_mbsnbcoll** and **_mbsnbicoll** collate the two multibyte-character strings according to the lexicographic order specified by the multibyte code page currently in use.

For some code pages and corresponding character sets, the order of characters in the character set may differ from the lexicographic character order. In the "C" locale, this is not the case: the order of characters in the ASCII character set is the same as the lexicographic order of the characters. However, in certain European code pages, for example, the character 'a' (value 0x61) precedes the character 'ä' (value 0xE4) in the character set, but the character 'ä' precedes the character 'a' lexicographically. To perform a lexicographic comparison of strings by bytes in such an instance, use **_mbsnbcoll** rather than **_mbsnbcmp**; to check only for string equality, use **_mbsnbcmp**.

Because the **coll** functions collate strings lexicographically for comparison, whereas the **cmp** functions simply test for string equality, the **coll** functions are much slower than the corresponding **cmp** versions. Therefore, the **coll** functions should be used only when there is a difference between the character set order and the lexicographic character order in the current code page and this difference is of interest for the comparison.

Generic-Text Routine Mappings

TCHAR.H Routine	_UNICODE & _MBCS Not Defined	_MBCS Defined	_UNICODE Defined
_tcsncoll	_strncoll	_mbsnbcoll	_wcsncoll
_tcsnicoll	_strnicoll	_mbsnbicoll	_wcsnicoll

See Also

_mbsnbcat, _mbsnbcmp, _mbsnbicmp, strcoll Functions, **strncmp, _strnicmp**

_mbsnbcpy

unsigned char * _mbsnbcpy(unsigned char *dest,
  const unsigned char *src, size_t count);

Routine	Required Header	Compatibility
_mbsnbcpy	<mbstring.h>	Win 95, Win NT

For additional compatibility information, see "Compatibility" in the Introduction.

Libraries

LIBC.LIB	Single thread static library, retail version
LIBCMT.LIB	Multithread static library, retail version
MSVCRT.LIB	Import library for MSVCRT.DLL, retail version

Return Value

_mbsnbcpy returns a pointer to the character string that is to be copied.

Parameters

dest
  Destination for character string to be copied

src
  Character string to be copied

count
  Number of bytes to be copied

Remarks

The **_mbsnbcpy** function copies count bytes from *src* to *dest*. If *src* is shorter than *dest*, the string is padded with null characters. If *dest* is less than or equal to *count* it is not terminated with a null character.

Generic-Text Routine Mappings

TCHAR.H Routine	_UNICODE & _MBCS Not Defined	_MBCS Defined	_UNICODE Defined
_tcsncpy	strncpy	_mbsnbcpy	wcsncpy

See Also

_mbsnbcat, _mbsnbcmp, _mbsnbcnt, _mbsnccnt, _mbsnbicmp, _mbsnbset, _mbsncpy

_mbsnbicmp

int _mbsnbicmp(const unsigned char *string1,
    const unsigned char *string2, size_t count);

Routine	Required Header	Compatibility
_mbsnbicmp	<mbstring.h>	Win 95, Win NT

For additional compatibility information, see "Compatibility" in the Introduction.

Libraries

LIBC.LIB	Single thread static library, retail version
LIBCMT.LIB	Multithread static library, retail version
MSVCRT.LIB	Import library for MSVCRT.DLL, retail version

Return Value

The return value indicates the relationship between the substrings.

Return Value	Description
< 0	string1 substring less than string2 substring
0	string1 substring identical to string2 substring
> 0	string1 substring greater than string2 substring

On an error, _mbsnbcmp returns _NLSCMPERROR, which is defined in STRING.H and MBSTRING.H.

Parameters

string1, string2
    Null-terminated strings to compare

count
    Number of bytes to compare

Remarks

The _mbsnbicmp function lexicographically compares, at most, the first count bytes of string1 and string2. The comparison is performed without regard to case; _mbsnbcmp is a case-sensitive version of _mbsnbicmp. The comparison ends if a terminating null character is reached in either string before count characters are compared. If the strings are equal when a terminating null character is reached in either string before count characters are compared, the shorter string is lesser.

_mbsnbicmp is similar to **_mbsnicmp**, except that it compares strings by bytes instead of by characters.

Two strings containing characters located between 'Z' and 'a' in the ASCII table ("[", "\", "]", "^", "_", and "`") compare differently, depending on their case. For example, the two strings "ABCDE" and "ABCD^" compare one way if the comparison is lowercase ("abcde" > "abcd^") and the other way ("ABCDE" < "ABCD^") if it is uppercase.

_mbsnbicmp recognizes multibyte-character sequences according to the multibyte code page currently in use. It is not affected by the current locale setting.

Generic-Text Routine Mappings

TCHAR.H Routine	_UNICODE & _MBCS Not Defined	_MBCS Defined	_UNICODE Defined
_tcsnicmp	_strnicmp	_mbsnbicmp	_wcsnicmp

Example

```
/* STRNBCMP.C */
#include <mbstring.h>
#include <stdio.h>

char string1[] = "The quick brown dog jumps over the lazy fox";
char string2[] = "The QUICK brown fox jumps over the lazy dog";

void main( void )
{
   char tmp[20];
   int result;
   printf( "Compare strings:\n\t\t%s\n\t\t%s\n\n", string1, string2 );
   printf( "Function:\t_mbsnbcmp (first 10 characters only)\n" );
   result = _mbsncmp( string1, string2 , 10 );
   if( result > 0 )
      _mbscpy( tmp, "greater than" );
   else if( result < 0 )
      _mbscpy( tmp, "less than" );
   else
      _mbscpy( tmp, "equal to" );
   printf( "Result:\t\tString 1 is %s string 2\n\n", tmp );
   printf( "Function:\t_mbsnicmp _mbsnicmp (first 10 characters only)\n" );
   result = _mbsnicmp( string1, string2, 10 );
   if( result > 0 )
      _mbscpy( tmp, "greater than" );
   else if( result < 0 )
      _mbscpy( tmp, "less than" );
   else
      _mbscpy( tmp, "equal to" );
   printf( "Result:\t\tString 1 is %s string 2\n\n", tmp );
}
```

```
Compare strings:
The quick brown dog jumps over the lazy fox
The QUICK brown fox jumps over the lazy dog

Function:_mbsnbcmp (first 10 characters only)
Result:   String 1 is greater than string 2

Function:_mbsnicmp (first 10 characters only)
Result:   String 1 is equal to string 2
```

See Also

_mbsnbcat, _mbsnbcmp, _stricmp

_mbsnbset

unsigned char *_mbsnbset(unsigned char **string***, unsigned int** *c*, **size_t** *count* **);**

Routine	Required Header	Compatibility
_mbsnbset	<mbstring.h>	Win 95, Win NT

For additional compatibility information, see "Compatibility" in the Introduction.

Libraries

LIBC.LIB	Single thread static library, retail version
LIBCMT.LIB	Multithread static library, retail version
MSVCRT.LIB	Import library for MSVCRT.DLL, retail version

Return Value

_mbsnbset returns a pointer to the altered string.

Parameters

string
    String to be altered

c
    Single-byte or multibyte character setting

count
    Number of bytes to be set

Remarks

The **_mbsnbset** function sets, at most, the first *count* bytes of *string* to *c*. If *count* is greater than the length of *string*, the length of *string* is used instead of *count*. If *c* is a multibyte character and cannot be set entirely into the last byte specified by *count*, then the last byte will be padded with a blank character. **_mbsnbset** does not place a terminating null at the end of *string*.

_mbsnbset is similar to **_mbsnset**, except that it sets *count* bytes rather than *count* characters of *c*.

Generic-Text Routine Mappings

TCHAR.H Routine	_UNICODE & _MBCS Not Defined	_MBCS Defined	_UNICODE Defined
_tcsnset	_strnset	_mbsnbset	_wcsnset

Example

```
/* MBSNBSET.C */
#include <mbstring.h>
#include <stdio.h>

void main( void )
{
    char string[15] = "This is a test";
    /* Set not more than 4 bytes of string to be *'s */
    printf( "Before: %s\n", string );
    _mbsnbset( string, '*', 4 );
    printf( "After:  %s\n", string );
}
```

Output

```
Before: This is a test
After:  **** is a test
```

See Also

_mbsnbcat, _mbsnset, _mbsset

_mbsnextc, _strnextc, _wcsnextc

unsigned int _mbsnextc(const unsigned char *string);

Routine	Required Header	Compatibility
_mbsnextc	<mbstring.h>	Win 95, Win NT
_strnextc	<tchar.h>	Win 95, Win NT
_wcsnextc	<tchar.h>	Win 95, Win NT

For additional compatibility information, see "Compatibility" in the Introduction.

Libraries

LIBC.LIB	Single thread static library, retail version
LIBCMT.LIB	Multithread static library, retail version
MSVCRT.LIB	Import library for MSVCRT.DLL, retail version

Return Value

Each of these functions returns the integer value of the next character in *string*.

Parameter

string
    Source string

Remarks

The **_mbsnextc** function returns the integer value of the next multibyte-character in *string*, without advancing the string pointer. **_mbsnextc** recognizes multibyte-character sequences according to the multibyte code page currently in use.

The generic-text function **_tcsnextc**, defined in TCHAR.H, maps to **_mbsnextc** if **_MBCS** has been defined, or to **_wcsnextc** if **_UNICODE** has been defined. Otherwise **_tcsnextc** maps to **_strnextc**. **_strnextc** and **_wcsnextc** are single-byte-character string and wide-character string versions of **_mbsnextc**. **_wcsnextc** returns the integer value of the next wide character in *string*; **_strnextc** returns the integer value of the next single-byte character in *string*. **_strnextc** and **_wcsnextc** are provided only for this mapping and should not be used otherwise. For more information, see "Using Generic-Text Mappings" in Chapter 1, "Run-Time Routines by Category," and see Appendix B, "Generic-Text Mappings."

See Also

_mbsdec, _mbsinc, _mbsninc

_mbsninc, _strninc, _wcsninc

unsigned char *_mbsninc(const unsigned char **string***, size_t** *count* **);**

Routine	Required Header	Compatibility
_mbsninc	<mbstring.h>	Win 95, Win NT
_strninc	<tchar.h>	Win 95, Win NT
_wcsninc	<tchar.h>	Win 95, Win NT

For additional compatibility information, see "Compatibility" in the Introduction.

Libraries

LIBC.LIB	Single thread static library, retail version
LIBCMT.LIB	Multithread static library, retail version
MSVCRT.LIB	Import library for MSVCRT.DLL, retail version

Return Value

Each of these routines returns a pointer to *string* after *string* has been incremented by *count* characters, or **NULL** if the supplied pointer is **NULL**. If *count* is greater than or equal to the number of characters in *string,* the result is undefined.

Parameters

string
   Source string

count
   Number of characters to increment string pointer

Remarks

The **_mbsninc** function increments *string* by *count* multibyte characters. **_mbsninc** recognizes multibyte-character sequences according to the multibyte code page currently in use.

The generic-text function **_tcsninc**, defined in TCHAR.H, maps to **_mbsninc** if **_MBCS** has been defined, or to **_wcsninc** if **_UNICODE** has been defined. Otherwise **_tcsninc** maps to **_strninc**. **_strninc** and **_wcsninc** are single-byte-character string and wide-character string versions of **_mbsninc**. **_wcsninc** and **_strninc** are provided only for this mapping and should not be used otherwise. For more information, see "Using Generic-Text Mappings" in Chapter 1, "Run-Time Routines by Category," and see Appendix B, "Generic-Text Mappings."

See Also

_mbsdec, _mbsinc, _mbsnextc

_mbsspnp, _strspnp, _wcsspnp

unsigned char *_mbsspnp(const unsigned char **string1***,**
   const unsigned char **string2***);**

Routine	Required Header	Compatibility
_mbsspnp	<mbstring.h>	Win 95, Win NT
_strspnp	<tchar.h>	Win 95, Win NT
_wcsspnp	<tchar.h>	Win 95, Win NT

For additional compatibility information, see "Compatibility" in the Introduction.

Libraries

LIBC.LIB	Single thread static library, retail version
LIBCMT.LIB	Multithread static library, retail version
MSVCRT.LIB	Import library for MSVCRT.DLL, retail version

Return Value

_strspnp, **_wcsspnp**, and **_mbsspnp** return a pointer to the first character in *string1* that does not belong to the set of characters in *string2*. Each of these functions returns **NULL** if *string1* consists entirely of characters from *string2*. For each of these routines, no return value is reserved to indicate an error.

Parameters

string1
  Null-terminated string to search

string2
  Null-terminated character set

Remarks

The **_mbsspnp** function returns a pointer to the multibyte character that is the first character in *string1* that does not belong to the set of characters in *string2*. **_mbsspnp** recognizes multibyte-character sequences according to the multibyte code page currently in use. The search does not include terminating null characters.

The generic-text function **_tcsspnp**, defined in TCHAR.H, maps to **_mbsspnp** if **_MBCS** has been defined, or to **_wcsspnp** if **_UNICODE** has been defined. Otherwise **_tcsspnp** maps to **_strspnp**. **_strspnp** and **_wcsspnp** are single-byte character and wide-character versions of **_mbsspnp**. **_strspnp** and **_wcsspnp** behave identically to **_mbsspnp** otherwise; they are provided only for this mapping and should not be used for any other reason. For more information, see "Using Generic-Text Mappings" in Chapter 1, "Run-Time Routines by Category," and see Appendix B, "Generic-Text Mappings."

Example

```
/* STRSPN.C: This program uses strspn to determine
 * the length of the segment in the string "cabbage"
 * consisting of a's, b's, and c's. In other words,
 * it finds the first non-abc letter.
 */

#include <string.h>
#include <stdio.h>
```

```
void main( void )
{
    char string[] = "cabbage";
    int  result;
    result = strspn( string, "abc" );
    printf( "The portion of '%s' containing only a, b, or c "
            "is %d bytes long\n", string, result );
}
```

Output

```
The portion of 'cabbage' containing only a, b, or c is 5 bytes long
```

See Also

strspn, strcspn, strncat, strncmp, strncpy, _strnicmp, strrchr

mbstowcs

Converts a sequence of multibyte characters to a corresponding sequence of wide characters.

size_t mbstowcs(wchar_t *_wcstr_, const char *_mbstr_, size_t _count_);

Routine	Required Header	Compatibility
mbstowcs	<stdlib.h>	ANSI, Win 95, Win NT

For additional compatibility information, see "Compatibility" in the Introduction.

Libraries

LIBC.LIB	Single thread static library, retail version
LIBCMT.LIB	Multithread static library, retail version
MSVCRT.LIB	Import library for MSVCRT.DLL, retail version

Return Value

If **mbstowcs** successfully converts the source string, it returns the number of converted multibyte characters. If the _wcstr_ argument is **NULL**, the function returns the required size of the destination string. If **mbstowcs** encounters an invalid multibyte character, it returns –1. If the return value is _count_, the wide-character string is not null-terminated.

Parameters

wcstr

   The address of a sequence of wide characters

mbstr
> The address of a sequence of multibyte characters

count
> The number of multibyte characters to convert

Remarks

The **mbstowcs** function converts *count* or fewer multibyte characters pointed to by *mbstr* to a string of corresponding wide characters that are determined by the current locale. It stores the resulting wide-character string at the address represented by *wcstr*. The result is similiar to a series of calls to **mbtowc**. If **mbstowcs** encounters the single-byte null character ('\0') either before or when *count* occurs, it converts the null character to a wide-character null character (L'\0') and stops. Thus the wide-character string at *wcstr* is null-terminated only if a null character is encountered during conversion. If the sequences pointed to by *wcstr* and *mbstr* overlap, the behavior is undefined.

If the *wcstr* argument is **NULL**, **mbstowcs** returns the required size of the destination string.

Example

```
/* MBSTOWCS.CPP illustrates the behavior of the mbstowcs function
 */

#include <stdlib.h>
#include <stdio.h>

void main( void )
{
    int i;
    char    *pmbnull  = NULL;
    char    *pmbhello = (char *)malloc( MB_CUR_MAX );
    wchar_t *pwchello = L"Hi";
    wchar_t *pwc      = (wchar_t *)malloc( sizeof( wchar_t ));

    printf( "Convert to multibyte string:\n" );
    i = wcstombs( pmbhello, pwchello, MB_CUR_MAX );
    printf( "\tCharacters converted: %u\n", i );
    printf( "\tHex value of first" );
    printf( " multibyte character: %#.4x\n\n", pmbhello );

    printf( "Convert back to wide-character string:\n" );
    i = mbstowcs( pwc, pmbhello, MB_CUR_MAX );
    printf( "\tCharacters converted: %u\n", i );
    printf( "\tHex value of first" );
    printf( " wide character: %#.4x\n\n", pwc );
}
```

```
Convert to multibyte string:
   Characters converted: 1
   Hex value of first multibyte character: 0x0e1a

Convert back to wide-character string:
   Characters converted: 1
   Hex value of first wide character: 0x0e1e
```

See Also

mblen, mbtowc, wcstombs, wctomb, MultiByteToWideChar

mbtowc

Convert a multibyte character to a corresponding wide character.

int mbtowc(wchar_t **wchar,* **const char** **mbchar,* **size_t** *count* **);**

Routine	Required Header	Compatibility
mbtowc	<stdlib.h>	ANSI, Win 95, Win NT

For additional compatibility information, see "Compatibility" in the Introduction.

Libraries

LIBC.LIB	Single thread static library, retail version
LIBCMT.LIB	Multithread static library, retail version
MSVCRT.LIB	Import library for MSVCRT.DLL, retail version

Return Value

If **mbchar** is not **NULL** and if the object that *mbchar* points to forms a valid multibyte character, **mbtowc** returns the length in bytes of the multibyte character. If *mbchar* is **NULL** or the object that it points to is a wide-character null character (L'\0'), the function returns 0. If the object that *mbchar* points to does not form a valid multibyte character within the first *count* characters, it returns −1.

Parameters

wchar
   Address of a wide character (type **wchar_t**)

mbchar
   Address of a sequence of bytes (a multibyte character)

count
   Number of bytes to check

Remarks

The **_open_osfhandle** function allocates a C run-time file handle and sets it to point to the operating-system file handle specified by *osfhandle*. The *flags* argument is an integer expression formed from one or more of the manifest constants defined in FCNTL.H. When two or more manifest constants are used to form the *flags* argument, the constants are combined with the bitwise-OR operator (|).

The FCNTL.H file defines the following manifest constants:

_O_APPEND
   Positions file pointer to end of file before every write operation.

_O_RDONLY
   Opens file for reading only

_O_TEXT
   Opens file in text (translated) mode

File Handling Routines

_outp, _outpw, _outpd

Output a byte(**_outp**), a word(**_outpw**), or a double word (**_outpd**) at a port.

int _outp(unsigned short *port*, **int** *databyte* **);**
unsigned short _outpw(unsigned short *port*, **unsigned short** *dataword* **);**
unsigned long _outpd(unsigned short *port*, **unsigned long** *dataword* **);**

Routine	Required Header	Compatibility
_outp	<conio.h>	Win 95
_outpw	<conio.h>	Win 95
_outpd	<conio.h>	Win 95

For additional compatibility information, see "Compatibility" in the Introduction.

Libraries

LIBC.LIB	Single thread static library, retail version
LIBCMT.LIB	Multithread static library, retail version
MSVCRT.LIB	Import library for MSVCRT.DLL, retail version

Return Value

The functions return the data output. There is no error return.

Parameters

port
   Port number

databyte, dataword
   Output values

Remarks

The **_outp**, **_outpw**, and **_outpd** functions write a byte, a word, and a double word, respectively, to the specified output port. The *port* argument can be any unsigned integer in the range 0–65,535; *databyte* can be any integer in the range 0–255; and *dataword* can be any value in the range of an integer, an unsigned short integer, and an unsigned long integer, respectively.

See Also

_inp

_pclose

Waits for new command processor and closes stream on associated pipe.

int _pclose(FILE *_stream_);

Routine	Required Header	Compatibility
_pclose	<stdio.h>	Win 95, Win NT

For additional compatibility information, see "Compatibility" in the Introduction.

Libraries

LIBC.LIB	Single thread static library, retail version
LIBCMT.LIB	Multithread static library, retail version
MSVCRT.LIB	Import library for MSVCRT.DLL, retail version

Return Value

_pclose returns the exit status of the terminating command processor, or –1 if an error occurs. The format of the return value is the same as that for **_cwait**, except the low-order and high-order bytes are swapped.

Parameter

stream
   Return value from previous call to **_popen**

Remarks

The **_pclose** function looks up the process ID of the command processor (CMD.EXE) started by the associated **_popen** call, executes a _cwait call on the new command processor, and closes the stream on the associated pipe.

See Also

_pipe, _popen

perror, _wperror

Print an error message.

void perror(const char *string* **);**
void _wperror(const wchar_t *string* **);**

Routine	Required Header	Compatibility
perror	<stdio.h> or <stdlib.h>	ANSI, Win 95, Win NT
_wperror	<stdio.h> or <wchar.h>	Win 95, Win NT

For additional compatibility information, see "Compatibility" in the Introduction.

Libraries

LIBC.LIB	Single thread static library, retail version
LIBCMT.LIB	Multithread static library, retail version
MSVCRT.LIB	Import library for MSVCRT.DLL, retail version

Return Value

None

Parameter

string
 String message to print

Remarks

The **perror** function prints an error message to **stderr**. **_wperror** is a wide-character version of **_perror**; the *string* argument to **_wperror** is a wide-character string. **_wperror** and **_perror** behave identically otherwise.

Generic-Text Routine Mappings

TCHAR.H Routine	_UNICODE & _MBCS Not Defined	_MBCS Defined	_UNICODE Defined
_tperror	perror	perror	_wperror

string is printed first, followed by a colon, then by the system error message for the last library call that produced the error, and finally by a newline character. If *string* is a null pointer or a pointer to a null string, **perror** prints only the system error message.

The error number is stored in the variable errno (defined in ERRNO.H). The system error messages are accessed through the variable _sys_errlist, which is an array of messages ordered by error number. **perror** prints the appropriate error message using the **errno** value as an index to **_sys_errlist**. The value of the variable _sys_nerr is defined as the maximum number of elements in the **_sys_errlist** array.

For accurate results, call **perror** immediately after a library routine returns with an error. Otherwise, subsequent calls can overwrite the **errno** value.

In Windows NT and Windows 95, some **errno** values listed in ERRNO.H are unused. These values are reserved for use by the UNIX operating system. See _doserrno, errno, _sys_errlist, and _sys_nerr for a listing of **errno** values used by Windows NT and Windows 95. **perror** prints an empty string for any **errno** value not used by these platforms.

Example

```
/* PERROR.C: This program attempts to open a file named
 * NOSUCHF.ILE. Because this file probably doesn't exist,
 * an error message is displayed. The same message is
 * created using perror, strerror, and _strerror.
 */

#include <fcntl.h>
#include <sys/types.h>
#include <sys/stat.h>
#include <io.h>
#include <stdlib.h>
#include <stdio.h>
#include <string.h>

void main( void )
{
    int   fh;

    if( (fh = _open( "NOSUCHF.ILE", _O_RDONLY )) == -1 )
    {
        /* Three ways to create error message: */
        perror( "perror says open failed" );
```

```
        printf( "strerror says open failed: %s\n", strerror( errno ) );
        printf( _strerror( "_strerror says open failed" ) );
    }
    else
    {
        printf( "open succeeded on input file\n" );
        _close( fh );
    }
}
```

Output

```
perror says open failed: No such file or directory

strerror says open failed: No such file or directory
_strerror says open failed: No such file or directory
```

See Also

clearerr, ferror, strerror

_pipe

Creates a pipe for reading and writing.

int _pipe(int *phandles, unsigned int psize, int textmode);

Routine	Required Header	Optional Headers	Compatibility
_pipe	<io.h>	<fcntl.h>,[1] <errno.h>[2]	Win 95, Win NT

[1] For _O_BINARY and _O_TEXT definitions.
[2] errno definitions.

For additional compatibility information, see "Compatibility" in the Introduction.

Libraries

LIBC.LIB	Single thread static library, retail version
LIBCMT.LIB	Multithread static library, retail version
MSVCRT.LIB	Import library for MSVCRT.DLL, retail version

Return Value

_pipe returns 0 if successful. It returns –1 to indicate an error, in which case **errno** is set to one of two values: **EMFILE**, which indicates no more file handles available, or **ENFILE**, which indicates a system file table overflow.

Parameters

phandles[2]
> Array to hold read and write handles

psize
> Amount of memory to reserve

textmode
> File mode

Remarks

The **_pipe** function creates a pipe. A *pipe* is an artificial I/O channel that a program uses to pass information to other programs. A pipe is similar to a file in that it has a file pointer, a file descriptor, or both, and can be read from or written to using the standard library's input and output functions. However, a pipe does not represent a specific file or device. Instead, it represents temporary storage in memory that is independent of the program's own memory and is controlled entirely by the operating system.

_pipe is similar to **_open** but opens the pipe for reading and writing, returning two file handles instead of one. The program can use both sides of the pipe or close the one it does not need. For example, the command processor in Windows NT creates a pipe when executing a command such as

```
PROGRAM1 | PROGRAM2
```

The standard output handle of PROGRAM1 is attached to the pipe's write handle. The standard input handle of PROGRAM2 is attached to the pipe's read handle. This eliminates the need for creating temporary files to pass information to other programs.

The **_pipe** function returns two handles to the pipe in the *phandles* argument. The element *phandles*[0] contains the read handle, and the element *phandles*[1] contains the write handle. Pipe file handles are used in the same way as other file handles. (The low-level input and output functions **_read** and **_write** can read from and write to a pipe.) To detect the end-of-pipe condition, check for a **_read** request that returns 0 as the number of bytes read.

The *psize* argument specifies the amount of memory, in bytes, to reserve for the pipe. The *textmode* argument specifies the translation mode for the pipe. The manifest constant **_O_TEXT** specifies a text translation, and the constant **_O_BINARY** specifies binary translation. (See fopen for a description of text and binary modes.) If the *textmode* argument is 0, **_pipe** uses the default translation mode specified by the default-mode variable _fmode.

In multithreaded programs, no locking is performed. The handles returned are newly opened and should not be referenced by any thread until after the **_pipe** call is complete.

In order to use the **_pipe** function to communicate between a parent and a child process, each process must have only one handle open on the pipe. The handles must be opposites: if the parent has a read handle open, then the child must have a write handle open. The easiest way to do this is to **OR** (|) the **_O_NOINHERIT** flag with *textmode*. Then, use **_dup** or **_dup2** to create an inheritable copy of the pipe handle you wish to pass to the child. Close the original handle, and spawn the child process. Upon returning from the spawn call, close the 'duplicate' handle in the parent process. See Example 2 below for more information.

In Windows NT and Windows 95, a pipe is destroyed when all of its handles have been closed. (If all read handles on the pipe have been closed, writing to the pipe causes an error.) All read and write operations on the pipe wait until there is enough data or enough buffer space to complete the I/O request.

Example 1

```
/* PIPE.C: This program uses the _pipe function to pass streams of
 * text to spawned processes.
 */

#include <stdlib.h>
#include <stdio.h>
#include <io.h>
#include <fcntl.h>
#include <process.h>
#include <math.h>

enum PIPES { READ, WRITE }; /* Constants 0 and 1 for READ and WRITE */
#define NUMPROBLEM 8

void main( int argc, char *argv[] )
{

    int hpipe[2];
    char hstr[20];
    int pid, problem, c;
    int termstat;

    /* If no arguments, this is the spawning process */
    if( argc == 1 )
    {

        setvbuf( stdout, NULL, _IONBF, 0 );

        /* Open a set of pipes */
        if( _pipe( hpipe, 256, O_BINARY ) == -1 )
            exit( 1 );
```

```
    /* Convert pipe read handle to string and pass as argument
     * to spawned program. Program spawns itself (argv[0]).
     */
    itoa( hpipe[READ], hstr, 10 );
    if( ( pid = spawnl( P_NOWAIT, argv[0], argv[0],
          hstr, NULL ) ) == -1 )
      printf( "Spawn failed" );

    /* Put problem in write pipe. Since spawned program is
     * running simultaneously, first solutions may be done
     * before last problem is given.
     */
    for( problem = 1000; problem <= NUMPROBLEM * 1000; problem += 1000)
    {

        printf( "Son, what is the square root of %d?\n", problem );
        write( hpipe[WRITE], (char *)&problem, sizeof( int ) );

    }

    /* Wait until spawned program is done processing. */
    _cwait( &termstat, pid, WAIT_CHILD );
    if( termstat & 0x0 )
      printf( "Child failed\n" );

    close( hpipe[READ] );
    close( hpipe[WRITE] );

  }

  /* If there is an argument, this must be the spawned process. */
  else
  {

    /* Convert passed string handle to integer handle. */
    hpipe[READ] = atoi( argv[1] );

    /* Read problem from pipe and calculate solution. */
    for( c = 0; c < NUMPROBLEM; c++ )
    {

        read( hpipe[READ], (char *)&problem, sizeof( int ) );
        printf( "Dad, the square root of %d is %3.2f.\n",
                problem, sqrt( ( double )problem ) );

    }
  }
}
```

```
Son, what is the square root of 1000?
Son, what is the square root of 2000?
Son, what is the square root of 3000?
Son, what is the square root of 4000?
Son, what is the square root of 5000?
Son, what is the square root of 6000?
Son, what is the square root of 7000?
Son, what is the square root of 8000?
Dad, the square root of 1000 is 31.62.
Dad, the square root of 2000 is 44.72.
Dad, the square root of 3000 is 54.77.
Dad, the square root of 4000 is 63.25.
Dad, the square root of 5000 is 70.71.
Dad, the square root of 6000 is 77.46.
Dad, the square root of 7000 is 83.67.
Dad, the square root of 8000 is 89.44.
```

Example 2

```cpp
// This is a simple filter application.  It will spawn
// the application on  command line. But before spawning
// the application, it will create a pipe that will direct the
// spawned application's stdout to the filter.  The filter
// will remove ASCII 7 (beep) characters.

// Beeper.Cpp

/* Compile options needed: None */
#include <stdio.h>
#include <string.h>

int main()
{
   inti;
   for(i=0;i<100;++i)
      {
          printf("\nThis is speaker beep number %d... \n\7", i+1);
      }
   return 0;
}


// BeepFilter.Cpp
/* Compile options needed: none
   Execute as: BeepFilter.exe <path>Beeper.exe
*/
```

```
#include <windows.h>
#include <process.h>
#include <memory.h>
#include <string.h>
#include <stdio.h>
#include <fcntl.h>
#include <io.h>

#define   OUT_BUFF_SIZE 512
#define   READ_HANDLE 0
#define   WRITE_HANDLE 1
#define   BEEP_CHAR 7

char szBuffer[OUT_BUFF_SIZE];

int Filter(char* szBuff, ULONG nSize, int nChar)
{
    char* szPos = szBuff + nSize -1;
    char* szEnd = szPos;
    int nRet = nSize;

    while (szPos > szBuff)
    {
        if (*szPos == nChar)
            {
                memmove(szPos, szPos+1, szEnd - szPos);
                --nRet;
            }
        --szPos;
    }
    return nRet;
}

int main(int argc, char** argv)
{
    int nExitCode = STILL_ACTIVE;
    if (argc >= 2)
    {
        HANDLE hProcess;
        int hStdOut;
        int hStdOutPipe[2];

        // Create the pipe
        if(_pipe(hStdOutPipe, 512, O_BINARY | O_NOINHERIT) == -1)
            return1;

        // Duplicate stdout handle (next line will close original)
        hStdOut = _dup(_fileno(stdout));
```

```
    // Duplicate write end of pipe to stdout handle
    if(_dup2(hStdOutPipe[WRITE_HANDLE], _fileno(stdout)) != 0)
        return2;

    // Close original write end of pipe
    close(hStdOutPipe[WRITE_HANDLE]);

    // Spawn process
    hProcess = (HANDLE)spawnvp(P_NOWAIT, argv[1],
    (const char* const*)&argv[1]);

    // Duplicate copy of original stdout back into stdout
    if(_dup2(hStdOut, _fileno(stdout)) != 0)
        return3;

    // Close duplicate copy of original stdout
    close(hStdOut);

    if(hProcess)
    {
        int nOutRead;
        while (nExitCode == STILL_ACTIVE)
        {
            nOutRead = read(hStdOutPipe[READ_HANDLE],
                szBuffer, OUT_BUFF_SIZE);
            if(nOutRead)
            {
                nOutRead = Filter(szBuffer, nOutRead, BEEP_CHAR);
                fwrite(szBuffer, 1, nOutRead, stdout);
            }

            if(!GetExitCodeProcess(hProcess,(unsigned long*)&nExitCode))
                return 4;
        }
    }
}

    printf("\nPress \'ENTER\' key to continue... ");
    getchar();
    return nExitCode;
}
```

See Also

_open

_popen, _wpopen

Creates a pipe and executes a command.

FILE *_popen(const char **command***, const char ****mode***);**
FILE *_wpopen(const wchar_t **command***, const wchar_t ****mode***);**

Routine	Required Header	Compatibility
_popen	<stdio.h>	Win 95, Win NT
_wpopen	<stdio.h> or <wchar.h>	Win NT

For additional compatibility information, see "Compatibility" in the Introduction.

Libraries

LIBC.LIB	Single thread static library, retail version
LIBCMT.LIB	Multithread static library, retail version
MSVCRT.LIB	Import library for MSVCRT.DLL, retail version

Return Value

Each of these functions returns a stream associated with one end of the created pipe. The other end of the pipe is associated with the spawned command's standard input or standard output. The functions return **NULL** on an error.

Parameters

command
    Command to be executed

mode
    Mode of returned stream

Remarks

The **_popen** function creates a pipe and asynchronously executes a spawned copy of the command processor with the specified string *command*. The character string *mode* specifies the type of access requested, as follows:

"r"
    The calling process can read the spawned command's standard output via the returned stream.

"w"
    The calling process can write to the spawned command's standard input via the returned stream.

"b"

Open in binary mode.

"t"

Open in text mode.

Note The **_popen** function returns an invalid file handle, if used in a Windows program, that will cause the program to hang indefinitely. **_popen** works properly in a Console application. To create a Windows application that redirects input and output, read the section "Creating a Child Process with Redirected Input and Output" in the *Platform SDK* online.

_wpopen is a wide-character version of **_popen**; the *path* argument to **_wpopen** is a wide-character string. **_wpopen** and **_popen** behave identically otherwise.

Generic-Text Routine Mappings

TCHAR.H Routine	_UNICODE & _MBCS Not Defined	_MBCS Defined	_UNICODE Defined
_tpopen	_popen	_popen	_wpopen

Example

```c
/* POPEN.C: This program uses _popen and _pclose to receive a
 * stream of text from a system process.
 */

#include <stdio.h>
#include <stdlib.h>

void main( void )
{

    char    psBuffer[128];
    FILE    *chkdsk;

    /* Run DIR so that it writes its output to a pipe. Open this
     * pipe with read text attribute so that we can read it
     * like a text file.
     */
    if( (chkdsk = _popen( "dir *.c /on /p", "rt" )) == NULL )
        exit( 1 );

    /* Read pipe until end of file. End of file indicates that
     * CHKDSK closed its standard out (probably meaning it
     * terminated).
     */
    while( !feof( chkdsk ) )
```

```
   {
      if( fgets( psBuffer, 128, chkdsk ) != NULL )
         printf( psBuffer );
   }

   /* Close pipe and print return value of CHKDSK. */
   printf( "\nProcess returned %d\n", _pclose( chkdsk ) );
}
```

Output

```
Volume in drive C is CDRIVE
Volume Serial Number is 0E17-1702

Directory of C:\dolphin\crt\code\pcode

05/02/94  01:05a                  805 perror.c
05/02/94  01:05a                2,149 pipe.c
05/02/94  01:05a                  882 popen.c
05/02/94  01:05a                  206 pow.c
05/02/94  01:05a                1,514 printf.c
05/02/94  01:05a                  454 putc.c
05/02/94  01:05a                  162 puts.c
05/02/94  01:05a                  654 putw.c
              8 File(s)          6,826 bytes
                     86,597,632 bytes free

Process returned 0
```

See Also

_pclose, _pipe

pow

Calculates x raised to the power of y.

double pow(double *x*, double *y*);

Routine	Required Header	Compatibility
pow	<math.h>	ANSI, Win 95, Win NT

For additional compatibility information, see "Compatibility" in the Introduction.

Libraries

LIBC.LIB	Single thread static library, retail version
LIBCMT.LIB	Multithread static library, retail version
MSVCRT.LIB	Import library for MSVCRT.DLL, retail version

Return Value

pow returns the value of x^y. No error message is printed on overflow or underflow.

Values of x and y	Return Value of pow
$x <> 0$ and y = 0.0	1
$x = 0.0$ and y = 0.0	1
$x = 0.0$ and y < 0	INF

Parameters

x

Base

y

Exponent

Remarks

The **pow** function computes *x* raised to the power of *y*.

pow does not recognize integral floating-point values greater than 2^{64}, such as `1.0E100`.

Example

```
/* POW.C
 *
 */

#include <math.h>
#include <stdio.h>

void main( void )
{
   double x = 2.0, y = 3.0, z;

   z = pow( x, y );
   printf( "%.1f to the power of %.1f is %.1f\n", x, y, z );
}
```

Output

```
2.0 to the power of 3.0 is 8.0
```

See Also

exp, log, sqrt

printf, wprintf

Print formatted output to the standard output stream.

int printf(const char **format* [**,** *argument*]... **);**
int wprintf(const wchar_t **format* [**,** *argument*]... **);**

Routine	Required Header	Compatibility
printf	<stdio.h>	ANSI, Win 95, Win NT
wprintf	<stdio.h> or <wchar.h>	ANSI, Win 95, Win NT

For additional compatibility information, see "Compatibility" in the Introduction.

Libraries

LIBC.LIB	Single thread static library, retail version
LIBCMT.LIB	Multithread static library, retail version
MSVCRT.LIB	Import library for MSVCRT.DLL, retail version

Return Value

Each of these functions returns the number of characters printed, or a negative value if an error occurs.

Parameters

format
    Format control

argument
    Optional arguments

Remarks

The **printf** function formats and prints a series of characters and values to the standard output stream, **stdout**. If arguments follow the *format* string, the *format* string must contain specifications that determine the output format for the arguments. **printf** and fprintf behave identically except that **printf** writes output to **stdout** rather than to a destination of type **FILE**.

wprintf is a wide-character version of **printf**; *format* is a wide-character string. **wprintf** and **printf** behave identically otherwise.

Generic-Text Routine Mappings

TCHAR.H Routine	_UNICODE & _MBCS Not Defined	_MBCS Defined	_UNICODE Defined
_tprintf	printf	printf	wprintf

The *format* argument consists of ordinary characters, escape sequences, and (if arguments follow *format*) format specifications. The ordinary characters and escape sequences are copied to **stdout** in order of their appearance. For example, the line

```
printf("Line one\n\t\tLine two\n");
```

produces the output

```
Line one
        Line two
```

Format specifications always begin with a percent sign (%) and are read left to right. When **printf** encounters the first format specification (if any), it converts the value of the first argument after *format* and outputs it accordingly. The second format specification causes the second argument to be converted and output, and so on. If there are more arguments than there are format specifications, the extra arguments are ignored. The results are undefined if there are not enough arguments for all the format specifications.

Example

```
/* PRINTF.C: This program uses the printf and wprintf functions
 * to produce formatted output.
 */

#include <stdio.h>

void main( void )
{
    char   ch = 'h', *string = "computer";
    int    count = -9234;
    double fp = 251.7366;
    wchar_t wch = L'w', *wstring = L"Unicode";

    /* Display integers. */
    printf( "Integer formats:\n"
            "\tDecimal: %d  Justified: %.6d  Unsigned: %u\n",
            count, count, count, count );

    printf( "Decimal %d as:\n\tHex: %Xh  C hex: 0x%x  Octal: %o\n",
            count, count, count, count );

    /* Display in different radixes. */
    printf( "Digits 10 equal:\n\tHex: %i  Octal: %i  Decimal: %i\n",
            0x10, 010, 10 );

    /* Display characters. */

    printf("Characters in field (1):\n%10c%5hc%5C%5lc\n", ch, ch, wch, wch);
    wprintf(L"Characters in field (2):\n%10C%5hc%5c%5lc\n", ch, ch, wch, wch);
```

```
    /* Display strings. */

    printf("Strings in field (1):\n%25s\n%25.4hs\n\t%S%25.3ls\n",
        string, string, wstring, wstring);
    wprintf(L"Strings in field (2):\n%25S\n%25.4hs\n\t%s%25.3ls\n",
        string, string, wstring, wstring);

    /* Display real numbers. */
    printf( "Real numbers:\n\t%f %.2f %e %E\n", fp, fp, fp, fp );

    /* Display pointer. */
    printf( "\nAddress as:\t%p\n", &count);

    /* Count characters printed. */
    printf( "\nDisplay to here:\n" );
    printf( "1234567890123456%n78901234567890\n", &count );
    printf( "\tNumber displayed: %d\n\n", count );
}
```

Output

```
Integer formats:
   Decimal: -9234  Justified: -009234  Unsigned: 4294958062
Decimal -9234 as:
   Hex: FFFFDBEEh  C hex: 0xffffdbee  Octal: 37777755756
Digits 10 equal:
   Hex: 16  Octal: 8  Decimal: 10
Characters in field (1):
        h     h     w     w
Characters in field (2):
        h     h     w     w
Strings in field (1):
                  computer
                       comp
   Unicode                     Uni
Strings in field (2):
                  computer
                       comp
   Unicode                     Uni
Real numbers:
   251.736600 251.74 2.517366e+002 2.517366E+002

Address as: 0012FFAC

Display to here:
123456789012345678901234567890
   Number displayed: 16
```

See Also

fopen, fprintf, scanf, sprintf, vprintf Functions

Format Specification Fields: printf and wprintf Functions

A format specification, which consists of optional and required fields, has the following form:

%[flags] [width] [.precision] [{**h** | **l** | **I64** | **L**}]type

Each field of the format specification is a single character or a number signifying a particular format option. The simplest format specification contains only the percent sign and a *type* character (for example, %s). If a percent sign is followed by a character that has no meaning as a format field, the character is copied to **stdout**. For example, to print a percent-sign character, use %%.

The optional fields, which appear before the *type* character, control other aspects of the formatting, as follows:

type
Required character that determines whether the associated *argument* is interpreted as a character, a string, or a number (see Table R.3).

flags
Optional character or characters that control justification of output and printing of signs, blanks, decimal points, and octal and hexadecimal prefixes (see Table R.4). More than one flag can appear in a format specification.

width
Optional number that specifies the minimum number of characters output. (See printf Width Specification.)

precision
Optional number that specifies the maximum number of characters printed for all or part of the output field, or the minimum number of digits printed for integer values (see Table R.5).

h | **l** | **I64** | **L**
Optional prefixes to *type*-that specify the size of *argument* (see Table R.6).

printf Type Field Characters

The *type* character is the only required format field ; it appears after any optional format fields. The *type* character determines whether the associated argument is interpreted as a character, string, or number. The types **C** and **S**, and the behavior of **c** and **s** with **printf** functions, are Microsoft extensions and are not ANSI-compatible.

Table R.3 printf Type Field Characters

Character	Type	Output Format
c	**int** or **wint_t**	When used with **printf** functions, specifies a single-byte character; when used with **wprintf** functions, specifies a wide character.
C	**int** or **wint_t**	When used with **printf** functions, specifies a wide character; when used with **wprintf** functions, specifies a single-byte character.
d	**int**	Signed decimal integer.
i	**int**	Signed decimal integer.
o	**int**	Unsigned octal integer.
u	**int**	Unsigned decimal integer.
x	**int**	Unsigned hexadecimal integer, using "abcdef."
X	**int**	Unsigned hexadecimal integer, using "ABCDEF."
e	**double**	Signed value having the form [−]d.dddd **e** [sign]ddd where d is a single decimal digit, dddd is one or more decimal digits, ddd is exactly three decimal digits, and sign is + or −.
E	**double**	Identical to the **e** format except that **E** rather than **e** introduces the exponent.
f	**double**	Signed value having the form [−]dddd.dddd, where dddd is one or more decimal digits. The number of digits before the decimal point depends on the magnitude of the number, and the number of digits after the decimal point depends on the requested precision.
g	**double**	Signed value printed in **f** or **e** format, whichever is more compact for the given value and precision. The **e** format is used only when the exponent of the value is less than −4 or greater than or equal to the precision argument. Trailing zeros are truncated, and the decimal point appears only if one or more digits follow it.
G	**double**	Identical to the **g** format, except that **E**, rather than **e**, introduces the exponent (where appropriate).
n	Pointer to integer	Number of characters successfully written so far to the stream or buffer; this value is stored in the integer whose address is given as the argument.
p	Pointer to **void**	Prints the address pointed to by the argument in the form xxxx:yyyy where xxxx is the segment and yyyy is the offset, and the digits x and y are uppercase hexadecimal digits.

Table R.3   printf Type Field Characters   *(continued)*

Character	Type	Output Format
s	String	When used with **printf** functions, specifies a single-byte-character string; when used with **wprintf** functions, specifies a wide-character string. Characters are printed up to the first null character or until the *precision* value is reached.
S	String	When used with **printf** functions, specifies a wide-character string; when used with **wprintf** functions, specifies a single-byte-character string. Characters are printed up to the first null character or until the *precision* value is reached.

Flag Directives

The first optional field of the format specification is *flags*. A flag directive is a character that justifies output and prints signs, blanks, decimal points, and octal and hexadecimal prefixes. More than one flag directive may appear in a format specification.

Table R.4   Flag Characters

Flag	Meaning	Default
–	Left align the result within the given field width.	Right align.
+	Prefix the output value with a sign (+ or –) if the output value is of a signed type.	Sign appears only for negative signed values (–).
0	If *width* is prefixed with **0**, zeros are added until the minimum width is reached. If 0 and – appear, the **0** is ignored. If **0** is specified with an integer format (**i, u, x, X, o, d**) the **0** is ignored.	No padding.
blank (' ')	Prefix the output value with a blank if the output value is signed and positive; the blank is ignored if both the blank and + flags appear.	No blank appears.
#	When used with the **o**, **x**, or **X** format, the # flag prefixes any nonzero output value with 0, 0x, or 0X, respectively.	No blank appears.
	When used with the **e**, **E**, or **f** format, the # flag forces the output value to contain a decimal point in all cases.	Decimal point appears only if digits follow it.
	When used with the **g** or **G** format, the # flag forces the output value to contain a decimal point in all cases and prevents the truncation of trailing zeros.	Decimal point appears only if digits follow it. Trailing zeros are truncated.
	Ignored when used with **c**, **d**, **i**, **u**, or **s**.	

printf Width Specification

The second optional field of the format specification is the width specification. The *width* argument is a nonnegative decimal integer controlling the minimum number of characters printed. If the number of characters in the output value is less than the specified width, blanks are added to the left or the right of the values — depending on whether the "–" flag (for left alignment) is specified — until the minimum width is reached. If *width* is prefixed with 0, zeros are added until the minimum width is reached (not useful for left-aligned numbers).

The width specification never causes a value to be truncated. If the number of characters in the output value is greater than the specified width, or if *width* is not given, all characters of the value are printed (subject to the precision specification).

If the width specification is an asterisk (*), an **int** argument from the argument list supplies the value. The *width* argument must precede the value being formatted in the argument list. A nonexistent or small field width does not cause the truncation of a field; if the result of a conversion is wider than the field width, the field expands to contain the conversion result.

Precision Specification

The third optional field of the format specification is the precision specification. It specifies a nonnegative decimal integer, preceded by a period (.), which specifies the number of characters to be printed, the number of decimal places, or the number of significant digits (see Table R.5). Unlike the width specification, the precision specification can cause either truncation of the output value or rounding of a floating-point value. If *precision* is specified as 0 and the value to be converted is 0, the result is no characters output, as shown below:

```
printf( "%.0d", 0 );       /* No characters output */
```

If the precision specification is an asterisk (*), an **int** argument from the argument list supplies the value. The precision argument must precede the value being formatted in the argument list.

The type determines the interpretation of *precision* and the default when *precision* is omitted, as shown in Table R.5.

Table R.5 How Precision Values Affect Type

Type	Meaning	Default
c, C	The precision has no effect.	Character is printed.
d, I, u, o, x, X	The precision specifies the minimum number of digits to be printed. If the number of digits in the argument is less than *precision*, the output value is padded on the left with zeros. The value is not truncated when the number of digits exceeds *precision*.	Default precision is 1.

Table R.5 How Precision Values Affect Type *(continued)*

Type	Meaning	Default
e, E	The precision specifies the number of digits to be printed after the decimal point. The last printed digit is rounded.	Default precision is 6; if *precision* is 0 or the period (.) appears without a number following it, no decimal point is printed.
f	The precision value specifies the number of digits after the decimal point. If a decimal point appears, at least one digit appears before it. The value is rounded to the appropriate number of digits.	Default precision is 6; if *precision* is 0, or if the period (.) appears without a number following it, no decimal point is printed.
g, G	The precision specifies the maximum number of significant digits printed.	Six significant digits are printed, with any trailing zeros truncated.
s, S	The precision specifies the maximum number of characters to be printed. Characters in excess of *precision* are not printed.	Characters are printed until a null character is encountered.

If the argument corresponding to a floating-point specifier is infinite, indefinite, or NaN, **printf** gives the following output.

Value	Output
+ infinity	**1.#INF***random-digits*
– infinity	**–1.#INF***random-digits*
Indefinite (same as quiet NaN)	*digit.***#IND***random-digits*
NAN	*digit.***#NAN***random-digits*

Size and Distance Specification

The optional prefixes to *type*, **h**, **l**, and **L**, specify the "size" of *argument* (long or short, single-byte character or wide character, depending upon the type specifier that they modify). These type-specifier prefixes are used with type characters in **printf** functions or **wprintf** functions to specify interpretation of arguments, as shown in the following table. These prefixes are Microsoft extensions and are not ANSI-compatible.

Table R.6 Size Prefixes for printf and wprintf Format-Type Specifiers

To Specify	Use Prefix	With Type Specifier
long int	**l**	**d, i, o, x,** or **X**
long unsigned int	**l**	**u**
short int	**h**	**d, i, o, x,** or **X**
short unsigned int	**h**	**u** *(continued)*

Table R.6   Size Prefixes for printf and wprintf Format-Type Specifiers *(continued)*

To Specify	Use Prefix	With Type Specifier
__int64	I64	d, i, o, u, x, or X
Single-byte character with **printf** functions	h	c or C
Single-byte character with **wprintf** functions	h	c or C
Wide character with **printf** functions	l	c or C
Wide character with **wprintf** functions	l	c or C
Single-byte–character string with **printf** functions	h	s or S
Single-byte–character string with **wprintf** functions	h	s or S
Wide-character string with **printf** functions	l	s or S
Wide-character string with **wprintf** functions	l	s or S

Thus to print single-byte or wide-characters with **printf** functions and **wprintf** functions, use format specifiers as follows.

To Print Character As	Use Function	With Format Specifier
single byte	printf	c, hc, or hC
single byte	wprintf	C, hc, or hC
wide	wprintf	c, lc, or lC
wide	printf	C, lc, or lC

To print strings with **printf** functions and **wprintf** functions, use the prefixes **h** and **l** analogously with format type-specifiers **s** and **S**.

putc, putwc, putchar, putwchar

Writes a character to a stream (**putc, putwc**) or to **stdout** (**putchar, putwchar**).

int putc(int *c*, **FILE** **stream* **);**
wint_t putwc(wint_t *c*, **FILE** **stream* **);**
int putchar(int *c* **);**
wint_t putwchar(wint_t *c* **);**

Routine	Required Header	Compatibility
putc	<stdio.h>	ANSI, Win 95, Win NT
putwc	<stdio.h> or <wchar.h>	ANSI, Win 95, Win NT

(continued)

Routine	Required Header	Compatibility
putchar	<stdio.h>	ANSI, Win 95, Win NT
putwchar	<stdio.h> or <wchar.h>	ANSI, Win 95, Win NT

For additional compatibility information, see "Compatibility" in the Introduction.

Libraries

LIBC.LIB	Single thread static library, retail version
LIBCMT.LIB	Multithread static library, retail version
MSVCRT.LIB	Import library for MSVCRT.DLL, retail version

Return Value

Each of these functions returns the character written. To indicate an error or end-of-file condition, **putc** and **putchar** return **EOF**; **putwc** and **putwchar** return **WEOF**. For all four routines, use ferror or feof to check for an error or end of file.

Parameters

c

    Character to be written

stream

    Pointer to **FILE** structure

Remarks

The **putc** routine writes the single character *c* to the output *stream* at the current position. Any integer can be passed to **putc**, but only the lower 8 bits are written. The **putchar** routine is identical to **putc**(*c*, **stdout**). For each routine, if a read error occurs, the error indicator for the stream is set. **putc** and **putchar** are similar to **fputc** and **_fputchar**, respectively, but are implemented both as functions and as macros (see "Choosing Between Functions and Macros" in the Introduction). **putwc** and **putwchar** are wide-character versions of **putc** and **putchar**, respectively.

Generic-Text Routine Mappings

TCHAR.H Routine	_UNICODE & _MBCS Not Defined	_MBCS Defined	_UNICODE Defined
_puttc	putc	putc	putwc
_puttchar	putchar	putchar	putwchar

Example

```
/* PUTC.C: This program uses putc to write buffer
 * to a stream. If an error occurs, the program
 * stops before writing the entire buffer.
 */

#include <stdio.h>

void main( void )
{
   FILE *stream;
   char *p, buffer[] = "This is the line of output\n";
   int  ch;

   ch = 0;
   /* Make standard out the stream and write to it. */
   stream = stdout;
   for( p = buffer; (ch != EOF) && (*p != '\0'); p++ )
      ch = putc( *p, stream );
}
```

Output

```
This is the line of output
```

See Also

fputc, getc

_putch

Writes a character to the console.

int _putch(int *c*);

Routine	Required Header	Compatibility
_putch	<conio.h>	Win 95, Win NT

For additional compatibility information, see "Compatibility" in the Introduction.

Libraries

LIBC.LIB	Single thread static library, retail version
LIBCMT.LIB	Multithread static library, retail version
MSVCRT.LIB	Import library for MSVCRT.DLL, retail version

Return Value

The function returns *c* if successful, and **EOF** if not.

Parameter

c

Character to be output

Remarks

The **_putch** function writes the character c directly (without buffering) to the console.

Example

```
/* GETCH.C: This program reads characters from
 * the keyboard until it receives a 'Y' or 'y'.
 */

#include <conio.h>
#include <ctype.h>

void main( void )
{
   int ch;

   _cputs( "Type 'Y' when finished typing keys: " );
   do
   {
      ch = _getch();
      ch = toupper( ch );
   } while( ch != 'Y' );

   _putch( ch );
   _putch( '\r' );    /* Carriage return */
   _putch( '\n' );    /* Line feed       */
}
```

Output

```
Type 'Y' when finished typing keys: Y
```

See Also

_cprintf, _getch

_putenv, _wputenv

Creates new environment variables; modifies or removes existing ones.

int _putenv(const char *envstring* **);**
int _wputenv(const wchar_t *envstring* **);**

Routine	Required Header	Compatibility
_putenv	<stdlib.h>	Win 95, Win NT
_wputenv	<stdlib.h> or <wchar.h>	Win NT

For additional compatibility information, see "Compatibility" in the Introduction.

Libraries

LIBC.LIB	Single thread static library, retail version
LIBCMT.LIB	Multithread static library, retail version
MSVCRT.LIB	Import library for MSVCRT.DLL, retail version

Return Value

_putenv and **_wputenv** return 0 if successful, or –1 in the case of an error.

Parameter

envstring
    Environment-string definition

Remarks

The **_putenv** function adds new environment variables or modifies the values of existing environment variables. Environment variables define the environment in which a process executes (for example, the default search path for libraries to be linked with a program). **_wputenv** is a wide-character version of **_putenv**; the *envstring* argument to **_wputenv** is a wide-character string.

Generic-Text Routine Mappings

TCHAR.H Routine	_UNICODE & _MBCS Not Defined	_MBCS Defined	_UNICODE Defined
_tputenv	_putenv	_putenv	_wputenv

The *envstring* argument must be a pointer to a string of the form *varname=string*, where *varname* is the name of the environment variable to be added or modified and string is the variable's value. If *varname* is already part of the environment, its value is replaced by string; otherwise, the new *varname* variable and its string value are added to the environment. You can remove a variable from the environment by specifying an empty string — in other words, by specifying only *varname=*.

_putenv and **_wputenv** affect only the environment that is local to the current process; you cannot use them to modify the command-level environment. That is, these functions operate only on data structures accessible to the run-time library and not on the environment "segment" created for a process by the operating system. When the current process terminates, the environment reverts to the level of the calling process (in most cases, the operating-system level). However, the modified environment can be passed to any new processes created by **_spawn**, **_exec**, or system, and these new processes get any new items added by **_putenv** and **_wputenv**.

With regard to environment entries, observe the following cautions:

• Do not change an environment entry directly; instead, use **_putenv** or **_wputenv** to change it. To modify the return value of **_putenv** or **_wputenv** without affecting the environment table, use **_strdup** or **strcpy** to make a copy of the string.

• Never free a pointer to an environment entry, because the environment variable will then point to freed space. A similar problem can occur if you pass **_putenv** or **_wputenv** a pointer to a local variable, then exit the function in which the variable is declared.

getenv and **_putenv** use the global variable **_environ** to access the environment table; **_wgetenv** and **_wputenv** use **_wenviron**. **_putenv** and **_wputenv** may change the value of **_environ** and **_wenviron**, thus invalidating the *envp* argument to **main** and the *wenvp* argument to **wmain**. Therefore, it is safer to use **_environ** or **_wenviron** to access the environment information. For more information about the relation of **_putenv** and **_wputenv** to global variables, see _environ, _wenviron.

Example

```
/* GETENV.C: This program uses getenv to retrieve
 * the LIB environment variable and then uses
 * _putenv to change it to a new value.
 */

#include <stdlib.h>
#include <stdio.h>

void main( void )
{
   char *libvar;

   /* Get the value of the LIB environment variable. */
   libvar = getenv( "LIB" );

   if( libvar != NULL )
      printf( "Original LIB variable is: %s\n", libvar );

   /* Attempt to change path. Note that this only affects the environment
   * variable of the current process. The command processor's environment
   * is not changed.
   */
```

```
    _putenv( "LIB=c:\\mylib;c:\\yourlib" );

    /* Get new value. */
    libvar = getenv( "LIB" );

    if( libvar != NULL )
        printf( "New LIB variable is: %s\n", libvar );
}
```

Output

```
Original LIB variable is: C:\progra~1\devstu~1\vc\lib
New LIB variable is: c:\mylib;c:\yourlib
```

See Also

getenv, _searchenv

puts, _putws

Write a string to stdout.

int puts(const char *string **);**
int _putws(const wchar_t *string **);**

Routine	Required Header	Compatibility
puts	<stdio.h>	ANSI, Win 95, Win NT
_putws	<stdio.h>	ANSI, Win 95, Win NT

For additional compatibility information, see "Compatibility" in the Introduction.

Libraries

LIBC.LIB	Single thread static library, retail version
LIBCMT.LIB	Multithread static library, retail version
MSVCRT.LIB	Import library for MSVCRT.DLL, retail version

Return Value

Each of these returns a nonnegative value if successful. If **puts** fails it returns **EOF**; if **_putws** fails it returns **WEOF**.

Parameter

string
    Output string

Remarks

The **puts** function writes *string* to the standard output stream **stdout**, replacing the string's terminating null character ('\0') with a newline character ('\n') in the output stream.

Generic-Text Routine Mappings

TCHAR.H Routine	_UNICODE & _MBCS Not Defined	_MBCS Defined	_UNICODE Defined
_putts	puts	puts	_putws

Example

```
/* PUTS.C: This program uses puts
 * to write a string to stdout.
 */

#include <stdio.h>

void main( void )
{
    puts( "Hello world from puts!" );
}
```

Output

```
Hello world from puts!
```

See Also

fputs, **gets**

_putw

Writes an integer to a stream.

int _putw(int *binint*, **FILE** **stream* **);**

Routine	Required Header	Compatibility
_putw	<stdio.h>	Win 95, Win NT

For additional compatibility information, see "Compatibility" in the Introduction.

Libraries

LIBC.LIB	Single thread static library, retail version
LIBCMT.LIB	Multithread static library, retail version
MSVCRT.LIB	Import library for MSVCRT.DLL, retail version

Return Value

_putw returns the value written. A return value of **EOF** may indicate an error. Because **EOF** is also a legitimate integer value, use **ferror** to verify an error.

Parameters

binint
    Binary integer to be output

stream
    Pointer to **FILE** structure

Remarks

The **_putw** function writes a binary value of type **int** to the current position of *stream*. **_putw** does not affect the alignment of items in the stream, nor does it assume any special alignment. **_putw** is primarily for compatibility with previous libraries. Portability problems may occur with **_putw** because the size of an **int** and the ordering of bytes within an **int** differ across systems.

Example

```
/* PUTW.C: This program uses _putw to write a
 * word to a stream, then performs an error check.
 */

#include <stdio.h>
#include <stdlib.h>

void main( void )
{
   FILE *stream;
   unsigned u;
   if( (stream = fopen( "data.out", "wb" )) == NULL )
      exit( 1 );
   for( u = 0; u << 10; u++ )
   {
      _putw( u + 0x2132, stdout );
      _putw( u + 0x2132, stream );   /* Write word to stream. */
      if( ferror( stream ) )         /* Make error check. */
      {
         printf( "_putw failed" );
         clearerr( stream );
         exit( 1 );
      }
   }
   printf( "\nWrote ten words\n" );
   fclose( stream );
}
```

Output

```
Wrote ten words
```

See Also

_getw

qsort

Performs a quick sort.

void qsort(void *base*, **size_t** *num*, **size_t** *width*, **int (__cdecl** **compare*)(**const void** **elem1*, **const void** **elem2*));

Routine	Required Header	Compatibility
qsort	<stdlib.h> and <search.h>	ANSI, Win 95, Win NT

For additional compatibility information, see "Compatibility" in the Introduction.

Libraries

LIBC.LIB	Single thread static library, retail version
LIBCMT.LIB	Multithread static library, retail version
MSVCRT.LIB	Import library for MSVCRT.DLL, retail version

Return Value

None

Parameters

base
Start of target array

num
Array size in elements

width
Element size in bytes

compare
Comparison function

elem1
Pointer to the key for the search

elem2
Pointer to the array element to be compared with the key

Remarks

The **qsort** function implements a quick-sort algorithm to sort an array of *num* elements, each of *width* bytes. The argument *base* is a pointer to the base of the array to be sorted. **qsort** overwrites this array with the sorted elements. The argument *compare* is a pointer to a user-supplied routine that compares two array elements and returns a value specifying their relationship. **qsort** calls the *compare* routine one or more times during the sort, passing pointers to two array elements on each call:

compare(**(void *)** *elem1*, **(void *)** *elem2*);

The routine must compare the elements, then return one of the following values:

Return Value	Description
< 0	*elem1* less than *elem2*
0	*elem1* equivalent to *elem2*
> 0	*elem1* greater than *elem2*

The array is sorted in increasing order, as defined by the comparison function. To sort an array in decreasing order, reverse the sense of "greater than" and "less than" in the comparison function.

Example

```
/* QSORT.C: This program reads the command-line
 * parameters and uses qsort to sort them. It
 * then displays the sorted arguments.
 */

#include <stdlib.h>
#include <string.h>
#include <stdio.h>

int compare( const void *arg1, const void *arg2 );

void main( int argc, char **argv )
{
    int i;
    /* Eliminate argv[0] from sort: */
    argv++;
    argc--;

    /* Sort remaining args using Quicksort algorithm: */
    qsort( (void *)argv, (size_t)argc, sizeof( char * ), compare );
```

```
   /* Output sorted list: */
   for( i = 0; i < argc; ++i )
      printf( "%s ", argv[i] );
   printf( "\n" );
}

int compare( const void *arg1, const void *arg2 )
{
   /* Compare all of both strings: */
   return _stricmp( * ( char** ) arg1, * ( char** ) arg2 );
}
```

Output

```
[C:\code]qsort every good boy deserves favor
boy deserves every favor good
```

See Also

bsearch, **_lsearch**

_query_new_handler

Returns address of current new handler routine.

_PNH _query_new_handler(void);

Routine	Required Header	Compatibility
_query_new_handler	<new.h>	Win 95, Win NT

For additional compatibility information, see "Compatibility" in the Introduction.

Libraries

LIBC.LIB	Single thread static library, retail version
LIBCMT.LIB	Multithread static library, retail version
MSVCRT.LIB	Import library for MSVCRT.DLL, retail version

Return Value

_query_new_handler returns the address of the current new handler routine as set by **_set_new_handler**.

Remarks

The C++ **_query_new_handler** function returns the address of the current exception-handling function set by the C++ _set_new_handler function. **_set_new_handler** is used to specify an exception-handling function that is to gain control if the **new** operator fails to allocate memory. For more information, see the discussions of the operator new and operator delete functions in the *C++ Language Reference* online.

See Also

free

_query_new_mode

Returns an integer indicating new handler mode set by **_set_new_mode** for **malloc**.

int _query_new_mode(void);

Routine	Required Header	Compatibility
_query_new_mode	<new.h>	Win 95, Win NT

For additional compatibility information, see "Compatibility" in the Introduction.

Libraries

LIBC.LIB	Single thread static library, retail version
LIBCMT.LIB	Multithread static library, retail version
MSVCRT.LIB	Import library for MSVCRT.DLL, retail version

Return Value

_query_new_mode returns the current new handler mode, namely 0 or 1, for **malloc**. A return value of 1 indicates that, on failure to allocate memory, **malloc** calls the new handler routine; a return value of 0 indicates that it does not.

Remarks

The C++ **_query_new_mode** function returns an integer that indicates the new handler mode that is set by the C++ _set_new_mode function for malloc. The new handler mode indicates whether, on failure to allocate memory, **malloc** is to call the new handler routine as set by _set_new_handler. By default, **malloc** does not call the new handler routine on failure. You can use **_set_new_mode** to override this behavior so that on failure **malloc** calls the new handler routine in the same way that the **new** operator does when it fails to allocate memory. For more information, see the operator delete and operator new functions in the *C++ Language Reference* online.

See Also

calloc, **free**, **realloc**, **_query_new_handler**

raise

Sends a signal to the executing program.

int raise(int *sig* **);**

Routine	Required Header	Compatibility
raise	<signal.h>	ANSI, Win 95, Win NT

For additional compatibility information, see "Compatibility" in the Introduction.

Libraries

LIBC.LIB	Single thread static library, retail version
LIBCMT.LIB	Multithread static library, retail version
MSVCRT.LIB	Import library for MSVCRT.DLL, retail version

Return Value

If successful, **raise** returns 0. Otherwise, it returns a nonzero value.

Parameter

sig
  Signal to be raised

Remarks

The **raise** function sends *sig* to the executing program. If a previous call to **signal** has
installed a signal-handling function for *sig*, **raise** executes that function. If no handler
function has been installed, the default action associated with the signal value *sig* is taken,
as follows.

Signal	Meaning	Default
SIGABRT	Abnormal termination	Terminates the calling program with exit code 3
SIGFPE	Floating-point error	Terminates the calling program
SIGILL	Illegal instruction	Terminates the calling program
SIGINT	CTRL+C interrupt	Terminates the calling program
SIGSEGV	Illegal storage access	Terminates the calling program
SIGTERM	Termination request sent to the program	Ignores the signal

See Also

abort, signal

rand

Generates a pseudorandom number.

int rand(void);

Routine	Required Header	Compatibility
rand	<stdlib.h>	ANSI, Win 95, Win NT

For additional compatibility information, see "Compatibility" in the Introduction.

Libraries

LIBC.LIB	Single thread static library, retail version
LIBCMT.LIB	Multithread static library, retail version
MSVCRT.LIB	Import library for MSVCRT.DLL, retail version

Return Value

rand returns a pseudorandom number, as described above. There is no error return.

Remarks

The **rand** function returns a pseudorandom integer in the range 0 to **RAND_MAX**. Use the srand function to seed the pseudorandom-number generator before calling **rand**.

Example

```
/* RAND.C: This program seeds the random-number generator
 * with the time, then displays 10 random integers.
 */

#include <stdlib.h>
#include <stdio.h>
#include <time.h>

void main( void )
{
   int i;

   /* Seed the random-number generator with current time so that
    * the numbers will be different every time we run.
    */
   srand( (unsigned)time( NULL ) );

   /* Display 10 numbers. */
   for( i = 0;   i < 10;i++ )
      printf( "  %6d\n", rand() );
}
```

```
 6929
 8026
21987
30734
20587
 6699
22034
25051
 7988
10104
```

See Also

srand

_read

Reads data from a file.

int _read(int *handle*, **void** **buffer*, **unsigned int** *count* **);**

Routine	Required Header	Compatibility
_read	<io.h>	Win 95, Win NT

For additional compatibility information, see "Compatibility" in the Introduction.

Libraries

LIBC.LIB	Single thread static library, retail version
LIBCMT.LIB	Multithread static library, retail version
MSVCRT.LIB	Import library for MSVCRT.DLL, retail version

Return Value

_read returns the number of bytes read, which may be less than count if there are fewer than count bytes left in the file or if the file was opened in text mode, in which case each carriage-return–linefeed (CR–LF) pair is replaced with a single linefeed character. Only the single linefeed character is counted in the return value. The replacement does not affect the file pointer.

If the function tries to read at end of file, it returns 0. If the handle is invalid, or the file is not open for reading, or the file is locked, the function returns –1 and sets **errno** to **EBADF**.

Parameters

handle
Handle referring to open file

buffer
Storage location for data

count
Maximum number of bytes

Remarks

The **_read** function reads a maximum of *count* bytes into *buffer* from the file associated with *handle*. The read operation begins at the current position of the file pointer associated with the given file. After the read operation, the file pointer points to the next unread character.

If the file was opened in text mode, the read terminates when **_read** encounters a CTRL+Z character, which is treated as an end-of-file indicator. Use _lseek to clear the end-of-file indicator.

Example

```
/* READ.C: This program opens a file named
 * READ.C and tries to read 60,000 bytes from
 * that file using _read. It then displays the
 * actual number of bytes read from READ.C.
 */

#include <fcntl.h>      /* Needed only for _O_RDWR definition */
#include <io.h>
#include <stdlib.h>
#include <stdio.h>

char buffer[60000];

void main( void )
{
    int fh;
    unsigned int nbytes = 60000, bytesread;

    /* Open file for input: */
    if( (fh = _open( "read.c", _O_RDONLY )) == -1 )
    {
        perror( "open failed on input file" );
        exit( 1 );
    }
```

```
   /* Read in input: */
   if( ( bytesread = _read( fh, buffer, nbytes ) ) <= 0 )
      perror( "Problem reading file" );
   else
      printf( "Read %u bytes from file\n", bytesread );

   _close( fh );
}
```

Output

```
Read 775 bytes from file
```

See Also

_creat, **fread**, **_open**, **_write**

realloc

Reallocate memory blocks.

void *realloc(void **memblock***, size_t** *size* **);**

Routine	Required Header	Compatibility
realloc	<stdlib.h> and <malloc.h>	ANSI, Win 95, Win NT

For additional compatibility information, see "Compatibility" in the Introduction.

Libraries

LIBC.LIB	Single thread static library, retail version
LIBCMT.LIB	Multithread static library, retail version
MSVCRT.LIB	Import library for MSVCRT.DLL, retail version

Return Value

realloc returns a **void** pointer to the reallocated (and possibly moved) memory block. The return value is **NULL** if the size is zero and the buffer argument is not **NULL**, or if there is not enough available memory to expand the block to the given size. In the first case, the original block is freed. In the second, the original block is unchanged. The return value points to a storage space that is guaranteed to be suitably aligned for storage of any type of object. To get a pointer to a type other than **void**, use a type cast on the return value.

Parameters

memblock
    Pointer to previously allocated memory block

size
    New size in bytes

Remarks

The **realloc** function changes the size of an allocated memory block. The *memblock* argument points to the beginning of the memory block. If *memblock* is **NULL**, **realloc** behaves the same way as **malloc** and allocates a new block of *size* bytes. If *memblock* is not **NULL**, it should be a pointer returned by a previous call to **calloc**, **malloc**, or **realloc**.

The *size* argument gives the new size of the block, in bytes. The contents of the block are unchanged up to the shorter of the new and old sizes, although the new block can be in a different location. Because the new block can be in a new memory location, the pointer returned by **realloc** is not guaranteed to be the pointer passed through the *memblock* argument.

realloc calls **malloc** in order to use the C++ _set_new_mode function to set the new handler mode. The new handler mode indicates whether, on failure, **malloc** is to call the new handler routine as set by _set_new_handler. By default, **malloc** does not call the new handler routine on failure to allocate memory. You can override this default behavior so that, when **realloc** fails to allocate memory, **malloc** calls the new handler routine in the same way that the **new** operator does when it fails for the same reason. To override the default, call

```
_set_new_mode(1)
```

early in your program, or link with NEWMODE.OBJ.

When the application is linked with a debug version of the C run-time libraries, **realloc** resolves to _realloc_dbg. For more information about how the heap is managed during the debugging process, see "Using C Run-Time Library Debugging Support" in the *Visual C++ Programmer's Guide* online.

Example

```
/* REALLOC.C: This program allocates a block of memory for
 * buffer and then uses _msize to display the size of that
 * block. Next, it uses realloc to expand the amount of
 * memory used by buffer and then calls _msize again to
 * display the new amount of memory allocated to buffer.
 */

#include <stdio.h>
#include <malloc.h>
#include <stdlib.h>

void main( void )
{
   long *buffer;
   size_t size;

   if( (buffer = (long *)malloc( 1000 * sizeof( long ) )) == NULL )
      exit( 1 );
```

```
    size = _msize( buffer );
    printf( "Size of block after malloc of 1000 longs: %u\n", size );

    /* Reallocate and show new size: */
    if( (buffer = realloc( buffer, size + (1000 * sizeof( long )) )) == NULL )exit( 1 );
    size = _msize( buffer );
    printf( "Size of block after realloc of 1000 more longs: %u\n", size );

    free( buffer );
    exit( 0 );
}
```

Output

```
Size of block after malloc of 1000 longs: 4000
Size of block after realloc of 1000 more longs: 8000
```

See Also

calloc, free, malloc

remove, _wremove

Delete a file.

int remove(const char *path **);**
int _wremove(const wchar_t *path **);**

Routine	Required Header	Compatibility
remove	<stdio.h> or <io.h>	ANSI, Win 95, Win NT
_wremove	<stdio.h> or <wchar.h>	Win NT

For additional compatibility information, see "Compatibility" in the Introduction.

Libraries

LIBC.LIB	Single thread static library, retail version
LIBCMT.LIB	Multithread static library, retail version
MSVCRT.LIB	Import library for MSVCRT.DLL, retail version

Return Value

Each of these functions returns 0 if the file is successfully deleted. Otherwise, it returns −1 and sets **errno** either to **EACCES** to indicate that the path specifies a read-only file, or to **ENOENT** to indicate that the filename or path was not found or that the path specifies a directory. This function fails and returns −1 if the file is open.

Parameter

path

Path of file to be removed

Remarks

The **remove** function deletes the file specified by *path*. **_wremove** is a wide-character version of **_remove**; the *path* argument to **_wremove** is a wide-character string. **_wremove** and **_remove** behave identically otherwise. All handles to a file must be closed before it can be deleted.

Generic-Text Routine Mappings

TCHAR.H Routine	_UNICODE & _MBCS Not Defined	_MBCS Defined	_UNICODE Defined
_tremove	remove	remove	_wremove

Example

```
/* REMOVE.C: This program uses remove to delete REMOVE.OBJ. */

#include <stdio.h>

void main( void )
{
    if( remove( "remove.obj" ) == -1 )
        perror( "Could not delete 'REMOVE.OBJ'" );
    else
        printf( "Deleted 'REMOVE.OBJ'\n" );
}
```

Output

```
Deleted 'REMOVE.OBJ'
```

See Also

_unlink

rename, _wrename

Rename a file or directory.

int rename(const char *oldname, const char *newname);
int _wrename(const wchar_t *oldname, const wchar_t *newname);

Routine	Required Header	Compatibility
rename	<io.h> or <stdio.h>	ANSI, Win 95, Win NT
_wrename	<stdio.h> or <wchar.h>	Win NT

For additional compatibility information, see "Compatibility" in the Introduction.

Libraries

LIBC.LIB	Single thread static library, retail version
LIBCMT.LIB	Multithread static library, retail version
MSVCRT.LIB	Import library for MSVCRT.DLL, retail version

Return Value

Each of these functions returns 0 if it is successful. On an error, the function returns a nonzero value and sets **errno** to one of the following values:

EACCES
File or directory specified by *newname* already exists or could not be created (invalid path); or *oldname* is a directory and *newname* specifies a different path.

ENOENT
File or path specified by *oldname* not found.

EINVAL
Name contains invalid characters.

For other possible return values, see _doserrno, _errno, syserrlist, and _sys_nerr.

Parameters

oldname
Pointer to old name

newname
Pointer to new name

Remarks

The **rename** function renames the file or directory specified by *oldname* to the name given by *newname*. The old name must be the path of an existing file or directory. The new name must not be the name of an existing file or directory. You can use **rename** to move a file from one directory or device to another by giving a different path in the *newname* argument. However, you cannot use **rename** to move a directory. Directories can be renamed, but not moved.

_wrename is a wide-character version of **_rename**; the arguments to **_wrename** are wide-character strings. **_wrename** and **_rename** behave identically otherwise.

Generic-Text Routine Mappings

TCHAR.H Routine	_UNICODE & _MBCS Not Defined	_MBCS Defined	_UNICODE Defined
_trename	rename	rename	_wrename

Example

```
/* RENAMER.C: This program attempts to rename a file
 * named RENAMER.OBJ to RENAMER.JBO. For this operation
 * to succeed, a file named RENAMER.OBJ must exist and
 * a file named RENAMER.JBO must not exist.
 */

#include <stdio.h>

void main( void )
{
   int  result;
   char old[] = "RENAMER.OBJ", new[] = "RENAMER.JBO";

   /* Attempt to rename file: */
   result = rename( old, new );
   if( result != 0 )
      printf( "Could not rename '%s'\n", old );
   else
      printf( "File '%s' renamed to '%s'\n", old, new );
}
```

Output

```
File 'RENAMER.OBJ' renamed to 'RENAMER.JBO'
```

rewind

Repositions the file pointer to the beginning of a file.

void rewind(FILE **stream* **);**

Routine	Required Header	Compatibility
rewind	<stdio.h>	ANSI, Win 95, Win NT

For additional compatibility information, see "Compatibility" in the Introduction.

Libraries

LIBC.LIB	Single thread static library, retail version
LIBCMT.LIB	Multithread static library, retail version
MSVCRT.LIB	Import library for MSVCRT.DLL, retail version

Return Value

None

Parameter

stream
    Pointer to **FILE** structure

Remarks

The **rewind** function repositions the file pointer associated with *stream* to the beginning of the file. A call to **rewind** is similar to

(void) fseek(*stream*, **0L, SEEK_SET);**

However, unlike **fseek**, **rewind** clears the error indicators for the stream as well as the end-of-file indicator. Also, unlike **fseek**, **rewind** does not return a value to indicate whether the pointer was successfully moved.

To clear the keyboard buffer, use **rewind** with the stream **stdin**, which is associated with the keyboard by default.

Example

```
/* REWIND.C: This program first opens a file named
 * REWIND.OUT for input and output and writes two
 * integers to the file. Next, it uses rewind to
 * reposition the file pointer to the beginning of
 * the file and reads the data back in.
 */

#include <stdio.h>

void main( void )
{
    FILE *stream;
    int data1, data2;

    data1 = 1;
    data2 = -37;

    if( (stream = fopen( "rewind.out", "w+" )) != NULL )
    {
        fprintf( stream, "%d %d", data1, data2 );
        printf( "The values written are: %d and %d\n", data1, data2 );
        rewind( stream );
        fscanf( stream, "%d %d", &data1, &data2 );
        printf( "The values read are: %d and %d\n", data1, data2 );
        fclose( stream );
    }
}
```

Output

```
The values written are: 1 and -37
The values read are: 1 and -37
```

_rmdir, _wrmdir

Delete a directory.

int _rmdir(const char *dirname* **);**
int _wrmdir(const wchar_t *dirname* **);**

Routine	Required Header	Compatibility
_rmdir	<direct.h>	Win 95, Win NT
_wrmdir	<direct.h> or <wchar.h>	Win NT

For additional compatibility information, see "Compatibility" in the Introduction.

Libraries

LIBC.LIB	Single thread static library, retail version
LIBCMT.LIB	Multithread static library, retail version
MSVCRT.LIB	Import library for MSVCRT.DLL, retail version

Return Value

Each of these functions returns 0 if the directory is successfully deleted. A return value of –1 indicates an error, and **errno** is set to one of the following values:

ENOTEMPTY
Given path is not a directory; directory is not empty; or directory is either current working directory or root directory.

ENOENT
Path is invalid.

Parameter

dirname
Path of directory to be removed

Remarks

The **_rmdir** function deletes the directory specified by *dirname*. The directory must be empty, and it must not be the current working directory or the root directory.

_wrmdir is a wide-character version of **_rmdir**; the *dirname* argument to **_wrmdir** is a wide-character string. **_wrmdir** and **_rmdir** behave identically otherwise.

Generic-Text Routine Mappings

TCHAR.H Routine	_UNICODE & _MBCS Not Defined	_MBCS Defined	_UNICODE Defined
_trmdir	_rmdir	_rmdir	_wrmdir

Example

```
/* MAKEDIR.C */

#include <direct.h>
#include <stdlib.h>
#include <stdio.h>

void main( void )
{
   if( _mkdir( "\\testtmp" ) == 0 )
   {
      printf( "Directory '\\testtmp' was successfully created\n" );
      system( "dir \\testtmp" );
      if( _rmdir( "\\testtmp" ) == 0 )
         printf( "Directory '\\testtmp' was successfully removed\n"  );
      else
         printf( "Problem removing directory '\\testtmp'\n" );
   }
   else
      printf( "Problem creating directory '\\testtmp'\n" );
}
```

Output

```
Directory '\testtmp' was successfully created
    Volume in drive C is CDRIVE
    Volume Serial Number is 0E17-1702

Directory of C:\testtmp

05/03/94  12:30p        <DIR>          .
05/03/94  12:30p        <DIR>          ..
             2 File(s)           0 bytes
                     17,358,848 bytes free
Directory '\testtmp' was successfully removed
```

See Also

_chdir, **_mkdir**

_rmtmp

Removes temporary files.

int _rmtmp(void);

Routine	Required Header	Compatibility
_rmtmp	<stdio.h>	Win 95, Win NT

For additional compatibility information, see "Compatibility" in the Introduction.

Libraries

LIBC.LIB	Single thread static library, retail version
LIBCMT.LIB	Multithread static library, retail version
MSVCRT.LIB	Import library for MSVCRT.DLL, retail version

Return Value

_rmtmp returns the number of temporary files closed and deleted.

Remarks

The **_rmtmp** function cleans up all temporary files in the current directory. The function removes only those files created by **tmpfile**; use it only in the same directory in which the temporary files were created.

Example

```
/* TMPFILE.C: This program uses tmpfile to create a
 * temporary file, then deletes this file with _rmtmp.
 */

#include <stdio.h>

void main( void )
{
   FILE *stream;
   char tempstring[] = "String to be written";
   int  i;

   /* Create temporary files. */
   for( i = 1; i <= 3; i++ )
   {
      if( (stream = tmpfile()) == NULL )
         perror( "Could not open new temporary file\n" );
      else
         printf( "Temporary file %d was created\n", i );
   }
```

```
    /* Remove temporary files. */
    printf( "%d temporary files deleted\n", _rmtmp() );
}
```

Output

```
Temporary file 1 was created
Temporary file 2 was created
Temporary file 3 was created
3 temporary files deleted
```

See Also

_flushall, **tmpfile**, **tmpnam**

_rotl, _rotr

Rotate bits to the left (_rotl) or right (_rotr).

unsigned int _rotl(unsigned int *value***, int** *shift* **);**
unsigned int _rotr(unsigned int *value***, int** *shift* **);**

Routine	Required Header	Compatibility
_rotl	<stdlib.h>	Win 95, Win NT
_rotr	<stdlib.h>	Win 95, Win NT

For additional compatibility information, see "Compatibility" in the Introduction.

Libraries

LIBC.LIB	Single thread static library, retail version
LIBCMT.LIB	Multithread static library, retail version
MSVCRT.LIB	Import library for MSVCRT.DLL, retail version

Return Value

Both functions return the rotated value. There is no error return.

Parameters

value
Value to be rotated

shift
Number of bits to shift

Remarks

The **_rotl** and **_rotr** functions rotate the unsigned *value* by *shift* bits. **_rotl** rotates the value left. **_rotr** rotates the value right. Both functions "wrap" bits rotated off one end of *value* to the other end.

Example

```
/* ROT.C: This program uses _rotr and _rotl with
 * different shift values to rotate an integer.
 */

#include <stdlib.h>
#include <stdio.h>

void main( void )
{
   unsigned val = 0x0fd93;
   printf( "0x%4.4x rotated left three times is 0x%4.4x\n",
           val, _rotl( val, 3 ) );
   printf( "0x%4.4x rotated right four times is 0x%4.4x\n",
           val, _rotr( val, 4 ) );
}
```

Output

```
0xfd93 rotated left three times is 0x7ec98
0xfd93 rotated right four times is 0x30000fd9
```

See Also

_lrotl

_scalb

Scales argument by a power of 2.

double _scalb(double *x*, long *exp*);

Routine	Required Header	Compatibility
_scalb	<float.h>	Win 95, Win NT

For additional compatibility information, see "Compatibility" in the Introduction.

Libraries

LIBC.LIB	Single thread static library, retail version
LIBCMT.LIB	Multithread static library, retail version
MSVCRT.LIB	Import library for MSVCRT.DLL, retail version

Return Value

_scalb returns an exponential value if successful. On overflow (depending on the sign of *x*), **_scalb** returns +/– **HUGE_VAL**; the **errno** variable is set to **ERANGE**.

Parameters

x

   Double-precision floating-point value

exp

   Long integer exponent

Remarks

The **_scalb** function calculates the value of $x * 2^{exp}$.

See Also

ldexp

scanf, wscanf

Read formatted data from the standard input stream.

int scanf(const char ***format** [,*argument*]...);
int wscanf(const wchar_t ***format** [,*argument*]...);

Routine	Required Header	Compatibility
scanf	<stdio.h>	ANSI, Win 95, Win NT
wscanf	<stdio.h> or <wchar.h>	ANSI, Win 95, Win NT

For additional compatibility information, see "Compatibility" in the Introduction.

Libraries

LIBC.LIB	Single thread static library, retail version
LIBCMT.LIB	Multithread static library, retail version
MSVCRT.LIB	Import library for MSVCRT.DLL, retail version

Return Value

Both **scanf** and **wscanf** return the number of fields successfully converted and assigned; the return value does not include fields that were read but not assigned. A return value of 0 indicates that no fields were assigned. The return value is **EOF** for an error or if the end of-file character or the end-of-string character is encountered in the first attempt to read a character.

Parameters

format
> Format control string

argument
> Optional arguments

Remarks

The **scanf** function reads data from the standard input stream **stdin** and writes the data into the location given by *argument*. Each *argument* must be a pointer to a variable of a type that corresponds to a type specifier in *format*. If copying takes place between strings that overlap, the behavior is undefined.

wscanf is a wide-character version of **scanf**; the *format* argument to **wscanf** is a wide-character string. **wscanf** and **scanf** behave identically otherwise.

Generic-Text Routine Mappings

TCHAR.H Routine	_UNICODE & _MBCS Not Defined	_MBCS Defined	_UNICODE Defined
_tscanf	scanf	scanf	wscanf

For more information, see "Format Specification Fields: scanf and wscanf Functions."

Example

```
/* SCANF.C: This program uses the scanf and wscanf functions
 * to read formatted input.
 */

#include <stdio.h>

void main( void )
{
   int   i, result;
   float fp;
   char  c, s[81];
   wchar_t wc, ws[81];

   printf( "\n\nEnter an int, a float, two chars and two strings\n");

   result = scanf( "%d %f %c %C %s %S", &i, &fp, &c, &wc, s, ws );
   printf( "\nThe number of fields input is %d\n", result );
   printf( "The contents are: %d %f %c %C %s %S\n", i, fp, c, wc, s, ws);

   wprintf( L"\n\nEnter an int, a float, two chars and two strings\n");

   result = wscanf( L"%d %f %hc %lc %S %ls", &i, &fp, &c, &wc, s, ws );
   wprintf( L"\nThe number of fields input is %d\n", result );
   wprintf( L"The contents are: %d %f %C %c %hs %s\n", i, fp, c, wc, s, ws);
}
```

Output

```
Enter an int, a float, two chars and two strings
71
98.6
h
z
Byte characters

The number of fields input is 6
The contents are: 71 98.599998 h z Byte characters

Enter an int, a float, two chars and two strings
36
92.3
y
n
Wide characters

The number of fields input is 6
The contents are: 456 92.300003 y n Wide characters
```

See Also

fscanf, printf, sprintf, sscanf

Format Specification Fields: scanf and wscanf Functions

A format specification has the following form:

%[*] [width] [{**h** | **l** | **I64** | **L**}]type

The *format* argument specifies the interpretation of the input and can contain one or more of the following:

- White-space characters: blank (' '); tab ('\t'); or newline ('\n'). A white-space character causes **scanf** to read, but not store, all consecutive white-space characters in the input up to the next non–white-space character. One white-space character in the format matches any number (including 0) and combination of white-space characters in the input.

- Non–white-space characters, except for the percent sign (%). A non–white-space character causes **scanf** to read, but not store, a matching non–white-space character. If the next character in **stdin** does not match, **scanf** terminates.

- Format specifications, introduced by the percent sign (%). A format specification causes **scanf** to read and convert characters in the input into values of a specified type. The value is assigned to an argument in the argument list.

The format is read from left to right. Characters outside format specifications are expected to match the sequence of characters in **stdin**; the matching characters in **stdin** are scanned but not stored. If a character in **stdin** conflicts with the format specification, **scanf** terminates, and the character is left in **stdin** as if it had not been read.

When the first format specification is encountered, the value of the first input field is converted according to this specification and stored in the location that is specified by the first *argument*. The second format specification causes the second input field to be converted and stored in the second *argument*, and so on through the end of the format string.

An input field is defined as all characters up to the first white-space character (space, tab, or newline), or up to the first character that cannot be converted according to the format specification, or until the field width (if specified) is reached. If there are too many arguments for the given specifications, the extra arguments are evaluated but ignored. The results are unpredictable if there are not enough arguments for the format specification.

Each field of the format specification is a single character or a number signifying a particular format option. The *type* character, which appears after the last optional format field, determines whether the input field is interpreted as a character, a string, or a number.

The simplest format specification contains only the percent sign and a *type* character (for example, %s). If a percent sign (%) is followed by a character that has no meaning as a format-control character, that character and the following characters (up to the next percent sign) are treated as an ordinary sequence of characters, that is, a sequence of characters that must match the input. For example, to specify that a percent-sign character is to be input, use %%.

An asterisk (*) following the percent sign suppresses assignment of the next input field, which is interpreted as a field of the specified type. The field is scanned but not stored.

scanf Width Specification

width is a positive decimal integer controlling the maximum number of characters to be read from **stdin**. No more than *width* characters are converted and stored at the corresponding *argument*. Fewer than *width* characters may be read if a white-space character (space, tab, or newline) or a character that cannot be converted according to the given format occurs before *width* is reached.

The optional prefixes **h, l, I64**, and **L** indicate the "size" of the *argument* (long or short, single-byte character or wide character, depending upon the type character that they modify). These format-specification characters are used with type characters in **scanf** or **wscanf** functions to specify interpretation of arguments as shown in Table R.7. The type prefixes **h, l, I64**, and **L** are Microsoft extensions and are not ANSI-compatible. The type characters and their meanings are described in Table R.8.

Table R.7 Size Prefixes for scanf and wscanf Format-Type Specifiers

To Specify	Use Prefix	With Type Specifier
double	l	e, E, f, g, or G
long int	l	d, i, o, x, or X
long unsigned int	l	u
short int	h	d, i, o, x, or X
short unsigned int	h	u
__int64	I64	d, i, o, u, x, or X
Single-byte character with **scanf**	h	c or C
Single-byte character with **wscanf**	h	c or C
Wide character with **scanf**	l	c or C
Wide character with **wscanf**	l	c, or C
Single-byte–character string with **scanf**	h	s or S
Single-byte–character string with **wscanf**	h	s or S
Wide-character string with **scanf**	l	s or S
Wide-character string with **wscanf**	l	s or S

Following are examples of the use of **h** and **l** with **scanf** functions and **wscanf** functions:

```
scanf( "%ls", &x );    // Read a wide-character string
wscanf( "%lC", &x );    // Read a single-byte character
```

To read strings not delimited by space characters, a set of characters in brackets ([ ]) can be substituted for the **s** (string) type character. The corresponding input field is read up to the first character that does not appear in the bracketed character set. If the first character in the set is a caret (^), the effect is reversed: The input field is read up to the first character that does appear in the rest of the character set.

Note that %[a-z] and %[z-a] are interpreted as equivalent to %[abcde...z]. This is a common **scanf** function extension, but note that the ANSI standard does not require it.

To store a string without storing a terminating null character ('\0'), use the specification %*nc* where *n* is a decimal integer. In this case, the **c** type character indicates that the argument is a pointer to a character array. The next *n* characters are read from the input stream into the specified location, and no null character ('\0') is appended. If *n* is not specified, its default value is 1.

The **scanf** function scans each input field, character by character. It may stop reading a particular input field before it reaches a space character for a variety of reasons:

- The specified width has been reached.

- The next character cannot be converted as specified.

- The next character conflicts with a character in the control string that it is supposed to match.

- The next character fails to appear in a given character set.

For whatever reason, when the **scanf** function stops reading an input field, the next input field is considered to begin at the first unread character. The conflicting character, if there is one, is considered unread and is the first character of the next input field or the first character in subsequent read operations on **stdin**.

scanf Type Field Characters

The *type* character is the only required format field; it appears after any optional format fields. The *type* character determines whether the associated argument is interpreted as a character, string, or number.

Table R.8 Type Characters for scanf functions

Character	Type of Input Expected	Type of Argument
c	When used with **scanf** functions, specifies single-byte character; when used with **wscanf** functions, specifies wide character. White-space characters that are ordinarily skipped are read when **c** is specified. To read next non–white-space single-byte character, use %**1s**; to read next non–white-space wide character, use %**1ws**.	Pointer to **char** when used with **scanf** functions, pointer to **wchar_t** when used with **wscanf** functions.
C	When used with **scanf** functions, specifies wide character; when used with **wscanf** functions, specifies single-byte character. White-space characters that are ordinarily skipped are read when **C** is specified. To read next non–white-space single-byte character, use %**1s**; to read next non–white-space wide character, use %**1ws**.	Pointer to **wchar_t** when used with **scanf** functions, pointer to **char** when used with **wscanf** functions.
d	Decimal integer.	Pointer to **int**.
I	Decimal, hexadecimal, or octal integer.	Pointer to **int**.
o	Octal integer.	Pointer to **int**.

Table R.8 Type Characters for scanf functions *(continued)*

Character	Type of Input Expected	Type of Argument
u	Unsigned decimal integer.	Pointer to **unsigned int**.
x	Hexadecimal integer.	Pointer to **int**.
e, E, f, g, G	Floating-point value consisting of optional sign (+ or –), series of one or more decimal digits containing decimal point, and optional exponent ("e" or "E") followed by an optionally signed integer value.	Pointer to **float**.
n	No input read from stream or buffer.	Pointer to **int**, into which is stored number of characters successfully read from stream or buffer up to that point in current call to **scanf** functions or **wscanf** functions.
s	String, up to first white-space character (space, tab or newline). To read strings not delimited by space characters, use set of square brackets ([ ]), as discussed following Table R.7.	When used with **scanf** functions, signifies single-byte character array; when used with **wscanf** functions, signifies wide-character array. In either case, character array must be large enough for input field plus terminating null character, which is automatically appended.
S	String, up to first white-space character (space, tab or newline). To read strings not delimited by space characters, use set of square brackets ([ ]), as discussed preceding this table.	When used with **scanf** functions, signifies wide-character array; when used with **wscanf** functions, signifies single-byte–character array. In either case, character array must be large enough for input field plus terminating null character, which is automatically appended.

The types **c**, **C**, **s**, and **S** are Microsoft extensions and are not ANSI-compatible.

Thus, to read single-byte or wide characters with **scanf** functions and **wscanf** functions, use format specifiers as follows.

To Read Character As	Use This Function	With These Format Specifiers
single byte	**scanf** functions	**c**, **hc**, or **hC**
single byte	**wscanf** functions	**C**, **hc**, or **hC**
wide	**wscanf** functions	**c**, **lc**, or **lC**
wide	**scanf** functions	**C**, **lc**, or **lC**

To scan strings with **scanf** functions, and **wscanf** functions, use the prefixes **h** and **l** analogously with format type-specifiers **s** and **S**.

_searchenv, _wsearchenv

Searches for a file using environment paths.

void _searchenv(const char *filename*, **const char** *varname*, **char** *pathname* **);**
void _wsearchenv(const wchar_t *filename*, **const wchar_t** *varname*, **wchar_t** *pathname* **);**

Routine	Required Header	Compatibility
_searchenv	<stdlib.h>	Win 95, Win NT
_wsearchenv	<stdlib.h> or <wchar.h>	Win NT

For additional compatibility information, see "Compatibility" in the Introduction.

Libraries

LIBC.LIB	Single thread static library, retail version
LIBCMT.LIB	Multithread static library, retail version
MSVCRT.LIB	Import library for MSVCRT.DLL, retail version

Return Value

None

Parameters

filename
   Name of file to search for

varname
   Environment to search

pathname
   Buffer to store complete path

Remarks

The **_searchenv** routine searches for the target file in the specified domain. The *varname* variable can be any environment or user-defined variable that specifies a list of directory paths, such as **PATH**, **LIB**, and **INCLUDE**. **_searchenv** is case sensitive, so *varname* should match the case of the environment variable.

The routine searches first for the file in the current working directory. If it does not find the file, it looks next through the directories specified by the environment variable. If the target file is in one of those directories, the newly created path is copied into *pathname*. If the *filename* file is not found, *pathname* contains an empty, null-terminated string.

The *pathname* buffer must be large enough to accomodate the full length of the constructed path name. Otherwise, **_searchenv** will overwite the *pathname* buffer resulting in unexpected behavior. This condition can be avoided by ensuring that the length of the constructed path name does not exceed the size of the *pathname* buffer, by calculating the maximum sum of the *filename* and *varname* lengths before calling **_searchenv**.

_wsearchenv is a wide-character version of **_searchenv**; the arguments to **_wsearchenv** are wide-character strings. **_wsearchenv** and **_searchenv** behave identically otherwise.

Generic-Text Routine Mappings

TCHAR.H Routine	_UNICODE & _MBCS Not Defined	_MBCS Defined	_UNICODE Defined
_tsearchenv	_searchenv	_searchenv	_wsearchenv

Example

```
/* SEARCHEN.C: This program searches for a file in
 * a directory specified by an environment variable.
 */

#include <stdlib.h>
#include <stdio.h>

void main( void )
{
   char pathbuffer[_MAX_PATH];
   char searchfile[] = "CL.EXE";
   char envvar[] = "PATH";

   /* Search for file in PATH environment variable: */
   _searchenv( searchfile, envvar, pathbuffer );
   if( *pathbuffer != '\0' )
      printf( "Path for %s: %s\n", searchfile, pathbuffer );
   else
      printf( "%s not found\n", searchfile );
}
```

Output

```
Path for CL.EXE: C:\msvcnt\c32\bin\CL.EXE
```

See Also

getenv, _putenv

setbuf

Controls stream buffering.

void setbuf(FILE **stream*, **char** **buffer* **);**

Routine	Required Header	Compatibility
setbuf	<stdio.h>	ANSI, Win 95, Win NT

For additional compatibility information, see "Compatibility" in the Introduction.

Libraries

LIBC.LIB	Single thread static library, retail version
LIBCMT.LIB	Multithread static library, retail version
MSVCRT.LIB	Import library for MSVCRT.DLL, retail version

Return Value

None

Parameters

stream
    Pointer to **FILE** structure

buffer
    User-allocated buffer

Remarks

The **setbuf** function controls buffering for *stream*. The *stream* argument must refer to an open file that has not been read or written. If the *buffer* argument is **NULL**, the stream is unbuffered. If not, the buffer must point to a character array of length **BUFSIZ**, where **BUFSIZ** is the buffer size as defined in STDIO.H. The user-specified buffer, instead of the default system-allocated buffer for the given stream, is used for I/O buffering. The **stderr** stream is unbuffered by default, but you can use **setbuf** to assign buffers to **stderr**.

setbuf has been replaced by setvbuf, which is the preferred routine for new code. **setbuf** is retained for compatibility with existing code.

Example

```
/* SETBUF.C: This program first opens files named DATA1 and
 * DATA2. Then it uses setbuf to give DATA1 a user-assigned
 * buffer and to change DATA2 so that it has no buffer.
 */
```

```
#include <stdio.h>

void main( void )
{
   char buf[BUFSIZ];
   FILE *stream1, *stream2;

   if( ((stream1 = fopen( "data1", "a" )) != NULL) &&
       ((stream2 = fopen( "data2", "w" )) != NULL) )
   {
      /* "stream1" uses user-assigned buffer: */
      setbuf( stream1, buf );
      printf( "stream1 set to user-defined buffer at: %Fp\n", buf );

      /* "stream2" is unbuffered              */
      setbuf( stream2, NULL );
      printf( "stream2 buffering disabled\n" );
      _fcloseall();
   }
}
```

Output

```
stream1 set to user-defined buffer at: 0013FDA0
stream2 buffering disabled
```

See Also

fclose, fflush, fopen, setvbuf

setjmp

Saves the current state of the program.

int setjmp(jmp_buf *env* **);**

Routine	Required Header	Compatibility
setjmp	<setjmp.h>	ANSI, Win 95, Win NT

For additional compatibility information, see "Compatibility" in the Introduction.

Libraries

LIBC.LIB	Single thread static library, retail version
LIBCMT.LIB	Multithread static library, retail version
MSVCRT.LIB	Import library for MSVCRT.DLL, retail version

Return Value

setjmp returns 0 after saving the stack environment. If **setjmp** returns as a result of a **longjmp** call, it returns the *value* argument of **longjmp,** or if the *value* argument of **longjmp** is 0, **setjmp** returns 1. There is no error return.

Parameter

env
　　Variable in which environment is stored

Remarks

The **setjmp** function saves a stack environment, which you can subsequently restore using **longjmp**. When used together, **setjmp** and **longjmp** provide a way to execute a "non-local goto." They are typically used to pass execution control to error-handling or recovery code in a previously called routine without using the normal calling or return conventions.

A call to **setjmp** saves the current stack environment in *env*. A subsequent call to **longjmp** restores the saved environment and returns control to the point just after the corresponding **setjmp** call. All variables (except register variables) accessible to the routine receiving control contain the values they had when **longjmp** was called.

setjmp and **longjmp** do not support C++ object semantics. In C++ programs, use the C++ exception-handling mechanism.

Example

```
/* FPRESET.C: This program uses signal to set up a
 * routine for handling floating-point errors.
 */

#include <stdio.h>
#include <signal.h>
#include <setjmp.h>
#include <stdlib.h>
#include <float.h>
#include <math.h>
#include <string.h>

jmp_buf mark;               /* Address for long jump to jump to */
int     fperr;              /* Global error number */

void __cdecl fphandler( int sig, int num );   /* Prototypes */
void fpcheck( void );
```

```
void main( void )
{
    double n1, n2, r;
    int jmpret;
    /* Unmask all floating-point exceptions. */
    _control87( 0, _MCW_EM );
    /* Set up floating-point error handler. The compiler
     * will generate a warning because it expects
     * signal-handling functions to take only one argument.
     */
    if( signal( SIGFPE, fphandler ) == SIG_ERR )
    {
        fprintf( stderr, "Couldn't set SIGFPE\n" );
        abort();    }

    /* Save stack environment for return in case of error. First
     * time through, jmpret is 0, so true conditional is executed.
     * If an error occurs, jmpret will be set to -1 and false
     * conditional will be executed.
     */
    jmpret = setjmp( mark );
    if( jmpret == 0 )
    {
        printf( "Test for invalid operation - " );
        printf( "enter two numbers: " );
        scanf( "%lf %lf", &n1, &n2 );
        r = n1 / n2;
        /* This won't be reached if error occurs. */
        printf( "\n\n%4.3g / %4.3g = %4.3g\n", n1, n2, r );

        r = n1 * n2;
        /* This won't be reached if error occurs. */
        printf( "\n\n%4.3g * %4.3g = %4.3g\n", n1, n2, r );
    }
    else
        fpcheck();
}


/* fphandler handles SIGFPE (floating-point error) interrupt. Note
 * that this prototype accepts two arguments and that the
 * prototype for signal in the run-time library expects a signal
 * handler to have only one argument.
 *
 * The second argument in this signal handler allows processing of
 * _FPE_INVALID, _FPE_OVERFLOW, _FPE_UNDERFLOW, and
 * _FPE_ZERODIVIDE, all of which are Microsoft-specific symbols
 * that augment the information provided by SIGFPE. The compiler
 * will generate a warning, which is harmless and expected.
 */
```

```
void fphandler( int sig, int num )
{
    /* Set global for outside check since we don't want
     * to do I/O in the handler.
     */
    fperr = num;
    /* Initialize floating-point package. */
    _fpreset();
    /* Restore calling environment and jump back to setjmp. Return
     * -1 so that setjmp will return false for conditional test.
     */
    longjmp( mark, -1 );
}
void fpcheck( void )
{
    char fpstr[30];
    switch( fperr )
    {
    case _FPE_INVALID:
        strcpy( fpstr, "Invalid number" );
        break;
    case _FPE_OVERFLOW:
        strcpy( fpstr, "Overflow" );

        break;
    case _FPE_UNDERFLOW:
        strcpy( fpstr, "Underflow" );
        break;
    case _FPE_ZERODIVIDE:
        strcpy( fpstr, "Divide by zero" );
        break;
    default:
        strcpy( fpstr, "Other floating point error" );
        break;
    }
    printf( "Error %d: %s\n", fperr, fpstr );
}
```

Output

```
Test for invalid operation - enter two numbers: 5 0
Error 131: Divide by zero
```

See Also

longjmp

setlocale, _wsetlocale

Define the locale.

char *setlocale(int *category*, **const char ****locale* **);**
wchar_t *_wsetlocale(int *category*, **const wchar_t ****locale* **);**

Routine	Required Header	Compatibility
setlocale	<locale.h>	ANSI, Win 95, Win NT
_wsetlocale	<locale.h> or <wchar.h>	Win 95, Win NT

For additional compatibility information, see "Compatibility" in the Introduction.

Libraries

LIBC.LIB	Single thread static library, retail version
LIBCMT.LIB	Multithread static library, retail version
MSVCRT.LIB	Import library for MSVCRT.DLL, retail version

Return Value

If a valid locale and category are given, the function returns a pointer to the string associated with the specified locale and category. If the locale or category is invalid, the function returns a null pointer and the current locale settings of the program are not changed.

For example, the call

```
setlocale( LC_ALL, "English" );
```

sets all categories, returning only the string `English_USA.1252`. If all categories are not explicitly set by a call to **setlocale**, the function returns a string indicating the current setting of each of the categories, separated by semicolons. If the *locale* argument is a null pointer, **setlocale** returns a pointer to the string associated with the *category* of the program's locale; the program's current locale setting is not changed.

The null pointer is a special directive that tells **setlocale** to query rather than set the international environment. For example, the sequence of calls

```
// Set all categories and return "English_USA.1252"
setlocale( LC_ALL, "English" );
// Set only the LC_MONETARY category and return "French_France.1252"
setlocale( LC_MONETARY, "French" );
setlocale( LC_ALL, NULL );
```

returns

```
LC_COLLATE=English_USA.1252;
LC_CTYPE=English_USA.1252;
LC_MONETARY=French_France.1252;
LC_NUMERIC=English_USA.1252;
LC_TIME=English_USA.1252
```

which is the string associated with the **LC_ALL** category.

You can use the string pointer returned by **setlocale** in subsequent calls to restore that part of the program's locale information, assuming that your program does not alter the pointer or the string. Later calls to **setlocale** overwrite the string; you can use _strdup to save a specific locale string.

Parameters

category
   Category affected by locale

locale
   Locale name

Remarks

Use the **setlocale** function to set, change, or query some or all of the current program locale information specified by *locale* and *category*. "Locale" refers to the locality (country and language) for which you can customize certain aspects of your program. Some locale-dependent categories include the formatting of dates and the display format for monetary values.

_wsetlocale is a wide-character version of **setlocale**; the *locale* argument and return value of **_wsetlocale** are wide-character strings. **_wsetlocale** and **setlocale** behave identically otherwise.

Generic-Text Routine Mappings

TCHAR.H Routine	_UNICODE & _MBCS Not Defined	_MBCS Defined	_UNICODE Defined
_tsetlocale	setlocale	setlocale	_wsetlocale

The *category* argument specifies the parts of a program's locale information that are affected. The macros used for *category* and the parts of the program they affect are as follows:

LC_ALL
   All categories, as listed below

LC_COLLATE
   The **strcoll, _stricoll, wcscoll, _wcsicoll,** and **strxfrm** functions

LC_CTYPE

> The character-handling functions (except **isdigit**, **isxdigit**, **mbstowcs**, and **mbtowc**, which are unaffected)

LC_MONETARY

> Monetary-formatting information returned by the **localeconv** function

LC_NUMERIC

> Decimal-point character for the formatted output routines (such as **printf**), for the data-conversion routines, and for the nonmonetary-formatting information returned by **localeconv**

LC_TIME

> The **strftime** and **wcsftime** functions

The *locale* argument is a pointer to a string that specifies the name of the locale. If *locale* points to an empty string, the locale is the implementation-defined native environment. A value of "C" specifies the minimal ANSI conforming environment for C translation. The "C" locale assumes that all **char** data types are 1 byte and that their value is always less than 256. The "C" locale is the only locale supported in Microsoft Visual C++ version 1.0 and earlier versions of Microsoft C/C++. Microsoft Visual C++ supports all the locales listed in Appendix A, "Language and Country Strings." At program startup, the equivalent of the following statement is executed:

```
setlocale( LC_ALL, "C" );
```

The *locale* argument takes the following form:

```
locale :: "lang[_country[.code_page]]"
          | ".code_page"
          | ""
          | NULL
```

The set of available languages, countries, and code pages includes all those supported by the Win32 NLS API. The set of language and country codes supported by **setlocale** is listed in Appendix A, "Language and Country Strings."

If *locale* is a null pointer, **setlocale** queries, rather than sets, the international environment, and returns a pointer to the string associated with the specified *category*. The program's current locale setting is not changed. For example,

```
setlocale( LC_ALL, NULL );
```

returns the string associated with *category*.

The following examples pertain to the **LC_ALL** category. Either of the strings ".OCP" and ".ACP" can be used in place of a code page number to specify use of the system default OEM code page and system-default ANSI code page, respectively.

```
setlocale( LC_ALL, "" );
```
Sets the locale to the default, which is the system-default ANSI code page obtained from the operating system.

```
setlocale( LC_ALL, ".OCP" );
```
Explicitly sets the locale to the current OEM code page obtained from the operating system.

```
setlocale( LC_ALL, ".ACP" );
```
Sets the locale to the ANSI code page obtained from the operating system.

```
setlocale( LC_ALL, "[lang_ctry]" );
```
Sets the locale to the language and country indicated, using the default code page obtained from the host operating system.

```
setlocale( LC_ALL, "[lang_ctry.cp]" );
```
Sets the locale to the language, country, and code page indicated in the [*lang_ctry.cp*] string. You can use various combinations of language, country, and code page. For example:

```
    setlocale( LC_ALL, "French_Canada.1252" );
    // Set code page to French Canada ANSI default
    setlocale( LC_ALL, "French_Canada.ACP" );
    // Set code page to French Canada OEM default
    setlocale( LC_ALL, "French_Canada.OCP" );
```

```
setlocale( LC_ALL, "[lang]" );
```
Sets the locale to the country indicated, using the default country for the language specified, and the system-default ANSI code page for that country as obtained from the host operating system. For example, the following two calls to **setlocale** are functionally equivalent:

```
    setlocale( LC_ALL, "English" );
    setlocale( LC_ALL, "English_United States.1252" );
```

```
setlocale( LC_ALL, "[.code_page]" );
```
Sets the code page to the value indicated, using the default country and language (as defined by the host operating system) for the specified code page.

The category must be either **LC_ALL** or **LC_CTYPE** to effect a change of code page. For example, if the default country and language of the host operating system are "United States" and "English," the following two calls to **setlocale** are functionally equivalent:

```
setlocale( LC_ALL, ".1252" );
setlocale( LC_ALL, "English_United States.1252");
```

For more information see the "setlocale pragma" in the *Preprocessor Reference* online.

Example

```
/* LOCALE.C: Sets the current locale to "Germany" using the
 * setlocale function and demonstrates its effect on the strftime
 * function.
 */

#include <stdio.h>
#include <locale.h>
#include <time.h>

void main(void)
{
      time_t ltime;
      struct tm *thetime;
      unsigned char str[100];

      setlocale(LC_ALL, "German");
      time (&ltime);
      thetime = gmtime(&ltime);

      /* %#x is the long date representation, appropriate to
       * the current locale
       */
      if (!strftime((char *)str, 100, "%#x",
          (const struct tm *)thetime))
        printf("strftime failed!\n");
      else
        printf("In German locale, strftime returns '%s'\n", str);

      /* Set the locale back to the default environment */
      setlocale(LC_ALL, "C");
      time (&ltime);
      thetime = gmtime(&ltime);

      if (!strftime((char *)str, 100, "%#x",
          (const struct tm *)thetime))
        printf("strftime failed!\n");
      else
        printf("In 'C' locale, strftime returns '%s'\n", str);
}
```

Output

```
In German locale, strftime returns 'Donnerstag, 22. April 1993'
In 'C' locale, strftime returns 'Thursday, April 22, 1993'
```

See Also

localeconv, mblen, _mbstrlen, mbstowcs, mbtowc, strcoll Functions, strftime, strxfrm, wcstombs, wctomb

_setmaxstdio

Sets a maximum for the number of simultaneously open files at the stdio level.

int _setmaxstdio(int *newmax* **);**

Routine	Required Header	Compatibility
_setmaxstdio	<stdio.h>	Win 95, Win NT

For additional compatibility information, see "Compatibility" in the Introduction.

Libraries

LIBC.LIB	Single thread static library, retail version
LIBCMT.LIB	Multithread static library, retail version
MSVCRT.LIB	Import library for MSVCRT.DLL, retail version

Return Value

Returns *newmax* if successful; –1 otherwise.

Parameter

newmax
    New maximum for number of simultaneously open files at the **stdio** level

Remarks

The **_setmaxstdio** function changes the maximum value for the number of files which may be simultaneously open at the stdio level.

C run-time I/O now supports many more open files on Win32 platforms than in previous versions. Up to 2,048 files may be open simultaneously at the lowio level (that is, opened and accessed by means of the **_open**, **_read**, **_write**, and so forth family of I/O functions). Up to 512 files may be open simultaneously at the stdio level (that is, opened and accessed by means of the **fopen**, **fgetc**, **fputc**, and so forth family of functions). The limit of 512 open files at the stdio level may be increased to a maximum of 2,048 by means of the **_setmaxstdio** function.

Since stdio level functions, such as **fopen**, are built on top of the lowio functions, the maximum of 2,048 is a hard upper limit for the number of simultaneously open files accessed through the C run-time library.

> **Note** This upper limit may be beyond what is supported by a particular Win32 platform and configuration. For example, Win32s only supports 255 open files.

_setmbcp

Sets a new multibyte code page.

int _setmbcp(int *codepage* **);**

Routine	Required Header	Compatibility
_setmbcp	<mbctype.h>	Win 95, Win NT

For additional compatibility information, see "Compatibility" in the Introduction.

Libraries

LIBC.LIB	Single thread static library, retail version
LIBCMT.LIB	Multithread static library, retail version
MSVCRT.LIB	Import library for MSVCRT.DLL, retail version

Return Value

_setmbcp returns 0 if the code page is set successfully. If an invalid code page value is supplied for *codepage*, the function returns –1 and the code page setting is unchanged.

Parameter

codepage
    New code page setting for locale-independent multibyte routines

Remarks

The **_setmbcp** function specifies a new multibyte code page. By default, the run-time system automatically sets the multibyte code page to the system-default ANSI code page. The multibyte code page setting affects all multibyte routines that are not locale-dependent. However, it is possible to instruct **_setmbcp** to use the code page defined for the current locale (see the following list of manifest constants and associated behavior results). For a list of the multibyte routines that are dependent on the locale code page rather than the multibyte code page, see "Interpretation of Multibyte-Character Sequences" in Chapter 1, "Run-Time Routines by Category."

The multibyte code page also affects multibyte-character processing by the following run-time library routines:

_exec functions	_mktemp	_stat
_fullpath	_spawn functions	_tempnam
_makepath	_splitpath	tmpnam

In addition, all run-time library routines that receive multibyte-character *argv* or *envp* program arguments as parameters (such as the **_exec** and **_spawn** families) process these strings according to the multibyte code page. Hence these routines are also affected by a call to **_setmbcp** that changes the multibyte code page.

The *codepage* argument can be set to any of the following values:

- **_MB_CP_ANSI** Use ANSI code page obtained from operating system at program startup

- **_MB_CP_LOCALE** Use the current locale's code page obtained from a previous call to setlocale

- **_MB_CP_OEM** Use OEM code page obtained from operating system at program startup

- **_MB_CP_SBCS** Use single-byte code page. When the code page is set to **_MB_CP_SBCS**, a routine such as _ismbblead always returns false.

- Any other valid code page value, regardless of whether the value is an ANSI, OEM, or other operating-sytem–supported code page.

See Also

_getmbcp, **setlocale**

_setmode

Sets the file translation mode.

int _setmode (int *handle*, **int** *mode* **);**

Routine	Required Header	Optional Headers	Compatibility
_setmode	<io.h>	<fcntl.h>	Win 95, Win NT

For additional compatibility information, see "Compatibility" in the Introduction.

Libraries

LIBC.LIB	Single thread static library, retail version
LIBCMT.LIB	Multithread static library, retail version
MSVCRT.LIB	Import library for MSVCRT.DLL, retail version

Return Value

If successful, **_setmode** returns the previous translation mode. A return value of –1 indicates an error, in which case **errno** is set to either **EBADF**, indicating an invalid file handle, or **EINVAL**, indicating an invalid *mode* argument (neither **_O_TEXT** nor **_O_BINARY**).

Parameters

handle
    File handle

mode
    New translation mode

Remarks

The **_setmode** function sets to *mode* the translation mode of the file given by *handle*. The mode must be one of two manifest constants, **_O_TEXT** or **_O_BINARY**. **_O_TEXT** sets text (translated) mode. Carriage-return–linefeed (CR–LF) combinations are translated into a single linefeed character on input. Linefeed characters are translated into CR–LF combinations on output. **_O_BINARY** sets binary (untranslated) mode, in which these translations are suppressed.

_setmode is typically used to modify the default translation mode of **stdin** and **stdout**, but you can use it on any file. If you apply **_setmode** to the file handle for a stream, call **_setmode** before performing any input or output operations on the stream.

Example

```
/* SETMODE.C: This program uses _setmode to change
 * stdin from text mode to binary mode.
 */

#include <stdio.h>
#include <fcntl.h>
#include <io.h>

void main( void )
{
   int result;

   /* Set "stdin" to have binary mode: */
   result = _setmode( _fileno( stdin ), _O_BINARY );
   if( result == -1 )
      perror( "Cannot set mode" );
   else
      printf( "'stdin' successfully changed to binary mode\n" );
}
```

Output

```
'stdin' successfully changed to binary mode
```

See Also

_creat, fopen, _open

_set_new_handler

Transfer control to your error-handling mechanism if the new operator fails to allocate memory.

_PNH _set_new_handler(_PNH *pNewHandler* **);**

Routine	Required Header	Compatibility
_set_new_handler	<new.h>	Win 95, Win NT

For additional compatibility information, see "Compatibility" in the Introduction.

Libraries

LIBC.LIB	Single thread static library, retail version
LIBCMT.LIB	Multithread static library, retail version
MSVCRT.LIB	Import library for MSVCRT.DLL, retail version

Return Value

_set_new_handler returns a pointer to the previous exception handling function registered by **_set_new_handler**, so that the previous function can be restored later. If no previous function has been set, the return value may be used to restore the default behavior; this value may be NULL.

Parameter

pNewHandler
    Pointer to the application-supplied memory handling function

Remarks

Call the C++ **_set_new_handler** function to specify an exception-handling function that is to gain control if the **new** operator fails to allocate memory. If **new** fails, the run-time system automatically calls the exception-handling function that was passed as an argument to **_set_new_handler**. **_PNH**, defined in NEW.H, is a pointer to a function that returns type **int** and takes an argument of type **size_t**. Use **size_t** to specify the amount of space to be allocated.

_set_new_handler is essentially a garbage-collection scheme. The run-time system retries allocation each time your function returns a nonzero value and fails if your function returns 0.

An occurrence of one of the **_set_new_handler** functions in a program registers the exception-handling function specified in the argument list with the run-time system:

```
#include <new.h>
int handle_program_memory_depletion( size_t )
```

```
{
    // Your code
}
void main( void )
{
    _set_new_handler( handle_program_memory_depletion );
    int *pi = new int[BIG_NUMBER];
}
```

You can save the function address that was last passed to the **_set_new_handler** function and reinstate it later:

```
_PNH old_handler = _set_new_handler( my_handler );
    // Code that requires my_handler
    _set_new_handler( old_handler )
    // Code that requires old_handler
```

The C++ _set_new_mode function sets the new handler mode for malloc. The new handler mode indicates whether, on failure, **malloc** is to call the new handler routine as set by **_set_new_handler**. By default, **malloc** does not call the new handler routine on failure to allocate memory. You can override this default behavior so that, when **malloc** fails to allocate memory, **malloc** calls the new handler routine in the same way that the **new** operator does when it fails for the same reason. To override the default, call

```
_set_new_mode(1)
```

early in your program, or link with NEWMODE.OBJ.

For more information, see **new** and **delete** in the *Language Quick Reference*.

Example

```
/* HANDLER.CPP: This program uses _set_new_handler to
 * print an error message if the new operator fails.
 */

#include <stdio.h>
#include <new.h>

/* Allocate memory in chunks of size MemBlock. */
const size_t MemBlock = 1024;

/* Allocate a memory block for the printf function to use in case
 * of memory allocation failure; the printf function uses malloc.
 * The failsafe memory block must be visible globally because the
 * handle_program_memory_depletion function can take one
 * argument only.
 */
char * failsafe = new char[128];
```

```
/* Declare a customized function to handle memory-allocation failure.
 * Pass this function as an argument to _set_new_handler.
 */
int handle_program_memory_depletion( size_t );

void main( void )
{
   // Register existence of a new memory handler.
   _set_new_handler( handle_program_memory_depletion );
   size_t *pmemdump = new size_t[MemBlock];
   for( ; pmemdump != 0; pmemdump = new size_t[MemBlock] );
}

int handle_program_memory_depletion( size_t size )
{
   // Release character buffer memory.
   delete failsafe;
   printf( "Allocation failed, " );
   printf( "%u bytes not available.\n", size );
   // Tell new to stop allocation attempts.
   return 0;
}
```

Output

```
Allocation failed %0 bytes not available.
```

See Also

calloc, free, realloc

_set_new_mode

Sets a new handler mode for **malloc**.

int _set_new_mode(int *newhandlermode* **);**

Routine	Required Header	Compatibility
_set_new_mode	<new.h>	Win 95, Win NT

For additional compatibility information, see "Compatibility" in the Introduction.

Libraries

LIBC.LIB	Single thread static library, retail version
LIBCMT.LIB	Multithread static library, retail version
MSVCRT.LIB	Import library for MSVCRT.DLL, retail version

Return Value

_set_new_mode returns the previous handler mode set for **malloc**. A return value of 1 indicates that, on failure to allocate memory, **malloc** previously called the new handler routine; a return value of 0 indicates that it did not. If the *newhandlermode* argument does not equal 0 or 1, **_set_new_mode** returns –1.

Parameter

newhandlermode
> New handler mode for **malloc**; valid value is 0 or 1

Remarks

The C++ **_set_new_mode** function sets the new handler mode for malloc. The new handler mode indicates whether, on failure, **malloc** is to call the new handler routine as set by _set_new_handler. By default, **malloc** does not call the new handler routine on failure to allocate memory. You can override this default behavior so that, when **malloc** fails to allocate memory, **malloc** calls the new handler routine in the same way that the **new** operator does when it fails for the same reason. For more information, see the **new** and **delete** operators in the *Language Quick Reference* online. To override the default, call

```
_set_new_mode(1)
```

early in your program, or link with NEWMODE.OBJ.

See Also

calloc, **free**, **realloc**, **_query_new_handler**, **_query_new_mode**

_set_sbh_threshold

Sets the upper limit for the size of a memory allocation that will be supported by the small-block heap.

int _set_sbh_threshold(size_t *size*);

Routine	Required Header	Compatibility
_set_sbh_threshold	<malloc.h>	Win 95, Win NT

For additional compatibility information, see "Compatibility" in the Introduction.

Libraries

LIBC.LIB	Single thread static library, retail version
LIBCMT.LIB	Multithread static library, retail version
MSVCRT.LIB	Import library for MSVCRT.DLL, retail version

Return Value

_set_sbh_threshold returns 1 if the operation of setting the small-block threshold size is successful. It returns 0 if the input threshold size is too big.

Parameter

size
    the new small-block threshold size to be set

Remarks

This function takes a user specified small-block threshold size as input, and sets the current small-block threshold size to that value. The small-block heap threshold size can be set to any multiples of 16, from 0 to 1920 bytes for Windows 95 and all Windows NT platforms except the DEC Alpha, and from 0 to 3616 bytes for DEC Alpha platforms.

See Also

_get_sbh_thresold

_set_se_translator

Handles Win32 exceptions (C structured exceptions) as C++ typed exceptions.

typedef void (*_se_translator_function)(unsigned int, struct _EXCEPTION_POINTERS*);
_se_translator_function _set_se_translator(_se_translator_function *se_trans_func* **);**

Routine	Required Header	Compatibility
_set_se_translator	<eh.h>	Win 95, Win NT

For additional compatibility information, see "Compatibility" in the Introduction.

Libraries

LIBC.LIB	Single thread static library, retail version
LIBCMT.LIB	Multithread static library, retail version
MSVCRT.LIB	Import library for MSVCRT.DLL, retail version

Return Value

_set_se_translator returns a pointer to the previous translator function registered by **_set_se_translator**, so that the previous function can be restored later. If no previous function has been set, the return value may be used to restore the default behavior; this value may be NULL.

er se_translator

Parameter

se_trans_func
   Pointer to a C structured exception translator function that you write

Remarks

The **_set_se_translator** function provides a way to handle Win32 exceptions (C structured
exceptions) as C++ typed exceptions. To allow each C exception to be handled by a C++
catch handler, first define a C exception "wrapper" class that can be used, or derived
from, in order to attribute a specific class type to a C exception. To use this class, install
a custom C exception translator function that is called by the internal exception-handling
mechanism each time a C exception is raised. Within your translator function, you can
throw any typed exception that can be caught by a matching C++ **catch** handler.

To specify a custom translation function, call **_set_se_translator** with the name of your
translation function as its argument. The translator function that you write is called once
for each function invocation on the stack that has **try** blocks. There is no default translator
function.

In a multithreaded environment, translator functions are maintained separately for each
thread. Each new thread needs to install its own translator function. Thus, each thread is
in charge of its own translation handling.

The *se_trans_func* function that you write must take an unsigned integer and a pointer to a
Win32 **_EXCEPTION_POINTERS** structure as arguments. The arguments are the return
values of calls to the Win32 API **GetExceptionCode** and **GetExceptionInformation**
functions, respectively.

Example

```
/*  SETRANS.CPP
 */

#include <stdio.h>
#include <windows.h>
#include <eh.h>

void SEFunc();
void trans_func( unsigned int, EXCEPTION_POINTERS* );

class SE_Exception
{
private:
   unsigned int nSE;
public:
   SE_Exception() {}
   SE_Exception( unsigned int n ) : nSE( n ) {}
   ~SE_Exception() {}
   unsigned int getSeNumber() { return nSE; }
};
```

Run-Time Library Reference **605**

```
void main( void )
{
    try
    {
        _set_se_translator( trans_func );
        SEFunc();
    }
    catch( SE_Exception e )
    {
        printf( "Caught a __try exception with SE_Exception.\n" );
    }
}
void SEFunc()
{
    __try
    {
        int x, y=0;
        x = 5 / y;
    }
    __finally
    {
        printf( "In finally\n" );
    }
}
void trans_func( unsigned int u, EXCEPTION_POINTERS* pExp )
{
    printf( "In trans_func.\n" );
    throw SE_Exception();
}
```

Output

```
In finally.
In trans_func.
Caught a __try exception with SE_Exception.
```

See Also

set_terminate, set_unexpected, terminate, unexpected

set_terminate

Installs your own termination routine to be called by terminate.

typedef void (*terminate_function)();
terminate_function set_terminate(terminate_function *term_func* **);**

Routine	Required Header	Compatibility
set_terminate	<eh.h>	ANSI, Win 95, Win NT

For additional compatibility information, see "Compatibility" in the Introduction.

Libraries

LIBC.LIB	Single thread static library, retail version
LIBCMT.LIB	Multithread static library, retail version
MSVCRT.LIB	Import library for MSVCRT.DLL, retail version

Return Value

set_terminate returns a pointer to the previous function registered by **set_terminate**, so that the previous function can be restored later. If no previous function has been set, the return value may be used to restore the default behavior; this value may be NULL.

Parameter

term_func
    Pointer to a terminate function that you write

Remarks

The **set_terminate** function installs *term_func* as the function called by **terminate**. **set_terminate** is used with C++ exception handling and may be called at any point in your program before the exception is thrown. **terminate** calls **abort** by default. You can change this default by writing your own termination function and calling **set_terminate** with the name of your function as its argument. **terminate** calls the last function given as an argument to **set_terminate**. After performing any desired cleanup tasks, *term_func* should exit the program. If it does not exit (if it returns to its caller), **abort** is called.

In a multithreaded environment, terminate functions are maintained separately for each thread. Each new thread needs to install its own terminate function. Thus, each thread is in charge of its own termination handling.

The **terminate_function** type is defined in EH.H as a pointer to a user-defined termination function, *term_func*, that returns **void**. Your custom function *term_func* can take no arguments and should not return to its caller. If it does, **abort** is called. An exception may not be thrown from within *term_func*.

Note The **set_terminate** function only works outside the debugger.

Example

```
/* TERMINAT.CPP:
 */
#include <eh.h>
#include <process.h>
#include <iostream.h>

void term_func();
```

```
void main()
{

    int i = 10, j = 0, result;
    set_terminate( term_func );
    try
    {
        if( j == 0 )
            throw "Divide by zero!";
        else
            result = i/j;
    }
    catch( int )
    {
        cout << "Caught some integer exception.\n";
    }
    cout << "This should never print.\n";
}
void term_func()
{

    cout << "term_func() was called by terminate().\n";

    // ... cleanup tasks performed here

    // If this function does not exit, abort is called.

    exit(-1);
}
```

Output

```
term_func() was called by terminate().
```

See Also

abort, **set_unexpected**, **terminate**, **unexpected**

set_unexpected

Installs your own termination function to be called by unexpected.

typedef void (*unexpected_function)();
unexpected_function set_unexpected(unexpected_function *unexp_func* **);**

Routine	Required Header	Compatibility
set_unexpected	<eh.h>	ANSI, Win 95, Win NT

For additional compatibility information, see "Compatibility" in the Introduction.

Libraries

LIBC.LIB	Single thread static library, retail version
LIBCMT.LIB	Multithread static library, retail version
MSVCRT.LIB	Import library for MSVCRT.DLL, retail version

Return Value

_set_unexpected returns a pointer to the previous termination function registered by **_set_unexpected**, so that the previous function can be restored later. If no previous function has been set, the return value may be used to restore the default behavior; this value may be NULL.

Parameter

unexp_func
    Pointer to a function that you write to replace the **unexpected** function

Remarks

The **set_unexpected** function installs *unexp_func* as the function called by **unexpected**. **unexpected** is not used in the current C++ exception-handling implementation. The **unexpected_function** type is defined in EH.H as a pointer to a user-defined unexpected function, *unexp_func*, that returns **void**. Your custom *unexp_func* function should not return to its caller.

By default, **unexpected** calls **terminate**. You can change this default behavior by writing your own termination function and calling **set_unexpected** with the name of your function as its argument. **unexpected** calls the last function given as an argument to **set_unexpected**.

Unlike the custom termination function installed by a call to **set_terminate**, an exception can be thrown from within *unexp_func*.

In a multithreaded environment, unexpected functions are maintained separately for each thread. Each new thread needs to install its own unexpected function. Thus, each thread is in charge of its own unexpected handling.

In the current Microsoft implementation of C++ exception handling, **unexpected** calls **terminate** by default and is never called by the exception-handling run-time library. There is no particular advantage to calling **unexpected** rather than **terminate**.

See Also

abort, **set_terminate**, **terminate**, **unexpected**

setvbuf

Controls stream buffering and buffer size.

int setvbuf(FILE **stream*, **char** **buffer*, **int** *mode*, **size_t** *size* **);**

Routine	Required Header	Compatibility
setvbuf	<stdio.h>	ANSI, Win 95, Win NT

For additional compatibility information, see "Compatibility" in the Introduction.

Libraries

LIBC.LIB	Single thread static library, retail version
LIBCMT.LIB	Multithread static library, retail version
MSVCRT.LIB	Import library for MSVCRT.DLL, retail version

Return Value

setvbuf returns 0 if successful, or a nonzero value if an illegal type or buffer size is specified.

Parameters

stream
   Pointer to **FILE** structure

buffer
   User-allocated buffer

mode
   Mode of buffering

size
   Buffer size in bytes. Allowable range: $2 < size < 32768$. Internally, the value supplied for *size* is rounded down to the nearest multiple of 2.

Remarks

The **setvbuf** function allows the program to control both buffering and buffer size for *stream*. *stream* must refer to an open file that has not undergone an I/O operation since it was opened. The array pointed to by *buffer* is used as the buffer, unless it is **NULL**, in which case **setvbuf** uses an automatically allocated buffer of length *size*/2 * 2 bytes.

The mode must be **_IOFBF**, **_IOLBF**, or **_IONBF**. If *mode* is **_IOFBF** or **_IOLBF**, then *size* is used as the size of the buffer. If *mode* is **_IONBF**, the stream is unbuffered and *size* and *buffer* are ignored. Values for *mode* and their meanings are:

_IOFBF

Full buffering; that is, *buffer* is used as the buffer and *size* is used as the size of the buffer. If *buffer* is **NULL**, an automatically allocated buffer *size* bytes long is used.

_IOLBF

With MS-DOS, the same as **_IOFBF**.

_IONBF

No buffer is used, regardless of *buffer* or *size*.

Example

```c
/* SETVBUF.C: This program opens two streams: stream1
 * and stream2. It then uses setvbuf to give stream1 a
 * user-defined buffer of 1024 bytes and stream2 no buffer.
 */

#include <stdio.h>

void main( void )
{
    char buf[1024];
    FILE *stream1, *stream2;

    if( ((stream1 = fopen( "data1", "a" )) != NULL) &&
        ((stream2 = fopen( "data2", "w" )) != NULL) )
    {
        if( setvbuf( stream1, buf, _IOFBF, sizeof( buf ) ) != 0 )
            printf( "Incorrect type or size of buffer for stream1\n" );
        else
            printf( "'stream1' now has a buffer of 1024 bytes\n" );
        if( setvbuf( stream2, NULL, _IONBF, 0 ) != 0 )
            printf( "Incorrect type or size of buffer for stream2\n" );
        else
            printf( "'stream2' now has no buffer\n" );
        _fcloseall();
    }
}
```

Output

```
'stream1' now has a buffer of 1024 bytes
'stream2' now has no buffer
```

See Also

fclose, fflush, fopen, setbuf

signal

Sets interrupt signal handling.

void (*signal(int *sig*, **void (__cdecl ****func*) **(int** *sig* **[, int** *subcode* **]))) (int** *sig* **);**

Routine	Required Header	Compatibility
signal	<signal.h>	ANSI, Win 95, Win NT

For additional compatibility information, see "Compatibility" in the Introduction.

Libraries

LIBC.LIB	Single thread static library, retail version
LIBCMT.LIB	Multithread static library, retail version
MSVCRT.LIB	Import library for MSVCRT.DLL, retail version

Return Value

signal returns the previous value of *func* associated with the given signal. For example, if the previous value of *func* was **SIG_IGN**, the return value is also **SIG_IGN**. A return value of **SIG_ERR** indicates an error, in which case **errno** is set to **EINVAL**.

Parameters

sig
   Signal value

func
   Function to be executed

subcode
   Optional subcode to the signal number

Remarks

The **signal** function allows a process to choose one of several ways to handle an interrupt signal from the operating system. The *sig* argument is the interrupt to which **signal** responds; it must be one of the following manifest constants, defined in SIGNAL.H.

sig Value	Description
SIGABRT	Abnormal termination
SIGFPE	Floating-point error
SIGILL	Illegal instruction
SIGINT	CTRL+C signal

(continued)

sig Value	Description
SIGSEGV	Illegal storage access
SIGTERM	Termination request

By default, **signal** terminates the calling program with exit code 3, regardless of the value of *sig*.

> **Note** **SIGINT** is not supported for any Win32 application including Windows NT and Windows 95. When a CTRL+C interrupt occurs, Win32 operating systems generate a new thread to specifically handle that interrupt. This can cause a single-thread application such as UNIX, to become multithreaded, resulting in unexpected behavior.

The *func* argument is an address to a signal handler that you write, or one of the manifest constants **SIG_DFL** or **SIG_IGN**, also defined in SIGNAL.H. If *func* is a function, it is installed as the signal handler for the given signal. The signal handler's prototype requires one formal argument, *sig*, of type **int**. The operating system provides the actual argument through *sig* when an interrupt occurs; the argument is the signal that generated the interrupt. Thus you can use the six manifest constants (listed in the preceding table) inside your signal handler to determine which interrupt occurred and take appropriate action. For example, you can call **signal** twice to assign the same handler to two different signals, then test the *sig* argument inside the handler to take different actions based on the signal received.

If you are testing for floating-point exceptions (**SIGFPE**), *func* points to a function that takes an optional second argument that is one of several manifest constants defined in FLOAT.H of the form **FPE_***xxx*. When a **SIGFPE** signal occurs, you can test the value of the second argument to determine the type of floating-point exception and then take appropriate action. This argument and its possible values are Microsoft extensions.

For floating-point exceptions, the value of *func* is not reset upon receiving the signal. To recover from floating-point exceptions, use setjmp with longjmp. If the function returns, the calling process resumes execution with the floating-point state of the process left undefined.

If the signal handler returns, the calling process resumes execution immediately following the point at which it received the interrupt signal. This is true regardless of the type of signal or operating mode.

Before the specified function is executed, the value of *func* is set to **SIG_DFL**. The next interrupt signal is treated as described for **SIG_DFL**, unless an intervening call to **signal** specifies otherwise. This feature lets you reset signals in the called function.

Because signal-handler routines are usually called asynchronously when an interrupt occurs, your signal-handler function may get control when a run-time operation is incomplete and in an unknown state. The list below summarizes restrictions that determine which functions you can use in your signal-handler routine.

- Do not issue low-level or STDIO.H I/O routines (such as **printf** and **fread**).

- Do not call heap routines or any routine that uses the heap routines (such as **malloc**, **_strdup**, and **_putenv**). See malloc for more information.

- Do not use any function that generates a system call (e.g., **_getcwd**, **time**).

- Do not use **longjmp** unless the interrupt is caused by a floating-point exception (i.e., *sig* is **SIGFPE**). In this case, first reinitialize the floating-point package with a call to **_fpreset**.

- Do not use any overlay routines.

A program must contain floating-point code if it is to trap the **SIGFPE** exception with the function. If your program does not have floating-point code and requires the run-time library's signal-handling code, simply declare a volatile double and initialize it to zero:

```
volatile double d = 0.0f;
```

The **SIGILL**, **SIGSEGV**, and **SIGTERM** signals are not generated under Windows NT. They are included for ANSI compatibility. Thus you can set signal handlers for these signals with **signal**, and you can also explicitly generate these signals by calling raise.

Signal settings are not preserved in spawned processes created by calls to **_exec** or **_spawn** functions. The signal settings are reset to the default in the new process.

See Also

abort, **_exec Functions**, **exit**, **_fpreset**, **_spawn Functions**

sin, sinh

Calculate sines and hyperbolic sines.

double sin(double x **);**
double sinh(double x **);**

Routine	Required Header	Compatibility
sin	\<math.h\>	ANSI, Win 95, Win NT
sinh	\<math.h\>	ANSI, Win 95, Win NT

For additional compatibility information, see "Compatibility" in the Introduction.

Libraries

LIBC.LIB	Single thread static library, retail version
LIBCMT.LIB	Multithread static library, retail version
MSVCRT.LIB	Import library for MSVCRT.DLL, retail version

Return Value

sin returns the sine of x. If x is greater than or equal to 2^{63}, or less than or equal to -2^{63}, a loss of significance in the result occurs, in which case the function generates a **_TLOSS** error and returns an indefinite (same as a quiet NaN).

sinh returns the hyperbolic sine of x. If the result is too large, **sinh** sets **errno** to **ERANGE** and returns ±**HUGE_VAL**. You can modify error handling with _matherr.

Parameter

x

    Angle in radians

Example

```
/* SINCOS.C: This program displays the sine, hyperbolic
 * sine, cosine, and hyperbolic cosine of pi / 2.
 */

#include <math.h>
#include <stdio.h>

void main( void )
{
    double pi = 3.1415926535;
    double x, y;

    x = pi / 2;
    y = sin( x );
    printf( "sin( %f ) = %f\n", x, y );
    y = sinh( x );
    printf( "sinh( %f ) = %f\n",x, y );
    y = cos( x );
    printf( "cos( %f ) = %f\n", x, y );
    y = cosh( x );
    printf( "cosh( %f ) = %f\n",x, y );
}
```

Output

```
sin( 1.570796 ) = 1.000000
sinh( 1.570796 ) = 2.301299
cos( 1.570796 ) = 0.000000
cosh( 1.570796 ) = 2.509178
```

See Also

acos, asin, atan, cos, tan

_snprintf, _snwprintf

Write formatted data to a string.

int _snprintf(char **buffer*, **size_t** *count*, **const char** **format* [**,** *argument*] ... **);**
int _snwprintf(wchar_t **buffer*, **size_t** *count*, **const wchar_t** **format* [**,** *argument*] ... **);**

Routine	Required Header	Compatibility
_snprintf	<stdio.h>	Win 95, Win NT
_snwprintf	<stdio.h> or <wchar.h>	Win 95, Win NT

For additional compatibility information, see "Compatibility" in the Introduction.

Libraries

LIBC.LIB	Single thread static library, retail version
LIBCMT.LIB	Multithread static library, retail version
MSVCRT.LIB	Import library for MSVCRT.DLL, retail version

Return Value

_snprintf returns the number of bytes stored in *buffer*, not counting the terminating null character. If the number of bytes required to store the data exceeds *count*, then *count* bytes of data are stored in *buffer* and a negative value is returned. **_snwprintf** returns the number of wide characters stored in *buffer*, not counting the terminating null wide character. If the storage required to store the data exceeds *count* wide characters, then *count* wide characters are stored in *buffer* and a negative value is returned.

Parameters

buffer
   Storage location for output

count
   Maximum number of characters to store

format
   Format-control string

argument
   Optional arguments

Remarks

The **_snprintf** function formats and stores *count* or fewer characters and values (including a terminating null character that is always appended unless *count* is zero or the formatted string length is greater than or equal to *count* characters) in *buffer*. Each *argument* (if any) is converted and output according to the corresponding format specification in *format*.

The format consists of ordinary characters and has the same form and function as the *format* argument for printf. If copying occurs between strings that overlap, the behavior is undefined.

_snwprintf is a wide-character version of **_snprintf**; the pointer arguments to **_snwprintf** are wide-character strings. Detection of encoding errors in **_snwprintf** may differ from that in **_snprintf**. **_snwprintf**, like **swprintf**, writes output to a string rather than to a destination of type **FILE**.

Generic-Text Routine Mappings

TCHAR.H Routine	_UNICODE & _MBCS Not Defined	_MBCS Defined	_UNICODE Defined
_sntprintf	_snprintf	_snprintf	_snwprintf

Example

```
/* SPRINTF.C: This program uses sprintf to format various
 * data and place them in the string named buffer.
 */

#include <stdio.h>

void main( void )
{
   char  buffer[200], s[] = "computer", c = '1';
   int   i = 35, j;
   float fp = 1.7320534f;

   /* Format and print various data: */
   j  = sprintf( buffer,     "\tString:    %s\n", s );
   j += sprintf( buffer + j, "\tCharacter: %c\n", c );
   j += sprintf( buffer + j, "\tInteger:   %d\n", i );
   j += sprintf( buffer + j, "\tReal:      %f\n", fp );

   printf( "Output:\n%s\ncharacter count = %d\n", buffer, j );
}
```

Output

```
Output:
   String:    computer
   Character: 1
   Integer:   35
   Real:      1.732053

character count = 71
```

See Also

sprintf, fprintf, printf, scanf, sscanf, vprintf Functions

_sopen, _wsopen

Open a file for sharing.

int _sopen(const char *_filename_, int _oflag_, int _shflag_ [, int _pmode_]);
int _wsopen(const wchar_t *_filename_, int _oflag_, int _shflag_ [, int _pmode_]);

Routine	Required Header	Optional Headers	Compatibility
_sopen	<io.h>	<fcntl.h>, <sys/types.h>, <sys/stat.h>, <share.h>	Win 95, Win NT
_wsopen	<io.h> or <wchar.h>	<fcntl.h>, <sys/types.h>, <sys/stat.h>, <share.h>	Win NT

For additional compatibility information, see "Compatibility" in the Introduction.

Libraries

LIBC.LIB	Single thread static library, retail version
LIBCMT.LIB	Multithread static library, retail version
MSVCRT.LIB	Import library for MSVCRT.DLL, retail version

Return Value

Each of these functions returns a file handle for the opened file. A return value of –1 indicates an error, in which case **errno** is set to one of the following values:

EACCES
Given path is a directory, or file is read-only, but an open-for-writing operation was attempted.

EEXIST
_O_CREAT and **_O_EXCL** flags were specified, but _filename_ already exists.

EINVAL
Invalid _oflag_ or _shflag_ argument.

EMFILE
No more file handles available.

ENOENT
File or path not found.

Parameters

filename
Filename

oflag
Type of operations allowed

shflag
>   Type of sharing allowed

pmode
>   Permission setting

Remarks

The **_sopen** function opens the file specified by *filename* and prepares the file for shared reading or writing, as defined by *oflag* and *shflag*. **_wsopen** is a wide-character version of **_sopen**; the *filename* argument to **_wsopen** is a wide-character string. **_wsopen** and **_sopen** behave identically otherwise.

Generic-Text Routine Mappings

TCHAR.H Routine	_UNICODE & _MBCS Not Defined	_MBCS Defined	_UNICODE Defined
_tsopen	_sopen	_sopen	_wsopen

The integer expression *oflag* is formed by combining one or more of the following manifest constants, defined in the file FCNTL.H. When two or more constants form the argument *oflag*, they are combined with the bitwise-OR operator (|).

_O_APPEND
>   Repositions file pointer to end of file before every write operation.

_O_BINARY
>   Opens file in binary (untranslated) mode. (See **fopen** for a description of binary mode.)

_O_CREAT
>   Creates and opens new file for writing. Has no effect if file specified by *filename* exists. The *pmode* argument is required when **_O_CREAT** is specified.

_O_CREAT | _O_SHORT_LIVED
>   Create file as temporary and if possible do not flush to disk. The *pmode* argument is required when **_O_CREAT** is specified.

_O_CREAT | _O_TEMPORARY
>   Create file as temporary; file is deleted when last file handle is closed. The *pmode* argument is required when **_O_CREAT** is specified.

_O_CREAT | _O_EXCL
>   Returns error value if file specified by *filename* exists. Applies only when used with **_O_CREAT**.

_O_NOINHERIT
>   Prevents creation of a shared file handle.

_O_RANDOM
>   Specifies primarily random access from disk.

_O_RDONLY
>   Opens file for reading only; cannot be specified with **_O_RDWR** or **_O_WRONLY**.

_O_RDWR

Opens file for both reading and writing; cannot be specified with **_O_RDONLY** or **_O_WRONLY**.

_O_SEQUENTIAL

Specifies primarily sequential access from disk

_O_TEXT

Opens file in text (translated) mode. (For more information, see "Text and Binary Mode File I/O," on page 16, and **fopen**.)

_O_TRUNC

Opens file and truncates it to zero length; the file must have write permission. You cannot specify this flag with **_O_RDONLY**. **_O_TRUNC** used with **_O_CREAT** opens an existing file or creates a new file.

> **Warning** The **_O_TRUNC** flag destroys the contents of the specified file.

_O_WRONLY

Opens file for writing only; cannot be specified with **_O_RDONLY** or **_O_RDWR**.

To specify the file access mode, you must specify either **_O_RDONLY**, **_O_RDWR**, or **_O_WRONLY**. There is no default value for the access mode.

The argument *shflag* is a constant expression consisting of one of the following manifest constants, defined in SHARE.H.

_SH_DENYRW

Denies read and write access to file

_SH_DENYWR

Denies write access to file

_SH_DENYRD

Denies read access to file

_SH_DENYNO

Permits read and write access

The *pmode* argument is required only when you specify **_O_CREAT**. If the file does not exist, *pmode* specifies the file's permission settings, which are set when the new file is closed the first time. Otherwise *pmode* is ignored. *pmode* is an integer expression that contains one or both of the manifest constants **_S_IWRITE** and **_S_IREAD**, defined in SYS\STAT.H. When both constants are given, they are combined with the bitwise-OR operator. The meaning of *pmode* is as follows:

_S_IWRITE

Writing permitted

_S_IREAD

Reading permitted

_S_IREAD | _S_IWRITE

Reading and writing permitted

If write permission is not given, the file is read-only. Under Windows NT and
Windows 95, all files are readable; it is not possible to give write-only permission.
Thus the modes **_S_IWRITE** and **_S_IREAD | _S_IWRITE** are equivalent.

_sopen applies the current file-permission mask to *pmode* before setting the permissions
(see **_umask**).

Example

```
/* LOCKING.C: This program opens a file with sharing. It locks
 * some bytes before reading them, then unlocks them. Note that the
 * program works correctly only if the file exists.
 */

#include <io.h>
#include <sys/types.h>
#include <sys/stat.h>
#include <sys/locking.h>
#include <share.h>
#include <fcntl.h>
#include <stdio.h>
#include <stdlib.h>

void main( void )
{
    int  fh, numread;
    char buffer[40];

    /* Quit if can't open file or system doesn't
     * support sharing.
     */
    fh = _sopen( "locking.c", _O_RDWR, _SH_DENYNO, _S_IREAD | _S_IWRITE );
    if( fh == -1 )
       exit( 1 );

    /* Lock some bytes and read them. Then unlock. */
    if( _locking( fh, LK_NBLCK, 30L ) != -1 )
    {
       printf( "No one can change these bytes while I'm reading them\n" );
       numread = _read( fh, buffer, 30 );
       printf( "%d bytes read: %.30s\n", numread, buffer );
       lseek( fh, 0L, SEEK_SET );
       _locking( fh, LK_UNLCK, 30L );
       printf( "Now I'm done. Do what you will with them\n" );
    }
    else
       perror( "Locking failed\n" );

    _close( fh );
}
```

Output

```
No one can change these bytes while I'm reading them
30 bytes read: /* LOCKING.C: This program ope
Now I'm done. Do what you will with them
```

See Also

_close, **_creat**, **fopen**, **_fsopen**, **_open**

_spawn, _wspawn Functions

Each of the **_spawn** functions creates and executes a new process.

_spawnl, _wspawnl	_spawnv, _wspawnv
_spawnle, _wspawnle	_spawnve, _wspawnve
_spawnlp, _wspawnlp	_spawnvp, _wspawnvp
_spawnlpe, _wspawnlpe	_spawnvpe, _wspawnvpe

The letter(s) at the end of the function name determine the variation.

_spawn Function Suffix	Description
e	*envp*, array of pointers to environment settings, is passed to new process.
l	Command-line arguments are passed individually to **_spawn** function. This suffix is typically used when number of parameters to new process is known in advance
p	**PATH** environment variable is used to find file to execute.
v	*argv,* array of pointers to command-line arguments, is passed to **_spawn** function. This suffix is typically used when number of parameters to new process is variable.

Remarks

The **_spawn** functions each create and execute a new process. They automatically handle multibyte-character string arguments as appropriate, recognizing multibyte-character sequences according to the multibyte code page currently in use. The **_wspawn** functions are wide-character versions of the **_spawn** functions; they do not handle multibyte-character strings. Otherwise, the **_wspawn** functions behave identically to their **_spawn** counterparts.

Generic-Text Routine Mappings

TCHAR.H Routine	_UNICODE & _MBCS Not Defined	_MBCS Defined	_UNICODE Defined
_tspawnl	_spawnl	_spawnl	_wspawnl
_tspawnle	_spawnle	_spawnle	_wspawnle
_tspawnlp	_spawnlp	_spawnlp	_wspawnlp
_tspawnlpe	_spawnlpe	_spawnlpe	_wspawnlpe
_tspawnv	_spawnv	_spawnv	_wspawnv
_tspawnve	_spawnve	_spawnve	_wspawnve
_tspawnvp	_spawnvp	_spawnvp	_wspawnvp
_tspawnvpe	_spawnvpe	_spawnvpe	_wspawnvpe

Enough memory must be available for loading and executing the new process. The *mode* argument determines the action taken by the calling process before and during **_spawn**. The following values for *mode* are defined in PROCESS.H:

_P_OVERLAY
Overlays calling process with new process, destroying the calling process (same effect as **_exec** calls).

_P_WAIT
Suspends calling thread until execution of new process is complete (synchronous **_spawn**).

_P_NOWAIT or _P_NOWAITO
Continues to execute calling process concurrently with new process (asynchronous **_spawn**).

_P_DETACH
Continues to execute the calling process; new process is run in the background with no access to the console or keyboard. Calls to **_cwait** against the new process will fail (asynchronous **_spawn**).

The *cmdname* argument specifies the file that is executed as the new process and can specify a full path (from the root), a partial path (from the current working directory), or just a filename. If *cmdname* does not have a filename extension or does not end with a period (.), the **_spawn** function first tries the .COM extension, then the .EXE extension, the .BAT extension, and finally the .CMD extension.

If *cmdname* has an extension, only that extension is used. If *cmdname* ends with a period, the **_spawn** call searches for *cmdname* with no extension. The **_spawnlp**, **_spawnlpe**, **_spawnvp**, and **_spawnvpe** functions search for *cmdname* (using the same procedures) in the directories specified by the **PATH** environment variable.

If *cmdname* contains a drive specifier or any slashes (that is, if it is a relative path), the **_spawn** call searches only for the specified file; no path searching is done.

> **Note** To ensure proper overlay initialization and termination, do not use the **setjmp** or **longjmp** function to enter or leave an overlay routine.

Arguments for the Spawned Process

To pass arguments to the new process, give one or more pointers to character strings as arguments in the **_spawn** call. These character strings form the argument list for the spawned process. The combined length of the strings forming the argument list for the new process must not exceed 1024 bytes. The terminating null character (`'\0'`) for each string is not included in the count, but space characters (automatically inserted to separate arguments) are included.

You can pass argument pointers as separate arguments (in **_spawnl**, **_spawnle**, **_spawnlp**, and **_spawnlpe**) or as an array of pointers (in **_spawnv**, **_spawnve**, **_spawnvp**, and **_spawnvpe**). You must pass at least one argument, *arg0* or *argv*[0], to the spawned process. By convention, this argument is the name of the program as you would type it on the command line. A different value does not produce an error.

The **_spawnl**, **_spawnle**, **_spawnlp**, and **_spawnlpe** calls are typically used in cases where the number of arguments is known in advance. The *arg0* argument is usually a pointer to *cmdname*. The arguments *arg1* through *argn* are pointers to the character strings forming the new argument list. Following *argn*, there must be a **NULL** pointer to mark the end of the argument list.

The **_spawnv**, **_spawnve**, **_spawnvp**, and **_spawnvpe** calls are useful when there is a variable number of arguments to the new process. Pointers to the arguments are passed as an array, *argv*. The argument *argv*[0] is usually a pointer to a path in real mode or to the program name in protected mode, and *argv*[1] through *argv*[*n*] are pointers to the character strings forming the new argument list. The argument *argv*[*n* +1] must be a **NULL** pointer to mark the end of the argument list.

Environment of the Spawned Process

Files that are open when a **_spawn** call is made remain open in the new process. In the **_spawnl**, **_spawnlp**, **_spawnv**, and **_spawnvp** calls, the new process inherits the environment of the calling process. You can use the **_spawnle**, **_spawnlpe**, **_spawnve**, and **_spawnvpe** calls to alter the environment for the new process by passing a list of environment settings through the *envp* argument. The argument *envp* is an array of character pointers, each element (except the final element) of which points to a null-terminated string defining an environment variable. Such a string usually has the form *NAME=value* where *NAME* is the name of an environment variable and *value* is the string value to which that variable is set. (Note that *value* is not enclosed in double quotation marks.) The final element of the *envp* array should be **NULL**. When *envp* itself is **NULL**, the spawned process inherits the environment settings of the parent process.

The **_spawn** functions can pass all information about open files, including the translation mode, to the new process. This information is passed in real mode through the **C_FILE_INFO** entry in the environment. The startup code normally processes this entry and then deletes it from the environment. However, if a **_spawn** function spawns a non-C process, this entry remains in the environment. Printing the environment shows graphics characters in the definition string for this entry because the environment information is passed in binary form in real mode. It should not have any other effect on normal operations. In protected mode, the environment information is passed in text form and therefore contains no graphics characters.

You must explicitly flush (using **fflush** or **_flushall**) or close any stream before calling a **_spawn** function.

You can control whether the open file information of a process is passed to its spawned processes. The external variable _fileinfo (declared in STDLIB.H) controls the passing of **C_FILE_INFO** information. If **_fileinfo** is 0 (the default), the **C_FILE_INFO** information is not passed to the new processes. If **_fileinfo** is not 0, **C_FILE_INFO** is passed to new processes. You can modify the default value of **_fileinfo** in one of two ways: link the supplied object file, FILEINFO.OBJ, into the program, or set the **_fileinfo** variable to a nonzero value directly in the C program.

New processes created by calls to **_spawn** routines do not preserve signal settings. Instead, the spawned process resets signal settings to the default.

Example

```
/* SPAWN.C: This program accepts a number in the range
 * 1-8 from the command line. Based on the number it receives,
 * it executes one of the eight different procedures that
 * spawn the process named child. For some of these procedures,
 * the CHILD.EXE file must be in the same directory; for
 * others, it only has to be in the same path.
 */

#include <stdio.h>
#include <process.h>

char *my_env[] =
{
   "THIS=environment will be",
   "PASSED=to child.exe by the",
   "_SPAWNLE=and",
   "_SPAWNLPE=and",
   "_SPAWNVE=and",
   "_SPAWNVPE=functions",
   NULL
};
```

```
void main( int argc, char *argv[] )
{
   char *args[4];

   /* Set up parameters to be sent: */
   args[0] = "child";
   args[1] = "spawn??";
   args[2] = "two";
   args[3] = NULL;

   if (argc <= 2)
   {
      printf( "SYNTAX: SPAWN <1-8> <childprogram>\n" );
      exit( 1 );
   }

   switch (argv[1][0])    /* Based on first letter of argument */
   {
case '1':
      _spawnl( _P_WAIT, argv[2], argv[2], "_spawnl", "two", NULL );
      break;
   case '2':
      _spawnle( _P_WAIT, argv[2], argv[2], "_spawnle", "two", NULL, my_env );
      break;
   case '3':
      _spawnlp( _P_WAIT, argv[2], argv[2], "_spawnlp", "two", NULL );
      break;
   case '4':
      _spawnlpe( _P_WAIT, argv[2], argv[2], "_spawnlpe", "two", NULL, my_env );
      break;
   case '5':
      _spawnv( _P_OVERLAY, argv[2], args );
      break;
   case '6':
      _spawnve( _P_OVERLAY, argv[2], args, my_env );
      break;
   case '7':
      _spawnvp( _P_OVERLAY, argv[2], args );
      break;
   case '8':
      _spawnvpe( _P_OVERLAY, argv[2], args, my_env );
      break;
   default:
      printf( "SYNTAX: SPAWN <1-8> <childprogram>\n" );
      exit( 1 );
   }
   printf( "from SPAWN!\n" );
}
```

Output

```
SYNTAX: SPAWN <1-8> <childprogram>
```

See Also

abort, atexit, _exec Functions, **exit, _flushall, _getmbcp, _onexit, _setmbcp, system**

_spawnl, _wspawnl

Create and execute a new process.

int _spawnl(int *mode***, const char** **cmdname***, const char** **arg0***,**
   const char **arg1***, ... const char** **argn***, NULL);**
int _wspawnl(int *mode***, const wchar_t** **cmdname***, const wchar_t** **arg0***,**
   const wchar_t **arg1***, ... const wchar_t** **argn***, NULL);**

Routine	Required Header	Compatibility
_spawnl	<process.h>	Win 95, Win NT
_wspawnl	<stdio.h> or <wchar.h>	Win NT

For additional compatibility information, see "Compatibility" in the Introduction.

Libraries

LIBC.LIB	Single thread static library, retail version
LIBCMT.LIB	Multithread static library, retail version
MSVCRT.LIB	Import library for MSVCRT.DLL, retail version

Return Value

The return value from a synchronous **_spawnl** or **_wspawnl** (**_P_WAIT** specified for *mode*) is the exit status of the new process. The return value from an asynchronous **_spawnl** or **_wspawnl** (**_P_NOWAIT** or **_P_NOWAITO** specified for *mode*) is the process handle. The exit status is 0 if the process terminated normally. You can set the exit status to a nonzero value if the spawned process specifically calls the **exit** routine with a nonzero argument. If the new process did not explicitly set a positive exit status, a positive exit status indicates an abnormal exit with an abort or an interrupt. A return value of –1 indicates an error (the new process is not started). In this case, **errno** is set to one of the following values:

E2BIG
   Argument list exceeds 1024 bytes

EINVAL
   mode argument is invalid

ENOENT

File or path is not found

ENOEXEC

Specified file is not executable or has invalid executable-file format

ENOMEM

Not enough memory is available to execute new process

Parameters

mode

Execution mode for calling process

cmdname

Path of file to be executed

arg0, ... argn

List of pointers to arguments

Remarks

Each of these functions creates and executes a new process, passing each command-line argument as a separate parameter.

See Also

abort, atexit, _exec Functions, exit, _flushall, _getmbcp, _onexit, _setmbcp, system

Example

```
/* SPAWN.C: This program accepts a number in the range
 * 1-8 from the command line. Based on the number it receives,
 * it executes one of the eight different procedures that
 * spawn the process named child. For some of these procedures,
 * the CHILD.EXE file must be in the same directory; for
 * others, it only has to be in the same path.
 */

#include <stdio.h>
#include <process.h>

char *my_env[] =
{
    "THIS=environment will be",
    "PASSED=to child.exe by the",
    "_SPAWNLE=and",
    "_SPAWNLPE=and",
    "_SPAWNVE=and",
    "_SPAWNVPE=functions",
    NULL
};
```

```
void main( int argc, char *argv[] )
{
    char *args[4];

    /* Set up parameters to be sent: */
    args[0] = "child";
    args[1] = "spawn??";
    args[2] = "two";
    args[3] = NULL;

    if (argc <= 2)
    {
        printf( "SYNTAX: SPAWN <1-8> <childprogram>\n" );
        exit( 1 );
    }

    switch (argv[1][0])    /* Based on first letter of argument */
    {
    case '1':
        _spawnl( _P_WAIT, argv[2], argv[2], "_spawnl", "two", NULL );
        break;
    case '2':
        _spawnle( _P_WAIT, argv[2], argv[2], "_spawnle", "two", NULL, my_env );
        break;
    case '3':
        _spawnlp( _P_WAIT, argv[2], argv[2], "_spawnlp", "two", NULL );
        break;
    case '4':
        _spawnlpe( _P_WAIT, argv[2], argv[2], "_spawnlpe", "two", NULL, my_env );
        break;
    case '5':
        _spawnv( _P_OVERLAY, argv[2], args );
        break;
    case '6':
        _spawnve( _P_OVERLAY, argv[2], args, my_env );
        break;
    case '7':
        _spawnvp( _P_OVERLAY, argv[2], args );
        break;
    case '8':
        _spawnvpe( _P_OVERLAY, argv[2], args, my_env );
        break;
    default:
        printf( "SYNTAX: SPAWN <1-8> <childprogram>\n" );
        exit( 1 );
    }
    printf( "from SPAWN!\n" );
}
```

Output

```
SYNTAX: SPAWN <1-8> <childprogram>
```

_spawnle, _wspawnle

Create and execute a new process.

int _spawnle(int *mode***, const char** **cmdname***, const char** **arg0***,**
    const char **arg1***, ... const char** **argn***, NULL, const char *const** **envp* **);**
int _wspawnle(int *mode***, const wchar_t** **cmdname***, const wchar_t** **arg0***,**
    const wchar_t **arg1***, ... const wchar_t** **argn***, NULL, const wchar_t *const** **envp* **);**

Routine	Required Header	Compatibility
_spawnle	<process.h>	Win 95, Win NT
_wspawnle	<stdio.h> or <wchar.h>	Win NT

For additional compatibility information, see "Compatibility" in the Introduction.

Libraries

LIBC.LIB	Single thread static library, retail version
LIBCMT.LIB	Multithread static library, retail version
MSVCRT.LIB	Import library for MSVCRT.DLL, retail version

Return Value

The return value from a synchronous **_spawnle** or **_wspawnle** (**_P_WAIT** specified for *mode*) is the exit status of the new process. The return value from an asynchronous **_spawnle** or **_wspawnle** (**_P_NOWAIT** or **_P_NOWAITO** specified for *mode*) is the process handle. The exit status is 0 if the process terminated normally. You can set the exit status to a nonzero value if the spawned process specifically calls the **exit** routine with a nonzero argument. If the new process did not explicitly set a positive exit status, a positive exit status indicates an abnormal exit with an abort or an interrupt. A return value of −1 indicates an error (the new process is not started). In this case, **errno** is set to one of the following values:

E2BIG
    Argument list exceeds 1024 bytes

EINVAL
    mode argument is invalid

ENOENT
    File or path is not found

ENOEXEC

Specified file is not executable or has invalid executable-file format

ENOMEM

Not enough memory is available to execute new process

Parameters

mode

Execution mode for calling process

cmdname

Path of file to be executed

arg0, ... argn

List of pointers to arguments

envp

Array of pointers to environment settings

Remarks

Each of these functions creates and executes a new process, passing each command-line argument as a separate parameter and also passing an array of pointers to environment settings.

See Also

abort, **atexit**, **_exec Functions**, **exit**, **_flushall**, **_getmbcp**, **_onexit**, **_setmbcp**, **system**

Example

```
/* SPAWN.C: This program accepts a number in the range
 * 1-8 from the command line. Based on the number it receives,
 * it executes one of the eight different procedures that
 * spawn the process named child. For some of these procedures,
 * the CHILD.EXE file must be in the same directory; for
 * others, it only has to be in the same path.
 */

#include <stdio.h>
#include <process.h>

char *my_env[] =
{
    "THIS=environment will be",
    "PASSED=to child.exe by the",
    "_SPAWNLE=and",
    "_SPAWNLPE=and",
    "_SPAWNVE=and",
    "_SPAWNVPE=functions",
    NULL
};
```

```
void main( int argc, char *argv[] )
{
    char *args[4];

    /* Set up parameters to be sent: */
    args[0] = "child";
    args[1] = "spawn??";
    args[2] = "two";
    args[3] = NULL;

    if (argc <= 2)
    {
        printf( "SYNTAX: SPAWN <1-8> <childprogram>\n" );
        exit( 1 );
    }

    switch (argv[1][0])    /* Based on first letter of argument */
    {
    case '1':
        _spawnl( _P_WAIT, argv[2], argv[2], "_spawnl", "two", NULL );
        break;
    case '2':
        _spawnle( _P_WAIT, argv[2], argv[2], "_spawnle", "two", NULL, my_env );
        break;
    case '3':
        _spawnlp( _P_WAIT, argv[2], argv[2], "_spawnlp", "two", NULL );
        break;
    case '4':
        _spawnlpe( _P_WAIT, argv[2], argv[2], "_spawnlpe", "two", NULL, my_env );
        break;
    case '5':
        _spawnv( _P_OVERLAY, argv[2], args );
        break;
    case '6':
        _spawnve( _P_OVERLAY, argv[2], args, my_env );
        break;
    case '7':
        _spawnvp( _P_OVERLAY, argv[2], args );
        break;
    case '8':
        _spawnvpe( _P_OVERLAY, argv[2], args, my_env );
        break;
    default:
        printf( "SYNTAX: SPAWN <1-8> <childprogram>\n" );
        exit( 1 );
    }
    printf( "from SPAWN!\n" );
}
```

Output

```
SYNTAX: SPAWN <1-8> <childprogram>
```

_spawnlp, _wspawnlp

Create and execute a new process.

int _spawnlp(int *mode,* **const char** **cmdname,* **const char** **arg0,*
const char **arg1,* ... **const char** **argn,* **NULL);**
int _wspawnlp(int *mode,* **const wchar_t** **cmdname,* **const wchar_t** **arg0,*
const wchar_t **arg1,* ... **const wchar_t** **argn,* **NULL);**

Routine	Required Header	Compatibility
_spawnlp	<process.h>	Win 95, Win NT
_wspawnlp	<stdio.h> or <wchar.h>	Win NT

For additional compatibility information, see "Compatibility" in the Introduction.

Libraries

LIBC.LIB	Single thread static library, retail version
LIBCMT.LIB	Multithread static library, retail version
MSVCRT.LIB	Import library for MSVCRT.DLL, retail version

Return Value

The return value from a synchronous **_spawnlp** or **_wspawnlp** (**_P_WAIT** specified
for *mode*) is the exit status of the new process. The return value from an asynchronous
_spawnlp or **_wspawnlp** (**_P_NOWAIT** or **_P_NOWAITO** specified for *mode*) is the
process handle. The exit status is 0 if the process terminated normally. You can set the exit
status to a nonzero value if the spawned process specifically calls the **exit** routine with a
nonzero argument. If the new process did not explicitly set a positive exit status, a positive
exit status indicates an abnormal exit with an abort or an interrupt. A return value of –1
indicates an error (the new process is not started). In this case, **errno** is set to one of the
following values:

E2BIG
Argument list exceeds 1024 bytes

EINVAL
mode argument is invalid

ENOENT
File or path is not found

ENOEXEC
Specified file is not executable or has invalid executable-file format

ENOMEM
Not enough memory is available to execute new process

Parameters

mode
Execution mode for calling process

cmdname
Path of file to be executed

arg0, ... argn
List of pointers to arguments

Remarks

Each of these functions creates and executes a new process, passing each command-line argument as a separate parameter and using the **PATH** environment variable to find the file to execute.

See Also

abort, **atexit**, **_exec Functions**, **exit**, **_flushall**, **_getmbcp**, **_onexit**, **_setmbcp**, **system**

Example

```
/* SPAWN.C: This program accepts a number in the range
 * 1-8 from the command line. Based on the number it receives,
 * it executes one of the eight different procedures that
 * spawn the process named child. For some of these procedures,
 * the CHILD.EXE file must be in the same directory; for
 * others, it only has to be in the same path.
 */

#include <stdio.h>
#include <process.h>

char *my_env[] =
{
    "THIS=environment will be",
    "PASSED=to child.exe by the",
    "_SPAWNLE=and",
    "_SPAWNLPE=and",
    "_SPAWNVE=and",
    "_SPAWNVPE=functions",
    NULL
};
```

```
void main( int argc, char *argv[] )
{
    char *args[4];

    /* Set up parameters to be sent: */
    args[0] = "child";
    args[1] = "spawn??";
    args[2] = "two";
    args[3] = NULL;

    if (argc <= 2)
    {
        printf( "SYNTAX: SPAWN <1-8> <childprogram>\n" );
        exit( 1 );
    }

    switch (argv[1][0])    /* Based on first letter of argument */
    {
    case '1':
        _spawnl( _P_WAIT, argv[2], argv[2], "_spawnl", "two", NULL );
        break;
    case '2':
        _spawnle( _P_WAIT, argv[2], argv[2], "_spawnle", "two", NULL, my_env );
        break;
    case '3':
        _spawnlp( _P_WAIT, argv[2], argv[2], "_spawnlp", "two", NULL );
        break;
    case '4':
        _spawnlpe( _P_WAIT, argv[2], argv[2], "_spawnlpe", "two", NULL, my_env );
        break;
    case '5':
        _spawnv( _P_OVERLAY, argv[2], args );
        break;
    case '6':
        _spawnve( _P_OVERLAY, argv[2], args, my_env );
        break;
    case '7':
        spawnvp( _P_OVERLAY, argv[2], args );
        break;
    case '8':
        _spawnvpe( _P_OVERLAY, argv[2], args, my_env );
        break;
    default:
        printf( "SYNTAX: SPAWN <1-8> <childprogram>\n" );
        exit( 1 );
    }
    printf( "from SPAWN!\n" );
}
```

Output

```
SYNTAX: SPAWN <1-8> <childprogram>
```

_spawnlpe, _wspawnlpe

Create and execute a new process.

int _spawnlpe(int *mode*, **const char** **cmdname*, **const char** **arg0*,
    const char **arg1*, ... **const char** **argn*, **NULL, const char *const** **envp*);
int _wspawnlpe(int *mode*, **const wchar_t** **cmdname*, **const wchar_t** **arg0*,
    const wchar_t **arg1*, ... **const wchar_t** **argn*, **NULL, const wchar_t *const** **envp*);

Routine	Required Header	Compatibility
_spawnlpe	<process.h>	Win 95, Win NT
_wspawnlpe	<stdio.h> or <wchar.h>	Win NT

For additional compatibility information, see "Compatibility" in the Introduction.

Libraries

LIBC.LIB	Single thread static library, retail version
LIBCMT.LIB	Multithread static library, retail version
MSVCRT.LIB	Import library for MSVCRT.DLL, retail version

Return Value

The return value from a synchronous **_spawnlpe** or **_wspawnlpe** (**_P_WAIT** specified
for *mode*) is the exit status of the new process. The return value from an asynchronous
_spawnlpe or **_wspawnlpe** (**_P_NOWAIT** or **_P_NOWAITO** specified for *mode*) is the
process handle. The exit status is 0 if the process terminated normally. You can set the exit
status to a nonzero value if the spawned process specifically calls the **exit** routine with a
nonzero argument. If the new process did not explicitly set a positive exit status, a positive
exit status indicates an abnormal exit with an abort or an interrupt. A return value of –1
indicates an error (the new process is not started). In this case, **errno** is set to one of the
following values:

E2BIG
    Argument list exceeds 1024 bytes

EINVAL
    mode argument is invalid

ENOENT
    File or path is not found

ENOEXEC
Specified file is not executable or has invalid executable-file format

ENOMEM
Not enough memory is available to execute new process

Parameters

mode
Execution mode for calling process

cmdname
Path of file to be executed

arg0, ... argn
List of pointers to arguments

envp
Array of pointers to environment settings

Remarks

Each of these functions creates and executes a new process, passing each command-line argument as a separate parameter and also passing an array of pointers to environment settings. These functions use the **PATH** environment variable to find the file to execute.

See Also

abort, **atexit**, **_exec Functions**, **exit**, **_flushall**, **_getmbcp**, **_onexit**, **_setmbcp**, **system**

Example

```
/* SPAWN.C: This program accepts a number in the range
 * 1-8 from the command line. Based on the number it receives,
 * it executes one of the eight different procedures that
 * spawn the process named child. For some of these procedures,
 * the CHILD.EXE file must be in the same directory; for
 * others, it only has to be in the same path.
 */

#include <stdio.h>
#include <process.h>

char *my_env[] =
{
    "THIS=environment will be",
    "PASSED=to child.exe by the",
    "_SPAWNLE=and",
    "_SPAWNLPE=and",
    "_SPAWNVE=and",
    "_SPAWNVPE=functions",
    NULL
};
```

```
void main( int argc, char *argv[] )
{
    char *args[4];

    /* Set up parameters to be sent: */
    args[0] = "child";
    args[1] = "spawn??";
    args[2] = "two";
    args[3] = NULL;

    if (argc <= 2)
    {
        printf( "SYNTAX: SPAWN <1-8> <childprogram>\n" );
        exit( 1 );
    }

    switch (argv[1][0])    /* Based on first letter of argument */
    {
    case '1':
        _spawnl( _P_WAIT, argv[2], argv[2], "_spawnl", "two", NULL );
        break;
    case '2':
        _spawnle( _P_WAIT, argv[2], argv[2], "_spawnle", "two", NULL, my_env );
        break;
    case '3':
        _spawnlp( _P_WAIT, argv[2], argv[2], "_spawnlp", "two", NULL );
        break;
    case '4':
        _spawnlpe( _P_WAIT, argv[2], argv[2], "_spawnlpe", "two", NULL, my_env );
        break;
    case '5':
        _spawnv( _P_OVERLAY, argv[2], args );
        break;
    case '6':
        _spawnve( _P_OVERLAY, argv[2], args, my_env );
        break;
    case '7':
        _spawnvp( _P_OVERLAY, argv[2], args );
        break;
    case '8':
        _spawnvpe( _P_OVERLAY, argv[2], args, my_env );
        break;
    default:
        printf( "SYNTAX: SPAWN <1-8> <childprogram>\n" );
        exit( 1 );
    }
    printf( "from SPAWN!\n" );
}
```

Output

```
SYNTAX: SPAWN <1-8> <childprogram>
```

_spawnv, _wspawnv

Create and execute a new process.

int _spawnv(int *mode,* **const char** **cmdname,* **const char *const** **argv* **);**
int _wspawnv(int *mode,* **const wchar_t** **cmdname,* **const wchar_t *const** **argv* **);**

Routine	Required Header	Compatibility
_spawnv	<stdio.h> or <process.h>	Win 95, Win NT
_wspawnv	<stdio.h> or <wchar.h>	Win NT

For additional compatibility information, see "Compatibility" in the Introduction.

Libraries

LIBC.LIB	Single thread static library, retail version
LIBCMT.LIB	Multithread static library, retail version
MSVCRT.LIB	Import library for MSVCRT.DLL, retail version

Return Value

The return value from a synchronous **_spawnv** or **_wspawnv** (**_P_WAIT** specified
for *mode*) is the exit status of the new process. The return value from an asynchronous
_spawnv or **_wspawnv** (**_P_NOWAIT** or **_P_NOWAITO** specified for *mode*) is the
process handle. The exit status is 0 if the process terminated normally. You can set the exit
status to a nonzero value if the spawned process specifically calls the **exit** routine with a
nonzero argument. If the new process did not explicitly set a positive exit status, a positive
exit status indicates an abnormal exit with an abort or an interrupt. A return value of –1
indicates an error (the new process is not started). In this case, **errno** is set to one of the
following values:

E2BIG
    Argument list exceeds 1024 bytes

EINVAL
    mode argument is invalid

ENOENT
    File or path is not found

ENOEXEC
    Specified file is not executable or has invalid executable-file format

ENOMEM
    Not enough memory is available to execute new process

Parameters

mode

> Execution mode for calling process

cmdname

> Path of file to be executed

argv

> Array of pointers to arguments

Remarks

Each of these functions creates and executes a new process, passing an array of pointers to command-line arguments.

See Also

abort, atexit, _exec Functions, exit, _flushall, _getmbcp, _onexit, _setmbcp, system

Example

```
/* SPAWN.C: This program accepts a number in the range
 * 1-8 from the command line. Based on the number it receives,
 * it executes one of the eight different procedures that
 * spawn the process named child. For some of these procedures,
 * the CHILD.EXE file must be in the same directory; for
 * others, it only has to be in the same path.
 */

#include <stdio.h>
#include <process.h>

char *my_env[] =
{
    "THIS=environment will be",
    "PASSED=to child.exe by the",
    "_SPAWNLE=and",
    "_SPAWNLPE=and",
    "_SPAWNVE=and",
    "_SPAWNVPE=functions",
    NULL
};

void main( int argc, char *argv[] )
{
    char *args[4];
```

```
    /* Set up parameters to be sent: */
    args[0] = "child";
    args[1] = "spawn??";
    args[2] = "two";
    args[3] = NULL;

    if (argc <= 2)
    {
        printf( "SYNTAX: SPAWN <1-8> <childprogram>\n" );
        exit( 1 );
    }

    switch (argv[1][0])    /* Based on first letter of argument */
    {
    case '1':
        _spawnl( _P_WAIT, argv[2], argv[2], "_spawnl", "two", NULL );
        break;
    case '2':
        _spawnle( _P_WAIT, argv[2], argv[2], "_spawnle", "two", NULL, my_env );
        break;
    case '3':
        _spawnlp( _P_WAIT, argv[2], argv[2], "_spawnlp", "two", NULL );
        break;
    case '4':
        _spawnlpe( _P_WAIT, argv[2], argv[2], "_spawnlpe", "two", NULL, my_env );
        break;
    case '5':
        _spawnv( _P_OVERLAY, argv[2], args );
        break;
    case '6':
        _spawnve( _P_OVERLAY, argv[2], args, my_env );
        break;
    case '7':
        _spawnvp( _P_OVERLAY, argv[2], args );
        break;
    case '8':
        _spawnvpe( _P_OVERLAY, argv[2], args, my_env );
        break;
    default:
        printf( "SYNTAX: SPAWN <1-8> <childprogram>\n" );
        exit( 1 );
    }
    printf( "from SPAWN!\n" );
}
```

Output

```
SYNTAX: SPAWN <1-8> <childprogram>
```

_spawnve, _wspawnve

Create and execute a new process.

int _spawnve(int *mode*, **const char** **cmdname*, **const char *const** **argv*, **const char *const** **envp* **);**
int _wspawnve(int *mode*, **const wchar_t** **cmdname*, **const wchar_t *const** **argv*,
  const wchar_t *const **envp* **);**

Routine	Required Header	Compatibility
_spawnve	<stdio.h> or <process.h>	Win 95, Win NT
_wspawnve	<stdio.h> or <wchar.h>	Win NT

For additional compatibility information, see "Compatibility" in the Introduction.

Libraries

LIBC.LIB	Single thread static library, retail version
LIBCMT.LIB	Multithread static library, retail version
MSVCRT.LIB	Import library for MSVCRT.DLL, retail version

Return Value

The return value from a synchronous **_spawnve** or **_wspawnve** (**_P_WAIT** specified for *mode*) is the exit status of the new process. The return value from an asynchronous **_spawnve** or **_wspawnve** (**_P_NOWAIT** or **_P_NOWAITO** specified for *mode*) is the process handle. The exit status is 0 if the process terminated normally. You can set the exit status to a nonzero value if the spawned process specifically calls the **exit** routine with a nonzero argument. If the new process did not explicitly set a positive exit status, a positive exit status indicates an abnormal exit with an abort or an interrupt. A return value of –1 indicates an error (the new process is not started). In this case, **errno** is set to one of the following values:

E2BIG
  Argument list exceeds 1024 bytes

EINVAL
  mode argument is invalid

ENOENT
  File or path is not found

ENOEXEC
  Specified file is not executable or has invalid executable-file format

ENOMEM
  Not enough memory is available to execute new process

Parameters

mode
Execution mode for calling process

cmdname
Path of file to be executed

argv
Array of pointers to arguments

envp
Array of pointers to environment settings

Remarks

Each of these functions creates and executes a new process, passing an array of pointers to command-line arguments and an array of pointers to environment settings.

See Also

abort, **atexit**, **_exec Functions**, **exit**, **_flushall**, **_getmbcp**, **_onexit**, **_setmbcp**, **system**

Example

```
/* SPAWN.C: This program accepts a number in the range
 * 1-8 from the command line. Based on the number it receives,
 * it executes one of the eight different procedures that
 * spawn the process named child. For some of these procedures,
 * the CHILD.EXE file must be in the same directory; for
 * others, it only has to be in the same path.
 */

#include <stdio.h>
#include <process.h>

char *my_env[] =
{
    "THIS=environment will be",
    "PASSED=to child.exe by the",
    "_SPAWNLE=and",
    "_SPAWNLPE=and",
    "_SPAWNVE=and",
    "_SPAWNVPE=functions",
    NULL
};

void main( int argc, char *argv[] )
{
    char *args[4];
```

```
        /* Set up parameters to be sent: */
        args[0] = "child";
        args[1] = "spawn??";
        args[2] = "two";
        args[3] = NULL;

        if (argc <= 2)
        {
            printf( "SYNTAX: SPAWN <1-8> <childprogram>\n" );
            exit( 1 );
        }

        switch (argv[1][0])   /* Based on first letter of argument */
        {
        case '1':
            _spawnl( _P_WAIT, argv[2], argv[2], "_spawnl", "two", NULL );
            break;
        case '2':
            _spawnle( _P_WAIT, argv[2], argv[2], "_spawnle", "two", NULL, my_env );
            break;
        case '3':
            _spawnlp( _P_WAIT, argv[2], argv[2], "_spawnlp", "two", NULL );
            break;
        case '4':
            _spawnlpe( _P_WAIT, argv[2], argv[2], "_spawnlpe", "two", NULL, my_env );
            break;
        case '5':
            _spawnv( _P_OVERLAY, argv[2], args );
            break;
        case '6':
            _spawnve( _P_OVERLAY, argv[2], args, my_env );
            break;
        case '7':
            _spawnvp( _P_OVERLAY, argv[2], args );
            break;
        case '8':
            _spawnvpe( _P_OVERLAY, argv[2], args, my_env );
            break;
        default:
            printf( "SYNTAX: SPAWN <1-8> <childprogram>\n" );
            exit( 1 );
        }
        printf( "from SPAWN!\n" );
    }
```

Output

```
SYNTAX: SPAWN <1-8> <childprogram>
```

_spawnvp, _wspawnvp

Create and execute a new process.

int _spawnvp(int *mode*, **const char ****cmdname*, **const char *const ****argv* **);**
int _wspawnvp(int *mode*, **const wchar_t ****cmdname*, **const wchar_t *const ****argv* **);**

Routine	Required Header	Compatibility
_spawnvp	<stdio.h> or <process.h>	Win 95, Win NT
_wspawnvp	<stdio.h> or <wchar.h>	Win NT

For additional compatibility information, see "Compatibility" in the Introduction.

Libraries

LIBC.LIB	Single thread static library, retail version
LIBCMT.LIB	Multithread static library, retail version
MSVCRT.LIB	Import library for MSVCRT.DLL, retail version

Return Value

The return value from a synchronous **_spawnvp** or **_wspawnvp** (**_P_WAIT** specified
for *mode*) is the exit status of the new process. The return value from an asynchronous
_spawnvp or **_wspawnvp** (**_P_NOWAIT** or **_P_NOWAITO** specified for *mode*) is the
process handle. The exit status is 0 if the process terminated normally. You can set the exit
status to a nonzero value if the spawned process specifically calls the **exit** routine with a
nonzero argument. If the new process did not explicitly set a positive exit status, a positive
exit status indicates an abnormal exit with an abort or an interrupt. A return value of –1
indicates an error (the new process is not started). In this case, **errno** is set to one of the
following values:

E2BIG
Argument list exceeds 1024 bytes

EINVAL
mode argument is invalid

ENOENT
File or path is not found

ENOEXEC
Specified file is not executable or has invalid executable-file format

ENOMEM
Not enough memory is available to execute new process

Parameters

mode
> Execution mode for calling process

cmdname
> Path of file to be executed

argv
> Array of pointers to arguments

Remarks

Each of these functions creates and executes a new process, passing an array of pointers to command-line arguments and using the the **PATH** environment variable to find the file to execute.

See Also

abort, atexit, _exec Functions, exit, _flushall, _getmbcp, _onexit, _setmbcp, system

Example

```
/* SPAWN.C: This program accepts a number in the range
 * 1-8 from the command line. Based on the number it receives,
 * it executes one of the eight different procedures that
 * spawn the process named child. For some of these procedures,
 * the CHILD.EXE file must be in the same directory; for
 * others, it only has to be in the same path.
 */

#include <stdio.h>
#include <process.h>

char *my_env[] =
{
   "THIS=environment will be",
   "PASSED=to child.exe by the",
   "_SPAWNLE=and",
   "_SPAWNLPE=and",
   "_SPAWNVE=and",
   "_SPAWNVPE=functions",
   NULL
};

void main( int argc, char *argv[] )
{
   char *args[4];
```

```
/* Set up parameters to be sent: */
args[0] = "child";
args[1] = "spawn??";
args[2] = "two";
args[3] = NULL;

if (argc <= 2)
{
    printf( "SYNTAX: SPAWN <1-8> <childprogram>\n" );
    exit( 1 );
}

switch (argv[1][0])    /* Based on first letter of argument */
{
case '1':
    _spawnl( _P_WAIT, argv[2], argv[2], "_spawnl", "two", NULL );
    break;
case '2':
    _spawnle( _P_WAIT, argv[2], argv[2], "_spawnle", "two", NULL, my_env );
    break;
case '3':
    _spawnlp( _P_WAIT, argv[2], argv[2], "_spawnlp", "two", NULL );
    break;
case '4':
    _spawnlpe( _P_WAIT, argv[2], argv[2], "_spawnlpe", "two", NULL, my_env );
    break;
case '5':
    _spawnv( _P_OVERLAY, argv[2], args );
    break;
case '6':
    _spawnve( _P_OVERLAY, argv[2], args, my_env );
    break;
case '7':
    _spawnvp( _P_OVERLAY, argv[2], args );
    break;
case '8':
    _spawnvpe( _P_OVERLAY, argv[2], args, my_env );
    break;
default:
    printf( "SYNTAX: SPAWN <1-8> <childprogram>\n" );
    exit( 1 );
}
printf( "from SPAWN!\n" );
}
```

Output

```
SYNTAX: SPAWN <1-8> <childprogram>
```

_spawnvpe, _wspawnvpe

Create and execute a new process.

int _spawnvpe(int *mode,* **const char ****cmdname,* **const char *const ****argv,* **const char *const ****envp* **);**

int _wspawnvpe(int *mode,* **const wchar_t ****cmdname,* **const wchar_t *const ****argv,*
const wchar_t *const *envp **);**

Routine	Required Header	Compatibility
_spawnvpe	<stdio.h> or <process.h>	Win 95, Win NT
_wspawnvpe	<stdio.h> or <wchar.h>	Win NT

For additional compatibility information, see "Compatibility" in the Introduction.

Libraries

LIBC.LIB	Single thread static library, retail version
LIBCMT.LIB	Multithread static library, retail version
MSVCRT.LIB	Import library for MSVCRT.DLL, retail version

Return Value

The return value from a synchronous **_spawnvpe** or **_wspawnvpe** (**_P_WAIT** specified for *mode*) is the exit status of the new process. The return value from an asynchronous **_spawnvpe** or **_wspawnvpe** (**_P_NOWAIT** or **_P_NOWAITO** specified for *mode*) is the process handle. The exit status is 0 if the process terminated normally. You can set the exit status to a nonzero value if the spawned process specifically calls the **exit** routine with a nonzero argument. If the new process did not explicitly set a positive exit status, a positive exit status indicates an abnormal exit with an abort or an interrupt. A return value of –1 indicates an error (the new process is not started). In this case, **errno** is set to one of the following values:

E2BIG
Argument list exceeds 1024 bytes

EINVAL
mode argument is invalid

ENOENT
File or path is not found

ENOEXEC
Specified file is not executable or has invalid executable-file format

ENOMEM
Not enough memory is available to execute new process

Parameters

mode
Execution mode for calling process

cmdname
Path of file to be executed

argv
Array of pointers to arguments

envp
Array of pointers to environment settings

Remarks

Each of these functions creates and executes a new process, passing an array of pointers to command-line arguments and an array of pointers to environment settings. These functions use the **PATH** environment variable to find the file to execute.

See Also

abort, atexit, _exec Functions, exit, _flushall, _getmbcp, _onexit, _setmbcp, system

Example

```
/* SPAWN.C: This program accepts a number in the range
 * 1-8 from the command line. Based on the number it receives,
 * it executes one of the eight different procedures that
 * spawn the process named child. For some of these procedures,
 * the CHILD.EXE file must be in the same directory; for
 * others, it only has to be in the same path.
 */

#include <stdio.h>
#include <process.h>

char *my_env[] =
{
    "THIS=environment will be",
    "PASSED=to child.exe by the",
    "_SPAWNLE=and",
    "_SPAWNLPE=and",
    "_SPAWNVE=and",
    "_SPAWNVPE=functions",
    NULL
};

void main( int argc, char *argv[] )
{
    char *args[4];
```

```
    /* Set up parameters to be sent: */
    args[0] = "child";
    args[1] = "spawn??";
    args[2] = "two";
    args[3] = NULL;

    if (argc <= 2)
    {
        printf( "SYNTAX: SPAWN <1-8> <childprogram>\n" );
        exit( 1 );
    }

switch (argv[1][0])    /* Based on first letter of argument */
    {
    case '1':
        _spawnl( _P_WAIT, argv[2], argv[2], "_spawnl", "two", NULL );
        break;
    case '2':
        _spawnle( _P_WAIT, argv[2], argv[2], "_spawnle", "two", NULL, my_env );
        break;
    case '3':
        _spawnlp( _P_WAIT, argv[2], argv[2], "_spawnlp", "two", NULL );
        break;
    case '4':
        _spawnlpe( _P_WAIT, argv[2], argv[2], "_spawnlpe", "two", NULL, my_env );
        break;
    case '5':
        _spawnv( _P_OVERLAY, argv[2], args );
        break;
    case '6':
        _spawnve( _P_OVERLAY, argv[2], args, my_env );
        break;
    case '7':
        _spawnvp( _P_OVERLAY, argv[2], args );
        break;
    case '8':
        _spawnvpe( _P_OVERLAY, argv[2], args, my_env );
        break;
    default:
        printf( "SYNTAX: SPAWN <1-8> <childprogram>\n" );
        exit( 1 );
    }
    printf( "from SPAWN!\n" );
}
```

Output

```
SYNTAX: SPAWN <1-8> <childprogram>
```

_splitpath, _wsplitpath

Break a path name into components.

void _splitpath(const char **path*, **char** **drive*, **char** **dir*, **char** **fname*, **char** **ext* **);**
void _wsplitpath(const wchar_t **path*, **wchar_t** **drive*, **wchar_t** **dir*, **wchar_t** **fname*, **wchar_t** **ext* **);**

Routine	Required Header	Compatibility
_splitpath	\<stdlib.h\>	Win 95, Win NT
_wsplitpath	\<stdlib.h\> or \<wchar.h\>	Win 95, Win NT

For additional compatibility information, see "Compatibility" in the Introduction.

Libraries

LIBC.LIB	Single thread static library, retail version
LIBCMT.LIB	Multithread static library, retail version
MSVCRT.LIB	Import library for MSVCRT.DLL, retail version

Return Value

None

Parameters

path
    Full path

drive
    Optional drive letter, followed by a colon (**:**)

dir
    Optional directory path, including trailing slash. Forward slashes (**/**), backslashes (****), or both may be used.

fname
    Base filename (no extension)

ext
    Optional filename extension, including leading period (**.**)

Remarks

The **_splitpath** function breaks a path into its four components. **_splitpath** automatically handles multibyte-character string arguments as appropriate, recognizing multibyte-character sequences according to the multibyte code page currently in use. **_wsplitpath** is a wide-character version of **_splitpath**; the arguments to **_wsplitpath** are wide-character strings. These functions behave identically otherwise.

Generic-Text Routine Mappings

TCHAR.H Routine	_UNICODE & _MBCS Not Defined	_MBCS Defined	_UNICODE Defined
_tsplitpath	_splitpath	_splitpath	_wsplitpath

Each argument is stored in a buffer; the manifest constants **_MAX_DRIVE**, **_MAX_DIR**, **_MAX_FNAME**, and **_MAX_EXT** (defined in STDLIB.H) specify the maximum size necessary for each buffer. The other arguments point to buffers used to store the path elements. After a call to **_splitpath** is executed, these arguments contain empty strings for components not found in *path*. You can pass a **NULL** pointer to **_splitpath** for any component you don't need.

Example

```
/* MAKEPATH.C */

#include <stdlib.h>
#include <stdio.h>

void main( void )
{
    char path_buffer[_MAX_PATH];
    char drive[_MAX_DRIVE];
    char dir[_MAX_DIR];
    char fname[_MAX_FNAME];
    char ext[_MAX_EXT];

    _makepath( path_buffer, "c", "\\sample\\crt\\", "makepath", "c" );
    printf( "Path created with _makepath: %s\n\n", path_buffer );
    _splitpath( path_buffer, drive, dir, fname, ext );
    printf( "Path extracted with _splitpath:\n" );
    printf( "  Drive: %s\n", drive );
    printf( "  Dir: %s\n", dir );
    printf( "  Filename: %s\n", fname );
    printf( "  Ext: %s\n", ext );
}
```

Output

```
Path created with _makepath: c:\sample\crt\makepath.c

Path extracted with _splitpath:
   Drive: c:
   Dir: \sample\crt\
   Filename: makepath
   Ext: .c
```

See Also

_fullpath, **_getmbcp**, **_makepath**, **_setmbcp**

sprintf, swprintf

Write formatted data to a string.

int sprintf(char **buffer*, **const char** **format* [, *argument*] ... **);**
int swprintf(wchar_t **buffer*, **const wchar_t** **format* [, *argument*] ... **);**

Routine	Required Header	Compatibility
sprintf	<stdio.h>	ANSI, Win 95, Win NT
swprintf	<stdio.h> or <wchar.h>	ANSI, Win 95, Win NT

For additional compatibility information, see "Compatibility" in the Introduction.

Libraries

LIBC.LIB	Single thread static library, retail version
LIBCMT.LIB	Multithread static library, retail version
MSVCRT.LIB	Import library for MSVCRT.DLL, retail version

Return Value

sprintf returns the number of bytes stored in *buffer,* not counting the terminating null character. **swprintf** returns the number of wide characters stored in *buffer,* not counting the terminating null wide character.

Parameters

buffer
    Storage location for output

format
    Format-control string

argument
    Optional arguments

For more information, see "Format Specification Fields: printf and #wprintf Functions" on page 543.

Remarks

The **sprintf** function formats and stores a series of characters and values in *buffer.* Each *argument* (if any) is converted and output according to the corresponding format specification in *format.* The format consists of ordinary characters and has the same form and function as the *format* argument for printf. A null character is appended after the last character written. If copying occurs between strings that overlap, the behavior is undefined.

swprintf is a wide-character version of **sprintf**; the pointer arguments to **swprintf** are wide-character strings. Detection of encoding errors in **swprintf** may differ from that in **sprintf**. **swprintf** and **fwprintf** behave identically except that **swprintf** writes output to a string rather than to a destination of type **FILE**.

Generic-Text Routine Mappings

TCHAR.H Routine	_UNICODE & _MBCS Not Defined	_MBCS Defined	_UNICODE Defined
_stprintf	sprintf	sprintf	swprintf

Example

```
/* SPRINTF.C: This program uses sprintf to format various
 * data and place them in the string named buffer.
 */

#include <stdio.h>
void main( void )
{
    char  buffer[200], s[] = "computer", c = '1';
    int   i = 35, j;
    float fp = 1.7320534f;

    /* Format and print various data: */
    j  = sprintf( buffer,     "\tString:    %s\n", s );
    j += sprintf( buffer + j, "\tCharacter: %c\n", c );
    j += sprintf( buffer + j, "\tInteger:   %d\n", i );
    j += sprintf( buffer + j, "\tReal:      %f\n", fp );

    printf( "Output:\n%s\ncharacter count = %d\n", buffer, j );
}
```

Output

```
Output:
    String:    computer
    Character: 1
    Integer:   35
    Real:      1.732053

character count = 71
```

See Also

_snprintf, **fprintf**, **printf**, **scanf**, **sscanf**, **vprintf** Functions

sqrt

Calculates the square root.

double sqrt(double *x* **);**

Routine	Required Header	Compatibility
sqrt	<math.h>	ANSI, Win 95, Win NT

For additional compatibility information, see "Compatibility" in the Introduction.

Libraries

LIBC.LIB	Single thread static library, retail version
LIBCMT.LIB	Multithread static library, retail version
MSVCRT.LIB	Import library for MSVCRT.DLL, retail version

Return Value

The **sqrt** function returns the square-root of *x*. If *x* is negative, **sqrt** returns an indefinite (same as a quiet NaN). You can modify error handling with _matherr.

Parameter

x

　　Nonnegative floating-point value

Example

```
/* SQRT.C: This program calculates a square root. */

#include <math.h>
#include <stdio.h>
#include <stdlib.h>

void main( void )
{
   double question = 45.35, answer;

   answer = sqrt( question );
   if( question < 0 )
      printf( "Error: sqrt returns %.2f\n, answer" );
   else
   printf( "The square root of %.2f is %.2f\n", question, answer );
}
```

Output

```
The square root of 45.35 is 6.73
```

See Also

exp, **log**, **pow**

srand

Sets a random starting point.

void srand(unsigned int *seed* **);**

Routine	Required Header	Compatibility
srand	<stdlib.h>	ANSI, Win 95, Win NT

For additional compatibility information, see "Compatibility" in the Introduction.

Libraries

LIBC.LIB	Single thread static library, retail version
LIBCMT.LIB	Multithread static library, retail version
MSVCRT.LIB	Import library for MSVCRT.DLL, retail version

Return Value

None

Parameter

seed
Seed for random-number generation

Remarks

The **srand** function sets the starting point for generating a series of pseudorandom integers. To reinitialize the generator, use 1 as the *seed* argument. Any other value for *seed* sets the generator to a random starting point. **rand** retrieves the pseudorandom numbers that are generated. Calling **rand** before any call to **srand** generates the same sequence as calling **srand** with *seed* passed as 1.

Example

```
/* RAND.C: This program seeds the random-number generator
 * with the time, then displays 10 random integers.
 */

#include <stdlib.h>
#include <stdio.h>
#include <time.h>
```

```
void main( void )
{
    int i;

    /* Seed the random-number generator with current time so that
     * the numbers will be different every time we run.
     */
    srand( (unsigned)time( NULL ) );
    /* Display 10 numbers. */
    for( i = 0;    i < 10;i++ )
        printf( "  %6d\n", rand() );
}
```

Output

```
 6929
 8026
21987
30734
20587
 6699
22034
25051
 7988
10104
```

See Also

rand

sscanf, swscanf

Read formatted data from a string.

int sscanf(const char *buffer, const char *format [, argument] ...);
int swscanf(const wchar_t *buffer, const wchar_t *format [, argument] ...);

Routine	Required Header	Compatibility
sscanf	<stdio.h>	ANSI, Win 95, Win NT
swscanf	<stdio.h> or <wchar.h>	ANSI, Win 95, Win NT

For additional compatibility information, see "Compatibility" in the Introduction.

Libraries

LIBC.LIB	Single thread static library, retail version
LIBCMT.LIB	Multithread static library, retail version
MSVCRT.LIB	Import library for MSVCRT.DLL, retail version

Return Value

Each of these functions returns the number of fields successfully converted and assigned; the return value does not include fields that were read but not assigned. A return value of 0 indicates that no fields were assigned. The return value is **EOF** for an error or if the end of the string is reached before the first conversion.

Parameters

buffer
    Stored data

format
    Format-control string

argument
    Optional arguments

For more information, see "Format Specification Fields" on page 543.

Remarks

The **sscanf** function reads data from *buffer* into the location given by each *argument*. Every *argument* must be a pointer to a variable with a type that corresponds to a type specifier in *format*. The *format* argument controls the interpretation of the input fields and has the same form and function as the *format* argument for the **scanf** function; see **scanf** for a complete description of *format*. If copying takes place between strings that overlap, the behavior is undefined.

swscanf is a wide-character version of **sscanf**; the arguments to **swscanf** are wide-character strings. **sscanf** does not handle multibyte hexadecimal characters. **swscanf** does not handle Unicode fullwidth hexadecimal or "compatibility zone" characters. Otherwise, **swscanf** and **sscanf** behave identically.

Generic-Text Routine Mappings

TCHAR.H Routine	_UNICODE & _MBCS Not Defined	_MBCS Defined	_UNICODE Defined
_stscanf	sscanf	sscanf	swscanf

Example

```
/* SSCANF.C: This program uses sscanf to read data items
 * from a string named tokenstring, then displays them.
 */

#include <stdio.h>

void main( void )
{
    char   tokenstring[] = "15 12 14...";
    char   s[81];
```

```
char   c;
int    i;
float fp;

/* Input various data from tokenstring: */
sscanf( tokenstring, "%s", s );
sscanf( tokenstring, "%c", &c );
sscanf( tokenstring, "%d", &i );
sscanf( tokenstring, "%f", &fp );

/* Output the data read */
printf( "String    = %s\n", s );
printf( "Character = %c\n", c );
printf( "Integer:  = %d\n", i );
printf( "Real:     = %f\n", fp );
}
```

Output

```
String    = 15
Character = 1
Integer:  = 15
Real:     = 15.000000
```

See Also

fscanf, scanf, sprintf, _snprintf

_stat, _wstat, _stati64, _wstati64

Get status information on a file.

int _stat(const char *path***, struct _stat** *buffer* **);**
__int64 _stati64(const char *path***, struct _stat** *buffer* **);**
int _wstat(const wchar_t *path***, struct _stat** *buffer* **);**
__int64 _wstati64(const wchar_t *path***, struct _stat** *buffer* **);**

Routine	Required Header	Optional Headers	Compatibility
_stat	<sys/types.h> followed by <sys/stat.h>	<errno.h>	Win 95, Win NT
_wstat	<sys/types.h> followed by <sys/stat.h> or <wchar.h>	<errno.h>	Win NT
_stati64	<sys/types.h> followed by <sys/stat.h>	<errno.h>	Win 95, Win NT
_wstati64	<sys/types.h> followed by <sys/stat.h> or <wchar.h>	<errno.h>	Win NT

For additional compatibility information, see "Compatibility" in the Introduction.

Libraries

LIBC.LIB	Single thread static library, retail version
LIBCMT.LIB	Multithread static library, retail version
MSVCRT.LIB	Import library for MSVCRT.DLL, retail version

Return Value

Each of these functions returns 0 if the file-status information is obtained. A return value of –1 indicates an error, in which case **errno** is set to **ENOENT**, indicating that the filename or path could not be found.

Parameters

path
   Path of existing file

buffer
   Pointer to structure that stores results

Remarks

The **_stat** function obtains information about the file or directory specified by *path* and stores it in the structure pointed to by *buffer*. **_stat** automatically handles multibyte-character string arguments as appropriate, recognizing multibyte-character sequences according to the multibyte code page currently in use.

_wstat is a wide-character version of **_stat**; the *path* argument to **_wstat** is a wide-character string. **_wstat** and **_stat** behave identically except that **_wstat** does not handle multibyte-character strings.

Generic-Text Routine Mappings

TCHAR.H Routine	_UNICODE & _MBCS Not Defined	_MBCS Defined	_UNICODE Defined
_tstat	_stat	_stat	_wstat
_tstati64	_stati64	_stati64	_wstati64

The **_stat** structure, defined in SYS\STAT.H, includes the following fields.

st_gid
   Numeric identifier of group that owns file (UNIX-specific) This field will always be zero on NT systems. A redirected file is classified as an NT file.

st_atime
   Time of last access of file.

st_ctime
   Time of creation of file.

st_dev

Drive number of the disk containing the file (same as **st_rdev**).

st_ino

Number of the information node (the *inode*) for the file (UNIX-specific). On UNIX file systems, the inode describes the file date and time stamps, permissions, and content. When files are hard-linked to one another, they share the same inode. The inode, and therefore **st_ino**, has no meaning in the FAT, HPFS, or NTFS file systems.

st_mode

Bit mask for file-mode information. The **_S_IFDIR** bit is set if *path* specifies a directory; the **_S_IFREG** bit is set if *path* specifies an ordinary file or a device. User read/write bits are set according to the file's permission mode; user execute bits are set according to the filename extension.

st_mtime

Time of last modification of file.

st_nlink

Always 1 on non-NTFS file systems.

st_rdev

Drive number of the disk containing the file (same as **st_dev**).

st_size

Size of the file in bytes; a 64-bit integer for **_stati64** and **_wstati64**

st_uid

Numeric identifier of user who owns file (UNIX-specific). This field will always be zero on NT systems. A redirected file is classified as an NT file.

If *path* refers to a device, the size, time, **_dev**, and **_rdev** fields in the **_stat** structure are meaningless. Because STAT.H uses the _dev_t type that is defined in TYPES.H, you must include TYPES.H before STAT.H in your code.

Example

```
/* STAT.C: This program uses the _stat function to
 * report information about the file named STAT.C.
 */

#include <time.h>
#include <sys/types.h>
#include <sys/stat.h>
#include <stdio.h>

void main( void )
{
    struct _stat buf;
    int result;
    char buffer[] = "A line to output";
```

```
/* Get data associated with "stat.c": */
result = _stat( "stat.c", &buf );

/* Check if statistics are valid: */
if( result != 0 )
   perror( "Problem getting information" );
else
{
   /* Output some of the statistics: */
   printf( "File size     : %ld\n", buf.st_size );
   printf( "Drive         : %c:\n", buf.st_dev + 'A' );
   printf( "Time modified : %s", ctime( &buf.st_atime ) );
}
}
```

Output

```
File size     : 745
Drive         : C:
Time modified : Tue May 03 00:00:00 1994
```

See Also

_access, **_fstat**, **_getmbcp**, **_setmbcp**

_status87, _statusfp

Get the floating point status word.

unsigned int _status87(void);
unsigned int _statusfp(void);

Routine	Required Header	Compatibility
_status87	<float.h>	Win 95, Win NT
_statusfp	<float.h>	Win 95, Win NT

For additional compatibility information, see "Compatibility" in the Introduction.

Libraries

LIBC.LIB	Single thread static library, retail version
LIBCMT.LIB	Multithread static library, retail version
MSVCRT.LIB	Import library for MSVCRT.DLL, retail version

Return Value

The bits in the value returned indicate the floating-point status. See the FLOAT.H include file for a complete definition of the bits returned by **_status87**.

Many math library functions modify the 8087/80287 status word, with unpredictable results. Return values from **_clear87** and **_status87** are more reliable if fewer floating-point operations are performed between known states of the floating-point status word.

Remarks

The **_status87** function gets the floating-point status word. The status word is a combination of the 8087/80287/80387 status word and other conditions detected by the 8087/80287/80387 exception handler, such as floating-point stack overflow and underflow. Unmasked exceptions are checked for before returning the contents of the status word. This means that the caller is informed of pending exceptions.

_statusfp is a platform-independent, portable version of **_status87**. It is identical to **_status87** on Intel (x86) platforms and is also supported by the MIPS platform. To ensure that your floating-point code is portable to MIPS, use **_statusfp**. If you are only targeting x86 platforms, use either **_status87** or **_statusfp**.

Example

```
/* STATUS87.C: This program creates various floating-point errors and
 * then uses _status87 to display messages indicating these problems.
 * Compile this program with optimizations disabled (/Od). Otherwise,
 * the optimizer removes the code related to the unused floating-
 * point values.
 */

#include <stdio.h>
#include <float.h>

void main( void )
{
    double a = 1e-40, b;
    float  x, y;

    printf( "Status = %.4x - clear\n",_status87() );

    /* Assignment into y is inexact & underflows: */
    y = a;
    printf( "Status = %.4x - inexact, underflow\n", _status87() );

    /* y is denormal: */
    b = y;
    printf( "Status = %.4x - inexact underflow, denormal\n", _status87() );
```

```
      /* Clear user 8087: */
      _clear87();
}
```

Output

```
Status = 0000 - clear
Status = 0003 - inexact, underflow
Status = 80003 - inexact underflow, denormal
```

See Also

_clear87, **_control87**

strcat, wcscat, _mbscat

Append a string.

char *strcat(char *strDestination**, const char ***strSource **);**
wchar_t *wcscat(wchar_t *strDestination**, const wchar_t ***strSource **);**
unsigned char *_mbscat(unsigned char *strDestination**, const unsigned char ***strSource **);**

Routine	Required Header	Compatibility
strcat	<string.h>	ANSI, Win 95, Win NT
wcscat	<string.h> or <wchar.h>	ANSI, Win 95, Win NT
_mbscat	<mbstring.h>	Win 95, Win NT

For additional compatibility information, see "Compatibility" in the Introduction.

Libraries

LIBC.LIB	Single thread static library, retail version
LIBCMT.LIB	Multithread static library, retail version
MSVCRT.LIB	Import library for MSVCRT.DLL, retail version

Return Value

Each of these functions returns the destination string (*strDestination*). No return value is reserved to indicate an error.

Parameters

strDestination
  Null-terminated destination string

strSource
  Null-terminated source string

Remarks

The **strcat** function appends *strSource* to *strDestination* and terminates the resulting string with a null character. The initial character of *strSource* overwrites the terminating null character of *strDestination*. No overflow checking is performed when strings are copied or appended. The behavior of **strcat** is undefined if the source and destination strings overlap.

wcscat and **_mbscat** are wide-character and multibyte-character versions of **strcat**. The arguments and return value of **wcscat** are wide-character strings; those of **_mbscat** are multibyte-character strings. These three functions behave identically otherwise.

Generic-Text Routine Mappings

TCHAR.H Routine	_UNICODE & _MBCS Not Defined	_MBCS Defined	_UNICODE Defined
_tcscat	strcat	_mbscat	wcscat

Example

```
/* STRCPY.C: This program uses strcpy
 * and strcat to build a phrase.
 */

#include <string.h>
#include <stdio.h>

void main( void )
{
   char string[80];
   strcpy( string, "Hello world from " );
   strcat( string, "strcpy " );
   strcat( string, "and " );
   strcat( string, "strcat!" );
   printf( "String = %s\n", string );
}
```

Output

```
String = Hello world from strcpy and strcat!
```

See Also

strncat, strncmp, strncpy, _strnicmp, strrchr, strspn

strchr, wcschr, _mbschr

Find a character in a string.

char *strchr(const char **string***, int** *c* **);**
wchar_t *wcschr(const wchar_t **string***, wint_t** *c* **);**
unsigned char *_mbschr(const unsigned char **string***, unsigned int** *c* **);**

Routine	Required Header	Compatibility
strchr	<string.h>	ANSI, Win 95, Win NT
wcschr	<string.h> or <wchar.h>	ANSI, Win 95, Win NT
_mbschr	<mbstring.h>	Win 95, Win NT

For additional compatibility information, see "Compatibility" in the Introduction.

Libraries

LIBC.LIB	Single thread static library, retail version
LIBCMT.LIB	Multithread static library, retail version
MSVCRT.LIB	Import library for MSVCRT.DLL, retail version

Return Value

Each of these functions returns a pointer to the first occurrence of *c* in *string*, or **NULL** if *c* is not found.

Parameters

string
    Null-terminated source string

c
    Character to be located

Remarks

The **strchr** function finds the first occurrence of *c* in *string*, or it returns **NULL** if *c* is not found. The null-terminating character is included in the search.

wcschr and **_mbschr** are wide-character and multibyte-character versions of **strchr**. The arguments and return value of **wcschr** are wide-character strings; those of **_mbschr** are multibyte-character strings. **_mbschr** recognizes multibyte-character sequences according to the multibyte code page currently in use. These three functions behave identically otherwise.

Generic-Text Routine Mappings

TCHAR.H Routine	_UNICODE & _MBCS Not Defined	_MBCS Defined	_UNICODE Defined
_tcschr	strchr	_mbschr	wcschr

Example

```
/* STRCHR.C: This program illustrates searching for a character
 * with strchr (search forward) or strrchr (search backward).
 */

#include <string.h>
#include <stdio.h>

int  ch = 'r';

char string[] = "The quick brown dog jumps over the lazy fox";
char fmt1[] =   "          1         2         3         4         5";
char fmt2[] =   "12345678901234567890123456789012345678901234567890";

void main( void )
{
   char *pdest;
   int result;

   printf( "String to be searched: \n\t\t%s\n", string );
   printf( "\t\t%s\n\t\t%s\n\n", fmt1, fmt2 );
   printf( "Search char:\t%c\n", ch );

   /* Search forward. */
   pdest = strchr( string, ch );
   result = pdest - string + 1;
   if( pdest != NULL )
      printf( "Result:\tfirst %c found at position %d\n\n", ch, result );
   else
      printf( "Result:\t%c not found\n" );

   /* Search backward. */
   pdest = strrchr( string, ch );
   result = pdest - string + 1;
   if( pdest != NULL )
      printf( "Result:\tlast %c found at position %d\n\n", ch, result );
   else
      printf( "Result:\t%c not found\n" );
}
```

Output

```
String to be searched:
    The quick brown dog jumps over the lazy fox
             1         2         3         4         5
    12345678901234567890123456789012345678901234567890

Search char:   r
Result:   first r found at position 12

Result:   last r found at position 30
```

See Also

strcspn, strncat, strncmp, strncpy, _strnicmp, strpbrk, strrchr, strstr

strcmp, wcscmp, _mbscmp

Compare strings.

int strcmp(const char *string1, const char *string2);
int wcscmp(const wchar_t *string1, const wchar_t *string2);
int _mbscmp(const unsigned char *string1, const unsigned char *string2);

Routine	Required Header	Compatibility
strcmp	<string.h>	ANSI, Win 95, Win NT
wcscmp	<string.h> or <wchar.h>	ANSI, Win 95, Win NT
_mbscmp	<mbstring.h>	Win 95, Win NT

For additional compatibility information, see "Compatibility" in the Introduction.

Libraries

LIBC.LIB	Single thread static library, retail version
LIBCMT.LIB	Multithread static library, retail version
MSVCRT.LIB	Import library for MSVCRT.DLL, retail version

Return Value

The return value for each of these functions indicates the lexicographic relation of *string1* to *string2*.

Value	Relationship of string1 to string2
< 0	*string1* less than *string2*
0	*string1* identical to *string2*
> 0	*string1* greater than *string2*

On an error, **_mbscmp** returns **_NLSCMPERROR**, which is defined in STRING.H and MBSTRING.H.

Parameters

string1, string2
    Null-terminated strings to compare

Remarks

The **strcmp** function compares *string1* and *string2* lexicographically and returns a value indicating their relationship. **wcscmp** and **_mbscmp** are wide-character and multibyte-character versions of **strcmp**. The arguments and return value of **wcscmp** are wide-character strings; those of **_mbscmp** are multibyte-character strings. **_mbscmp** recognizes multibyte-character sequences according to the current multibyte code page and returns **_NLSCMPERROR** on an error. (For more information, see "Code Pages" in Chapter 1, "Run-Time Routines by Category.") These three functions behave identically otherwise.

Generic-Text Routine Mappings

TCHAR.H Routine	_UNICODE & _MBCS Not Defined	_MBCS Defined	_UNICODE Defined
_tcscmp	strcmp	_mbscmp	wcscmp

The **strcmp** functions differ from the **strcoll** functions in that **strcmp** comparisons are not affected by locale, whereas the manner of **strcoll** comparisons is determined by the **LC_COLLATE** category of the current locale. For more information on the **LC_COLLATE** category, see **setlocale**.

In the "C" locale, the order of characters in the character set (ASCII character set) is the same as the lexicographic character order. However, in other locales, the order of characters in the character set may differ from the lexicographic order. For example, in certain European locales, the character 'a' (value 0x61) precedes the character 'ä' (value 0xE4) in the character set, but the character 'ä' precedes the character 'a' lexicographically.

In locales for which the character set and the lexicographic character order differ, use **strcoll** rather than **strcmp** for lexicographic comparison of strings according to the **LC_COLLATE** category setting of the current locale. Thus, to perform a lexicographic comparison of the locale in the above example, use **strcoll** rather than **strcmp**. Alternatively, you can use **strxfrm** on the original strings, then use **strcmp** on the resulting strings.

_stricmp, **_wcsicmp**, and **_mbsicmp** compare strings by first converting them to their lowercase forms.Two strings containing characters located between 'Z' and 'a' in the ASCII table ('[', '\', ']', '^', '_', and '`') compare differently, depending on their case. For example, the two strings "ABCDE" and "ABCD^" compare one way if the comparison is lowercase ("abcde" > "abcd^") and the other way ("ABCDE" < "ABCD^") if the comparison is uppercase.

Example

```
/* STRCMP.C */

#include <string.h>
#include <stdio.h>

char string1[] = "The quick brown dog jumps over the lazy fox";
char string2[] = "The QUICK brown dog jumps over the lazy fox";

void main( void )
{
   char tmp[20];
   int result;
   /* Case sensitive */
   printf( "Compare strings:\n\t%s\n\t%s\n\n", string1, string2 );
   result = strcmp( string1, string2 );
   if( result > 0 )
      strcpy( tmp, "greater than" );
   else if( result < 0 )
      strcpy( tmp, "less than" );
   else
      strcpy( tmp, "equal to" );
   printf( "\tstrcmp:   String 1 is %s string 2\n", tmp );
   /* Case insensitive (could use equivalent _stricmp) */
   result = _stricmp( string1, string2 );
   if( result > 0 )
      strcpy( tmp, "greater than" );
   else if( result < 0 )
      strcpy( tmp, "less than" );
   else
      strcpy( tmp, "equal to" );
   printf( "\t_stricmp:  String 1 is %s string 2\n", tmp );
}
```

Output

```
Compare strings:
   The quick brown dog jumps over the lazy fox
   The QUICK brown dog jumps over the lazy fox

   strcmp:   String 1 is greater than string 2
   _stricmp:  String 1 is equal to string 2
```

See Also

memcmp, _memicmp, strcoll Functions, **_stricmp, strncmp, _strnicmp, strrchr, strspn, strxfrm**

strcoll Functions

Each of the **strcoll** and **wcscoll** functions compares two strings according to the **LC_COLLATE** category setting of the locale code page currently in use. Each of the **_mbscoll** functions compares two strings according to the multibyte code page currently in use. Use the **coll** functions for string comparisons when there is a difference between the character set order and the lexicographic character order in the current code page and this difference is of interest for the comparison. Use the corresponding **cmp** functions to test only for string equality.

strcoll Functions

SBCS	Unicode	MBCS	Description
strcoll	wcscoll	_mbscoll	Collate two strings
_stricoll	_wcsicoll	_mbsicoll	Collate two strings (case insensitive)
_strncoll	_wcsncoll	_mbsncoll	Collate first *count* characters of two strings
_strnicoll	_wcsnicoll	_mbsnicoll	Collate first *count* characters of two strings (case-insensitive)

Remarks

The single-byte character (SBCS) versions of these functions (**strcoll**, **stricoll**, **_strncoll**, and **_strnicoll**) compare *string1* and *string2* according to the **LC_COLLATE** category setting of the current locale. These functions differ from the corresponding **strcmp** functions in that the **strcoll** functions use locale code page information that provides collating sequences. For string comparisons in locales in which the character set order and the lexicographic character order differ, the **strcoll** functions should be used rather than the corresponding **strcmp** functions. For more information on **LC_COLLATE**, see **setlocale**.

For some code pages and corresponding character sets, the order of characters in the character set may differ from the lexicographic character order. In the "C" locale, this is not the case: the order of characters in the ASCII character set is the same as the lexicographic order of the characters. However, in certain European code pages, for example, the character 'a' (value 0x61) precedes the character 'ä' (value 0xE4) in the character set, but the character 'ä' precedes the character 'a' lexicographically. To perform a lexicographic comparison in such an instance, use **strcoll** rather than **strcmp**. Alternatively, you can use **strxfrm** on the original strings, then use **strcmp** on the resulting strings.

strcoll, **stricoll**, **_strncoll**, and **_strnicoll** automatically handle multibyte-character strings according to the locale code page currently in use, as do their wide-character (Unicode) counterparts. The multibyte-character (MBCS) versions of these functions, however, collate strings on a character basis according to the multibyte code page currently in use.

Because the **coll** functions collate strings lexicographically for comparison, whereas the **cmp** functions simply test for string equality, the **coll** functions are much slower than the corresponding **cmp** versions. Therefore, the **coll** functions should be used only when there is a difference between the character set order and the lexicographic character order in the current code page and this difference is of interest for the string comparison.

See Also

localeconv, _mbsnbcoll, setlocale, strcmp, strncmp, _strnicmp, strxfrm

strcoll, wcscoll, _mbscoll

Compare strings using locale-specific information.

int strcoll(const char * *string1* **, const char *** *string2* **);**
int wcscoll(const wchar_t * *string1* **, const wchar_t *** *string2* **);**
int _mbscoll(const unsigned char * *string1* **, const unsigned char *** *string2* **);**

Routine	Required Header	Compatibility
strcoll	<string.h>	ANSI, Win 95, Win NT
wcscoll	<wchar.h>, <string.h>	ANSI, Win 95, Win NT
_mbscoll	<mbstring.h>	Win 95, Win NT

For additional compatibility information, see "Compatibility" in the Introduction.

Libraries

LIBC.LIB	Single thread static library, retail version
LIBCMT.LIB	Multithread static library, retail version
MSVCRT.LIB	Import library for MSVCRT.DLL, retail version

Return Value

Each of these functions returns a value indicating the relationship of *string1* to *string2*, as follows.

Return Value	Relationship of string1 to string2
< 0	*string1* less than *string2*
0	*string1* identical to *string2*
> 0	*string1* greater than *string2*

Each of these functions returns **_NLSCMPERROR** on an error. To use
_NLSCMPERROR, include either STRING.H or MBSTRING.H. **wcscoll** can fail if
either *string1* or *string2* contains wide-character codes outside the domain of the collating
sequence. When an error occurs, **wcscoll** may set **errno** to **EINVAL**. To check for an
error on a call to **wcscoll**, set **errno** to 0 and then check **errno** after calling **wcscoll**.

Parameters

string1, string2
    Null-terminated strings to compare

Remarks

Each of these functions performs a case-sensitive comparison of *string1* and *string2*
according to the code page currently in use. These functions should be used only when
there is a difference between the character set order and the lexicographic character order
in the current code page and this difference is of interest for the string comparison.

Generic-Text Routine Mappings

TCHAR.H Routine	_UNICODE & _MBCS Not Defined	_MBCS Defined	_UNICODE Defined
_tcscoll	strcoll	_mbscoll	wcscoll

See Also

localeconv, _mbsnbcoll, setlocale, strcmp, _stricmp, strncmp, _strnicmp, strxfrm

_stricoll, _wcsicoll, _mbsicoll

Compare strings using locale-specific information.

int _stricoll(const char **string1,* **const char** **string2* **);**
int _wcsicoll(const wchar_t **string1,* **const wchar_t** **string2* **);**
int _mbsicoll(const unsigned char **string1,* **const unsigned char** **string2* **);**

Routine	Required Header	Compatibility
_stricoll	<string.h>	Win 95, Win NT
_wcsicoll	<wchar.h>, <string.h>	Win 95, Win NT
_mbsicoll	<mbstring.h>	Win 95, Win NT

For additional compatibility information, see "Compatibility" in the Introduction.

Libraries

LIBC.LIB	Single thread static library, retail version
LIBCMT.LIB	Multithread static library, retail version
MSVCRT.LIB	Import library for MSVCRT.DLL, retail version

Return Value

Each of these functions returns a value indicating the relationship of *string1* to *string2*, as follows.

Return Value	Relationship of string1 to string2
< 0	*string1* less than *string2*
0	*string1* identical to *string2*
> 0	*string1* greater than *string2*

Each of these functions returns **_NLSCMPERROR**. To use **_NLSCMPERROR**, include either STRING.H or MBSTRING.H. **_wcsicoll** can fail if either *string1* or *string2* contains wide-character codes outside the domain of the collating sequence. When an error occurs, **_wcsicoll** may set **errno** to **EINVAL**. To check for an error on a call to **_wcsicoll**, set **errno** to 0 and then check **errno** after calling **_wcsicoll**.

Parameters

string1, string2
   Null-terminated strings to compare

Remarks

Each of these functions performs a case-insensitive comparison of *string1* and *string2* according to the code page currently in use. These functions should be used only when there is a difference between the character set order and the lexicographic character order in the current code page and this difference is of interest for the string comparison.

Generic-Text Routine Mappings

TCHAR.H Routine	_UNICODE & _MBCS Not Defined	_MBCS Defined	_UNICODE Defined
_tcsicoll	_stricoll	_mbsicoll	_wcsicoll

See Also

localeconv, _mbsnbcoll, setlocale, strcmp, _stricmp, strncmp, _strnicmp, strxfrm

_strncoll, _wcsncoll, _mbsncoll

Compare strings using locale-specific information.

int _strncoll(const char ***string1, const char ***string2**, size_t** *count* **);**
int _wcsncoll(const wchar_t ***string1, const wchar_t ***string2**, size_t** *count* **);**
int _mbsncoll(const unsigned char ***string1, const unsigned char ***string2**, size_t** *count* **);**

Routine	Required Header	Compatibility
_strncoll	<string.h>	Win 95, Win NT
_wcsncoll	<wchar.h> or <string.h>	Win 95, Win NT
_mbsncoll	<mbstring.h>	Win 95, Win NT

For additional compatibility information, see "Compatibility" in the Introduction.

Libraries

LIBC.LIB	Single thread static library, retail version
LIBCMT.LIB	Multithread static library, retail version
MSVCRT.LIB	Import library for MSVCRT.DLL, retail version

Return Value

Each of these functions returns a value indicating the relationship of the substrings of *string1* and *string2*, as follows.

Return Value	Relationship of string1 to string2
< 0	*string1* less than *string2*
0	*string1* identical to *string2*
> 0	*string1* greater than *string2*

Each of these functions returns **_NLSCMPERROR**. To use **_NLSCMPERROR**, include either STRING.H or MBSTRING.H. **_wcsncoll** can fail if either *string1* or *string2* contains wide-character codes outside the domain of the collating sequence. When an error occurs, **_wcsncoll** may set **errno** to **EINVAL**. To check for an error on a call to **_wcsncoll**, set **errno** to 0 and then check **errno** after calling **_wcsncoll**.

Parameters

string1, string2
   Null-terminated strings to compare

count
   Number of characters to compare

Remarks

Each of these functions performs a case-sensitive comparison of the first *count* characters in *string1* and *string2* according to the code page currently in use. These functions should be used only when there is a difference between the character set order and the lexicographic character order in the current code page and this difference is of interest for the string comparison.

Generic-Text Routine Mappings

TCHAR.H Routine	_UNICODE & _MBCS Not Defined	_MBCS Defined	_UNICODE Defined
_tcsnccoll	_strncoll	_mbsnbcoll	_wcsncoll
_tcsncoll	_strncoll	_mbsnbcoll	_wcsncoll

See Also

localeconv, _mbsnbcoll, setlocale, strcmp, _stricmp, strncmp, _strnicmp, strxfrm

_strnicoll, _wcsnicoll, _mbsnicoll

Compare strings using locale-specific information.

int _strnicoll(const char *string1***, const char** *string2***, size_t** *count* **);**
int _wcsnicoll(const wchar_t *string1***, const wchar_t** *string2* **, size_t** *count* **);**
int _mbsnicoll(const unsigned char *string1***, const unsigned char** *string2***, size_t** *count* **);**

Routine	Required Header	Compatibility
_strnicoll	<string.h>	Win 95, Win NT
_wcsnicoll	<wchar.h> or <string.h>	Win 95, Win NT
_mbsnicoll	<mbstring.h>	Win 95, Win NT

For additional compatibility information, see "Compatibility" in the Introduction.

Libraries

LIBC.LIB	Single thread static library, retail version
LIBCMT.LIB	Multithread static library, retail version
MSVCRT.LIB	Import library for MSVCRT.DLL, retail version

Return Value

Each of these functions returns a value indicating the relationship of the substrings of *string1* and *string2*, as follows.

Return Value	Relationship of string1 to string2
< 0	*string1* less than *string2*
0	*string1* identical to *string2*
> 0	*string1* greater than *string2*

Each of these functions returns **_NLSCMPERROR**. To use **_NLSCMPERROR**, include either STRING.H or MBSTRING.H. **_wcsnicoll** can fail if either *string1* or *string2* contains wide-character codes outside the domain of the collating sequence. When an error occurs, **_wcsnicoll** may set **errno** to **EINVAL**. To check for an error on a call to **_wcsnicoll**, set **errno** to 0 and then check **errno** after calling **_wcsnicoll**.

Parameters

string1, string2
 Null-terminated strings to compare

count
 Number of characters to compare

Remarks

Each of these functions performs a case-insensitive comparison of the first *count* characters in *string1* and *string2* according to the code page currently in use. These functions should be used only when there is a difference between the character set order and the lexicographic character order in the current code page and this difference is of interest for the string comparison.

Generic-Text Routine Mappings

TCHAR.H Routine	_UNICODE & _MBCS Not Defined	_MBCS Defined	_UNICODE Defined
_tcsncicoll	_strnicoll	_mbsnbicoll	_wcsnicoll
_tcsnicoll	_strnicoll	_mbsnbicoll	_wcsnicoll

See Also

localeconv, _mbsnbcoll, setlocale, strcmp, _stricmp, strncmp, _strnicmp, strxfrm

strcpy, wcscpy, _mbscpy

Copy a string.

char *strcpy(char **strDestination***, const char ****strSource***);**
wchar_t *wcscpy(wchar_t **strDestination***, const wchar_t ****strSource***);**
unsigned char *_mbscpy(unsigned char **strDestination***, const unsigned char ****strSource***);**

Routine	Required Header	Compatibility
strcpy	<string.h>	ANSI, Win 95, Win NT
wcscpy	<string.h> or <wchar.h>	ANSI, Win 95, Win NT
_mbscpy	<mbstring.h>	Win 95, Win NT

For additional compatibility information, see "Compatibility" in the Introduction.

Libraries

LIBC.LIB	Single thread static library, retail version
LIBCMT.LIB	Multithread static library, retail version
MSVCRT.LIB	Import library for MSVCRT.DLL, retail version

Return Value

Each of these functions returns the destination string. No return value is reserved to indicate an error.

Parameters

strDestination
  Destination string

strSource
  Null-terminated source string

Remarks

The **strcpy** function copies *strSource*, including the terminating null character, to the location specified by *strDestination*. No overflow checking is performed when strings are copied or appended. The behavior of **strcpy** is undefined if the source and destination strings overlap.

wcscpy and **_mbscpy** are wide-character and multibyte-character versions of **strcpy**. The arguments and return value of **wcscpy** are wide-character strings; those of **_mbscpy** are multibyte-character strings. These three functions behave identically otherwise.

Generic-Text Routine Mappings

TCHAR.H Routine	_UNICODE & _MBCS Not Defined	_MBCS Defined	_UNICODE Defined
_tcscpy	strcpy	_mbscpy	wcscpy

Example

```
/* STRCPY.C: This program uses strcpy
 * and strcat to build a phrase.
 */

#include <string.h>
#include <stdio.h>
```

```
void main( void )
{
   char string[80];
   strcpy( string, "Hello world from " );
   strcat( string, "strcpy " );
   strcat( string, "and " );
   strcat( string, "strcat!" );
   printf( "String = %s\n", string );
}
```

Output

```
String = Hello world from strcpy and strcat!
```

See Also

strcat, strcmp, strncat, strncmp, strncpy, _strnicmp, strrchr, strspn

strcspn, wcscspn, _mbscspn

Find a substring in a string.

size_t strcspn(const char **string***, const char ****strCharSet***);**
size_t wcscspn(const wchar_t **string***, const wchar_t ****strCharSet***);**
size_t _mbscspn(const unsigned char **string***, const unsigned char ****strCharSet***);**

Routine	Required Header	Compatibility
strcspn	<string.h>	ANSI, Win 95, Win NT
wcscspn	<string.h> or <wchar.h>	ANSI, Win 95, Win NT
_mbscspn	<mbstring.h>	Win 95, Win NT

For additional compatibility information, see "Compatibility" in the Introduction.

Libraries

LIBC.LIB	Single thread static library, retail version
LIBCMT.LIB	Multithread static library, retail version
MSVCRT.LIB	Import library for MSVCRT.DLL, retail version

Return Value

Each of these functions returns an integer value specifying the length of the initial
segment of *string* that consists entirely of characters not in *strCharSet*. If *string* begins
with a character that is in *strCharSet*, the function returns 0. No return value is reserved
to indicate an error.

Parameters

string
> Null-terminated searched string

strCharSet
> Null-terminated character set

Remarks

The **strcspn** function returns the index of the first occurrence of a character in *string* that belongs to the set of characters in *strCharSet*. Terminating null characters are included in the search.

wcscspn and **_mbscspn** are wide-character and multibyte-character versions of **strcspn.** The arguments of **wcscspn** are wide-character strings; those of **_mbscspn** are multibyte-character strings. These three functions behave identically otherwise.

Generic-Text Routine Mappings

TCHAR.H Routine	_UNICODE & _MBCS Not Defined	_MBCS Defined	_UNICODE Defined
_tcscspn	strcspn	_mbscspn	wcscspn

Example

```
/* STRCSPN.C */

#include <string.h>
#include <stdio.h>

void main( void )
{
    char string[] = "xyzabc";
    int  pos;

    pos = strcspn( string, "abc" );
    printf( "First a, b or c in %s is at character %d\n",
    ↪ string, pos );
}
```

Output

```
First a, b or c in xyzabc is at character 3
```

See Also

strncat, strncmp, strncpy, _strnicmp, strrchr, strspn

_strdate, _wstrdate

Copy a date to a buffer.

char *_strdate(char *datestr**);**
wchar_t *_wstrdate(wchar_t *datestr**);**

Routine	Required Header	Compatibility
_strdate	<time.h>	Win 95, Win NT
_wstrdate	<time.h> or <wchar.h>	Win 95, Win NT

For additional compatibility information, see "Compatibility" in the Introduction.

Libraries

LIBC.LIB	Single thread static library, retail version
LIBCMT.LIB	Multithread static library, retail version
MSVCRT.LIB	Import library for MSVCRT.DLL, retail version

Return Value

Each of these functions returns a pointer to the resulting character string *datestr*.

Parameter

datestr
   A pointer to a buffer containing the formatted date string

Remarks

The **_strdate** function copies a date to the buffer pointed to by *datestr,* formatted *mm/dd/yy*, where *mm* is two digits representing the month, *dd* is two digits representing the day, and *yy* is the last two digits of the year. For example, the string 12/05/99 represents December 5, 1999. The buffer must be at least 9 bytes long.

_wstrdate is a wide-character version of **_strdate**; the argument and return value of **_wstrdate** are wide-character strings. These functions behave identically otherwise.

Generic-Text Routine Mappings

TCHAR.H Routine	_UNICODE & _MBCS Not Defined	_MBCS Defined	_UNICODE Defined
_tstrdate	_strdate	_strdate	_wstrdate

Example

```
/* TIMES.C illustrates various time and date functions including:
 *      time            _ftime          ctime           asctime
 *      localtime       gmtime          mktime          _tzset
 *      _strtime        _strdate        strftime
 *
 * Also the global variable:
 *      _tzname
 */

#include <time.h>
#include <stdio.h>
#include <sys/types.h>
#include <sys/timeb.h>
#include <string.h>

void main()
{
    char tmpbuf[128], ampm[] = "AM";
    time_t ltime;
    struct _timeb tstruct;
    struct tm *today, *gmt, xmas = { 0, 0, 12, 25, 11, 93 };

    /* Set time zone from TZ environment variable. If TZ is not set,
     * the operating system is queried to obtain the default value
     * for the variable.
     */
    _tzset();

    /* Display operating system-style date and time. */
    _strtime( tmpbuf );
    printf( "OS time:\t\t\t\t%s\n", tmpbuf );
    _strdate( tmpbuf );
    printf( "OS date:\t\t\t\t%s\n", tmpbuf );

    /* Get UNIX-style time and display as number and string. */
    time( &ltime );
    printf( "Time in seconds since UTC 1/1/70:\t%ld\n", ltime );
    printf( "UNIX time and date:\t\t\t%s", ctime( &ltime ) );

    /* Display UTC. */
    gmt = gmtime( &ltime );
    printf( "Coordinated universal time:\t\t%s", asctime( gmt ) );

    /* Convert to time structure and adjust for PM if necessary. */
    today = localtime( &ltime );
    if( today->tm_hour > 12 )
```

```
{
strcpy( ampm, "PM" );
today->tm_hour -= 12;
}
if( today->tm_hour == 0 )  /* Adjust if midnight hour. */
today->tm_hour = 12;

/* Note how pointer addition is used to skip the first 11
 * characters and printf is used to trim off terminating
 * characters.
 */
printf( "12-hour time:\t\t\t\t%.8s %s\n", asctime( today ) + 11, ampm );

/* Print additional time information. */
_ftime( &tstruct );
printf( "Plus milliseconds:\t\t\t%u\n", tstruct.millitm );
printf( "Zone difference in seconds from UTC:\t%u\n", tstruct.timezone );
printf( "Time zone name:\t\t\t\t%s\n", _tzname[0] );
printf( "Daylight savings:\t\t\t%s\n", tstruct.dstflag ? "YES" : "NO" );

/* Make time for noon on Christmas, 1997. */
if( mktime( &xmas ) != (time_t)-1 )
printf( "Christmas\t\t\t\t%s\n", asctime( &xmas ) );

/* Use time structure to build a customized time string. */
today = localtime( &ltime );

/* Use strftime to build a customized time string. */
strftime( tmpbuf, 128, "Today is %A, day %d of %B in the year %Y.\n", today );
printf( tmpbuf );
}
```

Output

```
OS time:                              21:51:03
OS date:                              05/03/94
Time in seconds since UTC 1/1/70:     768027063
UNIX time and date:                   Tue May 03 21:51:03 1998
Coordinated universal time:           Wed May 04 04:51:03 1998
12-hour time:                         09:51:03 PM
Plus milliseconds:                    279
Zone difference in seconds from UTC:  480
Time zone name:
Daylight savings:                     YES
Christmas                             Sat Dec 25 12:00:00 1997

Today is Tuesday, day 03 of May in the year 1998.
```

See Also

asctime, ctime, gmtime, localtime, mktime, time, _tzset

_strdup, _wcsdup, _mbsdup

Duplicate strings.

char *_strdup(const char **strSource** **);**
wchar_t *_wcsdup(const wchar_t **strSource** **);**
unsigned char *_mbsdup(const unsigned char **strSource** **);**

Routine	Required Header	Compatibility
_strdup	<string.h>	Win 95, Win NT
_wcsdup	<string.h> or <wchar.h>	Win 95, Win NT
_mbsdup	<mbstring.h>	Win 95, Win NT

For additional compatibility information, see "Compatibility" in the Introduction.

Libraries

LIBC.LIB	Single thread static library, retail version
LIBCMT.LIB	Multithread static library, retail version
MSVCRT.LIB	Import library for MSVCRT.DLL, retail version

Return Value

Each of these functions returns a pointer to the storage location for the copied string or **NULL** if storage cannot be allocated.

Parameter

strSource
    Null-terminated source string

Remarks

The **_strdup** function calls malloc to allocate storage space for a copy of *strSource* and then copies *strSource* to the allocated space.

_wcsdup and **_mbsdup** are wide-character and multibyte-character versions of **_strdup**. The arguments and return value of **_wcsdup** are wide-character strings; those of **_mbsdup** are multibyte-character strings. These three functions behave identically otherwise.

Generic-Text Routine Mappings

TCHAR.H Routine	_UNICODE & _MBCS Not Defined	_MBCS Defined	_UNICODE Defined
_tcsdup	_strdup	_mbsdup	_wcsdup

Because **_strdup** calls **malloc** to allocate storage space for the copy of *strSource*, it is good practice always to release this memory by calling the **free** routine on the pointer returned by the call to **_strdup**.

Example

```
/* STRDUP.C */

#include <string.h>
#include <stdio.h>

void main( void )
{
   char buffer[] = "This is the buffer text";
   char *newstring;
   printf( "Original: %s\n", buffer );
   newstring = _strdup( buffer );
   printf( "Copy:     %s\n", newstring );
   free( newstring );
}
```

Output

```
Original: This is the buffer text
Copy:     This is the buffer text
```

See Also

memset, strcat, strcmp, strncat, strncmp, strncpy, _strnicmp, strrchr, strspn

strerror, _strerror

Get a system error message (**strerror**) or prints a user-supplied error message (**_strerror**).

char *strerror(int *errnum* **);**
char *_strerror(const char *strErrMsg **);**

Routine	Required Header	Compatibility
strerror	<string.h>	ANSI, Win 95, Win NT
_strerror	<string.h>	Win 95, Win NT

For additional compatibility information, see "Compatibility" in the Introduction.

Libraries

LIBC.LIB	Single thread static library, retail version
LIBCMT.LIB	Multithread static library, retail version
MSVCRT.LIB	Import library for MSVCRT.DLL, retail version

Return Value

strerror and **_strerror** return a pointer to the error-message string. Subsequent calls to **strerror** or **_strerror** can overwrite the string.

Parameters

errnum
> Error number

strErrMsg
> User-supplied message

Remarks

The **strerror** function maps *errnum* to an error-message string, returning a pointer to the string. Neither **strerror** nor **_strerror** actually prints the message: For that, you need to call an output function such as fprintf:

```
if (( _access( "datafile",2 )) == -1 )
    fprintf( stderr, strerror(NULL) );
```

If *strErrMsg* is passed as **NULL**, **_strerror** returns a pointer to a string containing the system error message for the last library call that produced an error. The error-message string is terminated by the newline character ('\n'). If *strErrMsg* is not equal to **NULL**, then **_strerror** returns a pointer to a string containing (in order) your string message, a colon, a space, the system error message for the last library call producing an error, and a newline character. Your string message can be, at most, 94 bytes long.

The actual error number for **_strerror** is stored in the variable errno. The system error messages are accessed through the variable _sys_errlist, which is an array of messages ordered by error number. **_strerror** accesses the appropriate error message by using the **errno** value as an index to the variable **_sys_errlist**. The value of the variable _sys_nerr is defined as the maximum number of elements in the **_sys_errlist** array. To produce accurate results, call **_strerror** immediately after a library routine returns with an error. Otherwise, subsequent calls to **strerror** or **_strerror** can overwrite the **errno** value.

_strerror is not part of the ANSI definition but is instead a Microsoft extension to it. Do not use it where portability is desired; for ANSI compatibility, use **strerror** instead.

Example

```
/* PERROR.C: This program attempts to open a file named
 * NOSUCHF.ILE. Because this file probably doesn't exist,
 * an error message is displayed. The same message is
 * created using perror, strerror, and _strerror.
 */

#include <fcntl.h>
#include <sys/types.h>
#include <sys/stat.h>
```

```
#include <io.h>
#include <stdlib.h>
#include <stdio.h>
#include <string.h>

void main( void )
{
   int  fh;

   if( (fh = _open( "NOSUCHF.ILE", _O_RDONLY )) == -1 )
   {
      /* Three ways to create error message: */
      perror( "perror says open failed" );
      printf( "strerror says open failed: %s\n", strerror( errno ) );
      printf( _strerror( "_strerror says open failed" ) );
   }
   else
   {
      printf( "open succeeded on input file\n" );
      _close( fh );
   }
}
```

Output

```
perror says open failed: No such file or directory

strerror says open failed: No such file or directory
_strerror says open failed: No such file or directory
```

See Also

clearerr, **ferror**, **perror**

strftime, wcsftime

Format a time string.

size_t strftime(char *****strDest, **size_t** *maxsize*, **const char *****format**, **const struct tm *****timeptr**);
size_t wcsftime(wchar_t *****strDest, **size_t** *maxsize*, **const wchar_t *****format**, **const struct tm *****timeptr**);

Routine	Required Header	Compatibility
strftime	<time.h>	ANSI, Win 95, Win NT
wcsftime	<time.h> or <wchar.h>	ANSI, Win 95, Win NT

For additional compatibility information, see "Compatibility" in the Introduction.

Libraries

LIBC.LIB	Single thread static library, retail version
LIBCMT.LIB	Multithread static library, retail version
MSVCRT.LIB	Import library for MSVCRT.DLL, retail version

Return Value

strftime returns the number of characters placed in *strDest* if the total number of resulting characters, including the terminating null, is not more than *maxsize*. **wcsftime** returns the corresponding number of wide characters. Otherwise, the functions return 0, and the contents of *strDest* is indeterminate.

Parameters

strDest
    Output string

maxsize
    Maximum length of string

format
    Format-control string

timeptr
    tm data structure

Remarks

The **strftime** and **wcsftime** functions format the **tm** time value in *timeptr* according to the supplied *format* argument and store the result in the buffer *strDest*. At most, *maxsize* characters are placed in the string. For a description of the fields in the *timeptr* structure, see asctime. **wcsftime** is the wide-character equivalent of **strftime**; its string-pointer argument points to a wide-character string. These functions behave identically otherwise.

> **Note**   Prior to this version of Visual C++, the documentation described the *format* parameter of **wcsftime** as having the datatype **const wchar_t ***, but the actual implementation of the *format* datatype was **const char ***. In this version, the implementation of the *format* datatype has been updated to reflect the previous and current documentation, that is: **const wchar_t ***.

Generic-Text Routine Mappings

TCHAR.H Routine	_UNICODE & _MBCS Not Defined	_MBCS Defined	_UNICODE Defined
_tcsftime	strftime	strftime	wcsftime

The *format* argument consists of one or more codes; as in **printf**, the formatting codes are preceded by a percent sign (%). Characters that do not begin with % are copied unchanged to *strDest*. The **LC_TIME** category of the current locale affects the output formatting of **strftime**.(For more information on **LC_TIME**, see **setlocale**.) The formatting codes for **strftime** are listed below:

%a
Abbreviated weekday name

%A
Full weekday name

%b
Abbreviated month name

%B
Full month name

%c
Date and time representation appropriate for locale

%d
Day of month as decimal number (01–31)

%H
Hour in 24-hour format (00–23)

%I
Hour in 12-hour format (01–12)

%j
Day of year as decimal number (001–366)

%m
Month as decimal number (01–12)

%M
Minute as decimal number (00–59)

%p
Current locale's A.M./P.M. indicator for 12-hour clock

%S
Second as decimal number (00–59)

%U
Week of year as decimal number, with Sunday as first day of week (00–53)

%w
Weekday as decimal number (0–6; Sunday is 0)

%W
Week of year as decimal number, with Monday as first day of week (00–53)

%x

Date representation for current locale

%X

Time representation for current locale

%y

Year without century, as decimal number (00–99)

%Y

Year with century, as decimal number

%z, %Z

Time-zone name or abbreviation; no characters if time zone is unknown

% %

Percent sign

As in the **printf** function, the **#** flag may prefix any formatting code. In that case, the meaning of the format code is changed as follows.

Format Code	Meaning
%#a, %#A, %#b, %#B, %#p, %#X, %#z, %#Z, %#%	# flag is ignored.
%#c	Long date and time representation, appropriate for current locale. For example: "Tuesday, March 14, 1995, 12:41:29."
%#x	Long date representation, appropriate to current locale. For example: "Tuesday, March 14, 1995."
%#d, %#H, %#I, %#j, %#m, %#M, %#S, %#U, %#w, %#W, %#y, %#Y	Remove leading zeros (if any).

Example

```
/* TIMES.C illustrates various time and date functions including:
 *
 *      time            _ftime          ctime           asctime
 *      localtime       gmtime          mktime          _tzset
 *      _strtime        _strdate        strftime
 *
 * Also the global variable:
 *      _tzname
 */

#include <time.h>
#include <stdio.h>
#include <sys/types.h>
#include <sys/timeb.h>
#include <string.h>
```

```
void main()
{
    char tmpbuf[128], ampm[] = "AM";
    time_t ltime;
    struct _timeb tstruct;
    struct tm *today, *gmt, xmas = { 0, 0, 12, 25, 11, 93 };

    /* Set time zone from TZ environment variable. If TZ is not set,
     * the operating system is queried to obtain the default value
     * for the variable.
     */
    _tzset();

    /* Display operating system-style date and time. */
    _strtime( tmpbuf );
    printf( "OS time:\t\t\t\t%s\n", tmpbuf );
    _strdate( tmpbuf );
    printf( "OS date:\t\t\t\t%s\n", tmpbuf );

    /* Get UNIX-style time and display as number and string. */
    time( &ltime );
    printf( "Time in seconds since UTC 1/1/70:\t%ld\n", ltime );
    printf( "UNIX time and date:\t\t\t%s", ctime( &ltime ) );

    /* Display UTC. */
    gmt = gmtime( &ltime );
    printf( "Coordinated universal time:\t\t%s", asctime( gmt ) );

    /* Convert to time structure and adjust for PM if necessary. */
    today = localtime( &ltime );
    if( today->tm_hour > 12 )
    {
    strcpy( ampm, "PM" );
    today->tm_hour -= 12;
    }
    if( today->tm_hour == 0 )  /* Adjust if midnight hour. */
    today->tm_hour = 12;

    /* Note how pointer addition is used to skip the first 11
     * characters and printf is used to trim off terminating characters.
     */
    printf( "12-hour time:\t\t\t\t%.8s %s\n", asctime( today ) + 11, ampm );

    /* Print additional time information. */
    _ftime( &tstruct );
    printf( "Plus milliseconds:\t\t\t%u\n", tstruct.millitm );
    printf( "Zone difference in seconds from UTC:\t%u\n", tstruct.timezone );
    printf( "Time zone name:\t\t\t\t%s\n", _tzname[0] );
    printf( "Daylight savings:\t\t\t%s\n", tstruct.dstflag ? "YES" : "NO" );
```

```
/* Make time for noon on Christmas, 1993. */
if( mktime( &xmas ) != (time_t)-1 )
printf( "Christmas\t\t\t\t%s\n", asctime( &xmas ) );

/* Use time structure to build a customized time string. */
today = localtime( &ltime );

/* Use strftime to build a customized time string. */
strftime( tmpbuf, 128,
    "Today is %A, day %d of %B in the year %Y.\n", today );
printf( tmpbuf );
}
```

Output

```
OS time:                              21:51:03
OS date:                              05/03/94
Time in seconds since UTC 1/1/70:     768027063
UNIX time and date:                   Tue May 03 21:51:03 1994
Coordinated universal time:           Wed May 04 04:51:03 1994
12-hour time:                         09:51:03 PM
Plus milliseconds:                    279
Zone difference in seconds from UTC:  480
Time zone name:
Daylight savings:                     YES
Christmas                             Sat Dec 25 12:00:00 1993

Today is Tuesday, day 03 of May in the year 1994.
```

See Also

localeconv, setlocale, strcoll, _stricoll, strxfrm

_stricmp, _wcsicmp, _mbsicmp

Perform a lowercase comparison of strings.

int _stricmp(const char **string1***, const char ****string2***);**
int _wcsicmp(const wchar_t **string1***, const wchar_t ****string2***);**
int _mbsicmp(const unsigned char **string1***, const unsigned char_t ****string2***);**

Routine	Required Header	Compatibility
_stricmp	<string.h>	Win 95, Win NT
_wcsicmp	<string.h> or <wchar.h>	Win 95, Win NT
_mbsicmp	<mbstring.h>	Win 95, Win NT

For additional compatibility information, see "Compatibility" in the Introduction.

Libraries

LIBC.LIB	Single thread static library, retail version
LIBCMT.LIB	Multithread static library, retail version
MSVCRT.LIB	Import library for MSVCRT.DLL, retail version

Return Value

The return value indicates the relation of *string1* to *string2* as follows.

Return Value	Description
< 0	*string1* less than *string2*
0	*string1* identical to *string2*
> 0	*string1* greater than *string2*

On an error, **_mbsicmp** returns **_NLSCMPERROR**, which is defined in STRING.H and MBSTRING.H.

Parameters

string1, *string2*
   Null-terminated strings to compare

Remarks

The **_stricmp** function lexicographically compares lowercase versions of *string1* and *string2* and returns a value indicating their relationship. **_stricmp** differs from **_stricoll** in that the **_stricmp** comparison is not affected by locale, whereas the **_stricoll** comparison is according to the **LC_COLLATE** category of the current locale. For more information on the **LC_COLLATE** category, see **setlocale**.

The **_strcmpi** function is equivalent to **_stricmp** and is provided for backward compatibility only.

_wcsicmp and **_mbsicmp** are wide-character and multibyte-character versions of **_stricmp**. The arguments and return value of **_wcsicmp** are wide-character strings; those of **_mbsicmp** are multibyte-character strings. **_mbsicmp** recognizes multibyte-character sequences according to the current multibyte code page and returns **_NLSCMPERROR** on an error. (For more information, see "Code Pages" in Chapter 1, "Run-Time Routines by Category.") These three functions behave identically otherwise.

_wcsicmp and **wcscmp** behave identically except that **wcscmp** does not convert its arguments to lowercase before comparing them. **_mbsicmp** and **_mbscmp** behave identically except that **_mbscmp** does not convert its arguments to lowercase before comparing them.

Generic-Text Routine Mappings

TCHAR.H Routine	_UNICODE & _MBCS Not Defined	_MBCS Defined	_UNICODE Defined
_tcsicmp	_stricmp	_mbsicmp	_wcsicmp

Example

```
/* STRCMP.C */

#include <string.h>
#include <stdio.h>

char string1[] = "The quick brown dog jumps over the lazy fox";
char string2[] = "The QUICK brown dog jumps over the lazy fox";

void main( void )
{
   char tmp[20];
   int result;
   /* Case sensitive */
   printf( "Compare strings:\n\t%s\n\t%s\n\n", string1, string2 );
   result = strcmp( string1, string2 );
   if( result > 0 )
      strcpy( tmp, "greater than" );
   else if( result < 0 )
      strcpy( tmp, "less than" );
   else
      strcpy( tmp, "equal to" );
   printf( "\tstrcmp:   String 1 is %s string 2\n", tmp );
   /* Case insensitive (could use equivalent _stricmp) */
   result = _stricmp( string1, string2 );
   if( result > 0 )
      strcpy( tmp, "greater than" );
   else if( result < 0 )
      strcpy( tmp, "less than" );
   else
      strcpy( tmp, "equal to" );
   printf( "\t_stricmp:  String 1 is %s string 2\n", tmp );
}
```

Output

```
Compare strings:
   The quick brown dog jumps over the lazy fox
   The QUICK brown dog jumps over the lazy fox

   strcmp:   String 1 is greater than string 2
   _stricmp:  String 1 is equal to string 2
```

See Also

memcmp, **_memicmp**, **strcmp**, **strcoll Functions**, **strncmp**, **_strnicmp**, **strrchr**, **_strset**, **strspn**

strlen, wcslen, _mbslen, _mbstrlen

Get the length of a string.

size_t strlen(const char **string* **);**
size_t wcslen(const wchar_t **string* **);**
size_t _mbslen(const unsigned char **string* **);**
size_t _mbstrlen(const char **string* **);**

Routine	Required Header	Compatibility
strlen	<string.h>	ANSI, Win 95, Win NT
wcslen	<string.h> or <wchar.h>	ANSI, Win 95, Win NT
_mbslen	<mbstring.h>	Win 95, Win NT
_mbstrlen	<stdlib.h>	Win 95, Win NT

For additional compatibility information, see "Compatibility" in the Introduction.

Libraries

LIBC.LIB	Single thread static library, retail version
LIBCMT.LIB	Multithread static library, retail version
MSVCRT.LIB	Import library for MSVCRT.DLL, retail version

Return Value

Each of these functions returns the number of characters in *string*, excluding the terminal **NULL**. No return value is reserved to indicate an error.

Parameter

string
    Null-terminated string

Remarks

Each of these functions returns the number of characters in *string*, not including the terminating null character. **wcslen** is a wide-character version of **strlen**; the argument of **wcslen** is a wide-character string. **wcslen** and **strlen** behave identically otherwise.

Generic-Text Routine Mappings

TCHAR.H Routine	_UNICODE & _MBCS Not Defined	_MBCS Defined	_UNICODE Defined
_tcslen	strlen	strlen	wcslen
_tcsclen	strlen	_mbslen	wcslen

_mbslen and **_mbstrlen** return the number of multibyte characters in a multibyte-character string. **_mbslen** recognizes multibyte-character sequences according to the multibyte code page currently in use; it does not test for multibyte-character validity. **_mbstrlen** tests for multibyte-character validity and recognizes multibyte-character sequences according to the **LC_CTYPE** category setting of the current locale. For more information about the **LC_CTYPE** category, see **setlocale**.

Example

```
/*  STRLEN.C */

#include <string.h>
#include <stdio.h>
#include <conio.h>
#include <dos.h>

void main( void )
{
    char buffer[61] = "How long am I?";
    int  len;
    len = strlen( buffer );
    printf( "'%s' is %d characters long\n", buffer, len );
}
```

Output

```
'How long am I?' is 14 characters long
```

See Also

setlocale, strcat, strcmp, strcoll Functions, strcpy, strrchr, _strset, strspn

_strlwr, _wcslwr, _mbslwr

Convert a string to lowercase.

char *_strlwr(char *_string_);
wchar_t *_wcslwr(wchar_t *_string_);
unsigned char *_mbslwr(unsigned char *_string_);

Routine	Required Header	Compatibility
_strlwr	<string.h>	Win 95, Win NT
_wcslwr	<string.h> or <wchar.h>	Win 95, Win NT
_mbslwr	<mbstring.h>	Win 95, Win NT

For additional compatibility information, see "Compatibility" in the Introduction.

Libraries

LIBC.LIB	Single thread static library, retail version
LIBCMT.LIB	Multithread static library, retail version
MSVCRT.LIB	Import library for MSVCRT.DLL, retail version

Return Value

Each of these functions returns a pointer to the converted string. Because the modification is done in place, the pointer returned is the same as the pointer passed as the input argument. No return value is reserved to indicate an error.

Parameter

string
    Null-terminated string to convert to lowercase

Remarks

The **_strlwr** function converts any uppercase letters in *string* to lowercase as determined by the **LC_CTYPE** category setting of the current locale. Other characters are not affected. For more information on **LC_CTYPE**, see **setlocale**.

The **_wcslwr** and **_mbslwr** functions are wide-character and multibyte-character versions of **_strlwr**. The argument and return value of **_wcslwr** are wide-character strings; those of **_mbslwr** are multibyte-character strings. These three functions behave identically otherwise.

Generic-Text Routine Mappings

TCHAR.H Routine	_UNICODE & _MBCS Not Defined	_MBCS Defined	_UNICODE Defined
_tcslwr	_strlwr	_mbslwr	_wcslwr

Example

```
/* STRLWR.C: This program uses _strlwr and _strupr to create
 * uppercase and lowercase copies of a mixed-case string.
 */

#include <string.h>
#include <stdio.h>
```

```
void main( void )
{
    char string[100] = "The String to End All Strings!";
    char *copy1, *copy2;
    copy1 = _strlwr( _strdup( string ) );
    copy2 = _strupr( _strdup( string ) );
    printf( "Mixed: %s\n", string );
    printf( "Lower: %s\n", copy1 );
    printf( "Upper: %s\n", copy2 );
}
```

Output

```
Mixed: The String to End All Strings!
Lower: the string to end all strings!
Upper: THE STRING TO END ALL STRINGS!
```

See Also

_strupr

strncat, wcsncat, _mbsncat

Append characters of a string.

char *strncat(char *_strDest_, const char *_strSource_, size_t _count_);
wchar_t *wcsncat(wchar_t *_strDest_, const wchar_t *_strSource_, size_t _count_);
unsigned char *_mbsncat(unsigned char *_strDest_, const unsigned char *_strSource_, size_t _count_);

Routine	Required Header	Compatibility
strncat	<string.h>	ANSI, Win 95, Win NT
wcsncat	<string.h> or <wchar.h>	ANSI, Win 95, Win NT
_mbsncat	<mbstring.h>	Win 95, Win NT

For additional compatibility information, see "Compatibility" in the Introduction.

Libraries

LIBC.LIB	Single thread static library, retail version
LIBCMT.LIB	Multithread static library, retail version
MSVCRT.LIB	Import library for MSVCRT.DLL, retail version

Return Value

Each of these functions returns a pointer to the destination string. No return value is reserved to indicate an error.

Parameters

strDest
  Null-terminated destination string

strSource
  Null-terminated source string

count
  Number of characters to append

Remarks

The **strncat** function appends, at most, the first *count* characters of *strSource* to *strDest*.
The initial character of *strSource* overwrites the terminating null character of *strDest*. If a
null character appears in *strSource* before *count* characters are appended, **strncat** appends
all characters from *strSource*, up to the null character. If *count* is greater than the length
of *strSource*, the length of *strSource* is used in place of *count*. The resulting string is
terminated with a null character. If copying takes place between strings that overlap,
the behavior is undefined.

wcsncat and **_mbsncat** are wide-character and multibyte-character versions of **strncat**.
The string arguments and return value of **wcsncat** are wide-character strings; those of
_mbsncat are multibyte-character strings. These three functions behave identically
otherwise.

Generic-Text Routine Mappings

TCHAR.H Routine	_UNICODE & _MBCS Not Defined	_MBCS Defined	_UNICODE Defined
_tcsncat	strncat	_mbsnbcat	wcsncat

Example

```
/* STRNCAT.C */

#include <string.h>
#include <stdio.h>

void main( void )
{
    char string[80] = "This is the initial string!";
    char suffix[] = " extra text to add to the string...";
    /* Combine strings with no more than 19 characters of suffix: */
    printf( "Before: %s\n", string );
    strncat( string, suffix, 19 );
    printf( "After:  %s\n", string );
}
```

Output

```
Before: This is the initial string!
After:  This is the initial string! extra text to add
```

See Also

_mbsnbcat, strcat, strcmp, strcpy, strncmp, strncpy, _strnicmp, strrchr, _strset, strspn

strncmp, wcsncmp, _mbsncmp

Compare characters of two strings.

int strncmp(const char *_string1_, const char *_string2_, size_t _count_);
int wcsncmp(const wchar_t *_string1_, const wchar_t *_string2_, size_t _count_);
int _mbsncmp(const unsigned char *_string1_, const unsigned char _string2_, size_t _count_);

Routine	Required Header	Compatibility
strncmp	<string.h>	ANSI, Win 95, Win NT
wcsncmp	<string.h> or <wchar.h>	ANSI, Win 95, Win NT
_mbsncmp	<mbstring.h>	Win 95, Win NT

For additional compatibility information, see "Compatibility" in the Introduction.

Libraries

LIBC.LIB	Single thread static library, retail version
LIBCMT.LIB	Multithread static library, retail version
MSVCRT.LIB	Import library for MSVCRT.DLL, retail version

Return Value

The return value indicates the relation of the substrings of _string1_ and _string2_ as follows.

Return Value	Description
< 0	_string1_ substring less than _string2_ substring
0	_string1_ substring identical to _string2_ substring
> 0	_string1_ substring greater than _string2_ substring

On an error, **_mbsncmp** returns **_NLSCMPERROR**, which is defined in STRING.H and MBSTRING.H.

Parameters

string1, *string2*
> Strings to compare

count
> Number of characters to compare

Remarks

The **strncmp** function lexicographically compares, at most, the first *count* characters in *string1* and *string2* and returns a value indicating the relationship between the substrings. **strncmp** is a case-sensitive version of **_strnicmp**. Unlike **strcoll**, **strncmp** is not affected by locale. For more information on the **LC_COLLATE** category, see **setlocale**.

wcsncmp and **_mbsncmp** are wide-character and multibyte-character versions of **strncmp**. The arguments and return value of **wcsncmp** are wide-character strings; those of **_mbsncmp** are multibyte-character strings. **_mbsncmp** recognizes multibyte-character sequences according to the current multibyte code page and returns **_NLSCMPERROR** on an error. For more information, see "Code Pages" in Chapter 1, "Run-Time Routines by Category." These three functions behave identically otherwise. **wcsncmp** and **_mbsncmp** are case-sensitive versions of **_wcsnicmp** and **_mbsnicmp**.

Generic-Text Routine Mappings

TCHAR.H Routine	_UNICODE & _MBCS Not Defined	_MBCS Defined	_UNICODE Defined
_tcsnccmp	strncmp	_mbsnbcmp	wcsncmp
_tcsncmp	strncmp	_mbsnbcmp	wcsncmp

Example

```
/* STRNCMP.C */
#include <string.h>
#include <stdio.h>

char string1[] = "The quick brown dog jumps over the lazy fox";
char string2[] = "The QUICK brown fox jumps over the lazy dog";

void main( void )
{
   char tmp[20];
   int result;
   printf( "Compare strings:\n\t\t%s\n\t\t%s\n\n", string1, string2 );
   printf( "Function:\tstrncmp (first 10 characters only)\n" );
   result = strncmp( string1, string2 , 10 );
   if( result > 0 )
      strcpy( tmp, "greater than" );
   else if( result < 0 )
      strcpy( tmp, "less than" );
```

```
        else
           strcpy( tmp, "equal to" );
        printf( "Result:\t\tString 1 is %s string 2\n\n", tmp );
        printf( "Function:\tstrnicmp _strnicmp (first 10 characters only)\n" );
        result = _strnicmp( string1, string2, 10 );
        if( result > 0 )
           strcpy( tmp, "greater than" );
        else if( result < 0 )
           strcpy( tmp, "less than" );
        else
           strcpy( tmp, "equal to" );
        printf( "Result:\t\tString 1 is %s string 2\n\n", tmp );
     }
```

Output

```
Compare strings:
        The quick brown dog jumps over the lazy fox
        The QUICK brown fox jumps over the lazy dog

Function:    strncmp (first 10 characters only)
Result:      String 1 is greater than string 2

Function:    _strnicmp (first 10 characters only)
Result:      String 1 is equal to string 2
```

See Also

_mbsnbcmp, _mbsnbicmp, strcmp, strcoll Functions, _strnicmp, strrchr, _strset, strspn

strncpy, wcsncpy, _mbsncpy

Copy characters of one string to another.

char *strncpy(char *strDest**, const char ***strSource**, size_t** count **);**
wchar_t *wcsncpy(wchar_t *strDest**, const wchar_t ***strSource**, size_t** count **);**
unsigned char *_mbsncpy(unsigned char *strDest**, const unsigned char ***strSource**, size_t** count **);**

Routine	Required Header	Compatibility
strncpy	<string.h>	ANSI, Win 95, Win NT
wcsncpy	<string.h> or <wchar.h>	ANSI, Win 95, Win NT
_mbsncpy	<mbstring.h>	Win 95, Win NT

For additional compatibility information, see "Compatibility" in the Introduction.

Libraries

LIBC.LIB	Single thread static library, retail version
LIBCMT.LIB	Multithread static library, retail version
MSVCRT.LIB	Import library for MSVCRT.DLL, retail version

Return Value

Each of these functions returns *strDest*. No return value is reserved to indicate an error.

Parameters

strDest
   Destination string

strSource
   Source string

count
   Number of characters to be copied

Remarks

The **strncpy** function copies the initial *count* characters of *strSource* to *strDest* and returns *strDest*. If *count* is less than or equal to the length of *strSource*, a null character is not appended automatically to the copied string. If *count* is greater than the length of *strSource*, the destination string is padded with null characters up to length *count*. The behavior of **strncpy** is undefined if the source and destination strings overlap.

wcsncpy and **_mbsncpy** are wide-character and multibyte-character versions of **strncpy**. The arguments and return value of **wcsncpy** and **_mbsncpy** vary accordingly. These three functions behave identically otherwise.

Generic-Text Routine Mappings

TCHAR.H Routine	_UNICODE & _MBCS Not Defined	_MBCS Defined	_UNICODE Defined
_tcsncpy	strncpy	_mbsnbcpy	wcsncpy

Example

```
/* STRNCPY.C */

#include <string.h>
#include <stdio.h>

void main( void )
{
    char string[100] = "Cats are nice usually";
    printf ( "Before: %s\n", string );
    strncpy( string, "Dogs", 4 );
```

```
        strncpy( string + 9, "mean", 4 );
        printf ( "After:  %s\n", string );
}
```

Output

```
Before: Cats are nice usually
After:  Dogs are mean usually
```

See Also

_mbsnbcpy, strcat, strcmp, strcpy, strncat, strncmp, _strnicmp, strrchr, _strset, strspn

_strnicmp, _wcsnicmp, _mbsnicmp

Compare characters of two strings without regard to case.

int _strnicmp(const char **string1*, **const char** **string2*, **size_t** *count* **);**
int _wcsnicmp(const wchar_t **string1*, **const wchar_t** **string2*, **size_t** *count* **);**
int _mbsnicmp(const unsigned char **string1*, **const unsigned char** **string2*, **size_t** *count* **);**

Routine	Required Header	Compatibility
_strnicmp	<string.h>	Win 95, Win NT
_wcsnicmp	<string.h> or <wchar.h>	Win 95, Win NT
_mbsnicmp	<mbstring.h>	Win 95, Win NT

For additional compatibility information, see "Compatibility" in the Introduction.

Libraries

LIBC.LIB	Single thread static library, retail version
LIBCMT.LIB	Multithread static library, retail version
MSVCRT.LIB	Import library for MSVCRT.DLL, retail version

Return Value

The return value indicates the relationship between the substrings as follows.

Return Value	Description
< 0	*string1* substring less than *string2* substring
0	*string1* substring identical to *string2* substring
> 0	*string1* substring greater than *string2* substring

On an error, **_mbsnicmp** returns **_NLSCMPERROR**, which is defined in STRING.H and MBSTRING.H.

Parameters

string1, *string2*
  Null-terminated strings to compare

count
  Number of characters to compare

Remarks

The **_strnicmp** function lexicographically compares, at most, the first *count* characters of *string1* and *string2*. The comparison is performed without regard to case; **_strnicmp** is a case-insensitive version of **strncmp**. The comparison ends if a terminating null character is reached in either string before *count* characters are compared. If the strings are equal when a terminating null character is reached in either string before *count* characters are compared, the shorter string is lesser.

Two strings containing characters located between 'Z' and 'a' in the ASCII table ('[', '\', ']', '^', '_', and '`') compare differently, depending on their case. For example, the two strings "ABCDE" and "ABCD^" compare one way if the comparison is lowercase ("abcde" > "abcd^") and the other way ("ABCDE" < "ABCD^") if it is uppercase.

_wcsnicmp and **_mbsnicmp** are wide-character and multibyte-character versions of **_strnicmp**. The arguments and return value of **_wcsnicmp** are wide-character strings; those of **_mbsnicmp** are multibyte-character strings. **_mbsnicmp** recognizes multibyte-character sequences according to the current multibyte code page and returns **_NLSCMPERROR** on an error. For more information, see "Code Pages" in Chapter 1, Run-Time Routines by Category." These three functions behave identically otherwise. These functions are not affected by the current locale setting.

Generic-Text Routine Mappings

TCHAR.H Routine	_UNICODE & _MBCS Not Defined	_MBCS Defined	_UNICODE Defined
_tcsncicmp	_strnicmp	_mbsnbicmp	_wcsnicmp
_tcsnicmp	_strnicmp	_mbsnbicmp	_wcsnicmp

Example

```
/* STRNCMP.C */
#include <string.h>
#include <stdio.h>

char string1[] = "The quick brown dog jumps over the lazy fox";
char string2[] = "The QUICK brown fox jumps over the lazy dog";
```

```
void main( void )
{
    char tmp[20];
    int result;
    printf( "Compare strings:\n\t\t%s\n\t\t%s\n\n", string1, string2 );
    printf( "Function:\tstrncmp (first 10 characters only)\n" );
    result = strncmp( string1, string2 , 10 );
    if( result > 0 )
        strcpy( tmp, "greater than" );
    else if( result < 0 )
        strcpy( tmp, "less than" );
    else
        strcpy( tmp, "equal to" );
    printf( "Result:\t\tString 1 is %s string 2\n\n", tmp );
    printf( "Function:\tstrnicmp _strnicmp (first 10 characters only)\n" );
    result = _strnicmp( string1, string2, 10 );
    if( result > 0 )
        strcpy( tmp, "greater than" );
    else if( result < 0 )
        strcpy( tmp, "less than" );
    else
        strcpy( tmp, "equal to" );
    printf( "Result:\t\tString 1 is %s string 2\n\n", tmp );
}
```

Output

```
Compare strings:
        The quick brown dog jumps over the lazy fox
        The QUICK brown fox jumps over the lazy dog

Function:   strncmp (first 10 characters only)
Result:     String 1 is greater than string 2

Function:   _strnicmp (first 10 characters only)
Result:     String 1 is equal to string 2
```

See Also

strcat, strcmp, strcpy, strncat, strncmp, strncpy, strrchr, _strset, strspn

_strnset, _wcsnset, _mbsnset

Initialize characters of a string to a given format.

char *_strnset(char *string, int c, size_t count);
wchar_t *_wcsnset(wchar_t *string, wchar_t c, size_t count);
unsigned char *_mbsnset(unsigned char *string, unsigned int c, size_t count);

Routine	Required Header	Compatibility
_strnset	<string.h>	Win 95, Win NT
_wcsnset	<string.h> or <wchar.h>	Win 95, Win NT
_mbsnset	<mbstring.h>	Win 95, Win NT

For additional compatibility information, see "Compatibility" in the Introduction.

Libraries

LIBC.LIB	Single thread static library, retail version
LIBCMT.LIB	Multithread static library, retail version
MSVCRT.LIB	Import library for MSVCRT.DLL, retail version

Return Value

Each of these functions returns a pointer to the altered string.

Parameters

string
    String to be altered

c
    Character setting

count
    Number of characters to be set

Remarks

The **_strnset** function sets, at most, the first *count* characters of *string* to *c* (converted to **char**). If *count* is greater than the length of *string*, the length of *string* is used instead of *count*.

_wcsnset and **_mbsnset** are wide-character and multibyte-character versions of **_strnset**. The string arguments and return value of **_wcsnset** are wide-character strings; those of **_mbsnset** are multibyte-character strings. These three functions behave identically otherwise.

Generic-Text Routine Mappings

TCHAR.H Routine	_UNICODE & _MBCS Not Defined	_MBCS Defined	_UNICODE Defined
_tcsnset	_strnset	_mbsnbset	_wcsnset

Example

```
/* STRNSET.C */

#include <string.h>
#include <stdio.h>

void main( void )
{
   char string[15] = "This is a test";
   /* Set not more than 4 characters of string to be *'s */
   printf( "Before: %s\n", string );
   _strnset( string, '*', 4 );
   printf( "After:  %s\n", string );
}
```

Output

```
Before: This is a test
After:  **** is a test
```

See Also

strcat, strcmp, strcpy, _strset

strpbrk, wcspbrk, _mbspbrk

Scan strings for characters in specified character sets.

char *strpbrk(const char **string***, const char ****strCharSet* **);**
wchar_t *wcspbrk(const wchar_t **string***, const wchar_t ****strCharSet* **);**
unsigned char *_mbspbrk(const unsigned char**string***, const unsigned char ****strCharSet* **);**

Routine	Required Header	Compatibility
strpbrk	<string.h>	ANSI, Win 95, Win NT
wcspbrk	<string.h> or <wchar.h>	ANSI, Win 95, Win NT
_mbspbrk	<mbstring.h>	Win 95, Win NT

For additional compatibility information, see "Compatibility" in the Introduction.

Libraries

LIBC.LIB	Single thread static library, retail version
LIBCMT.LIB	Multithread static library, retail version
MSVCRT.LIB	Import library for MSVCRT.DLL, retail version

Return Value

Each of these functions returns a pointer to the first occurrence of any character from *strCharSet* in *string*, or a **NULL** pointer if the two string arguments have no characters in common.

Parameters

string
   Null-terminated, searched string

strCharSet
   Null-terminated character set

Remarks

The **strpbrk** function returns a pointer to the first occurrence of a character in *string* that belongs to the set of characters in *strCharSet*. The search does not include the terminating null character.

wcspbrk and **_mbspbrk** are wide-character and multibyte-character versions of **strpbrk**. The arguments and return value of **wcspbrk** are wide-character strings; those of **_mbspbrk** are multibyte-character strings. These three functions behave identically otherwise. **_mbspbrk** is similar to **_mbscspn** except that **_mbspbrk** returns a pointer rather than a value of type size_t.

Generic-Text Routine Mappings

TCHAR.H Routine	_UNICODE & _MBCS Not Defined	_MBCS Defined	_UNICODE Defined
_tcspbrk	strpbrk	_mbspbrk	wcspbrk

Example

```
/* STRPBRK.C */

#include <string.h>
#include <stdio.h>

void main( void )
{
    char string[100] = "The 3 men and 2 boys ate 5 pigs\n";
    char *result;
    /* Return pointer to first 'a' or 'b' in "string" */
    printf( "1: %s\n", string );
    result = strpbrk( string, "0123456789" );
    printf( "2: %s\n", result++ );
    result = strpbrk( result, "0123456789" );
    printf( "3: %s\n", result++ );
    result = strpbrk( result, "0123456789" );
    printf( "4: %s\n", result );
}
```

```
1: The 3 men and 2 boys ate 5 pigs

2: 3 men and 2 boys ate 5 pigs

3: 2 boys ate 5 pigs

4: 5 pigs
```

See Also

strcspn, strchr, strrchr

strrchr, wcsrchr, _mbsrchr

Scan a string for the last occurrence of a character.

char *strrchr(const char **string***, int** *c* **);**
char *wcsrchr(const wchar_t **string***, int** *c* **);**
int _mbsrchr(const unsigned char **string***, unsigned int** *c* **);**

Routine	Required Header	Compatibility
strrchr	<string.h>	ANSI, Win 95, Win NT
wcsrchr	<string.h> or <wchar.h>	ANSI, Win 95, Win NT
_mbsrchr	<mbstring.h>	Win 95, Win NT

For additional compatibility information, see "Compatibility" in the Introduction.

Libraries

LIBC.LIB	Single thread static library, retail version
LIBCMT.LIB	Multithread static library, retail version
MSVCRT.LIB	Import library for MSVCRT.DLL, retail version

Return Value

Each of these functions returns a pointer to the last occurrence of *c* in *string*, or **NULL** if *c* is not found.

Parameters

string
    Null-terminated string to search

c
    Character to be located

Remarks

The **strchr** function finds the last occurrence of *c* (converted to **char**) in *string*. The search includes the terminating null character.

wcsrchr and **_mbsrchr** are wide-character and multibyte-character versions of **strchr**. The arguments and return value of **wcsrchr** are wide-character strings; those of **_mbsrchr** are multibyte-character strings. These three functions behave identically otherwise.

Generic-Text Routine Mappings

TCHAR.H Routine	_UNICODE & _MBCS Not Defined	_MBCS Defined	_UNICODE Defined
_tcsrchr	strchr	_mbsrchr	wcsrchr

Example

```
/* STRCHR.C: This program illustrates searching for a character
 * with strchr (search forward) or strrchr (search backward).
 */

#include <string.h>
#include <stdio.h>

int  ch = 'r';

char string[] = "The quick brown dog jumps over the lazy fox";
char fmt1[] =   "         1         2         3         4         5";
char fmt2[] =   "12345678901234567890123456789012345678901234567890";

void main( void )
{
   char *pdest;
   int result;

   printf( "String to be searched: \n\t\t%s\n", string );
   printf( "\t\t%s\n\t\t%s\n\n", fmt1, fmt2 );
   printf( "Search char:\t%c\n", ch );

   /* Search forward. */
   pdest = strchr( string, ch );
   result = pdest - string + 1;
   if( pdest != NULL )
      printf( "Result:\tfirst %c found at position %d\n\n",
              ch, result );
   else
      printf( "Result:\t%c not found\n" );

   /* Search backward. */
   pdest = strrchr( string, ch );
   result = pdest - string + 1;
```

```
    if( pdest != NULL )
        printf( "Result:\tlast %c found at position %d\n\n", ch, result );
    else
        printf( "Result:\t%c not found\n" );
}
```

Output

```
String to be searched:
     The quick brown dog jumps over the lazy fox
             1         2         3         4         5
     12345678901234567890123456789012345678901234567890

Search char:   r
Result:   first r found at position 12

Result:   last r found at position 30
```

See Also

strchr, strcspn, _strnicmp, strpbrk, strspn

_strrev, _wcsrev, _mbsrev

Reverse characters of a string.

char *_strrev(char *_string_**);**
wchar_t *_wcsrev(wchar_t *_string_**);**
unsigned char *_mbsrev(unsigned char *_string_**);**

Routine	Required Header	Compatibility
_strrev	<string.h>	Win 95, Win NT
_wcsrev	<string.h> or <wchar.h>	Win 95, Win NT
_mbsrev	<mbstring.h>	Win 95, Win NT

For additional compatibility information, see "Compatibility" in the Introduction.

Libraries

LIBC.LIB	Single thread static library, retail version
LIBCMT.LIB	Multithread static library, retail version
MSVCRT.LIB	Import library for MSVCRT.DLL, retail version

Return Value

Each of these functions returns a pointer to the altered string. No return value is reserved to indicate an error.

Parameter

string
   Null-terminated string to reverse

Remarks

The **_strrev** function reverses the order of the characters in *string*. The terminating null character remains in place. **_wcsrev** and **_mbsrev** are wide-character and multibyte-character versions of **_strrev**. The arguments and return value of **_wcsrev** are wide-character strings; those of **_mbsrev** are multibyte-character strings. For **_mbsrev**, the order of bytes in each multibyte character in *string* is not changed. These three functions behave identically otherwise.

Generic-Text Routine Mappings

TCHAR.H Routine	_UNICODE & _MBCS Not Defined	_MBCS Defined	_UNICODE Defined
_tcsrev	_strrev	_mbsrev	_wcsrev

Example

```
/* STRREV.C: This program checks an input string to
 * see whether it is a palindrome: that is, whether
 * it reads the same forward and backward.
 */

#include <string.h>
#include <stdio.h>

void main( void )
{
    char string[100];
    int result;

    printf( "Input a string and I will tell you if it is a palindrome:\n" );
    gets( string );

    /* Reverse string and compare (ignore case): */
    result = _stricmp( string, _strrev( _strdup( string ) ) );
    if( result == 0 )
        printf( "The string \"%s\" is a palindrome\n\n", string );
    else
        printf( "The string \"%s\" is not a palindrome\n\n", string );
}
```

Output

```
Input a string and I will tell you if it is a palindrome:
Able was I ere I saw Elba
The string "Able was I ere I saw Elba" is a palindrome
```

See Also

strcpy, _strset

_strset, _wcsset, _mbsset

Set characters of a string to a character.

char *_strset(char **string***, int** *c* **);**
wchar_t *_wcsset(wchar_t **string***, wchar_t** *c* **);**
unsigned char *_mbsset(unsigned char **string***, unsigned int** *c* **);**

Routine	Required Header	Compatibility
_strset	<string.h>	Win 95, Win NT
_wcsset	<string.h> or <wchar.h>	Win 95, Win NT
_mbsset	<mbstring.h>	Win 95, Win NT

For additional compatibility information, see "Compatibility" in the Introduction.

Libraries

LIBC.LIB	Single thread static library, retail version
LIBCMT.LIB	Multithread static library, retail version
MSVCRT.LIB	Import library for MSVCRT.DLL, retail version

Return Value

Each of these functions returns a pointer to the altered string. No return value is reserved to indicate an error.

Parameters

string

Null-terminated string to be set

c

Character setting

Remarks

The **_strset** function sets all the characters of *string* to *c* (converted to **char**), except
the terminating null character. **_wcsset** and **_mbsset** are wide-character and multibyte-
character versions of **_strset**. The data types of the arguments and return values vary
accordingly. These three functions behave identically otherwise.

Generic-Text Routine Mappings

TCHAR.H Routine	_UNICODE & _MBCS Not Defined	_MBCS Defined	_UNICODE Defined
_tcsset	_strset	_mbsset	_wcsset

Example

```
/* STRSET.C */

#include <string.h>
#include <stdio.h>

void main( void )
{
    char string[] = "Fill the string with something";
    printf( "Before: %s\n", string );
    _strset( string, '*' );
    printf( "After:  %s\n", string );
}
```

Output

```
Before: Fill the string with something
After:  ******************************
```

See Also

_mbsnbset, memset, strcat, strcmp, strcpy, _strnset

strspn, wcsspn, _mbsspn

Find the first substring.

```
size_t strspn( const char *string, const char *strCharSet );
size_t wcsspn( const wchar_t *string, const wchar_t *strCharSet );
size_t _mbsspn( const unsigned char *string, const unsigned char *strCharSet );
```

Routine	Required Header	Compatibility
strspn	<string.h>	ANSI, Win 95, Win NT
wcsspn	<string.h> or <wchar.h>	ANSI, Win 95, Win NT
_mbsspn	<mbstring.h>	Win 95, Win NT

For additional compatibility information, see "Compatibility" in the Introduction.

Libraries

LIBC.LIB	Single thread static library, retail version
LIBCMT.LIB	Multithread static library, retail version
MSVCRT.LIB	Import library for MSVCRT.DLL, retail version

Return Value

strspn, **wcsspn**, and **_mbsspn** return an integer value specifying the length of the substring in *string* that consists entirely of characters in *strCharSet*. If *string* begins with a character not in *strCharSet,* the function returns 0. No return value is reserved to indicate an error. For each of these routines, no return value is reserved to indicate an error.

Parameters

string
　　Null-terminated string to search

strCharSet
　　Null-terminated character set

Remarks

The **strspn** function returns the index of the first character in *string* that does not belong to the set of characters in *strCharSet*. The search does not include terminating null characters.

wcsspn and **_mbsspn** are wide-character and multibyte-character versions of **strspn.** The arguments of **wcsspn** are wide-character strings; those of **_mbsspn** are multibyte-character strings. These three functions behave identically otherwise.

Generic-Text Routine Mappings

TCHAR.H Routine	_UNICODE & _MBCS Not Defined	_MBCS Defined	_UNICODE Defined
_tcsspn	strspn	_mbsspn	wcsspn

Example

```
/* STRSPN.C: This program uses strspn to determine
 * the length of the segment in the string "cabbage"
 * consisting of a's, b's, and c's. In other words,
 * it finds the first non-abc letter.
 */

#include <string.h>
#include <stdio.h>
```

```
void main( void )
{
    char string[] = "cabbage";
    int  result;
    result = strspn( string, "abc" );
    printf( "The portion of '%s' containing only a, b, or c "
            "is %d bytes long\n", string, result );
}
```

Output

```
The portion of 'cabbage' containing only a, b, or c is 5 bytes long
```

See Also

_mbsspnp, strcspn, strncat, strncmp, strncpy, _strnicmp, strrchr

strstr, wcsstr, _mbsstr

Find a substring.

char *strstr(const char **string***, const char ****strCharSet** **);**
wchar_t *wcsstr(const wchar_t **string***, const wchar_t ****strCharSet** **);**
unsigned char *_mbsstr(const unsigned char **string***, const unsigned char ****strCharSet** **);**

Routine	Required Header	Compatibility
strstr	<string.h>	ANSI, Win 95, Win NT
wcsstr	<string.h> or <wchar.h>	ANSI, Win 95, Win NT
_mbsstr	<mbstring.h>	Win 95, Win NT

For additional compatibility information, see "Compatibility" in the Introduction.

Libraries

LIBC.LIB	Single thread static library, retail version
LIBCMT.LIB	Multithread static library, retail version
MSVCRT.LIB	Import library for MSVCRT.DLL, retail version

Return Value

Each of these functions returns a pointer to the first occurrence of *strCharSet* in *string*,
or **NULL** if *strCharSet* does not appear in *string*. If *strCharSet* points to a string of zero
length, the function returns *string*.

Parameters

string
> Null-terminated string to search

strCharSet
> Null-terminated string to search for

Remarks

The **strstr** function returns a pointer to the first occurrence of *strCharSet* in *string*. The search does not include terminating null characters. **wcsstr** and **_mbsstr** are wide-character and multibyte-character versions of **strstr**. The arguments and return value of **wcsstr** are wide-character strings; those of **_mbsstr** are multibyte-character strings. These three functions behave identically otherwise.

Generic-Text Routine Mappings

TCHAR.H Routine	_UNICODE & _MBCS Not Defined	_MBCS Defined	_UNICODE Defined
_tcsstr	strstr	_mbsstr	wcsstr

Example

```
/* STRSTR.C */

#include <string.h>
#include <stdio.h>

char str[] =    "lazy";
char string[] = "The quick brown dog jumps over the lazy fox";
char fmt1[] =   "         1         2         3         4         5";
char fmt2[] =   "12345678901234567890123456789012345678901234567890";

void main( void )
{
    char *pdest;
    int  result;
    printf( "String to be searched:\n\t%s\n", string );
    printf( "\t%s\n\t%s\n\n", fmt1, fmt2 );
    pdest = strstr( string, str );
    result = pdest - string + 1;
    if( pdest != NULL )
        printf( "%s found at position %d\n\n", str, result );
    else
        printf( "%s not found\n", str );
}
```

Output

```
String to be searched:
   The quick brown dog jumps over the lazy fox
            1         2         3         4         5
   12345678901234567890123456789012345678901234567890

lazy found at position 36
```

See Also

strcspn, strcmp, strpbrk, strrchr, strspn

_strtime, _wstrtime

Copy the time to a buffer.

char *_strtime(char *timestr**);**
wchar_t *_wstrtime(wchar_t *timestr**);**

Routine	Required Header	Compatibility
_strtime	<time.h>	Win 95, Win NT
_wstrtime	<time.h> or <wchar.h>	Win 95, Win NT

For additional compatibility information, see "Compatibility" in the Introduction.

Libraries

LIBC.LIB	Single thread static library, retail version
LIBCMT.LIB	Multithread static library, retail version
MSVCRT.LIB	Import library for MSVCRT.DLL, retail version

Return Value

Each of these functions returns a pointer to the resulting character string *timestr*.

Parameter

timestr
   Time string

Remarks

The **_strtime** function copies the current local time into the buffer pointed to by *timestr*. The time is formatted as *hh:mm:ss* where *hh* is two digits representing the hour in 24-hour notation, *mm* is two digits representing the minutes past the hour, and *ss* is two digits representing seconds. For example, the string 18:23:44 represents 23 minutes and 44 seconds past 6 P.M. The buffer must be at least 9 bytes long.

_wstrtime is a wide-character version of **_strtime**; the argument and return value of **_wstrtime** are wide-character strings. These functions behave identically otherwise.

Generic-Text Routine Mappings

TCHAR.H Routine	_UNICODE & _MBCS Not Defined	_MBCS Defined	_UNICODE Defined
_tstrtime	_strtime	_strtime	_wstrtime

Example

```
/* STRTIME.C */

#include <time.h>
#include <stdio.h>

void main( void )
{
    char dbuffer [9];
    char tbuffer [9];
    _strdate( dbuffer );
    printf( "The current date is %s \n", dbuffer );
    _strtime( tbuffer );
    printf( "The current time is %s \n", tbuffer );
}
```

Output

```
The current date is 03/23/93
The current time is 13:40:40
```

See Also

asctime, ctime, gmtime, localtime, mktime, time, _tzset

strtod, strtol, strtoul Functions

Return Value

strtod returns the value of the floating-point number, except when the representation would cause an overflow, in which case the function returns +/–**HUGE_VAL**. The sign of **HUGE_VAL** matches the sign of the value that cannot be represented. **strtod** returns 0 if no conversion can be performed or an underflow occurs.

strtol returns the value represented in the string *nptr*, except when the representation would cause an overflow, in which case it returns **LONG_MAX** or **LONG_MIN**. **strtoul** returns the converted value, if any, or **ULONG_MAX** on overflow. Each of these functions returns 0 if no conversion can be performed.

wcstod, **wcstol**, and **wcstoul** return values analogously to **strtod**, **strtol**, and **strtoul,** respectively.

For all six functions in this group, **errno** is set to **ERANGE** if overflow or underflow occurs.

Parameters

nptr
Null-terminated string to convert

endptr
Pointer to character that stops scan

base
Number base to use

Remarks

The **strtod**, **strtol**, and **strtoul** functions convert *nptr* to a double-precision value, a long-integer value, or an unsigned long-integer value, respectively.

The input string *nptr* is a sequence of characters that can be interpreted as a numerical value of the specified type. Each function stops reading the string *nptr* at the first character it cannot recognize as part of a number. This may be the terminating null character. For **strtol** or **strtoul**, this terminating character can also be the first numeric character greater than or equal to *base*.

For all six functions in the **strtod** group, the current locale's **LC_NUMERIC** category setting determines recognition of the radix character in *nptr;* for more information, see setlocale. If *endptr* is not **NULL**, a pointer to the character that stopped the scan is stored at the location pointed to by *endptr*. If no conversion can be performed (no valid digits were found or an invalid base was specified), the value of *nptr* is stored at the location pointed to by *endptr*.

strtod expects *nptr* to point to a string of the following form:

[*whitespace*] [*sign*] [*digits*] [*.digits*] [{**d** | **D** | **e** | **E**}[*sign*]*digits*]

A *whitespace* may consist of space or tab characters, which are ignored; *sign* is either plus (**+**) or minus (**–**); and *digits* are one or more decimal digits. If no digits appear before the radix character, at least one must appear after the radix character. The decimal digits can be followed by an exponent, which consists of an introductory letter (**d**, **D**, **e**, or **E**) and an optionally signed integer. If neither an exponent part nor a radix character appears, a radix character is assumed to follow the last digit in the string. The first character that does not fit this form stops the scan.

The **strtol** and **strtoul** functions expect *nptr* to point to a string of the following form:

[*whitespace*] [{**+** | **–**}] [**0** [{ **x** | **X** }]] [*digits*]

If *base* is between 2 and 36, then it is used as the base of the number. If *base* is 0, the initial characters of the string pointed to by *nptr* are used to determine the base. If the first character is 0 and the second character is not 'x' or 'X', the string is interpreted as an octal integer; otherwise, it is interpreted as a decimal number. If the first character is '0' and the second character is 'x' or 'X', the string is interpreted as a hexadecimal integer. If the first character is '1' through '9', the string is interpreted as a decimal integer. The letters 'a' through 'z' (or 'A' through 'Z') are assigned the values 10 through 35; only letters whose assigned values are less than *base* are permitted. **strtoul** allows a plus (**+**) or minus (**–**) sign prefix; a leading minus sign indicates that the return value is negated.

wcstod, **wcstol**, and **wcstoul** are wide-character versions of **strtod**, **strtol**, and **strtoul,** respectively; the *nptr* argument to each of these wide-character functions is a wide-character string. Otherwise, each of these wide-character functions behaves identically to its single-byte–character counterpart.

Example

```
/* STRTOD.C: This program uses strtod to convert a
 * string to a double-precision value; strtol to
 * convert a string to long integer values; and strtoul
 * to convert a string to unsigned long-integer values.
 */

#include <stdlib.h>
#include <stdio.h>

void main( void )
{
    char    *string, *stopstring;
    double  x;
    long    l;
    int     base;
    unsigned long ul;
    string = "3.1415926This stopped it";
    x = strtod( string, &stopstring );
    printf( "string = %s\n", string );
    printf("   strtod = %f\n", x );
    printf("   Stopped scan at: %s\n\n", stopstring );
    string = "-10110134932This stopped it";
    l = strtol( string, &stopstring, 10 );
    printf( "string = %s", string );
    printf("   strtol = %ld", l );
    printf("   Stopped scan at: %s", stopstring );
    string = "10110134932";
    printf( "string = %s\n", string );
    /* Convert string using base 2, 4, and 8: */
    for( base = 2; base <= 8; base *= 2 )
```

```
    {
        /* Convert the string: */
        ul = strtoul( string, &stopstring, base );
        printf( "    strtol = %ld (base %d)\n", ul, base );
        printf( "    Stopped scan at: %s\n", stopstring );
    }
}
```

Output

```
string = 3.1415926This stopped it
    strtod = 3.141593
    Stopped scan at: This stopped it

string = -10110134932This stopped it
    strtol = -2147483647
    Stopped scan at: This stopped it

string = 10110134932
    strtol = 45 (base 2)
    Stopped scan at: 34932
    strtol = 4423 (base 4)
    Stopped scan at: 4932
    strtol = 2134108 (base 8)
    Stopped scan at: 932
```

See Also

atof, **localeconv**, **setlocale**

strtod, wcstod

Convert strings to a double-precision value.

double strtod(const char **nptr*, **char** ***endptr* **);**
double wcstod(const wchar_t **nptr*, **wchar_t** ***endptr* **);**

Each of these functions converts the input string *nptr* to a **double**.

Routine	Required Header	Compatibility
strtod	<stdlib.h>	ANSI, Win 95, Win NT
wcstod	<stdlib.h> or <wchar.h>	ANSI, Win 95, Win NT

For additional compatibility information, see "Compatibility" in the Introduction.

Libraries

LIBC.LIB	Single thread static library, retail version
LIBCMT.LIB	Multithread static library, retail version
MSVCRT.LIB	Import library for MSVCRT.DLL, retail version

Return Value

strtod returns the value of the floating-point number, except when the representation would cause an overflow, in which case the function returns +/–**HUGE_VAL**. The sign of **HUGE_VAL** matches the sign of the value that cannot be represented. **strtod** returns 0 if no conversion can be performed or an underflow occurs.

wcstod returns values analogously to **strtod.** For both functions, **errno** is set to **ERANGE** if overflow or underflow occurs.

Parameters

nptr
  Null-terminated string to convert

endptr
  Pointer to character that stops scan

Remarks

The **strtod** function converts *nptr* to a double-precision value. **strtod** stops reading the string *nptr* at the first character it cannot recognize as part of a number. This may be the terminating null character. **wcstod** is a wide-character version of **strtod**; its *nptr* argument is a wide-character string. Otherwise these functions behave identically.

Generic-Text Routine Mappings

TCHAR.H Routine	_UNICODE & _MBCS Not Defined	_MBCS Defined	_UNICODE Defined
_tcstod	strtod	strtod	wcstod

The **LC_NUMERIC** category setting of the current locale determines recognition of the radix character in *nptr;* for more information, see setlocale. If *endptr* is not **NULL**, a pointer to the character that stopped the scan is stored at the location pointed to by *endptr.* If no conversion can be performed (no valid digits were found or an invalid base was specified), the value of *nptr* is stored at the location pointed to by *endptr.*

strtod expects *nptr* to point to a string of the following form:

[*whitespace*] [*sign*] [*digits*] [*.digits*] [{**d** | **D** | **e** | **E**}[*sign*]*digits*]

A *whitespace* may consist of space and tab characters, which are ignored; *sign* is either plus (+) or minus (–); and *digits* are one or more decimal digits. If no digits appear before the radix character, at least one must appear after the radix character. The decimal digits can be followed by an exponent, which consists of an introductory letter (**d**, **D**, **e**, or **E**) and an optionally signed integer. If neither an exponent part nor a radix character appears, a radix character is assumed to follow the last digit in the string. The first character that does not fit this form stops the scan.

Example

```
/* STRTOD.C: This program uses strtod to convert a
 * string to a double-precision value; strtol to
 * convert a string to long integer values; and strtoul
 * to convert a string to unsigned long-integer values.
 */

#include <stdlib.h>
#include <stdio.h>

void main( void )
{
    char    *string, *stopstring;
    double x;
    long    l;
    int     base;
    unsigned long ul;
    string = "3.1415926This stopped it";
    x = strtod( string, &stopstring );
    printf( "string = %s\n", string );
    printf("   strtod = %f\n", x );
    printf("   Stopped scan at: %s\n\n", stopstring );
    string = "-10110134932This stopped it";
    l = strtol( string, &stopstring, 10 );
    printf( "string = %s", string );
    printf("   strtol = %ld", l );
    printf("   Stopped scan at: %s", stopstring );
    string = "10110134932";
    printf( "string = %s\n", string );
    /* Convert string using base 2, 4, and 8: */
    for( base = 2; base <= 8; base *= 2 )
    {
        /* Convert the string: */
        ul = strtoul( string, &stopstring, base );
        printf( "   strtol = %ld (base %d)\n", ul, base );
        printf( "   Stopped scan at: %s\n", stopstring );
    }
}
```

Output

```
string = 3.1415926This stopped it
    strtod = 3.141593
    Stopped scan at: This stopped it

string = -10110134932This stopped it
    strtol = -2147483647
    Stopped scan at: This stopped it

string = 10110134932
    strtol = 45 (base 2)
    Stopped scan at: 34932
    strtol = 4423 (base 4)
    Stopped scan at: 4932
    strtol = 2134108 (base 8)
    Stopped scan at: 932
```

See Also

strtol, **strtoul**, **atof**, **localeconv**, **setlocale**

strtok, wcstok, _mbstok

Find the next token in a string.

char *strtok(char *strToken**, const char ***strDelimit **);**
wchar_t *wcstok(wchar_t *strToken**, const wchar_t ***strDelimit **);**
unsigned char *_mbstok(unsigned char*strToken**, const unsigned char ***strDelimit **);**

Routine	Required Header	Compatibility
strtok	<string.h>	ANSI, Win 95, Win NT
wcstok	<string.h> or <wchar.h>	ANSI, Win 95, Win NT
_mbstok	<mbstring.h>	Win 95, Win NT

For additional compatibility information, see "Compatibility" in the Introduction.

Libraries

LIBC.LIB	Single thread static library, retail version
LIBCMT.LIB	Multithread static library, retail version
MSVCRT.LIB	Import library for MSVCRT.DLL, retail version

Return Value

All of these functions return a pointer to the next token found in *strToken*. They return **NULL** when no more tokens are found. Each call modifies *strToken* by substituting a NULL character for each delimiter that is encountered.

Parameters

strToken
  String containing token(s)

strDelimit
  Set of delimiter characters

Remarks

The **strtok** function finds the next token in *strToken*. The set of characters in *strDelimit* specifies possible delimiters of the token to be found in *strToken* on the current call. **wcstok** and **_mbstok** are wide-character and multibyte-character versions of **strtok**. The arguments and return value of **wcstok** are wide-character strings; those of **_mbstok** are multibyte-character strings. These three functions behave identically otherwise.

Generic-Text Routine Mappings

TCHAR.H Routine	_UNICODE & _MBCS Not Defined	_MBCS Defined	_UNICODE Defined
_tcstok	strtok	_mbstok	wcstok

On the first call to **strtok**, the function skips leading delimiters and returns a pointer to the first token in *strToken*, terminating the token with a null character. More tokens can be broken out of the remainder of *strToken* by a series of calls to **strtok**. Each call to **strtok** modifies *strToken* by inserting a null character after the token returned by that call. To read the next token from *strToken*, call **strtok** with a **NULL** value for the *strToken* argument. The **NULL** *strToken* argument causes **strtok** to search for the next token in the modified *strToken*. The *strDelimit* argument can take any value from one call to the next so that the set of delimiters may vary.

> **Warning** Each of these functions uses a static variable for parsing the string into tokens. If multiple or simultaneous calls are made to the same function, a high potential for data corruption and inaccurate results exists. Therefore, do not attempt to call the same function simultaneously for different strings and be aware of calling one of these function from within a loop where another routine may be called that uses the same function. However, calling this function simultaneously from multiple threads does not have undesirable effects.

Example

```
/* STRTOK.C: In this program, a loop uses strtok
 * to print all the tokens (separated by commas
 * or blanks) in the string named "string".
 */

#include <string.h>
#include <stdio.h>

char string[] = "A string\tof ,,tokens\nand some  more tokens";
char seps[]   = " ,\t\n";
char *token;
```

```
void main( void )
{
   printf( "%s\n\nTokens:\n", string );
   /* Establish string and get the first token: */
   token = strtok( string, seps );
   while( token != NULL )
   {
      /* While there are tokens in "string" */
      printf( " %s\n", token );
      /* Get next token: */
      token = strtok( NULL, seps );
   }
}
```

Output

```
A string    of ,,tokens
and some   more tokens

Tokens:
   A
   string
   of
   tokens
   and
   some
   more
   tokens
```

See Also

strcspn, strspn, setlocale

strtol, wcstol

Convert strings to a long-integer value.

long strtol(const char *nptr*, **char** ***endptr*, **int** *base* **);**
long wcstol(const wchar_t *nptr*, **wchar_t** ***endptr*, **int** *base* **);**

Routine	Required Header	Compatibility
strtol	<stdlib.h>	ANSI, Win 95, Win NT
wcstol	<stdlib.h> or <wchar.h>	ANSI, Win 95, Win NT

For additional compatibility information, see "Compatibility" in the Introduction.

Libraries

LIBC.LIB	Single thread static library, retail version
LIBCMT.LIB	Multithread static library, retail version
MSVCRT.LIB	Import library for MSVCRT.DLL, retail version

Return Value

strtol returns the value represented in the string *nptr*, except when the representation would cause an overflow, in which case it returns **LONG_MAX** or **LONG_MIN**. **strtol** returns 0 if no conversion can be performed. **wcstol** returns values analogously to **strtol**. For both functions, **errno** is set to **ERANGE** if overflow or underflow occurs.

Parameters

nptr
   Null-terminated string to convert

endptr
   Pointer to character that stops scan

base
   Number base to use

Remarks

The **strtol** function converts *nptr* to a **long**. **strtol** stops reading the string *nptr* at the first character it cannot recognize as part of a number. This may be the terminating null character, or it may be the first numeric character greater than or equal to *base*.

wcstol is a wide-character version of **strtol**; its *nptr* argument is a wide-character string. Otherwise these functions behave identically.

Generic-Text Routine Mappings

TCHAR.H Routine	_UNICODE & _MBCS Not Defined	_MBCS Defined	_UNICODE Defined
_tcstol	strtol	strtol	wcstol

The current locale's **LC_NUMERIC** category setting determines recognition of the radix character in *nptr;* for more information, see setlocale. If *endptr* is not **NULL**, a pointer to the character that stopped the scan is stored at the location pointed to by *endptr*. If no conversion can be performed (no valid digits were found or an invalid base was specified), the value of *nptr* is stored at the location pointed to by *endptr*.

strtol expects *nptr* to point to a string of the following form:

[*whitespace*] [{**+** | **−**}] [**0** [{ **x** | **X** }]] [*digits*]

A *whitespace* may consist of space and tab characters, which are ignored; *digits* are one or more decimal digits. The first character that does not fit this form stops the scan. If *base* is between 2 and 36, then it is used as the base of the number. If *base* is 0, the initial characters of the string pointed to by *nptr* are used to determine the base. If the first character is 0 and the second character is not 'x' or 'X', the string is interpreted as an octal integer; otherwise, it is interpreted as a decimal number. If the first character is '0' and the second character is 'x' or 'X', the string is interpreted as a hexadecimal integer. If the first character is '1' through '9', the string is interpreted as a decimal integer. The letters 'a' through 'z' (or 'A' through 'Z') are assigned the values 10 through 35; only letters whose assigned values are less than *base* are permitted.

Example

```
/* STRTOD.C: This program uses strtod to convert a
 * string to a double-precision value; strtol to
 * convert a string to long integer values; and strtoul
 * to convert a string to unsigned long-integer values.
 */

#include <stdlib.h>
#include <stdio.h>

void main( void )
{
    char    *string, *stopstring;
    double x;
    long    l;
    int     base;
    unsigned long ul;
    string = "3.1415926This stopped it";
    x = strtod( string, &stopstring );
    printf( "string = %s\n", string );
    printf("    strtod = %f\n", x );
    printf("    Stopped scan at: %s\n\n", stopstring );
    string = "-10110134932This stopped it";
    l = strtol( string, &stopstring, 10 );
    printf( "string = %s", string );
    printf("    strtol = %ld", l );
    printf("    Stopped scan at: %s", stopstring );
    string = "10110134932";
    printf( "string = %s\n", string );
    /* Convert string using base 2, 4, and 8: */
    for( base = 2; base <= 8; base *= 2 )
    {
        /* Convert the string: */
        ul = strtoul( string, &stopstring, base );
        printf( "    strtol = %ld (base %d)\n", ul, base );
        printf( "    Stopped scan at: %s\n", stopstring );
    }
}
```

Output

```
string = 3.1415926This stopped it
    strtod = 3.141593
    Stopped scan at: This stopped it

string = -10110134932This stopped it
    strtol = -2147483647
    Stopped scan at: This stopped it

string = 10110134932
    strtol = 45 (base 2)
    Stopped scan at: 34932
    strtol = 4423 (base 4)
    Stopped scan at: 4932
    strtol = 2134108 (base 8)
    Stopped scan at: 932
```

See Also

strtod, **strtoul**, **atof**, **localeconv**, **setlocale**

strtoul, wcstoul

Convert strings to an unsigned long-integer value.

unsigned long strtoul(const char **nptr*, **char** ***endptr*, **int** *base* **);**
unsigned long wcstoul(const wchar_t **nptr*, **wchar_t** ***endptr*, **int** *base* **);**

Routine	Required Header	Compatibility
strtoul	<stdlib.h>	ANSI, Win 95, Win NT
wcstoul	<stdlib.h> or <wchar.h>	ANSI, Win 95, Win NT

For additional compatibility information, see "Compatibility" in the Introduction.

Libraries

LIBC.LIB	Single thread static library, retail version
LIBCMT.LIB	Multithread static library, retail version
MSVCRT.LIB	Import library for MSVCRT.DLL, retail version

Return Value

strtoul returns the converted value, if any, or **ULONG_MAX** on overflow. **strtoul** returns 0 if no conversion can be performed. **wcstoul** returns values analogously to **strtoul**. For both functions, **errno** is set to **ERANGE** if overflow or underflow occurs.

Parameters

nptr
 Null-terminated string to convert

endptr
 Pointer to character that stops scan

base
 Number base to use

Remarks

Each of these functions converts the input string *nptr* to an **unsigned long**.

strtoul stops reading the string *nptr* at the first character it cannot recognize as part of a number. This may be the terminating null character, or it may be the first numeric character greater than or equal to *base*. The **LC_NUMERIC** category setting of the current locale determines recognition of the radix character in *nptr;* for more information, see setlocale. If *endptr* is not **NULL**, a pointer to the character that stopped the scan is stored at the location pointed to by *endptr*. If no conversion can be performed (no valid digits were found or an invalid base was specified), the value of *nptr* is stored at the location pointed to by *endptr*.

wcstoul is a wide-character version of **strtoul**; its *nptr* argument is a wide-character string. Otherwise these functions behave identically.

Generic-Text Routine Mappings

TCHAR.H Routine	_UNICODE & _MBCS Not Defined	_MBCS Defined	_UNICODE Defined
_tcstoul	strtoul	strtoul	wcstoul

strtoul expects *nptr* to point to a string of the following form:

[*whitespace*] [{**+** | **–**}] [**0** [{ **x** | **X** }]] [*digits*]

A *whitespace* may consist of space and tab characters, which are ignored; *digits* are one or more decimal digits. The first character that does not fit this form stops the scan. If *base* is between 2 and 36, then it is used as the base of the number. If *base* is 0, the initial characters of the string pointed to by *nptr* are used to determine the base. If the first character is 0 and the second character is not 'x' or 'X', the string is interpreted as an octal integer; otherwise, it is interpreted as a decimal number. If the first character is '0' and the second character is 'x' or 'X', the string is interpreted as a hexadecimal integer. If the first character is '1' through '9', the string is interpreted as a decimal integer. The letters 'a' through 'z' (or 'A' through 'Z') are assigned the values 10 through 35; only letters whose assigned values are less than *base* are permitted. **strtoul** allows a plus (**+**) or minus (**–**) sign prefix; a leading minus sign indicates that the return value is negated.

Example

```
/* STRTOD.C: This program uses strtod to convert a
 * string to a double-precision value; strtol to
 * convert a string to long integer values; and strtoul
 * to convert a string to unsigned long-integer values.
 */

#include <stdlib.h>
#include <stdio.h>

void main( void )
{
    char    *string, *stopstring;
    double x;
    long    l;
    int     base;
    unsigned long ul;
    string = "3.1415926This stopped it";
    x = strtod( string, &stopstring );
    printf( "string = %s\n", string );
    printf(" strtod = %f\n", x );
    printf(" Stopped scan at: %s\n\n", stopstring );
    string = "-10110134932This stopped it";
    l = strtol( string, &stopstring, 10 );
    printf( "string = %s", string );
    printf(" strtol = %ld", l );
    printf(" Stopped scan at: %s", stopstring );
    string = "10110134932";
    printf( "string = %s\n", string );
    /* Convert string using base 2, 4, and 8: */
    for( base = 2; base <= 8; base *= 2 )
    {
        /* Convert the string: */
        ul = strtoul( string, &stopstring, base );
        printf( " strtol = %ld (base %d)\n", ul, base );
        printf( " Stopped scan at: %s\n", stopstring );
    }

}
```

Output

```
string = 3.1415926This stopped it
    strtod = 3.141593
    Stopped scan at: This stopped it

string = -10110134932This stopped it
    strtol = -2147483647
    Stopped scan at: This stopped it
```

```
string = 10110134932
   strtol = 45 (base 2)
   Stopped scan at: 34932
   strtol = 4423 (base 4)
   Stopped scan at: 4932
   strtol = 2134108 (base 8)
   Stopped scan at: 932
```

See Also

strtod, **strtol**, **atof**, **localeconv**, **setlocale**

_strupr, _wcsupr, _mbsupr

Convert a string to uppercase.

char *_strupr(char **string**);**
wchar_t *_wcsupr(wchar_t **string**);**
unsigned char *_mbsupr(unsigned char **string**);**

Routine	Required Header	Compatibility
_strupr	<string.h>	Win 95, Win NT
_wcsupr	<string.h> or <wchar.h>	Win 95, Win NT
_mbsupr	<mbstring.h>	Win 95, Win NT

For additional compatibility information, see "Compatibility" in the Introduction.

Libraries

LIBC.LIB	Single thread static library, retail version
LIBCMT.LIB	Multithread static library, retail version
MSVCRT.LIB	Import library for MSVCRT.DLL, retail version

Return Value

These functions return a pointer to the altered string. Because the modification is done in place, the pointer returned is the same as the pointer passed as the input argument. No return value is reserved to indicate an error.

Parameter

string
   String to capitalize

Remarks

The **_strupr** function converts, in place, each lowercase letter in *string* to uppercase.
The conversion is determined by the **LC_CTYPE** category setting of the current locale.
Other characters are not affected. For more information on **LC_CTYPE**, see setlocale.

_wcsupr and **_mbsupr** are wide-character and multibyte-character versions of **_strupr**.
The argument and return value of **_wcsupr** are wide-character strings; those of **_mbsupr**
are multibyte-character strings. These three functions behave identically otherwise.

Generic-Text Routine Mappings

TCHAR.H Routine	_UNICODE & _MBCS Not Defined	_MBCS Defined	_UNICODE Defined
_tcsupr	_strupr	_mbsupr	_wcsupr

Example

```
/* STRLWR.C: This program uses _strlwr and _strupr to create
 * uppercase and lowercase copies of a mixed-case string.
 */

#include <string.h>
#include <stdio.h>

void main( void )
{
    char string[100] = "The String to End All Strings!";
    char *copy1, *copy2;
    copy1 = _strlwr( _strdup( string ) );
    copy2 = _strupr( _strdup( string ) );
    printf( "Mixed: %s\n", string );
    printf( "Lower: %s\n", copy1 );
    printf( "Upper: %s\n", copy2 );
}
```

Output

```
Mixed: The String to End All Strings!
Lower: the string to end all strings!
Upper: THE STRING TO END ALL STRINGS!
```

See Also

_strlwr

strxfrm, wcsxfrm

Transform a string based on locale-specific information.

size_t strxfrm(char *strDest***, const char** *strSource***, size_t** *count* **);**
size_t wcsxfrm(wchar_t *strDest***, const wchar_t** *strSource***, size_t** *count* **);**

Routine	Required Header	Compatibility
strxfrm	<string.h>	ANSI, Win 95, Win NT
wcsxfrm	<string.h> or <wchar.h>	ANSI, Win 95, Win NT

For additional compatibility information, see "Compatibility" in the Introduction.

Libraries

LIBC.LIB	Single thread static library, retail version
LIBCMT.LIB	Multithread static library, retail version
MSVCRT.LIB	Import library for MSVCRT.DLL, retail version

Return Value

Each of these functions returns the length of the transformed string, not counting the terminating null character. If the return value is greater than or equal to *count*, the content of *strDest* is unpredictable. On an error, each of the functions sets **errno** and returns **(size_t)** − 1.

Parameters

strDest
  Destination string

strSource
  Source string

count
  Maximum number of characters to place in *strDest*

Remarks

The **strxfrm** function transforms the string pointed to by *strSource* into a new collated form that is stored in *strDest*. No more than *count* characters, including the null character, are transformed and placed into the resulting string. The transformation is made using the current locale's **LC_COLLATE** category setting. For more information on **LC_COLLATE**, see setlocale.

After the transformation, a call to **strcmp** with the two transformed strings yields results identical to those of a call to **strcoll** applied to the original two strings. As with **strcoll** and **stricoll**, **strxfrm** automatically handles multibyte-character strings as appropriate.

wcsxfrm is a wide-character version of **strxfrm**; the string arguments of **wcsxfrm** are wide-character pointers. For **wcsxfrm**, after the string transformation, a call to **wcscmp** with the two transformed strings yields results identical to those of a call to **wcscoll** applied to the original two strings. **wcsxfrm** and **strxfrm** behave identically otherwise.

Generic-Text Routine Mappings

TCHAR.H Routine	_UNICODE & _MBCS Not Defined	_MBCS Defined	_UNICODE Defined
_tcsxfrm	strxfrm	strxfrm	wcsxfrm

In the "C" locale, the order of the characters in the character set (ASCII character set) is the same as the lexicographic order of the characters. However, in other locales, the order of characters in the character set may differ from the lexicographic character order. For example, in certain European locales, the character 'a' (value 0x61) precedes the character 'ä' (value 0xE4) in the character set, but the character 'ä' precedes the character 'a' lexicographically.

In locales for which the character set and the lexicographic character order differ, use **strxfrm** on the original strings and then **strcmp** on the resulting strings to produce a lexicographic string comparison according to the current locale's **LC_COLLATE** category setting. Thus, to compare two strings lexicographically in the above locale, use **strxfrm** on the original strings, then **strcmp** on the resulting strings. Alternatively, you can use **strcoll** rather than **strcmp** on the original strings.

The value of the following expression is the size of the array needed to hold the **strxfrm** transformation of the source string:

```
1 + strxfrm( NULL, string, 0 )
```

In the "C" locale only, **strxfrm** is equivalent to the following:

```
strncpy( _string1, _string2, _count );
return( strlen( _string1 ) );
```

See Also

localeconv, setlocale, strcmp, strncmp

_swab

Swaps bytes.

void _swab(char *_src_, char *_dest_, int _n_);

Routine	Required Header	Compatibility
_swab	<stdlib.h>	Win 95, Win NT

For additional compatibility information, see "Compatibility" in the Introduction.

Libraries

LIBC.LIB	Single thread static library, retail version
LIBCMT.LIB	Multithread static library, retail version
MSVCRT.LIB	Import library for MSVCRT.DLL, retail version

Return Value

None

Parameters

src
  Data to be copied and swapped

dest
  Storage location for swapped data

_n_
  Number of bytes to be copied and swapped

Remarks

The **_swab** function copies _n_ bytes from _src_, swaps each pair of adjacent bytes, and stores the result at _dest_. The integer _n_ should be an even number to allow for swapping. **_swab** is typically used to prepare binary data for transfer to a machine that uses a different byte order.

Example

```
/* SWAB.C illustrates:
 *      _swab
 */

#include <stdlib.h>
#include <stdio.h>

char from[] = "BADCFEHGJILKNMPORQTSVUXWZY";
char to[] =   "........................";
```

```
void main()
{
    printf( "Before:\t%s\n\t%s\n\n", from, to );
    _swab( from, to, sizeof( from ) );
    printf( "After:\t%s\n\t%s\n\n", from, to );
}
```

Output

```
Before:   BADCFEHGJILKNMPORQTSVUXWZY
          . . . . . . . . . . . . . . . . . . . . . . . .

After:    BADCFEHGJILKNMPORQTSVUXWZY
          ABCDEFGHIJKLMNOPQRSTUVWXYZ
```

system, _wsystem

Execute a command.

int system(const char *command* **);**
int _wsystem(const wchar_t *command* **);**

Routine	Required Header	Compatibility
system	<process.h> or <stdlib.h>	ANSI, Win 95, Win NT
_wsystem	<process.h> or <stdlib.h> or <wchar.h>	Win NT

For additional compatibility information, see "Compatibility" in the Introduction.

Libraries

LIBC.LIB	Single thread static library, retail version
LIBCMT.LIB	Multithread static library, retail version
MSVCRT.LIB	Import library for MSVCRT.DLL, retail version

Return Value

If *command* is **NULL** and the command interpreter is found, the function returns a nonzero value. If the command interpreter is not found, it returns 0 and sets **errno** to **ENOENT**. If *command* is not **NULL**, **system** returns the value that is returned by the command interpreter. It returns the value 0 only if the command interpreter returns the value 0. A return value of −1 indicates an error, and **errno** is set to one of the following values:

E2BIG
   Argument list (which is system-dependent) is too big.

ENOENT
   Command interpreter cannot be found.

ENOEXEC

Command-interpreter file has invalid format and is not executable.

ENOMEM

Not enough memory is available to execute command; or available memory has been corrupted; or invalid block exists, indicating that process making call was not allocated properly.

Parameter

command

Command to be executed

Remarks

The **system** function passes *command* to the command interpreter, which executes the string as an operating-system command. **system** refers to the **COMSPEC** and **PATH** environment variables that locate the command-interpreter file (the file named CMD.EXE in Windows NT). If *command* is NULL, the function simply checks to see whether the command interpreter exists.

You must explicitly flush (using **fflush** or **_flushall**) or close any stream before calling **system**.

_wsystem is a wide-character version of **system**; the *command* argument to **_wsystem** is a wide-character string. These functions behave identically otherwise.

Generic-Text Routine Mappings

TCHAR.H Routine	_UNICODE & _MBCS Not Defined	_MBCS Defined	_UNICODE Defined
_tsystem	system	system	_wsystem

Example

```
/* SYSTEM.C: This program uses
 * system to TYPE its source file.
 */

#include <process.h>

void main( void )
{
    system( "type system.c" );
}
```

Output

```
/* SYSTEM.C: This program uses
 * system to TYPE its source file.
 */
```

```
#include <process.h>
void main( void )
{
    system( "type system.c" );
}
```

See Also

_exec Functions, exit, _flushall, _spawn Functions

tan, tanh

Calculate the tangent (**tan**) or hyperbolic tangent (**tanh**).

double tan(double x **);**
double tanh(double x **);**

Routine	Required Header	Compatibility
tan	<math.h>	ANSI, Win 95, Win NT
tanh	<math.h>	ANSI, Win 95, Win NT

For additional compatibility information, see "Compatibility" in the Introduction.

Libraries

LIBC.LIB	Single thread static library, retail version
LIBCMT.LIB	Multithread static library, retail version
MSVCRT.LIB	Import library for MSVCRT.DLL, retail version

Return Value

tan returns the tangent of x. If x is greater than or equal to 2^{63}, or less than or equal to -2^{63}, a loss of significance in the result occurs, in which case the function generates a **_TLOSS** error and returns an indefinite (same as a quiet NaN). You can modify error handling with _matherr.

tanh returns the hyperbolic tangent of x. There is no error return.

Parameter

x

   Angle in radians

Example

```
/* TAN.C:  This program displays the tangent of pi / 4
 * and the hyperbolic tangent of the result.
 */

#include <math.h>
#include <stdio.h>

void main( void )
{
    double pi = 3.1415926535;
    double x, y;

    x = tan( pi / 4 );
    y = tanh( x );
    printf( "tan( %f ) = %f\n", pi/4, x );
    printf( "tanh( %f ) = %f\n", x, y );
}
```

Output

```
tan( 0.785398 ) = 1.000000
tanh( 1.000000 ) = 0.761594
```

See Also

acos, asin, atan, cos, sin

_tell, _telli64

Get the position of the file pointer.

long _tell(int *handle* **);**
__int64 _telli64(int *handle* **);**

Routine	Required Header	Compatibility
_tell	<io.h>	Win 95, Win NT
_telli64	<io.h>	Win 95, Win NT

For additional compatibility information, see "Compatibility" in the Introduction.

Libraries

LIBC.LIB	Single thread static library, retail version
LIBCMT.LIB	Multithread static library, retail version
MSVCRT.LIB	Import library for MSVCRT.DLL, retail version

Return Value

A return value of –1L indicates an error, and **errno** is set to **EBADF** to indicate an invalid file-handle argument. On devices incapable of seeking, the return value is undefined.

Parameter

handle
   Handle referring to open file

Remarks

The **_tell** function gets the current position of the file pointer (if any) associated with the *handle* argument. The position is expressed as the number of bytes from the beginning of the file. For the **_telli64** function, this value is expressed as a 64-bit integer.

Example

```
/* TELL.C:  This program uses _tell to tell the
 * file pointer position after a file read.
 */

#include <io.h>
#include <stdio.h>
#include <fcntl.h>

void main( void )
{
   int  fh;
   char buffer[500];

   if( (fh = _open( "tell.c", _O_RDONLY )) != -1 )
   {
      if( _read( fh, buffer, 500 ) > 0 )
         printf( "Current file position is: %d\n", _tell( fh ) );
      _close( fh );
   }
}
```

Output

```
Current file position is: 434
```

See Also

ftell, **_lseek**

_tempnam, _wtempnam, tmpnam, _wtmpnam

Create temporary filenames.

char *_tempnam(char **dir***, char ****prefix***);**
wchar_t *_wtempnam(wchar_t **dir***, wchar_t ****prefix***);**
char *tmpnam(char **string***);**
wchar_t *_wtmpnam(wchar_t **string***);**

Routine	Required Header	Compatibility
_tempnam	<stdio.h>	Win 95, Win NT
_wtempnam	<stdio.h> or <wchar.h>	Win 95, Win NT
tmpnam	<stdio.h>	ANSI, Win 95, Win NT
_wtmpnam	<stdio.h> or <wchar.h>	Win 95, Win NT

For additional compatibility information, see "Compatibility" in the Introduction.

Libraries

LIBC.LIB	Single thread static library, retail version
LIBCMT.LIB	Multithread static library, retail version
MSVCRT.LIB	Import library for MSVCRT.DLL, retail version

Return Value

Each of these functions returns a pointer to the name generated, unless it is impossible to create this name or the name is not unique. If the name cannot be created or if a file with that name already exists, **tmpnam** and **_tempnam** return **NULL**. **_tempnam** and **_wtempnam** also return **NULL** if the file search fails.

Note The pointer returned by **tmpnam** points to an internal static buffer. **free** does not need to be called to deallocate this pointer.

Parameters

prefix
 Filename prefix

dir
 Target directory to be used if TMP not defined

string
 Pointer to temporary name

Remarks

The **tmpnam** function generates a temporary filename that can be used to open a temporary file without overwriting an existing file.

This name is stored in *string*. If *string* is **NULL**, then **tmpnam** leaves the result in an internal static buffer. Thus any subsequent calls destroy this value. If *string* is not **NULL**, it is assumed to point to an array of at least **L_tmpnam** characters — or 2***L_tmpnam** bytes. The value of **L_tmpnam** is defined in STDIO.H. The function generates unique filenames for up to **TMP_MAX** calls.

The character string that **tmpnam** creates consists of the path prefix, defined by the entry **P_tmpdir** in the file STDIO.H, followed by a sequence consisting of the digit characters '0' through '9'; the numerical value of this string is in the range 1–65,535. Changing the definitions of **L_tmpnam** or **P_tmpdir** in STDIO.H does not change the operation of **tmpnam**.

_tempnam creates a temporary filename for use in another directory. This filename is different from that of any existing file. The *prefix* argument is the prefix to the filename. **_tempnam** uses malloc to allocate space for the filename; the program is responsible for freeing this space when it is no longer needed. **_tempnam** looks for the file with the given name in the following directories, listed in order of precedence.

Directory Used	Conditions
Directory specified by **TMP**	**TMP** environment variable is set, and directory specified by **TMP** exists.
dir argument to **_tempnam**	**TMP** environment variable is not set, or directory specified by **TMP** does not exist.
P_tmpdir in STDIO.H	*dir* argument is **NULL**, or *dir* is name of nonexistent directory.
Current working directory	**P_tmpdir** does not exist.

_tempnam and **tmpnam** automatically handle multibyte-character string arguments as appropriate, recognizing multibyte-character sequences according to the OEM code page obtained from the operating system. **_wtempnam** is a wide-character version of **_tempnam**; the arguments and return value of **_wtempnam** are wide-character strings. **_wtempnam** and **_tempnam** behave identically except that **_wtempnam** does not handle multibyte-character strings. **_wtmpnam** is a wide-character version of **tmpnam**; the argument and return value of **_wtmpnam** are wide-character strings. **_wtmpnam** and **tmpnam** behave identically except that **_wtmpnam** does not handle multibyte-character strings.

Generic-Text Routine Mappings

TCHAR.H Routine	_UNICODE & _MBCS Not Defined	_MBCS Defined	_UNICODE Defined
_ttmpnam	tmpnam	tmpnam	_wtmpnam
_ttempnam	_tempnam	_tempnam	_wtempnam

Example

```
/* TEMPNAM.C: This program uses tmpnam to create a unique
 * filename in the current working directory, then uses
 * _tempnam to create a unique filename with a prefix of stq.
 */

#include <stdio.h>

void main( void )
{
    char *name1, *name2;

    /* Create a temporary filename for the current working directory: */
    if( ( name1 = tmpnam( NULL ) ) != NULL )
        printf( "%s is safe to use as a temporary file.\n", name1 );
    else
        printf( "Cannot create a unique filename\n" );

    /* Create a temporary filename in temporary directory with the
     * prefix "stq". The actual destination directory may vary
     * depending on the state of the TMP environment variable and
     * the global variable P_tmpdir.
     */
    if( ( name2 = _tempnam( "c:\\tmp", "stq" ) ) != NULL )
        printf( "%s is safe to use as a temporary file.\n", name2 );
    else
        printf( "Cannot create a unique filename\n" );
}
```

Output

```
\s5d. is safe to use as a temporary file.
C:\temp\stq2 is safe to use as a temporary file.
```

See Also

_getmbcp, malloc, _setmbcp, tmpfile

terminate

Calls **abort** or a function you specify using **set_terminate**.

void terminate(void);

Routine	Required Header	Compatibility
terminate	<eh.h>	ANSI, Win 95, Win NT

For additional compatibility information, see "Compatibility" in the Introduction.

Libraries

LIBC.LIB	Single thread static library, retail version
LIBCMT.LIB	Multithread static library, retail version
MSVCRT.LIB	Import library for MSVCRT.DLL, retail version

Return Value

None

Remarks

The **terminate** function is used with C++ exception handling and is called in the following cases:

- A matching catch handler cannot be found for a thrown C++ exception.

- An exception is thrown by a destructor function during stack unwind.

- The stack is corrupted after throwing an exception.

terminate calls **abort** by default. You can change this default by writing your own termination function and calling **set_terminate** with the name of your function as its argument. **terminate** calls the last function given as an argument to **set_terminate**.

Example

```
/* TERMINAT.CPP:
 */
#include <eh.h>
#include <process.h>
#include <iostream.h>

void term_func();

void main()
{
    int i = 10, j = 0, result;
    set_terminate( term_func );
    try
    {
        if( j == 0 )
            throw "Divide by zero!";
        else
            result = i/j;
    }
    catch( int )
    {
        cout << "Caught some integer exception.\n";
    }
```

```
   cout << "This should never print.\n";

}
void term_func()
{
   cout << "term_func() was called by terminate().\n";

   // ... cleanup tasks performed here

   // If this function does not exit, abort is called.

   exit(-1);
}
```

Output

```
term_func() was called by terminate().
```

See Also

abort, _set_se_translator, set_terminate, set_unexpected, unexpected

time

Gets the system time.

time_t time(time_t *timer);

Routine	Required Header	Compatibility
time	<time.h>	ANSI, Win 95, Win NT

For additional compatibility information, see "Compatibility" in the Introduction.

Libraries

LIBC.LIB	Single thread static library, retail version
LIBCMT.LIB	Multithread static library, retail version
MSVCRT.LIB	Import library for MSVCRT.DLL, retail version

Return Value

time returns the time in elapsed seconds. There is no error return.

Parameter

timer
   Storage location for time

Remarks

The **time** function returns the number of seconds elapsed since midnight (00:00:00),
January 1, 1970, coordinated universal time, according to the system clock. The return
value is stored in the location given by *timer*. This parameter may be **NULL**, in which
case the return value is not stored.

Example

```
/* TIMES.C illustrates various time and date functions including:
 *      time            _ftime          ctime           asctime
 *      localtime       gmtime          mktime          _tzset
 *      _strtime        _strdate        strftime
 *
 * Also the global variable:
 *      _tzname
 */

#include <time.h>
#include <stdio.h>
#include <sys/types.h>
#include <sys/timeb.h>
#include <string.h>

void main()
{
    char tmpbuf[128], ampm[] = "AM";
    time_t ltime;
    struct _timeb tstruct;
    struct tm *today, *gmt, xmas = { 0, 0, 12, 25, 11, 93 };

    /* Set time zone from TZ environment variable. If TZ is not set,
     * the operating system is queried to obtain the default value
     * for the variable.
     */
    _tzset();

    /* Display operating system-style date and time. */
    _strtime( tmpbuf );
    printf( "OS time:\t\t\t\t%s\n", tmpbuf );
    _strdate( tmpbuf );
    printf( "OS date:\t\t\t\t%s\n", tmpbuf );

    /* Get UNIX-style time and display as number and string. */
    time( &ltime );
    printf( "Time in seconds since UTC 1/1/70:\t%ld\n", ltime );
    printf( "UNIX time and date:\t\t\t%s", ctime( &ltime ) );
```

```
    /* Display UTC. */
    gmt = gmtime( &ltime );
    printf( "Coordinated universal time:\t\t%s", asctime( gmt ) );

    /* Convert to time structure and adjust for PM if necessary. */
    today = localtime( &ltime );
    if( today->tm_hour > 12 )
    {
    strcpy( ampm, "PM" );
    today->tm_hour -= 12;
    }
    if( today->tm_hour == 0 )   /* Adjust if midnight hour. */
    today->tm_hour = 12;

    /* Note how pointer addition is used to skip the first 11
     * characters and printf is used to trim off terminating
     * characters.
     */
    printf( "12-hour time:\t\t\t\t%.8s %s\n",
       asctime( today ) + 11, ampm );

    /* Print additional time information. */
    _ftime( &tstruct );
    printf( "Plus milliseconds:\t\t\t%u\n", tstruct.millitm );
    printf( "Zone difference in seconds from UTC:\t%u\n",
            tstruct.timezone );
    printf( "Time zone name:\t\t\t\t%s\n", _tzname[0] );
    printf( "Daylight savings:\t\t\t%s\n",
            tstruct.dstflag ? "YES" : "NO" );

    /* Make time for noon on Christmas, 1993. */
    if( mktime( &xmas ) != (time_t)-1 )
    printf( "Christmas\t\t\t\t%s\n", asctime( &xmas ) );

    /* Use time structure to build a customized time string. */
    today = localtime( &ltime );

    /* Use strftime to build a customized time string. */
    strftime( tmpbuf, 128,
        "Today is %A, day %d of %B in the year %Y.\n", today );
    printf( tmpbuf );
}
```

Output

```
OS time:                            21:51:03
OS date:                            05/03/94
Time in seconds since UTC 1/1/70:   768027063
UNIX time and date:                 Tue May 03 21:51:03 1994
```

```
Coordinated universal time:              Wed May 04 04:51:03 1994
12-hour time:                            09:51:03 PM
Plus milliseconds:                       279
Zone difference in seconds from UTC:     480
Time zone name:
Daylight savings:                        YES
Christmas                                Sat Dec 25 12:00:00 1993

Today is Tuesday, day 03 of May in the year 1994.
```

See Also

asctime, **_ftime**, **gmtime**, **localtime**, **_utime**

tmpfile

Creates a temporary file.

FILE *tmpfile(void);

Routine	Required Header	Compatibility
tmpfile	<stdio.h>	ANSI, Win 95, Win NT

For additional compatibility information, see "Compatibility" in the Introduction.

Libraries

LIBC.LIB	Single thread static library, retail version
LIBCMT.LIB	Multithread static library, retail version
MSVCRT.LIB	Import library for MSVCRT.DLL, retail version

Return Value

If successful, **tmpfile** returns a stream pointer. Otherwise, it returns a **NULL** pointer.

Remarks

The **tmpfile** function creates a temporary file and returns a pointer to that stream. If the file cannot be opened, **tmpfile** returns a **NULL** pointer. This temporary file is automatically deleted when the file is closed, when the program terminates normally, or when **_rmtmp** is called, assuming that the current working directory does not change. The temporary file is opened in **w+b** (binary read/write) mode.

Example

```
/* TMPFILE.C: This program uses tmpfile to create a
 * temporary file, then deletes this file with _rmtmp.
 */
```

```
#include <stdio.h>

void main( void )
{
    FILE *stream;
    char tempstring[] = "String to be written";
    int  i;

    /* Create temporary files. */
    for( i = 1; i <= 3; i++ )
    {
        if( (stream = tmpfile()) == NULL )
            perror( "Could not open new temporary file\n" );
        else
            printf( "Temporary file %d was created\n", i );
    }

    /* Remove temporary files. */
    printf( "%d temporary files deleted\n", _rmtmp() );
}
```

Output

```
Temporary file 1 was created
Temporary file 2 was created
Temporary file 3 was created
3 temporary files deleted
```

See Also

_rmtmp, _tempnam

to Functions

Each of the **to** functions and its associated macro, if any, converts a single character to another character.

| __toascii | tolower, _tolower, towlower | toupper, _toupper, towupper |

Remarks

The **to** functions and macro conversions are as follows.

Routine	Macro	Description
__toascii	**__toascii**	Converts c to ASCII character
tolower	**tolower**	Converts c to lowercase if appropriate
_tolower	**_tolower**	Converts c to lowercase

(continued)

Routine	Macro	Description
towlower	None	Converts *c* to corresponding wide-character lowercase letter
toupper	**toupper**	Converts *c* to uppercase if appropriate
_toupper	**_toupper**	Converts *c* to uppercase
towupper	None	Converts c to corresponding wide-character uppercase letter

To use the function versions of the **to** routines that are also defined as macros, either remove the macro definitions with **#undef** directives or do not include CTYPE.H. If you use the /Za compiler option, the compiler uses the function version of **toupper** or **tolower**. Declarations of the **toupper** and **tolower** functions are in STDLIB.H.

The __**toascii** routine sets all but the low-order 7 bits of *c* to 0, so that the converted value represents a character in the ASCII character set. If *c* already represents an ASCII character, *c* is unchanged.

The **tolower** and **toupper** routines:

- Are dependent on the **LC_CTYPE** category of the current locale (**tolower** calls **isupper** and **toupper** calls **islower**).

- Convert *c* if *c* represents a convertible letter of the appropriate case in the current locale and the opposite case exists for that locale. Otherwise, *c* is unchanged.

The **_tolower** and **_toupper** routines:

- Are locale-independent, much faster versions of **tolower** and **toupper.**

- Can be used only when **isascii**(*c*) and either **isupper**(*c*) or **islower**(*c*), respectively, are true.

- Have undefined results if *c* is not an ASCII letter of the appropriate case for converting.

The **towlower** and **towupper** functions return a converted copy of *c* if and only if both of the following conditions are true. Otherwise, *c* is unchanged.

- *c* is a wide character of the appropriate case (that is, for which **iswupper** or **iswlower,** respectively, is true).

- There is a corresponding wide character of the target case (that is, for which **iswlower** or **iswupper,** respectively, is true).

Example

```
/* TOUPPER.C: This program uses toupper and tolower to
 * analyze all characters between 0x0 and 0x7F. It also
 * applies _toupper and _tolower to any code in this
 * range for which these functions make sense.
 */
```

```
#include <conio.h>
#include <ctype.h>
#include <string.h>

char msg[] = "Some of THESE letters are Capitals\r\n";
char *p;

void main( void )
{
   _cputs( msg );

   /* Reverse case of message. */
   for( p = msg; p < msg + strlen( msg ); p++ )
   {
      if( islower( *p ) )
         _putch( _toupper( *p ) );
      else if( isupper( *p ) )
         _putch( _tolower( *p ) );
      else
         _putch( *p );
   }
}
```

Output

```
Some of THESE letters are Capitals
sOME OF these LETTERS ARE cAPITALS
```

See Also

is Routines

__toascii

Converts characters.

int __toascii(int *c*);

Routine	Required Header	Compatibility
__toascii	<ctype.h>	Win 95, Win NT

For additional compatibility information, see "Compatibility" in the Introduction.

Libraries

LIBC.LIB	Single thread static library, retail version
LIBCMT.LIB	Multithread static library, retail version
MSVCRT.LIB	Import library for MSVCRT.DLL, retail version

Return Value

__**toascii** converts a copy of *c* if possible, and returns the result. There is no return value reserved to indicate an error.

Parameter

c

Character to convert

Remarks

The __**toascii** routine converts the given character to an ASCII character.

See Also

is Routines, to Functions Overview

Example

```
/* TOUPPER.C: This program uses toupper and tolower to
 * analyze all characters between 0x0 and 0x7F. It also
 * applies _toupper and _tolower to any code in this
 * range for which these functions make sense.
 */

#include <conio.h>
#include <ctype.h>
#include <string.h>

char msg[] = "Some of THESE letters are Capitals\r\n";
char *p;

void main( void )
{
    _cputs( msg );

    /* Reverse case of message. */
    for( p = msg; p < msg + strlen( msg ); p++ )
    {
        if( islower( *p ) )
            _putch( _toupper( *p ) );
        else if( isupper( *p ) )
            _putch( _tolower( *p ) );
        else
            _putch( *p );
    }
}
```

Output

```
Some of THESE letters are Capitals
sOME OF these LETTERS ARE cAPITALS
```

tolower, _tolower, towlower

Convert character to lowercase.

int tolower(int *c* **);**
int _tolower(int *c* **);**
int towlower(wint_t *c* **);**

Routine	Required Header	Compatibility
tolower	<stdlib.h> and <ctype.h>	ANSI, Win 95, Win NT
_tolower	<ctype.h>	Win 95, Win NT
towlower	<ctype.h> or <wchar.h>	ANSI, Win 95, Win NT

For additional compatibility information, see "Compatibility" in the Introduction.

Libraries

LIBC.LIB	Single thread static library, retail version
LIBCMT.LIB	Multithread static library, retail version
MSVCRT.LIB	Import library for MSVCRT.DLL, retail version

Return Value

Each of these routines converts a copy of *c,* if possible, and returns the result. There is no return value reserved to indicate an error.

Parameter

c

Character to convert

Remarks

Each of these routines converts a given uppercase letter to a lowercase letter if possible and appropriate.

See Also

is Routines, to Functions Overview

Example

```
/* TOUPPER.C: This program uses toupper and tolower to
 * analyze all characters between 0x0 and 0x7F. It also
 * applies _toupper and _tolower to any code in this
 * range for which these functions make sense.
 */
```

```
#include <conio.h>
#include <ctype.h>
#include <string.h>

char msg[] = "Some of THESE letters are Capitals\r\n";
char *p;

void main( void )
{
   _cputs( msg );

   /* Reverse case of message. */
   for( p = msg; p < msg + strlen( msg ); p++ )
   {
      if( islower( *p ) )
         _putch( _toupper( *p ) );
      else if( isupper( *p ) )
         _putch( _tolower( *p ) );
      else
         _putch( *p );
   }
}
```

Output

```
Some of THESE letters are Capitals
sOME OF these LETTERS ARE cAPITALS
```

toupper _toupper, towupper

Convert character to uppercase.

int toupper(int c);
int _toupper(int c);
int towupper(wint_t c);

Routine	Required Header	Compatibility
toupper	<stdlib.h> and <ctype.h>	ANSI, Win 95, Win NT
_toupper	<ctype.h>	Win 95, Win NT
towupper	<ctype.h> or <wchar.h>	ANSI, Win 95, Win NT

For additional compatibility information, see "Compatibility" in the Introduction.

Libraries

LIBC.LIB	Single thread static library, retail version
LIBCMT.LIB	Multithread static library, retail version
MSVCRT.LIB	Import library for MSVCRT.DLL, retail version

Return Value

Each of these routines converts a copy of *c,* if possible, and returns the result.

If *c* is a wide character for which **iswlower** is true and there is a corresponding wide character for which **iswupper** is true, **towupper** returns the corresponding wide character; otherwise, **towupper** returns *c* unchanged.

There is no return value reserved to indicate an error.

Parameter

c

Character to convert

Remarks

Each of these routines converts a given lowercase letter to an uppercase letter if possible and appropriate.

See Also

is Routines, to Functions Overview

Example

```
/* TOUPPER.C: This program uses toupper and tolower to
 * analyze all characters between 0x0 and 0x7F. It also
 * applies _toupper and _tolower to any code in this
 * range for which these functions make sense.
 */

#include <conio.h>
#include <ctype.h>
#include <string.h>

char msg[] = "Some of THESE letters are Capitals\r\n";
char *p;

void main( void )
{
    _cputs( msg );
```

```
/* Reverse case of message. */
for( p = msg; p < msg + strlen( msg ); p++ )
{
    if( islower( *p ) )
        _putch( _toupper( *p ) );
    else if( isupper( *p ) )
        _putch( _tolower( *p ) );
    else
        _putch( *p );
}
}
```

Output

```
Some of THESE letters are Capitals
sOME OF these LETTERS ARE cAPITALS
```

towctrans

Transforms a wide character.

wint_t towctrans(wint_t c, wctrans_t category);

Routine	Required Header	Compatibility
towctrans	<wctype.h>	Win 95, Win NT

For additional compatibility information, see "Compatibility" in the Introduction.

Libraries

LIBCP.LIB	Single thread static library, retail version
LIBCPMT.LIB	Multithread static library, retail version
MSVCPRT.LIB	Import library for MSVCRT.DLL, retail version

Return Value

The transformation of the character *c*, using the transform in *category*.

Remarks

The value of *category* must have been returned by an earlier successful call to wctrans.

_tzset

Sets time environment variables.

void _tzset(void);

Routine	Required Header	Compatibility
_tzset	<time.h>	Win 95, Win NT

For additional compatibility information, see "Compatibility" in the Introduction.

Libraries

LIBC.LIB	Single thread static library, retail version
LIBCMT.LIB	Multithread static library, retail version
MSVCRT.LIB	Import library for MSVCRT.DLL, retail version

Return Value

None

Remarks

The **_tzset** function uses the current setting of the environment variable **TZ** to assign values to three global variables: **_daylight**, **_timezone**, and **_tzname**. These variables are used by the _ftime and localtime functions to make corrections from coordinated universal time (UTC) to local time, and by the **time** function to compute UTC from system time. Use the following syntax to set the **TZ** environment variable:

set TZ=_tzn_[+ | –]_hh_[:_mm_[:_ss_]][_dzn_]

tzn
>   Three-letter time-zone name, such as PST. You must specify the correct offset from local time to UTC.

hh
>   Difference in hours between UTC and local time. Optionally signed.

mm
>   Minutes. Separated from *hh* by a colon (**:**).

ss
>   Seconds. Separated from *mm* by a colon (**:**).

dzn
>   Three-letter daylight-saving-time zone such as PDT. If daylight saving time is never in effect in the locality, set **TZ** without a value for *dzn*. The C run-time library assumes the United States's rules for implementing the calculation of Daylight Saving Time (DST).

For example, to set the **TZ** environment variable to correspond to the current time zone in Germany, you can use one of the following statements:

```
set TZ=GST-1GDT
set TZ=GST+1GDT
```

These strings use GST to indicate German standard time, assume that Germany is one hour ahead of UTC, and assume that daylight savings time is in effect.

If the **TZ** value is not set, **_tzset** attempts to use the time zone information specified by the operating system. Under Windows NT and Windows 95, this information is specified in the Control Panel's Date/Time application. If **_tzset** cannot obtain this information, it uses PST8PDT by default, which signifies the Pacific time zone.

Based on the **TZ** environment variable value, the following values are assigned to the global variables **_daylight**, **_timezone**, and **_tzname** when **_tzset** is called:

Global Variable	Description	Default Value
_daylight	Nonzero value if a daylight-saving-time zone is specified in **TZ** setting; otherwise, 0	1
_timezone	Difference in seconds between UTC and local time	28800 (28800 seconds equals 8 hours)
_tzname[0]	String value of time-zone name from **TZ** environmental variable; empty if **TZ** has not been set	PST
_tzname[1]	String value of daylight-saving-time zone; empty if daylight-saving-time zone is omitted from **TZ** environmental variable	PDT

The default values shown in the preceding table for **_daylight** and the **_tzname** array correspond to "PST8PDT." If the DST zone is omitted from the **TZ** environmental variable, the value of **_daylight** is 0 and the **_ftime**, **gmtime**, and **localtime** functions return 0 for their DST flags.

Example

```
/* TZSET.C: This program first sets up the time zone by
 * placing the variable named TZ=EST5 in the environment
 * table. It then uses _tzset to set the global variables
 * named _daylight, _timezone, and _tzname.
 */

#include <time.h>
#include <stdlib.h>
#include <stdio.h>

void main( void )
{
    if( _putenv( "TZ=EST5EDT" ) == -1 )
```

```
    {
        printf( "Unable to set TZ\n" );
        exit( 1 );
    }
    else
    {
        _tzset();
        printf( "_daylight = %d\n", _daylight );
        printf( "_timezone = %ld\n", _timezone );
        printf( "_tzname[0] = %s\n", _tzname[0] );
    }
    exit( 0 );
}
```

Output

```
_daylight = 1
_timezone = 18000
_tzname[0] = EST
```

See Also

asctime, **_ftime**, **gmtime**, **localtime**, **time**, **_utime**

_ultoa, _ultow

Convert an unsigned long integer to a string.

char *_ultoa(unsigned long *value*, **char** *string, **int** *radix* **);**
wchar_t *_ultow(unsigned long *value*, **wchar_t** *string, **int** *radix* **);**

Routine	Required Header	Compatibility
_ultoa	<stdlib.h>	Win 95, Win NT
_ultow	<stdlib.h> or <wchar.h>	Win 95, Win NT

For additional compatibility information, see "Compatibility" in the Introduction.

Libraries

LIBC.LIB	Single thread static library, retail version
LIBCMT.LIB	Multithread static library, retail version
MSVCRT.LIB	Import library for MSVCRT.DLL, retail version

Return Value

Each of these functions returns a pointer to *string*. There is no error return.

Parameters

value
Number to be converted

string
String result

radix
Base of *value*

Remarks

The **_ultoa** function converts *value* to a null-terminated character string and stores the result (up to 33 bytes) in *string*. No overflow checking is performed. *radix* specifies the base of *value*; *radix* must be in the range 2–36. **_ultow** is a wide-character version of **_ultoa**.

Generic-Text Routine Mappings

TCHAR.H Routine	_UNICODE & _MBCS Not Defined	_MBCS Defined	_UNICODE Defined
_ultot	_ultoa	_ultoa	_ultow

Example

```
/* ITOA.C: This program converts integers of various
 * sizes to strings in various radixes.
 */

#include <stdlib.h>
#include <stdio.h>

void main( void )
{
    char buffer[20];
    int  i = 3445;
    long l = -344115L;
    unsigned long ul = 1234567890UL;

    _itoa( i, buffer, 10 );
    printf( "String of integer %d (radix 10): %s\n", i, buffer );
    _itoa( i, buffer, 16 );
    printf( "String of integer %d (radix 16): 0x%s\n", i, buffer );
    _itoa( i, buffer, 2 );
    printf( "String of integer %d (radix 2): %s\n", i, buffer );

    _ltoa( l, buffer, 16 );
    printf( "String of long int %ld (radix 16): 0x%s\n", l, buffer );

    _ultoa( ul, buffer, 16 );
    printf( "String of unsigned long %lu (radix 16): 0x%s\n", ul, buffer );
}
```

Output

```
String of integer 3445 (radix 10): 3445
String of integer 3445 (radix 16): 0xd75
String of integer 3445 (radix 2): 110101110101
String of long int -344115 (radix 16): 0xfffabfcd
String of unsigned long 1234567890 (radix 16): 0x499602d2
```

See Also

_itoa, **_ltoa**

_umask

Sets the default file-permission mask.

int _umask(int *pmode* **);**

Routine	Required Header	Compatibility
_umask	<io.h> and <sys/stat.h> and <sys/types.h>	Win 95, Win NT

For additional compatibility information, see "Compatibility" in the Introduction.

Libraries

LIBC.LIB	Single thread static library, retail version
LIBCMT.LIB	Multithread static library, retail version
MSVCRT.LIB	Import library for MSVCRT.DLL, retail version

Return Value

_umask returns the previous value of *pmode*. There is no error return.

Parameter

pmode
    Default permission setting

Remarks

The **_umask** function sets the file-permission mask of the current process to the mode specified by *pmode*. The file-permission mask modifies the permission setting of new files created by **_creat**, **_open**, or **_sopen**. If a bit in the mask is 1, the corresponding bit in the file's requested permission value is set to 0 (disallowed). If a bit in the mask is 0, the corresponding bit is left unchanged. The permission setting for a new file is not set until the file is closed for the first time.

The argument *pmode* is a constant expression containing one or both of the manifest constants **_S_IREAD** and **_S_IWRITE**, defined in SYS\STAT.H. When both constants are given, they are joined with the bitwise-OR operator (|). If the *pmode* argument is **_S_IREAD**, reading is not allowed (the file is write-only). If the *pmode* argument is **_S_IWRITE**, writing is not allowed (the file is read-only). For example, if the write bit is set in the mask, any new files will be read-only. Note that with MS-DOS, Windows NT, and Windows 95, all files are readable; it is not possible to give write-only permission. Therefore, setting the read bit with **_umask** has no effect on the file's modes.

Example

```
/* UMASK.C: This program uses _umask to set
 * the file-permission mask so that all future
 * files will be created as read-only files.
 * It also displays the old mask.
 */

#include <sys/stat.h>
#include <sys/types.h>
#include <io.h>
#include <stdio.h>

void main( void )
{
    int oldmask;

    /* Create read-only files: */
    oldmask = _umask( _S_IWRITE );
    printf( "Oldmask = 0x%.4x\n", oldmask );
}
```

Output

```
Oldmask = 0x0000
```

See Also

_chmod, _creat, _mkdir, _open

unexpected

Calls **terminate** or function you specify using **set_unexpected**.

void unexpected(void);

Routine	Required Header	Compatibility
unexpected	<eh.h>	ANSI, Win 95, Win NT

For additional compatibility information, see "Compatibility" in the Introduction.

Libraries

LIBC.LIB	Single thread static library, retail version
LIBCMT.LIB	Multithread static library, retail version
MSVCRT.LIB	Import library for MSVCRT.DLL, retail version

Return Value

None

Remarks

The **unexpected** routine is not used with the current implemenation of C++ exception handling. **unexpected** calls **terminate** by default. You can change this default behavior by writing a custom termination function and calling **set_unexpected** with the name of your function as its argument. **unexpected** calls the last function given as an argument to **set_unexpected**.

See Also

abort, **_set_se_translator**, **set_terminate**, **set_unexpected**, **terminate**

ungetc, ungetwc

Pushes a character back onto the stream.

int ungetc(int *c*, **FILE** **stream* **);**
wint_t ungetwc(wint_t *c*, **FILE** **stream* **);**

Routine	Required Header	Compatibility
ungetc	<stdio.h>	ANSI, Win 95, Win NT
ungetwc	<stdio.h> or <wchar.h>	ANSI, Win 95, Win NT

For additional compatibility information, see "Compatibility" in the Introduction.

Libraries

LIBC.LIB	Single thread static library, retail version
LIBCMT.LIB	Multithread static library, retail version
MSVCRT.LIB	Import library for MSVCRT.DLL, retail version

Return Value

If successful, each of these functions returns the character argument *c*. If *c* cannot be pushed back or if no character has been read, the input stream is unchanged and **ungetc** returns **EOF**; **ungetwc** returns **WEOF**.

Parameters

c

  Character to be pushed

stream

  Pointer to **FILE** structure

Remarks

The **ungetc** function pushes the character *c* back onto *stream* and clears the end-of-file indicator. The stream must be open for reading. A subsequent read operation on *stream* starts with *c*. An attempt to push **EOF** onto the stream using **ungetc** is ignored.

Characters placed on the stream by **ungetc** may be erased if **fflush**, **fseek**, **fsetpos**, or **rewind** is called before the character is read from the stream. The file-position indicator will have the value it had before the characters were pushed back. The external storage corresponding to the stream is unchanged. On a successful **ungetc** call against a text stream, the file-position indicator is unspecified until all the pushed-back characters are read or discarded. On each successful **ungetc** call against a binary stream, the file-position indicator is decremented; if its value was 0 before a call, the value is undefined after the call.

Results are unpredictable if **ungetc** is called twice without a read or file-positioning operation between the two calls. After a call to **fscanf**, a call to **ungetc** may fail unless another read operation (such as **getc**) has been performed. This is because **fscanf** itself calls **ungetc**.

ungetwc is a wide-character version of **ungetc**. However, on each successful **ungetwc** call against a text or binary stream, the value of the file-position indicator is unspecified until all pushed-back characters are read or discarded.

Generic-Text Routine Mappings

TCHAR.H Routine	_UNICODE & _MBCS Not Defined	_MBCS Defined	_UNICODE Defined
_ungettc	ungetc	ungetc	ungetwc

Example

```
/* UNGETC.C: This program first converts a character
 * representation of an unsigned integer to an integer. If
 * the program encounters a character that is not a digit,
 * the program uses ungetc to replace it in the  stream.
 */

#include <stdio.h>
#include <ctype.h>
```

```
void main( void )
{
   int ch;
   int result = 0;

   printf( "Enter an integer: " );

   /* Read in and convert number: */
   while( ((ch = getchar()) != EOF) && isdigit( ch ) )
      result = result * 10 + ch - '0';   /* Use digit. */
   if( ch != EOF )
      ungetc( ch, stdin );                /* Put nondigit back. */
   printf( "Number = %d\nNextcharacter in stream = '%c'",
           result, getchar() );
}
```

Output

```
Enter an integer: 521a
Number = 521
Nextcharacter in stream = 'a'
```

See Also

getc, **putc**

_ungetch

Pushes back the last charcter read from the console.

int _ungetch(int *c* **);**

Routine	Required Header	Compatibility
_ungetch	<conio.h>	Win 95, Win NT

For additional compatibility information, see "Compatibility" in the Introduction.

Libraries

LIBC.LIB	Single thread static library, retail version
LIBCMT.LIB	Multithread static library, retail version
MSVCRT.LIB	Import library for MSVCRT.DLL, retail version

Return Value

_ungetch returns the character *c* if it is successful. A return value of **EOF** indicates an error.

Parameter

c

Character to be pushed

Remarks

The **_ungetch** function pushes the character *c* back to the console, causing *c* to be the next character read by **_getch** or **_getche**. **_ungetch** fails if it is called more than once before the next read. The *c* argument may not be **EOF**.

Example

```c
/* UNGETCH.C: In this program, a white-space delimited
 * token is read from the keyboard. When the program
 * encounters a delimiter, it uses _ungetch to replace
 * the character in the keyboard buffer.
 */

#include <conio.h>
#include <ctype.h>
#include <stdio.h>

void main( void )
{
    char buffer[100];
    int count = 0;
    int ch;
    ch = _getche();
    while( isspace( ch ) )    /* Skip preceding white space. */
        ch = _getche();
    while( count < 99 )       /* Gather token. */
    {
        if( isspace( ch ) )   /* End of token. */
            break;
        buffer[count++] = (char)ch;
        ch = _getche();
    }
    _ungetch( ch );           /* Put back delimiter. */
    buffer[count] = '\0';     /* Null terminate the token. */
    printf( "\ntoken = %s\n", buffer );
}
```

Output

```
White
token = White
```

See Also

_cscanf, _getch

_unlink, _wunlink

Delete a file.

int _unlink(const char *****filename* **);
int _wunlink(const wchar_t *****filename* **);

Routine	Required Header	Compatibility
_unlink	<io.h> and <stdio.h>	Win 95, Win NT
_wunlink	<io.h> or <wchar.h>	Win NT

For additional compatibility information, see "Compatibility" in the Introduction.

Libraries

LIBC.LIB	Single thread static library, retail version
LIBCMT.LIB	Multithread static library, retail version
MSVCRT.LIB	Import library for MSVCRT.DLL, retail version

Return Value

Each of these functions returns 0 if successful. Otherwise, the function returns –1 and sets **errno** to **EACCES**, which means the path specifies a read-only file, or to **ENOENT**, which means the file or path is not found or the path specified a directory.

Parameter

filename
    Name of file to remove

Remarks

The **_unlink** function deletes the file specified by *filename*. **_wunlink** is a wide-character version of **_unlink**; the *filename* argument to **_wunlink** is a wide-character string. These functions behave identically otherwise.

Generic-Text Routine Mappings

TCHAR.H Routine	_UNICODE & _MBCS Not Defined	_MBCS Defined	_UNICODE Defined
_tunlink	_unlink	_unlink	_wunlink

Example

```
/* UNLINK.C: This program uses _unlink to delete UNLINK.OBJ. */

#include <stdio.h>
```

```
void main( void )
{
   if( _unlink( "unlink.obj" ) == -1 )
      perror( "Could not delete 'UNLINK.OBJ'" );
   else
      printf( "Deleted 'UNLINK.OBJ'\n" );
}
```

Output

```
Deleted 'UNLINK.OBJ'
```

See Also

_close, remove

_utime, _wutime

Set the file modification time.

int _utime(unsigned char *_filename_, struct _utimbuf *_times_);
int _wutime(wchar_t *_filename_, struct _utimbuf *_times_);

Routine	Required Headers	Optional Headers	Compatibility
_utime	<sys/utime.h>	<errno.h>	Win 95, Win NT
_wutime	<utime.h> or <wchar.h>	<errno.h>	Win 95, Win NT

For additional compatibility information, see "Compatibility" in the Introduction.

Libraries

LIBC.LIB	Single thread static library, retail version
LIBCMT.LIB	Multithread static library, retail version
MSVCRT.LIB	Import library for MSVCRT.DLL, retail version

Return Value

Each of these functions returns 0 if the file-modification time was changed. A return value
of –1 indicates an error, in which case **errno** is set to one of the following values:

EACCES
   Path specifies directory or read-only file

EINVAL
   Invalid _times_ argument

EMFILE

Too many open files (the file must be opened to change its modification time)

ENOENT

Path or filename not found

Parameters

filename

Path or filename

times

Pointer to stored time values

Remarks

The **_utime** function sets the modification time for the file specified by *filename*. The process must have write access to the file in order to change the time. Under Windows NT and Windows 95, you can change the access time and the modication time in the **_utimbuf** structure. If *times* is a **NULL** pointer, the modification time is set to the current local time. Otherwise, *times* must point to a structure of type **_utimbuf**, defined in SYS\UTIME.H.

The **_utimbuf** structure stores file access and modification times used by **_utime** to change file-modification dates. The structure has the following fields, which are both of type **time_t**:

actime

Time of file access

modtime

Time of file modification

_utime is identical to **_futime** except that the *filename* argument of **_utime** is a filename or a path to a file, rather than a handle to an open file.

_wutime is a wide-character version of **_utime**; the *filename* argument to **_wutime** is a wide-character string. These functions behave identically otherwise.

Generic-Text Routine Mappings

TCHAR.H Routine	_UNICODE & _MBCS Not Defined	_MBCS Defined	_UNICODE Defined
_tutime	_utime	_utime	_wutime

Example

```
/* UTIME.C: This program uses _utime to set the
 * file-modification time to the current time.
 */

#include <stdio.h>
#include <stdlib.h>
#include <sys/types.h>
#include <sys/utime.h>
```

```
void main( void )
{
   /* Show file time before and after. */
   system( "dir utime.c" );
   if( _utime( "utime.c", NULL ) == -1 )
      perror( "_utime failed\n" );
   else
      printf( "File time modified\n" );
   system( "dir utime.c" );
}
```

Output

```
Volume in drive C is ALDONS
Volume Serial Number is 0E17-1702

Directory of C:\dolphin\crt\code

05/03/94  10:00p                   451 utime.c
            1 File(s)              451 bytes
                          83,320,832 bytes free
Volume in drive C is ALDONS
Volume Serial Number is 0E17-1702

Directory of C:\dolphin\crt\code

05/03/94  10:00p                   451 utime.c
            1 File(s)              451 bytes
                          83,320,832 bytes free
File time modified
```

See Also

asctime, ctime, _fstat, _ftime, _futime, gmtime, localtime, _stat, time

va_arg, va_end, va_start

Access variable-argument lists.

type **va_arg**(**va_list** *arg_ptr*, *type*);
void va_end(**va_list** *arg_ptr*);
void va_start(**va_list** *arg_ptr*);   (UNIX version)
void va_start(**va_list** *arg_ptr*, *prev_param*);   (ANSI version)

Routine	Required Header	Optional Headers	Compatibility
va_arg	<stdio.h> and <stdarg.h>	<varargs.h>[*]	ANSI, Win 95, Win NT
va_end	<stdio.h> and <stdarg.h>	<varargs.h>[*]	ANSI, Win 95, Win NT
va_start	<stdio.h> and <stdarg.h>	<varargs.h>[*]	ANSI, Win 95, Win NT

* Required for UNIX V compatibility.

For additional compatibility information, see "Compatibility" in the Introduction.

Libraries

LIBC.LIB	Single thread static library, retail version
LIBCMT.LIB	Multithread static library, retail version
MSVCRT.LIB	Import library for MSVCRT.DLL, retail version

Return Value

va_arg returns the current argument; **va_start** and **va_end** do not return values.

Parameters

type
  Type of argument to be retrieved

arg_ptr
  Pointer to list of arguments

prev_param
  Parameter preceding first optional argument (ANSI only)

Remarks

The **va_arg**, **va_end**, and **va_start** macros provide a portable way to access the arguments to a function when the function takes a variable number of arguments. Two versions of the macros are available: The macros defined in STDARG.H conform to the ANSI C standard, and the macros defined in VARARGS.H are compatible with the UNIX System V definition. The macros are:

va_alist
  Name of parameter to called function (UNIX version only)

va_arg
  Macro to retrieve current argument

va_dcl
  Declaration of **va_alist** (UNIX version only)

va_end
  Macro to reset *arg_ptr*

va_list
  typedef for pointer to list of arguments defined in STDIO.H

va_start
  Macro to set *arg_ptr* to beginning of list of optional arguments (UNIX version only)

Both versions of the macros assume that the function takes a fixed number of required arguments, followed by a variable number of optional arguments. The required arguments are declared as ordinary parameters to the function and can be accessed through the parameter names. The optional arguments are accessed through the macros in STDARG.H or VARARGS.H, which set a pointer to the first optional argument in the argument list, retrieve arguments from the list, and reset the pointer when argument processing is completed.

The ANSI C standard macros, defined in STDARG.H, are used as follows:

- All required arguments to the function are declared as parameters in the usual way. **va_dcl** is not used with the STDARG.H macros.

- **va_start** sets *arg_ptr* to the first optional argument in the list of arguments passed to the function. The argument *arg_ptr* must have **va_list** type. The argument *prev_param* is the name of the required parameter immediately preceding the first optional argument in the argument list. If *prev_param* is declared with the register storage class, the macro's behavior is undefined. **va_start** must be used before **va_arg** is used for the first time.

- **va_arg** retrieves a value of *type* from the location given by *arg_ptr* and increments *arg_ptr* to point to the next argument in the list, using the size of *type* to determine where the next argument starts. **va_arg** can be used any number of times within the function to retrieve arguments from the list.

- After all arguments have been retrieved, **va_end** resets the pointer to **NULL**.

The UNIX System V macros, defined in VARARGS.H, operate somewhat differently:

- Any required arguments to the function can be declared as parameters in the usual way.

- The last (or only) parameter to the function represents the list of optional arguments. This parameter must be named **va_alist** (not to be confused with **va_list**, which is defined as the type of **va_alist**).

- **va_dcl** appears after the function definition and before the opening left brace of the function. This macro is defined as a complete declaration of the **va_alist** parameter, including the terminating semicolon; therefore, no semicolon should follow **va_dcl**.

- Within the function, **va_start** sets *arg_ptr* to the beginning of the list of optional arguments passed to the function. **va_start** must be used before **va_arg** is used for the first time. The argument *arg_ptr* must have **va_list** type.

- **va_arg** retrieves a value of *type* from the location given by *arg_ptr* and increments *arg_ptr* to point to the next argument in the list, using the size of *type* to determine where the next argument starts. **va_arg** can be used any number of times within the function to retrieve the arguments from the list.

- After all arguments have been retrieved, **va_end** resets the pointer to **NULL**.

Example

```
/* VA.C: The program below illustrates passing a variable
 * number of arguments using the following macros:
 *      va_start            va_arg              va_end
 *      va_list             va_dcl (UNIX only)
 */

#include <stdio.h>
#define ANSI               /* Comment out for UNIX version    */
#ifdef ANSI                /* ANSI compatible version         */
#include <stdarg.h>
int average( int first, … );
#else                      /* UNIX compatible version         */
#include <varargs.h>
int average( va_list );
#endif

void main( void )
{
   /* Call with 3 integers (-1 is used as terminator). */
   printf( "Average is: %d\n", average( 2, 3, 4, -1 ) );

   /* Call with 4 integers. */
   printf( "Average is: %d\n", average( 5, 7, 9, 11, -1 ) );

   /* Call with just -1 terminator. */
   printf( "Average is: %d\n", average( -1 ) );
}

/* Returns the average of a variable list of integers. */
#ifdef ANSI                     /* ANSI compatible version    */
int average( int first, … )
{
   int count = 0, sum = 0, I = first;
   va_list marker;

   va_start( marker, first );     /* Initialize variable arguments. */
   while( I != -1 )
   {
      sum += I;
      count++;
      I = va_arg( marker, int);
   }
   va_end( marker );                  /* Reset variable arguments.    */
   return( sum ? (sum / count) : 0 );
}
```

```
#else         /* UNIX compatible version must use old-style definition.  */
int average( va_alist )
va_dcl
{
   int I, count, sum;
   va_list marker;

   va_start( marker );              /* Initialize variable arguments. */
   for( sum = count = 0; (I = va_arg( marker, int)) != -1; count++ )
      sum += I;
   va_end( marker );                /* Reset variable arguments.      */
   return( sum ? (sum / count) : 0 );
}
#endif
```

Output

```
Average is: 3
Average is: 8
Average is: 0
```

See Also

vfprintf

vprintf Functions

Each of the **vprintf** functions takes a pointer to an argument list, then formats and writes
the given data to a particular destination.

vfprintf, vfwprintf	_vsnprintf, _vsnwprintf
vprintf, vwprintf	vsprintf, vswprintf

Remarks

The **vprintf** functions are similar to their counterpart functions as listed in the following
table. However, each **vprintf** function accepts a pointer to an argument list, whereas each
of the counterpart functions accepts an argument list.

These functions format data for output to destinations as follows.

Function	Counterpart Function	Output Destination	
vfprintf	fprintf	*stream*	
vfwprintf	fwprintf	*stream*	
vprintf	printf	**stdout**	
vwprintf	wprintf	**stdout**	*(continued)*

(continued)

Function	Counterpart Function	Output Destination
vsprintf	sprintf	memory pointed to by *buffer*
vswprintf	swprintf	memory pointed to by *buffer*
_vsnprintf	_snprintf	memory pointed to by *buffer*
_vsnwprintf	_snwprintf	memory pointed to by *buffer*

The *argptr* argument has type **va_list**, which is defined in VARARGS.H and STDARG.H. The *argptr* variable must be initialized by **va_start,** and may be reinitialized by subsequent **va_arg** calls; *argptr* then points to the beginning of a list of arguments that are converted and transmitted for output according to the corresponding specifications in the *format* argument. *format* has the same form and function as the *format* argument for printf. None of these functions invokes **va_end**. For a more complete description of each **vprintf** function, see the description of its counterpart function as listed in the preceding table.

_vsnprintf differs from **vsprintf** in that it writes no more than *count* bytes to *buffer*.

vfwprintf, **_vsnwprintf**, **vswprintf**, and **vwprintf** are wide-character versions of **vfprintf**, **_vsnprintf**, **vsprintf,** and **vprintf**, respectively; in each of these wide-character functions, *buffer* and *format* are wide-character strings. Otherwise, each wide-character function behaves identically to its SBCS counterpart function.

For **vsprintf**, **vswprintf**, **_vsnprintf** and **_vsnwprintf**, if copying occurs between strings that overlap, the behavior is undefined.

See Also

fprintf, **printf**, **sprintf**, **va_arg**

vfprintf, vfwprintf

Write formatted output using a pointer to a list of arguments.

int vfprintf(FILE **stream***, const char ****format*, **va_list** *argptr* **);**
int vfwprintf(FILE **stream***, const wchar_t ****format***, va_list** *argptr* **);**

Routine	Required Header	Optional Headers	Compatibility
vfprintf	<stdio.h> and <stdarg.h>	<varargs.h>[*]	ANSI, Win 95
vfwprintf	<stdio.h> or <wchar.h>, and <stdarg.h>	<varargs.h>[*]	ANSI, Win 95, Win NT

[*] Required for UNIX V compatibility.

For additional compatibility information, see "Compatibility" in the Introduction.

Libraries

LIBC.LIB	Single thread static library, retail version
LIBCMT.LIB	Multithread static library, retail version
MSVCRT.LIB	Import library for MSVCRT.DLL, retail version

Return Value

vfprintf and **vfwprintf** return the number of characters written, not including the terminating null character, or a negative value if an output error occurs.

Parameters

stream
   Pointer to **FILE** structure

format
   Format specification

argptr
   Pointer to list of arguments

For more information, see "Format Specification Fields: printf and wprintf Functions" on page 543.

Remarks

Each of these functions takes a pointer to an argument list, then formats and writes the given data to *stream*.

Generic-Text Routine Mappings

TCHAR.H Routine	_UNICODE & _MBCS Not Defined	_MBCS Defined	_UNICODE Defined
_vftprintf	vfprintf	vfprintf	vfwprintf

See Also

fprintf, **printf**, **sprintf**, **va_arg**

vprintf, vwprintf

Write formatted output using a pointer to a list of arguments.

int vprintf(const char *_format_, va_list _argptr_);
int vwprintf(const wchar_t *_format_, va_list _argptr_);

Routine	Required Header	Optional Headers	Compatibility
vprintf	<stdio.h> and <stdarg.h>	<varargs.h>*	ANSI, Win 95, Win NT
vwprintf	<stdio.h> or <wchar.h>, and <stdarg.h>	<varargs.h>*	ANSI, Win 95, Win NT

* Required for UNIX V compatibility.

For additional compatibility information, see "Compatibility" in the Introduction.

Libraries

LIBC.LIB	Single thread static library, retail version
LIBCMT.LIB	Multithread static library, retail version
MSVCRT.LIB	Import library for MSVCRT.DLL, retail version

Return Value

vprintf and **vwprintf** return the number of characters written, not including the terminating null character, or a negative value if an output error occurs.

Parameters

format
  Format specification

argptr
  Pointer to list of arguments

Remarks

Each of these functions takes a pointer to an argument list, then formats and writes the given data to **stdout**.

Generic-Text Routine Mappings

TCHAR.H Routine	_UNICODE & _MBCS Not Defined	_MBCS Defined	_UNICODE Defined
_vtprintf	vprintf	vprintf	vwprintf

See Also

fprintf, **printf**, **sprintf**, **va_arg**

_vsnprintf, _vsnwprintf

Write formatted output using a pointer to a list of arguments.

int _vsnprintf(char **buffer*, **size_t** *count*, **const char** **format*, **va_list** *argptr* **);**
int _vsnwprintf(wchar_t **buffer*, **size_t** *count*, **const wchar_t** **format*, **va_list** *argptr* **);**

Routine	Required Header	Optional Headers	Compatibility
_vsnprintf	<stdio.h> and <stdarg.h>	<varargs.h>*	Win 95, Win NT
_vsnwprintf	<stdio.h> or <wchar.h>, and <stdarg.h>	<varargs.h>*	Win 95, Win NT

* Required for UNIX V compatibility.

For additional compatibility information, see "Compatibility" in the Introduction.

Libraries

LIBC.LIB	Single thread static library, retail version
LIBCMT.LIB	Multithread static library, retail version
MSVCRT.LIB	Import library for MSVCRT.DLL, retail version

Return Value

_vsnprintf and **_vsnwprintf** return the number of characters written, not including the terminating null character, or a negative value if an output error occurs. For **_vsnprintf**, if the number of bytes to write exceeds *buffer,* then *count* bytes are written and −1 is returned.

Parameters

buffer
    Storage location for output

count
    Maximum number of characters to write

format
    Format specification

argptr
    Pointer to list of arguments

Remarks

Each of these functions takes a pointer to an argument list, then formats and writes the given data to the memory pointed to by *buffer*.

Generic-Text Routine Mappings

TCHAR.H Routine	_UNICODE & _MBCS Not Defined	_MBCS Defined	_UNICODE Defined
_vsntprintf	_vsnprintf	_vsnprintf	_vsnwprintf

See Also

fprintf, **printf**, **sprintf**, **va_arg**

vsprintf, vswprintf

Write formatted output using a pointer to a list of arguments.

int vsprintf(char **buffer***, const char** **format***, va_list** *argptr* **);**
int vswprintf(wchar_t **buffer***, const wchar_t** **format***, va_list** *argptr* **);**

Routine	Required Header	Optional Headers	Compatibility
vsprintf	<stdio.h> and <stdarg.h>	<varargs.h>[*]	ANSI, Win 95, Win NT
vswprintf	<stdio.h> or <wchar.h>, and <stdarg.h>	<varargs.h>[*]	ANSI, Win 95, Win NT

* Required for UNIX V compatibility.

For additional compatibility information, see "Compatibility" in the Introduction.

Libraries

LIBC.LIB	Single thread static library, retail version
LIBCMT.LIB	Multithread static library, retail version
MSVCRT.LIB	Import library for MSVCRT.DLL, retail version

Return Value

vsprintf and **vswprintf** return the number of characters written, not including the terminating null character, or a negative value if an output error occurs. For **vswprintf**, a negative value is also returned if *count* or more wide characters are requested to be written.

Parameters

buffer
Storage location for output

format
Format specification

argptr
Pointer to list of arguments

count
Maximum number of bytes to write

Remarks

Each of these functions takes a pointer to an argument list, then formats and writes the given data to the memory pointed to by *buffer*.

Generic-Text Routine Mappings

TCHAR.H Routine	_UNICODE & _MBCS Not Defined	_MBCS Defined	_UNICODE Defined
_vstprintf	vsprintf	vsprintf	vswprintf

See Also

fprintf, **printf**, **sprintf**, **va_arg**

wcstombs

Converts a sequence of wide characters to a corresponding sequence of multibyte characters.

size_t wcstombs(char *mbstr*, **const wchar_t** *wcstr*, **size_t** *count* **);**

Routine	Required Header	Compatibility
wcstombs	<stdlib.h>	ANSI, Win 95, Win NT

For additional compatibility information, see "Compatibility" in the Introduction.

Libraries

LIBC.LIB	Single thread static library, retail version
LIBCMT.LIB	Multithread static library, retail version
MSVCRT.LIB	Import library for MSVCRT.DLL, retail version

Return Value

If **wcstombs** successfully converts the multibyte string, it returns the number of bytes written into the multibyte output string, excluding the terminating **NULL** (if any). If the *mbstr* argument is **NULL**, **wcstombs** returns the required size of the destination string. If **wcstombs** encounters a wide character it cannot be convert to a multibyte character, it returns –1 cast to type **size_t**.

Parameters

mbstr
   The address of a sequence of multibyte characters

wcstr
   The address of a sequence of wide characters

count
   The maximum number of bytes that can be stored in the multibyte output string

Remarks

The **wcstombs** function converts the wide-character string pointed to by *wcstr* to the corresponding multibyte characters and stores the results in the *mbstr* array. The *count* parameter indicates the maximum number of bytes that can be stored in the multibyte output string (that is, the size of *mbstr*). In general, it is not known how many bytes will be required when converting a wide-character string. Some wide characters will require only one byte in the output string; others require two. If there are two bytes in the multibyte output string for every wide character in the input string (including the wide character **NULL**), the result is guaranteed to fit.

If **wcstombs** encounters the wide-character null character (L'\0') either before or when *count* occurs, it converts it to an 8-bit 0 and stops. Thus, the multibyte character string at *mbstr* is null-terminated only if **wcstombs** encounters a wide-character null character during conversion. If the sequences pointed to by *wcstr* and *mbstr* overlap, the behavior of **wcstombs** is undefined.

If the *mbstr* argument is **NULL**, **wcstombs** returns the required size of the destination string.

Example

```
/* WCSTOMBS.C illustrates the behavior of the wcstombs function. */

#include <stdio.h>
#include <stdlib.h>

void main( void )
{
    int     i;
    char    *pmbbuf   = (char *)malloc( MB_CUR_MAX );
    wchar_t *pwchello = L"Hello, world.";

    printf( "Convert wide-character string:\n" );
    i = wcstombs( pmbbuf, pwchello, MB_CUR_MAX );
    printf( "\tCharacters converted: %u\n", i );
    printf( "\tMultibyte character: %s\n\n", pmbbuf );
}
```

Output

```
Convert wide-character string:
    Characters converted: 1
    Multibyte character: H
```

See Also

mblen, mbstowcs, mbtowc, wctomb, WideCharToMultiByte

wctomb

Converts a wide character to the corresponding multibyte character.

int wctomb(char **mbchar***, wchar_t** *wchar* **);**

Routine	Required Header	Compatibility
wctomb	<stdlib.h>	ANSI, Win 95, Win NT

For additional compatibility information, see "Compatibility" in the Introduction.

Libraries

LIBC.LIB	Single thread static library, retail version
LIBCMT.LIB	Multithread static library, retail version
MSVCRT.LIB	Import library for MSVCRT.DLL, retail version

Return Value

If **wctomb** converts the wide character to a multibyte character, it returns the number of bytes (which is never greater than **MB_CUR_MAX**) in the wide character. If *wchar* is the wide-character null character (L'\0'), **wctomb** returns 1. If the conversion is not possible in the current locale, **wctomb** returns –1.

Parameters

mbchar
   The address of a multibyte character

wchar
   A wide character

Remarks

The **wctomb** function converts its *wchar* argument to the corresponding multibyte character and stores the result at *mbchar*. You can call the function from any point in any program.

Example

```
/* WCTOMB.CPP illustrates the behavior of the wctomb function */

#include <stdio.h>
#include <stdlib.h>
```

```
void main( void )
{
   int i;
   wchar_t wc = L'a';
   char *pmbnull = NULL;
   char *pmb = (char *)malloc( sizeof( char ) );

   printf( "Convert a wide character:\n" );
   i = wctomb( pmb, wc );
   printf( "\tCharacters converted: %u\n", i );
   printf( "\tMultibyte character: %.1s\n\n", pmb );

   printf( "Attempt to convert when target is NULL:\n" );
   i = wctomb( pmbnull, wc );
   printf( "\tCharacters converted: %u\n", i );
   printf( "\tMultibyte character: %.1s\n", pmbnull );
}
```

Output

```
Convert a wide character:
   Characters converted: 1
   Multibyte character: a

Attempt to convert when target is NULL:
   Characters converted: 0
   Multibyte character: (
```

See Also

mblen, mbstowcs, mbtowc, wcstombs, WideCharToMultiByte

wctrans

Determines a mapping from one set of wide-character codes to another.

wctrans_t wctrans(const char *property* **);**

Routine	Required Header	Compatibility
wctrans	<wctype.h>	Win 95, Win NT

For additional compatibility information, see "Compatibility" in the Introduction.

Libraries

LIBCP.LIB	Single thread static library, retail version
LIBCPMT.LIB	Multithread static library, retail version
MSVCPRT.LIB	Import library for MSVCRT.DLL, retail version

Return Value

If the LC_CTYPE category of the current locale does not define a mapping whose name matches the property string *property*, the function returns zero. Otherwise, it returns a nonzero value suitable for use as the second argument to a subsequent call to **towctrans**.

Parameters

property
  property string

Remarks

This function determines a mapping from one set of wide-character codes to another.

The following pairs of calls have the same behavior in all locales (but an implementation can define additional mappings even in the "C" locale):

tolower(*c* **)** same as **towctrans(** *c,* **wctrans("towlower"))**

towupper(*c* **)** same as **towctrans(** *c,* **wctrans("toupper"))**

See Also

setlocale

wctype

Determines a classification rule for wide-character codes.

wctype_t wctype(const char * *property* **);**

Routine	Required Header	Compatibility
wctype	<wctype.h>	Win 95, Win NT

For additional compatibility information, see "Compatibility" in the Introduction.

Libraries

LIBCP.LIB	Single thread static library, retail version
LIBCPMT.LIB	Multithread static library, retail version
MSVCPRT.LIB	Import library for MSVCRT.DLL, retail version

Return Value

If the **LC_CTYPE** category of the current locale does not define a classification rule whose name matches the property string *property*, the function returns zero. Otherwise, it returns a nonzero value suitable for use as the second argument to a subsequent call to **towctrans**.

Parameters

property
>   property string

Remarks

The function determines a classification rule for wide-character codes. The following pairs of calls have the same behavior in all locales (but an implementation can define additional classification rules even in the "C" locale):

iswalnum(*c* **)** same as **iswctype(** *c*, **wctype(** "alnum" **))**

iswalpha(*c* **)** same as **iswctype(** *c*, **wctype(** "alpha" **))**

iswcntrl(*c* **)** same as **iswctype(** *c*, **wctype(** "cntrl" **))**

iswdigit(*c* **)** same as **iswctype(** *c*, **wctype(** "digit" **))**

iswgraph(*c* **)** same as **iswctype(** *c*, **wctype(** "graph" **))**

iswlower(*c* **)** same as **iswctype(** *c*, **wctype(** "lower" **))**

iswprint(*c* **)** same as **iswctype(** *c*, **wctype(** "print" **))**

iswpunct(*c* **)** same as **iswctype(** *c*, **wctype(** "punct" **))**

iswspace(*c* **)** same as **iswctype(** *c*, **wctype(** "space" **))**

iswupper(*c* **)** same as **iswctype(** *c*, **wctype(** "upper" **))**

iswxdigit(*c* **)** same as **iswctype(** *c*, **wctype(** "xdigit" **))**

See Also

setlocale

_write

Writes data to a file.

int _write(int *handle*, **const void** **buffer*, **unsigned int** *count* **);**

Routine	Required Header	Compatibility
_write	<io.h>	Win 95, Win NT

For additional compatibility information, see "Compatibility" in the Introduction.

Libraries

LIBC.LIB	Single thread static library, retail version
LIBCMT.LIB	Multithread static library, retail version
MSVCRT.LIB	Import library for MSVCRT.DLL, retail version

Return Value

If successful, **_write** returns the number of bytes actually written. If the actual space remaining on the disk is less than the size of the buffer the function is trying to write to the disk, **_write** fails and does not flush any of the buffer's contents to the disk. A return value of –1 indicates an error. In this case, **errno** is set to one of two values: **EBADF**, which means the file handle is invalid or the file is not opened for writing, or **ENOSPC**, which means there is not enough space left on the device for the operation.

If the file is opened in text mode, each linefeed character is replaced with a carriage return–linefeed pair in the output. The replacement does not affect the return value.

Parameters

handle
    Handle of file into which data is written

buffer
    Data to be written

count
    Number of bytes

Remarks

The **_write** function writes *count* bytes from *buffer* into the file associated with *handle*. The write operation begins at the current position of the file pointer (if any) associated with the given file. If the file is open for appending, the operation begins at the current end of the file. After the write operation, the file pointer is increased by the number of bytes actually written.

When writing to files opened in text mode, **_write** treats a CTRL+Z character as the logical end-of-file. When writing to a device, **_write** treats a CTRL+Z character in the buffer as an output terminator.

Example

```
/* WRITE.C: This program opens a file for output
 * and uses _write to write some bytes to the file.
 */

#include <io.h>
#include <stdio.h>
#include <stdlib.h>
#include <fcntl.h>
#include <sys/types.h>
#include <sys/stat.h>

char buffer[] = "This is a test of '_write' function";
```

```
void main( void )
{
    int fh;
    unsigned byteswritten;

    if( (fh = _open( "write.o", _O_RDWR | _O_CREAT, _S_IREAD | _S_IWRITE )) != -1 )
    {
        if(( byteswritten = _write( fh, buffer, sizeof( buffer ))) == -1 )
            perror( "Write failed" );
        else
            printf( "Wrote %u bytes to file\n", byteswritten );

        _close( fh );
    }
}
```

Output

```
Wrote 36 bytes to file
```

See Also

fwrite, **_open**, **_read**

_wtoi, _wtoi64, _wtol

Converts a wide-character string to an integer (**_wtoi** and **_wtoi64**) or to a long integer (**_wtol**).

int _wtoi(const wchar_t *_string_);
__int64 _wtoi64(wchar_t *_string_);
long _wtol(const wchar_t *_string_);

Routine	Required Header	Compatibility
_wtoi	<stdlib.h> or <wchar.h>	Win 95, Win NT
_wtoi64	<stdlib.h> or <wchar.h>	Win 95, Win NT
_wtol	<stdlib.h> or <wchar.h>	Win 95, Win NT

For additional compatibility information, see "Compatibility" in the Introduction.

Libraries

LIBC.LIB	Single thread static library, retail version
LIBCMT.LIB	Multithread static library, retail version
MSVCRT.LIB	Import library for MSVCRT.DLL, retail version

Return Value

Each function returns the **int**, **__int64**, or **long** value produced by interpreting the input characters as a number. If the input cannot be converted to a value of the appropriate type, **_wtoi** and **_wtoi64** return 0 and **_wtol** returns 0L. The return value is undefined in case of overflow.

Parameter

string
    String to be converted

Remarks

The **_wtoi** and **_wtoi64** function converts a wide-character string to an integer value. **_wtol** converts a wide-character string to a long integer value. The input string is a sequence of characters that can be interpreted as a numerical value of the specified type. The output value is affected by the setting of the **LC_NUMERIC** category of the current locale. (For more information on the **LC_NUMERIC** category, see **setlocale**. The function stops reading the input string at the first character that it cannot recognize as part of a number. This character may be the null character (L'\0') terminating the string.

The *string* argument for these functions has the form

[*whitespace*] [*sign*]*digits*

A *whitespace* consists of space and/or tab characters, which are ignored. *sign* is either plus (**+**) or minus (**−**). *digits* is one or more decimal digits. **_wtoi**, **_wtoi64**, and **_wtol** do not recognize decimal points or exponents.

Example

```
/* ATOF.C: This program shows how numbers stored
 * as strings can be converted to numeric values
 * using the atof, atoi, and atol functions.
 */

#include <stdlib.h>
#include <stdio.h>

void main( void )
{
    char *s; double x; int i; long l;

    s = "  -2309.12E-15";    /* Test of atof */
    x = atof( s );
    printf( "atof test: ASCII string: %s\tfloat:  %e\n", s, x );

    s = "7.8912654773d210";  /* Test of atof */
    x = atof( s );
    printf( "atof test: ASCII string: %s\tfloat:  %e\n", s, x );
```

```
        s = "  -9885 pigs";        /* Test of atoi */
        i = atoi( s );
        printf( "atoi test: ASCII string: %s\t\tinteger: %d\n", s, i );

        s = "98854 dollars";        /* Test of atol */
        l = atol( s );
        printf( "atol test: ASCII string: %s\t\tlong: %ld\n", s, l );
}
```

Output

```
atof test: ASCII string:  -2309.12E-15 float:  -2.309120e-012
atof test: ASCII string: 7.8912654773d210  float:  7.891265e+210
atoi test: ASCII string:  -9885 pigs    integer: -9885
atol test: ASCII string: 98854 dollars    long: 98854
```

See Also

atoi, **_ecvt**, **_fcvt**, **_gcvt**

Language and Country Strings

The *locale* argument to the setlocale function takes the following form:

```
locale  "lang[_country[.code_page]]"
        | ".code_page"
        | ""
        | NULL
```

This appendix lists the language strings and country strings available to **setlocale**. All country and language codes currently supported by the Win32 NLS API are supported by **setlocale**. For information on code pages, see "Code Pages" in Chapter 1, "Run-Time Routines by Categories."

Language Strings

The following language strings are recognized by **setlocale**. Any language not supported by the operating system is not accepted by **setlocale**. The three-letter language-string codes are only valid in Windows NT and Windows 95.

Primary Language	Sublanguage	Language String
Chinese	Chinese	"chinese"
Chinese	Chinese (simplified)	"chinese-simplified" or "chs"
Chinese	Chinese (traditional)	"chinese-traditional" or "cht"
Czech	Czech	"csy" or "czech"
Danish	Danish	"dan"or "danish"
Dutch	Dutch (Belgian)	"belgian," "dutch-belgian," or "nlb"
Dutch	Dutch (default)	"dutch" or "nld"
English	English (Australian)	"australian," "ena," or "english-aus"
English	English (Canadian)	"canadian," "enc," or "english-can"
English	English (default)	"english"

(continued)

(continued)

Primary Language	Sublanguage	Language String
English	English (New Zealand)	"english-nz" or "enz"
English	English (UK)	"eng," "english-uk," or "uk"
English	English (USA)	"american," "american english," "american-english," "english-american," "english-us," "english-usa," "enu," "us," or "usa"
Finnish	Finnish	"fin" or "finnish"
French	French (Belgian)	"frb" or "french-belgian"
French	French (Canadian)	"frc" or "french-canadian"
French	French (default)	"fra"or "french"
French	French (Swiss)	"french-swiss" or "frs"
German	German (Austrian)	"dea" or "german-austrian"
German	German (default)	"deu" or "german"
German	German (Swiss)	"des," "german-swiss," or "swiss"
Greek	Greek	"ell" or "greek"
Hungarian	Hungarian	"hun" or "hungarian"
Icelandic	Icelandic	"icelandic" or "isl"
Italian	Italian (default)	"ita" or "italian"
Italian	Italian (Swiss)	"italian-swiss" or "its"
Japanese	Japanese	"japanese" or "jpn"
Korean	Korean	"kor" or "korean"
Norwegian	Norwegian (Bokmal)	"nor" or "norwegian-bokmal"
Norwegian	Norwegian (default)	"norwegian"
Norwegian	Norwegian (Nynorsk)	"non" or "norwegian-nynorsk"
Polish	Polish	"plk" or "polish"
Portuguese	Portuguese (Brazilian)	"portuguese-brazilian" or "ptb"
Portuguese	Portuguese (default)	"portuguese" or "ptg"
Russian	Russian (default)	"rus" or "russian"

(continued)

Primary Language	Sublanguage	Language String
Slovak	Slovak	"sky" or "slovak"
Spanish	Spanish (default)	"esp" or "spanish"
Spanish	Spanish (Mexican)	"esm" or "spanish-mexican"
Spanish	Spanish (Modern)	"esn" or "spanish-modern"
Swedish	Swedish	"sve" or "swedish"
Turkish	Turkish	"trk" or "turkish"

Country Strings

The following is a list of country strings recognized by **setlocale**. Strings for countries that are not supported by the operating system are not accepted by **setlocale**. Three-letter country-name codes are from ISO/IEC (International Organization for Standardization, International Electrotechnical Commission) specification 3166.

Country/Region	Country/Region String
Australia	"aus" or "australia"
Austria	"austria" or "aut"
Belgium	"bel" or "belgium"
Brazil	"bra" or "brazil"
Canada	"can" or "canada"
Czech Republic	"cze" or "czech"
Denmark	"denmark" or "dnk"
Finland	"fin" or "finland"
France	"fra" or "france"
Germany	"deu" or "germany"
Greece	"grc" or "greece"
Hong Kong	"hkg", "hong kong", or "hong-kong"
Hungary	"hun" or "hungary"
Iceland	"iceland" or "isl"

(continued)

(continued)

Country/Region	Country/Region String
Ireland	"ireland" or "irl"
Italy	"ita" or "italy"
Japan	"japan" or "jpn"
Mexico	"mex" or "mexico"
Netherlands	"nld," "holland," or "netherlands"
New Zealand	"new zealand," "new-zealand," "nz," or "nzl"
Norway	"nor" or "norway"
People's Republic of China	"china," "chn," "pr china," or "pr-china"
Poland	"pol" or "poland"
Portugal	"prt" or "portugal"
Russia	"rus" or "russia"
Singapore	"sgp" or "singapore"
Slovak Repubic	"svk" or "slovak"
South Korea	"kor," "korea," "south korea," or "south-korea"
Spain	"esp" or "spain"
Sweden	"swe" or "sweden"
Switzerland	"che" or "switzerland"
Taiwan	"taiwan" or "twn"
Turkey	"tur" or "turkey"
United Kingdom	"britain," "england," "gbr," "great britain," "uk," "united kingdom," or "united-kingdom"
United States of America	"america," "united states," "united-states," "us," or "usa"

Generic-Text Mappings

To simplify writing code for international markets, generic-text mappings are defined in TCHAR.H for:

- Data types
- Constants and global variables
- Routine mappings

For more information, see "Using Generic-Text Mappings" in Chapter 1, "Run-Time Routines by Category." Generic-text mappings are Microsoft extensions that are not ANSI-compatible.

See Also

Data Type Mappings, Constants and Global Variables, Routine Mappings, A Sample Generic-Text Program, Using Generic-Text Mappings

Data Type Mappings

These data-type mappings are defined in TCHAR.H and depend on whether the constant **_UNICODE** or **_MBCS** has been defined in your program.

For related information, see "Using TCHAR.H Data Types with _MBCS Code" in the *Visual C++ Programmer's Guide* online.

Generic-Text Data Type Mappings

Generic-Text Data Type Name	SBCS (_UNICODE, _MBCS Not Defined)	_MBCS Defined	_UNICODE Defined
_TCHAR	char	char	wchar_t
_TINT	int	int	wint_t
_TSCHAR	signed char	signed char	wchar_t
_TUCHAR	unsigned char	unsigned char	wchar_t
_TXCHAR	char	unsigned char	wchar_t
_T or **_TEXT**	No effect (removed by preprocessor)	No effect (removed by preprocessor)	**L** (converts following character or string to its Unicode counterpart)

See Also

Generic-Text Mappings, Constants and Global Variable Mappings, Routine Mappings, A Sample Generic-Text Program, Using Generic-Text Mappings

Constant and Global Variable Mappings

These generic-text constant, global variable, and standard-type mappings are defined in TCHAR.H and depend on whether the constant **_UNICODE** or **_MBCS** has been defined in your program.

Generic-Text Constant and Global Variable Mappings

Generic-Text – Object Name	SBCS (_UNICODE, _MBCS Not Defined)	_MBCS Defined	_UNICODE Defined
_TEOF	**EOF**	**EOF**	**WEOF**
_tenviron	**_environ**	**_environ**	**_wenviron**
_tfinddata_t	**_finddata_t**	**_finddata_t**	**_wfinddata_t**

See Also

Generic-text mappings, Data type mappings, Routine mappings, A sample generic-text program, Using generic-text mappings

Routine Mappings

The generic-text routine mappings are defined in TCHAR.H. **_tccpy** and **_tclen** map to functions in the MBCS model; they are mapped to macros or inline functions in the SBCS and Unicode models for completeness. For information on a generic text routine, see the help topic about the corresponding SBCS-, _MBCS-, or _UNICODE-related routine.

More specific information about individual routines listed in the left column below is not available in this documentation. However, you can easily look up the information on a corresponding SBCS-, _MBCS-, or _UNICODE-related routine. Use the Search command on the Help menu to look up any generic-text routine listed below.

For related information, see "Generic-Text Mappings" in the *Visual C++ Programmer's Guide* online.

Generic-Text Routine Mappings

Generic-Text Routine Name	SBCS (_UNICODE & MBCS Not Defined)	_MBCS Defined	_UNICODE Defined
_fgettc	fgetc	fgetc	fgetwc
_fgettchar	fgetchar	fgetchar	_fgetwchar
_fgetts	fgets	fgets	fgetws
_fputtc	fputc	fputc	fputwc
_fputtchar	fputchar	fputchar	_fputwchar
_fputts	fputs	fputs	fputws
_ftprintf	fprintf	fprintf	fwprintf
_ftscanf	fscanf	fscanf	fwscanf
_gettc	getc	getc	getwc
_gettchar	getchar	getchar	getwchar
_getts	gets	gets	getws
_istalnum	isalnum	_ismbcalnum	iswalnum
_istalpha	isalpha	_ismbcalpha	iswalpha
_istascii	__isascii	__isascii	iswascii
_istcntrl	iscntrl	iscntrl	iswcntrl
_istdigit	isdigit	_ismbcdigit	iswdigit
_istgraph	isgraph	_ismbcgraph	iswgraph
_istlead	Always returns false	_ismbblead	Always returns false
_istleadbyte	Always returns false	isleadbyte	Always returns false
_istlegal	Always returns true	_ismbclegal	Always returns true
_istlower	islower	_ismbclower	iswlower
_istprint	isprint	_ismbcprint	iswprint
_istpunct	ispunct	_ismbcpunct	iswpunct
_istspace	isspace	_ismbcspace	iswspace
_istupper	isupper	_ismbcupper	iswupper
_istxdigit	isxdigit	isxdigit	iswxdigit

(continued)

Generic-Text Routine Mappings *(continued)*

Generic-Text Routine Name	SBCS (_UNICODE & MBCS Not Defined)	_MBCS Defined	_UNICODE Defined
_itot	_itoa	_itoa	_itow
_ltot	_ltoa	_ltoa	_ltow
_puttc	putc	putc	putwc
_puttchar	putchar	putchar	putwchar
_putts	puts	puts	putws
_tmain	main	main	wmain
_sntprintf	_snprintf	_snprintf	_snwprintf
_stprintf	sprintf	sprintf	swprintf
_stscanf	sscanf	sscanf	swscanf
_taccess	_access	_access	_waccess
_tasctime	asctime	asctime	_wasctime
_tccpy	Maps to macro or inline function	_mbccpy	Maps to macro or inline function
_tchdir	_chdir	_chdir	_wchdir
_tclen	Maps to macro or inline function	_mbclen	Maps to macro or inline function
_tchmod	_chmod	_chmod	_wchmod
_tcreat	_creat	_creat	_wcreat
_tcscat	strcat	_mbscat	wcscat
_tcschr	strchr	_mbschr	wcschr
_tcsclen	strlen	_mbslen	wcslen
_tcscmp	strcmp	_mbscmp	wcscmp
_tcscoll	strcoll	_mbscoll	wcscoll
_tcscpy	strcpy	_mbscpy	wcscpy
_tcscspn	strcspn	_mbscspn	wcscspn
_tcsdec	_strdec	_mbsdec	_wcsdec
_tcsdup	_strdup	_mbsdup	_wcsdup

Generic-Text Routine Mappings   *(continued)*

Generic-Text Routine Name	SBCS (_UNICODE & MBCS Not Defined)	_MBCS Defined	_UNICODE Defined
_tcsftime	strftime	strftime	wcsftime
_tcsicmp	_stricmp	_mbsicmp	_wcsicmp
_tcsicoll	_stricoll	_stricoll	_wcsicoll
_tcsinc	_strinc	_mbsinc	_wcsinc
_tcslen	strlen	strlen	wcslen
_tcslwr	_strlwr	_mbslwr	_wcslwr
_tcsnbcnt	_strncnt	_mbsnbcnt	_wcsncnt
_tcsncat	strncat	_mbsnbcat	wcsncat
_tcsnccat	strncat	_mbsncat	wcsncat
_tcsncmp	strncmp	_mbsnbcmp	wcsncmp
_tcsnccmp	strncmp	_mbsncmp	wcsncmp
_tcsnccnt	_strncnt	_mbsnccnt	_wcsncnt
_tcsnccpy	strncpy	_mbsncpy	wcsncpy
_tcsncicmp	_strnicmp	_mbsnicmp	_wcsnicmp
_tcsncpy	strncpy	_mbsnbcpy	wcsncpy
_tcsncset	_strnset	_mbsnset	_wcsnset
_tcsnextc	_strnextc	_mbsnextc	_wcsnextc
_tcsnicmp	_strnicmp	_mbsnicmp	_wcsnicmp
_tcsnicoll	_strnicoll	_strnicoll	_wcsnicoll
_tcsninc	_strninc	_mbsninc	_wcsninc
_tcsnccnt	_strncnt	_mbsnccnt	_wcsncnt
_tcsnset	_strnset	_mbsnbset	_wcsnset
_tcspbrk	strpbrk	_mbspbrk	wcspbrk
_tcsspnp	_strspnp	_mbsspnp	_wcsspnp
_tcsrchr	strrchr	_mbsrchr	wcsrchr
_tcsrev	_strrev	_mbsrev	_wcsrev

(continued)

Generic-Text Routine Mappings *(continued)*

Generic-Text Routine Name	SBCS (_UNICODE & MBCS Not Defined)	_MBCS Defined	_UNICODE Defined
_tcsset	_strset	_mbsset	_wcsset
_tcsspn	strspn	_mbsspn	wcsspn
_tcsstr	strstr	_mbsstr	wcsstr
_tcstod	strtod	strtod	wcstod
_tcstok	strtok	_mbstok	wcstok
_tcstol	strtol	strtol	wcstol
_tcstoul	strtoul	strtoul	wcstoul
_tcsupr	_strupr	_mbsupr	_wcsupr
_tcsxfrm	strxfrm	strxfrm	wcsxfrm
_tctime	ctime	ctime	_wctime
_texecl	_execl	_execl	_wexecl
_texecle	_execle	_execle	_wexecle
_texeclp	_execlp	_execlp	_wexeclp
_texeclpe	_execlpe	_execlpe	_wexeclpe
_texecv	_execv	_execv	_wexecv
_texecve	_execve	_execve	_wexecve
_texecvp	_execvp	_execvp	_wexecvp
_texecvpe	_execvpe	_execvpe	_wexecvpe
_tfdopen	_fdopen	_fdopen	_wfdopen
_tfindfirst	_findfirst	_findfirst	_wfindfirst
_tfindnext	_findnext	_findnext	_wfindnext
_tfopen	fopen	fopen	_wfopen
_tfreopen	freopen	freopen	_wfreopen
_tfsopen	_fsopen	_fsopen	_wfsopen
_tfullpath	_fullpath	_fullpath	_wfullpath
_tgetcwd	_getcwd	_getcwd	_wgetcwd
_tgetenv	getenv	getenv	_wgetenv

Generic-Text Routine Mappings   *(continued)*

Generic-Text Routine Name	SBCS (_UNICODE & MBCS Not Defined)	_MBCS Defined	_UNICODE Defined
_tmain	main	main	wmain
_tmakepath	_makepath	_makepath	_wmakepath
_tmkdir	_mkdir	_mkdir	_wmkdir
_tmktemp	_mktemp	_mktemp	_wmktemp
_tperror	perror	perror	_wperror
_topen	_open	_open	_wopen
_totlower	tolower	_mbctolower	towlower
_totupper	toupper	_mbctoupper	towupper
_tpopen	_popen	_popen	_wpopen
_tprintf	printf	printf	wprintf
_tremove	remove	remove	_wremove
_trename	rename	rename	_wrename
_trmdir	_rmdir	_rmdir	_wrmdir
_tsearchenv	_searchenv	_searchenv	_wsearchenv
_tscanf	scanf	scanf	wscanf
_tsetlocale	setlocale	setlocale	_wsetlocale
_tsopen	_sopen	_sopen	_wsopen
_tspawnl	_spawnl	_spawnl	_wspawnl
_tspawnle	_spawnle	_spawnle	_wspawnle
_tspawnlp	_spawnlp	_spawnlp	_wspawnlp
_tspawnlpe	_spawnlpe	_spawnlpe	_wspawnlpe
_tspawnv	_spawnv	_spawnv	_wspawnv
_tspawnve	_spawnve	_spawnve	_wspawnve
_tspawnvp	_spawnvp	_spawnvp	_tspawnvp
_tspawnvpe	_spawnvpe	_spawnvpe	_tspawnvpe
_tsplitpath	_splitpath	_splitpath	_wsplitpath

(continued)

Generic-Text Routine Mappings *(continued)*

Generic-Text Routine Name	SBCS (_UNICODE & MBCS Not Defined)	_MBCS Defined	_UNICODE Defined
_tstat	_stat	_stat	_wstat
_tstrdate	_strdate	_strdate	_wstrdate
_tstrtime	_strtime	_strtime	_wstrtime
_tsystem	system	system	_wsystem
_ttempnam	_tempnam	_tempnam	_wtempnam
_ttmpnam	tmpnam	tmpnam	_wtmpnam
_ttoi	atoi	atoi	_wtoi
_ttol	atol	atol	_wtol
_tutime	_utime	_utime	_wutime
_tWinMain	WinMain	WinMain	wWinMain
_ultot	_ultoa	_ultoa	_ultow
_ungettc	ungetc	ungetc	ungetwc
_vftprintf	vfprintf	vfprintf	vfwprintf
_vsntprintf	_vsnprintf	_vsnprintf	_vsnwprintf
_vstprintf	vsprintf	vsprintf	vswprintf
_vtprintf	vprintf	vprintf	vwprintf

See Also

Generic-Text Mappings, Data Type Mappings, Constants and Global Variable Mappings, A Sample Generic-Text Program, Using Generic-Text Mappings

Index

A

_A_ARCH constant 60
_A_HIDDEN constant 60
_A_NORMAL constant 60
_A_RDONLY constant 60
_A_SUBDIR constant 60
_A_SYSTEM constant 60
abort function 161
aborting
   abort function 161
   assert macro 172
abs function 163
absolute values, calculating
   abs function 163
   fabs function 275
   labs function 427
access constants, file read/write 62–63
_access function 164
accessing variable-argument lists,
   va_arg, va_end, va_start functions 773
acos function 166
adding memory to heaps,
   _heapadd function 374
_alloca function 167
allocating memory *See* memory allocation
_amblksiz variable 43
ANSI C compatibility ix
ANSI code pages 24
API compatibility ix
appending
   bytes of strings, _mbsnbcat function 475
   characters of strings, strncat, wcsncat,
     _mbsncat functions 698
   strings, strcat, wcscat,
     _mbscat functions 664
arccosines, calculating with acos function 166
arcsines, calculating with asin function 171
arctangents, calculating with atan function 174
argument lists, using
   pointer to write formatted output to,
     vprintf functions (list) 777
   routines for accessing variable length 1

arguments
   floating point
     calculating absolute value with
       fabs function 275
     reversing sign of double-precision,
       _chgsign function 201
   type checking
     described xiii
     (list) xiii
   variable, accessing lists with va_arg,
     va_end, va_start functions 773
arrays
   searching
     binary, bsearch function 189
     for keys, _lfind function 431
     for values, _lsearch function 448
   sorting, qsort function 557
ASCII, converting characters to
  lowercase or uppercase with _ _toascii,
  tolower, toupper functions 752
asctime function 168
asin function 171
assert macro 172
_ASSERT, _ASSERTE macros 77
atan, atan2 functions 174
atexit function 175
atof, atoi, atol functions 177
attribute constants, file
   See file attribute constants

B

backward compatibility, structure names x
_beginthread, _beginthreadex functions 180
bessel functions 184
binary and text file-translation modes 16
bits, rotating
   _lrotl, _lrotr functions 446
   _rotl, _rotr functions 575
bsearch function 189
buffer-manipulation routines
   described by category 2
   (list) 2

S

_S_IEXEC constant 73
_S_IFCHR constant 73
_S_IFDIR constant 73
_S_IFMT constant 73
_S_IFREG constant 73
_S_IREAD constant 62, 73
_S_IWRITE constant 62, 73
saving current state of program,
  setjmp function 587
_scalb function 576
scanf function
    described 577
    format specification fields 579
    type field characters 582
    width specification 580
scanf function family,
  floating-point support for 12
scanning strings
    for characters in specified character sets,
      strpbrk, wcspbrk, _mbspbrk functions 708
    for last occurrence of characters, strrchr,
      wcsrchr, _mbsrchr functions 710
SCHAR_MAX constant 55
SCHAR_MIN constant 55
_searchenv function 584
searching
    arrays
        for keys, _lfind function 431
        for values, _lsearch function 448
        with binary search, bsearch function 189
    for files using environment paths,
      _searchenv, _wsearchenv functions 584
searching and sorting routines (list) 37
SEEK_CUR constant 65
SEEK_END constant 65
SEEK_SET constant 65
sending signal to executing programs,
  raise function 561
_set_error_mode function 159
_set_new_handler function 600
_set_new_mode function 602
_set_sbh_threshold function 603
_set_se_translator function 604
set_terminate function 606
set_unexpected function 608
setbuf function 586
setjmp function 587
setlocale function 591
setlocale, language and country strings (list) 793
_setmaxstdio function 596
_setmbcp function 597
_setmode function 598

setting
    buffers to specified character,
      memset function 505
    characters of strings to character,
      _strset, _wcsset, _mbsset functions 714
    code pages for multibyte functions,
      _setmbcp function 597
    file default permission mask,
      _umask function 764
    file translation modes,
      _setmode function 598
    file-position indicators, fsetpos function 336
    floating-point control word,
      _control187, _controlfp functions 214
    interrup, signal handling, signal function 612
    locales, setlocale, _wsetlocale functions 591
    number of open files,
      _setmaxstdio function 596
setvbuf constants
    _IOFBF 70
    _IOLBF 70
    _IONBF 70
    (list) 70
setvbuf function 610
_SH_COMPAT constant 71
_SH_DENYNO constant 71
_SH_DENYRD constant 71
_SH_DENYRW constant 71
_SH_DENYWR constant 71
sharing constants
    (list) 70
    _SH_COMPAT 71
    _SH_DENYNO 71
    _SH_DENYRD 71
    _SH_DENYRW 71
    _SH_DENYWR 71
Shift JIS (Japan Industry Standard) characters,
  _mbcjistojms, _mbcjmstojis functions 466
SHRT_MAX constant 55
SHRT_MIN constant 55
sig_atomic_t standard type 51
SIG_IGN constant 72
SIGFPE constant 71
SIGILL constant 71
SIGINT constant 71
signal action constants
    (list) 72
    SIG_DFL 72
    SIG_IGN 72
signal constants
    (list) 71
    SIGABRT 71
    SIGFPE 71
    SIGILL 71

X

Finish faster.

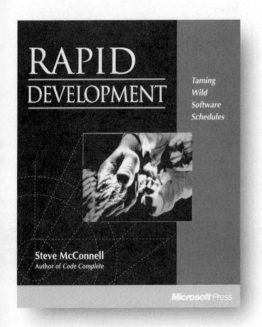

U.S.A. **$35.00**
U.K. £32.49
Canada $46.95
ISBN 1-55615-900-5

"An indispensable road map for those who wish to write code as fast as humanly possible..."
— *G. Pascal Zachary,* author of SHOWSTOPPER!:The Breakneck Race to Create Windows NT and the Next Generation at Microsoft

In RAPID DEVELOPMENT, award-winning author Steve McConnell reveals the secrets to taming wild software schedules. He analyzes the development-speed implications of many traditional development practices, pointing out which are effective and which are harmful. The book alerts you to 36 classic mistakes—practices intended to shorten the development process that lengthen it instead. McConnell counters with 27 proven ways to shorten schedules and reduce the risk of schedule overruns. RAPID DEVELOPMENT has a hard-headed, practical focus—with the emphasis on suggestions you can use right away to finish your next development project faster.

Microsoft Press

Microsoft Press has titles to help everyone— from new users to seasoned developers—

Step by Step Series
Self-paced tutorials for classroom instruction or individualized study

Starts Here™ Series
Interactive instruction on CD-ROM that helps students learn by doing

Field Guide Series
Concise, task-oriented A–Z references for quick, easy answers— anywhere

Official Series
Timely books on a wide variety of Internet topics geared for advanced users

All User Training   All User Reference

Quick Course® Series
Fast, to-the-point instruction for new users

Running Series
A comprehensive curriculum alternative to standard documentation books

At a Glance Series
Quick visual guides for task-oriented instruction

Microsoft Press® products are available worldwide wherever quality computer books are sold. For more information, contact your book or computer retailer, software reseller, or local Microsoft Sales Office, or visit our Web site at mspress.microsoft.com. To locate your nearest source for Microsoft Press products, or to order directly, call 1-800-MSPRESS in the U.S. (in Canada, call 1-800-268-2222).

Prices and availability dates are subject to change.

start faster
and go farther!

The wide selection of books and CD-ROMs published by Microsoft Press contain something for every level of user and every area of interest, from just-in-time online training tools to development tools for professional programmers. Look for them at your bookstore or computer store today!

Professional Select Editions Series
Advanced titles geared for the system administrator or technical support career path

Microsoft® Certified Professional Training
The Microsoft Official Curriculum for certification exams

Best Practices Series
Candid accounts of the new movement in software development

Microsoft Programming Series
The foundations of software development

Professional   Developers

Strategic Technology Series
Easy-to-read overviews for decision makers

Solution Developer Series
Comprehensive titles for intermediate to advanced developers

Microsoft Press® Interactive
Integrated multimedia courseware for all levels

Microsoft Professional Editions
Technical information straight from the source

Microsoft Press

mspress.microsoft.com